Conflict and Consensus
in
Early American History

Conflict and Consensus
in
Early American History

FIFTH EDITION

Edited and with Introductions by

Allen F. Davis
Temple University

Harold D. Woodman
Purdue University

D.C. HEATH AND COMPANY
Lexington, Massachusetts   Toronto

Acknowledgment is made to the following sources for permission to reproduce material from their collections:

Cover: The Metropolitan Museum of Art, Purchase, 1959, The Ella Morris de Peyster Bequest.

p. 1: Courtesy, American Antiquarian Society.

p. 51: The Metropolitan Museum of Art, Bequest of Charles Allen Munn, 1924.

p. 153: Courtesy of The New York Historical Society, New York City.

p. 233: Barry Donahue / Schlesinger Library, Radcliffe College.

p. 273: The New York Public Library, Astor, Lenox and Tilden Foundations.

p. 425: The New York Public Library, Astor, Lenox and Tilden Foundations.

International Standard Book Number: 0-669-02489-9

Library of Congress Catalog Card Number: 79-87594

For Gregory and Paul
and
Allan and David

Preface

We are pleased that the continued success of *Conflict and Consensus in Early American History* has warranted the publication of this fifth edition. We have retained the basic organization of the earlier editions, as well as the emphasis on the themes of conflict and consensus. We remain convinced that the presentation of conflicting views of particular periods and problems, shown within the context of general interpretations, allows students to deepen their understanding of the historical details and provides them with the means for interpreting the broad sweep of the country's history.

We have made a number of changes for this edition. In order to make the book more useful in the introductory course, we have introduced some new readings; this new material incorporates the changing approaches to the themes of conflict and consensus. The new material includes more emphasis on social history and the history of women and minorities. We have also given more attention to the history of the United States since World War II. At the same time, however, we have retained some of the good work that has appeared in earlier editions.

In this edition, as in the previous ones, we have avoided presenting only two extreme positions on each problem raised. Such an either/or approach is artificial, and forces students to choose one extreme or another or to conclude, without adequate evidence, that the truth must be midway between the two extremes. We have, therefore, included at least three selections dealing with the same problem in order to illustrate the subtleties of interpretation.

Our main concern has not been with historiography, although we do direct interested students to relevant historiographical discussions. Beginning students are not especially interested in tracing shifting interpretations, nor should they be at this stage. They should be stimulated to learn *what* happened and *why* it happened, by seeing how different historians, viewing the same event, have attempted to answer these questions. We have therefore concentrated not on the evolution of historical writing but on the historical problems themselves. We hope to leave students with a heightened under-standing of how various issues in American history are interpreted and at the same time to provide the ammunition for thoughtful and spirited discussions. Brief, annotated bibliographies are provided at the end of each section for those who wish to do further reading on a particular interpretation.

In the third edition we added an introduction that was designed to help the beginning student to understand why historians disagree. We found that readers were often confused rather than enlightened when presented with conflicting interpretations of the same events. Too often they lacked the skills needed to discern the bases of historical disagreements. Because of the favorable response, we have retained (with revisions) this brief introduction to his-torical methods and philosophy.

Allen F. Davis
Harold D. Woodman

Acknowledgments

We wish to thank the various publishers and authors for permission to reprint copyrighted material. This book had its origin in our introductory course in American history at the University of Missouri; our former teaching assistants and students will recognize many of the ideas. We are grateful for their aid and recognize that in a real sense they have been collaborators.

We would also like to thank the many teachers and students who have made useful comments on the earlier editions. Their candid evaluations and suggestions for change have been invaluable. We are especially grateful for the aid of the following: John Lankford of the University of Missouri, Columbia; Robert L. Branyan and Lawrence H. Larsen of the University of Missouri, Kansas City; Thomas C. Barrow of Clark University; Franklin Mitchell of the University of Southern California; Lyle Dorsett of the University of Denver; James F. Watts of the City College of the City University of New York; John Burnham of Ohio State University; J. Stanley Lemons of Rhode Island College; William Cutler, Herbert Ershkowitz, Charles Hardy, Robert Miller, and Howard Ohline of Temple University; Richard S. Kirkendall of Indiana University; Alonzo Hamby of Ohio University; William O. Wagnon, Jr., of Washburn University of Topeka; Alice Kessler-Harris of Hofstra University; Kenneth Wayne Mixon and Henry R. Warnock of Mercer University; Ross Webb of Winthrop College; Joe P. Dunn of Converse College; Alton Hornsby of Morehouse College; Juliet Walker of the University of Illinois at Urbana-Champaign; Anita Goodstein of the University of the South; and Sharon Alter of William Rainey Harper College.

Finally, we want to express a special debt to our wives, Roberta Davis and Leonora Woodman, who offered aid and encouragement at every step in the preparation of this book.

Contents

4
Jeffersonians and Federalists

5
The Era of Andrew Jackson

6
Women in Antebellum Society

7
The Black Response to Slavery

8
The Abolitionists

9
The Civil War

10
Reconstruction

Introduction: History and Historians

Most students are usually introduced to the study of history by way of a fat textbook and become quickly immersed in a vast sea of names, dates, events, and statistics. The students' skills are then tested by examinations that require them to show how much of the data they remember; the more they remember, the higher their grades. From this experience a number of conclusions seem obvious: the study of history is the study of "facts" about the past; the more "facts" you know, the better you are as a student of history. The professional historian, be he teacher or textbook writer, is simply one who brings together a very large number of "facts."

Of course, only the most naive of students fail to see that the data of history, the "facts," are presented in an organized manner. Textbooks describe not only what happened, but also why it happened. For example, students learn that Puritans began coming from England to the Massachusetts Bay Colony in the New World in 1630, but they also learn why the Puritans came when they read about the religious persecutions in seventeenth-century England. Similarly, they read of the steady trek of people westward during the nineteenth century; however, at the same time they learn details that explain this movement of people—the availability of fertile lands in the West, the discovery of gold in California, the improvement of roads and other transportation facilities.

But beginning students, even as they come to recognize that their teacher and their textbook are explaining as well as describing events in the past, still have no reason to alter their notion as to what history is all about. They are still working in the realm of "fact." The "fact" of the movement of people into Ohio is explained by the "fact" that fertile land was available there. They may learn more details about the event—how many people went to Ohio, when they arrived, where they settled—and about the explanation—the cost of land in Ohio, the availability of credit, the exhaustion of soils in the eastern states. Or they may be introduced to a fuller explanation when they read that some people came to Ohio to escape their creditors or to seek adventure or to speculate in land. In either case, they are simply learning more "facts." An advanced course in American history in high school differs from the sixth-grade course in American history in that it gives more detail; the older student must remember more "facts."

Students who have been introduced to history in this way may become confused upon discovering in a book like this one that historians often disagree sharply. To be sure, historians present their material in familiar ways; they tell us what happened and why it happened by presenting a mass of historical data. But students soon discover that two or three or more historians dealing with the same event may come to quite different conclusions about it. Sometimes two historians will use two very different sets of "facts" in describing an event and this leads them to different conclusions. At other times, however, the same "facts" are given different meanings by different historians and their conclusions therefore differ.

The common-sense reaction to this state of affairs is to conclude that one historian is right while the other is wrong. But common sense will take students no further than this. Presumably, historians who are wrong will have their "facts" wrong. This is seldom the case, however. Students find that all historians argue reasonably—and persuasively. And the "facts"—the names, dates, events, figures—usually turn out to be correct. Moreover, to complicate matters, they often find that contending historians more or less agree on the facts; that is, they use much the same data to come to different conclusions. To state that all are right when they say different things seems irrational; in any case, such an approach is often unacceptable to teachers who expect their students to take a position. The only way out for the baffled students is to choose one point of view for reasons they cannot fully explain. History, which had seemed to be a cut-and-dried matter of memorizing "facts," now becomes a matter of choosing one good interpretation from among many. Historical truth becomes a matter of personal preference, like the choice of one brand-named item over another in a supermarket.

This position is hardly satisfying. And when their teachers inform them that the controversy over historical interpretations is what lends excitement to the study of history, they can only respond that they feel more confusion than excitement. They cannot help but feel that two diametrically opposed points of view about an event cannot both be right; yet they lack the ability to decide between them.

Obviously, there is no easy solution to this problem. Indeed, if there were, the problem would not be a problem at all because historians would not differ in their interpretations. Historians do not disagree in order to provide the raw material for "problems" books such as this one; they disagree because each historian views the past from a particular perspective. Once students grasp this, they have taken the first step toward being able to evaluate the work of various historians. But before they can take this first step, students must consider a problem they have more or less taken for granted. They must ask themselves what history really is.

The word *history* has several meanings. In its broadest sense, it denotes the whole of the human past. More restricted is the notion that history is the *recorded* past, that is, that part of human life which has left some sort of record such as folk tales, artifacts, or written documents. Finally, history may be defined as that which historians write about the past.

Of course, the three meanings are related. Historians writing about the past base their accounts on the remains of the past, on the artifacts and documents left by people. Obviously they cannot know everything for the simple reason that not every event, every happening, was fully and completely recorded. And the further back one goes in time, the fewer are the records that remain. In this sense, then, the historian can only approximate history in the first meaning above, that is, history as the entire human past.

But this does not say enough. If historians cannot know everything because not everything was recorded, neither do they use all the records that are available to them. Rather, historians *select* from the total those records they deem most significant. Moreover, to complicate matters a bit more, they also re-create parts of the past for which they have no recorded evidence. Like detectives, they piece together evidence to fill in the gaps in the available records.

Historians are able to select evidence and to create evidence by using some theory or idea of human motivation and behavior. Sometimes this appears to be easy, requiring very little sophistication and subtlety. Thus, for example, historians investigating America's entry into World War I would probably find that the sinking of American merchant ships on the high seas by German submarines was relevant to their discussion. At the same time, they would most likely not use evidence that President Woodrow Wilson was dissatisfied with a new hat he bought during the first months of 1917. The choice as to which fact to use is based on a theory—admittedly, in this case a rather crude theory, but a theory nonetheless. It would go something like this: National leaders contemplating war are more likely to be influenced by belligerent acts against their countries than by their unhappiness with their haberdashers.

The choice, of course, is not always so obvious. But, before pursuing the problem further, it is important to note that a choice must be made. Historians do not just present facts; they present *some* facts and not others. They choose those facts that seem significant and reject others. This is one of the reasons why historians disagree. They have different views or different theories concerning human behavior and therefore find different kinds of information significant.

Perhaps it might appear that it is the subject matter being investigated rather than any theory held by the historian that dictates which facts are significant. But this is not really so. With a little imagination—and poetic license—one could conceive of a psychological explanation for Wilson's actions that would include mounting frustration and anger fed in part, at least, by his strong disappointment with his new hat. In this case the purchase of a new hat would be a relevant fact in explaining Wilson's decision to ask Congress for a declaration of war. If the reader finds this outlandish, it is only because his notion of presidential motivation does not include this kind of personal reaction as an influence in determining matters of state.

If the choices were always as simple as choosing between German submarines and President Wilson's new hat, the problem would be easily resolved. But usually the choices are not so easy to make. Historians investigating United States' entry into World War I will find in addition to German submarine warfare a whole series of other facts that could be relevant to the event under study. For instance, they will find that the British government had a propaganda machine at work in the United States that did its best to win public support for the British cause. They will discover that American bankers had made large loans to the British, loans that would not be repaid in the event of a British defeat. They will read of the interception of the "Zimmerman Note," in which the German foreign secretary ordered the German minister in Mexico, in the event of war, to suggest an alliance between Germany and Mexico whereby Mexico, with German support, could win back territory taken from Mexico by the United States in the Mexican War. They will also find among many American political leaders a deep concern over the balance of power in Europe, a balance that would be destroyed—to America's disadvantage—if the Germans were able to defeat the French and the British and thereby emerge as the sole major power in Europe.

What then are the historians investigating America's entry into World War I to make of these facts? One group could simply conclude that America entered the war for several reasons and then list the facts they have discovered. By doing so, they would be making two important assumptions: (1) those facts they put on their list—in this case, German submarine warfare, British propaganda, American loans, the Zimmerman Note, and concern over the balance of power—are the main reasons, while those they do not list are not important; and (2) those things they put on their list are of equal importance in explaining the U.S. role. But another group of historians might argue that the list is incomplete in that it does not take into account the generally pro-British views of Woodrow Wilson, views that stemmed from the President's background and education. The result will be a disagreement among the historians. Moreover, because the second group raise the question of Wilson's views, they will find a number of relevant facts that the first group would ignore. They will concern themselves with Wilson's education, the influence of his teachers, the books he read, and the books he wrote. In short, although both groups of historians are dealing with the same subject—America's entry into World War I—they will come to different conclusions and use different facts to support their points of view. The facts selected, and those ignored, will depend not on the problem studied but on the points of view of the historians.

Similarly, a third group of historians might maintain that the various items on the list should not be given equal weight, that one of the reasons listed, say bankers' loans, was most important and that the others seemed to be significant only because of the overwhelming power of the bankers to influence American policy. The theory here would be that economic matters are the key to human motivation and that a small number of wealthy bankers have a disproportionate ability to influence government. Again, these historians will disagree with the first two groups, and they will find relevant certain facts that the others overlook—for example, bankers' opinions, the lobbying activities of bankers, financial and political connections between bankers and politicians, and the like.

In the examples given, historians disagree and use different facts or give different emphasis to the same facts because they begin from different premises; in other words, they have different theories of human motivation. But there is still another realm of disagreement which, although it often appears similar to that just discussed, in fact stems from something rather different. Historians sometimes disagree because they are not really discussing the same thing. Often they are merely considering different levels of cause and effect. A few examples will illustrate this point.

The simplest level of analysis of cause and effect is to recognize what may be called proximate cause. "I was late for class," you explain, "because I overslept." Or, to use an historical example, "The Civil War began because South Carolina shore batteries under the command of General Beauregard opened fire on the federal garrison at Fort Sumter on April 12, 1861." Neither statement can be faulted on the grounds that it is inaccurate; at the same time, however, neither is sufficient as an explanation of the event being considered. The next question is obvious: Why did you oversleep, or why did relations between one state and the federal government reach the point where differences had to be settled by war? To this you may answer that you were out very late last night at a party, and the historian may respond that the authorities in South Carolina concluded that the election of Abraham Lincoln and his subsequent actions in threatening to supply the federal garrison at Fort Sumter were a clear menace to the well-being of South Carolina.

We have now dug more deeply into the problems, but the answers may still not be sufficient to satisfy us. Again we ask the question why and the answer takes us more deeply into the causes of the events under consideration. As we probe further, of course, the answers become more difficult and more complex. The problems discussed earlier—a theory of motivation and the selection of facts—begin to become increasingly important, and disagreements among historians will begin to emerge. But the potential for another kind of disagreement also arises. The further back or the deeper the historian goes, the more factors there are to be considered and the more tenuous the connection between cause and effect becomes. Historians may disagree about the point at which to begin their analysis, that is, about the location of a point beyond which the causal connection becomes so tenuous as to be meaningless. You might argue that the ultimate cause of your being late to class was the fact that you were born, but obviously this goes back too far to be meaningful. That you were born is, of course, a *necessary* factor—unless that had happened, you could not have been late—but is not a *sufficient* factor; it does not really tell enough to explain your behavior today. Similarly, we could trace the cause of the Civil War back to the discovery of America, but again, this is a necessary but not a sufficient cause.

The point at which causes are both necessary and sufficient is not self-evident. In part, the point is determined by the theoretical stance of historians. If they decide that slavery is the key to understanding the coming of the Civil War, the point will be located somewhere along the continuum of the history of slavery in the United States. But even those historians who agree that slavery is the key to the war will not necessarily agree at what point slavery becomes both necessary and sufficient. The historians who believe that slavery was a constant irritant driving the North and South apart might begin their discussion with the introduction of blacks into Virginia in 1619. They would find relevant the antislavery attitudes of Northerners during the colonial period, the conflict over slavery in the Constitutional Convention, the Missouri Compromise, the militant abolitionist movement of the 1830s, and the Compromise of 1850. But other historians might argue that the slavery issue did not become really significant until it was associated with the settlement of the western lands. They would probably begin their discussion with the Missouri Compromise, and the facts they would find most relevant would be those that illustrated the fear many people had of the expansion of slavery into the new western lands.

Ostensibly, both groups of historians would be discussing the role of slavery in the coming of the Civil War, but actually they would be discussing two different things. For the first group, the expansion of slavery to the West would be only part of a longer and more complex story; for the second group, slavery and the West would be the whole story. Sometimes the same facts would be used by both, with each giving them different weight and significance; at other times one group would find some facts relevant that the other would not.

The reader should now be in a position to understand something of the sources of disagreement among historians. Historians arrive at different conclusions because they have different notions about human motivation and different ideas about what constitutes necessary and sufficient cause. Historical facts as such have no intrinsic meaning; they take on meaning and significance only when they are organized and presented by historians with a particular point of view. The well-used phrase "let the facts speak for themselves" therefore has no real meaning. The facts do *not* speak for themselves; historians use the facts in a particular way and therefore they, and not the facts, are doing the speaking.

By shifting our analysis from the historians' conclusions to their assumptions (from which the conclusions flow), we are in a better position to evaluate their work. To be sure, we still cannot "solve" the problem of disagreement; that is, we cannot, merely by understanding the theoretical stance of the historian, eliminate all disagreement. If the state of our knowledge were such that it provided us with a model of unquestioned validity that completely explained human behavior, we could employ this model to explain our data, our historical facts. Any analysis that began by assuming a different model or explanation would therefore be wrong.*

But since we do not have such a complete and foolproof explanation, disagreements are destined to remain. For the readers who have been patient enough to follow the argument to this point, the conclusions stated here may appear somewhat dismal and unrewarding. In convincing them that evaluating an historical interpretation is not like picking an item off a supermarket shelf, have we done more than move them to another store with a different stock on its shelves? If there are many explanatory models to choose from, and if no one of them is complete, foolproof, and guaranteed true, then it would appear that we are simply in another store with different merchandise on display.

Such a conclusion is unwarranted. In the first place, students who are able to understand the premises from which historians begin will be able to comprehend the way historians work and the process by which they fashion interpretation. Moreover, this understanding will enable them to evaluate the work of the historians. For at this stage students are no longer simply memorizing details; nor are they attempting to evaluate an historical essay by trying to discover whether each of the facts presented is true. They can now ask more important questions of the material before them. Are the premises from which historians begin adequate explanations of human behavior? Do the facts they present really flow from their premises and support their conclusions? Are there other data historians ignored that would tend to undermine their arguments and throw doubt on the adequacy of their premises?

As students attempt to answer these questions, they begin to learn history by thinking and acting like historians. And, as they do, they begin to accumulate knowledge, understanding, and insight in much the same ways that historians do. Historians are constantly discovering new information: diaries, letters, business records, and family Bibles are always being found in attics, basements, and even in remote corners of large research libraries. Historians are also gaining new insights from the research of social scientists such as economists, political scientists, sociologists, and psychologists. Investigations by these

---

* It should be noted in passing that even if we had such a theory, there would be much room for disagreement because we would often lack the required data. Some essential information would be lost through deliberate or accidental destruction. Other information might leave no record. Records of births, deaths, income, and so forth are now required by law, but in earlier days these records were not kept or were kept only sporadically. And telephone and personal conversations might leave no concrete record even though they could have a profound influence on behavior.

scholars into such problems as family relationships, the influence of propaganda on behavior, the effects of the money supply on economic change, the relationship between voting patterns and racial and ethnic origin, and the psychological effects of racism all provide insights that may be of value to historians investigating the past. Historians are also mastering and using new techniques. For example, the computer now permits the historian to handle huge masses of data quickly and accurately.

Historians also learn from one another. For example, when one historian discovers the existence of certain political, social, and economic relationships in a given city at a certain time, he or she provides other historians studying other cities, either at the same or different times, with what may be important and enlightening insights. International comparisons of similar events and institutions can also reveal important features that will be invisible or obscure when these events and institutions are viewed from the perspective of a single nation's history. Finally, and perhaps most important, historians are influenced by their own experiences and by the events of their own time. Scholars cannot be entirely objective (nor should they be); they interpret the past through a frame of reference that is influenced by the world in which they live. During World War II, for instance, historians reexamined the causes and consequences of World War I, just as the war in Vietnam provided a new perspective on the Cold War years. The civil rights movement and black radicalism in the 1960s inspired a number of historians to reinterpret the role of abolitionists in the events leading up to the Civil War and to give more attention to race, prejudice, and class conflict in American life. In a similar way the feminist movement is causing a reexamination of the role of women and the family in the American past, while urban violence, the black revolution, and increasing ethnic identity are causing a reassessment of the importance of violence, slavery, and ethnic groups in American history. Their own experiences often help historians to relate the past to the present, but the exact nature of that relationship remains controversial.

At first it may seem frustrating to realize that there is no one easy answer to the problems historians raise and that "truth" is but an elusive yet intriguing goal in a never-ending quest. But when students realize this, they have *begun* their education. At that point, they will find the study of history to be a significant, exhilarating, and useful part of their education. For coming to grips with conflicting interpretations of the past is more than an interesting classroom game; it is part of a larger process of coming to terms with the world around us. Every day we are asked to evaluate articles in newspapers and magazines or reports of events provided by friends or radio commentators. A knowledge of history provides a background for interpreting these accounts; but more than that, the past and the present are so interconnected that one's interpretation of the American Revolution, slavery, the progressive movement, or American foreign policy after World War II are intimately related to one's views toward civil rights and domestic and foreign policy today.

The discussion thus far has emphasized the element of disagreement among historians and has attempted to show beginning students how these disagreements arise and how they should deal with them. But if disagreements arise because historians often start their analyses from different perspectives, it does not follow that there is no agreement at all among historians. On the contrary, groups of historians have tended to assume similar theoretical postures, and the result has been the emergence of "schools" of historical writing. All differences among members of a particular school do not disappear, but their approaches remain similar enough to differentiate them from members of other schools.

Identifying schools and placing historians in them is seldom easy and is always somewhat arbitrary. The reasons are obvious enough: the amount and complexity of works about America's past are so great that it is possible to identify a large number of schools. Moreover, since few historians begin with an explicit ideology or philosophy of history, their work may fit into a number of possible schools. Finally, most good historians do not cling dogmatically to a particular approach. As their research and writing proceeds, as they learn more, or as contemporary events alter their perspectives, their interpretations tend to change.

In organizing this book we have chosen two recurrent and important schools, or interpretive themes, in the writings on American history: conflict and consensus. Admittedly, the choice, in one sense at least, is arbitrary; we could have chosen from a number of other unifying themes. On the other hand, the choice has not been completely arbitrary in that these themes— conflict and consensus—expressed either explicitly or implicitly, may be found in virtually all major interpretations of our country's past. The student who reads the following pages and attempts to evaluate the arguments presented will be faced with two real and meaningful ways to understand the American past and, indeed, to judge the contemporary American scene.

Stripped to its essentials, the task of historians is to deal with change. And nowhere do historians find change more manifest than when they study the United States. Almost in the twinkling of an eye a vast, scarcely populated continent was transformed into a major industrial power of phenomenal complexity. Overnight, virgin forests became fertile farms; Indian trails became roads, highways, and railroads; and empty spaces became bustling cities. Matching this transformation of the physical face of the continent were equally momentous changes in politics, social relations, ideas, and attitudes. For most Americans, constant and rapid change was inevitable if only because it was so obvious. "Ten years in America are like a century in Spain," wrote the German immigrant Francis Leiber soon after his arrival in the United States early in the nineteenth century. "The United States really changes in some respects more within ten years than a country like Spain has within a hundred."

But who could argue that Europe was static and unchanging? True enough, Europe had little in the way of trackless wilderness to be discovered, settled, and transformed; and, true also, Europe was crowded with the remnants of what might appear to be an unchanging past—cathedrals and monuments, aristocratic and royal institutions, and ways of doing things that seemed to have existed time out of mind. But at the same time, Europe periodically exploded into change. Indeed, time after time, Americans saw Europe swept by rebellion and war as one group after another sought, often successfully, to revolutionize European lives and institutions.

Generations of American historians have tried to describe and to explain the vast alterations that have taken place on the North American continent. As they did so, many kept one eye on the changes in European institutions, seeking to compare and to contrast the nature of changes in the Old World with those of the New. But even as they read the historical documents, often in the light of European history and experience, the historians themselves were living through vast and rapid changes taking place around them in the United States.

The writings by American historians have been varied and rich. But from this variety two rather distinct traditions have emerged, each of which has sought to provide an explanation for the course of American history.

One tradition or point of view holds that the key to American history, like that of Europe, is conflict. Historians who adhere to this point of view speak in terms of revolution and class and sectional conflict. They stress the differences among Americans—class differences, social differences, political differences. Their emphasis is on fundamental·conflicts: democrats versus aristocrats, debtors versus creditors, workers versus businessmen, North versus South, farmers versus railroads, blacks versus whites. Change, they argue, is a function of this never-ending conflict; it arises from the efforts of particular groups and classes to impose their hegemony over American society, or at least to increase their influence over that society.

The other tradition stresses the uniqueness of the American experience by finding a basic consensus in American society. According to this tradition, all Americans of whatever class or station shared what was essentially a common outlook. To be sure, Americans did not all live alike nor did they always agree with one another. But their disagreements, especially when compared with the dissensions that divided European society, were not fundamental. Consensus historians do not ignore class and sectional differences, and they do not deny conflicts between groups such as workers and employers; but they do deny that these conflicts were basic. Americans, they argue, achieved a consensus on fundamentals; if they disagreed, their disagreements were minor differences within an underlying consensus. Change then is the result of a fundamental agreement that change is required and does not arise from a struggle for power.

Although both these themes can be found in the earliest writings on American history, they became dominant interpretive themes only during the twentieth century. The theme of conflict was central to the writings of those Richard Hofstadter has called the "Progressive Historians": Frederick Jackson Turner, Charles A. Beard, and Vernon L. Parrington. Growing up in the midst of the nation's rapid industrialization and living in a time of growing protest against the problems created by that industrialization, these historians saw the past in terms of bitter conflict. Their influence, as the reader of the following pages will discover, was profound. The theme of consensus was in part a reaction to what was considered to be the overstatements of the conflict school and in part a reaction to the world of the 1950s. At that time, European wars and revolutionary conflicts seemed strangely alien to American society, as did historical interpretations cast in the European mold. Looking at the past, these historians discovered that America had always been different from Europe; Americans had, for the most part, been spared the bitter conflicts that plagued Europe. Like the conflict historians of an earlier generation, the new consensus historians had a great influence on American historical thought.

But the consensus historians were not without their critics. John Higham argued that they were "homogenizing" American history; he accused them of "carrying out a massive grading operation to smooth over America's social convulsions." He and other critics did not simply call for a return to the history of the progressive historians. They argued that the consensus historians had made the American past bland and meaningless, because they ignored real and significant differences that produced sharp conflicts.

There was the danger that the debate would degenerate into nothing more than an argument over the meaning given to the words *conflict* and *consensus*. Indeed, often this was exactly what happened. Usually, however, historians attempted to use insights drawn from the work of their predecessors in the two schools in order to develop new and more meaningful interpretations.

The new work was marked by a number of new techniques and fresh approaches. Quantitative historians, aided by the computer and modern statistical methods and using theories borrowed from economics, sociology, political science, linguistics, anthropology, and psychology, conducted massive investigations of such matters as economic growth patterns, voting behavior, family life, and social mobility. Social historians, using both quantitative and other methods, attempted to write history from the "bottom-up," giving major emphasis to the lives of ordinary people rather than to those at the top. Similarly, they turned their attention to the role and status of women, creating an important dimension of this new history. Social historians also studied local developments in great detail, concerning themselves with small communities, villages, ethnic groups, and local religious and political institutions. The "New Left" historians, although they encompassed a quite diverse group, sought variously to find a radical tradition in American history or to explain the absence of such a tradition.

Although these and other new approaches enriched historical writing and often provided a more subtle and complex story of the nation's past, the themes of conflict and consensus continued to be relevant in the new work.

The problems of historical interpretation were not resolved, despite historians' ability to amass more data by using new techniques to mine huge sources of information and by utilizing insights from the social sciences. New methods and techniques could provide new "facts," but the question of which facts to use and what meaning to give them remained.

The lines that divide the conflict from the consensus historians are not so sharp as they once were, and many contemporary historians are drawing from both in their analyses of America's past. Nevertheless, the differences remain and will continue to do so, to the benefit of our persistent search for understanding. In the readings that follow, the reader is introduced to the two traditions of conflict and consensus and their variations through the words of some of their most able exponents.

SUGGESTIONS FOR FURTHER READING

The literature on the philosophy and practice of history comes from the pens of both philosophers and practicing historians. A few recent volumes have been written specifically for the beginning student; examples are Walter T. K. Nugent, *Creative History* (Philadelphia, 1967), and Allan J. Lichtman and Valerie French, *Historians and the Living Past* (Arlington Heights, Ill., 1978). More sophisticated but eminently readable are E. H. Carr, *What Is History?* (New York, 1964), Louis Gottschalk, *Understanding History* (New York, 1963), Allan Nevins, *The Gateway to History* (Garden City, N.Y., 1962), and Marc Bloch, *The Historian's Craft* (New York, 1953). An illuminating and superbly written guide to historical research and writing that will show readers how historians work is Jacques Barzun and Henry F. Graff, *The Modern Researcher* (New York, 1970). A splendid anthology prefaced by an illuminating introduction is Hans Meyerhoff, ed., *The Philosophy of History in Our Time* (Garden City, N.Y., 1959). Another good collection of readings on the philosophy of history is Patrick Gardiner, ed., *Theories of History* (New York, 1959). The books listed have bibliographies that will take the interested student as far as he might wish to go in the field.

Students wishing to pursue the historiography (that is, the history of historical writing) of the conflict-consensus theme should begin with the progressive historians. Charles A. Beard was a prolific writer, but the best approach to him is through Charles and Mary Beard, *The Rise of American Civilization* (New York, 1927, 1930), a lively and interesting interpretation of the whole course of American history, with an emphasis on class and economic conflict. Beard's *An Economic Interpretation of the Constitution* (New York, 1913, 1935) must be read by any serious student. Vernon Parrington's three-volume *Main Currents in American Thought* (New York, 1927, 1930) complements Beard's work and deals with the relationship of literature and ideas to society and social movements. Frederick Jackson Turner's essays may be found in *The Frontier in American History* (New York, 1920), and *The Significance of Sections in American History* (New York, 1932). There are many discussions of the work and influence of these

* Available in paperback edition.

historians; the reader can do no better than to begin with Richard Hofstadter, *The Progressive Historians* (New York, 1968), the work of a perceptive and sensitive critic. This book's great value is enhanced by an outstanding "bibliographical essay" that will lead the student deep into the literature on the subject.

Any serious student of the consensus historians must read and study Louis Hartz, *The Liberal Tradition in America* (New York, 1955) and the key works of Daniel J. Boorstin: *The Genius of American Politics* (Chicago, 1953), *The Americans: The Colonial Experience* (New York, 1958); *The Americans: The Democratic Experience* (New York, 1973); and *The Americans: The National Experience* (New York, 1965). A perceptive discussion of these books as well as of the entire consensus school along with good bibliographical information may be found in the Hofstadter volume cited above. An important and provocative critique of the consensus approach is John Higham, "The Cult of the American Consensus," *Commentary*, 27 (February 1959), pp. 93–100. See also J. Rogers Hollingsworth, "Consensus and Continuity in Recent American Historical Writing," *South Atlantic Quarterly*, 61 (Winter 1962), pp. 40–50, and Gene Wise, "Political 'Reality' in Recent American Scholarship: Progressives versus Symbolists," *American Quarterly*, 22, Part 2 (Summer 1967), pp. 303–28.

A good introduction to the work of the "new left" in much of its variety is Barton J. Bernstein, ed., *Towards a New Past: Dissenting Essays in American History* (New York, 1968). A critical evaluation of the work of this group, which can also serve as an introductory bibliography, is Irwin Unger, "The 'New Left' and American History: Some Recent Trends in United States Historiography," *American Historical Review*, 77 (July 1967), pp. 1237–63. Quantitative history is difficult for the uninitiated, but for those who want a taste of it, a good introduction is William O. Adydelotte, Allan G. Bogue, and Robert William Fogel, eds., *The Dimensions of Quantitative Research in History* (Princeton, N.Y., 1972).

Two examples of the more subtle and complex interpretation that emphasize unity and diversity as well as conflict and consensus are John Higham, "Hanging Together: Divergent Unities in American History," *Journal of American History*, 61 (June 1974), pp. 5–28, and Robert H. Wiebe, *The Segmented Society: An Historical Preface to the Meaning of America* (New York, 1975). Gene Wise, *American Historical Explanations* (Homewood, Ill., 1973) discusses three paradigms in recent historical writing that he defines as Progressive, Consensus, and New Left. A convenient collection of examples of new approaches and methods may be found in Felix Gilbert and Stephen R. Graubard, eds., *Historical Studies Today* (New York, 1972). Bernard Sternsher, *Consensus, Conflict and American Historians* (Bloomington, Ind., 1975), examines the theme of this book in great detail.

Conflict and Consensus in
Early American History

1

Society
and Politics in
Colonial America

In the spring of 1607 three small ships, the Susan Constant, the Godspeed, and the Discovery, sailed up Chesapeake Bay. In May a small group of travel-weary colonists disembarked at what they thought was a suitable site and founded Jamestown, which was to be the first permanent English settlement in the New World. The decades that followed witnessed the establishment of other English colonies—the Pilgrims at Plymouth, a group including many Catholics at Maryland, and the Puritans at Massachusetts Bay. In these and other early settlements the colonists' first task became simple survival in an often inhospitable and always unfamiliar environment.

Survival required more than clearing the land, planting crops, and building shelters. The settlers left behind not only their homes and fields but also the institutions and laws that had governed their lives. They carried with them memories of the past and visions of the future that they would build, but these were merely ideas that had to be given substance if they were to become real in the New World. First, they had to work out rules and regula-tions to govern their relationships with one another and with the authorities back home in the Old World.

In the early years when the new societies were small, relatively homo-geneous, and mainly concerned with survival in the wilderness, the colonists had little trouble agreeing with one another. But success soon brought prob-lems. Newcomers often did not share the ideas of the first settlers, and some-times even those who did agree (or thought they did) in principle found that they sharply disagreed when it came time to put principles into practice. Differences arose over such matters as the distribution of land, church doc-trine, the manner in which leaders were to be chosen, and, once chosen, the powers such leaders should have. Moreover, successful expansion helped create social classes and divisions as some colonials grew wealthier than their neigh-bors by amassing more land, by buying slaves and indentured servants to increase their production, and by engaging in trade and commerce.

All these differences were reflected in the political life of the colonies. Each colony had a representative assembly, a council, and a governor; some had even more political agencies: town meetings, county administrators, and church assemblies. Because these official governmental bodies were so impor-tant in dealing with differences among them, the colonists were naturally concerned with such matters as how representatives should be chosen, who could hold office, and what regions and interests should be represented.

Behind these official governmental agencies were the unofficial, but nonetheless politically important, aspects of colonial life. Newspapers and pamphlets could be (and were) used to mobilize opinion to pressure political leaders through petitions or, at times, through armed intervention.

By the 1770s, the handful of settlers at Jamestown had swelled to over two million people who lived in an area stretching from present-day Maine to southern Georgia. The farming population—more than 90 percent of the total—ranged from tobacco planters and grain growers with hundreds (or even thousands) of acres and hundreds of slaves or indentured servants working the land to small farmers working small plots with their own labor and that of their family. The colonies boasted a number of thriving cities such as Boston, New York, and Philadelphia, with a population of prosperous merchants, skilled artisans, and propertyless laborers. Although divided politically into thirteen separate colonies and economically and socially by class, status, wealth, and religion, the colonies were able to achieve the unity necessary to engage Britain in a long and successful war for independence.

The building of a new society in America was obviously a remarkable achievement. Some historians viewing the colonial experience emphasize a basic unity or consensus among Americans during this long period in their history and tend to find this unity arising from the peculiar experiences of life in the New World. Others, however, argue that whatever final unity was achieved was the result of bitter conflict during the colonial era, conflict that arose from sharp differences in wealth and status among the people and that was reflected in politics. The selections that follow illustrate these differences among historians.

Michael Kammen, in the first selection, points to what he calls the "unstable pluralism" in the American colonies. The great social, religious, and political variation among and within the colonies (along with the uncertainties concerning imperial relations) created instability (dangerous and worrisome because of its potential for conflict) that leading colonials tried to overcome by creating "legitimate," that is, generally accepted, institutions.

In the second selection, James A. Henretta points to growing class divisions based on wealth, which carried the potential—and sometimes the reality—of sharp conflict. But, he adds, the aristocratic society of the South and the entrepreneurial society of the North molded personality types and created institutional structures that mitigated the conflict. Yet tensions and the potential for conflict remained.

In the final selection, Gary Nash gives much greater emphasis to the conflicts arising from sharp differences in wealth in colonial cities during the eighteenth century. He finds deep resentments and the beginnings of a "radical ideology" among the poor.

As the American colonies became more populous, richer, and more diverse, did they at the same time become more unstable and prone to conflict? Or did the development of peculiarly American social and political institutions serve to create an overriding unity in the midst of growing diversity? The answers to these questions not only give insight into the nature of the colonial experience but also they provide a starting point for an evaluation of the American Revolution.

Michael Kammen

Unstable Pluralism and the Quest for Legitimacy

I would like to suggest that an inquiry into the problem of legitimacy—the need to create and validate viable public institutions, statuses, and relationships—helps to clarify our conception of the colonies' relationship to England, helps to explain patterns of behavior, belief, instability, and subsequent events after Independence. It should also bring into meaningful juxtaposition various themes and issues—concerning religion, law, politics, and society—which have hitherto been regarded in compartmentalized fashion. . . .

The most basic conception of legitimacy is "the condition of being in accordance with law, rule, or principle." Legitimate power is derived from some source of established authority that clearly allocates the right to command and the duty to obey. Compliance of the community is obtained when it affirms the belief that the rulers and their requirements constitute an acceptable order of custom and authority. Insofar as legitimacy is a psychological phenomenon, it depends upon the assumption that a particular set of institutions is appropriate for a certain society and that they function in a manner accepted or understood by the society.

There are various ways in which power may be legitimized and stability achieved: through personal confidence in the qualities of a charismatic leader; through the traditionalism which emanates over a long period of time from a system larger than any individual and faithful to "original principles"—what Max Weber called "the authority of the eternal yesterday"; and through belief in the validity of legal statute and functional competence based on rationally created rules.[1]

[1] See H. H. Gerth and C. Wright Mills, eds.: *From Max Weber: Essays in Sociology* (New

The sources of legitimacy in political society may be hereditary, aristo-cratic, democratic, elective, or a combination thereof. Significantly, legitimacy in the English colonies inhered increasingly in democratic and elective sources, rather than in hereditary and titled origins. Nevertheless, the colonists recognized this reality with great reluctance because it signaled a serious departure from traditional European standards. In consequence, a considerable number of colonial governments and institutions achieved a condition of only quasi-legitimacy. They were necessary in order to prevent anarchy, and they were able to gain sufficiently wide acceptance so as not to be obliged to rely exclusively upon deception, corruption, and physical constraint; yet their acceptance was incomplete, grudging, and accompanied by mistrust. The reasons run deep in the American colonial experience, and were present from the outset.

Many of the seventeenth-century settlers found themselves living beyond the reach of sanctioned government, without charters or with patents of questionable validity. The Pilgrims held tenaciously but tenuously to their rock at Plymouth for three generations, unable to obtain a patent from the Crown; in 1692 they were absorbed by the Bay Colony. Connecticut and Rhode Island anxiously sought valid and valued charters, sending John Winthrop, Jr., and Roger Williams, their best men, repeatedly to London for that purpose. Even the patriarchal Puritan statesman, John Winthrop of Massachusetts, declared in 1635 that "we should do nothing hereafter but by commission out of England."[2] During the final quarter of the seventeenth century, a number of the early colonial charters—joint-stock as well as proprietary—came under attack by officials in London and were interpreted in contradictory ways. These challenges to the legitimacy of government in New England, New Jersey, Pennsylvania, Maryland, and Bermuda created and exacerbated severe political tensions. . . .

Because the nations of western Europe had conflicting claims in the New World, colonial boundaries and territorial hegemony were often unclear. Witness the conflicts between Dutch and English over lands between the Hudson and Connecticut rivers. Pioneers of each nationality commonly charged their enemies with settling beyond the sanctions of clear title. In part, such moralistic-legalistic utterances served to assuage the colonizers' anxieties about visible lawlessness within their own precincts, or to disguise the disintegration of local governmental authority.

In early seventeenth-century England, the legal system stood in desperate need of rationalization and reform. The complexities and confusion of English law were transported to the colonies, however, ineluctably blurring even further the dimensions of legitimacy abroad. In addition, the Puritans of New

---

York, 1958), 78–9, 294–5; Guglielmo Ferrero: *The Principles of Power* (New York, 1942); Robert A. Kann: *The Problem of Restoration: A Study in Comparative Political History* (Berkeley, 1968), 46–54.

[2] William Bradford: *Of Plymouth Plantation, 1620–1647*, ed. Samuel Eliot Morison (New York, 1952), 75; James K. Hosmer, ed.: *Winthrop's Journal, History of New England, 1630–1649* (New York, 1908), I, 164.

England were charged with building a body of private, nonconstitutional law of their own—a code of laws out of line with English standards. Since no other seventeenth-century colony had so complete a compilation of law as Massachusetts, law was clearly a greater source of ambiguity than of well-defined orthodoxy. Common law simply could not function in the colonies in the same way it did in England. There were no trained lawyers, little attention to previous case law, and written judicial opinions virtually did not exist.[3]

Just as English lawyers had Sir Edward Coke's *Institutes of the Laws of England*, English Puritans had the *Institutes* of John Calvin. But European institutes were inadequate sources of intellectual legitimacy in the New World. The emphasis in American Puritanism upon an elaborate structure of covenants—between God and man, man and man, God and his chosen community of saints—indicates a form of ecclesiastical constitutionalism, or legalism, symptomatic of a quest for spiritual legitimacy. Having challenged the sanctity and propriety of the Church of England, New England's elect were doubly obliged to establish canons of orthodoxy. In this context, the Half-Way Covenant of 1662 constituted a crisis of legitimacy in which elders, ministers, and churches were accused of being "irregular, illegal, & disorderly." Hence the periodic need of New England Congregationalists to convene synods, even though they smelled suspiciously Presbyterian. And all too often in all the colonies there were congregations without regular clergymen at all— "sheep without a shepherd," the Mennonites called themselves in the 1680's. "Since they had no preacher, they endeavored to admonish one another."[4]

Most of the public institutions which developed in the seventeenth-century colonies underwent this quest for integrity and recognition. The early assemblies, for example, existed on sufferance in many cases: Virginia's burgesses went unrecognized by the Crown from 1619 until 1639. The complex system of great and small burgher rights in New Netherland was designed to provide social legitimacy for the most important magistrates, officers, and ministers. Massachusetts Bay established Harvard College strictly on its own authority; therefore, whenever the colony's constitutional identity came under attack, Harvard's legal status fell into jeopardy as well. When the Bay Colony lost its charter in 1684, it was assumed that Harvard's charter of 1650 was also null and void. The failure of towns to develop in the Chesapeake colonies indicated to many—who judged by Old World standards—a lack of social legitimacy. Men associated towns with the presence of social control and good order. Cities would supposedly facilitate "good Discipline and careful tending . . . under faithful Teachers and Magistrates."

In 1689, when the constitutional kettle boiled to rebellion in many colonies, both the established governments *and* the insurrectionists seemed to

---

[3] See Mark DeWolfe Howe: "The Sources and Nature of Law in Colonial Massachusetts," in *Law and Authority in Colonial America*, ed. George A. Billias (Barre, 1965), 11, 14; Davis H. Flaherty, ed.: *Essays in the History of Early American Law* (Chapel Hill, 1969), esp. chs. 2 and 3.
[4] H. Shelton Smith, et al., eds.: *American Christianity. An Historical Interpretation with Representative Documents* (New York, 1960), I, 272.

lack proper credentials. Certainly the Dominion of New England, established by King James II in 1686, lacked integrity in the eyes of most New Englanders. And when word of the Glorious Revolution in Britain reached Virginia, the news precipitated widespread chatter about the illegitimacy of royal government and sparked uprisings in the Northern Neck—"saying there was neither King, Laws nor Government."[5] In such unstable societies as these were, merely the menace of governmental illegitimacy posed a danger to public order. In Maryland, men in rebellion complained that "the Lawes are soe uncertaine and unknown that the people canot stere their Course with safetie in respect of them, which is a great greevance."[6]

The provisional governments established by various groups of malcontents, however, lacked legitimacy even more visibly than their predecessors. Jacob Leisler's twenty-month régime in New York had scarcely a shred of serious claim to exercise authority there; and Gershom Bulkeley's *Will and Doom*, the most important piece of political philosophy to emerge in response to the colonial rebellions, was explicitly designed to expose the new government of Connecticut as an illegitimate usurper. "They have no shadow of any warrant from their majesties," Bulkeley insisted, "for the exercise of this government to which they now pretend."[7]

The manifold crises of legitimacy in late seventeenth-century America were crises of change. At a time when new groups were seeking access to the political process, and at a time when new social assumptions were taking shape, countervailing legitimacy could not be located in the continuity of traditional integrative institutions. For some years prior to 1689, repeated deterioration in governmental effectiveness had made the stability of legitimate systems precarious at best. In the years immediately following the rebellions, the most effective (albeit illegitimate) régimes proved to be even less stable than their predecessors. . . .

Look for a moment at the fragility of all three major instruments of government. The royal governors lacked leverage. Their tenure was insecure and their decisions might easily be reversed "at home." They suffered, as Bernard Bailyn has remarked, from "swollen claims and shrunken powers." Whether a governor's royal instructions were in fact part of the law of the land was unclear, especially after 1715 when it was decided in London that an act passed by a provincial legislature and approved by the Crown took precedence over a royal instruction.[8] Then, too, no one really knew how to define the proper role and identity of the colonial council. It was not quite

---

[5] H. R. McIlwaine, ed.: *Executive Journals of the Council of Colonial Virginia, 1680–1699* (Richmond, 1925), I, 104–7.

[6] Michael G. Hall, et al., eds.: *The Glorious Revolution in America. Documents on the Colonial Crisis of 1689* (Chapel Hill, 1964), 54–5, 180.

[7] Bulkeley: *Will and Doom, or the Miseries of Connecticut by and Under an Usurped and Arbitrary Power* (1692), in *Collections of the Connecticut Historical Society* (Hartford, 1895), III, 82, 94.

[8] Bailyn: *The Origins of American Politics* (New York, 1968), 69, 88, 96; Leonard W. Labaree, ed.: *The Autobiography of Benjamin Franklin* (New Haven, 1964), 261–2.

a cabinet, but not quite a counterpart of the House of Lords either. Because it had multiple functions, most of them were unclearly defined. And finally, the provincial assemblies' "quest for power" may be considered as simultaneously having been a quest for legitimacy as well. Endless squabbles between governors and burgesses over parliamentary privilege reveal the insecure bases on which both institutions rested.[9]

Every colonial assembly faced (or else self-consciously avoided) the difficult problem of relating the laws it passed to the legal system of Great Britain. And throughout the eighteenth century there was considerable ambiguity as to which English statutes were in effect overseas. In 1706, for example, the complex trial of the Reverend Francis Makemie threw New York into confusion over whether the penal laws of England did or did not extend to the plantations.[10]. . .

At intervals during the first half of the eighteenth century, Whitehall requested and insisted that the several colonies codify their laws and make clear digests available for use on both sides of the water. The colonies remained diffident, however, reluctant to expose their statutory deviations from the law of the realm. Finally, between 1750 and 1753 most of the colonies complied by compiling an up-to-date digest of laws in force. Only then, near the end of the colonial period, were provincial laws dignified and clarified by being given explicit public expression. In the process, however, indigenous alternatives to imperial authority were sanctified and publicized.[11]

The concept of legitimacy, and the legitimacy of law, have much to do with *who* can make, or discover, or apply the law. They also depend upon *how* the law is made, discovered, and applied, and upon the procedures which are used to bring the law into force. It is well known that the people of colonial America were a litigious lot, "on every little difference at law," as Cadwallader Colden said. Their litigiousness was a function and a symptom of the lack of clear criteria of legitimacy.[12] Characteristically, the famous Zenger case of 1735 hinged upon the validity of traditional interpretations of seditious libel; and the Morrisite faction in that affair took as its slogan "King

9 Leonard W. Labaree: *Royal Government in America. A Study of the British Colonial System* (New York, 1958), 3, 167, 192–3; *Journals of the House of Representatives of Massachusetts, 1727–1729* and *1729–31* (Boston, 1927–28), VIII, 245–436, IX, 3–80 passim; Robert Zemsky: *Merchants, Farmers, and River Gods. An Essays on Eighteenth-Century American Politics* (Boston, 1971), 69–70, 239–40.

10 St. George L. Sioussat: "The Theory of the Extension of English Statutes to the Plantations," in *Select Essays in Anglo-American Legal History* (Boston, 1907), I, 418, 420, 422, 425–6, 429; William Smith, Jr.: *The History of the Province of New-York* (London, 1757); 113, 247–9.

11 See *The Charlemagne Tower Collection of American Colonial Laws* (n.p., 1890), passim; Leonard W. Lebaree, ed.: *Royal Instructions to British Colonial Governors, 1670–1776* (New York, 1935), I, 166–7.

12 There was considerable litigiousness in England and France, too, during the seventeenth and eighteenth centuries, in part a surrogate for the personal violence by which so many disputes were settled previously. In a sense, right replaced might as the criterion of legitimacy. What made colonial litigiousness special in this context was their unwillingness to accept adjudication as binding. Again and again the colonists ignored court decisions, or appealed them interminably.

George, Liberty, and Law." Authors of *The Independent Reflector*, an opposition weekly in New York in 1752–3, remarked upon the failure of magistrates to execute their public duties and enforce the laws. "Can it be presumed, that Persons sworn to execute the Laws, should openly counteract and violate them?"[13]

In addition to the laws and their manner of enforcement, other regulations and reagents of human relationships also functioned in ways regarded as queer and unacceptable by European measures of judgment. The great problem with paper currency and banks of credit in colonial America was their apparent lack of legitimacy. The early American obsession with land titles and with surveying reveals their desperate concern with legitimizing property holdings and provincial boundaries. "We have, from the beginning," wrote an eighteenth-century historian, "been exposed to controversies about limits." Both the substantive and symbolic significance of boundaries in early America have been grossly neglected by modern historians. The quest for accurate boundaries—between New York and New Jersey, Massachusetts and New Hampshire, New Hampshire and New York, New York and Connecticut, Massachusetts and Rhode Island—was part and parcel of the quest for social and cultural norms and for stable political institutions. Accepted boundaries provide territorial hegemony at the least and geo-political legitimacy at best. Once the seventeenth century's sense of boundlessness has passed, men became deeply involved in the search for determinative land settlements. Thus Dr. William Douglass devoted the first chapter of his *Summary . . . and Present State of the Settlements* to a discussion of Anglo-French boundaries, and later passages to problems of provincial territoriality. Governor Thomas Hutchinson happened to write his *History of Massachusetts-Bay* because of work he did earlier on boundary commissions. William Byrd II wrote a classic essay, "The History of the Dividing Line," as a result of surveying the boundary between Virginia and North Carolina. Charles Mason and Jeremiah Dixon have been immortalized in American history because they spent the years from 1763 until 1768 demarcating the long-disputed border between Pennsylvania, Maryland, and Delaware.[14] Although Americans have usually cared more about saving face than space, they have been passionately concerned about the destiny and domination of space. Never more so than in the eighteenth century.

---

[13] *Collections of the New-York Historical Society for the Year 1869*, 208; James Alexander: *A Brief Narrative of the Case and Trial of John Peter Zenger*, ed. Stanley N. Katz (Cambridge, Mass., 1963), 7, 26, 28, 33, 53, 82; William Livingston, et al.: *The Independent Reflector, or, Weekly Essays on Sundry Important Subjects More Particularly Adopted to the Province of New-York* [1753], ed. Milton M. Klein (Cambridge, Mass., 1963), 59, 85, 115–16, 148, 185–6, 195–7, 266–7.

[14] Smith: *History of the Province of New-York*, 186; Douglass: *Summary, Historical and Political . . . and Present State of the British Settlements in North America*, I, ch. 1, and 398–404, 415–19, 421–5; Byrd: "The History of the Dividing Line," in *The Prose Works of William Byrd of Westover*, ed. Louis B. Wright (Cambridge, Mass., 1966), 157–336; A. Hughlett Mason, ed.: *The Journal of Charles Mason and Jeremiah Dixon*, in *Memoirs of the American Philosophical Society* (Philadelphia, 1969), LXXVI.

If we turn our attention to the social institutions and assumptions of provincial America, we find that comparable conditions obtained. Although all of the colonies but three had established churches, they were not very securely established by European standards, and their legitimacy was therefore suspect. The recurrent episcopacy question in the eighteenth-century colonies —involving the Anglican quest for an American bishop—was profoundly symptomatic of the problem. In the absence of an American bishop, the Bishop of London had the colonies as part of his jurisdiction; but the nature and extent of his supervision remained unclear in practice, and ambiguous even in theory. A significant number of colonial religious groups looked to their European hierarchies as ultimate sources of authority. This was especially true of the Anglicans and Roman Catholics. The Dutch Reformed Church so relied upon the Classis of Amsterdam to supply colonial clergy that the Classis became accepted as the only source of legitimate ministerial authority. That assumption remained unchallenged until 1737, and operative until 1791 when the Dutch Reformed group in America finally asserted its independence.[15]

Clearly, there must have been for many denominations an awkward dichotomy between the formal locus of legitimate religious authority and the immediacy of religious truth as each sect saw it. During the eighteenth century, dissenting groups in the southern colonies engaged in a long and arduous struggle to obtain an acceptable status in public law. Indeed, this issue was really the prime secular ingredient in the southern variant of the Great Awakening. In the middle colonies and in New England, Old Lights leveled the accusation at New Lights that they lacked theological legitimacy, and that they fostered "Disorders and Errors." New Lights, in their turn, accused the Old of lacking spiritual legitimacy: that was the great danger of an "unconverted ministry." Today we expect a psychoanalyst to have undergone analysis himself; in those days devout men expected their ministers to be converted.[16]

Understandably, matters of self-image and social legitimacy were especially complex in colonial times. "In order to secure my Credit and Character as a Tradesman, I took care not only to be in *Reality* Industrious and frugal, but to avoid all *Appearances* of the Contrary." So wrote Benjamin Franklin in his *Autobiography*.[17] Certainly, there is something very American about Franklin's emphasis upon industriousness and self-help; but most of all it is his quest for personal legitimacy—the attempt to make appearance and reality coincide—that rings true. Over the years England had dumped some of her most lawless inhabitants into the plantations. Not without cause were respectable Americans anxious to overcome the common view that most early colonists had been criminals. Even so, many servants had indeed ar-

15 John P. Luidens: "The Americanization of the Dutch Reformed Church" (unpublished Ph.D. dissertation, University of Oklahoma, 1969), 40, 47, 118–19, 122, 321.
16 See Smith, *et al.*, eds.: *American Christianity . . . Representative Documents*, I, 262–3.
17 Labaree, ed.: *Autobiography*, 125–6.

rived in the seventeenth-century settlements without written indentures, thereby creating a serious problem of ambiguous legal and social identities. Eventually, each colony had to develop some standard, known as the "custom of the country," in order to specify the length of time which servants arriving without indenture should serve. Sooner or later this "custom" became statutory law.[18] The momentum ran from expedience to acceptance to perpetuation.

The inevitable inflation of statuses in the colonies contributed to the quirkiness of social legitimacy there. In some situations, provincial governments tried to create artificial class distinctions by fiat, and in others they tried sumptuary laws. Governor Bernard of Massachusetts even proposed the establishment of an American nobility. None of these devices worked, of course; and as customary patterns of deference began to break down after 1740, the last real bulwark of traditional hierarchy crumbled. In consequence, the social order from mid-eighteenth to mid-nineteenth century was extremely fluid. Many Americans learned acceptable behavior from etiquette books, and symbols of status became important because they helped to make apparent the otherwise invisible ligaments of social order. Similarly, ceremonial and pageantry were important in the colonies in order to inform the populace that this office and that holiday were invested with special cachet. Hence the need for trumpets and cannons, or reading commissions aloud in public assemblies.

Europeans living primitively in the New World recognized that they faced a problem of maintaining traditional standards of "civilization." But with the passage of time it became difficult to determine just what the minimal or suitable standards were. For many, the lowest measure of civility became the American Indian. Colonists castigated one another with the admonition that they might sink to the barbaric level of the heathen. Positive criteria of social excellence and achievement, however, were much more difficult to ascertain. Eventually, and happily, personal qualities of merit became for many the critical test. "There is, perhaps, not a more dangerous Error, than to believe that we are bound to reverence Men for the Offices they sustain, without any Regard to their virtuous Qualities, or useful Actions." So wrote William Livingston in 1753. "So in civil Life, nothing occurs more frequently, than to see an eminent Knave demanding the popular Esteem on Account of his Elevation. This ridiculous Respect paid to Men of superior Rank, without any Regard to their moral Character, is the Source of the most pernicious Consequences."[19]

Then too, the problem of social legitimacy in the colonies came down to the most literal levels, such as marriage and the family. In the seventeenth century, owing to the paucity of ministers, there were an extraordinary number of common law marriages—possibly more proportionately than in England. In consequence, some colonies passed legislation designed to legitimize

[18] Abbot E. Smith: *Colonists in Bondage. White Servitude and Convict Labor in America, 1607–1776* (Chapel Hill, 1947), 19, 226–7, 229, 285–7.
[19] Livingston, *et al.*: *The Independent Reflector*, 360, 363.

retroactively common law marriages entered into during unsettled periods. In the Fundamental Constitutions of Carolina, first drafted in 1669, care was taken that "the Chamberlain's Court . . . shall have the care of all Ceremonies, Precedency, Heraldry . . . and Pedigrees; the Registries of all Births, Burials, and Marriages; legitimization and all cases concerning Matrimony or arising from it." All through the eighteenth century, clandestine and common law marriages remained commonplace despite the attendant ambiguities about the children of such relationships. Moreover, many believed that the religious enthusiasm of the Great Awakening had the unfortunate effect of stimulating unholy hormones. The Anglican Timothy Cutler called the Awakening a time when "our presses are forever teeming with books and our women with bastards." Cutler most likely was wrong about the erotic effects of enthusiasm, but merely the *belief* in rising illegitimacy caused social and psychological repercussions in colonial society.[20]. . .

Insecure people are quickest to find fault with others. Given the various crises of legitimacy in English America, therefore, and given the inevitable quest for constitutional, institutional, and social integrity, it is not surprising that colonists seized eagerly upon opportunities to challenge the rightfulness of Britain's dominion. They did so in a limited way in 1689, and would do so again more fully between 1765 and 1776. The prelude to the American Revolution first involved rejection of Parliament as an imperial legislative body, and ultimately even the moral legitimacy of the Crown. Until 1774, colonists tried to distinguish between legitimate powers of Parliament and those of the provincial assemblies. When Parliament denied the validity of such distinctions, the ideological crisis passed beyond the point of no return. Quite logically, the question of sovereignty became a vital issue of the American Revolution, for sovereignty is a critical quality of constitutional legitimacy. . . .

The quest for legitimacy in early America was complicated by the presence of a kind of multi-dimensional pluralism. Adapting the phrase of Ortega y Gasset, I find it useful to envision the colonies, particularly in the period 1660–1760, as invertebrate America: "a series of water-tight compartments," none of which felt very much "curiosity toward events in the domain of the others." Taken together, the plantations lacked a figurative spinal column. All too easily they slipped in and out of relation to one another because they were not firmly connected. They had not yet achieved the kind of collective individualism whose motto would be struck by Theodore Parker in 1848: "You are as good as I, and let us help one another."[21]

English colonial society, almost from the outset, underwent both a remarkable degree of "horizontal" or simultaneous pluralism (prodigious clus-

---

20 James H. Cassedy: *Demography in Early America. Beginnings of the Statistical Mind, 1600–1800* (Cambridge, Mass., 1969), 53, 57, 97n, 151–2, 155; Smith: *History of the Province of New-York*, 228; Labaree, ed.: *Autobiography of Benjamin Franklin*, 129–30.
21 Parker: "The Political Destination of America and the Signs of the Times," in *The Transcendentalists*, ed. Perry Miller (Garden City, 1957), 357.

ters of private groups, factionalism, a fairly complex governmental apparatus) and of "vertical" or sequential pluralism. By the latter I mean simply the recurring nature of the transplantation experience, the repeated shocks to social relationships as wave after wave of swirling groups washed up along the eastern shores. Add the fact that many who came had already led disordered lives in Europe, and then note that the vastness of available space provided yet another major stimulus to heterogeneity in America. It has always been easier to deviate from canons of orthodoxy in this country, both because the canons have been so unclear and uncodified, and because people who thought "otherwise," like Roger Williams or Brigham Young, could go "elsewhere" and do so with impunity. Each sort of pluralism—the simultaneous and the sequential—intensified and reinforced the other, as new people from unstable situations added their uneasy presence to the fluidity of colonial society, and thereby made it even more so.

The depth and breadth of pluralism in America's experience have had many sources. Certainly, and unparadoxically, economic individualism has been a contributory factor, as well as the commitment (intermittently fulfilled) to uphold the dignity of individual persons and groups. Material opportunity has pushed sons toward an early independence, and disrupted the vocational and locational continuities of traditional European families. American fathers have held great expectations for their sons (and sometimes daughters), have wanted them to "do better than I did." Moreover, instability is especially likely to occur in a heterogeneous society where rapid change or improvement occurs in one sphere—in wealth, for example—without equally rapid change in other spheres, such as services, status, freedom, and power. . . .

I am most comfortable with an ordinary-language definition in which "plural society" connotes a polity containing distinct cleavages amongst diverse population groups. Often there will be a dispersion of power among groups bound together by cross-cutting loyalties, common values, and a competitive equilibrium or balance of power. Equally often there will be conflict between racial, tribal, religious, and regional groups, to such a degree that the whole must be maintained by regulation and force. Because of the role of authority in any system of domination, there is commonly a psychological pressure upon subordinate cultural segments to deny legitimacy to the imposed order, and to reject law and authority as such. Finally, I think it is particularly important to note that pluralism in less repressive societies has a built-in dynamic toward uncontrolled change. Certainly that has been true in the United States.

From the very beginning of American history, one might argue, our governmental and cultural impulses have been in the direction of uniformity and away from multiplicity. Yet our economic and social imperatives—the labor shortage, military requirements, and recruitment patterns for colonization—as well as geographical expanse, have all fostered pluralism. But why has pluralism been any more of a factor in the North American colonies than in many other settings? The answer, I think, is that ours has been *unstable* pluralism, and that the adjective here makes quite a difference. So many of the immigrants to the colonies came for anti-authoritarian reasons, came with hostilities against restraint already well formed. Moreover, plural societies gain in stability where major political parties cut across ethnic lines. Such has been the case in nineteenth- and twentieth-century America, where the history of party is remarkable for continuity and longevity. But such was not the case in colonial America, where there were Quaker parties, German parties, Presbyterian parties—where each group might have its own faction, each sect its own school, each dogmatist his own ideology.

Therefore, I must insist upon the fragile condition of unstable pluralism as being critical to an understanding of early, especially eighteenth-century, America. . . .

Nonetheless, despite the eighteenth-century emphasis of this phenomenon, we ought to begin with some notion of earliest origins and anticipations. For the facts are that while Massachusetts, Connecticut, Virginia, and perhaps South Carolina were founded on the premise of stable homogeneity, and while Rhode Island, New York, New Jersey, Pennsylvania, Maryland, and Georgia were established with the expectation of stable heterogeneity, both sets of assumptions failed to be fulfilled.

The congregational churches of New England were to have enjoyed a kind of co-operative autonomy, an ecclesiastical polity of plural equilibrium. Serious doctrinal differences and dissension, however, emerged with effervescence by the 1640's, and synods were required irregularly for decades thereafter in order to prevent the full fragmentation of New England's orthodoxy. The Puritans of Massachusetts, moreover, as well as Quaker and German sectarians scattered elsewhere, acquired a state of mind and underwent a social process known as "tribalism." In becoming so exclusive and withdrawn, they were demonstrating one kind of defense mechanism against an unexpectedly plural society. They coped by refusing to cope, by abandoning all sense of mission save the salvation of their very own kind.

Ambiguities about the legitimacy of religious diversity in New Netherland were abundantly present from the very beginning. Dutch Reformed dominies insisted that the preservation of social stability required the strict enforcement of laws regulating religious practices. An orderly polity required religious orthodoxy and uniformity. Officials of the West India Company, however, took the side of Amsterdam's merchant aristocracy and supported *de facto* toleration. The Reverend John Megapolensis complained of "these godless rascals . . . Papists, Mennonites and Lutherans among the Dutch; also many Puritans or Independents, and many Atheists and various other servants of Baal among the English under this Government, who conceal themselves under the name of Christians; it would create a still greater confusion, if the obstinate and immovable Jews came to settle here.". . .

In the colony of East Jersey, developed a decade after this correspondence, the same imperatives obtained, with comparable results: Quakers and anti-Quakers, Scottish Quakers and Scottish Presbyterians, Puritans from

Long Island in Elizabethtown, Puritans from New Hampshire in Piscataway, Dutch Calvinists in Bergen, Baptists and Quakers in Middletown and Navesink—a cacophony of discordant sectarians.

Sectarianism. The word should carry a heavy freight of import, and yet it has been strangely neglected by American cultural historians. We have long assumed that denominationalism is America's peculiar contribution to the history of religion, and that there is continuity in the configuration of American denominations from the colonial to the national period. I would like to suggest instead that sectarianism preceded denominationalism in American history, and that the differences are significant.

If I may be forgiven for defining what is Christ's in terms of what is Caesar's, a sect is to a political faction as a denomination is to a party. Sects and factions tend to be unstable and impermanent, they lack the longevity, institutional apparatus, and coalition qualities of denominations and parties. Sects fluctuate, fragment, and feud among themselves. George Keith, the great Quaker controversialist of the 1690's, became an Anglican priest in 1702, while other erstwhile Keithian Quakers became Baptists. Francis Daniel Pastorius, the prominent Lutheran pietist, became a Quaker; and Count Zinzendorf, the German evangelical leader in Pennsylvania, was oft-criticized for constantly shifting his sectarian affiliation. Francis Makemie almost achieved martyrdom in fighting for Presbyterian liberties after 1700, yet he hated the Quakers who were waging the self-same struggle.[22]

Paradoxically, as one student has remarked, "the New World vision of the group and of group society entails an affirmation rather than a negation of individualism." America's pluralistic experience owes much to the enthusiastic and expansive drives of effulgent colonial communities. Inevitably, of course, pluralistic individualism would lead to sectarian cooperation, and ultimately to the stability of institutionalized denominationalism.[23] But not until after the Great Awakening had irrevocably shattered the remaining coherence of colonial Christendom. The religious revival was explicitly opposed as a threat to social and political stability. Connecticut's government claimed that revivals had a "natural tendency to disturb and destroy the peace and order" of the colony; and in 1743 the *Boston Evening Post* looked upon them as "the grand Engine of fomenting Divisions, and making Separations in our Churches." In New York the Awakening merely aggravated a condition of unstable pluralism long since out of control. . . .

The sources, processes, and expressions of cultural pluralism all contributed to the creative variability of colonial life. Even New England, the most homogeneous of regions, received Huguenots by the 1680's, Irish after 1708, and significant numbers of non-English immigrants by the 1720's. By

---

[22] See H. Shelton Smith, et al., eds.: *American Christianity. An Historical Interpretation with Representative Documents, 1607–1820* (New York, 1960), I, 252–3, 285, 296–7.
[23] Darryl Baskin: "The Congregationalist Origins of American Pluralism," *Journal of Church and State*, XI (1969), 278, 280; Leonard W. Labaree, ed.: *The Autobiography of Benjamin Franklin* (New Haven, 1964), 194.

the 1690's, immigrants could no longer be easily absorbed by Puritan society; between 1690 and 1740, sharp class differences and hostility emerged between established families and newcomers. Moreover, whereas British naturalization laws were designed to *minimize* immigration, protect the hegemony of the Church of England, and avert threats to political stability at home, colonial naturalization laws were intended to *encourage* immigration. Their permissiveness was an invitation to unstable pluralism: their openness to foreign Protestants, relatively liberal (albeit limited) welcome to Jews, growing acceptance of Roman Catholics, absence of religious rites, simpler procedures, and lower costs were all symptomatic and stimulating.[24]

Similarly, the proliferation of provincial newspapers after the 1720's was both a response to and a generator of unstable pluralism. They reprinted news from abroad as well as from other colonies, and thereby provided the beginnings of a more unified outlook. At the same time, however, newspapers were organs of factionalism and sectarianism, parochial, petty, and vituperative in their unsettling attacks. The famous case and trial of John Peter Zenger in 1734–5 arose from precisely these origins; and Zenger's canny lawyer, Andrew Hamilton, invoked a new kind of legal relativism appropriate to the circumstances of plural societies: "What is good law at one time and in one place," he contended, "is not so at another time and in another place."[25]

By the 1720's and 1730's there were also demographic changes which intensified mobility and contributed to change. People achieved physical maturity at a younger age, established economic independence and married earlier, were divorced more easily, and left their communities of origin with greater frequency.[26] Because of economic growth and social diversity, the eighteenth-century colonies became less egalitarian and more stratified than the seventeenth had been. And when men moved, they moved to and through a plurality of ever-changing frontiers surrounding discrete and discontinuous areas of settlement.[27]

Because stability of any sort, homogeneous or heterogeneous, was so elusive to find and tenuous to keep, the settlers' public rhetoric played incessantly on themes of union and unity. "Union is the source of public happiness," Jonathan Mayhew insisted; "unity must subside and then it's plain what will follow," fumed the selectmen of Worcester, Massachusetts.

24 Clifford K. Shipton: "Immigration to New England, 1680–1740," *Journal of Political Economy*, XLIV (1936), 225–39; Edward A. Hoyt: "Naturalization Under the American Colonies," *Political Science Quarterly*, LXVII (1952), 248–66.
25 James Alexander: *A Brief Narrative of the Case and Trial of John Peter Zenger, Printer of the New York Weekly Journal*, ed. Stanley N. Katz (Cambridge, Mass., 1963), 67–8.
26 Greven: *Four Generations*, 272–3; Lockridge: *A New England Town*, 172–3; Cadwallader Colden to Alexander Colden, June 15, 1759, *Collections of the New-York Historical Society for the Year 1868* (New York, 1868), 187.
27 James A. Henretta: "Economic Development and Social Structure in Colonial Boston," *William and Mary Quarterly*, 3d series, XXII (1965), 75–92; James T. Lemon and Gary B. Nash: "The Distribution of Wealth in 18th-Century America: A Century of Change in Chester County, Pennsylvania, 1693–1802," *Journal of Social History*, II (1968), 1–24; Fulmer Mood: "Studies in the History of American Settled Areas and Frontier Lines, 1625–1790," *Agricultural History*, XXVI (1952), 16–34.

"Our Ennemies never fail to take advantage of intestine divisions & confusion," wrote Cadwallader Colden in 1759, and the purpose of his exhortatory plea was clear.[28]

. It had been equally manifest ever since the first generation that intercolonial co-operation was ephemeral at best and nonexistent at worst. Material and religious differences kept the colonies at loggerheads except during moments of mutual crisis. Even then, conflicting interests and factions within each colony made joint military action difficult. In the eighteenth century, Virginia and Pennsylvania were at odds over trade rights in the Ohio Valley; Pennsylvania and New York over the Lake Erie trade; almost all of the colonies over boundary disputes, claims to western lands, and proper Indian policies. The Albany Congress, called in 1754 to organize a united front, ended in bickering and dissension. . . .

For nearly a century, English officials had been bothered by the diversity, untidiness, and instability they saw in colonial life, laws, and polities. Again and again abortive efforts were made to impose uniformity. Hence the Dominion of New England, the sporadic revocation of colonial charters, repeated requests for codification of colonial laws, resentment of provincial paper currencies, parliamentary passage of the Naturalization Act of 1740, creation of the entire navigation system, and the administrative reforms which came in 1764–5 and caused so much trouble. Hence one imperial official's denunciation in 1752 of the "false Policy, that calls Factions and Parties, and Checks, and independent Interests, and such Stuff Constitutional." Hence Thomas Hutchinson's lament in 1767 that "we shall never be all of one mind in our political principles." Hence Daniel Leonard, the polemical opponent of John Adams, wrote in 1775 that "the provincial constitutions, considered as subordinate, are generally well adapted to those purposes of government, for which they were intended, that is, to regulate the internal police of the several colonies; but [they] *have no principle of stability within themselves.*"[29]. . .

We might well pause for a moment in order to reflect upon some interconnections between the quest for legitimacy and the problem of unstable pluralism. It has been strategically useful, I think, to isolate both and examine them *in vacuo*. Nevertheless, they must historically have had a synergistic relationship—the mutual action of agents which, when taken together, increase each other's effectiveness.

A congruence of legitimacy and stability is basic to the life of any sound political society. Stability will be more easily achieved where members of a community, large or small, approve of the institutional arrangements

---

[28] Michael Zuckerman: *Peaceable Kingdoms. New England Towns in the Eighteenth Century* (New York, 1970), 67; Colden to Alexander Colden, July 5, 1759, in William Smith, Jr.: *The History of the Province of New-York*, ed. Michael Kammen (Cambridge, Mass., 1972), I, 295.

[29] Thomas Pownall: *Principles of Polity, being the Grounds and Reasons of Civil Empire* (London, 1752), 37; Hutchinson: *The History of the Colony and Province of Massachusetts-Bay*, ed. L. S. Mayo (London, 1764).

which determine their lives. A government will be more viable if its pattern of authority dovetails with the other, parallel patterns in the society of which it is a part. Where there is uncertainty about norms and forms of legitimacy, various options are opened which encourage or aggravate unstable pluralism. . . .

The concept of liberty is felt less urgently in a homogeneous society where the values of the individual are predominantly those of the social order also. Freedom becomes a cherished ideal, however, in a complex society where the individual may hold conflicting values derived from various sources.

In colonial America, the spiritual communities—"churches" in the original meaning of that word—ceased rather early to coincide with the physical communities of citizens and inhabitants. That disjunction contributed to a particularly heady sort of pluralism which undermined one of the traditional canons of legitimacy in the Old World.

Moreover, especially in the eighteenth century, a remarkable degree of geographical mobility intensified the condition of unstable pluralism, and thereby contributed to confusion about the legitimacy of provincial social structures and statuses. Physical fluidity and upward mobility tended to undermine older criteria of constitutional government, as well. Where discrete social classes were difficult to identify, assumptions about "mixed government" —their time-honored formula for the proper relationship between Estates and political power—were thrown into confusion, and eventually forced a major adjustment in American political theory.

I find it strikingly symptomatic that the colonists so often sought specific demographic data about their societies. The presence of many diverse and energetic people made it imperative to keep reasonably good vital records, as well as census and immigration information. Significantly, the leading exponents of early American demography were residents of two of the most heterogeneous colonies: Benjamin Franklin of Pennsylvania and Ezra Stiles of Rhode Island.[30]

Equally interesting is the way in which social diversity forced provincials to legitimize the formal statuses of individual immigrants on an ad hoc basis. The several settlements simply assumed the right to naturalize aliens, since none of their royal charters granted that right explicitly. The interpenetration of points of legitimacy and pluralism on this matter would cause problems in defining allegiance and national identity, and eventually lead to unpleasant forms of xenophobia. . . .

Stable pluralism requires a strong underpinning of legitimacy. A plural society is best insured by the rule of law—law made within the framework of an explicit constitution by elected representatives, executed by a partially autonomous administrative staff, and adjudicated by an independent judiciary. Insofar as all of these were created in 1787 and achieved in 1789, those dates do distinguish a genuine watershed in American history.

[30] See James H. Cassedy: Demography in Early America. Beginnings of the Statistical Mind, 1600–1800 (Cambridge, Mass., 1969), 107, 110–13, 167–8.

But stable pluralism in a democracy also requires a strong and lasting inventory of psychological legitimacy: understanding, acceptance, and pervasive confidence in the composite system necessary to make it run smoothly rather than by fits and starts. Americans continue to celebrate pluralism in the past, but are reluctant to honor it in the present. Have we fully accepted the legitimacy of pluralism? How highly do we value cultural, moral, and regional autonomy, absolute toleration, community control over education, the continued integrity of divergent groups? Partially: some of us, some of these, in some places, at some times. Our ambiguity about the implications of our own system—"the huge, unrecorded hum of implication"—ought to prompt us to look more closely than we have at the historical background of our ambivalence.

James A. Henretta

Wealth, Authority, and Power

The Evolution of the Southern Aristocracy

The presence of black slaves at the bottom of the social scale had a large, perhaps even a determinative, effect on the nature of white society. Before 1670 there had been relatively few blacks resident in the Chesapeake region, certainly not more than 5 percent of the total population, and not all of them were bound to hereditary lifetime service. From the very first, Africans had been perceived by whites as racially distinct and culturally different; but initially they had been treated in law in much the same manner as indentured servants from Europe. Then, rather suddenly, their status was completely undermined. A series of laws passed between 1667 and 1671 stated that conversion to Christianity did not relieve a black of his bondage. At the same time it became clear that Africans, and their children, served for life rather than for a specific period of years; and that color was the single defining feature of their status as slaves. By the end of the seventeenth century all of the southern American colonies had outlawed miscegenation: to be black or brown was to be a chattel slave, the personal property of one who was white and free.

Just at the time that this general debasement of blacks was taking place, the lines of class and status in white society were taking on a more coherent and a more permanent form. The high prices paid for Chesapeake tobacco during the first half-century of settlement had brought quick fortunes to those privileged colonists, many of them the younger sons of London merchants and bureaucrats, with large land grants and many indentured servants. The growing economic cleavages in Chesapeake society were accentuated by the falling price of tobacco after 1660, which struck particularly hard at the small yeoman farmers with limited capital resources, and by the attempts

Reprinted by permission of the publisher, from James A. Henretta, The Evolution of American Society, 1700–1815: An Interdisciplinary Analysis (Lexington, Mass.: D.C. Heath, 1973).

of certain leading families to appropriate control of government on the local and provincial levels.

In 1675 social discontent helped to precipitate an armed uprising led by Nathaniel Bacon, an ambitious planter of good connections and considerable means. The laws passed by Bacon's Assembly sought to limit the political power of important families on the county level by broadening the suffrage to include tenants and by creating elective posts to offset the power of appointed magistrates. Other laws, conceived and supported by the very families whose local predominance was under attack from below, attempted to combat the growing influence of the provincial council and its domination by a few families favored by the royal governor. The appointive powers of the governor were drastically limited while provincial councillors were excluded from the county courts and their tax exemptions were revoked.

Bacon's Assembly was ousted within a year, and the reform programs (especially on the local level) were as abortive as the revolt itself. Within a few decades it became generally accepted that certain established families were destined to be preeminent in wealth and power. During these same years the once-prevalent fear among the landed classes that white and black servants would rise together in rebellion gradually vanished; the fastening of a subordinate status on Africans had ensured that all white men would stand together. Subsequently, the social distance between black and white was to appear far greater than the social or economic inequalities among the classes of the white population.

The reasons for the simultaneous emergence of a caste and a class society in the Chesapeake are not completely clear, but this much is certain: In 1700, as throughout southern history, the extensive ownership of slaves and the expropriation of the produce of their labor was the prerogative of a privileged minority. There were about 3,000 slaves in Maryland at the beginning of the eighteenth century, but they were owned by only about 1,000 to 1,250 whites—less than one-fourth of the 5,000–6,000 white households in the province. The probate records in Maryland during the 1690s reveal that 75 percent of the planters whose wills were probated held property assessed at less than £100 sterling. Not only were these men too poor to own a slave or an indentured servant, but over one-third of them were landless and had to lease the very soil they worked. Shipping 1,200 to 3,000 pounds of tobacco each year (worth £6 to £15 sterling), this tarnished residue of the once-proud yeoman class scraped along at a subsistence level, often deeply in debt to the local storekeeper or moneylender.

A second distinct group in the white population was that 20 percent whose estates at probate were valued at £100 to £500 sterling. During their lifetimes most of these men had owned slaves—usually from one to five—and so had a vested interest in the perpetuation of the system. The labor of their black workers or, less often, investment in land or in a store had lifted these families above the majority of poor white planters. But social prestige and political power eluded these men as well. These honors were reserved, in the main, for the wealthiest 5 percent of the white population, the members of the 250 households who owned from a quarter to a third of all the slaves and who controlled the bulk of the wealth of the society.

During the first half of the eighteenth century the proportion of slaves in the total population increased dramatically (from 20 to 40 percent in Virginia and from 11 to 30 percent in Maryland). This development, the result of high rates of natural increase and of a significant increase in slave importation, had an important effect on the social structure of the white community. A greater proportion of whites employed slave labor. By the 1730s only 55 percent of the probated estates were assessed at less than £100 sterling, as compared to 75 percent a generation before. Nearly half of the white planters now had sufficient resources to own a slave (although not this many actually did). Even taking into account the rise in prices—which meant that £100 sterling was worth less in actual purchasing power—there had been a significant increase in the prosperity of the white population, but (interestingly enough) this general improvement had not resulted in greater equality within the white community.

Indeed, just the opposite, for the dimensions of the upper class expanded—in numbers and in wealth. In the 1690s the Great Planters of Maryland, those who at their deaths had estates worth £1,000 or more, constituted only 1.5 percent of those whose wills were probated. This proportion rose steadily: to 2.2 percent during the 1720s; to 3.6 percent during the 1730s; and to 3.9 percent of the total sample during the 1750s. The white population of Maryland had increased four-fold during these six decades, but the number of Great Planters had grown by a factor of ten. The wealth generated by the use of more slaves and the expansion of the tobacco industry had not been diffused equally among the members of the white community but had helped to create a relatively large class of wealthy planters.

Many of the members of this elite group were related by blood or marriage to those Great Planters who had established their predominance during the last quarter of the seventeenth century. The unique feature of the landed aristocracy of the Chesapeake was its ability to perpetuate its control over a society that was rapidly expanding, both in numbers and in geographic area. The total number of white households in Virginia increased from about 6,000 in 1700 to 80,000 in 1790, but economic wealth and political power resided in the hands of the same family clans at the end of this period as at the beginning. In the decades preceding the war for independence no less than 70 percent of the 110 leaders of the Virginia House of Burgesses were drawn from families resident in Virginia before 1690.

The remarkable success of the Great Planters of Virginia in preserving and extending the power of their families was the result of high rates of reproduction (which provided an ample supply of sons to take over family lands and of daughters to marry into established or rapidly rising families) and also of the system by which the resources of the family were transmitted from one generation to the next. The estate of the father did not pass to the eldest son (as among the aristocracy of eighteenth century England) leaving younger sons to find their fortunes in law, government, or the church. It was, instead, distributed among all of his male and female offspring. . . .

As these sons and daughters took up residence on the lands accumulated for them by the economic success and political acumen of their father, the family extended its influence into new localities. And this expansion more than matched the numerical and geographical growth of the colony as a whole. In the end, the weight of these established families came to press, like the atmosphere itself, evenly over the whole face of Virginia. (A similar proliferation of the upper classes had taken place in England during the sixteenth century, also during a period of rapid population growth.) Of the 100 wealthiest men in the state in 1787, all except four owned lands in at least two counties, and more than half had estates in at least four counties. There was a certain irony in this development; for the practice of partible inheritance had produced both a greater equality within the ranks of the wealthy families and a greater disparity between the resources of these clans and the rest of the population. Seven members of the Carter family, the richest of all of the clans, owned a total of 170,000 acres of land and 2,300 slaves scattered over seven different counties. They were joined, as members of the privileged one hundred, by nine members of Cocke family, eight Fitzhughs, seven Harrisons, eight Lees, seven Randolphs, and eight Washingtons.

It was this small homogeneous elite—English by descent, Anglican in religion, and linked to one another by ties of kinship and bonds of economic interest—which monopolized the political life of Virginia during the eighteenth century. There were seven members of the Lee family, all of the same generation, sitting in the Virginia assembly in the 1750s and representing five different counties. And the majority of all of the leaders of the House of Burgesses between 1720 and 1775, the men who sat on the important committees and dominated the debates, were related by blood or marriage to one or another of the dozen or so great family clans. That 60 percent of the white adult males had sufficient property to vote and that 45 percent of them regularly exercised the franchise was irrelevant given this concentration of hereditary power. In this deferential society the mass of poor white planters acquiesced in the decisions of their betters and submitted meekly to their rule. . . .

The children of the poor white planter sensed what their parents knew all too well: that they occupied an inferior place in the social hierarchy and should act accordingly. "We were accustomed to look upon, what were called *gentle folks*, as beings of a superior order," recalled the Reverend Devereux Jaratt, the son of a carpenter who eventually rose to a position of authority within the Church of England. . . . The consciousness of social inferiority, inculcated in childhood to such an extent that it induced physical fear, became an enduring part of the behavior patterns (and perhaps even the personalities) of thousands of poor whites. Wherever they went, in the town or in the fields, in public or private, these men and women carried the stigma of subordinate rank with them: in their halting speech, gnarled hands, and emaciated faces. They were deferential to those above them and—especially when emboldened by drink or by numbers—harshly demanded respect from slaves and servants, whom they could consider as their social inferiors.

A hierarchical and authoritarian pattern of personal relationships had come to characterize southern colonial society by 1700, and it persisted for more than a century and a half because the conduct it sanctioned corresponded to the actual distribution of power and influence in the community. The existence of these established role expectations, these shared experiences and assumptions, also helped to perpetuate that system. The "difference between gentle and simple" which Jaratt testified was "universal among all of my age and rank," had become part of the social environment, accepted by the inhabitants as immutable and correct. Anchored in the child-training and socialization process and solidified by the institutionalized roles of adult life, this pattern of relationships came to form an integral part of the sense of identity of thousands of adult individuals. The congruence between the social structure and the personalities of those who composed it was not exact; in this, as in any society, there was a great deal of "slippage," as the mobility achieved by Jaratt himself clearly demonstrated. And, yet, the strength and pervasiveness of these role expectations and values worked constantly to inhibit any widespread intellectual or personal challenge to the existing system. They became, in a very real sense, the social chains which bound this stratified society together. The shackles of psychological dependence and subordination had come to bind the minds of poor whites as tightly as iron chains bound the limbs of blacks.

Entrepreneurial Capitalism and Social Differentiation

It is not inequality itself, but its extent and the mode of its institutionalization, that differentiates one society from another. In the northern colonies women were placed in a position legally, socially, and economically inferior to men. The male population itself was divided by age, abilities, and accomplishments. Yet the spectrum of wealth and power in the agricultural sector of the North was much narrower than in the South and the hierarchy of social prestige was not based on the ownership of other men and women. The relative parity among the rural inhabitants of Pennsylvania, Benjamin Franklin suggested in 1759, arose

first from a more equal distribution of land by the assemblies . . . and secondly, from the nature of their occupation; husbandmen with small tracts of land, though they may by industry maintain themselves and families in mediocrity, [have] few means of acquiring great wealth. . . .

"The hopes of having land of their own and becoming independent of Landlords," observed another writer, "is what chiefly induces people into America." This commitment to independence as a prime social value had an important effect on the political life of the local community. Only those who were not dependent on others—in practical terms, those who controlled property—could hope to have a voice in the affairs of the town. This sharp line of demarcation excluded all married women, whose real and personal possessions belonged to their husbands. It also severely restricted the rights of children and of servants, who were the dependents of the male parent in the household in which they lived and worked.

During the seventh century the institution of bonded servitude had functioned as a means of introducing children into adult society, training them for their life's work on the farms or in the shops of others, or exposing them to good manners (and a steady diet) in the homes of the well-to-do. The system of indenture also served as a means of providing employment for adult immigrants who did not have resources sufficient to support themselves. In either case, bonded servitude was a step on the bottom of the social or agricultural ladder. . . .

By the middle of the eighteenth century the system of indentured servitude was breaking down as a method of social control. The family unit was unable to assimilate or control the culturally distinct groups which now composed the servant class. Moreover, in the large colonial cities, the majority of the dependent white population was no longer encompassed within the bounds of family government. In Boston in 1771, 29 percent of the adult male population were neither property owners nor the dependents of taxpaying members of the community.

These propertyless men, mostly laborers, seamen, or journeymen artisans who bargained their services for wages, introduced an element of instability into the bottom of the urban social order. Apart from the economic sanctions exercised by employers during the hours of work, there was no institutional method for controlling the activities of these men and their families, many of whom moved from town to town in search of economic subsistence. Of the 188 propertyless men resident in Boston in 1687, only 64 (or 35 percent) were resident in the town eight years later. This rate of persistence was less than half of that of the wealthiest portion of the population, those who were tied to the community by bonds of kinship and of economic investment. A century later the relationship between occupational status and permanence of residence was much the same; of the 546 proletarians in Boston in 1780 only 228 (or 42 percent) remained a decade later.

Given the differing material condition and life style of this floating population of workers, an increase in social disorder was only to be expected. Until the agitation against British rule gave an ideological edge to the anti-authoritarian and unruly activities of this lumpenproletariat, most of its violent energies were directed at other members of the class or against the black population. . . .

The members of this turbulent section of the population were not, as a rule, master mechanics or master craftsmen with established businesses or even the less affluent but stable and respected workingmen who were members of the dozens of private clubs and societies which had appeared among the urban lower classes. They were, rather, the drifters, the undesirables, the part-time workers, the unfortunate men who lacked the family background or class advantages or individual psychological resources to compete success-fully in the harsh and impersonal world of a market economy. To survive, prosper, and thrive in a system based on commercial exchange demanded a very different set of moral and mental attitudes from those required in a culture founded on personal dependence. Life in a contractual society necessi-tated more calculating behavior than that in a community divided along the lines of inherited or ascribed status; sociability was suddenly less important than self-reliance. The way was open here for a man of great ambition and exceptional abilities to rise in his own lifetime to a position of great wealth. And yet, both individual initiative and the opportunity to exploit it were socially determined; the same opportunities were simply not open to all men.

The career of Thomas Hancock was a prime example of the cumulative advantages bestowed by social class and childhood training. Born in Lexington, Massachusetts, in 1703, Hancock was the third son of a Congregationalist minister. Although his two older brothers had been sent to Harvard, Thomas was apprenticed at the age of fourteen to a bookseller. This was a relatively humble, but not an insignificant, beginning. His father's status and educa-tional background had given the young man expectations and aspirations which went far beyond those of most children in the community. The acci-dent of birth gave him greater opportunities as well. . . . After setting up his own business at the end of his seven-year indenture, he made a "good" marriage to the daughter of an established dealer in books and general merchandise.

The solid advantages bestowed by his class background explain only a part of Hancock's subsequent career. The traits of character fashioned during his childhood and young adult years also played a crucial role. He did not—indeed could not—rest content as an ordinary shopkeeper; his ambition was too strong, always prompting him to expand and to diversify his activities. Within a few years he was trading molasses for fish in Newfoundland; importing Dutch tea through St. Eustatius in the West Indies; working on a commission basis for English merchants with interests in Boston; investing in trading ventures; and accumulating his own fleet of merchant ships. Only in 1737, when his fortune was well established, did Hancock pause to erect a testimonial to his success in the form of a mansion on Beacon Hill.

The acquisitive mentality and the capitalistic activities which raised Hancock far above his already substantial origins were, to some extent, merely the latest manifestation of an ethos characteristic of the commercial classes in European society for hundreds of years. The only unique feature of the ap-pearance of these values in America was in the extent of their influence and in the relative absence of a countervailing (if not predominant) ethic of aristocratic leisure and gentility. "The only principle of life propagated among the young people is to get money," Cadwallader Colden reported from New

York in 1748, "and men are only esteemed according to what they are worth—that is, the money they are possessed of.". . .

The existence of these values and these patterns of behavior had a profound meaning. They hinted at the existence, on an extensive scale, of a new type of modal personality in the northern areas of colonial America. This was the dynamic character structure of the rational entrepreneur, an individual who is at once intensely ambitious, compulsively motivated, and yet cautious and calculating in his business activities.

The roots of this personality structure extended backward to an earlier phase of American (and English) history, to the religious upheavals in the mother country which, during the seventeenth century, led to the migration of dissenting Protestants to the new world. There was, in the communities formed in the American wilderness, a strange blend of old and new ideas, values, and institutions—an accurate reflection of the fact that Puritanism itself represented a key transitional phase in the long and slow evolution from a traditional to a modern conception of life, authority, and personality.

Initially, the transplantation of Puritanism to American soil accentuated the more traditional and conservative elements of this complex and contradictory social movement. In the small isolated agricultural settlements of seventeenth century New England, the father stood at the head of the family, exacting obedience from all those dependent on him; the village leaders, men dignified by age and experience, filled the offices of government and dominated political affairs; the minister directed the spiritual lives of his congregation, arranging their seating in church to reflect before God their standing among men. The pattern of authority and the institutions that gave it expression were one and the same. The key to the Puritan character as it developed in this environment "can be found in the responses of individuals to the series of stern fathers who stood over them in the homes of their childhood, in the church, in society, and in the state.". . .

Children raised in this type of home developed a hyperactive conscience. Charged with personal responsibility for their actions and deeply concerned to avoid offense, they were forced to discriminate for themselves between what their parents would approve or disapprove, between what was "right" and what was "wrong." With the development of full moral autonomy, this process of discrimination became divorced from the system of reinforcement that had engendered it: The individual's conscience (or superego) warned him against moral transgression and urged him on to a continual reform of himself.

This inner psychological dynamic pushed men and women onward in the pursuit of higher standards and demanded excellence and achievement, however those terms were defined. . . . Here then in the childtraining practices and the social values of certain dissenting Protestant sects (and perhaps also a certain class within those religious groups) was an important source of the entrepreneurial character structure. Here also was the threat of boundless discontent—a compulsiveness which could be harnessed only by a strict organization of activity. "The order which the Quakers are accustomed from childhood to apply to the distribution of their tasks, their thoughts, and every moment of their lives," a percipient French visitor to Philadelphia observed, "economizes time, activity and money."

ˑThere were many differences between the Congregational creed of Thomas Hancock's father and the Quakerism of the Philadelphia Friends, but their members practiced a similar method of childtraining: a middle path which kept well clear of the extremes of authoritarian repression and parental neglect. Not all of their children became self-reliant adults imbued with a deep need for achievement. Sex roles, birth order, and the wider environment also affected the socialization process; and, in any event, inherited propensities could only be influenced within certain limits. Nonetheless, the results were impressive. Quakers constituted less than one-seventh of the population of Philadelphia in 1769, but they accounted for more than half of those who paid taxes in excess of £100. Of the seventeen wealthiest men in the city, twelve had been raised as Friends. . . .

The new entrepreneurial personality was most prevalent in urban centers and among particular classes and religious groups, but the economic behavior patterns and materialistic values which accompanied (and/or reinforced) it knew no geographic or social limits. . . .

The key elements, in rural and urban areas alike, were the growing scarcity of certain factors of production (which increased the economic leverage of those who controlled them) and the opportunities offered to merchants and creditors to provide processed goods and financial services to an expanding population. In Chester County, for example, the number of taxpayers tripled in the half century following 1730. By 1782 between 25 percent and 35 percent of all taxpayers were either tenant farmers or "inmates" —married artisans or laborers living in dwellings owned by others—who, each month, paid a part of their income in rent to the land- and house-owning members of the community, and yet another part to storekeepers and other creditors in return for services. The established property owners and middle-men thus amassed a disproportionate share of the growing wealth of the county. Because of their position they were able to secure—through rents, commission and interest charges, retail markups, and the like—a part of the income of many others.

This method of accumulating wealth was different from that practiced in the slave colonies, where the *entire* surplus product of the black slave was expropriated by his master. It was, rather, a system of agrarian and commercial capitalism in which a *part* of the output of many free men was funneled into the hands of a few. By 1774 the poorest 50 percent of all the adults who were potential wealth holders in the colonies of New Jersey, Delaware, and Pennsylvania owned only 13 percent of the total wealth of this region, as against the 40 percent held by the richest tenth of the population. But because of the general increase in prosperity (the result, in part, of the entrepreneurial activities of the affluent taxpayers), the standard of living of many members of the poorer half of the society was higher than that of their parents or grandparents. Concealed behind the increase in inequality (but part of the same process of economic development and social differentiation) was a significant rise in the absolute wealth of the community.

Indeed, it was this facet of the total evolutionary process that was the subject of most contemporary comment. "One half of the wealth of this city is owned by men who wear leather aprons," a contributor to a Philadelphia newspaper claimed in the 1770s, "and the other half by those whose fathers or grandfathers wore leather aprons." However valid as a statement of personal belief, the logic was deceptive and the remark misleading. Those who had benefited substantially from the labor of their parents numbered only 10 percent of the population, and this small group of wealthy taxpayers controlled 54 percent of the city's wealth in 1774. Moreover, even the present generation of artisans and shopkeepers constituted only half of the residents of the community. Below both of these relatively privileged groups were 40 percent of the free adult inhabitants; the members of this sizeable fraction of the society owned a pitiful 4 percent of the total wealth.

It was not this depressed section of the population, however, who controlled the development of Philadelphia or who conceived its myths and values. This was the prerogative of the successful, those long-time residents who saw about them only those craftsmen and storekeepers who had succeeded and not the great numbers who had failed and floated away to other settlements. The descriptions of social reality composed by the members of this literate and articulate section of the community were optimistic not only because of the actual growth and prosperity of the city but also because they assumed that their own experience reflected that of the society as a whole. As always, the myths of the ruling class propagated a distorted, if attractive, version of social existence.

However skewed in their depiction of reality, these myths of social mobility and economic affluence were of crucial importance. They expressed, in an intangible, abstract form, the values and aspirations of the leading part of the community. Grudgingly acquiesced in by ordinary laborers; tacitly accepted by tenant farmers; and wholeheartedly embraced by small landowners, newly arrived indentured servants, hardworking artisans, and ambitious storekeepers, they constituted a set of shared beliefs which obscured (or perhaps justified) the acute differences in their respective material conditions.

Insofar as these elite and entrepreneurial values were internalized by the populace at large or assumed institutionalized form as role expectations of the adult members of the society, they bound this stratified community together and facilitated its continued economic expansion. Thus the White Oaks of Philadelphia—a society of relatively poor if respectable ship carpenters—instituted, as the high point of their year's social activity, an Annual Fishery which was modeled directly on the more elaborate and more prestigious festival celebrated by the gentry of the town. This conscious emulation of the social habits of their betters, this cultural mimesis, testified to the hold exercised on the minds and emotions of the lower status groups by the values and way of life of the wealthy merchants and gentry. Freer than the black slave, more prosperous than the poor white planter, blessed with a genuine opportunity for social mobility, the urban mechanic was, nevertheless, encompassed in a mental world not entirely of his own making.

The Social Basis of Provincial Politics

There were several levels of political activity in the colonies, each concerned with a different array of problems and each subject to a separate constituency. On the highest plane, the politics of empire were conducted primarily in London by aristocratic Englishmen and imperial bureaucrats with little personal knowledge of American affairs and by merchants and commercial groups with interests of their own to defend. Through their agents or allies in England the colonists in America had a voice in the deliberations that took place in the Palace, in Parliament, and in the Plantation Office but it was weak and not often heard.

Local politics in America was equally impervious to imperial direction. In hundreds of towns, townships, and counties officials were elected and taxes levied by the resident inhabitants without direction or interference from London. These essentially autonomous systems of political power intersected on the provincial level: in the clash between the royal governor and the representative assemblies of the various colonies. The governor's task was to secure local support for imperial edicts and parliamentary legislation, if possible by persuasion but by patronage, threat, or bribery if necessary. All too often the weapons at his disposal (a few offices and military contracts, his own personal prestige and political abilities) were inadequate to the task.

These difficulties increased over time. No comprehensive and coherent colonial policy was conceived in London for implementation in America, and the patronage at the disposal of the governors was gradually appropriated by English ministers anxious to reward their own friends and supporters. An even more important factor in bringing about a slow decline in imperial authority was the appearance of an indigenous political elite. In the first generations of settlement most of the colonies lacked a distinct governing class or group of political leaders at the provincial level. Successful families might predominate in a given locality and royal governors might gather a small clique of supporters, but the ingredients of a functioning political system—a complex web of interest groups, family alliances, and regional factions —was completely lacking. Thus there was a period of "chaotic" factionalism in which there was "a ruthless competition for dominance, power, and economic advantage among rival groups of leading men, groups which were largely ad hoc and impermanent."

This type of political activity—uncertain, constantly shifting, based on temporary alliances over specific issues—was the mark of a polity in which there was no sure center of social gravity. This chaotic state was characteristic of government throughout the colonies, except in the special circumstances created by the existence of the Puritan oligarchy in New England, during the first decades of settlement. It was true in Virginia until 1660 and in Maryland until 1689; it appeared as well upon the colonization of Pennsylvania, New Hampshire, and the Carolinas lasting, in each instance, for thirty or forty years. These conditions magnified the importance of the royal or proprietary governors, giving them effective authority out of proportion to the inherent powers of their office. This kaleidoscopic system of politics mirrored, on the governmental level, the unsettled social and economic structure of the community.

As social fluidity crystallized into coherent form, atomistic factionalism gave way to more stable and more predictable types of political activity. This evolution took two forms. In Virginia after 1720 and in South Carolina after 1740 the monopolization of wealth by a group of interrelated families with similar social interests and cultural values brought about the creation of a powerful political elite. . . . There were differences of opinion among individuals and struggles for power among families, but these contests were muted in tone and essentially superficial in character. They hinged on personal differences among men and not on deep economic, social, or religious cleavages in society.

The second, and more common, evolutionary political form was the emergence of a polity characterized by "stable" factionalism, with two or more relatively permanent interest groups contending for power. The classic case of this process of development was Rhode Island. Until the 1750s provincial politics in this small corporate colony had been virtually nonexistent, in part because of the absence of a strong executive branch of government. Each year the men selected by local communities of farmers predominated in the General Assembly and, in conjunction with the representatives from mercantile Newport, passed the few tax laws and general ordinances that were required. On nine occasions between 1710 and 1751 the agricultural interest enacted paper money bills designed to stimulate trade and relieve agrarian indebtedness; but apart from this particular schism between Newport and its hinterland, there were few permanent divisions within the assembly.

The emergence of Providence as a port city in competition with Newport effected a realignment of economic ties and created a system of factional politics based on sectional advantage. The spread of credit facilities and market contacts inward from the two urban centers prompted an intense civic rivalry which took political form in a bitter contest for control of the elective governorship. In 1755 the post was won by Stephen Hopkins, a merchant of Providence; this victory inaugurated a struggle for the governorship between the Hopkins family and the Ward family of Newport which lasted until the outbreak of the war for independence. The two family factions were agreed on questions of financial policy (succeeding finally in 1763 in winning assembly approval for a bill to control the value of currency) but differed sharply over the grant of monopolies, the apportionment of taxes, the bestowal of patronage, and other governmental actions which could be turned to sectional advantage. It was the prevailing strength of the Hopkins faction, guaranteed finally in the election of 1767, which resulted in the establishment of the College of Rhode Island (Brown University) in Providence rather than in Newport.

Thus the atomistic factionalism of provincial government in Rhode Island, based on the autonomy of small farming communities, had given way under the pressure of economic development to a more coherent political system dominated by merchants, lawyers, and their commercial allies resident in the urban centers. There were similar centralizing and stabilizing forces at work in other colonies as successful families translated their wealth and social prestige into political power on the provincial level. In New York a faction led by the Livingston family and based on support from the Hudson River aristocracy and dissenting religious sects battled for political hegemony with the Delanceys—Episcopalian in religion, mercantile in sympathy, and allied to the landowners of Westchester County. In the absence of political "parties," these family alliances based on social and religious interest groups had come to constitute the structural basis of provincial politics. Here also the diversity of the population made political activity open, competitive, and abusive—not at all conducive to the inculcation of habits of deference among the mass of the voters.

This emergence of an indigenous American polity, based solidly on the accumulated wealth and achieved status of a native-born elite, undermined the power of the royal governor. The deflation of imperial authority was greatest in those colonies, such as Virginia, where there were few differences among the representatives which could be exploited to the advantage of the Crown, but the process was everywhere the same. Only the socially and politically undeveloped colonies could be easily managed in the interest of the mother country. . . .

As old families and established groups tightened their grip on the institutions of government during the first three-quarters of the eighteenth century, American politics became more elitist and oligarchic. Fewer and fewer settlers could justly observe, with Cadwallader Colden, that "the most opulent families, in our own memory, have risen from the lowest ranks of the people." Even in relatively democratic Connecticut the 600 offices above town level were filled by only 400 different men (because of plural officeholding) in the 1750s; and in any one year over half of these officials were members of the one hundred most prominent families. A few decades later, John Adams remarked:

Go into every village in New England and you will find that the office of justice of the peace, and even the place of representative, which has ever depended only on the freest election of the people, have generally descended from generation to generation, in three or four families at most.

Politics had become predictable. The great mass of ordinary men voted for the members of those families who had proved their astuteness in economic affairs and whose large houses and social prestige clearly marked them out for the management of the affairs of state.

The difference between the politics of the northern colonies and those in the South did not lie primarily in the extent of the franchise, but rather in the proportion of men who were genuinely eligible for office. In Virginia, Maryland, and much of South Carolina all of the black population and 75 percent of the white inhabitants were automatically excluded, by color or condition, from an active role in the decision making process. Political life was the prerogative of the privileged members of this quasi-aristocratic society: capable, well-read men who were, in a very real sense, born to rule. In these regions of colonial America a place in the county court or the legislature was effectively limited to nominees chosen from among the top 10 percent of the total adult male population.

The social spectrum of political representation and active participation in the North was about twice as large. The absence of a large slave population and a cultural heritage of independence had resulted in a less highly stratified society; and the greater diversity of economic activities had brought moderate affluence to a greater proportion of the total population, especially in the predominant rural sector. There were the glimmerings of an established oligarchy in New York, with its mass of tenant farmers presided over by members of the Livingston, Van Courtland, or Van Rensselaer families— and even in Massachusetts, where 40 percent of the top officials in thirteen towns were drawn from their four leading families. But there was also more competition for office among men of considerable property and less deference paid to them by those of ordinary means, especially in the heterogeneous middle colonies. If its abusive tone, open character, and social, religious, and sectional diversity occasionally gave the royal or proprietary governor greater leverage and more room to maneuver, the emphasis on local autonomy and the democratic thrust of the provincial politics of the North rendered it as impervious to imperial direction and control as that of the less internally divided colonies to the south.

Conflict and Consensus

Common allegiance to the British Crown produced similarities in language, culture, and political institutions in the various American colonies, but it could not prevent (or conceal) their fundamental divergences in social development. The economic base and the composition of the population varied from one region to another; and so also did the value systems, behavior patterns, and character structures of their inhabitants. Within each area, however, the fragments, or facets, of social life formed a coherent and interdependent whole. Each of these social systems had a number of functionally critical qualities; and these can be isolated, as a set of abstractions, for comparison and contrast. . . .

Despite reliance on force and a strict caste division between the races, the society of the southern American colonies was not plural in character. The widely dispersed black population was unable to maintain a viable religion and culture of its own. Moreover, the gradual acculturization of native-born slaves through the total-institution of slavery gradually lessened the crude dependence on force. As time passed, elements of "consensus" and of moral persuasion began to infuse the system of social control. This was especially the case among the poor white planters who quickly learned to accept their subordinate place in the social hierarchy. Thus, although sharply divided along the lines of race and class, this society (except in the back-country) was relatively stable; conflict was latent, not manifest.

By contrast, New England society was a model of the consensus made possible by homogeneity. British troops were never stationed in these settlements until 1768 and their presence then was an important factor in bringing about armed revolt by the xenophobic resident population. There had been previous outbreaks of violence against customs officials and other royal bureaucrats, likewise the agents of an alien and external power. There had also been a good many uprisings which were extrainstitutional in character: "mobs" composed of a fair cross-section of the population took action, for example, against deviant elements (such as prostitutes, carriers of contagious diseases, and those who sought to hoard food or manipulate its price) who seemed to constitute a danger to the moral or physical health of the community. As a rule these mass police actions received the tacit support of the local officials. Lacking a powerful constabulary and overwhelmingly white, Anglo-Saxon, and dissenting Protestant in composition, these communities mobilized the entire body politic for the task of preserving order.

This system of social self-control was possible because of the relative uniformity of thought and condition among the members of these towns. Access to many communities in New England was strictly regulated by the resident population, and undesirable aliens were constantly "warned out." These rigid standards of social (and often religious) selection were designed to insure that these settlements remained restricted to like-minded inhabitants. This quest for unanimity was bolstered by a religious ideology which stressed self-restraint and selflessness in dealings with others; by a system of childtraining which fostered a strong moral conscience and an acute sense of right and wrong; and by cultural habits and social expectations which placed a high value on conformity to accepted standards. Once the members of a town meeting had achieved consensus on a given issue, their decision assumed an ethical significance all were bound to respect.

Those who would not heed the voice of the community were encouraged to leave or, upon occasion, actually expelled. There was no toleration of diversity in this homogeneous region; no philosophical commitment to the rule of the majority. "The major part of those who were present were [farmers]," the merchants of Salem, Massachusetts, argued when protesting against a tax schedule which imposed high rates on their financial assets, "and the vote then passed was properly their vote and not the vote of the whole body of the town." The metaphor—with its implication of a mutually dependent and interconnected polity in which the well-being of one member affected the condition of all—was completely appropriate. It reflected the social and cultural homogeneity of most of rural New England and the intuitive rejection by most of its inhabitants of a world in which there was a diversity of value systems; they had no historical experience of such complexity.

The cultural difference between the original Dutch settlers and their English conquerors had helped to provoke Leisler's rebellion in New York in 1689; and the result had been permanent stationing of a detachment of British troops in the colony. Subsequent migration of thousands of Germans and Scotch-Irish Presbyterians into Dutch New York (and the neighboring provinces of New Jersey and Pennsylvania, which were already the home of a sizable Quaker population) introduced even more diversity into the social complexity of this region. And yet these colonies never degenerated into plural societies ruled only by naked force.

New England democracy, a "democracy devoid of legitimate difference, dissent, and conflict," had a very different character from that developed by the more heterogeneous society of the middle colonies. A political system based on compromise and accommodation gradually (and grudgingly) emerged in this area during the course of the eighteenth century, giving institutional legitimacy and an encompassing constitutional form to its cultural diversity. Political factionalism was rife in these provinces—was perhaps more intense here than anywhere in the British empire—but these legislative struggles served to prevent a resort to physical force and political coercion. All religious and cultural factions, even eventually the rough Scotch-Irish Presbyterians of the frontier regions, were accepted into the polity on the basis of equality. Consensus was limited to representation and participation; not, as in New England, to the substance of politics. But this was sufficient to preserve social stability while generating a competitive type of politics which eventually produced (in the persons of Aaron Burr, DeWitt Clinton, and Martin Van Buren) the first really professional politicians in American history.

If the middle colonies lacked the homogeneous solidarity of New England or the enforced stability of southern slave society during the eighteenth century, these provinces were also spared their rigorous psychological or martial systems of social control. The internal coherence of the middle colonies did not derive from the existence of dependent personalities created by huge disparities in wealth and status or from the institutionalized violence of slavery; nor did it rely on invocation of a conformity in thought and action which stultified individual self-expression by channeling it into accepted forms. It was not completely accidental that the freedom of the press to criticize government officials was first clearly enunciated in New York—in the Zenger case of 1735. And the grounds of defense, which admitted the libel but justified it as being true, adumbrated a new principle of law. Forced by the contingencies of history to deal with diversity, the inhabitants of the middle colonies were slowly accommodating their laws, political systems, and personal mental outlooks to their unpredictable new world of social and cultural complexity.

At midcentury these problems had assumed a new sense of urgency, not only in the middle colonies, but also in areas less well-equipped by experience or inclination to deal with them. Beginning in 1740 there were a series of interrelated crises in American society as the inherent tendencies of two generations of rapid population growth, extensive economic development, and increased social diversity rushed forward to fulfillment. In more than one colony these new tensions were to pull the inherited web of social authority and political power to the breaking point.

Gary B. Nash

Social Change and the Growth of Prerevolutionary Urban Radicalism

*   *   *

I

The most generally recognized alteration in eighteenth-century urban social structures is the long-range trend toward a less even distribution of wealth. Tax lists for Boston, Philadelphia, and New York, ranging over nearly a century prior to the Revolution, make this clear. By the early 1770s the top 5 percent of Boston's taxpayers controlled 49 percent of the taxable assets of the community, whereas they had held only 30 percent in 1687. In Philadelphia the top twentieth increased its share of wealth from 33 to 55 percent between 1693 and 1774. Those in the lower half of society, who in Boston in 1687 had commanded 9 percent of the taxable wealth, were left collectively with a mere 5 percent in 1771. In Philadelphia, those in the lower half of the wealth spectrum saw their share of wealth drop from 10.1 to 3.3 percent in the same period. It is now evident that the concentration of wealth had proceeded very far in the eighteenth-century cities.

Though city dwellers from the middle and lower ranks could not measure this redistribution of economic resources with statistical precision, they could readily discern the general trend. No one could doubt that upper-class merchants were amassing fortunes when four-wheeled coaches, manned by liveried Negro slaves, appeared in Boston's crooked streets, or when urban mansions, lavishly furnished in imitation of the English aristocracy, rose in

Reprinted from "Social Change and the Growth of Prerevolutionary Urban Radicalism" by Gary B. Nash, in The American Revolution: Explorations in the History of American Radicalism, edited by Alfred F. Young, copyright © 1976 by Northern Illinois University Press. By permission of the publisher.

Philadelphia and New York. Colonial probate records reveal that personal estates of £5,000 sterling were rare in the northern cities before 1730, but by 1750 the wealthiest town dwellers were frequently leaving assets of £20,000 sterling, exclusive of real estate, and sometimes fortunes of more than £50,000 sterling—equivalent in purchasing power to about 2.5 million dollars today. Wealth of this magnitude was not disguised in cities with populations ranging from about 16,000 in Boston to about 25,000 in New York and Philadelphia and with geographical expanses half as large as public university campuses today.

While urban growth produced a genuinely wealthy upper class, it simultaneously created a large class of impoverished city dwellers. All of the cities built almshouses in the 1730s in order to house under one roof as many of the growing number of poor as possible. This was the beginning of a long trend toward substituting confinement in workhouses and almshouses for the older familial system of direct payments to the poor at home. The new system was designed to reduce the cost of caring for a growing number of marginal persons—people who, after the 1730s, were no longer simply the aged, widowed, crippled, incurably ill, or orphaned members of society, but also the seasonally unemployed, war veterans, new immigrants, and migrants from inland areas seeking employment in the cities. These persons, whose numbers grew impressively in the 1750s and 1760s, were now expected to contribute to their own support through cloth weaving, shoemaking, and oakum picking in city workhouses.

Beginning in Boston in the 1740s and in New York and Philadelphia somewhat later, poverty scarred the lives of a growing part of the urban populations. Among its causes were periodic unemployment, rising prices that outstripped wage increases, and war taxes which fell with unusual severity on the lower classes. In Boston, where the Overseers of the Poor had expended only £25–35 sterling per thousand inhabitants in the 1720s and 1730s, per capita expenditures for the poor more than doubled in the 1740s and 1750s, and then doubled again in the last fifteen years of the colonial period. Poor relief rose similarly in Philadelphia and New York after 1750.

In the third quarter of the eighteenth century poverty struck even harder at Boston's population and then blighted the lives of the New York and Philadelphia laboring classes to a degree unparalleled in the first half of the century. In New York, the wartime boom of 1755–1760 was followed by postwar depression. High rents and unemployment brought hundreds of families to the edge of indigency. The incidence of poverty jumped more than fourfold between 1750 and 1775. By 1772 a total of 425 persons jostled for space in the city's almshouse, which had been built to accommodate about 100 indigents. In Philadelphia, in the decade before the Revolution, more than 900 persons each year were admitted to the city's institutions for the impoverished—the almshouse, workhouse, and Hospital for the Sick Poor. The data on poor relief leaves little room for doubt that the third quarter of the eighteenth century was an era of severe economic and social dislocation in the cities, and that by the end of the colonial period a large number of urban dwellers were without property, without opportunity, and, except for public aid, without the means of obtaining the necessities of life.

The economic changes that redistributed wealth, filled the almshouses to overflowing, and drove up poor rates, also hit hard at the lower part of the middle class in the generation before the Revolution. These people—master artisans rather than laborers, skilled shipwrights rather than merchant seamen, shopkeepers rather than peddlers—were financially humbled in substantial numbers in Boston beginning in the 1740s and in Philadelphia and New York a dozen years later.

In Boston, this crumbling of middle-class economic security can be traced in individual cases through the probate records and in aggregate form in the declining number of "taxables." In that city, where the population remained nearly static, at about 15,500 from 1735 to the Revolution, the number of "rateable polls" declined from a high of more than 3,600 in 1735, when the city's economy was at its peak, to a low of about 2,500 around mid-century. By 1771, Boston's taxables still numbered less than 2,600. This decline of more than a thousand taxable adults was not caused by loss of population but by the sagging fortunes of more than 1,000 householders—almost one third of the city's taxpaying population. Boston's selectmen made this clear in 1757 when they pointed out that "besides a great Number of Poor . . . who are either wholly or in part maintained by the Town, & so are exempt from being Taxed, there are many who are Rateable according to Law . . . who are yet in such poor Circumstances that Considering how little business there is to be done in Boston they can scarcely procure from day to day daily Bread for themselves & Families."

In Philadelphia, the decay of a substantial part of the "middling sort" similarly altered the urban scene, though the trend began later and did not proceed as far as in Boston. City tax collectors reported the names of each taxable inhabitant from whom they were unable to extract a tax, and the survival of their records allows for some precision in tracing this phenomenon. Taxpayers dropped from the rolls because of poverty represented less than 3 percent of the taxables in the period before 1740, but they increased to about 6 to 7 percent in the two decades beginning in 1740, and then to one in every ten taxpayers in the fifteen years before the Revolution.

The probate records of Boston and Philadelphia tell a similar tale of economic insecurity hovering over the middle ranges of urban society. Among these people in Boston, median wealth at death dropped sharply between 1685 and 1735 and then made a partial but uneven recovery as the Revolution approached. The average carpenter, baker, shopkeeper, shipwright, or tavern-keeper dying in Boston between 1735 and 1765 had less to show for a lifetime's work than his counterpart of a half century before. In Philadelphia, those in the lower ranges of the middle class also saw the value of their assets, accumulated over a lifetime's labor, slowly decline during the first half of the eighteenth century, though not so severely as in Boston. The startling conclusion that must be drawn from a study of nearly 4,500 Boston and Philadelphia inventories of estates at probate is that population growth and economic development in the colonial cities did not raise the standard of living and broaden opportunities for the vast majority of people, but instead conferred benefits primarily upon those at the top of the social pyramid. The long-range effect of growth was to erode the personal assets held at death by those in the lower 75 percent of Boston society and the lower 60 percent of Philadelphia society. Though many city dwellers had made spectacular individual ascents from the bottom, in the manner of Benjamin Franklin of Philadelphia or Isaac Sears of New York, the statistical chances of success for those beginning beneath the upper class were considerably less after the first quarter of the eighteenth century than before. The dominating fact of late colonial life for many middle-class as well as most lower-class city folk was not economic achievement but economic frustration.

II

Understanding that the cities were becoming centers of frustrated ambition, propertylessness, genuine distress for those in the lower strata, and stagnating fortunes for many in the middle class makes comprehensible much of the violence, protest, and impassioned rhetoric that occurred in the half-generation before the colonial challenge to British regulations began in 1764. Upper-class colonists typically condemned these verbal attacks and civil disorders as the work of the "rabble," the "mob," the "canaille," or individuals "of turbulent disposition." These labels were used to discredit crowd activity, and historians have only recently recognized that the "rabble" often included a broad range of city dwellers, from slaves and servants through laborers and seamen to artisans and shopkeepers—all of whom were directly or indirectly expressing grievances. Cutting across class lines, and often unified by economic conditions that struck at the welfare of both the lower and middle classes, these crowds began to play a larger role in a political process that grew more heated as the colonial period came to an end. This developing consciousness and political sophistication of ordinary city dwellers came rapidly to fruition in the early 1760s and thereafter played a major role in the advent of the Revolution.

Alienation and protest had been present in the northern cities, especially during periods of economic difficulty, since the early eighteenth century. In Boston, between 1709 and 1713, townspeople protested vigorously and then took extralegal action when Andrew Belcher, a wealthy merchant, refused to stop exporting grain during a bread shortage in the city. Belcher had grown fat on war contracts during Queen Anne's War, and when he chose to export grain to the Caribbean, at a handsome profit, rather than sell it for a smaller profit to hungry townspeople, his ships were attacked and his warehouses emptied by an angry crowd. Rank had no privileges, as even the lieutenant-governor was shot when he tried to intervene. Bostonians of meagre means learned that through concerted action, the powerless could become powerful, if only for the moment. Wealthy merchants who would not listen to pleas from the community could be forced through collective action to subordinate profits to the public need.

After the end of Queen Anne's War, in 1713, Boston was troubled by postwar recession and inflation, which cut into the wages of working people. Attempts to organize a land bank in order to increase the scarce circulating medium in Boston were opposed by wealthy men, many of them former war contractors. Gathering around the unpopular governor, Paul Dudley, these fiscal conservatives blamed the hard times on the extravagant habits of "the Ordinary sort" of people, who squandered their money on a "foolish fondness of Foreign Commodities & Fashions" and on too frequent tippling in the town's taverns. But such explanations did not deceive returning war veterans, the unemployed, or those caught in an inflationary squeeze. They protested openly against men who made their fortunes "by grinding the poor," as one writer expressed it, and who studied "how to oppress, cheat, and overreach their neighbours." "The Rich, Great, and Potent," stormed this angry spokesman, "with rapacious violence bear down all before them, who have not wealth, or strength to encounter or avoid their fury." Although the land bank movement failed in 1720, it was out of this defeat that the Boston Caucus, the political organization designed to mobilize the middle- and lower-class electorate in the decades to come, arose.

In Philadelphia, economic issues also set the mechanic and laborer against the rich as early as the 1720s. When a business recession brought unemployment and a severe shortage of specie (the only legal circulating medium), leading merchant-politicians argued that the problem was moral in nature. If the poor were unemployed or hungry, they had their own lack of industry and prudence to thank, wrote James Logan, a thriving merchant and land speculator. "The Sot, the Rambler, the Spendthrift, and the Slip Season," he charged, were at the heart of the slump. Schemes for reviving the economy with emissions of paper money were reckless attempts to cheat those who worked for their money instead of drinking their time away.

But, as in Boston, the majority of people were not fooled by such high-toned arguments. Angry tracts appeared on both sides of the debate concerning the causes and cure for recession. Those who favored paper money and called for restrictions on land speculators and monopolizers of the money market made an attack on wealth itself an important theme. Logan found bricks flying through his windows and a crowd threatening to level his house. Meanwhile, he looked on in disgust as Governor William Keith organized a political caucus, encouraged laboring men to participate in politics, and conducted a campaign aimed at discrediting Logan and other wealthy merchants. "It is neither the Great, the Rich, nor the Learned, that compose the Body of any People, and . . . civil Government ought carefully to protect the poor, laborious and industrious Part of Mankind," Keith cautioned the Assembly in 1723. Logan, formerly respected as William Penn's chief proprietary officeholder, a member of council, a judge of the colony's highest court, and Pennsylvania's most educated man, now found himself reviled in widely distributed tracts as "Pedagogus Mathematicus"—an ambitious, ruthless elitist. He and his henchmen, cried the pamphleteers, deserved to be called "petty Tyrants of this Province," "Serpents in the Grass," "Rich Misers," "Phenomena of Aristocracy," "Infringers of our Priviledges," and "Understrappers of Government."

In a striking inversion of the conventional eighteenth-century thinking that only the rich and educated were equipped to hold high political offices, the Keithian faction urged the voters to recognize that "a mean Man, of small Interest, devoted to the faithful Discharge of his Trust and Duty to the Government" was far more to be valued than rich and learned men. For the rest of the decade the anti-Logan forces, organized into political clubs in Philadelphia, held sway at the annual elections and passed legislation to relieve the distress of the lower-class unemployed and middle-class debtors. Members of the Philadelphia elite, such as Logan and merchant Isaac Norris, hated the "new vile people [who] may be truly called a mob," and deplored Keith's "doctrine of reducing all to a level." But they could no longer manage politics from the top. The "moral economy of the crowd," as E. P. Thompson has called it— the people's sense that basic rules of equity in social relations had been breached—had intervened when the rich would do nothing to relieve suffering in a period of economic decline.

When an economic slump beset New York in the 1730s, causing unemployment and an increase in suits for debt, the reaction was much the same as in the other cities. The John Peter Zenger trial of this era is best remembered as a chapter in the history of the freedom of the press. But central to the campaign organized by Zenger's supporters were the indictment of the rich and the mobilization of the artisanry against them. A 1734 election tract reminded the New York electorate that the city's strength—and its future—lay with the fortunes of "Shuttle" the weaver, "Plane" the joiner, "Drive" the carter, "Mortar" the mason, "Tar" the mariner, "Snip" the tailor, "Smallrent" the fair-minded landlord, and "John Poor" the tenant. Pitted against them were "Gripe the Merchant, Squeeze the Shopkeeper, Spintext and Quible the Lawyer." In arguments reminiscent of those in Philadelphia a decade before, the Lewis Morris faction counseled the people that "A poor honest Man [is] preferable to a rich Knave." Only by electing men responsive to the needs of the whole community, the Morrisites advised, could New Yorkers arrest the forces that were impoverishing the artisan class while fattening the purses of merchants and moneylenders. The conservative clergy of the city advised working people to pray harder in difficult times, but the Morrisite pamphleteers urged the electorate to throw out of office those "people in Exalted Stations" who looked with disdain upon "those they call the Vulgar, the Mob, the herd of Mechanicks."

Attacks on wealth and concentrated power continued in New York through 1737. The opulent and educated of the city were exposed as self-interested and oppressive men, not the public-minded community servants that conventional political philosophy prescribed. Though the leaders of the Morris faction were themselves men of substantial wealth, and though they never advocated a truly popular form of politics, their attacks on the rich and their organization of artisan voters became imbedded in the structure and ideology of politics.

A decade later, political contention broke out again in New York City and attacks on the wealthy and well-born were revived. To some extent the political factionalism in the period from 1747 to 1755 represented a competition for power and profit between different elements of the elite. DeLanceys were pitted against Coldens, and Alexanders against Bayards, in a game where the stakes were control of land in neighboring New Jersey, the profits of the Iroquois fur trade, and the power of the assembly in opposition to the governor and his clique of officeholders. But as in earlier decades, the success of these intra-elite struggles depended upon gaining support from below. In appealing to the artisans and tradesmen, especially during periods of economic decline, bitter charges surfaced about the selfishness of wealthy men and the social inequities in society which they promoted. Cadwallader Colden's *Address to the Freeholders* in 1747 inveighed against the rich, who did not build their fortunes "by the honestest means" and who had no genuine concern for the "publick spirit." Colden attacked the wealthy, among whose ranks he figured importantly, as tax dodgers who indulged in wanton displays of wealth and gave little thought to the welfare of those below them. "The midling rank of mankind," argued Colden, was far more honest, dependable, sober, and public spirited "in all Countries," and it was therefore best to trust "our Liberty & Property" to them rather than to New York's "rich jolly or swaggering companions."

In Boston, resentment against the rich, focusing on specific economic grievances, continued to find voice in the middle third of the century. Moreover, since the forming of the caucus a generation before, well-coordinated street action channeled the wrath of townspeople against those who were thought to act against the interest of the commonality. In the 1730s an extended debate erupted on establishing a public market where prices and marketing conditions would be controlled. Many Bostonians in the lower and middle strata regarded a regulated public market as a device of merchants and fiscal conservatives to drive small retailers from the field and reap the profits of victualing Boston themselves. Though they lost their cause after a number of bitter debates and close votes at the town meeting in the mid-1730s, these humbler people, who probably included many without a vote, ultimately prevailed by demolishing the public market on Dock Square in 1737. The attack was accompanied by much "murmuring agt the Government & the rich people," lamented Benjamin Colman, an advocate of the regulated market and a member of the conservative faction. Worse yet, "none of the Rioters or Mutineers" could be discovered. Their support was so broad that they promised that any attempt to arrest or arraign the saboteurs would be met by "Five Hundred Men in Solemn League and Covenant," who would resist the sheriff and destroy any other markets erected by wealthy merchants. The timbers of the public market which fell before the night raiders in 1737 showed how widely held was the conviction that only this kind of civil disobedience would "deliver the poor oppressed and distressed People out of the Hands of the Rich and Mighty."

The Land Bank controversy from 1740 to 1742 further inflamed a wide segment of Boston society. Most of the colony, including Boston, favored a land bank which would relieve the economic distress of the period by issuing more paper money and thus continuing the inflationist policies of the last twenty years. In opposition stood a group of Boston merchants, who "had railed against the evils of paper money" for years and now "damned the Bank as merely a more invidious form of the soft money panacea typically favored by the province's poor and unsuccessful." One of their spokesman, William Douglass, reflected the elitist view by characterizing the dispute as a struggle between the "Idle & Extravagant who want to borrow money at any bad lay" and "our considerable Foreign Traders and rich Men."

Even though the inflationists swept the Massachusetts assembly elections of 1740 and 1741, they could not overcome the combined opposition of Governor Jonathan Belcher, a group of wealthy merchants, and officials in England. In the end, the Land Bank movement was thwarted. The defeat was not lightly accepted or quickly forgotten by debtors and Bostonians of modest means. Three years later, a committee of the Boston town meeting, which had consistently promoted inflated paper currency as a means of relief for Boston's numerous debtors, exploded with angry words at another deflationist proposal of the mercantile elite: "We cannot suppose, because in some extraordinary Times when a Party Spirit has run high there have been some Abuses of Our Liberties and Priviledges, that therefore We should in a Servile Manner give them all up. And have our Bread & Water measured out to Us by those Who Riot in Luxury & Wantonness on Our Sweat & Toil and be told by them that we are too happy, because we are not reduced to Eat Grass with the Cattle."

The crowning blow to ordinary Bostonians came in 1748 when Thomas Hutchinson, the principal architect of the monetary policy favored by the wealthiest merchants, engineered a merciless devaluation of Massachusetts currency as a cure to the continuing inflation, which by now had reduced the value of paper money to a fraction of its face value. With many persons unemployed, with poverty afflicting hundreds of families, and with Hutchinson personifying the military contractors who had reaped fortunes from King George's War (1739–1747) while common people suffered, popular sentiment exploded. The newspapers carried a rancorous debate on the proposed devaluation, street fights broke out when the new policy was instituted, and Hutchinson was personally threatened on several occasions. An anonymous pamphleteer put into words the sentiment of many in the city who had watched the gap widen between rich and poor during hard times. "Poverty and Discontent appear in every Face, (except the Countenances of the Rich), and dwell upon every Tongue." A few men, fed by "Lust of Power, Lust of Fame, Lust of Money," had grown rich by supplying military expeditions during the last war and had now cornered the paper money market and manipulated the rates of exchange for English sterling to their own profit. "No Wonder such Men can build Ships, Houses, buy Farms, set up their Coaches, Chariots, live very splendidly, purchase Fame, Posts of Honour," railed the pamphleteer. But such "Birds of prey . . . are Enemies to all Communities—wherever they live."

The growing sentiment in the cities against the wealthy was nourished by the Great Awakening—the outbreak of religious enthusiasm throughout the colonies beginning in the late 1730s. Although this eruption of evangelical fervor is primarily identified as a rural phenomenon, it also had powerful effects in the cities, where fiery preachers such as George Whitefield and Gilbert Tennant had their greatest successes. We have no study as yet of the Great Awakening in the cities, but clues abound that one important reason for its urban appeal was the fact that the evangelists took as one of their primary targets the growth of wealth and extravagance, accompanied by a dwindling of social concern in colonial America. Nowhere was this manifested more noticeably than in the cities.

The urban dwellers who thronged to hear George Whitefield in Philadelphia in 1739 and 1741 and those who crowded the Common in Boston to hear Whitefield and the vituperative James Davenport in the early 1740s were overwhelmingly from the "lower orders," so far as we can tell. What accounts for their "awakening" is the evangelists' presentation of a personal religion where humble folk might find succor from debt, daily toil, sickness, and want, and might express deeply felt emotions in an equality of fellowship. At the same time, the revivalist preachers spread a radical message concerning established authority. City dwellers were urged to partake in mass revivals, where the social distance between clergyman and parishioner and among worshippers themselves was obliterated. They were exhorted to be skeptical toward dogma and to participate in ecclesiastical affairs rather than bow passively to established hierarchy.

Through the Great Awakening, doctrinal controversy and attacks on religious leaders became widely accepted in the 1740s. In Boston the itinerant preacher James Davenport hotly indicted the rich and powerful and advised ordinary people to break through the crust of tradition in order to right the wrongs of a decaying society. It was the spectre of unlearned artisans and laborers assuming authority in this manner that frightened many upper-class city dwellers and led them to charge the revivalists with preaching levelism and anarchy. "It is . . . an exceedingly difficult, gloomy time with us . . . ," wrote one conservative clergyman from Boston. "Such an enthusiastic, factious, censorious Spirit was never known here. . . . Every low-bred, illiterate Person can resolve Cases of Conscience and settle the most difficult Points of Divinity better than the most learned Divines."

Such charges were heard repeatedly during the Great Awakening, revealing the fears of those who trembled to see the "unthinking multitude" invested with a new dignity and importance. Nor could the passing of the

Awakening reverse the tide, for this new sense of power remained a part of the social outlook of ordinary people. In fact, the radical transformation of religious feeling overflowed into civil affairs. The new feeling of autonomy and importance was bred in the churches, but now it was carried into the streets. Laboring people in the city learned "to identify the millenium with the establishment of governments which derived their power from the people, and which were free from the great disparities of wealth which characterized the old world."

III

The crescendo of urban protest and extralegal activity in the prerevolutionary decades cannot be separated from the condition of people's lives. Of course those who authored attacks on the growing concentration of wealth and power were rarely artisans or laborers; usually they were men who occupied the middle or upper echelons of society, and sometimes they were men who sought their own gain—installment in office, or the defeat of a competitor for government favors. But whatever their motives, their sharp criticisms of the changes in urban society were widely shared among humbler townspeople. It is impossible to say how much they shaped rather than reflected the views of those in the lower half of the social structure—urban dwellers whose opportunities and daily existence had been most adversely affected by the structural changes overtaking the colonial cities. But the willingness of broad segments of urban society to participate in attacks on narrowly concentrated wealth and power—both at the polls where the poor and propertyless were excluded, and in the streets where everyone, including women, apprentices, indentured servants, and slaves, could engage in action—should remind us that a rising tide of class antagonism and political consciousness, paralleling important economic changes, was a distinguishing feature of the cities at the end of the colonial period.

*   *   *

IV

The growing resentment of wealth, the rejection of an elitist conception of politics, and the articulation of artisan- and laboring-class interests also gained momentum after 1765. These were vital developments in the revolutionary period. Indeed, it was the extraordinary new vigor of urban laboring people in defining and pursuing their goals that raised the frightening spectre of a radicalized form of politics and a radically changed society in the minds of many upper-class city dwellers, who later abandoned the resistance movement against England that they had initially supported and led.

That no full-fledged proletarian radical ideology emerged in the decade before the Revolution should not surprise us, for this was a preindustrial society in which no proletariat yet existed. Instead, we can best understand the long movement of protest against concentrated wealth and power, building powerfully as social and economic conditions changed in the cities, as a reflection of the disillusionment of laborers, artisans, and many middle-class city dwellers against a system that no longer delivered equitable rewards to the industrious. "Is it equitable that 99, rather 999, should suffer for the Extravagance or Grandeur of one," asked a New Yorker in 1765, "especially when it is considered that Men frequently owe their Wealth to the impoverishment of their Neighbors?" Such thoughts, cutting across class lines, were gaining force among large parts of the urban population in the late colonial period. They were directed squarely at outmoded notions that only the idle and profligate could fail in America and that only the educated and wealthy were entitled to manage political affairs.

But the absence of clearly identifiable class consciousness and of organized proletarian radicalism does not mean that a radical ideology, nurtured within the matrix of preindustrial values and modes of thought, failed to emerge during the Revolution. Though this chapter in the history of the Revolution is largely unwritten, current scholarship is making it clear that the radicalization of thought in the cities, set in motion by economic and social change, advanced very rapidly once the barriers of traditional thought were broken down. A storm of demands, often accompanied by crowd action to insure their implementation, rose from the urban "tradesmen" and "mechanicks": for the end of closed assembly debates and the erection of public galleries in the legislative houses; for published roll-call votes which would indicate how faithfully elected legislators followed the wishes of their constituents; for open-air meetings where laboring men could help devise and implement public policy; for more equitable laying of taxes; for price controls instituted by and for the laboring classes to shield them from avaricious men of wealth; and for the election of mechanics and other ordinary people at all levels of government.

How rapidly politics and political ideology could be transformed, as colonists debated the issue of rebellion, is well illustrated by the case of Philadelphia. In one brief decade preceding the Revolution the artisanry and laboring poor of the city moved from a position of clear political inferiority to a position of political control. They took over the political machinery of the city, pushed through the most radical state constitution of the period, and articulated concepts of society and political economy that would have stunned their predecessors. By mid-1776, laborers, artisans, and small tradesmen, employing extralegal measures when electoral politics failed, were in clear command in Philadelphia. Working with middle-class leaders such as James Cannon, Timothy Matlack, Thomas Young, and Thomas Paine, they launched a full-scale attack on wealth and even on the right to acquire unlimited private property. By the summer of 1776 the militant Privates Committee, which probably represented the poorest workers, became the foremost carrier of radical ideology in Pennsylvania. It urged the voters, in electing delegates for the constitutional convention, to shun "great and overgrown rich men [who] will be improper to be trusted, [for] they will be too apt to be framing distinctions in society, because they will reap the benefits of all such distinctions." Going even further, they drew up a bill of rights for consideration by the convention, which included the proposition that "an enormous proportion of property vested in a few individuals is dangerous to the rights, and destructive of the common happiness, of mankind; and therefore every free state hath a right by its laws to discourage the possession of such property." For four years, in an extremely fluid political scene, a radicalized artisanry shaped—and sometimes dominated—city and state politics, while setting forth the most fully articulated ideology of reform yet heard in America.

These calls for reform varied from city to city, depending on differing conditions, past politics, and the qualities of particular leaders. Not all the reforms were implemented, especially those that went to the heart of the structural problems in the economy. Pennsylvania, for example, did not adopt the radical limitation on property holding. But that we know from hindsight that the most radical challenges to the existing system were thwarted, or enjoyed only a short period of success, does not mean that they are not a vital part of the revolutionary story. At the time, the disaffected in the cities were questioning some of the most fundamental tenets of colonial thought. Ordinary people, in bold opposition to their superiors, to whom custom required that they defer, were creating power and suggesting solutions to problems affecting their daily lives. . . . How far these calls for radical reform extended and the success they achieved are matters that historians have begun to investigate only lately. But this much is clear: even though many reforms were defeated or instituted briefly and then abandoned, political thought and behavior would never again be the same in America.

SUGGESTIONS FOR FURTHER READING

A splendid general survey of the colonial period is Clarence L. Ver Steeg, *The Formative Years, 1607–1763* (New York, 1964). Ver Steeg argues that the growth and expansion of the colonies led to great instability and even armed conflict in the late seventeenth and early eighteenth centuries. This conflict was a sign of the disruptiveness of change as "English colonies became American provinces." But the result was a new, American consensus. Wesley Frank Craven, **The Southern Colonies in the Seventeenth Century, 1607–1689* (Baton Rouge, 1949) finds conflict in the form of an attack on economic and political abuses. He calls Nathaniel Bacon, who led an uprising in Virginia in 1676, one of the many "who have shaped the long tradition of political liberalism in America." Daniel J. Boorstin, **The Americans: The Colonial Experience* (New York, 1958) perceptively traces the evolution of a peculiarly American society in the New World. On this point see also Sigmund Diamond, "From Organization to Society: Virginia in the Seventeenth Century," *American Journal of Sociology*, 63 (March 1958), pp. 457–75. Curtis P. Nettels, *The Roots of American Civilization* (New York, 1963) puts far more emphasis on class conflict, which, he says, arises from the unequal

* Available in paperback edition.

distribution of wealth and power in the colonies. Sharp class conflict is also stressed by Herbert Aptheker, *The Colonial Era* (New York, 1959). The nature and extent of class differences is surveyed in Jackson Turner Main, *The Social Structure of Revolutionary America* (Princeton, 1965).

In recent years historians have undertaken a number of local studies that shed considerable light on the political and social structure of individual towns. Among these are Charles S. Grant, *Democracy in the Connecticut Frontier Town of Kent* (New York, 1961); Sumner Chilton Powell, *Puritan Village: The Formation of a New Town* (Middletown, Conn., 1963); Kenneth A. Lockridge, *A New England Town: The First Hundred Years, Dedham, Massachusetts, 1636–1736* (New York, 1970); G. B. Warden, *Boston, 1689–1776* (Boston, 1970). Broader in scope is Michael Zuckerman, *Peaceable Kingdoms: New England Towns in the Eighteenth Century* (New York, 1970).

An outstanding discussion of the development of the business mentality in the colonies may be found in Part I of Thomas C. Cochran, *Business in American Life: A History* (New York, 1972). Richard Hofstadter, *America at 1750: A Social Portrait* (New York, 1971), describes the colonies as a "middle-class world" that developed from the modernizing tendencies already evident in the old world. Bernard Bailyn, *The New England Merchants in the Seventeenth Century* (Cambridge, Mass., 1955), traces the conflict between merchants and religious leaders for political and economic hegemony, a conflict that ended with merchant victory. Pictures of urban development differing from that of Nash may be found in Carl Bridenbaugh's two studies: *Cities in the Wilderness: The First Century of Urban Life in America, 1625–1742* (New York, 1938) and *Cities in Revolt: Urban Life in America, 1743–1776* (New York, 1955).

Edmund S. Morgan, *American Slavery American Freedom: The Ordeal of Colonial Virginia* (New York, 1975), finds the growth of freedom (for whites) and the blunting of class conflict (among whites) to be the result of the enslavement and debasement of blacks. On slavery and the colonial attitudes toward blacks, see also Winthrop Jordan, *White Over Black: American Attitudes Toward the Negro, 1550–1812* (Chapel Hill, N.C., 1968).

2

The
American Revolution

The basic question that must be asked about the American Revolution is, "What was it?" At first glance, the answer to this question seems obvious; a more important problem, it would appear, would deal with the causes of the Revolution. Yet, the question is not so easy to answer as it might seem, and the causes of the Revolution cannot be dealt with without first seeking its answer.

Writing in 1909, the historian Carl Becker argued that the American Revolution was really two revolutions in one—a dual revolution: "The American Revolution was the result of two general movements: The contests for home-rule and independence, and the democratization of American politics and society. Of these movements, the latter was fundamental." In addition to the antagonism toward the British, Becker saw conflicts within America during the Revolutionary period, conflicts arising from sharp class cleavages in American society. The Revolution, then, arose from the desire to reform the British empire—by separating from it—and the desire to reform society at home—by instituting democratic and libertarian reforms and by undermining the power of the local aristocracy. Conflict, not consensus, is the theme of this interpretation.

Not all historians accept Becker's answer to the question "What was the American Revolution?" While granting that there were differences among Americans before and during the Revolutionary period, some historians maintain that to emphasize these differences is to distort the true picture of American society in the eighteenth century. Becker's stress on conflict, they argue, obscures the fact that there was a general agreement among Americans which was stronger and more significant than the differences dividing them. In a variety of ways the experience in the New World had created a new man with new ideas; the Revolution was simply the attempt to maintain what Americans had already rather uniformly accepted. The Revolution was not revolutionary at all, concludes historian Daniel J. Boorstin; it was merely a "conservative colonial rebellion." Obviously, the theme of this interpretation is consensus, not conflict.

The selections that follow illustrate the lack of agreement among historians concerning the nature of the American Revolution. Quoting John Adams, Clinton Rossiter maintains that the "real American Revolution" took place during the colonial period. The change was "in the minds and hearts of the people," and it occurred before the outbreak of hostilities. While Rossiter does not deny that there were differences among the colonial Americans, he finds that these very differences resulted in a general consensus in America.

Merrill Jensen also quotes John Adams. He, too, returns to the pre-Revolutionary period as a means of understanding the American Revolution; but Jensen sees conflict, not consensus, in the period. He argues that colonial society was marked by vigorous class conflict and that the agitation during the Revolutionary period allowed the democratic, radical elements in America to achieve ascendancy over the aristocratic classes that had ruled colonial society. For Jensen, the Declaration of Independence and the Articles of Confederation were the embodiments of the radical philosophy that had become dominant.

Many scholars have evaluated the nature of the American Revolution in terms of similar developments elsewhere in the world; indeed this comparison is implicit in the selections by Rossiter and Jensen. The third selection approaches this problem explicitly. Thomas C. Barrow argues that the modern colonial liberation struggles provide apt comparisons and contrasts to the American Revolution.

In the final selection, Edmund S. Morgan describes the conflicts that divided Americans and then traces the ways in which these conflicts were resolved, creating a consensus that "invited conflicts" and provided new means to resolve them.

It is evident that the American Revolution was a colonial rebellion resulting in the independence of thirteen of the English colonies in the New World. Had the colonial experience resulted in the creation of an American consensus, making the Revolution merely the culmination of generations of gradual change? If so, then perhaps the greatest significance of the American Revolution was that it was not revolutionary!

But such an interpretation may tell only half the story. Was the American Revolution also a bitter social conflict on the order of the French Revolution of 1789 or the Russian Revolution of 1917? Perhaps class conflict within the colonies transformed the colonial rebellion into a revolutionary turning point in American history. Or would it be more accurate to see the Revolution as a colonial liberation movement much like the Algerian struggle against the French?

How important were the differences that divided Americans? How were these conflicts dealt with to create the unity necessary to fight the Revolution?

Clinton Rossiter

A Revolution to Conserve

In the year 1765 there lived along the American seaboard 1,450,000 white and 400,000 Negro subjects of King George III of England. The area of settlement stretched from the Penobscot to the Altamaha and extended inland, by no means solidly, to the Appalachian barrier. Within this area flourished thirteen separate political communities, subject immediately or ultimately to the authority of the Crown, but enjoying in fact large powers of self-government. Life was predominantly rural, the economy agrarian, religion Protestant, descent English, and politics the concern of men of property.

To the best of the average man's knowledge, whether his point of observation was in the colonies or England, all but a handful of these Americans were contented subjects of George III. It was hard for them to be continually enthusiastic about a sovereign or mother country so far away, yet there were few signs that the imperial bonds were about to chafe so roughly. Occasionally statements appeared in print or official correspondence accusing the colonists of republicanism, democracy, and a hankering for independence, but these could be written off as the scoldings of overfastidious travelers or frustrated agents of the royal will. Among the ruling classes sentiments of loyalty to the Crown were strongly held and eloquently expressed, while the attitude of the mass of men was not much different from that of the plain people of England: a curious combination of indifference and obeisance. Benjamin Franklin, who had more firsthand information about the colonies than any other man, could later write in all sincerity, "I never had heard in any Conversation from any Person drunk or sober, the least Expression of a wish for a Separation, or Hint that such a Thing would be advantageous to America."

From The First American Revolution, © *1953, 1956 by Clinton Rossiter. Reprinted by permission of Harcourt Brace Jovanovich, Inc.*

Yet in the summer and fall of this same year the colonists shook off their ancient habits of submission in the twinkling of an eye and stood revealed as almost an alien people. The passage of the Stamp Act was greeted by an overwhelming refusal to obey, especially among colonial leaders who saw ruin in its provisions—lawyers, merchants, planters, printers, and ministers. Although the flame of resistance was smothered by repeal of the obnoxious act, the next ten years were at best a smoldering truce. In 1775 the policies of Lord North forced a final appeal to arms, and enough Americans answered it to bring off a successful war of independence.

Dozens of able historians have inquired into the events and forces that drove this colonial people to armed rebellion. Except among extreme patriots and equally extreme economic determinists, fundamental agreement now prevails on the immediate causes of the American Revolution. Less attention has been devoted to the question: What made this people ripe for rebellion, or, more exactly, what was there about the continental colonies in 1765 that made them so willing to engage in open defiance of a major imperial policy?

One answer, perhaps the best and certainly the best-known, was volunteered in 1818 by John Adams, himself a cause of the American Revolution: "The Revolution was effected before the war commenced. The Revolution was in the minds and hearts of the people. . . . This radical change in the principles, opinions, sentiments, and affections of the people, was the real American Revolution." What Adams seems to have argued was that well before Lexington and Concord there existed a collective outlook called the American mind, a mind whose chief characteristics, so we learn in other parts of his writings, were self-reliance, patriotism, practicality, and love of liberty, with liberty defined as freedom from alien dictation. It was the alien dictation of North, Townshend, Grenville, and the other shortsighted ministers of a shortsighted king that forced the American mind to assert itself boldly for the first time.

Adams did not find it necessary to describe in detail the long-range forces that had produced this mind, perhaps because that extraordinary student of political realities, Edmund Burke, had already given so perceptive a description. In his magnificent speech on conciliation with the colonies March 22, 1775, Burke singled out "six capital sources" to account for the American "love of freedom," that "fierce spirit of liberty" which was "stronger in the English colonies probably than in any other people of the earth": their English descent; their popular forms of government; "religion in the northern provinces"; "manners in the southern"; education, especially in the law; and "the remoteness of the situation from the first mover of government." Implicit in Burke's praise of the American spirit of liberty, as in Adams's recollection of it, was a recognition that this liberty rested on firm and fertile ground, that the colonists enjoyed in fact as well as in spirit a measure of opportunity and self-direction almost unique in the annals of mankind.

The grand thesis of American history toward which Adams and Burke were groping, not altogether blindly, was rounded off by Alexis de Tocqueville a half-century after the Revolution. With one of his most brilliant flashes of insight De Tocqueville revealed the unique nature of the American Republic: "The great advantage of the Americans is that they have arrived at a state of democracy without having to endure a democratic revolution" or, to state the thesis in terms of 1776, the Americans, unlike most revolutionists in history, already enjoyed the liberty for which they were fighting. The "real American Revolution" was over and done with before the Revolution began. The first revolution alone made the second possible.

My purpose . . . is to provide an extended commentary in support of Adams, Burke, and De Tocqueville—not that this glorious threesome needs support from anyone. I accept with practically no reservations the notion that the American Revolution was wholly different in character and purpose from the French, Russian, and almost all other revolutions, and I ascribe this difference largely to the plain truth that the Americans had no need and thus no intention to "make the world over." By 1765 their world had already been made over as thoroughly as most sensible men—most sensible white men, to be sure—could imagine or expect. Americans had never known or had long since begun to abandon feudal tenures, a privilege-ridden economy, centralized and despotic government, religious intolerance, and hereditary stratification. Americans had achieved and were prepared to defend with their blood a society more open, an economy more fluid, a religion more tolerant, and a government more popular than anything Europeans would know for decades to come. The goal of the rebellious colonists was largely to consolidate, then expand by cautious stages, the large measure of liberty and prosperity that was already part of their way of life. . . .

I think it necessary to point to four all-pervading features of the colonial experience that were hastening the day of liberty, independence, and democracy. Over only one of these massive forces did the colonists or English authorities have the slightest degree of control, and the political wisdom that was needed to keep it in tight rein simply did not exist in empires of that time.

I

The first ingredient of American liberty was the heritage from England. Burke acknowledged this "capital source" in words that his countrymen could understand but apparently not act upon.

The people of the colonies are descendants of Englishmen. England, Sir, is a nation which still I hope respects, and formerly adored, her freedom. The colonists emigrated from you when this part of your character was most predominant; and they took this bias and direction the moment they parted from your lands. They are therefore not only devoted to liberty, but to liberty according to English ideas, and on English principles.

"Wee humbly pray," wrote the General Assembly of Rhode Island to the Board of Trade in 1723, "that their Lordships will believe wee have a Tincture of the ancient British Blood in our veines." The colonists had considerably more than a tincture: at least seven in ten were English in blood, and virtually all their institutions, traditions, ideas, and laws were English in origin and inspiration. The first colonists had brought over both the good and evil of seventeenth-century England. The good had been toughened and in several instances improved; much of the bad had been jettisoned under frontier conditions. As a result of this interaction of heredity and environment, the eighteenth-century American was simply a special brand of Englishman. When it pleased him he could be more English than the English, and when it pleased him most was any occurrence in which questions of liberty and self-government were at issue. In a squabble over the question of a fixed salary between Governor Joseph Dudley and the Massachusetts Assembly, the latter could state without any sense of pretension:

It hath been the Priviledge from Henry the third & confirmed by Edward the first, & in all Reigns unto this Day, granted, & is now allowed to be the just & unquestionable Right of the Subject, to raise when & dispose of how they see Cause, any Sums of money by Consent of Parliament, the which Priviledge We her Majesty's Loyal and Dutiful Subjects have lived in the Enjoym^t of, & do hope always to enjoy the same, under Our most gracious Queen Ann & Successors, & shall ever endeavour to discharge the Duty incumbent on us; But humbly conceive the Stating of perpetual Salaries not agreable to her Majesty's Interests in this Province, but prejudicial to her Majesty's good Subjects.

Southerners were, if anything, more insistent. In 1735 the South Carolina legislature resolved:

That His Majesty's subjects in this province are entitled to all the liberties and privileges of Englishmen . . . [and] that the Commons House of Assembly in South Carolina, by the laws of England and South Carolina, and ancient usage and custom, have all the rights and privileges pertaining to Money bills that are enjoyed by the British House of Commons.

And the men of the frontier, who were having the same trouble with assemblies that assemblies were having with governors, made the echo ring.

1st. We apprehend, as Free-Men and English Subjects, we have an indisputable Title to the same Privileges and Immunities with his Majesty's other Subjects, who reside in the interior Counties of Philadelphia, Chester and Bucks, and therefore ought not to be excluded from an equal Share with them in the very important Privilege of Legislation.

These were the words of men who made much of the English tie, even when, as in the last of these instances, most of them were Scotch-Irish or German. Their traditions—representative government, supremacy of law, constitutionalism, liberty of the subject—belonged to them as Englishmen. Their institutions, especially the provincial assembly, were often looked upon as sound to the extent that they conformed to English models, or at least to colonial interpretations or recollections of those models. The rights for which they contended were not the natural rights of all men but the ancient rights of Englishmen. "It is no Little Blessing of God," said Cotton Mather to the Massachusetts Assembly in 1700, "that we are a part of the *English Nation.*"

Throughout the colonial period the English descent and attitudes of the great majority of Americans gave impetus to their struggles for liberty. It is a momentous fact of American history that until 1776 it was a chapter in English history as well. Just as England in 1765 was ahead of the Continent in the struggle for law and liberty, so America, this extraordinary part of England, was even further ahead, not least because most of its leading inhabitants thought of themselves as Englishmen. Such men would not easily be cheated or argued out of their heritage—a truth that Burke did his best to advertise:

The temper and character which prevail in our colonies are, I am afraid, unalterable by any human act. We cannot, I fear, falsify the pedigree of this fierce people, and persuade them that they are not sprung from a nation in whose veins the blood of freedom circulates. The language in which they would hear you tell them this tale would detect the imposition; your speech would betray you. An Englishman is the unfittest person on earth to argue another Englishman into slavery.

The clash of imperial policy and colonial self-reliance is almost always productive of the spirit of liberty. This is especially true if the policy of the parent state is conceived purely in its own interests, and if the colonists are men of high political aptitude and proud descent. Such was the pattern of Anglo-American relations in the colonial period. From the time of the earliest settlement, which like all the important settlements was the result of private initiative, English and American opinions on the political and economic status of the colonies were in sharp conflict.

The conduct of colonial affairs by the English government rested on these assumptions: The colonies were dependents of the parent state. Since their interests were subordinate to those of England, the welfare of the latter was to be the one concern of all agencies charged with governing them. They were therefore to serve, apparently forever, as a source of wealth and support for the land out of which their inhabitants had departed. If the English government had acted on these assumptions consistently throughout the colonial period, the contrasting ideas of the colonists would have had less chance to strike deep root. But confusion at the beginning, domestic troubles in the middle, and "salutary neglect" throughout most of this period permitted the colonists to build not only a theory but a condition of self-government. And it was this condition, of course, as some perceptive Englishmen were aware, that helped the colonies develop into prizes worth retaining by force of arms. The interests of England were, in this important sense, fatally self-contradictory.

The views of the colonists on their place in the imperial structure were somewhat mixed, ranging from the arrogant independence asserted by Massachusetts in the seventeenth century to the abject dependence argued by a handful of Tory apologists in the eighteenth. In general, the colonial attitude was one looking to near-equality in the present and some sort of full partnership in the future, all within the confines of a benevolent and protecting empire. The colonist acknowledged that for certain diplomatic and commercial purposes his destiny would rest for some time to come in the hands of men in London. But in all other matters, especially in that of political self-determination, he considered himself a "freeborn subject of the Crown of England." Theories of the origin and nature of the colonial assemblies are a good example of these divergent views. In English eyes the assemblies were founded by royal grant and existed at royal pleasure; in American eyes they existed as a matter of right. The Board of Trade looked upon them as inferior bodies enjoying rule-making powers under the terms of their charters; the men of Virginia and Massachusetts looked upon them as miniature Houses of Commons with power to make all laws they could get away with in practice. The struggle between these assemblies and the royal governors sent to control them was the focus of conflict of colonial and imperial interests.

Had Parliament not decided to intrude its authority into colonial affairs, the old-fashioned imperial views of the English authorities and the prophetic self-governing claims of the American colonists might have co-existed for decades without producing a violent break. The tardy policies of stern control initiated by the Grenville ministry brought this long-standing conflict fully into the open. In the years before 1765 the push-and-pull of imperialism and home rule had been a spur to the growth of liberty in the colonies. In the next decade it ignited a rebellion.

II

Let us hear again from the member for Bristol.

The last cause of this disobedient spirit in the colonies is hardly less powerful than the rest, as it is not merely moral, but laid deep in the natural constitution of things. Three thousand miles of ocean lie between you and them. No contrivance can prevent the effect of this distance in weakening government. Seas roll, and months pass, between the order and the execution; and the want of a speedy explanation of a single point is enough to defeat a whole system. . . . In large bodies, the circulation of power must be less vigorous at the extremities. Nature has said it. . . . This is the immutable condition, the eternal law, of extensive and detached empire.

This harsh fact of geography, the remoteness of the colonies, squared the difference between imperial purpose and colonial aspiration. The early colonists, thrown willy-nilly on their own devices, developed habits of self-government and passed them on to their descendants. The descendants, still just as far if not farther from London, fell naturally into an attitude of provincialism well suited to their condition but corrosive of empire. The lack of contact between one colony and another, the result of distance and unbelievably bad roads, allowed each to develop on its own. The diversity in character of the key colonies of Virginia, Massachusetts, New York, and Pennsylvania made a mockery of any notion of uniform imperial policy.

Worst of all from the imperial point of view, the ill effects of the inconsistency, inefficiency, corruption, stupidity, arrogance, and ignorance displayed to some degree at all times and to a perilous degree at some times by the English authorities were doubled and redoubled by the rolling seas and passing months. English laxity in enforcing the Navigation Acts and colonial habits of disobeying them were one instance of the extent to which three thousand miles of ocean could water down a policy of strict control. The technique of royal disallowance, which seemed so perfectly designed to keep the colonial assemblies in check, was likewise weakened by the mere fact of distance. For example, the disallowance in 1706 of two New Hampshire judiciary acts passed in 1699 and 1701 was never reported properly to the province, and the judiciary in that colony continued to function under these laws for a half century. And the royal governor, the linchpin of empire, was a far more accommodating fellow in Boston or Charleston than he appeared in his commissions and instructions issued from London. A governor like Sir Matthew Johnson of North Carolina, whose reports to the Board of Trade went astray four years in a row, could not have been much of a buffer against colonial urges to independence. When we realize that no regular mail-service of any kind existed until 1755, and that war disrupted communications more than one-third of the time between 1689 and 1763, we can understand how the ocean was at once a highway to freedom and a barrier to imperialism. Rarely in history have the laws of geopolitics worked so powerfully for liberty.

Had Burke ever lived in the colonies, he might have listed still another "capital source" to explain the rise of liberty in America, and thus have anticipated Frederick Jackson Turner and his celebrated thesis. We need not go all the way with Turner—"American democracy is fundamentally the out-

come of the experiences of the American people in dealing with the West"—
to acknowledge the significance of the frontier in early American history.
Whatever the extent of that influence in the nineteenth century, in the seventeenth and eighteenth centuries—when America was one vast frontier and
perhaps one in three Americans a frontiersman at some time in his life—it
was clearly of the first importance. If we may take the word "frontier" to
mean not only the line of farthest settlement to the west, but also the primitive conditions of life and thought which extended throughout the colonies
in the seventeenth century and continued to prevail in many areas east of the
Appalachians during most of the eighteenth, we may point to at least a half-
dozen indications of the influence of the American environment.

First, the frontier impeded the transfer to America of outworn attitudes
and institutions. The wilderness frustrated completely such attempts to plant
feudalism in America as the schemes of Sir Ferdinando Gorges and the still-
born Fundamental Constitutions of Carolina, and everywhere archaic laws
and customs were simplified, liberalized, or rudely abandoned. In the matter
of church-state relations the frontier was especially influential as a decentral-
izing and democratizing force. The positive result of this process of sloughing
off the old ways was an increase in mobility, experimentation, and self-reliance
among the settlers.

The wilderness demanded of those who would conquer it that they
spend their lives in unremitting toil. Unable to devote any sizable part of their
energies to government, the settlers insisted that government let them alone
and perform its severely limited tasks at the amateur level. The early American definition of liberty as freedom *from* government was given added popularity and meaning by frontier conditions. It was a new and invigorating
experience for tens of thousands of Englishmen, Germans, and Scotch-Irish
to be able to build a home where they would at last be "let alone."

The frontier produced, in ways that Turner and his followers have made
clear, a new kind of individual and new doctrines of individualism. The wilderness did not of itself create democracy; indeed, it often encouraged the
growth of ideas and institutions hostile to it. But it did help produce some of
the raw materials of American democracy—self-reliance, social fluidity, simplicity, equality, dislike of privilege, optimism, and devotion to liberty. At the
same time, it emphasized the importance of voluntary co-operation. The
group, too, had its uses on the frontier, whether for defense or barn-raising or
cornhusking. The phrases "free association," "mutual subjection," and "the
consent of the governed" were given new content in the wilderness.

Next, the fact that wages were generally higher and working conditions
better in the colonies than in England did much to advance the cause of liberty. The reason for this happy condition was a distinct shortage of labor, and
a prime reason for the shortage was land for the asking. The frontier population was made up of thousands of men who had left the seaboard to toil for

themselves in the great forest. The results of this constant migration were as important for the seaboard as they were for the wilderness.

From the beginning the frontier was an area of protest and thus a nursery of republican notions. Under-represented in assemblies that made a habit of overtaxing them, scornful of the privileges and leadership assumed by the tidewater aristocracy, resentful of attempts to saddle them with unwanted ministers and officials, the men of the back country were in fact if not in print the most determined radicals of the colonial period. If their quaint and strangely deferential protests contributed very little to the literature of a rising democracy, they nevertheless made more popular the arguments for liberty and self-government.

Finally, all these factors combined to give new force to the English heritage of law, liberty, and self-government. The over-refined and often archaic institutions that the settlers brought along as part of their intellectual baggage were thrust once again into the crucible of primitive conditions. If these institutions emerged in shapes that horrified royal governors, they were nevertheless more simple, workable, and popular than they had been for several centuries in England. The laws and institutions of early Rhode Island or North Carolina would not have worked in more civilized societies, but they had abandoned most of their outworn features and were ready to develop along American lines. The hardworking, long-suffering men and women of the frontier—"People a litle wilful Inclined to doe when and how they please or not at al"—were themselves a primary force in the rise of colonial self-government.

The English descent and heritage of the colonists, the conflict of imperial and colonial interests, the rolling ocean, the all-pervading frontier—these were the "forces-behind-the-forces" that shaped the history of the colonies and spurred the peaceful revolution that preceded the bloody one of 1776. . . .

III

The colonists were not completely at the mercy of their environment. Much of the environment was of their own making; and if circumstances were favorable to the rise of liberty, they did not relieve the colonists of the formidable task of winning it for themselves. The condition of liberty in 1765 was in large part the work of men determined to be free, and the questions thus arise: Who were these men who talked so much of their rights and privileges? Whence came they to America, and how did they fare? . . .

It is now generally agreed that almost all immigrants to the colonies came from the middle and lower classes. "The rich stay in Europe," wrote Crèvecoeur; "it is only the middling and the poor that emigrate." The myths of aristocratic lineage die hard, especially in Cavalier country, but diaries, shipping lists, and court minutes tell us in no uncertain terms of the simple origins of even the most haughty families of New York and Virginia. This does not mean that early America was a land of rogues and poor servant-girls. England and the Continent sent over thousands upon thousands of substantial, intelligent, propertied men and women. Yet fully half the people who came to the colonies could not pay their own passage, and gentleman immigrants, even in the seventeenth century, were amazingly few.

As a matter of fact, those twentieth-century Americans who like to go searching for an ancestor among the gentry of East Anglia may wind up with three or four among the riffraff of Old Bailey. Probably thirty to forty thousand convicts were shipped from England to the colonies in the eighteenth century, a fact that inspired Dr. Johnson's famous growl: "Sir, they are a race of convicts, and ought to be content with anything we allow them short of hanging." Their behavior in the colonies, especially in unhappy Virginia and Maryland, moved Franklin to offer America's rattlesnakes to England as the only appropriate return. Not only did transported convicts commit a large proportion of the crimes in eighteenth-century America, but their presence did much to degrade the servant class and make a callous society even more callous. The mother country's insistence on dumping "the dregs, the excrescence of England" in the colonies was a major item in the catalogue of American grievances, especially since the Privy Council vetoed repeatedly the acts through which the colonies sought to protect themselves.

Well before 1765 the colonies had begun to take on a pattern of national origins that was "characteristically American": They looked to one country for their language, institutions, and paramount culture, but to many for their population. Americans were predominantly English in origin, but they were also Scotch, Irish, German, French, Swiss, Dutch, Swedish, and African. It is impossible to fix precisely the proportions of each nationality in the total white population of 1765; the necessary statistics are simply not available. These general percentages are about as accurate as can be expected: English, 65 to 70 percent; Scots and Scotch-Irish, 12 to 15 percent; Germans, 6 to 9 percent; Irish, 3 to 5 percent; Dutch, 3 percent; all others, 3 to 5 percent. Out of a total population of 1,850,000, probably 400,000 were Negroes and mulattoes. . . .

What was the total effect on society, culture, and government of this influx of nationalities into the American settlement? . . .

First, the melting pot had only just begun to heat up in the latter part of the eighteenth century. Crèvecoeur's example of the English-French-Dutch family "whose present four sons have now four wives of four different nations" was a phenomenon more prophetic of the Republic than typical of the colonies. The great process of national fusion had made little progress by 1765. Assimilation into the English stock rather than the creation of a new people was the result of such intermarriage as took place in colonial times. Nor were all the ingredients yet in the pot; the essential racial (Teutonic-Celtic) and religious (Protestant) unity of the population must not be overlooked.

The arrival of non-English immigrants did much to weaken the hold of the mother country. The newcomer wanted to be as loyal as anyone else, but his allegiance to the Crown could have little real emotional content. The Germans were inclined to be conservatively neutral about English dominion; the Scots and Irish were, for all the loyal humility that oozed from their petitions, innately hostile to the Georges and their agents. They lacked, as one traveler put it, the "same filial attachment" to England "which her own immediate offspring have."

Next, the influx of aliens did much to strengthen the Protestant, dissenting, individualistic character of colonial religion. The Presbyterian, Lutheran, Baptist, and German Pietist churches were the chief beneficiaries of this immigration. The numbers and enthusiasm of these dissenting groups gave a tremendous lift to the cause of religious liberty in the colonies south of Pennsylvania.

The eighteenth-century immigrants helped democratize the political institutions that had been brought over from England and put to work in the wilderness. This was especially true of the Scotch-Irish, whose only quarrel with the representative governments of their adopted colonies was that they were not representative enough. The Germans were inclined to be politically passive; their major contribution to the coming democracy was the support they brought to the middle-class creed of industry, frugality, and self-reliance. The Scotch-Irish, on the other hand, were more politically conscious. If the controlling groups of the coastal counties refused to honor their legitimate claims to participation in public life, this rebuff served only to make their radicalism more insistent. They had little intention of altering the English-American scheme of government, but they did mean to show the world how democratic it could be. The sentiments of "leveling republicanism" were especially active on the Scotch-Irish frontier; here the "real American Revolution" went on apace.

Finally, the mere volume of immigration from Germany and Ireland had a pronounced effect on colonial life. The swarming of these industrious peoples made possible the remarkable expansion in territory and population that marked the eighteenth century in America. If the Scotch-Irishman was America's typical frontiersman, the German was its typical farmer; and between them they made it possible for cities like Philadelphia and towns like Lancaster to grow and flourish. Though they were men of different natures, both sought the same blessing. "And what but LIBERTY, charming LIBERTY, is the resistless Magnet that attracts so many different Nations into that flourishing Colony?" . . .

The Second American Revolution Succeeds the First

On March 22, 1765, George III gave his royal assent to the Stamp Act, a stick of imperial dynamite so harmless in appearance that it had passed both houses of Parliament as effortlessly as "a common Turnpike Bill." Eleven years later, July 2, 1776, the Continental Congress resolved after "the greatest and most solemn debate":

That these United Colonies are, and, of right, ought to be, Free and Independent States; that they are absolved from all allegiance to the British crown, and that all political connexion between them, and the state of Great Britain, is, and ought to be totally dissolved.

In the tumultuous years between these two fateful acts the American colonists, at least a sufficient number of them, stumbled and haggled their way to a heroic decision: to found a new and independent nation upon political and social principles that were a standing reproach to almost every other nation in the world. Not for another seven years could they be certain that their decision had been sound as well as bold; only then would the mother country admit reluctantly that the new nation was a fact of life rather than an act of treason. The colonists were to learn at Brooklyn and Valley Forge that it was one thing to resolve for independence and another to achieve it.

Yet the resolution for independence, the decision to fight as a "separate and equal" people rather than as a loose association of remonstrating colonials, was as much the climax of a revolution as the formal beginning of one, and it is this revolution—the "real American Revolution"—that I have sought to describe. . . . By way of conclusion, I would think it useful to point briefly to those developments in the decade after 1765 that speeded up and brought to bloody conclusion "this radical change in the principles, opinions, sentiments, and affections" of the hitherto loyal American subjects of George III.

The progress of the colonies in these years was nothing short of astounding. Thanks to the fecundity of American mothers and the appeal of the American land, population increased from 1,850,000 in 1765 to more than 2,500,000 in 1776. America's troubles seemed only to make America more alluring; immigrants arrived in especially large numbers between 1770 and 1773. The westward pressure of 650,000 new colonists was, of course, enormous, and many new towns and settlements were planted in frontier lands east of the proclamation line of 1763. The sharp increase in population of the continental colonies lent support to arguments, especially popular after 1774, that Americans would some day outnumber Englishmen, and that there was "something absurd in supposing a continent to be perpetually governed by an island." Signs of increased wealth and well-being inspired other Americans to sing the glories of "a commerce out of all proportion to our numbers."

Far more significant than this material progress was the quickened influence of the "forces-behind-the-forces." . . . The English heritage, the ocean, the frontier, and imperial tension never worked so positively for political liberty as in this decade of ferment. Until the last days before independence the colonists continued to argue as Englishmen demanding English rights. The more they acted like Americans, the more they talked like Englishmen. Heirs of a tradition that glorified resistance to tyranny, they moved into political combat as English Whigs rather than American democrats, reminding the world that "it is the peculiar Right of Englishmen to complain when injured." The other basic forces were no less favorable to the swift advance of the spirit of liberty. In a situation that called desperately for accurate information, firm decisions, and resolute administration, the very distance between London and Boston frustrated the development of a viable imperial policy. In a situation that called no less desperately for colonial understanding of the imperial difficulties facing Crown and Parliament, the push to the frontier weakened the bonds of loyalty to an already too-distant land. And the Stamp Act and Townshend Acts forced most articulate colonists to reduce the old conflict of English and American interests to the simplest possible terms. Since some Englishmen proposed to consign other Englishmen to perpetual inferiority, was it not simply a question of liberty or slavery?

The forces that had long been working for political freedom underwent a sharp increase in influence. The ancient struggle between royal governor and popular assembly took on new vigor and meaning. The depths of ill feeling were plumbed in the maneuvers and exchanges of Governors Bernard and Hutchinson and the Massachusetts legislature. The colonial press engaged in more political reporting and speculation in the single year between June, 1765, and June, 1766, than in all the sixty-odd years since the founding of the *Boston News-Letter*. In early 1765 there were twenty-three newspapers in the colonies, only two or three of which were politically conscious; in early 1775 there were thirty-eight, only two or three of which were not. The spirit of constitutionalism and the demand for written constitutions also quickened in the course of the far-ranging dispute over the undetermined boundaries of imperial power and colonial rights. The word "unconstitutional," an essential adjunct of constitutionalism, became one of America's favorite words. Most important, the Stamp Act was a healthy spur to political awareness among all ranks of men. Wrote John Adams in 1766:

> The people, even to the lowest ranks, have become more attentive to their liberties, more inquisitive about them, and more determined to defend them, than they were ever before known or had occasion to be; innumerable have been the monuments of wit, humor, sense, learning, spirit, patriotism, and heroism, erected in the several provinces in the course of this year. Their counties, towns, and even private clubs and sodalities have voted and determined; their merchants have agreed to sacrifice even their bread to the cause of liberty; their legislatures have resolved; the united colonies have remonstrated; the presses have everywhere groaned; and the pulpits have thundered.

The thundering pulpit, an old and faithful servant of American freedom, set out to demonstrate anew the affinity of religious and political liberty. Bumptious Protestantism vied with temperate rationalism as spurs to disestablishment and liberty of conscience. Conditions for the final triumph of unqualified religious liberty grew more favorable in this unsettled decade. So, too, did conditions of economic independence. The over-all state of the American economy lent impressive support to radical claims that the colonies would get along just as well, if not better, outside the protecting confines of British mercantilism. In wealth, resources, production, ingenuity, and energy the Americans were fast approaching the end of the colonial line. . . .

In every colony the middle class formed the nucleus of the patriot party, and in Boston it attained a position of commanding political influence. The aristocracy split into opposing camps, but the Lees of Virginia and Livingstons of New York are reminders that a decisive share of patriotic leadership fell to the American aristocrat. The political storms of the decade, which deposited power in new hands in almost every colony, did much to stimulate social mobility and class conflict. The career of the Sons of Liberty attests the growing fluidity of colonial society; the uprisings of the "Paxton Boys" in Pennsylvania and the Regulators in North Carolina attest the heightened tensions of class and section.

Finally, the colonial mind took rapid strides forward in this period, not alone in the field of political thought. Deism, rationalism, and the scientific spirit claimed increasing numbers of men in positions of leadership. The cult of virtue enjoyed a vogue even more intense than in the colonial period. The arts showed new signs of indigenous strength. The sharp increase in the number of newspapers was matched by an even sharper increase in the output of books and pamphlets. Three new colleges opened their doors to eager students, and King's and the Philadelphia Academy instituted the first American medical schools. Despite all the shouting about English rights and ways, the colonial mind was growing steadily less English and more American. By the standards of the old world, it was a mind not especially attractive, not least because it was setting out at last to find standards of its own.

The American colonies moved fast and far between 1765 and 1776. While the King fumed, the ministry blundered, assemblies protested, mobs rioted, and Samuel Adams plotted, the people of the colonies, however calm or convulsed the political situation, pushed steadily ahead in numbers, wealth, self-reliance, and devotion to liberty. The peaceful revolution that had been gathering momentum from the time of the first settlements moved irresistibly to conclusion, and the fighting revolution could now begin. It could begin, moreover, with high hopes for its success. Blessed by a way of life that knew much freedom and held the promise of much more, the Americans, like the Englishmen who unseated James II, could make their revolution "a parent to settlement, and not a nursery of future revolutions." This was one colonial people that went to war for liberty knowing in its bones what liberty was.

Merrill Jensen

Radicals vs. Conservatives

The American Revolution was far more than a war between the colonies and Great Britain; it was also a struggle between those who enjoyed political privileges and those who did not. Yet the conclusions which may be drawn from the history of social conflict within the colonies and applied to such matters of mutual concern as the writing of a common constitution are seldom drawn and applied. Ordinarily the Revolution is treated as the end of one age and the beginning of another; a new country was born; political parties sprang into being; political leaders, full of wisdom learned during the Revolution, sought to save the new nation from the results of ignorance and inexperience. So runs the story.

But the story is true only in an external sense. The basic social forces in colonial life were not eliminated by the Declaration of Independence. There was no break in the underlying conflict between party and party representing fundamental divisions in American society. Those divisions had their roots in the very foundation of the colonies, and by the middle of the eighteenth century there had arisen broad social groupings based on economic and political conditions. More and more, wealth and political power were concentrated along the coast, in the hands of planters in the South and of merchants in the North. There were exceptions, of course, but by and large the colonial governments were in the hands of the economic upper classes. Exceedingly conscious of its local rights, the ruling aristocracy was willing to use democratic arguments to defeat the centralizing policies of Great Britain, but it had no intention of widening the base of political power within the colonies to accord with the conclusions which could be, and were, drawn from those

Reprinted with permission of the copyright owners, the Regents of the University of Wisconsin, from Merrill Jensen, The Articles of Confederation, 1959, the University of Wisconsin Press.

arguments. On the contrary, it had kept itself in power through the use of a number of political weapons. As wealth accumulated and concentrated along the coast, as the frontier moved westward and became debtor and alien in character, and as the propertyless element in the colonial towns grew larger, the owners of property demanded "a political interpretation of their favored position"—that is, political supremacy—as a protection against the economic programs of debtor agrarians and the town poor. Encouraged by the British government, they gradually secured the political safeguards they demanded— property qualifications for participation in government and representation disproportionate to their numbers. The imposition of property qualifications for the suffrage and of even higher qualifications for office effectively quelled the political ambitions of the greater part of the town population, and the denial of proportional representation to the newly settled areas prevented the growing West from capturing control of colonial governments. Laws of entail and primogeniture insured the economic basis of colonial society, so much so that Thomas Jefferson believed that their abolition in Virginia would annul the privileges of an "aristocracy of wealth."

But the economic-political aristocracy which Jefferson hoped to abolish had not always been characteristic of the American colonies. In early Virginia and Maryland every free man, whether holding property or not, could vote. The first serious attempt to impose a property qualification for the suffrage came with the Restoration and it met with bitter opposition. One of the significant acts of Bacon's Assembly in 1676 was the abolition of the property qualification imposed by the Berkeley regime. But the victory of the poorer elements was short-lived at best, and in Virginia, as elsewhere in the colonies by the end of the seventeenth century, the property qualification was an integral part of the political system. During the eighteenth century the tendency was in the direction of ever higher qualifications, and colonial assemblies continued to refuse adequate representation to the expanding West. By the middle of the century a small minority of the colonial population wielded economic and political powers which could not be taken from them by any legal means. This political oligarchy was able to ignore most of the popular demands, and when smoldering discontent did occasionally flare up in a violent outburst, it was forcibly suppressed. Thus democracy was decreasingly a characteristic of constitutional development in the American colonies.

Opposition to the oligarchical rule of the planters and merchants came from the agrarian and proletarian elements which formed the vast majority of the colonial population. Probably most of them were politically inert, but from their ranks nevertheless came some of the effective leadership and much of the support for revolutionary activity after 1763. In the towns the poorer people, although a small part of the colonial population, far outnumbered the large property-owners. Most of them—laborers, artisans, and small tradesmen —were dependent on the wealthy merchants, who ruled them economically and socially. Agrarian discontent, too, was the product of local developments:

of exploitation by land speculators, "taxation without representation," and the denial of political privileges, economic benefits, and military assistance. The farmer's desire for internal revolution had already been violently expressed in Bacon's Rebellion and in the Regulator Movement, events widely separated in time but similar in cause and consequence.

To a large extent, then, the party of colonial radicalism was composed of the masses in the towns and on the frontier. In Charleston, Philadelphia, New York, and Boston the radical parties were the foundation of the revolutionary movement in their towns and colonies.[1] It was they who provided the organization for uniting the dispersed farming population, which had not the means of organizing, but which was more than ready to act and which became the bulwark of the Revolution once it had started. Located at the center of things, the town radicals were able to seize upon issues as they arose and to spread propaganda by means of circular letters, committees of correspondence, and provincial congresses. They brought to a focus forces that would otherwise have spent themselves in sporadic outbursts easily suppressed by the established order.

Colonial radicalism did not become effective until after the French and Indian War. Then, fostered by economic depression and aided by the bungling policy of Great Britain and the desire of the local governing classes for independence within the empire, it became united in an effort to throw off its local and international bonds. The discontented were given an opportunity to express their discontent when the British government began to enforce restrictions upon the colonies after 1763. The colonial merchants used popular demonstrations to give point to their more orderly protests against such measures as the Stamp Act, and it was only a step from such riots, incited and controlled by the merchants, to the organization of radical parties bent on the redress of local grievances which were of far more concern to the masses than the more remote and less obvious effects of British policy. Furthermore, there arose, in each of the colonies, leaders of more than ordinary ability, men who were able to create issues when none were furnished by Great Britain, and

[1] The terms "radical" and "conservative" in this discussion are not synonymous with "revolutionist" and "loyalist." That they are not interchangeable is obvious from the easily demonstrable fact that there were in internal colonial politics radicals who became loyalists, and conservatives who became revolutionists.

The interpretation of the Revolution is too often confused by the insistence that all revolutionists were radicals. Probably most radicals were revolutionists, but a large number of revolutionists were not radicals. The conservatives were those who—whether they desired independence or not—wanted to maintain the aristocratic order in the American colonies and states. The radicals were those who wanted changes in the existing order, changes which can be best described as democratic, though the term is necessarily relative.

By and large the majority of the colonial aristocracy was opposed to independence. This attitude was due partly to training, partly to self-interest, and partly—increasingly after 1774—to the fear that independence would result in an internal revolution. The radicals, on the other hand, shifted from mere opposition to British measures to a demand for independence as they came to realize that only independence would make possible the internal revolution which radicalism in the colonies had come more and more to demand.

who seized on British acts as heaven-sent opportunities to attack the local aristocracy—too strongly entrenched to be overthrown on purely local issues —under the guise of a patriotic defense of American liberties. Thus, used as tools at first, the masses were soon united under capable leadership in what became as much a war against the colonial aristocracy as a war for independence.

The American Revolution thus marks the ascendancy of the radicals of the colonies, for the first time effectively united. True, this radical ascendancy was of brief duration, but while it lasted an attempt was made to write democratic ideals and theories of government into the laws and constitutions of the American states. Fulfillment was not complete, for the past was strong and in some states the conservatives retained their power and even strengthened it. And once independence was won, the conservatives soon united in undoing, so far as they could, such political and economic democracy as had resulted from the war. Nevertheless it is significant that the attempt at democratization was made and that it was born of colonial conditions. The participation of the radicals in the creation of a common government is all-important, for they as well as the conservatives believed that a centralized government was essential to the maintenance of conservative rule. Naturally the radicals who exercised so much power in 1776 refused to set up in the Articles of Confederation a government which would guarantee the position of the conservative interests they sought to remove from power.

The conservatives gradually became aware that internal revolution might be the result of continued disputes between themselves and Great Britain, but they were not agreed on the measures necessary to retain both "home rule" and the power to "rule at home." Some of them, like Joseph Galloway, sought to tighten the bonds between the colonies and the mother country and thus to consolidate the power and bulwark the position of the colonial aristocracy. Other conservatives, like John Dickinson, denied that Parliament had any authority over the colonies and cared little for a close tie with the mother country; what they demanded was a status that was in effect home rule within the British Empire. Complete independence was to be avoided if possible, for it was fraught with the danger of social revolution within the colonies. As these men became aware that conservative rule had as much or more to fear from the people of the colonies as from British restrictions, they sought more and more for reconciliation with the mother country, in spite of her obvious intention to enforce her laws by means of arms. But they made the fatal yet unavoidable error of uniting with the radicals in meeting force with force. They made themselves believe that it was neither traitorous nor illegal to resist with arms the British measures they disliked.

When independence could no longer be delayed, the conservatives were forced to choose between England and the United States. Some became "Tories," or "Loyalists." Others, the victims of circumstances partly of their own creation, fearfully and reluctantly became revolutionists. But in so doing they did not throw away their ideals of government. They were too cool, too well versed in checkmating radicalism and in administering governments in their own interest, to be misled by the democratic propaganda of the radicals. Not even John Adams, one of the few conservatives who worked for independence, was willing to stomach the ideas of Tom Paine when it came to the task of forming governments within the American colonies.

The continued presence of groups of conservatives in all the states, weakened though they were by the Revolution, is of profound importance in the constitutional history of the United States. They appeared in strength in the first Continental Congress. In it their ideas and desires were expressed. They were still powerful at the beginning of the second Continental Congress, but gradually their hold was weakened by the growing revolutionary movement in the various states. They were strong enough, however, to obstruct the radical program during 1775 and to delay a declaration of independence in 1776 until long after the radicals believed that independence was an accomplished fact. In the bitter controversies which occurred the conservatives stated their ideas of government. In its simplest form their objection to independence was that it involved internal revolution. When forced to accept independence, they demanded the creation of a central government which would be a bulwark against internal revolution, which would aid the merchant classes, which would control Western lands, which would, in short, be a "national" government. In this they were opposed by the radicals, who created a "federal" government in the Articles of Confederation and who resisted the efforts of the conservatives to shape the character of those Articles while they were in process of writing and ratification.

It is against such a background of internal conflict that the Articles of Confederation must be considered. Naturally any statement of the issues or principles of the Revolution, however broad the terminology, is likely to be misleading, for, as John Adams wrote, "the principles of the American Revolution may be said to have been as various as the thirteen states that went through it, and in some sense almost as diversified as the individuals who acted in it." There are inconsistencies and contradictions that cannot be forced into a logical pattern. Generalizations must therefore be understood as statements of tendencies and of presumed predominance rather than as unexceptionable statements of fact. Thus when the Revolution is interpreted in the following pages as predominantly an internal revolution carried on by the masses of the people against the local aristocracy, it is not without recognition of the fact that there were aristocratic revolutionists and proletarian loyalists; that probably the majority of the people were more or less indifferent to what was taking place; and that British policy after 1763 drove many conservatives into a war for independence.

Any interpretation of the American Revolution is subject to such qualifications, discomforting as it is to those who want complexities reduced to simple formulas. Any collection of facts must, however, be grouped around a theme, and particularly is this true of a movement having so many aspects as the American Revolution. Such grouping is unavoidable if one seeks to understand how the course of events, how the course of social revolution within the several states, often played a far more important role in determining political attitudes than did the more remote dangers of British policy.

In spite of the paradoxes involved one may still maintain that the Revolution was essentially, though relatively, a democratic movement within the thirteen American colonies, and that its significance for the political and constitutional history of the United States lay in its tendency to elevate the political and economic status of the majority of the people. The Articles of Confederation were the constitutional expression of this movement and the embodiment in governmental form of the philosophy of the Declaration of Independence.

The Internal Revolution

The Articles of Confederation were written by men many of whom rose to leadership as a result of the tempestuous local political battles fought in the years before the Revolution. Most of these new leaders gained power because they voiced the animosities and thus won the support of the discontented—the masses in the towns and the farmers of the back country—, who in most of the states won the right to express themselves politically, or were able to force concessions where the conservative element remained in control of the new governments created.

When it came to the formation of a common government for all the states, the radicals were guided by experience and by certain political ideas. Experience had taught them to dislike the colonial governing classes and to fear the concentration of wealth and political power. Their political philosophy taught that governments exercising power over wide areas were inherently undemocratic in action. This distrust of the concentration and centralization of unchecked political authority was deepened by the fact that most of the revolutionary leaders were essentially local leaders whom necessity had forced into an international movement for independence but who continued to be guided and controlled by the exigencies of local politics. It is necessary, therefore, to turn to the revolutionary history of the individual colonies for an explanation of the many exceptions one must make to any generalizations regarding the revolutionary movement as a whole and the constitution it produced.

* * *

Pennsylvania offers the clearest illustration of some of the basic issues upon which the course of the American Revolution turned. In no other colony were the racial-political-economic lines so sharply drawn, nowhere was the ruling class so opposed to change or to concession, and nowhere was the political revolution so complete in 1776.

As the colony had grown in wealth and population, political control had been retained by the three old counties of Philadelphia, Bucks, and Chester, and the city of Philadelphia. By the middle of the century an oligarchy of Quaker merchants and lawyers was dictating most of the policies of government. Their instrument was the colonial assembly, control of which they retained by denying representation to the ever-growing west. Even when new counties were created, they were made so vast in extent and were allotted so few representatives in the Assembly that the rule of the east was never endangered. In the east itself the masses were prevented from threatening oligarchical rule by suffrage laws which excluded all but a small minority of the population. The right to vote was contingent upon the possession of fifty pounds in personal property or a freehold. Neither was easy to secure, at least in the east. In Philadelphia in 1775 only 335 of 3,452 taxable males had estates large enough to give them the vote.

Opposition to the oligarchy was centered in the Susquehanna Valley and in the city of Philadelphia. The Susquehanna Valley, peopled largely by Scotch-Irish and Germans, was separated from the east by geography, by economic interest, by race, and by religion. Its natural market was the city of Baltimore, which very early improved roads to attract the trade of its northern neighbors, while the Pennsylvania Assembly refused to build roads or in any way to tie the west to the east.

Aside from racial and religious animosities, the grievances of the west against the east were very specific. It carried a burden of taxation without adequate representation, which in 1771, when an excise tax on hard liquor was instituted, was opposed in a manner prophetic of the later Whiskey Rebellion. The Presbyterian Scotch-Irish were driven to desperation by the refusal of the Quaker Assembly to aid them in their ever-continuing war with the Indians. The Proclamation line of 1763, which threatened to dispossess many westerners of lands already settled, was blamed on the Quakers. The pacifism of the Quaker merchants enraged frontiersmen, who suspected them of being moved more by a desire to maintain the fur trade than by humanitarian concern over the fate of the Indians.

The western farmer could meet the eastern merchant on terms of approximate equality only if he could secure adequate representation in the Assembly. This too was the demand of the populace of Philadelphia, where government was in the hands of the same wealthy class as controlled the colony. The sources of urban discontent were even more immediate than those of the west. All through the century the merchants had tried by various means to overthrow the system of markets and auctions in order to get a monopoly of the retail trade. Finally, in 1771, they devised a scheme which led to the most startling outburst of popular feeling that occurred before the Revolution. They agreed among themselves to buy from none but vendue masters who would agree to sell in large quantities. It was obvious that to continue in business the vendue masters would have to meet the demands of the big merchants. It was equally obvious that the poor could not afford to buy in large quantities and would thus be forced to buy from the merchants, who had long shown a disposition to take a more than "reasonable" profit in fixing retail prices. The merchants likewise tried to check the activity of wandering peddlers. Fishing rights in the navigable rivers were restricted, a measure which the poor felt to be aimed directly at them. In the face of such events it was natural that the lawyer-agents of the merchants should be bitterly attacked by the masses of the population.

The attempt of the Quaker element in the east to convert Pennsylvania from a proprietary into a crown colony was fought bitterly by the Presbyterians in both east and west. Though they had none too great a love for the Penn family, they knew full well that the creation of a crown colony would place them entirely at the mercy of the oligarchy. In this struggle John Dickinson led the proprietary party, which had the support of the west. Franklin, who, oddly enough, has since acquired a reputation as a democrat, was the agent of the oligarchy in England. A future loyalist, Joseph Galloway, led its forces in the Pennsylvania Assembly.

British policy was at once the occasion and the excuse for action in Pennsylvania. As in the other colonies, the propertied classes were strongly opposed to any acts of Parliament infringing upon their local independence or interfering with the profits of trade. But the arguments they advanced in support of their rights were a double-edged weapon that cut in favor of the unrepresented classes as well as colonial self-government. By 1755 the oligarchy began to realize that it was caught between the hammer and the anvil. This became increasingly clear as a revolutionary organization was developed wherein the old restrictions on the franchise and county representation no longer held. The creation of a provincial congress gave the west a dominance in the colony and deprived the three old counties of the hold they had had over the majority of the others. Yet the old Assembly continued to meet and to refuse concessions that would have weakened the radical program and enabled the Assembly to assume the leadership itself. By thus refusing either to lead or to guide, the conservative party was thrown from power in June, 1776. The radical party, temporarily unhampered, was able to write the most democratic constitution any American state has ever had.

The conservatives, led by James Wilson, Robert Morris, John Dickinson, and others, opposed the new order so bitterly that they very nearly wrecked the government of the state and did in fact render it largely ineffective in fighting the Revolution. The unicameral legislature, which they had considered satisfactory so long as it had been in their own control, they now criticized as the worst of all possible forms of government. Their proposal of a system of "checks and balances" as the remedy for all political ills was a thin disguise for their desire to regain control of the state. By 1779 they had made some political gains, but since they were a minority their control of a democratic government was bound to be precarious. Recognizing this to be so, they turned more and more to "nationalism" in the hope of gaining power and protection in another political sphere. They became more and more insistent upon the creation of a "national" government. Their program involved strengthening the Articles of Confederation, but when this failed they participated in a conservative political revolution which ignored the legal methods of constitutional change and created a government in harmony with conservative ideas and experience. . . .

* * *

The calling of the first Continental Congress wrought a fundamental change in the growing revolutionary movement. No longer were the scattered revolutionary forces, feeding upon the vacillations of British policy and the exigencies of local politics, the center of the movement. When Congress outlined general policies which achieved the status of law as a result of popular support, it took the lead in the Revolution, although its effectiveness as a revolutionary organization was determined ultimately by the political character of the state organizations sending delegates to it. As the local radical parties gained power and sent radicals to Congress, it changed its policies. The history of those changing policies is the history of the outbreak of the American Revolution.

Thomas C. Barrow

The American Revolution
as a Colonial War
for Independence

The current historiographical controversies over the American Revolution owe much to Carl Becker. From Becker's day to the present, historians have debated the question of the existence or non-existence of an "internal revolution" in American society. Some historians, following Becker's lead, search for traces of internal social or political turmoil. Others, disagreeing with Becker, stress the continuity of institutions and traditions during the Revolution. At issue is the basic question of just "how revolutionary was the American Revolution," and in the failure of historians to agree on an answer to that question lies the source of controversy. And so the great debate continues.

Unfortunately, there is no adequate definition of a "revolution." The dictionary description of a revolution as a "total or radical change" certainly provides no effective guideline. Since history is the study of change in human society, locating a revolution according to that formula becomes a matter of appraising just how much change is involved in a given event, which inevitably comes down to a question of where one wants to place the emphasis. In any case, precise definitions are somewhat beside the point. When the word *revolution* is used today in connection with a political system, its meaning, if not its precise definition, is abundantly clear. The image called to mind is inescapably that of the French and Russian revolutions, which have provided us with our classic formulas for revolutionary re-structurings of society. A revolution in these terms represents the replacement of an archaic, repressive regime or regimes with something new, something more

From Thomas C. Barrow, "The American Revolution as a Colonial War for Independence," William and Mary Quarterly, 3rd ser., XXV (July 1968), pp, 452–464.

open, more flexible, more adaptable. In effect, in the interests of "progress," within the political system stability is replaced by instability until some new synthesis is achieved. Only then is stability restored, at which point the revolutionary drama is closed.

For generations now American historians have struggled to fit their "revolution" into this classic mold. The difficulties they have encountered in doing so are reflected in the present historiographical impasse. It is a problem that might have been avoided had we remembered that the American people were, until 1776, colonials. By its very nature, a colonial society must be, in certain vital ways, unstable. Unable to exercise complete political control, subject to continual external intervention and negative interference, a colonial society cannot achieve effective "maturity"—that is, cannot create and control a political system that will be suited to the requirements of the interests indigenous to that society. A colonial society is an "incomplete" society, and consequently an inherently unstable society. This was as true of American society prior to 1776 as it is today of the colonial societies left in our world. And, consequently, if instability is the given fact in American society at the beginning of the imperial crisis, it is hard to see how the classic pattern of "stability replaced by instability" can be imposed upon it. The answer, of course, is that it cannot, that in fact colonial wars for independence or "liberation," are generically different from revolutions of the French or Russian variety. And, after all, the American Revolution was just that—a colonial war of liberation. Given the widespread existence of such wars in today's world, it is odd that for so long a time we have overlooked the full implications of this fact.

Colonial wars for independence have an inner logic of their own. The first problem is to achieve self-determination. Once that is accomplished, it then becomes a matter of organization, about which, naturally, there always will be fundamental disagreement. What course this disagreement will take, and how bitter it will be, will be determined by the nature of the particular society. In former colonies which have emerged into nationhood in this century, the determining factor has largely been the heterogeneous nature of their societies; with little internal unity or coherence, these new nations generally have fallen back at first on authoritarian centralism. When this has proved incapable of solving the complex problems confronting the society, it has been replaced usually by some kind of collective leadership, often based on the only effective national organization in existence, the military. It is at this point that many of the emergent nations of today find themselves.

Americans were more fortunate in their escape from colonialism. Thanks to the nature of the First British Empire, with its emphasis on commercial growth rather than on imperial efficiency, its loose organization, and the high degree of self-government allowed to the colonists, Americans had developed effective political units which commanded the allegiance of most inhabitants and served as adequate vehicles for the transition from colonial status to nationhood. Given a common English inheritance and a common struggle against British "tyranny," these states made the transition with a minimum of disagreement and dissension. In effect, by 1760 self-government in America, while still incomplete, had gone far. A tightening of English imperial authority after the last war with France brought about a reaction within the colonies toward complete self-determination, which was achieved finally through military success.

Yet, whatever the difference of the American experience from other colonial wars of liberation, certain elements were of necessity shared in common. Within any colonial society there exists an establishment, a group of men whose interests and situation tie them to the existing structure and whose orientation is towards the preservation of the colonial status. When the issue of independence or self-determination begins to be debated, these men are caught in powerful crosscurrents. As natives to the society, they identify to some degree with its problems. At the same time, as beneficiaries of their privileged position within the existing colonial structure, they are not enthusiastic for change. Such men fall back on arguments of moderation, particularly stressing the economic benefits of association with the dominant country and also emphasizing the immaturity of their own society. The gains associated with independence are outweighed for them by the prospects of social and political disorganization. So these men cast their lot with their colonial rulers. Such a man was Thomas Hutchinson. So, too, were many of his Tory associates.

And men like Hutchinson found much to disturb them within American society. Actually, not only was American colonial society subjected to the instability normally inherent in colonial status but there were certain peculiar circumstances which complicated matters further. The melting-pot aspects of American society, the diversity of ethnic, religious, and cultural backgrounds to be found within it, created problems of communication. And, of equal importance, American colonial society was, after all, an artificial creation. Unlike most other historic colonial episodes, the American case was not a matter of an indigenous native society being expropriated and exploited by outsiders. In such instances, the pre-existing patterns of such native societies provide a degree of internal continuity and stability. But the English colonies in North America had at their disposal no such pre-existence. They were created specifically and artificially to perform certain functions in relation to the mother country. Most particularly, from the very beginning their economy was geared to production for distant markets over which they had no control and little influence.

At the same time, while there were sizeable non-English elements within the colonial population which created special problems, nevertheless the majority of the colonists were of the same national origin as their "rulers." It was not an instance of a conquered native population forced to bow fatalistically before the superior skills and power of an alien culture. Rather, it was a case in large part of Englishmen being governed and exploited by Englishmen. The result was a high degree of friction between governed and governors—an insistence by the colonists on their rights as Englishmen—that gave a special flavor and complexity to colonial politics.

Thoughtful colonials were well aware of and influenced by these problems. Thomas Hutchinson and John Adams—Tory and Whig—disagreed not so much on the question of the eventual independence of the American colonies as on the question of timing. Hutchinson's toryism sprang in part from his conviction that American society was too immature, too unstable, to stand alone. External force and authority, it seemed to him, would be required for many years to maintain internal order and stability in America. Realistically, he understood that eventually independence was probable: "It is not likely that the American Colonies will remain part of the Dominions of Great Britain another Century." But, Hutchinson added, until then, "as we cannot otherwise subsist I am consulting the best interest of my country when I propose measures for maintaining this subjection [to England]." What particularly disturbed Hutchinson about the changes in English policy after 1760 was that they tended to increase the instability and disorder inherent within American society: "Sieur Montesquieu is right in supposing men good or bad according to the Climate where they live. In less than two centuries Englishmen by change of country are become more barbarous and fierce than the Savages who inhabited the country before they extirpated them, the Indians themselves."

John Adams viewed American development in a different way. Contrasting the New World with the Old, he found the former far superior. The settlement of America had produced men who "knew that government was a plain, simple, intelligible thing, founded in nature and reason, and quite comprehensible by common sense. They detested all the base services and servile dependencies of the feudal system . . . and they thought all such slavish subordinations were equally inconsistent with the constitution of human nature and that religious liberty with which Jesus had made them free." The problem was that this purity of mind and behavior was always threatened by contact with the corruption of the Old World. Specifically, subordination of Americans to a distant Parliament which knew little of their needs and desires was not only frustrating but dangerous to the American experiment: "A legislature that has so often discovered a want of information concerning us and our country; a legislature interested to lay burdens upon us; a legislature, two branches of which, I mean the lords and commons, neither love nor fear us! Every American of fortune and common sense, must look upon his property to be sunk downright one half of its value, the moment such an absolute subjection to parliament is established." Independence was a logical capstone to such reasoning, although it took Adams some time to take that final step.

The differences between Hutchinson and Adams suggest that the divisions in American society between conservatives and radicals on the question of separation from Great Britain were related in part to a disagreement over the means to achieve coherence or stability within American society. For one side, continued tutelage under English authority was a necessity until such a time as maturity was achieved. For the other, it seemed that the major roadblock to maturity, to internal harmony and unity, was that self-same English authority. In effect, it was a disagreement on means, not ends. And disagreements similar to that between Hutchinson and Adams can be found within any society—whether in the eighteenth or twentieth century—which is in the process of tearing itself loose from its colonial ties.

It is possible, too, to suggest certain similarities between American intellectual development in these years and the experience of other colonial peoples. From his study of politics in eighteenth-century America and particularly from his analysis of the pamphlet literature of the Revolutionary years, Bernard Bailyn has concluded that the "configuration of ideas and attitudes" which comprised the "Revolutionary ideology could be found intact—completely formed—as far back as the 1730's" and that these ideas had their origin in the "transmission from England to America of the literature of political opposition that furnished the substance of the ideology of the Revolution." Colonial societies are both fascinated and yet antagonized by the culture of the dominant exploiting nation. They tend to borrow much from their rulers. The English background of a majority of the American colonists in their case made such borrowing a natural and easy process, particularly for those who, for one reason or another, identified themselves with British rule.

However, in colonial societies even many of those who are anxious to assert, or preserve, their native interests or culture cannot resist that fascination exerted by the dominant "mother country." These "patriots" borrow, too, but they are likely to borrow from the dissenting tradition within the dominant culture, from the literature of "opposition," to utilize in their own defense the language and literature of those elements within the ruling society which are critical, or subversive, of the governing traditions. In this way the prestige of the "superior" society can be used against that society itself. On the evidence of Bailyn's research, it seems that the Americans followed just such a line of development, fitting the "opposition" tradition into the framework of their own evolving institutions and traditions—a process which was facilitated by the natural connections between the American religious dissenting traditions and the "opposition" traditions of eighteenth-century English society.

Again, once the movement for independence enters its final phase within a colonial society and becomes an open contest of strength, other divisions tend to become obscured. The most determined supporters of the colonial rule are silenced or forced to rely increasingly on the military strength of their rulers to maintain their position. On the other side, the advocates of independence submerge momentarily whatever differences they may have and present a common front. It is a time of common effort, of mutual support within the forces interested in achieving self-determination. At the same time the "patriot" groups develop special organizations capable of coercing those elements within society, often a majority of the population, which are inclined towards neutrality or moderation. Such were the Sons of Liberty in the American Revolution, and the evidence suggests that they performed their work effectively. Partly because of their efforts, and more generally because of the peculiar character of American colonial society and the nature of the imperial conflict, American society weathered the crisis with relative stability and harmony. As John Adams put it, "The zeal and ardor of the people during the revolutionary war, supplying the place of government, commanded a degree of order, sufficient at least for the temporary preservation of society."

With independence come altered circumstances for a former colonial society. Victorious patriots, confronted with the task of creating a permanent political structure, gradually begin to disagree among themselves as to how it can best be done. Since the only effective central direction came previously from the colonial rulers, the problem in each newly independent society is to fit the surviving local units into some coherent national structure. Here the forces of localism and centralism come into conflict. Those men or interests firmly entrenched in their positions at the local level see in increased centralism a threat to their existence and power. On the other hand, those men or interests of a more cosmopolitan nature, geared to extra-local activities and contacts, can see the benefits that would accrue to them through the introduction of the smoother flow of communications and transactions that effective centralization would bring. The disagreement pits the particularism of the entrenched local interests and individuals against the nationalism of the cosmopolitan interests and individuals. In most contemporary emergent societies these latter groups are by far the weaker. Fortunately, in America the cosmopolitan groups were stronger and more effective, partly again because of the unusual origin and nature of American colonial society. From the beginning the English colonies had been geared to production for European markets; it was the reason for their existence. The result was the development of an economy which had geographical variations but a common external orientation. Merchants and large-scale producers of items for export dominated this society. In the period after independence was achieved, these men provided a firm base for the construction of an effective national political system. Their success came with the substitution of the Constitution of 1787 for the Articles of Confederation.

Historians following the Becker-Beard approach put a different interpretation on the period following the achievement of de facto independence. For them, it was the moment of the triumph of radical democratic elements within American society. The wording of the Declaration of Independence, the constitutions of the new state governments, and particularly the drawing up of the Articles of Confederation represent for these historians the influence of a form of "radicalism." Yet, as Elisha Douglass has noted, in the formation of the governments for the new states, rather puzzlingly the one political reorganization that was subjected to the most democratic method of discussion and adoption—that of Massachusetts—turned out to be not only the most conservative of all the state constitutions but more conservative, in fact, than the previous system. Somehow in Massachusetts, at least, an excess of democracy seems to have led to an enthronement of conservatism. And, indeed, the new constitutions or systems adopted in all the states were remarkable generally for their adherence to known and familiar forms and institutions.

Obviously, given the disruption of the traditional ties to England, the interruption of the natural economic dependence on English markets, the division of American society into opposing Whig and Tory camps, and the presence on American soil of enemy troops (which occupied at different moments the most important commercial centers), some confusion and dissension was inevitable within American society. What is remarkable is how little upheaval and disagreement there actually was. Had American society been ripe for a social upheaval, had it been comprised of oppressing and oppressed classes, no better opportunity could have been offered. The conservative nature of the American response suggests that something other than a radical re-structuring of society was what was debated or desired.

Again, some historians have interpreted the decentralized political system created under the Articles of Confederation as a "triumph" of radical democracy. However, if instability, associated with colonial status and with the peculiar character of American colonial society, was a recurrent problem, and if inability to achieve positive control of their own political system was a major irritant, then the decentralization of the Articles was a logical development. In effect, if home rule was the issue and the cure, it was only natural that each local unit should seek as much autonomy within the national framework as possible. Seemingly, decentralization was the best method to bring coherence and stability, or maturity, to American society. Each local unit could look to its own needs, could arrange for the effective solution of its own special problems, could work to create that internal balance and harmony of conflicting interests that are the earmark of stability and maturity.

The problem with the Articles was not an excess of democracy. What brought about an effective opposition to them was their failure to achieve their purpose. The history of the states under the Articles, at least in the eyes of many contemporaries, suggested that decentralization, rather than being a source of stability, was a source of confusion and turmoil. James Madison explained the nature of the mistake in his Tenth Federalist. In spite of independence, under the system created by the Articles, wrote Madison, "complaints are everywhere heard from our most considerate and virtuous citizens . . . that our governments are too unstable." The problem, for Madison, was to control faction within society, and the most dangerous type of faction is that which includes a majority. Unfortunately, the "smaller the society, the fewer probably will be the distinct parties and interests composing it; the fewer the distinct parties and interests, the more frequently will a majority be found of the same party; and the smaller the number of individuals composing a majority, and the smaller the compass within which they are placed, the more easily will they concert and execute their plans of oppression." The solution is to enlarge the sphere, because if "you take in a greater variety of parties and interests," then "you make it less probable that a majority of the whole will have a common motive to invade the rights of other citizens. . . . The influence of factious leaders may kindle a flame within their particular States, but will be unable to spread a general conflagration through the other States."

Nor was the opposition to the Constitution less concerned than Madison about order and stability within society. Again, disagreement was fundamentally over means, not ends. The anti-Federalists clung to the former ideas of local autonomy. They were, in fact, not more democratic than their opponents but more conservative. They were afraid of change: "If it were not for the stability and attachment which time and habit gives to forms of government, it would be in the power of the enlightened and aspiring few, if they should combine, at any time to destroy the best establishments, and even make the people the instruments of their own subjugation." The trouble was that the system created under the Articles was not yet sanctified by time: "The late revolution having effaced in a great measure all former habits, and the present institutions are so recent, that there exists not that great reluctance to innovation, so remarkable in old communities . . . it is the genius of the common law to resist innovation." George Clinton agreed with Madison on the dangers of faction: "The people, when wearied with their distresses, will in the moment of frenzy, be guilty of the most imprudent and desperate measures. . . . I know the people are too apt to vibrate from one extreme to another. The effects of this disposition are what I wish to guard against." It was on the solution to the problem, not on the nature of the problem, that Clinton differed from Madison. For Clinton, the powerful central government created by the Constitution might too easily become a vehicle for popular tyranny. It was this same sentiment which led eventually to the adoption of the first ten amendments, the Bill of Rights, with their reservations of basic rights and powers to local units and individuals.

It would not do to carry the comparison between the American Revolution and other colonial wars of liberation, particularly those of the twentieth century, too far. But there is enough evidence to suggest certain basic similarities between the American experience and that of other emergent colonial peoples—enough evidence, at least, to suggest that the efforts of historians to impose on the American Revolution the classic pattern of the French and Russian revolutions have led to a distorted view of our national beginnings. A French Revolution is the product of unbearable tensions within a society. The purpose of such a revolution is to destroy society as it exists, or at least to destroy its most objectionable aspects, and to replace the old with something new. In contrast, a colonial "revolution" or war of liberation has as its purpose the achievement of self-determination, the "completion" or fulfillment of an existing society, rather than its destruction. A French Revolution is first of all destructive; a colonial revolution, first of all constructive. In either case the process may not be completed. In the instance of the French Revolution, the re-constructed society may contain more of the old than the original revolutionaries desired. And in the case of the colonial revolution, the process of winning independence and the difficulties of organizing an effective national political structure may open the gates to change, may create a radicalism that carries the original society far from its former course; the result may be more destruction than was originally envisaged. Yet, the goals of these two revolutions are fundamentally different, and their different goals determine a different process of fulfillment. The unfolding of the revolutionary drama, the "stages" of revolution, will be quite different, if not opposite.

For John Adams, the American Revolution was an epochal event, a moment of wonder for the world to behold and consider. At times his rhetoric carried him beyond the confines of his innate caution, and he sounded like a typical revolutionary: "The progress of society will be accelerated by centuries by this revolution. . . . Light spreads from the day-spring in the west, and may it shine more and more until the perfect day." But, as Edward Handler has noted, "The truth is that if Adams was a revolutionary, he was so in a sense very different than that produced by the other great modern revolutions." Adams did indeed feel that his revolution had a meaning for the world but it was not related to the violent re-structurings of society. Rather its message, for Adams, was that free men can decide voluntarily to limit their freedom in the interests of mutual association, that rational men can devise a system that can at once create order and preserve liberty. The American success was in contrast to the traditional authoritarian systems of the Old World: "Can authority be more amiable or respectable, when it descends from accidents or institutions established in remote antiquity, than when it springs fresh from the hearts and judgments of an honest and enlightened people?"

Most wars of liberation are not so orderly as that of the American Revolution. Most, at least in this century, have led to increasing radicalism and division within the liberated society. National unity has not been easily achieved. That the American emergence from colonialism had a different ending is significant. A firm basis for unity obviously existed within American society, which, naturally, suggests that the reverse too, was true—that such tensions and divisions as did exist within American society were relatively minor and harmless. It is no wonder that historians determined to find an internal social or political revolution of the French variety within the American Revolution have encountered such difficulties. Nor is it a wonder that the Revolution has become so beclouded with historiographical debates and arguments. The problem has been in our approach. We have been studying, it would seem, the wrong revolution.

Edmund S. Morgan

Conflict and Consensus in the American Revolution

During the past fifteen or twenty years a division has emerged among historians of the American Revolution, a division between those who emphasize the consensus achieved by the revolting colonists and those who emphasize conflicts among them. The division has excited attention and has perhaps been exaggerated because of the special position occupied by the Revolution in our national consciousness. As the noises of the approaching bicentennial grow louder, it is scarcely necessary to point out that most Americans, including historians, seem to think the Revolution was a good thing. If any episode in our past is enshrined in our consciousness, this is it. By consequence any group or cause that can affiliate itself with the Revolution may hope to have some goodness rub off on it. As an example, some of us can remember vividly the campaign of the 1930s to make the Revolution and its Founding Fathers rise to the support of Stalinism. Under the slogan "Communism is twentieth-century Americanism," Washington, Jefferson, and Franklin were enrolled posthumously in the popular front. We have similarly had, long since, Catholic interpretations of the Revolution and Calvinist interpretations, Massachusetts interpretations and Virginia interpretations, and a host of others, each somehow concerned with reflecting American-Revolutionary glory on Catholicism or Calvinism, on Massachusetts or Virginia, or whatever.

The alacrity with which the current division among scholars has been recognized, if not promoted, I believe, lies in this sanctifying power of the Revolution and its Founding Fathers. Those who contend that the Revolution bore few marks of social conflict or social upheaval seem to be denying the blessing of the Founding Fathers to present-day struggles against the establish-

From Stephen G. Kurtz and James H. Hutson, eds., Essays on the American Revolution (Chapel Hill: University of North Carolina Press, 1973), pp. 289–309. Reprinted by permission of Edmund S. Morgan.

ment, while those who emphasize conflicts seem to be suggesting that conflicts, or at least conflicts against an upper class or established system, are sponsored by the Founding Fathers, consecrated in the fires at Valley Forge. No such power attaches to other episodes in our history. The New Deal, for example, has not achieved sanctifying power in the national memory. Hence no one would think to classify as conservative those historians who deny that the New Deal achieved or aimed at radical social change. But to say that the Revolution did not achieve or aim at radical social change and lacked the conflicts that generally accompany such change is taken as a denial that radical social change is a good thing. Hence those who give the Founding Fathers failing grades as social revolutionaries are greeted, sometimes to their astonishment, as conservative.

But conservative and radical are relative terms, and so are consensus and conflict; and relative terms, if I may be allowed to follow for a moment the logic of Peter Ramus, can be understood only in relation to each other. Those impressed by the achievement of consensus among the Revolutionists can scarcely hope to understand the nature of that consensus without understanding the conflicts that had to be overcome or repressed in order to arrive at it. Nor can those who emphasize conflict gauge the force of the movements they examine without considering the kind of consensus that later grew out of those movements or that succeeded in subduing them. Therefore, in attempting to assess the meaning of the American Revolution, it may be worthwhile to survey the various points of consensus and conflict that can be discerned in the Revolutionary period, to weigh their effect on the Revolution, and then to examine the kind of consensus that emerged at the end, even if that consensus is thought to be no more than a sullen acquiescence in the measures of a ruling class.

The type of internal conflict that historians have most eagerly searched for among Americans of the Revolutionary period is class conflict. The search is handicapped by a problem of identification. With the struggle of the colonies against the mother country dominating the scene, how does one distinguish a class conflict within that larger conflict?

Not by the side a man chose to support. Although the first historians of the loyalists did assume that they represented an upper if not a ruling class, subsequent investigations have revealed that loyalists, like patriots, were drawn from all classes. That a man sided with the mother country or against her tells us little about his social position. Although it seems altogether likely on the latest evidence that a larger percentage of the well-to-do could be found among the loyalists than among the Revolutionists, the Revolution cut sharply across nearly all previous divisions, whether regional, ethnic, religious, or class. It was not a conflict in which one side was predominantly upper class and the other predominantly lower class.

If, then, we look only at one side, at the Americans who supported the Revolution, or who did not oppose it, can we there find that lower-class rebels were bent on the overthrow or reduction of ruling-class rebels? A moment's reflection on the nature of the Revolutionary War may moderate our expectations. The Revolutionary effort against Great Britain tended to suppress or encompass social conflicts. Where it did not, where hostility between social groups rose to a level of intensity approximating that of the conflict with the mother country, one group or the other would be likely to join with the loyalists. Some merchants in New York City, for example, felt that the local Revolutionary leaders threatened their interests more than the mother country did; and similarly some tenant farmers of the Hudson Valley felt more bitter toward their patriot landlords than they did toward king and Parliament. But these men, whether merchants or tenants, by joining the loyalist side deprived themselves of a part in any contest about who should rule at home. Loyalism in this way tended to absorb social groups that felt endangered or oppressed by the Revolutionary party. It operated as a safety valve to remove from the American side men who felt a high degree of social discontent. Or to change the figure, it drew off men at either end of the political spectrum, reducing the range of disagreements. It removed from the scene the intransigents, of whatever persuasion, who might have prevented the achievement of consensus.

Disputes did occur, of course, among those who remained on the Revolutionary side, but the extraordinary social mobility characteristic of eighteenth-century American society usually prevented such disputes from hardening along class lines. Although recent statistical samplings point to a narrowing of economic opportunity in the latter half of the eighteenth century, Americans still enjoyed an upward mobility unknown in other societies. In a land of rising men a political group formed along lower-class lines had little prospect of endurance.

The Revolution probably increased social mobility temporarily both upward and downward, ruining the fortunes of many established families and opening opportunities for speedy ascent by daring upstarts. This very mobility engendered, as it always has, political disputes, but seldom along class lines. An American who had moved up from the lower ranks carried with him the expectation of sharing with those who had already arrived the offices of government traditionally exercised by the economically and socially successful. If he found himself excluded, he could call upon a wide electorate of his former equals but present inferiors to help him achieve the kind of office that they, no less than he, considered proper for successful men. But the fact that the lower ranks were involved in the contest should not obscure the fact that the contest itself was generally a struggle for office and power between members of an upper class: the new against the established. We must be wary of seeing such struggles, like Patrick Henry's successful bid for power in Virginia, as a rising of the oppressed against their masters.

I do not mean to argue that hostility between classes did not exist at all among those who supported the Revolution or that it cannot be discerned or recognized. In the antirent riots of 1766, for example, New York tenant farmers expressed a hostility to their landlords that was not entirely absorbed by loyalism after 1775. More than one scholar has found clear expressions of class conflict in the conduct of the war and of politics in Revolutionary New York. But in assessing class conflict as a Revolutionary force, we shall be hard pressed to find many instances outside New York in which antagonism rose to the level of actual fighting or even to openly expressed hostility of the kind that might be expected to lead to fighting.

American social structure was so fluid that to talk about social classes at all in most colonies or states requires the use of very loose economic categories such as rich, poor, and middle class, or contemporary designations like "the better sort" or "the poorer sort," or occupational categories like merchant, planter, lawyer, farmer, artisan, and seaman. Americans were no less skilled than other peoples in measuring the degree of deference due to each of their neighbors for the host of reasons and prejudices that confer honor or contempt on the members of any community. But such distinctions were local, seldom negotiable beyond the neighborhood where a man was known, and not always easy to discern even there.

Nevertheless, one absolute, clearly defined, and easily recognized division did exist, that between freeman and slave. Half a million Americans, perhaps a fifth of the total population, were slaves, and slavery is so direct an assault by one group of men on another that it can properly be considered as a form of class conflict in itself. In the American Revolution, however, slaves were unable to mount any serious uprising against their masters. Although the armies of both sides sooner or later made use of slaves and gave some of them freedom for their services, neither side provided the help necessary for large-scale insurrection. Both felt more need to woo masters than slaves. Perhaps the possibility of insurrection was even lessened by the few efforts of the British to promote it. When Lord Dunmore invited the slaves of Virginia to desert their masters and join his forces, he probably drew off many of the bolder individuals, leaving behind those who were less likely to rise in revolt later. Again loyalism tended to absorb men who might otherwise have directed their energies more radically against a local ruling class.

That the American Revolution did not produce an uprising of the group in colonial society that was most visibly and legally oppressed, and oppressed with the explicit or tacit approval of the rest of the society, is itself an instructive comment on the nature of social conflict and consensus during the Revolution.

The absence of any massive revolt, white or black, may perhaps be put in perspective if we compare the labor force of the Revolutionary period with that a century earlier, when Bacon's Rebellion had terrorized the first families of Virginia. In the seventeenth century as in the eighteenth the greater part of the colonial labor force, that is, of men who worked for other men, was concentrated in the South and especially in Virginia. In 1676, when Bacon's Rebellion occurred, the laborers were mostly imported servants, English, Irish, Scottish, or Welsh, whose terms of service generally expired when they reached the age of twenty-four. They were imported at the rate of eight hundred to a thousand or perhaps as many as fifteen hundred or two thousand annually;

they were mostly male, and they had come in expectation of a better life once their terms of service were up.

For a variety of reasons, in the ten or fifteen years before 1676, Virginia underwent a depression that severely curtailed the opportunities for a newly freed servant to make his way in the world. Tobacco prices were low. Land in the settled areas had been taken up in large quantities by earlier comers, and men either had to rent land at prices that left no room for profit or else they had to move to the frontiers, where Indians mounted guerrilla attacks on them. The officers of government lived high off the hog in spite of depression, by levying high taxes and voting each other generous fees, salaries, and sinecures. The result was the presence of a clearly distinguishable privileged class and a clearly distinguishable lower class, composed not merely of servants who made tobacco for their betters but of former servants who were trying to make it for themselves. These freedmen were likely to be single. They were likely to be without land of their own. But they were not likely to be without guns, especially those who had moved, as many had, to the frontier.

As early as 1673 Governor Berkeley recognized the dangers of this situation. At least one-third of Virginia's militia, he estimated, were single freedmen, who would have nothing to lose by turning their arms against their superiors for the sake of plunder. Three years later, goaded by Indian raids, they did it. Bacon's Rebellion swept across Virginia, starting among the penniless pioneers of the frontier counties and gathering momentum from the adherence of other men who had nothing to lose in a free-for-all scramble for the accumulated wealth of the privileged few. In the midst of it Berkeley wrote to England, understandably raising his estimate of the numbers of the disaffected. "How miserable that man is," he complained, "that Governes a People wher six parts of seaven at least are Poore Endebted Discontented and Armed."

A hundred years later the situation had changed radically in at least one important respect. In the South, where a large labor force still furnished the way to wealth for plantation owners, the laborers were not continually emerging into the status of independent, poverty-stricken, discontented freemen trying to make a start against heavy odds. By the middle of the eighteenth century the majority of the entire labor force in the plantation colonies was held in permanent slavery. The development of slavery is perhaps the key to the consensus that prevailed in colonial America, for slavery meant the substitution of a helpless, closely guarded lower class for a dangerous, armed lower class that would fight if exploited too ruthlessly. The slave had more reason to revolt than the servant or the new freedman. But he was less able to. He had no hope, no rising expectations, and no arms. On top of that he was black. His status in the community was proclaimed by his color and maintained by a tyranny in which white men of all ranks and regions consented and approved. The consensus on which colonial society rested was a racist consensus.

Had the southern plantations not shifted from free to slave labor, had the planters continued to import masses of indentured servants and continued to pour them into their own and other colonies a few years later as indigent freedmen, then the picture of social mobility in the colonial period and of class conflict in the Revolution might have been quite different. The minutemen of 1775 might have been truly a rabble in arms, ready to turn from fighting the British to fighting their well-to-do neighbors, just as Bacon's men turned from fighting the Indians to fighting Berkeley and his crew. But in the century between 1676 and 1776 the growth of slavery had curbed the growth of a free, depressed lower class and correspondingly magnified the social and economic opportunities of whites. It is perhaps the greatest irony of a Revolution fought in the name of freedom, a Revolution that indeed advanced the cause of freedom throughout the world, that the men who carried it out were able to unite against British oppression because they had so completely and successfully oppressed the largest segment of their own laboring population.

To be sure, there were those among the Revolutionists who felt uncomfortable about rebelling against what they chose to call the threat of slavery, while they themselves held some 20 percent of their own population in slavery. But such feelings were translated into legal action only in states where slaves were few in number. Those were not the states where an enslaved labor force grew the country's principal exports. And if northerners freed their own slaves, they did not propose at this time to free their neighbors'. The racial consensus on which colonial society had rested was shaken a little but not broken by the Revolution.

There of course continued to be indentured servants and servants who worked for wages both in the plantation colonies and in the North. But the great majority of men who worked for other men were probably the slaves of the plantation colonies. The growing economy, in spite of periodic depressions like that of the 1670s, could absorb the number of indentured servants who turned free each year and could offer most of them an independent and comfortable if not affluent existence on the land. Only a small minority fell permanently into the servant class, like some of the sailors whom Jesse Lemisch has described, and even they reacted more visibly, violently, and vociferously against iniquities of the British government than against whatever oppression was visited upon them by their compatriots.

In sum, the evidence of Revolutionary class conflict is scanty, and for good reason. With a majority of laborers in chains and with the most discontented freemen venting their discontent in loyalism, the struggle over who should rule at home was unlikely to bear many of the marks of class conflict. Class conflict was indubitably present, but it did not surface with an effective intensity until a later day, after the Revolution had built a consensus that could both nourish and contain it, and after social, political, and economic change had produced greater provocations to it.

Let us turn now to another kind of conflict that was more intense and also, I believe, more significant for the Revolution. If we examine the occasions when Americans fought with one another or came very close to fighting between 1763 and 1789, excluding battles between loyalists and patriots, we find a number of episodes, all of them involving men who had moved from the older coastal regions into the interior: the march of the Paxton Boys against Philadelphia, the Regulator movement in the Carolinas with its Battle of Alamance, the activities of the Green Mountain Boys in Vermont, the skirmishes of Pennamite and Yankee in the Wyoming Valley of Pennsylvania, and Shays's Rebellion in Massachusetts. However diverse in immediate cause and attendant circumstance, these conflicts had one thing in common: they were all manifestations of the discontent of western settlers or settlers on new lands against governments dominated by or subservient to the interests of older or eastern regions.

Americans of the Revolutionary period were less successful in repressing sectional conflicts than conflicts arising from class or race. Though this fact is obvious and though the westward movement has received its full share of attention, historians considering the Revolution as a social movement have not always borne in mind two conspicuous conditions of life in eighteenth-century America, conditions that lay at the root of East-West conflict: first, the extraordinary rate of population growth and, second, the abundance of land, unoccupied or only thinly occupied by the native Indians.

Although the rate of population growth in the colonies varied a good deal from place to place and from year to year, the overall long-range trend is clear. The total population of the thirteen colonies that participated in the Revolution more than doubled every twenty-five years during the eighteenth century. Beginning at about 250,000 in 1700, it rose to over 5,000,000 by 1800. As we learn more about the role of population growth in history, it may ultimately appear that the most significant social fact about America in the eighteenth century was this fearful growth, unlike anything that had been known in Europe in recorded history. Every twenty-five years the colonies had to absorb numbers equal to their total population. The result by the last quarter of the eighteenth century was explosive emigration out of the older settled regions into the West. Consider the westward thrust into the Kentucky-Tennessee area alone: the population there could scarcely have amounted to 10,000 in 1781; by 1790 it had soared to 110,000. If we note that this migration over the mountains in the 1780s by itself dwarfed the so-called Great Migration over the ocean in the 1630s, when probably no more than 50,000 left England for all parts of the New World, if we note also that migration was simultaneously occurring into other western areas, then we may begin to appreciate the magnitude of a western factor in the Revolutionary period.

The westward population explosion probably relieved the East from social conflicts that might have arisen from overcrowding; but it generated other conflicts potentially as dangerous. It set rival groups of speculators into contests for control of the richest western lands, contests that drew in and corrupted state governments and the national government. And it created a block of Americans who by moving west acquired different needs and interests from eastern Americans, but who by the same move lost their political ability to make their needs heard or attended to. People moved west so rapidly that even with the best of intentions a government could scarcely have kept up with them in furnishing the town or parish or county organization that formed the units of representation in the legislature. Because representation did not keep up with the expansion of population into new territory, governments remained under the domination of easterners and frequently neglected the needs of westerners. Even where representation was fairly proportioned, the location of the legislature subjected it to eastern influences that could bring it into serious conflict with the West.

Eastern insensitivity to western needs was the source of the Paxton incident, as it had been in part of Bacon's Rebellion. The prime western need in the early years of a settlement was to cope with the Indians, who gathered to attack the invaders of their land. Indian raids were no longer part of life in the East. The very existence of westerners furnished a buffer zone to easterners, enabling them to view the rights and wrongs of the situation with an objectivity that westerners could not achieve or afford. We need not assume that the Paxton Boys were righteous. Benjamin Franklin called them "Christian White Savages," and the epithet was deserved. They were armed thugs, terrorists, murderers; but they were also westerners, and as westerners they had grievances against an eastern-dominated legislature that spent its time arguing about who would pay the bills while it neglected the defense of the frontier.

The Regulator movement represents another phase of the same East-West conflict: the eastern-dominated governments of South Carolina and North Carolina failed to extend the machinery of law enforcement into the West as rapidly as the needs of the settlers required, and so the West took the law in its own hands. In Shays's Rebellion the Shaysites, who also called themselves Regulators, hoped to gain by direct action what the government in Boston had denied them. The Pennamite-Yankee conflict and the activities of the Green Mountain Boys offer a variation on the theme. In these cases two colonial governments, representing different speculative interests, were engaged in a contest for western lands, and the actual settlers fought with each other. The significance of the frontier in early American history, if we may borrow that phrase, was that it kept Americans in conflict. Movement of the exploding population into new lands was continually generating new communities with interests differing from those of the older communities that retained, or at least claimed, control over them.

This kind of internal conflict among Americans was far more visible during the Revolutionary period than was class conflict. Although there were overtones of class conflict in any contest between established eastern interests and the interests of pioneer western farmers, the contest was primarily geographical, created by the problem of stretching the social and political apparatus that bound one group of people to another in the expanding American universe.

That this form of conflict produced more active hostility in the Revolutionary period will seem no more than natural if we view the Revolution itself from the same perspective. The English colonies in America stood to England in the way that the western parts of the colonies stood to the eastern parts, but with even stronger grievances and correspondingly stronger hostility. The institutions that England devised for her overseas emigrants in the wake of the Great Migration were even more inadequate by 1776 than the institutions that they had devised for themselves. While many colonial legislatures had too few representatives from their western areas, Parliament, which could legislate for all the colonies, had not a single representative from them. When the colonists cried out that Parliament without American representatives knew nothing about their needs and had no right to tax them, they spoke to England in the voice of westerners speaking to easterners. In the Declaration of Independence they announced that the social and political bonds that tied them to an eastern government were severed. The American Revolution was itself a revolt of settlers in a new land against a government that by its location and composition could not be properly acquainted with their needs and could not keep up with their growth.

After 1776, in seeking to sustain the new nation they had just proclaimed themselves to be, the Americans had to contain the very force that had impelled their revolt against the mother country. If the colonies could secede from England, the West could secede from the East for the same reasons. The danger was aggravated by the fact that slavery and loyalism, which helped to lower tension between classes, perversely heightened tension between East and West. Since slavery did not move westward as rapidly as freedom, the much higher concentration of slaves in the East served to emphasize the difference in sectional interests. And since loyalism had as much appeal for disaffected regions as for disaffected individuals, it could become a catastrophic ingredient in sectional conflicts. If an entire region became sufficiently hostile to a government dominated by easterners, it might choose to rejoin the mother country. The result, as in the defection of individuals or groups, might be a greater harmony among those remaining. But the defection of a whole region could have jeopardized the viability of the Union; and a consensus formed by the secession of all dissident elements would scarcely deserve the name.

The British were not slow to recognize the advantages for them of sectional conflict and kept hoping for it after the war was over. In violation of the treaty they clung to their northwest trading posts, flirted with the disgruntled leaders of Vermont, and made plans for detaching the whole Northwest. Nor was Britain the only recourse for discontented westerners: Spain had eyes on the whole Southwest. She came uncomfortably close to detaching Kentucky when the Spanish minister maneuvered the Continental Congress into what appeared to westerners as a gross display of eastern indifference to western interests. If Congress had actually ratified the Jay-Gardoqui Treaty, with its seeming recognition of Spanish control of the Mississippi, the Americans who marched across the mountains into Kentucky and Tennessee in the 1780s might well have marched right into the arms of Spain.

In sum, while class conflict tended to be muted during the Revolutionary period by social mobility among whites, by the enslavement of blacks, and by loyalism, sectional conflict was aggravated. The gravest form of sectional conflict was East-West, but it was not the only form. The greater North-South conflict had already cast its ominous shadow in congressional voting alignments, in the uneasiness of both northerners and southerners over the continuance of slavery, and in steps taken toward abolition of slavery in the North, but not in the South. The most farsighted Americans sensed already that North-South differences as well as East-West differences might one day lead to secession. Indeed in the late 1780s so many sectional disagreements were festering that men who had led their states to a united independence fifteen years earlier now predicted the breakup of the American nation.

We know that it did not break up. What, then, other than the superior wisdom of the Founding Fathers, prevented the breakup? What sort of consensus enabled Americans to contain not only the immediate threats to their Union perceived in the 1780s but also the threats that grew with time from sectional and class conflict? The question in some measure answers itself. The Americans did achieve nationality during the Revolutionary period, and nationalism has proved to be the most powerful, if the least understood, social force of modern times. In the shrinking world of the twentieth century it has often been a sinister force, confining the vision of its devotees to a single country when they should be looking at the entire globe. But for Americans of the Revolutionary period the world was expanding instead of shrinking, and nationalism exerted a cohesive influence among the people of the several states, stretching instead of confining their political horizons. Even Jefferson, whose state loyalties proved particularly strong, urged his fellow Virginians to send their best young men to Congress, so that they could acquire the continental vision early. That vision extended not merely up and down the Atlantic seaboard but westward to the areas where Americans were moving so rapidly in the 1780s. It scarcely occurred to Jefferson that the United States might not one day reach to the Pacific and indeed occupy the whole of North America, and perhaps the Caribbean and South America too. If not everyone felt this way, there were enough who did to give American nationalism an expansive quality and to make her statesmen conscious of the need to retain the westward migrants within the national community.

Nationalism was in itself the strongest force binding Americans of the Revolutionary generation together. Devotion to the nation helped to keep both sides in any conflict on speaking terms, helped to make disagreements negotiable within the framework of national politics, and even made possible the creation of a new and stronger framework in 1787 when the old one proved unsatisfactory. But nationalism was not the only force disposing Americans to bury their conflicts. The racial consensus of colonial times, though challenged and diminished, still prevailed and helped to keep the North-South conflict from coming to center stage. The Revolutionists were not prepared to allow the issue of freedom for blacks to threaten the union of whites. By the consent of white Americans the American labor force, concentrated in the South, remained for the most part in slavery, outside the arena where American quarrels and conflicts were expected to take place. Contending factions, whether of class, region, or party, were agreed in not seeking or expecting the participation of men in chains.

The exclusion of most laborers meant that the participants on both sides of any conflict were men who possessed formidable powers, powers that were carefully withheld from slaves. Both sides could negotiate from strength and demand compromise. Although repression might be an effective mode of dealing with discontent or insubordination from slaves, it did not recommend itself as a way of handling men who had the means to fight back either politically or, if necessary, with force. Unlike the peasants of the Old World, Americans, or at least those Americans without black skin, possessed two palpable sources of power: most of them owned the land on which they lived, and a very large number of them owned guns. Land gave them economic and political power; and guns, we may as well admit, gave them firepower.

In the events that led up to the Revolution, England had failed to recognize the strength that these two kinds of power gave to her colonists. The colonists themselves knew at first hand that the ownership of land enabled a man to bid defiance to those who had traditionally controlled society through control of its lands. They had developed a society in which deference to birth and wealth was tempered by constant reminders to the rich and wellborn that their authority rested on the consent of ordinary property owners. Most adult male Americans owned property and could vote for the men who made the laws that affected their property. If they generally voted for a local bigwig, a man who held more property than they did, they did not hesitate to dump him if he neglected their interests. Similarly, within the legislative assemblies lesser men bowed to the leadership of bigger ones. As Robert Zemsky has shown, social status counted for more than seniority in at least one colonial assembly. But when the leaders of the assembly brought in a bill that looked oppressive to the back-benchers, they voted it down and even substituted impromptu measures of their own from the floor.

What alarmed Americans about taxation by Parliament was that they could not vote it down. The program that seemed so conventional and so reasonable from the standpoint of Whitehall appeared to the Americans as a threat to the power that enabled them to direct their own lives. If a legislature to which they elected no member could take their property in taxes, that legislature could ultimately take all their property and reduce them to the impotence of which they had such visible examples in the slaves at their feet. It was consensus on this point that enabled the colonies to unite so suddenly and so successfully against parliamentary taxation. The American reaction to parliamentary taxation seemed to England too hysterical and wicked to be genuine, and her statesmen failed to deal with it adequately, partly because they failed to recognize its existence.

The British failed also to recognize the existence of American firepower. It would perhaps be an exaggeration to say that most Americans had guns and knew how to use them. But it seems likely that nowhere else in the world at the time was there a population so well armed as the Americans. Governor Berkeley had perceived and experienced the implications of this fact in 1676, and as early as 1691 William Blathwayt, the English auditor general for the colonies, who was more conversant in colonial affairs than any other Englishman of the time, recorded with admiration the familiarity of the colonists with guns. "There is no Custom more generally to be observed among the young Virginians," he noted, "than that they all learn to keep and use a gun with a Marvellous dexterity as soon as ever they have strength enough to lift it to their heads." Had Lord North been as keenly aware as Blathwayt of the skills thus acquired, he and George III might not have underestimated so badly the American capacity for resistance.

In order to maintain themselves as a single nation, Americans had to recognize the economic power and firepower that Britain ignored. By the time of the Revolution the proportion of the population owning land in the East may have been somewhat reduced from what it had been fifty or a hundred years earlier, but the westerner by definition was a man who had broken out of the limited acreage of the East. Whether or not he held a secure title, he knew how to make his living from the land and to make life uncomfortable for anyone who tried to stop him. And he was even more likely than the easterner to be armed. The westerner in our history has always been a man with a gun. Eastern-dominated governments simply did not have sufficient power of their own in the long run to impose on the West conditions that armed westerners would not agree to, any more than the Continental Congress could have imposed its edicts on the states, as some members proposed, by the use of military force. American nationalism was obliged to start with the assumption that the population was armed and that no group within it, slaves excepted, could be pushed very hard in any direction it did not want to go.

With a population already equalized to a large degree by firepower and economic power, the United States began its independence appropriately with the declaration that all men are created equal. The immediate purpose was to affirm the equality of England's transatlantic colonists with Englishmen in England, who were taxed only by their elected representatives. But the simplicity of the declaration of equality endowed it with a resonance that was momentous for the whole subsequent history of the nation whose existence it announced.

It could not have been predicted at the time that this would become a national creed. The men who adopted the declaration in 1776 would scarcely have been unanimous if they had been obliged to state precisely what they meant by "created equal." Many of them, including the author of the phrase, held slaves. If the preceding analysis is correct, the fact that they were able to unite at all depended in part on their denial of equality to black Americans. Even when applied only to white Americans, the meaning of equality was hardly as self-evident as Congress declared the proposition itself to be. The equality promulgated by the Congress at Philadelphia had no power to dissolve at once the conflicts and tensions in American society. Westerners were

obliged for several years to flirt with Spain and England, while eastern speculators, many of them in Congress, quarreled over the profits they hoped to gain
from western settlement if the West could be kept under eastern domination.
James Madison tried in vain to secure a guarantee in the Federal Constitution
of the equality of western states. Instead the principle was precariously acknowledged only as a result of a shady bargain during the last weeks of the
expiring Continental Congress.

But acknowledged it was in the end. The Northwest Ordinance, by
stipulating that western states should be admitted to the Union on equal
terms with the existing states, saved the nation from future attempts to make
subordinate colonists out of its western emigrants. As the Revolutionists gradually became aware of the implications of the creed to which they had committed themselves, they also whittled down, albeit even more gradually, the
inequities in their laws governing religion, representation, and inheritance.
And as the social structure of the nation changed in subsequent generations,
Americans probed further into the meaning of equality.

It has generally taken more than the chanting of the creed to bring about
the social justice that it promises. Our history is not the chronicle of steady
and continuous application of the principle of equality to match the continuous expansion of the population. The reluctance of easterners to grant equal
rights to westerners was prophetic of later contests. Those who have claimed
the benefits of equality in America have usually had to press their own claims
against stubborn opposition. Men with power over other men have often
affirmed their dedication to the principle while denying it by their actions,
masters denying it to slaves, employers to workmen, natives to immigrants,
whites to blacks, men to women.

Is it fair, then, to call this a point of consensus? Was it not mere rhetoric? Perhaps, if by rhetoric is meant the terms on which men can agree to
speak together. An alternative rhetoric and an alternative social creed prevailed
before the Revolution both in America and Europe and continued to prevail
in most of Europe. That creed also offered a way to consensus, but of a quite
different sort. It affirmed divine sanction for a social hierarchy in which every
man knew his place and was expected to keep it. The old creed was designed
to suppress the aspirations of lower classes, to make them content with their
lot. Redress of grievances was not impossible, if superiors failed in their acknowledged obligations to inferiors; but the likelihood was much greater that
oppression would go unchecked and that resentment would build into an explosive, revolutionary situation before redress could be obtained. The American Revolution itself was brought on by a British minister who had rejected
what he called "the absurd opinion that all men are equal." That absurd
opinion became the basis of the American consensus that grew out of the
Revolution.

It may indeed seem an absurd sort of consensus that rests upon an invitation to conflict. The creed of equality did not give men equality, but invited
them to claim it, invited them, not to know their place and keep it, but to seek

and demand a better place. Yet the conflicts resulting from such demands have generally, though not always, stopped short of large-scale violence and have generally eventuated in a greater degree of actual equality. After each side has felt out the other's strengths and weaknesses, some bargain, some equivalent to a Northwest Ordinance, is agreed upon, leaving demands not quite fulfilled, leaving the most radical still discontented with remaining inequalities, but keeping the nation still committed to the creed of equality and bound to move, if haltingly, in the direction it signals.

While the creed invites resistance by the oppressed, it also enjoins accommodation by the oppressor. If it is mere rhetoric, it is a rhetoric that has kept conservatism in America on the defensive. The power that the consensus of equality has wielded over the minds of Americans ever since the Revolution is in fact nowhere more clearly exhibited than in the posture it has imposed on conservatism. To Europeans it may seem odd for conservatism to be garbed in the language of human equality, but conservatives in America quickly learned that this was the only acceptable dress in which they could appear in public. In order to argue for special privilege in the United States it was necessary to show—and it sometimes required considerable legerdemain—that special privilege was somehow the outcome of equality or a device to protect equality. John Adams, for example, contended that Americans should reserve a special place in their governments for the rich, the talented, and the well-born, on the grounds that it was necessary to isolate and thus ostracize and disarm these dangerous men in order to preserve equality. A century later William Graham Sumner argued against every kind of social legislation on the grounds that all Americans were created equal, so that every American who attained wealth and position had done so by his own efforts and therefore deserved to keep what he had earned, while the poor equally deserved their poverty. To aid the poor would threaten equality.

If these arguments today seem ludicrous, it is because conservatism in the United States has often been reduced to the ludicrous by the national commitment to equality. A conservatism based on a more congenial premise can make little headway. When the South, long after the Revolution, attempted to defend slavery on another premise, the attempt generated the greatest crisis American nationality has faced. The resulting conflict did not really destroy the racial consensus among whites and did not achieve equality for Negroes, but it did destroy slavery and it did preserve the national commitment to equality. That commitment is gradually eroding racism. And it continues to serve the oppressed, both black and white, in their efforts to attain what the nation has promised them, just as it also serves to keep most of the oppressed from totally rejecting a society that admits their right to an equal treatment not yet received.

If, then, the American Revolution produced a consensus among the victorious Americans, it was not a static consensus but one with the genius to serve changing times and needs. It was a consensus that invited conflicts and still invites them, a consensus peculiarly adapted to a growing people, a people on the move both geographically and socially. It could not have contained, but it did not produce, the kind of conflict that gave Charles I his Cromwell. It made instead for a society where a Hamilton had his Jefferson, a Hoover his Roosevelt, and a Nixon—might profit by their example. If this be conservatism, it is radicals who have made the most of it.

SUGGESTIONS FOR FURTHER READING

Carl Becker's argument that the American Revolution was a conflict within the colonies as well as a struggle against England may be found in his *History of Political Parties in the Province of New York, 1760–1776* (Madison, 1909). Arthur M. Schlesinger, *Colonial Merchants and the American Revolution* (New York, 1918) gives support to Becker's position by showing how merchants sought to protect their interests against both England and other groups in colonial society. A classic little study showing the social upheaval resulting from the revolutionary struggle is J. Franklin Jameson, *The American Revolution Considered as a Social Movement* (Princeton, N.J., 1926). These views are generally upheld in a more recent study by Elisha P. Douglass, *Rebels and Democrats* (Chapel Hill, 1955). Michael Kammen, *A Season of Youth: The American Revolution and the Historical Imagination* (New York, 1978) traces the meaning of the Revolution over two hundred years.

Edmund S. Morgan, *The Birth of the Republic, 1763–89* (Chicago, 1956) disputes the contention that there were sharp divisions among the colonists and instead finds a basic consensus among the revolutionaries. A different emphasis emerges in a study of many of the same events in Merrill Jensen, *The Founding of a Nation: A History of the American Revolution, 1763–1776* (New York, 1968). Louis Hartz, "Democracy Without a Democratic Revolution," *American Political Science Review*, 46 (June 1952), pp. 321–42, argues that because in America there was no aristocratic or feudal tradition to overthrow, the Revolution was no revolution at all. In Chapter III of his *Genius of American Politics* (Chicago, 1953), Daniel J. Boorstin uses very different evidence to come to conclusions similar to those of Louis Hartz.

Bernard Bailyn, *The Ideological Origins of the American Revolution* (Cambridge, Mass, 1967), rejects the concept of a social or internal revolution, suggesting instead that revolutionary ideas, accepted by the colonists for more than a century before the actual conflict, are what made the American Revolution truly revolutionary. On this point see also Gordon S. Wood, *The Creation of the American Republic, 1776–1787* (Chapel Hill, N.C., 1969). In his "A Note on Mobs in the American Revolution," *William and Mary Quarterly*, XXIII (October 1966), pp. 635–42, Wood compares American and European revolutionary mobs. Jesse Lemisch, "Jack Tar in the Streets: Merchant Seamen in the Politics of Revolutionary America," *William and Mary Quarterly*, 3rd ser., 25 (July 1968), pp. 371–407, arguing that the Revolution should be seen from the point of view of the common man, gives support to the conflict interpretation and adds another dimension to the discussion of the mob in revolutionary America. Pauline Maier, *From Resistance to Revolution: Colonial Radicals and The Development of*

* Available in paperback edition.

American Opposition to Britain, 1765–1776 (New York, 1972), describes popular uprisings and violence as the path to the Revolution. Alfred F. Young, ed., *The American Revolution: Explorations in the History of American Radicalism* (De-Kalb, Ill., 1976), includes many essays that support the conflict interpretation. The nature of the differences that divided Americans (as well as differences that divide historians) may be found in the following studies of a loyalist, Thomas Hutchinson, and a radical, Thomas Paine: Bernard Bailyn, *The Ordeal of Thomas Hutchinson* (Cambridge, Mass., 1974); Eric Foner, *Tom Paine and Revolutionary America* (New York, 1976).

Useful bibliographical articles surveying the literature on the Revolution are Edmund S. Morgan, "The American Revolution: Revisions in Need of Revising," *William and Mary Quarterly*, 14 (January 1957), pp. 3–15, and Frederick B. Tolles, "The American Revolution Considered as a Social Movement: A Re-Evaluation," *American Historical Review*, 60 (October 1954), pp. 1–12.

3

The
Constitution

There was widespread unrest and dissatisfaction with government under the Articles of Confederation. With thirteen states often going thirteen different ways, many feared for the future of the new nation. Men of property lamented the inability of Congress to collect taxes, to regulate interstate commerce, and to negotiate a favorable trade treaty with England. Widespread depression following the end of the war compounded the difficulties. In the summer of 1786 a group of farmers in western Massachusetts, hard hit by depression and angered by the state legislature's failure to heed their demands for a paper money issue and debtors' stay laws, took matters into their own hands. Led by Daniel Shays, they organized an army, marched on several courthouses, and threatened to take over the government. The governor called out the militia, which easily crushed the uprising; but the specter of rebellion remained and had a significant influence on those who wanted a stronger, more centralized national government.

Even as rebellion raged in Massachusetts, a small group of delegates met at Annapolis to discuss the conflicting regulations regarding interstate commerce. The Annapolis convention went beyond problems of trade, however, issuing a call for another convention to meet the following year in Philadelphia to consider remedies for the defects in the Articles of Confederation. Delegates to the Philadelphia convention quickly scrapped the idea of revising the Articles and instead drafted a new Constitution of the United States.

The American people have come to venerate, indeed, almost to worship their constitution. For many, the founding fathers are godlike; their handiwork almost divine. The student of history, however, quickly discovers that the Constitution was very controversial at the time it was drafted, and that its ratification was hotly contested. He also discovers that there has been a lively controversy among historians regarding the meaning and significance of the Constitution.

Some scholars have argued that the Constitution was the work of a political and economic minority striving to create a government that would limit the power of the majority. Opposed to this wealthy aristocracy of large property owners were the small farmers and artisans, men such as those who had followed Daniel Shays in Massachusetts. The struggle over the Constitution, therefore, was essentially a class struggle, exhibiting a basic conflict in American society.

Others have strongly contested this interpretation of the Constitution. Disputes over the ratification of the Constitution, they maintain, did not represent basic differences based on property and class. On fundamentals most Americans agreed. They knew why they had fought the Revolution and what kind of government they wanted. But they had no precedents to follow; they were feeling their way, searching for the best means to institutionalize the goals for which they had fought. Differences over means rested on the solid foundation of a basic consensus on ends.

Variations on these two interpretations are illustrated in the selections that follow. Charles A. Beard argues that the Constitution was written by men of property who feared democracy and who sought to create a government that would promote and protect their economic interests. For Beard, the Constitution is an economic document designed to protect the interests of a privileged class. Henry Steele Commager disputes Beard directly. The Constitution, he maintains, was written with political, not economic, goals in mind. He denies that the founding fathers were aiming to promote the interests of property owners; rather, their goal was to create a government "capable of extending to its citizens the blessings of liberty and happiness." Staughton Lynd, in the next selection, returns to the theme of conflict. Like Beard, he stresses propertied interests, but for Lynd the key conflict was over slave property. Taking his clue from the abolitionist critique of the Constitution, he argues that the major conflict in the Constitutional Convention was not between rich and poor, small states and large, but rather between North and South over the question of slavery.

Few historians would deny that many of the founding fathers were brilliant men; the Philadelphia convention brought together one of the most remarkable group of men ever assembled. Yet when they probe further, historians begin to disagree. Whom did these men represent, and what were they trying to accomplish? Did the men who gathered in Philadelphia in the summer of 1787 represent a cross-section of the American people, or did they represent particular classes or property interests? There were sharp differences among the founding fathers themselves and even sharper differences divided the founding fathers from other political leaders in the new nation. What was the nature of these differences? And how important were they?

Charles Beard

The Constitution: A Minority Document

The Economic Interests of Members of the Convention

A survey of the economic interests of the members of the Convention presents certain conclusions:

A majority of the members were lawyers by profession.

Most of the members came from towns, on or near the coast, that is, from the regions in which personalty was largely concentrated.

Not one member represented in his immediate personal economic interests the small farming or mechanic classes.

The overwhelming majority of members, at least five-sixths, were immediately, directly, and personally interested in the outcome of their labors at Philadelphia, and were to a greater or less extent economic beneficiaries from the adoption of the Constitution.

1. Public security interests were extensively represented in the Convention. Of the fifty-five members who attended no less than forty appear on the Records of the Treasury Department for sums varying from a few dollars up to more than one hundred thousand dollars. . . .

It is interesting to note that, with the exception of New York, and possibly Delaware, each state had one or more prominent representatives in the Convention who held more than a negligible amount of securities, and who could therefore speak with feeling and authority on the question of providing in the new Constitution for the full discharge of the public debt. . . .

Reprinted with permission of Macmillan Publishing Co., Inc., from An Economic Interpretation of the Constitution by Charles Beard. Copyright 1925 by Macmillan Publishing Co., Inc., renewed 1963 by William Beard and Miriam Vagts.

2. Personalty invested in lands for speculation was represented by at least fourteen members. . . .

3. Personalty in the form of money loaned at interest was represented by at least twenty-four members. . . .

4. Personalty in mercantile, manufacturing, and shipping lines was represented by at least eleven members. . . .

5. Personalty in slaves was represented by at least fifteen members. . . .

It cannot be said, therefore, that the members of the Convention were "disinterested." On the contrary, we are forced to accept the profoundly significant conclusion that they knew through their personal experiences in economic affairs the precise results which the new government that they were setting up was designed to attain. As a group of doctrinaires, like the Frankfort assembly of 1848, they would have failed miserably; but as practical men they were able to build the new government upon the only foundations which could be stable: fundamental economic interests.[1]

The Constitution as an Economic Document

It is difficult for the superficial student of the Constitution, who has read only the commentaries of the legists, to conceive of that instrument as an economic document. It places no property qualifications on voters or officers; it gives no outward recognition of any economic groups in society; it mentions no special privileges to be conferred upon any class. It betrays no feeling, such as vibrates through the French constitution of 1791; its language is cold, formal, and severe.

The true inwardness of the Constitution is not revealed by an examination of its provisions as simple propositions of law; but by a long and careful study of the voluminous correspondence of the period, contemporary newspapers and pamphlets, the records of the debates in the Convention at Philadelphia and in the several state conventions, and particularly, *The Federalist*, which was widely circulated during the struggle over ratification. The correspondence shows the exact character of the evils which the Constitution was intended to remedy; the records of the proceedings in the Philadelphia Convention reveal the successive steps in the building of the framework of the government under the pressure of economic interests; the pamphlets and newspapers disclose the ideas of the contestants over the ratification; and *The Federalist* presents the political science of the new system as conceived by three of the profoundest thinkers of the period, Hamilton, Madison, and Jay.

Doubtless, the most illuminating of these sources on the economic

[1] The fact that a few members of the Convention, who had considerable economic interests at stake, refused to support the Constitution does not invalidate the general conclusions here presented. In the cases of Yates, Lansing, Luther Martin, and Mason, definite economic reasons for their action are forthcoming; but this is a minor detail.

character of the Constitution are the records of the debates in the Convention, which have come down to us in fragmentary form; and a thorough treatment of material forces reflected in the several clauses of the instrument of government created by the grave assembly at Philadelphia would require a rewriting of the history of the proceedings in the light of the great interests represented there. But an entire volume would scarcely suffice to present the results of such a survey, and an undertaking of this character is accordingly impossible here.

The Federalist, on the other hand, presents in a relatively brief and systematic form an economic interpretation of the Constitution by the men best fitted, through an intimate knowledge of the ideals of the framers, to expound the political science of the new government. This wonderful piece of argumentation by Hamilton, Madison, and Jay is in fact the finest study in the economic interpretation of politics which exists in any language; and whoever would understand the Constitution as an economic document need hardly go beyond it. It is true that the tone of the writers is somewhat modified on account of the fact that they are appealing to the voters to ratify the Constitution, but at the same time they are, by the force of circumstances, compelled to convince large economic groups that safety and strength lie in the adoption of the new system.

Indeed, every fundamental appeal in it is to some material and substantial interest. Sometimes it is to the people at large in the name of protection against invading armies and European coalitions. Sometimes it is to the commercial classes whose business is represented as prostrate before the follies of the Confederation. Now it is to creditors seeking relief against paper money and the assaults of the agrarians in general; now it is to the holders of federal securities which are depreciating toward the vanishing point. But above all, it is to the owners of personalty anxious to find a foil against the attacks of levelling democracy, that the authors of *The Federalist* address their most cogent arguments in favor of ratification. It is true there is much discussion of the details of the new frame-work of government, to which even some friends of reform took exceptions; but Madison and Hamilton both knew that these were incidental matters when compared with the sound basis upon which the superstructure rested.

In reading the pages of this remarkable work as a study in political economy, it is important to bear in mind that the system, which the authors are describing, consisted of two fundamental parts—one positive, the other negative:

I. A government endowed with certain positive powers, but so constructed as to break the force of majority rule and prevent invasions of the property rights of minorities.

II. Restrictions on the state legislatures which had been so vigorous in their attacks on capital.

Under some circumstances, action is the immediate interest of the dominant party; and whenever it desires to make an economic gain through governmental functioning, it must have, of course, a system endowed with the requisite powers.

Examples of this are to be found in protective tariffs, in ship subsidies, in railway land grants, in river and harbor improvements, and so on through the catalogue of so-called "paternalistic" legislation. Of course it may be shown that the "general good" is the ostensible object of any particular act; but the general good is a passive force, and unless we know who are the several individuals that benefit in its name, it has no meaning. When it is so analyzed, immediate and remote beneficiaries are discovered; and the former are usually found to have been the dynamic element in securing the legislation. Take for example, the economic interests of the advocates who appear in tariff hearings at Washington.

On the obverse side, dominant interests quite as often benefit from the prevention of governmental action as from positive assistance. They are able to take care of themselves if let alone within the circle of protection created by the law. Indeed, most owners of property have as much to fear from positive governmental action as from their inability to secure advantageous legislation. Particularly is this true where the field of private property is already extended to cover practically every form of tangible and intangible wealth. This was clearly set forth by Hamilton:

> It may perhaps be said that the power of preventing bad laws includes that of preventing good ones. . . . But this objection will have little weight with those who can properly estimate the mischiefs of that inconstancy and mutability in the laws which form the greatest blemish in the character and genius of our governments. They will consider every institution calculated to restrain the excess of law-making, and to keep things in the same state in which they happen to be at any given period, as more likely to do good than harm. . . . The injury which may possibly be done by defeating a few good laws will be amply compensated by the advantage of preventing a number of bad ones.

The Underlying Political Science of the Constitution

Before taking up the economic implications of the structure of the federal government, it is important to ascertain what, in the opinion of *The Federalist*, is the basis of all government. The most philosophical examination of the foundations of political science is made by Madison in the tenth number. Here he lays down, in no uncertain language, the principle that the first and elemental concern of every government is economic.

1. "The first object of government," he declares, is the protection of "the diversity in the faculties of men, from which the rights of property originate." The chief business of government, from which, perforce, its essential nature must be derived, consists in the control and adjustment of conflicting economic interests. After enumerating the various forms of propertied

interests which spring up inevitably in modern society, he adds: "The regulation of these various and interfering interests forms the principal task of modern legislation, and involves the spirit of party and faction in the ordinary operations of the government."

2. What are the chief causes of these conflicting political forces with which the government must concern itself? Madison answers. Of course fanciful and frivolous distinctions have sometimes been the cause of violent conflicts;

but the most common and durable source of factions has been the various and unequal distribution of property. Those who hold and those who are without property have ever formed distinct interests in society. Those who are creditors, and those who are debtors, fall under a like discrimination. A landed interest, a manufacturing interest, a mercantile interest, a moneyed interest, with many lesser interests grow up of necessity in civilized nations, and divide them into different classes actuated by different sentiments and views.

3. The theories of government which men entertain are emotional reactions to their property interests. "From the protection of different and unequal faculties of acquiring property, the possession of different degrees and kinds of property immediately results; *and from the influence of these on the sentiments and views of the respective proprietors, ensues a division of society into different interests and parties.*" Legislatures reflect these interests. "What," he asks, "are the different classes of legislators but advocates and parties to the causes which they determine." There is no help for it. "The causes of faction cannot be removed," and "we well know that neither moral nor religious motives can be relied on as an adequate control."

4. Unequal distribution of property is inevitable, and from it contending factions will rise in the state. The government will reflect them, for they will have their separate principles and "sentiments"; but the supreme danger will arise from the fusion of certain interests into an overbearing majority, which Madison, in another place, prophesied would be the landless proletariat,—an overbearing majority which will make its "rights" paramount, and sacrifice the "rights" of the minority. "To secure the public good," he declares, "and private rights against the danger of such a faction and at the same time preserve the spirit and the form of popular government is then the great object to which our inquiries are directed."

5. How is this to be done? Since the contending classes cannot be eliminated and their interests are bound to be reflected in politics, the only way out lies in making it difficult for enough contending interests to fuse into a majority, and in balancing one over against another. The machinery for doing this is created by the new Constitution and by the Union. (a) Public views are to be refined and enlarged "by passing them through the medium of a chosen body of citizens." (b) The very size of the Union will

enable the inclusion of more interests so that the danger of an overbearing majority is not so great.

The smaller the society, the fewer probably will be the distinct parties and interests composing it; the fewer the distinct parties and interests, the more frequently will a majority be found of the same party. . . . Extend the sphere, and you take in a greater variety of parties and interests; you make it less probable that a majority of the whole will have a common motive to invade the rights of other citizens; or if such a common motive exists, it will be more difficult for all who feel it to discover their strength and to act in unison with each other.

Q. E. D., "in the extent and proper structure of the Union, therefore, we behold a republican remedy for the diseases most incident to republican government."

The Structure of Government or the Balance of Powers

The fundamental theory of political economy thus stated by Madison was the basis of the original American conception of the balance of powers which is formulated at length in four numbers of *The Federalist* and consists of the following elements:

1. No mere parchment separation of departments of government will be effective. "The legislative department is everywhere extending the sphere of its activity, and drawing all power into its impetuous vortex. The founders of our republic . . . seem never for a moment to have turned their eyes from the danger to liberty from the overgrown and all-grasping prerogative of an hereditary magistrate, supported and fortified by an hereditary branch of the legislative authority. They seem never to have recollected the danger from legislative usurpations, which, by assembling all power in the same hands, must lead to the same tyranny as is threatened by executive usurpations."

2. Some sure mode of checking usurpations in the government must be provided, other than frequent appeals to the people. "There appear to be insuperable objections against the proposed recurrence to the people as a provision in all cases for keeping the several departments of power within their constitutional limits." In a contest between the legislature and the other branches of the government, the former would doubtless be victorious on account of the ability of the legislators to plead their cause with the people.

3. What then can be depended upon to keep the government in close rein?

The only answer that can be given is, that as all these exterior provisions are found to be inadequate, the defect must be supplied by so contriving the interior structure of the government as that its several constituent parts may, by their mutual relations, be the means of keeping each other in their proper places. . . . It

*is of great importance in a republic not only to guard the society against the op-
pression of its rulers, but to guard one part of the society against the injustice of the
other part. Different interests necessarily exist in different classes of citizens. If a
majority be united by a common interest, the rights of the minority will be insecure.*

There are two ways of obviating this danger: one is by establishing a monarch independent of popular will, and the other is by reflecting these contending interests (so far as their representatives may be enfranchised) in the
very structure of the government itself so that a majority cannot dominate
the minority—which minority is of course composed of those who possess
property that may be attacked. "Society itself will be broken into so many
parts, interests, and classes of citizens, that the rights of individuals, or of
the minority, will be in little danger from interested combinations of the
majority."

4. The structure of the government as devised at Philadelphia reflects
these several interests and makes improbable any danger to the minority
from the majority. "The House of Representatives being to be elected immediately by the people, the Senate by the State legislatures, the President
by electors chosen for that purpose by the people, there would be little
probability of a common interest to cement these different branches in a
predilection for any particular class of electors."

5. All of these diverse interests appear in the amending process but
they are further reinforced against majorities. An amendment must receive a
two-thirds vote in each of the two houses so constituted and the approval of
three-fourths of the states.

6. The economic corollary of this system is as follows: Property interests may, through their superior weight in power and intelligence, secure
advantageous legislation whenever necessary, and they may at the same time
obtain immunity from control by parliamentary majorities.

If we examine carefully the delicate instrument by which the framers
sought to check certain kinds of positive action that might be advocated to
the detriment of established and acquired rights, we cannot help marvelling
at their skill. Their leading idea was to break up the attacking forces at the
starting point: the source of political authority for the several branches of the
government. This disintegration of positive action at the source was further
facilitated by the differentiation in the terms given to the respective departments of the government. And the crowning counterweight to "an interested
and over-bearing majority," as Madison phrased it, was secured in the peculiar position assigned to the judiciary, and the use of the sanctity and mystery
of the law as a foil to democratic attacks.

It will be seen on examination that no two of the leading branches of
the government are derived from the same source. The House of Representatives springs from the mass of the people whom the states may see fit to
enfranchise. The Senate is elected by the legislatures of the states, which

were, in 1787, almost uniformly based on property qualifications, sometimes with a differentiation between the sources of the upper and lower houses. The President is to be chosen by electors selected as the legislatures of the states may determine—at all events by an authority one degree removed from the voters at large. The judiciary is to be chosen by the President and the Senate, both removed from direct popular control and holding for longer terms than the House.

A sharp differentiation is made in the terms of the several authorities, so that a complete renewal of the government at one stroke is impossible. The House of Representatives is chosen for two years; the Senators for six, but not at one election, for one-third go out every two years. The President is chosen for four years. The judges of the Supreme Court hold for life. Thus "popular distempers," as eighteenth-century publicists called them, are not only restrained from working their havoc through direct elections, but they are further checked by the requirement that they must last six years in order to make their effects felt in the political department of the government, providing they can break through the barriers imposed by the indirect election of the Senate and the President. Finally, there is the check of judicial control that can be overcome only through the manipulation of the appointing power which requires time, or through the operation of a cumbersome amending system.

The keystone of the whole structure is, in fact, the system provided for judicial control—the most unique contribution to the science of government which has been made by American political genius. It is claimed by some recent writers that it was not the intention of the framers of the Constitution to confer upon the Supreme Court the power of passing upon the constitutionality of statutes enacted by Congress; but in view of the evidence on the other side, it is incumbent upon those who make this assertion to bring forward positive evidence to the effect that judicial control was not a part of the Philadelphia programme. Certainly, the authors of *The Federalist* entertained no doubts on the point, and they conceived it to be such an excellent principle that they were careful to explain it to the electors to whom they addressed their arguments.

After elaborating fully the principle of judicial control over legislation under the Constitution, Hamilton enumerates the advantages to be derived from it. Speaking on the point of tenure during good behavior, he says:

In a monarchy it is an excellent barrier to the despotism of the prince; in a republic it is no less an excellent barrier to the encroachments and oppressions of the representative body. . . . If, then, the courts of justice are to be considered as the bulwarks of a limited Constitution against legislative encroachments, this consideration will afford a strong argument for the permanent tenure of judicial offices, since nothing will contribute so much as this to that independent spirit in the judges which must be essential to the faithful performance of so arduous a duty. . . .

But it is not with a view to infractions of the Constitution only that the independence of the judges may be an essential safeguard against the effects of occasional ill humors in the society. These sometimes extend no farther than to the injury of private rights of particular classes of citizens, by unjust and partial laws. Here also severity and confining the operation of such laws. It not only serves to moderate the the firmness of the judicial magistracy is of vast importance in mitigating the immediate mischiefs of those which may have been passed, but it operates as a check upon the legislative body in passing them; who, perceiving that obstacles to the success of iniquitous intention are to be expected from the scruples of the courts, are in a manner compelled, by the very motives of injustice they meditate, to qualify their attempts. This is a circumstance calculated to have more influence upon the character of our governments than but few may be aware of.

Nevertheless, it may be asked why, if the protection of property rights lay at the basis of the new system, there is in the Constitution no provision for property qualifications for voters or for elected officials and representatives. This is, indeed, peculiar when it is recalled that the constitutional history of England is in a large part a record of conflict over the weight in the government to be enjoyed by definite economic groups, and over the removal of the property qualifications early imposed on members of the House of Commons and on the voters at large. But the explanation of the absence of property qualifications from the Constitution is not difficult.

The members of the Convention were, in general, not opposed to property qualifications as such, either for officers or voters. "Several propositions," says Mr. S. H. Miller,

were made in the federal Convention in regard to property qualifications. A motion was carried instructing the committee to fix upon such qualifications for members of Congress. The committee could not agree upon the amount and reported in favor of leaving the matter to the legislature. Charles Pinckney objected to this plan as giving too much power to the first legislature. . . . Ellsworth objected to a property qualification on account of the difficulty of fixing the amount. If it was made high enough for the South, it would not be applicable to the Eastern States. Franklin was the only speaker who opposed the proposition to require property on principle, saying that "some of the greatest rogues he was ever acquainted with were the richest rogues." A resolution was also carried to require a property qualification for the Presidency. Hence it was evident that the lack of all property requirements for office in the United States Constitution was not owing to any opposition of the convention to such qualifications per se.

Propositions to establish property restrictions were defeated, not because they were believed to be inherently opposed to the genius of American government, but for economic reasons—strange as it may seem. These economic reasons were clearly set forth by Madison in the debate over landed qualifications for legislators in July, when he showed, first, that slight property qualifications would not keep out the small farmers whose paper money schemes had been so disastrous to personalty; and, secondly, that landed property qualifications would exclude from Congress the representatives of "those classes of citizens who were not landholders," *i.e.*, the personalty interests. This was true, he thought, because the mercantile and manufacturing classes would hardly be willing to turn their personalty into sufficient quantities of landed property to make them eligible for a seat in Congress.

The other members also knew that they had most to fear from the very electors who would be enfranchised under a slight freehold restriction, for the paper money party was everywhere bottomed on the small farming class. As Gorham remarked, the elections at Philadelphia, New York, and Boston, "where the merchants and mechanics vote, are at least as good as those made by freeholders only." The fact emerges, therefore, that the personalty interests reflected in the Convention could, in truth, see no safeguard at all in a freehold qualification against the assaults on vested personalty rights which had been made by the agrarians in every state. And it was obviously impossible to establish a personalty test, had they so desired, for there would have been no chance of securing a ratification of the Constitution at the hands of legislatures chosen by freeholders, or at the hands of conventions selected by them.

A very neat example of this antagonism between realty and personalty in the Convention came out on July 26, when Mason made, and Charles Pinckney supported, a motion imposing landed qualifications on members of Congress and excluding from that body "persons having unsettled accounts with or being indebted to the United States." In bringing up this motion Mason "observed that persons of the latter descriptions had frequently got into the state legislatures in order to promote laws that might shelter their delinquencies; and that this evil had crept into Congress if report was to be regarded."

Gouverneur Morris was on his feet in an instant. If qualifications were to be imposed, they should be laid on electors, not elected persons. The disqualification would fall upon creditors of the United States, for there were but few who owed the government anything. He knew that under this rule very few members of the Convention could get into the new government which they were establishing.

As to persons having unsettled accounts, he believed them to be pretty many. He thought, however, that such a discrimination would be both odious and useless and in many instances unjust and cruel. The delay of settlement had been more the fault of the public than of individuals. What will be done with those patriotic Citizens who have lent money or services or property to their country, without having been yet able to obtain a liquidation of their claims? Are they to be excluded?

On thinking it over, Morris added to his remarks on the subject, saying, "It was a precept of great antiquity as well as of high authority that we should not be righteous overmuch. He thought we ought to be equally on our guard against being wise overmuch. . . . The parliamentary qualifications quoted by Colonel Mason had been disregarded in practice; and was but a scheme of the landed against the monied interest."

Gerry thought that the inconvenience of excluding some worthy creditors and debtors was of less importance than the advantages offered by the resolution, but, after some reflection, he added that "if property be one object of government, provisions for securing it cannot be improper." King sagely remarked that there might be a great danger in imposing a landed qualification, because "it would exclude the monied interest, whose aids may be essential in particular emergencies to the public safety."

Madison had no confidence in the effectiveness of the landed qualification and moved to strike it out, adding,

Landed possessions were no certain evidence of real wealth. Many enjoyed them to a great extent who were more in debt than they were worth. The unjust laws of the states had proceeded more from this class of men than any others. It had often happened that men who had acquired landed property on credit got into the Legislatures with a view of promoting an unjust protection against their Creditors. In the next place, if a small quantity of land should be made the standard, it would be no security; if a large one, it would exclude the proper representatives of those classes of Citizens who were not landholders.

For these and other reasons he opposed the landed qualifications and suggested that property qualifications on the voters would be better.

The motion to strike out the "landed" qualification for legislators was carried by a vote of ten to one; the proposition to strike out the disqualification of persons having unsettled accounts with the United States was carried by a vote of nine to two. Finally the proposition to exclude persons who were indebted to the United States was likewise defeated by a vote of nine to two, after Pinckney had called attention to the fact that "it would exclude persons who had purchased confiscated property or should purchase Western territory of the public and might be some obstacle to the sale of the latter."

Indeed, there was little risk to personalty in thus allowing the Constitution to go to the states for approval without any property qualifications on voters other than those which the state might see fit to impose. Only one branch of new government, the House of Representatives, was required to be elected by popular vote; and, in case popular choice of presidential electors might be established, a safeguard was secured by the indirect process. Two controlling bodies, the Senate and Supreme Court, were removed altogether from the possibility of popular election except by constitutional amendment. Finally, the conservative members of the Convention were doubly fortified in the fact that nearly all of the state constitutions then in force provided real or personal property qualifications for voters anyway, and radical democratic changes did not seem perilously near.

The Powers Conferred upon the Federal Government

1. The powers for positive action conferred upon the new government were few, but they were adequate to the purposes of the framers. They included, first, the power to lay and collect taxes; but here the rural interests were conciliated by the provision that direct taxes must be apportioned among the states according to population, counting three-fifths of the slaves. This, in the opinion of contemporaries eminently qualified to speak, was designed to prevent the populations of the manufacturing states from shifting the burdens of taxation to the sparsely settled agricultural regions.

In a letter to the governor of their state, three delegates from North Carolina, Blount, Spaight, and Williamson, explained the advantage of this safeguard on taxation to the southern planters and farmers:

We had many things to hope from a National Government and the chief thing we had to fear from such a Government was the risque of unequal or heavy Taxation, but we hope you will believe as we do that the Southern states in general and North Carolina in particular are well secured on that head by the proposed system. It is provided in the 9th section of article the first that no Capitation or direct Tax shall be laid except in proportion to the number of inhabitants, in which number five blacks are only counted as three. If a land tax is laid, we are to pay the same rate; for example, fifty citizens of North Carolina can be taxed no more for all their Lands than fifty Citizens in one of the Eastern States. This must be greatly in our favour, for as most of their farms are small and many of them live in Towns we certainly have, one with another, land of twice the value that they possess. When it is also considered that five Negroes are only to be charged the same Poll Tax as three whites, the advantage must be considerably increased under the proposed Form of Government. The Southern states have also a better security for the return of slaves who might endeavour to escape than they had under the original Confederation.

The taxing power was the basis of all other positive powers, and it afforded the revenues that were to discharge the public debt in full. Provision was made for this discharge in Article VI to the effect that "All debts contracted and engagements entered into before the adoption of this Constitution shall be valid against the United States under this Constitution as under the Confederation."

But the cautious student of public economy, remembering the difficulties which Congress encountered under the Articles of Confederation in its attempts to raise the money to meet the interest on the debt, may ask how the framers of the Constitution could expect to overcome the hostile economic forces which had hitherto blocked the payment of the requisitions. The answer is short. Under the Articles, Congress had no power to lay and collect taxes immediately; it could only make requisitions on the state legislatures. Inasmuch as most of the states relied largely on direct taxes for their revenues, the demands of Congress were keenly felt and stoutly resisted. Under the new system, however, Congress is authorized to lay taxes on its own account, but it is evident that the framers contemplated placing practically all of the national burden on the consumer. The provision requiring the apportionment of direct taxes on a basis of population obviously implied that such taxes were to be viewed as a last resort when indirect taxes failed to provide the required revenue.

With his usual acumen, Hamilton conciliates the freeholders and property owners in general by pointing out that they will not be called upon to support the national government by payments proportioned to their wealth. Experience has demonstrated that it is impracticable to raise any considerable sums by direct taxation. Even where the government is strong, as in Great Britain, resort must be had chiefly to indirect taxation. The pockets of the farmers "will reluctantly yield but scanty supplies, in the unwelcome shape of impositions on their houses and lands; and personal property is too precarious and invisible a fund to be laid hold of in any other way than by the imperceptible agency of taxes on consumption." Real and personal property are thus assured a generous immunity from such burdens as Congress had attempted to impose under the Articles; taxes under the new system will, therefore, be less troublesome than under the old.

2. Congress was given, in the second place, plenary power to raise and support military and naval forces, for the defence of the country against foreign and domestic foes. These forces were to be at the disposal of the President in the execution of national laws; and to guard the states against renewed attempts of "desperate debtors" like Shays, the United States guaranteed to every commonwealth a republican form of government and promised to aid in quelling internal disorder on call of the proper authorities.

The army and navy are considered by the authors of *The Federalist* as genuine economic instrumentalities. . . . They regarded trade and commerce as the fundamental cause of wars between nations; and the source of domestic insurrection they traced to class conflicts within society. "Nations in general," says Jay, "will make war whenever they have a prospect of getting anything by it," and it is obvious that the United States dissevered and discordant will be the easy prey to the commercial ambitions of their neighbors and rivals.

The material gains to be made by other nations at the expense of the United States are so apparent that the former cannot restrain themselves from aggression. France and Great Britain feel the pressure of our rivalry in the fisheries; they and other European nations are our competitors in navigation and the carrying trade; our independent voyages to China interfere with the monopolies enjoyed by other countries there; Spain would like to shut the Mississippi against us on one side and Great Britain fain would close the St. Lawrence on the other. The cheapness and excellence of our productions will excite their jealousy, and the enterprise and address of our merchants will not be consistent with the wishes or policy of the sovereigns of Europe. But, adds the commentator, by way of clinching the argument, "if they see that our national government is efficient and well administered, our trade prudently regulated, our militia properly organized and disciplined, our resources and finances discreetly managed, our credit re-established, our people free, contented, and united, they will be much more disposed to cultivate our friendship than provoke our resentment."

All the powers of Europe could not prevail against us. "Under a vigorous national government the natural strength and resources of the country, directed to a common interest, would baffle all the combinations of European jealousy to restrain our growth. . . . An active commerce, an extensive navigation, and a flourishing marine would then be the offspring of moral and physical necessity. We might defy the little arts of the little politicians to control or vary the irresistible and unchangeable course of nature." In the present state of disunion the profits of trade are snatched from us; our commerce languishes; and poverty threatens to overspread a country which might outrival the world in riches.

The army and navy are to be not only instruments of defence in protecting the United States against the commercial and territorial ambitions of other countries; but they may be used also in forcing open foreign markets. What discriminatory tariffs and navigation laws may not accomplish the sword may achieve. The authors of *The Federalist* do not contemplate that policy of mild and innocuous isolation which was later made famous by Washington's farewell address. On the contrary—they do not expect the United States to change human nature and make our commercial classes less ambitious than those of other countries to extend their spheres of trade. A strong navy will command the respect of European states.

There can be no doubt that the continuance of the Union under an efficient government would put it within our power, at a period not very distant, to create a navy which, if it could not vie with those of the great maritime powers, would at least be of respectable weight if thrown into the scale of either of two contending parties. . . . A few ships of the line sent opportunely to the reinforcement of either side, would often be sufficient to decide the fate of a campaign, on the event of which interests of the greatest magnitude were suspended. Our position is, in this respect, a most commanding one. And if to this consideration we add that of the usefulness of supplies from this country, in the prosecution of military operations in the West Indies, it will be readily perceived that a situation so favorable would enable us to bargain with great advantage for commercial privileges. A price would be set not only upon our friendship, but upon our neutrality. By a steady adherence to the Union, we may hope, ere long, to become the arbiter of Europe in America, and to be able to incline the balance of European competitions in this part of the world as our interest may dictate.

As to dangers from class wars within particular states, the authors of *The Federalist* did not deem it necessary to make extended remarks: the recent events in New England were only too vividly impressed upon the public mind. "The tempestuous situation from which Massachusetts has scarcely emerged," says Hamilton, "evinces that dangers of this kind are not merely speculative. Who can determine what might have been the issue of her late convulsions, if the malcontents had been headed by a Caesar or by a Cromwell." The strong arm of the Union must be available in such crises.

In considering the importance of defence against domestic insurrection, the authors of *The Federalist* do not overlook an appeal to the slave-holders' instinctive fear of a servile revolt. Naturally, it is Madison whose interest catches this point and drives it home, by appearing to discount it. In dealing with the dangers of insurrection, he says: "I take no notice of an unhappy species of population abounding in some of the states who, during the calm of regular government are sunk below the level of men; but who, in the tempestuous scenes of civil violence, may emerge into human character and give a superiority of strength to any party with which they may associate themselves."

3. In addition to the power to lay and collect taxes and raise and maintain armed forces on land and sea, the Constitution vests in Congress plenary control over foreign and interstate commerce, and thus authorizes it to institute protective and discriminatory laws in favor of American interests, and to create a wide sweep for free trade throughout the whole American empire. A single clause thus reflects the strong impulse of economic forces in the towns and young manufacturing centres. In a few simple words the mercantile and manufacturing interests wrote their *Zweck im Recht*; and they paid for their victory by large concessions to the slave-owning planters of the south.

While dealing with commerce in *The Federalist* Hamilton does not neglect the subject of interstate traffic and intercourse. He shows how free trade over a wide range will be to reciprocal advantage, will give diversity to commercial enterprise, and will render stagnation less liable by offering more distant markets when local demands fall off. "The speculative trader," he concludes, "will at once perceive the force of these observations and will acknowledge that the aggregate balance of the commerce of the United States would bid fair to be much more favorable than that of the thirteen states without union or with partial unions."

4. Another great economic antagonism found its expression in the clause conferring upon Congress the power to dispose of the territories and make rules and regulations for their government and admission to the Union. In this contest, the interests of the states which held territories came prominently to the front; and the ambiguity of the language used in the Constitution on this point may be attributed to the inability of the contestants to reach precise conclusions. The leaders were willing to risk the proper man-

agement of the land problem after the new government was safely launched; and they were correct in their estimate of their future political prowess.

These are the great powers conferred on the new government: taxation, war, commercial control, and disposition of western lands. Through them public creditors may be paid in full, domestic peace maintained, advantages obtained in dealing with foreign nations, manufactures protected, and the development of the territories go forward with full swing. The remaining powers are minor and need not be examined here. What implied powers lay in the minds of the framers likewise need not be inquired into; they have long been the subject of juridical speculation.

None of the powers conferred by the Constitution on Congress permits a direct attack on property. The federal government is given no general authority to define property. It may tax, but indirect taxes must be uniform, and these are to fall upon consumers. Direct taxes may be laid, but resort to this form of taxation is rendered practically impossible, save on extraordinary occasions, by the provision that they must be apportioned according to population—so that numbers cannot transfer the burden to accumulated wealth. The slave trade may be destroyed, it is true, after the lapse of a few years; but slavery as a domestic institution is better safeguarded than before.

Even the destruction of the slave trade had an economic basis, although much was said at the time about the ethics of the clause. In the North where slavery, though widespread, was of little economic consequence, sympathy with the unfortunate negroes could readily prevail. Maryland and Virginia, already overstocked with slaves beyond the limits of land and capital, had prohibited the foreign trade in negroes, because the slave-holders, who predominated in the legislatures, were not willing to see the value of their chattels reduced to a vanishing point by excessive importations. South Carolina and Georgia, where the death rate in the rice swamps and the opening of adjoining territories made a strong demand for the increase of slave property, on the other hand, demanded an open door for slave-dealers.

South Carolina was particularly determined, and gave northern representatives to understand that if they wished to secure their commercial privileges, they must make concessions to the slave trade. And they were met half way. Ellsworth said: "As slaves multiply so fast in Virginia and Maryland that it is cheaper to raise than import them, whilst in the sickly rice swamps foreign supplies are necessary, if we go no farther than is urged, we shall be unjust towards South Carolina and Georgia. Let us not intermeddle. As population increases; poor laborers will be so plenty as to render slaves useless."

General Pinckney taunted the Virginia representatives in the Convention, some of whom were against slavery as well as importation, with disingenuous interestedness.

South Carolina and Georgia cannot do without slaves. As to Virginia she will gain by stopping the importations. Her slaves will rise in value and she has more than she wants. It would be unequal to require South Carolina and Georgia to con-federate on such unequal terms.

Restrictions Laid upon State Legislatures

Equally important to personalty as the positive powers conferred upon Congress to tax, support armies, and regulate commerce were the restrictions imposed on the states. Indeed, we have the high authority of Madison for the statement that of the forces which created the Constitution, those property interests seeking protection against omnipotent legislatures were the most active.

In a letter to Jefferson, written in October, 1787, Madison elaborates the principle of federal judicial control over state legislation, and explains the importance of this new institution in connection with the restrictions laid down in the Constitution on laws affecting private rights. "The mutability of the laws of the States," he says,

is found to be a serious evil. The injustice of them has been so frequent and so flagrant as to alarm the most steadfast friends of Republicanism. I am persuaded I do not err in saying that the evils issuing from these sources contributed more to that uneasiness which produced the Convention, and prepared the public mind for a general reform, than those which accrued to our national character and interest from the inadequacy of the Confederation to its immediate objects. A reform, therefore, which does not make provision for private rights must be materially defective.

Two small clauses embody the chief demands of personalty against agrarianism: the emission of paper money is prohibited and the states are forbidden to impair the obligation of contract. The first of these means a return to a specie basis—when coupled with the requirement that the gold and silver coin of the United States shall be the legal tender. The Shays and their paper money legions, who assaulted the vested rights of personalty by the process of legislative depreciation, are now subdued forever, and money lenders and security holders may be sure of their operations. Contracts are to be safe, and whoever engages in a financial operation, public or private, may know that state legislatures cannot destroy overnight the rules by which the game is played.

A principle of deep significance is written in these two brief sentences. The economic history of the states between the Revolution and the adoption of the Constitution is compressed in them. They appealed to every money lender, to every holder of public paper, to every man who had any personalty at stake. The intensity of the economic interests reflected in these two pro-hibitions can only be felt by one who has spent months in the study of American agrarianism after the Revolution. In them personalty won a sig-nificant battle in the conflict of 1787–1788.

*　　*　　*

To carry the theory of the economic interpretation of the Constitution out into its ultimate details would require a monumental commentary, such as lies completely beyond the scope of this volume. But enough has been said to show that the concept of the Constitution as a piece of abstract legislation reflecting no group interests and recognizing no economic antagonisms is entirely false. It was an economic document drawn with superb skill by men whose property interests were immediately at stake; and as such it appealed directly and unerringly to identical interests in the country at large.

* * *

At the close of this long and arid survey—partaking of the nature of catalogue—it seems worth while to bring together the important conclusions for political science which the data presented appear to warrant.

The movement for the Constitution of the United States was originated and carried through principally by four groups of personalty interests which had been adversely affected under the Articles of Confederation: money, public securities, manufactures, and trade and shipping.

The first firm steps toward the formation of the Constitution were taken by a small and active group of men immediately interested through their personal possessions in the outcome of their labors.

No popular vote was taken directly or indirectly on the proposition to call the Convention which drafted the Constitution.

A large propertyless mass was, under the prevailing suffrage qualifications, excluded at the outset from participation (through representatives) in the work of framing the Constitution.

The members of the Philadelphia Convention which drafted the Constitution were, with a few exceptions, immediately, directly, and personally interested in, and derived economic advantages from, the establishment of the new system.

The Constitution was essentially an economic document based upon the concept that the fundamental private rights of property are anterior to government and morally beyond the reach of popular majorities.

The major portion of the members of the Convention are on record as recognizing the claim of property to a special and defensive position in the Constitution.

In the ratification of the Constitution, about three-fourths of the adult males failed to vote on the question, having abstained from the elections at which delegates to the state conventions were chosen, either on account of their indifference or their disfranchisement by property qualifications.

The Constitution was ratified by a vote of probably not more than one-sixth of the adult males.

It is questionable whether a majority of the voters participating in the elections for the state conventions in New York, Massachusetts, New Hampshire, Virginia, and South Carolina, actually approved the ratification of the Constitution.

The leaders who supported the Constitution in the ratifying conventions represented the same economic groups as the members of the Philadelphia Convention; and in a large number of instances they were also directly and personally interested in the outcome of their efforts.

In the ratification, it became manifest that the line of cleavage for and against the Constitution was between substantial personalty interests on the one hand and the small farming and debtor interests on the other.

The Constitution was not created by "the whole people" as the jurists have said; neither was it created by "the states" as Southern nullifiers long contended; but it was the work of a consolidated group whose interests knew no state boundaries and were truly national in their scope.

Henry Steele Commager

A Constitution for All the People

By June 26, 1787, tempers in the Federal Convention were already growing short, for gentlemen had come to the explosive question of representation in the upper chamber. Two days later Franklin moved to invoke divine guidance, and his motion was shunted aside only because there was no money with which to pay a chaplain and the members were unprepared to appeal to Heaven without an intermediary. It was not surprising that when James Madison spoke to the question of representation in the proposed legislature, he was conscious of the solemnity of the occasion. We are, he said, framing a system "which we wish to last for ages" and one that might "decide forever the fate of Republican Government."

It was an awful thought, and when, a few days later, Gouverneur Morris spoke to the same subject he felt the occasion a most solemn one: even the irrepressible Morris could be solemn. "He came here," he observed (so Madison noted),

as a Representative of America; he flattered himself he came here in some degree as a Representative of the whole human race: for the whole human race will be affected by the proceedings of this Convention. He wished gentlemen to extend their views beyond the present moment of time: beyond the narrow limits . . . from which they derive their political origin. . . .

Much has been said of the sentiments of the people. They were unknown. They could not be known. All that we can infer is that if the plan we recommend be reasonable & right: all who have reasonable minds and sound intentions will embrace it . . . .

These were by no means occasional sentiments only. They were senti-

From Henry Steele Commager, "The Constitution: Was It an Economic Document?," American Heritage, X (December 1958), pp. 58–61, 100–103. Reprinted by permission of author.

ments that occurred again and again throughout the whole of that long hot summer, until they received their final, eloquent expression from the aged Franklin in that comment on the rising, not the setting, sun. Even during the most acrimonious debates members were aware that they were framing a constitution for ages to come, that they were creating a model for people everywhere on the globe; there was a lively sense of responsibility and even of destiny. Nor can we now, as we contemplate that Constitution which is the oldest written national constitution, and that federal system which is one of the oldest and the most successful in history, regard these appeals to posterity as merely rhetorical.

That men are not always conscious either of what they do or of the motives that animate them is a familiar rather than a cynical observation. Some 45 years ago Charles A. Beard propounded an economic interpretation of the Constitution—an interpretation which submitted that the Constitution was *essentially* (that is a crucial word) an economic document—and that it was carried through the Convention and the state ratifying conventions by interested economic groups for economic reasons. "The Constitution," Mr. Beard concluded, "was essentially an economic document based upon the concept that the fundamental private rights of property are anterior to government and morally beyond the reach of popular majorities."

At the time it was pronounced, that interpretation caused something of a sensation, and Mr. Beard was himself eventually to comment with justifiable indignation on the meanness and the vehemence of the attacks upon it—and him. Yet the remarkable thing about the economic interpretation is not the criticism it inspired but the support it commanded. For within a few years it had established itself as the new orthodoxy, and those who took exception to it were stamped either as professional patriots—perhaps secret Sons or Daughters of the Revolution—or naïve academicians who had never learned the facts of economic life.

The attraction that the economic interpretation had for the generation of the twenties and thirties—and that it still exerts even into the fifties—is one of the curiosities of our cultural history, but it is by no means an inexplicable one. To a generation of materialists Beard's thesis made clear that the stuff of history was material. To a generation disillusioned by the exploitations of big business it discovered that the past, too, had been ravaged by economic exploiters. To a generation that looked with skeptical eyes upon the claims of Wilsonian idealism and all but rejoiced in their frustration, it suggested that all earlier idealisms and patriotisms—even the idealism and patriotism of the framers—had been similarly flawed by selfishness and hypocrisy.

Yet may it not be said of An Economic Interpretation of the Constitution that it is not a conclusion but a point of departure? It explains a great deal about the forces that went into the making of the Constitution, and a great deal, too, about the men who assembled in Philadelphia in 1787, but it tells us extraordinarily little about the document itself. And it tells us even less about the historical meaning of that document.

What were the objects of the Federal Convention? The immediate objects were to restore order; to strengthen the public credit; to enable the United States to make satisfactory commercial treaties and agreements; to provide conditions in which trade and commerce could flourish; to facilitate management of the western lands and of Indian affairs. All familiar enough. But what, in the light of history, were the grand objects of the Convention? What was it that gave Madison and Morris and Wilson and King and Washington himself a sense of destiny?

There were two grand objects—objects inextricably interrelated. The first was to solve the problem of federalism, that is, the problem of the distribution of powers among governments. Upon the wisdom with which members of the Convention distinguished between powers of a general and powers of a local nature, and assigned these to their appropriate governments, would depend the success or failure of the new experiment.

But it was impossible for the children of the eighteenth century to talk or think of powers without thinking of power, and this was a healthy realism. No less troublesome—and more fundamental—than the problem of the distribution of powers, was the problem of sanctions. How were they to enforce the terms of the distribution and impose limits upon all the governments involved? It was one thing to work out the most ideal distribution of general and local powers. It was another thing to see to it that the states abided by their obligations under the Articles of Union and that the national government respected the autonomy of the states and the liberty of individuals.

Those familiar with the Revolutionary era know that the second of these problems was more difficult than the first. Americans had, indeed, learned how to limit government: the written constitutions, the bills of rights, the checks and balances, and so forth. They had not yet learned (nor had anyone) how to "substitute the mild magistracy of the law for the cruel and violent magistracy of force." The phrase is Madison's.

Let us return to the *Economic Interpretation*. The correctness of Beard's analysis of the origins and backgrounds of the membership of the Convention, of the arguments in the Convention, and of the methods of assuring ratification, need not be debated. But these considerations are, in a sense, irrelevant and immaterial. For though they are designed to illuminate the document itself, in fact they illuminate only the processes of its manufacture.

The idea that property considerations were paramount in the minds of those assembled in Philadelphia is misleading and unsound and is borne out neither by the evidence of the debates·in the Convention nor by the Constitution itself. The Constitution was not *essentially* an economic document. It was, and is, *essentially* a political document. It addresses itself to the great and fundamental question of the distribution of powers between governments. The Constitution was—and is—a document that attempts to provide sanctions behind that distribution; a document that sets up, through law, a standing rule to live by and provides legal machinery for the enforcement of that rule. These are political, not economic functions.

Not only were the principles that animated the framers political rather than economic; the solutions that they formulated to the great questions that confronted them were dictated by political, not by economic considerations.

Here are two fundamental challenges to the Beard interpretation: first, the Constitution is primarily a document in federalism; and second, the Constitution does not in fact confess or display the controlling influence of those who held that "the fundamental private rights of property are anterior to government and morally beyond the reach of popular majorities."

Let us look more closely at these two contentions. The first requires little elaboration or vindication, for it is clear to all students of the Revolutionary era that the one pervasive and overbranching problem of that generation was the problem of imperial organization. How to get the various parts of any empire to work together for common purposes? How to get central control—over war, for example, or commerce or money—without impairing local autonomy? How, on the other hand, to preserve personal liberty and local self-government without impairing the effectiveness of the central government? This was one of the oldest problems in political science, and it is one of the freshest—as old as the history of the Greek city-states; as new as the recent debate over Federal aid to education or the Bricker amendment.

The British failed to solve the problem of imperial order; when pushed to the wall they had recourse to the hopelessly doctrinaire Declaratory Act, which was, in fact, a declaration of political bankruptcy; as Edmund Burke observed, no people is going to be argued into slavery. The Americans then took up the vexatious problem. The Articles of Confederation were satisfactory enough as far as the distribution of powers was concerned, but wholly wanting in sanctions. The absence of sanctions spelled the failure of the Articles—and this failure led to the Philadelphia Convention.

Now it will be readily conceded that many, if not most, of the questions connected with federalism were economic in character. Involved were such practical matters as taxation, the regulation of commerce, coinage, western lands, slavery, and so forth. Yet the problem that presented itself to the framers was not whether government should exercise authority over such matters as these; it was which government should exercise such authority—and how should it be exercised?

There were, after all, no anarchists at the Federal Convention. Everyone agreed that some government had to have authority to tax, raise armies, regulate commerce, coin money, control contracts, enact bankruptcy legislation, regulate western territories, make treaties, and do all the things that government must do. But where should these authorities be lodged—with the state governments or with the national government they were about to erect, or with both?

This question was a political, not an economic, one. And the solution at which the framers arrived was based upon a sound understanding of politics, and need not be explained by reference to class attachments or security interests.

Certainly if the framers were concerned primarily or even largely with protecting property against popular majorities, they failed signally to carry out their purposes. It is at this point in our consideration of the *Economic Interpretation of the Constitution* that we need to employ what our literary friends call *explication du texte*. For the weakest link in the Beard interpretation is precisely the crucial one—the document itself. Mr. Beard makes amply clear that those who wrote the Constitution were members of the propertied classes, and that many of them were personally involved in the outcome of what they were about to do; he makes out a persuasive case that the division over the Constitution was along economic lines. What he does not make clear is how or where the Constitution itself reflects all these economic influences.

Much is made of the contract clause and the paper money clause of the Constitution. No state may impair the obligations of a contract—whatever those words mean, and they apparently did not mean to the framers quite what Chief Justice Marshall later said they meant in *Fletcher v. Peck* or *Dartmouth College v. Woodward*. No state may emit bills of credit or make anything but gold and silver coin legal tender in payment of debts.

These are formidable prohibitions, and clearly reflect the impatience of men of property with the malpractices of the states during the Confederation. Yet quite aside from what the states may or may not have done, who can doubt that these limitations upon the states followed a sound principle—the principle that control of coinage and money belonged to the central, not the local governments, and the principle that local jurisdictions should not be able to modify or overthrow contracts recognized throughout the Union?

What is most interesting in this connection is what is so often overlooked; that the framers did not write any comparable prohibitions upon the United States government. The United States was not forbidden to impair the obligation of its contracts, not at least in the Constitution as it came from the hands of its property-conscious framers. Possibly the Fifth Amendment may have squinted toward such a prohibition; we need not determine that now, for the Fifth Amendment was added by the *states* after the Constitution had been ratified. So, too, the emission of bills of credit and the making of other than gold and silver legal tender were limitations on the states, but not on the national government. There was, in fact, a lively debate over the question of limiting the authority of the national government in the matter of bills of credit. When the question came up on August 16, Gouverneur Morris threatened that "The Monied interest will oppose the plan of Government, if paper emissions be not prohibited." In the end the Convention dropped out a specific authorization to emit bills of credit, but pointedly did not prohibit such action. Just where this left the situation troubled Chief Justice Chase's Court briefly three-quarters of a century later; the Court recovered its balance, and the sovereign power of the government over money was not again *successfully* challenged.

Nor were there other specific limitations of an economic character upon the powers of the new government that was being erected on the ruins of the old. The framers properly gave the Congress power to regulate commerce with foreign nations and among the states. The term commerce —as Hamilton and Adair (and Crosskey, too!) have made clear—was broadly meant, and the grant of authority, too, was broad. The framers gave Congress the power to levy taxes and, again, wrote no limitations into the Constitution except as to the apportionment of direct taxes; it remained for the most conservative of Courts to reverse itself, and common sense, and discover that the framers had intended to forbid an income tax! Today, organizations that invoke the very term "constitutional" are agitating for an amendment placing a quantitative limit upon income taxes that may be levied; fortunately, Madison's generation understood better the true nature of governmental power.

The framers gave Congress—in ambiguous terms, to be sure—authority to make "all needful Rules and Regulations respecting the Territory or other Property" of the United States, and provided that "new states may be admitted." These evasive phrases gave little hint of the heated debates in the Convention over western lands. Those who delight to find narrow and undemocratic sentiments in the breasts of the framers never cease to quote a Gouverneur Morris or an Elbridge Gerry on the dangers of the West, and it is possible to compile a horrid catalogue of such statements. But what is significant is not what framers said, but what they did. They did not place any limits upon the disposition of western territory, or establish any barriers against the admission of western states.

The fact is that we look in vain *in the Constitution itself* for any really effective guarantee for property or any effective barriers against what Beard calls "the reach of popular majorities."

It will be argued, however, that what the framers feared was the *states*, and that the specific prohibitions against state action, together with the broad transfer of economic powers from state to nation, were deemed sufficient guarantee against state attacks upon property. As for the national government, care was taken to make that sufficiently aristocratic, sufficiently the representative of the propertied classes, and sufficiently checked and limited so that it would not threaten basic property interests.

It is at this juncture that the familiar principle of limitation on governmental authority commands our attention. Granted the wisest distribution of powers among governments, what guarantee was there that power would be properly exercised? What guarantees were there against the abuse of power? What assurance was there that the large states would not ride roughshod over the small, that majorities would not crush minorities or minorities abuse majorities? What protection was there against mobs, demagogues, dangerous combinations of interests or of states? What protection was there for the commercial interest, the planter interest, the slave interest, the securities interests, the land speculator interests?

It was Madison who most clearly saw the real character of this problem and who formulated its solution. It was not that the people as such were dangerous; "The truth was," he said on July 11, "that all men having power ought to be distrusted to a certain degree." Long before Lord Acton coined the aphorism, the Revolutionary leaders had discovered that power corrupts. They understood, too, the drive for power on the part of individuals and groups. All this is familiar to students of *The Federalist*, No. 10. It should be familiar to students of the debates in Philadelphia, for there, too, Madison set forth his theory and supported it with a wealth of argument. Listen to him on one of the early days of the Convention, June 6, when he is discussing the way to avoid abuses of republican liberty—abuses which "prevailed in the largest as well as the smallest [states] . . ."

. . . *And were we not thence admonished [he continued] to enlarge the sphere as far as the nature of the Government would admit. This was the only defence against the inconveniences of democracy consistent with the democratic form of Government [our emphasis]. All civilized Societies would be divided into different Sects. Factions & interests, as they happened to consist of rich & poor, debtors and creditors, the landed, the manufacturing, the commercial interests, the inhabitants of this district or that district, the followers of this political leader or that political leader, the disciples of this religious Sect or that religious Sect. In all cases where a majority are united by a common interest or passion, the rights of the minority are in danger. . . . In a Republican Govt. the Majority if united have always an opportunity [to oppress the minority. What is the remedy?] The only remedy is to enlarge the sphere, & thereby divide the community into so great a number of interests & parties, that in the first place a majority will not be likely at the same moment to have a common interest separate from that of the whole or of the minority; and in the second place, that in case they should have such an interest, they may not be apt to unite in the pursuit of it. It was incumbent on us then to try this remedy, and . . . to frame a republican system on such a scale & in such a form as will controul all the evils which have been experienced.*

This long quotation is wonderfully eloquent of the attitude of the most sagacious of the framers. Madison, Wilson, Mason, Franklin, as well as Gerry, Morris, Pinckney, and Hamilton feared power. They feared power whether exercised by a monarch, an aristocracy, an army, or a majority, and they were one in their determination to write into fundamental law limitations on the arbitrary exercise of that power. To assume, as Beard so commonly does, that the fear of the misuse of power by majorities was either peculiar to the Federalists or more ardent with them than with their opponents, is mistaken. Indeed it was rather the anti-Federalists who were most deeply disturbed by the prospect of majority rule; they, rather than the Federalists, were the "men of little faith." Thus it was John Lansing, Jr., of New York (he who left the Convention rather than have any part in its dangerous work) who said that "all free constitutions are formed with two views—to deter the governed from crime, and the governors from tyranny." And the ardent Patrick Henry, who led the attack on the Constitution in the Virginia Convention—and almost defeated it—complained not of too little democracy in that document, but too much.

The framers, to be sure, feared the powers of the majority, as they feared all power unless controlled. But they were insistent that, in the last analysis, there must be government by majority; even conservatives like Morris and Hamilton made this clear. Listen to Hamilton, for example, at the very close of the Convention. Elbridge Gerry, an opponent of the Constitution, had asked for a reconsideration of the provision for calling a constitutional convention, alleging that this opened the gate to a majority that could "bind the union to innovations that may subvert the State-Constitutions altogether." To this Hamilton replied that

There was no greater evil in subjecting the people of the U.S. to the major voice than the people of a particular State. . . . It was equally desirable now that an easy mode should be established for supplying defects which will probably appear in the New System. . . . There could be no danger in giving this power, as the people would finally decide in the case.

And on July 13, James Wilson, another staunch Federalist, observed that "The majority of people wherever found ought in all questions to govern the minority."

But we need not rely upon what men said; there is too much of making history by quotation anyway. Let us look rather at what men did. We can turn again to the Constitution itself. Granted the elaborate system of checks and balances: the separation of powers, the bicameral legislature, the executive veto, and so forth—checks found in the state constitutions as well, and in our own democratic era as in the earlier one—what provision did the framers make against majority tyranny? What provisions did they write into the Constitution against what Randolph called "democratic licentiousness"?

They granted equality of representation in the Senate. If this meant that conservative Delaware would have the same representation in the upper chamber as democratic Pennsylvania, it also meant that democratic Rhode Island would have the same representation as conservative South Carolina. But the decision for equality of representation was not dictated by considerations either economic or democratic, but rather by the recalcitrance of the small states. Indeed, though it is difficult to generalize here, on the whole it is true that it was the more ardent Federalists who favored proportional representation in both houses.

They elaborated a most complicated method of electing a Chief Executive, a method designed to prevent the easy expression of any majority will. Again the explanation is not simple. The fact was that the framers did not envision the possibility of direct votes for presidential candidates which would not conform to state lines and interests and thus lead to dissension and confusion. Some method, they thought, must be designated to overcome the force of state prejudices (or merely of parochialism) and get an election; the method they anticipated was a preliminary elimination contest by the electoral college and then eventual election by the House. This, said George Mason, was what would occur nineteen times out of twenty. There is no evidence in the debates that the complicated method finally hit upon for electing a President was designed either to frustrate popular majorities or to protect special economic interests; its purpose was to overcome state pride and particularism.

Senators and Presidents, then, would not be the creatures of democracy. But what guarantee was there that senators would be representatives of property interests, or that the President himself would recognize the "priority of property"? Most states had property qualifications for office holding, but there are none in the Federal Constitution. As far as the Constitution is concerned, the President, congressmen, and Supreme Court justices can all be paupers.

Both General Charles Cotesworth Pinckney and his young cousin Charles, of South Carolina, were worried about this. The latter proposed a property qualification of $100,000 (a tidy sum in those days) for the Presidency, half that for the judges, and substantial sums for members of Congress. Franklin rebuked him. He was distressed, he said, to hear anything "that tended to debase the spirit of the common people." More surprising was the rebuke from that stout conservative, John Dickinson. "He doubted," Madison reports, "the policy of interweaving into a Republican constitution a veneration for wealth. He had always understood that a veneration for poverty & virtue were the objects of republican encouragement." Pinckney's proposal was overwhelmingly rejected.

What of the members of the lower house? When Randolph opened "the main business" on May 29 he said the remedy for the crisis that men faced must be "the republican principle," and two days later members were discussing the fourth resolution, which provided for election to the lower house by the people. Roger Sherman of Connecticut thought that "the people should have as little to do as may be about the Government," and Gerry hastened to agree in words now well-worn from enthusiastic quotation that "The evils we experience flow from the excess of democracy." These voices were soon drowned out, however. Mason "argued strongly for an election . . . by the people. It was to be the grand depository of the democratic principle of the Govt." And the learned James Wilson, striking the note to which he was to recur again and again, made clear that he was for "raising the federal pyramid to a considerable altitude, and for that reason wished to give it as broad a basis as possible." He thought that both branches of the legislature—and the President as well, for that matter—should be elected by the people. "The Legislature," he later observed, "ought to be the most exact transcript of the whole Society."

A further observation is unhappily relevant today. It was a maxim with John Adams that "where annual elections end, there tyranny begins," and the whole Revolutionary generation was committed to a frequent return to the source of authority. But the framers put into the Constitution no limits on the number of terms which Presidents or congressmen could serve. It was not that the question was ignored; it received elaborate attention. It was rather that the generation that wrote the Constitution was better grounded in political principles than is our own; that it did not confuse, as we so often do, quantitative and qualitative limitations; and that—in a curious way—it had more confidence in the intelligence and the good will of the people than we seem to have today. It is, in any event, our own generation that has the dubious distinction of writing into the Constitution the first quantitative limitation on the right of the majority to choose their President. It is not the generation of the framers that was undemocratic; it is our generation that is undemocratic.

It is relevant to note, too, that the Constitution contains no property qualification for voting. Most states, to be sure, had such qualifications—in general a freehold or its equivalent—and the Constitution assimilated such qualifications as states might establish. Yet the framers, whether for reasons practical or philosophical we need not determine, made no serious efforts to write any property qualifications for voting into the Constitution itself.

The question of popular control came up clearly in one other connection as well: the matter of ratification. Should the Constitution be ratified by state legislatures, or by conventions? The practical arguments for the two methods were nicely balanced. The decisive argument was not, however, one of expediency but of principle. "To the people with whom all power remains that has not been given up in the Constitutions derived from them" we must resort, said Mason. Madison put the matter on principle, too. "He considered the difference between a system founded on the Legislatures only, and one founded on the people, to be the true difference between a *league* or *treaty* and a *Constitution."* Ellsworth's motion to refer the Constitution to legislatures was defeated by a vote of eight to two, and the resolution to refer it to conventions passed with only Delaware in the negative.

Was the Constitution designed to place private property beyond the reach of majorities? If so, the framers did a very bad job. They failed to write into it the most elementary safeguards for property. They failed to write into it limitations on the tax power, or prohibitions against the abuse of the money power. They failed to provide for rule by those whom Adams was later to call the wise and the rich and the well-born. What they did succeed in doing was to create a system of checks and balances and adjustments and accommodations that would effectively prevent the suppression of most minorities by majorities. They took advantage of the complexity, the diversity, the pluralism, of American society and economy to encourage a balance of interests. They worked out sound and lasting political solutions to the problems of class, interest, section, race, religion, party.

Perhaps the most perspicacious comment on this whole question of the threat from turbulent popular majorities against property and order came, *mirabile dictu,* from the dashing young Charles Pinckney of South Carolina—he of the "lost" Pinckney Plan. On June 25 Pinckney made a major speech and thought it important enough to write out and give to Madison. The point of departure was the hackneyed one of the character of the second branch of the legislature, but the comments were an anticipation of De Tocqueville and Lord Bryce. We need not, Pinckney asserted, fear the rise of class conflicts in America, nor take precautions against them.

The genius of the people, their mediocrity of situation & the prospects which are afforded their industry in a Country which must be a new one for centuries are unfavorable to the rapid distinction of ranks. . . . If equality is . . . the leading feature of the U. States [he asked], where then are the riches & wealth whose representation & protection is the peculiar province of this permanent body [the Senate]. Are they in the hands of the few who may be called rich; in the possession of less than a hundred citizens? certainly not. They are in the great body of the people . . . . [There was no likelihood that a privileged body would ever develop in the United States, he added, either from the landed interest, the moneyed interest, or the mercantile.] Besides, Sir, I apprehend that on this point the policy of the U. States has been much mistaken. We have unwisely considered ourselves as the inhabitants of an old instead of a new country. We have adopted the maxims of a State full of people . . . . The people of this country are not only very different from the inhabitants of any State we are acquainted with in the modern world; but I assert that their situation is distinct from either the people of Greece or of Rome . . . . Our true situation appears to me to be this—a new extensive Country containing within itself the materials for forming a Government capable of extending to its citizens all the blessings of civil & religious liberty—capable of making them happy at home. This is the great end of Republican Establishments. . . .

Not a government cunningly contrived to protect the interests of property, but one capable of extending to its citizens the blessings of liberty and happiness—was that not, after all, what the framers created?

Staughton Lynd

The Conflict over Slavery

I

According to the abolitionist critique, slavery helped to shape the Constitution because slavery was the basis of conflict between North and South, and compromising that conflict was the main work of the Constitutional Convention.

Both in the nineteenth and twentieth centuries, one line of argument against the significance of slavery in the genesis of the Constitution has stressed the fact that the words "slave" and "slavery" do not appear in the Constitution, and contended that, to quote Farrand, "there was comparatively little said on the subject [of slavery] in the convention." This might be called the argument from silence.

But we know why the Founders did not use the words "slave" and "slavery" in the Constitution. Paterson of New Jersey stated in the Convention that when, in 1783, the Continental Congress changed its eighth Article of Confederation so that slaves would henceforth be included in apportioning taxation among the States, the Congress "had been ashamed to use the term 'Slaves' and had substituted a description." Iredell, in the Virginia ratifying convention, said similarly that the fugitive slave clause of the proposed Constitution did not use the word "slave" because of the "particular scruples" of the "northern delegates"; and in 1798 Dayton of New Jersey, who had been a member of the Convention, told the House of Representatives that the purpose was to avoid any "stain" on the new government. If for Northern delegates the motive was shame, for Southern

From Staughton Lynd, "The Abolitionist Critique of the United States Constitution," in The Anti-Slavery Vanguard: New Essays on the Abolitionists, ed. Martin Duberman, pp. 215–235. Copyright © 1965 by Princeton University Press; Princeton Paperback, 1968. Omission of footnotes. Reprinted by permission of Princeton University Press.

members of the Convention it was prudence. Madison wrote to Lafayette in 1830, referring to emancipation: "I scarcely express myself too strongly in saying, that any allusion in the Convention to the subject you have so much at heart would have been a spark to a mass of gunpowder." Madison's metaphor hardly suggests that the subject of slavery was of secondary importance to the Convention.

Farrand's own magnificent edition of the Convention records amply refutes his contention that the subject of slavery was little discussed. The South Carolinians in particular were often on their feet demanding security for what one of them called "this species of property." And yet the role of slavery in the Convention went much further than this. For we have it on Madison's authority that it was "pretty well understood" that the "institution of slavery and its consequences formed the line of discrimination" between the contending groups of States in the Convention. Slavery, that is to say, was recognized as the basis of sectionalism; and it is not a difficult task to show that sectional conflict between North and South was the major tension in the Convention.

According to Franklin, debate in the Convention proceeded peaceably ("with great coolness and temper") until on June 11, the rule of suffrage in the national legislature was discussed. Farrand would have us believe that the three-fifths ratio which resulted was not a compromise in the Convention, that it had been recommended by Congress in 1783, adopted by eleven states before the Convention met, and was part of the original New Jersey Plan. Farrand's statement is misleading, however, for all the above remarks refer to counting three-fifths of the slaves *in apportioning taxation.* What was at issue in Convention was the *extension of this ratio to representation:* what George Ticknor Curtis called "the naked question whether the slaves should be included as persons, and in the proportion of three fifths, in the census for the future apportionment of representatives among the States." The two applications were very different. As Luther Martin told the Maryland legislature, taxing slaves discouraged slavery, while giving them political representation encouraged it. Thus tempers rose in the Convention from the moment that Rutledge and Butler of South Carolina asserted that representation in the House should be according to quotas of contribution; years later Rufus King observed that the three-fifths clause "was, at the time, believed to be a great" concession, "and has proved to have been the greatest which was made to secure the adoption of the constitution."

On June 25 there occurred the first perfectly sectional vote of the Convention, the five States from Maryland to Georgia voting to postpone consideration of the election of the Senate until the three-fifths clause regarding elections for the House had been settled. On June 29, Madison made the first of many statements as to the sectional nature of the issue:

If there was real danger, I would give the smaller states the defensive weap-

ons.—*But there is none from that quarter. The great danger to our general government is the great southern and northern interests of the continent, being opposed to each other. Look to the votes in congress, and most of them stand divided by the geography of the country, not according to the size of the states.*

The next day Madison reiterated that "the States were divided into different interests not by their difference of size, but by other circumstances; the most material of which resulted partly from climate, but principally from their having or not having slaves." Farrand comments on these observations that "Madison was one of the very few men who seemed to appreciate the real division of interests in the country." Yet Madison's emphasis on sectional conflict at the Convention was echoed by Pinckney on July 2, by King on July 10, by Mason on July 11, and, with reluctance, by Gouverneur Morris on July 13; and when on July 14 Madison once more asserted that slavery, not size, formed the line of discrimination between the States, as previously remarked, he said that this was "pretty well understood" by the Convention. Slavery was thus the basis of the great Convention crisis, when, as Gouverneur Morris later said, the fate of America was suspended by a hair.

But this crisis, and the crisis which followed over the import of slaves, cannot be understood from the records of the Convention alone. The great Convention compromises involving slavery were attempts to reconcile disputes which had been boiling up for years in the Continental Congress.

II

Sectional conflict, like the ghost in *Hamlet*, was there from the beginning. When in September 1774 at the first Continental Congress Patrick Henry made his famous declaration "I am not a Virginian, but an American," the point he was making was that Virginia would not insist on counting slaves in apportioning representation; Henry's next sentence was: "Slaves are to be thrown out of the Question, and if the freemen can be represented according to their Numbers I am satisfyed." The next speaker, Lynch of South Carolina, protested, and the question was left unsettled. Thus early did South Carolinian intransigence overbear Virginian liberalism.

Again in July 1776, the month of the Declaration of Independence, the problem of slave representation was brought before Congress in the debate over the proposed Articles of Confederation. The Dickinson draft of the Articles produced three controversies, strikingly similar to the three great compromises of the subsequent Constitutional Convention: "The equal representation of all the states in Congress aroused the antagonism of the larger states. The apportionment of common expenses according to total population aroused the bitter opposition of the states with large slave populations. The grant to Congress of broad powers over Western lands and boundaries was resisted stubbornly by the states whose charters gave them large claims to the West." In its ten-year existence the Continental Congress succeeded in solving only the last of these controversies, the question of Western lands, and accordingly emphasis has tended to fall on it in histories of the Confederation. But the other two problems were just as hotly debated, in much the same language as in 1787; and on these questions, as Channing observes, there was a "different alignment in Congress" than on the matter of Western lands: a sectional alignment.

The eleventh Article of the Dickinson draft stated that money contributions from the States should be "in Proportion to the Number of Inhabitants of every Age, Sex and Quality, except Indians not paying Taxes." On July 30, 1776, Samuel Chase of Maryland (later a prominent Antifederalist) moved the insertion of the word "white," arguing that "if Negroes are taken into the Computation of Numbers to ascertain Wealth, they ought to be in settling the Representation"; Gouverneur Morris would use this same formula in July 1787 to resolve the deadlock over representation in the House. In the debate which followed the changes were rung upon several themes of the Constitutional Convention. Wilson of Pennsylvania said that to exempt slaves from taxation would encourage slaveholding; in response to the observation that if slaves were counted, Northern sheep should also be counted, Benjamin Franklin remarked that "sheep will never make any Insurrections"; Rutledge of South Carolina anticipated the August 1787 debate on navigation laws by warning that "the Eastern Colonies will become the Carriers for the Southern. They will obtain Wealth for which they will not be taxed"; and his colleague Lynch again threw down a South Carolina ultimatum: "If it is debated, whether their Slaves are their Property, there is an end of the Confederation."

The war had scarcely ended when the sectional debate resumed. We tend to think of Thomas Jefferson as a national statesman, and of the controversy over whether new states would be slave or free as something subsequent to 1820. How striking, then, to find Jefferson writing from Congress to Governor Benjamin Harrison of Virginia in November 1783 about the Northwest Territory: "If a state be first laid off on the [Great] lakes it will add a vote to the Northern scale, if on the Ohio it will add one to the Southern." This concern would never be out of the minds of Southern politicians until the Civil War. Jefferson did, of course, attempt to exclude slavery from the Territories. But on the ninth anniversary of Lexington and Concord, Congress, on motion of Spaight of North Carolina, seconded by Read of South Carolina, struck this provision from Jefferson's draft proposals.

A principal issue between North and South in these first years of the Critical Period was financial. Southern resistance to Northern financial manipulations did not wait until the 1790's: it began, if one must choose a date, when Delaware, Maryland, Virginia, and both the Carolinas voted against the devaluation plan of March 18, 1780, with every Northern state except divided New Hampshire voting Aye. After the war the issue became still more intense. The Revolutionary campaigns in the South took place largely in the last three years of the war "when neither Congress nor the states," in the words of E. James Ferguson, "had effective money and the troops were supported by impressment." The result was that of the three major categories of public debt—Quartermaster and Commissary certificates issued to civilians; loan certificates; and final settlement certificates issued to the Continental army—the South held only 16 percent. The public debt of the South was a state debt, while the various kinds of Federal debt were held by Northerners: as Spaight of North Carolina put it, "the Eastern [i.e., Northern] States . . . have got Continental Securities for all monies loaned, services done or articles impressed, while to the southward, it has been made a State debt." Hence when Congress sought to tax all the states to repay the Federal debt, the South protested; and when Congress further provided that Northern states could meet their Congressional requisitions with securities, so that only the South need pay coin, the South was furious. Madison told Edmund Randolph in 1783 that unless the public accounts were speedily adjusted and discharged "a dissolution of the Union will be inevitable." "The pious New-Englanders," Read of South Carolina wrote in April 1785, "think tis time to carry their long projected Scheme into Execution and make the southern states bear the burthen of furnishing all the actual money."

Sectional considerations underlay many an action of the early 1780's where they might not, at first glance, seem evident. Jefferson's appointment as United States representative in France is an example. Jefferson had been appointed to the commission to negotiate a peace, as had Laurens of South Carolina; but Jefferson did not go and Laurens was captured by the British en route to Europe, so that three Northerners—John Jay, John Adams, and Benjamin Franklin—carried the burden of the peace talks. The treaty completed, the same three men stayed on in Europe to represent American interests there, and it was this that aroused Southern concern. James Monroe expressed it in March 1784, writing to Governor Harrison. Monroe pointed out that Virginia owed British merchants £2,800,000 in debts, which according to the peace treaty must now be paid. "It is important to the southern States to whom the negotiation of these treaties are committed; for except the fishery and the fur-trade (the latter of w'h Mr. Jeff'n thinks . . . may be turn'd down the Potow'k); the southern States, are as States, almost alone interested in it." In May, with Jefferson's appointment achieved, the Virginia delegates in Congress wrote the governor: "It was an object with us, in order to render the Commission as agreable as possible to the Southern States to have Mr. Jefferson placed in the room of Mr. Jay." The previous arrangement, the Virginians went on, involved "obvious inequality in the Representation of these States in Europe"; had it continued, it would have presented "an insurmountable obstacle" to giving the commission such great powers.

Here in microcosm was the problem of the South until its victory at the 1787 Convention: recognizing the need for stronger Federal powers, it feared to create them until it was assured that the South could control their use.

III

Even as early as the 1780's the South felt itself to be a conscious minority. This was evident, for example, in the comment of Virginia delegates as to the location of the national capital. "The votes in Congress as they stand at present," wrote the delegates from the Old Dominion, "are unfavorable to a Southern situation and untill the admission of Western States into the Union, we apprehend it will be found impracticable to retain that Body [Congress], any length of time, Southward of the middle States." In the fall of 1786, when the clash over shutting the Mississippi to American commerce was at its height, Timothy Bloodworth of North Carolina remarked that "it is wel known that the ballance of Power is now in the Eastern States, and they appear determined to keep it in that Direction." This was why such Southerners as Richard Henry Lee, later the nation's leading Antifederalist pamphleteer, were already opposing stronger Federal powers in 1785. "It seems to me clear, beyond doubt," Lee wrote to Madison, "that the giving Congress a power to Legislate over the Trade of the Union would be dangerous in the extreme to the 5 Southern or Staple States, whose want of ships and seamen would expose their freightage and their produce to a most pernicious and destructive Monopoly." This was a strong argument, which would be heard throughout the South till 1861; it was this fear which in all probability caused George Mason and Edmund Randolph of Virginia to refuse to sign the Constitution in 1787. Recognizing the force of Lee's argument, Madison wrote to Jefferson in the summer and fall of 1785 that commercial distress was causing a call for stronger powers in Congress throughout the North, but that the South was divided. Lee was "an inflexible adversary, Grayson [William Grayson, another Virginia Antifederalist in 1788] unfriendly." Animosity against Great Britain would push the South toward commercial regulation, but the high price of tobacco would work against it. "S. Carolina I am told is deliberating on the distresses of her commerce and will probably concur in some general plan; with a proviso, no doubt against any restraint from importing slaves, of which they have received from Africa since the peace about twelve thousand." Madison concluded by telling his comrade in France that he trembled to think what would happen should the South not join the other states in strengthening Congress.

Others beside Madison trembled at this thought: the possibility of disunion was openly and seriously discussed in the 1780's, particularly by those who knew of the fiercely sectional debates in Congress. And if disunion was only the speculation of a few in 1785, the great controversy over the Mississippi in 1786 shook many more from their complacence.

The Mississippi question of the 1780's was a part of the larger question of the destiny of the West which, ultimately, would be the immediate cause of the Civil War. Farrand is less than accurate in his attempt to disengage the question of the admission of new states at the Constitutional Convention from sectional strife. For if there is a single key to the politics of Congress and the Convention in the Critical Period, it is that the South expected the West to be slave rather than free and to tilt the balance of power southward, while in Bancroft's words "an ineradicable dread of the coming power of the Southwest lurked in New England, especially in Massachusetts." That group in Congress recognized as "the Southern Interest" (1786), "the Southern party" (1787) or "the Southern Delegation" (1788) fought throughout the 1780's to forestall the admission of Vermont until at least one Southern state could be added simultaneously, to hasten the development of the West, and to remove all obstacles to its speedy organization into the largest possible number of new states. It was here that the Mississippi question entered. What was feared if America permitted Spain to close New Orleans to American commerce was not only a separation of the Western states, but a slackening of the southwestward migration which Southerners counted on to assure their long-run predominance in the Union.

"The southern states," wrote the French minister to his superior in Europe,

> are not in earnest when they assert that without the navigation of the Mississippi the inhabitants of the interior will seek an outlet by way of the lakes, and will throw themselves into the arms of England. . . . The true motive of this vigorous opposition is to be found in the great preponderance of the northern states, eager to incline the balance toward their side; the southern neglect no opportunity of increasing the population and importance of the western territory, and of drawing thither by degrees the inhabitants of New England. . . . These new territories will gradually form themselves into separate governments; they will have their representatives in congress, and will augment greatly the mass of the southern states.

Otto is abundantly confirmed by the debates of the Virginia ratifying convention, and still more by Monroe's correspondence of late 1786. On August 12, 1786, Monroe wrote from Congress to Patrick Henry:

> P.S. The object in the occlusion of the Mississippi on the part of these people so far as it is extended to the interest of their States (for those of a private kind gave birth to it): is to break up so far as this will do it, the settlements on the western waters, prevent any in future, and thereby keep the States Southward as they now are—or if settlements will take place, that they shall be on such principles as to make it the interest of the people to separate from the Confederacy, so as effectually to exclude any new State from it. To throw the weight of population eastward and keep it there. . . .

Like many another Southerner in the next seventy-five years, Monroe ended by saying that, if it came to separation, it was essential that Pennsylvania join the South. So forceful was the effect of his letter on Henry, Madison wrote Washington in December, that Henry, who had hitherto advocated a stronger Union, began to draw back. By 1788 he, like Lee, Grayson, and Monroe, would be an Antifederalist.

The upshot of the Mississippi squabble was that the long efforts to vest Congress with power over commerce were threatened with failure at the very brink of success. As delegates made their way to the Annapolis Convention in the fall of 1786, Bloodworth of North Carolina wrote that because of the Mississippi controversy "all other Business seems out of View at present." "Should the measure proposed be pursued," Grayson told the Congress, "the Southern States would never grant those powers which were acknowledged to be essential to the existence of the Union." When Foreign Secretary Jay attempted to have instructions, authorizing him to give up American insistence on using the river, adopted by a simple Congressional majority of seven states, it stirred in many Southern breasts the fear of being outvoted. Even before the Mississippi question came before Congress Southerners like Monroe had insisted that, if Congress were to regulate commerce, commercial laws should require the assent of nine or even eleven states. Jay's attempt (as Southerners saw it) to use a simple majority to push through a measure fundamentally injurious to the South greatly intensified this apprehension. When the Constitutional Convention met, the so-called Pinckney Plan suggested a two-thirds Congressional majority for commercial laws, and both the Virginia ratifying convention (which voted to ratify by a small majority) and the North Carolina convention (which rejected ratification) recommended the same amendment.

In the midst of the Mississippi controversy, men hopeful for stronger government saw little prospect of success. Madison wrote Jefferson in August 1786 that he almost despaired of strengthening Congress through the Annapolis Convention or any other; in September, Otto wrote to Vergennes: "It is to be feared that this discussion will cause a great coolness between the two parties, and may be the germ of a future separation of the southern states."

IV

Why then did the South consent to the Constitutional Convention? If the South felt itself on the defensive in the 1780's, and particularly so in the summer and fall of 1786, why did its delegates agree to strengthen Federal powers in 1787? If a two-thirds majority for commercial laws seemed essential to Southerners in August of one year, why did they surrender it in August of the next? Were Madison and Washington, as they steadfastly worked to strengthen the national government, traitors to the interests of their section, or was there some view of the future which nationalist Southerners then entertained which enabled them to be good Southerners and good Federalists at the same time?

It is Madison, once more, who provides the clue. He saw that if the South were to agree in strengthening Congress, the plan which gave each state one vote would have to be changed in favor of the South. And in letters to Jefferson, to Randolph, and to Washington in the spring of 1787 he foretold in a sentence the essential plot of the Convention drama. The basis of representation would be changed to allow representation by numbers as well as by states, because a change was "recommended to the Eastern States by the actual superiority of their populousness, and to the Southern by their expected superiority."

So it fell out. Over and over again members of the Convention stated, as of something on which all agreed, that "as soon as the Southern & Western population should predominate, which must happen in a few years," the South would be compensated for any advantages wrung from it by the North in the meantime. When Northerners insisted on equality of votes in the Senate, it was partly because they feared what would happen when the South gained its inevitable (as they supposed) majority. "He must be short sighted indeed," declared King on July 12,

who does not foresee that whenever the Southern States shall be more numerous than the Northern, they can & will hold a language that will awe them [the Northern States] into justice. If they threaten to separate now in case injury shall be done them, will their threats be less urgent or effectual, when force shall back their demands?

Gouverneur Morris echoed this gloomy prophecy the next day. "The consequence of such a transfer of power from the maritime to the interior & landed interest," Madison quoted him,

will he foresees be such an oppression of commerce, that he shall be obliged to vote for ye. vicious principle of equality in the 2d. branch in order to provide some defence for the N. States agst. it.

"It has been said," Morris added, "that N.C. [,] S.C. and Georgia only will in a little time have a majority of the people in America. They must in that case include the great interior Country, and every thing was to be apprehended from their getting the power into their hands."

This false expectation explains why Georgia and the Carolinas who (as Gunning Bedford noted) should by present population have been "small" states, considered themselves "large" states at the Convention. This expectation clarifies, it seems to me, why the South gave way in its demand that commercial laws require a two-thirds majority; for would not time and the flow of migration soon provide such a majority without written stipulation?

At the crucial Virginia ratifying convention no one questioned that the South would soon be the most populous section of the country. The difference lay between those who thought this inevitable event made it safe to strengthen the Federal government now, and those, like Henry and Mason, who counseled waiting until the Southern Congressional majority made absolutely safe a transfer of power.

The irony, of course, was that the expectation was completely erroneous. The expected Southern majority in the House never materialized, and the Senate, not the House, became the bulwark of the South. In 1790, the population of the South had been growing more rapidly than the North's population for several decades, and was within 200,000 of the population north of the Potomac. True to the general expectation in 1787, the Southwest filled up more rapidly than the area north of the Ohio River. In 1820, Ohio, Indiana, Illinois, and Michigan contained a population of almost 800,000, but Missouri, Kentucky, Tennessee, Alabama, Mississippi, Louisiana, and Arkansas held over 1,300,000 persons. Nevertheless, in the original thirteen states the Northern population pulled so far ahead of the Southern that in 1820 the white population of Northern states and territories was almost twice that of Southern states and territories. Thus the South never obtained the Congressional majority which statesmen of both sections had anticipated at the time of the Constitutional Convention.

When the dream of a Southern majority in Congress and the nation collapsed, there fell together with it the vision of a Southern commercial empire, drawing the produce of the West down the Potomac and the James to "a Philadelphia or a Baltimore" on the Virginia coast. It was not, as it so often seems, an accident that the Convention of 1787 grew from the Annapolis Convention, or that Virginians were the prime movers in calling both. Throughout the 1780's Madison, Jefferson, Monroe, and to an almost fanatical degree, Washington, were intent on strengthening the commercial ties between Virginia and the West. As early as 1784, Jefferson suggested to Madison cooperation with Maryland in opening communication to the West, and during that year and the next both Washington and Monroe toured the Western country with their grand plan in mind. Jefferson and Monroe pushed a Potomac location for the national capital partly with the hope that it would "cement us to our Western friends when they shall be formed into separate states" and help Virginia to beat out Pennsylvania and New York in the race for Western trade. Virginia had given up its claims to Western land, but its leaders hoped for a commercial dominion just as satisfactory: as Jefferson put it, "almost a monopoly of the Western and Indian trade." "But smooth the road once," wrote the enraptured Washington, "and make easy the way for them, and then see what an influx of articles will be poured upon us; how amazingly our exports will be increased by them, and how amply we shall be compensated for any trouble and expense we may encounter to effect it." The West, then, would not only give the South political predominance but also, as Madison wrote Jefferson, "double the value of half the land within the Commonwealth . . . extend its commerce, link with its interests those of the Western States, and lessen the immigration of its Citizens." This was the castle-in-the-air which Virginians pictured as they worked to bring about the Constitutional Convention, this was the plan for economic development so abruptly and traumatically shattered by Secretary of the Treasury Alexander Hamilton.

In the Spring and Summer of 1788, however, as the South with the North moved to ratify the Constitution, few foresaw the clouds on the horizon. The Constitutional Convention, with a Southern majority (in Bancroft's words) "from its organization to its dissolution," seemed to have wrought well for the South. Madison alone, from his vantage-point in Congress, fretted about that body's continued preoccupation with sectional issues. After wrangling all Spring about the admission of Kentucky, Congress turned to that old favorite, the location of the capital. "It is truly mortifying," Madison wrote to Washington, to see such "a display of locality," of "local and state considerations," at the very "outset of the new Government." The behavior of Congress would give "countenance to some of the most popular arguments which have been inculcated by the southern anti-federalists," and "be regarded as at once a proof of the preponderancy of the Eastern strength." "I foresee contentions," he wrote the next Spring, "first between federal and anti-federal parties, and then between northern and southern parties." Before long he would be leading the opposition.

V

Even this sampling of the printed sources suggests that sectional conflict based (to quote Madison once more) on "the institution of slavery and its consequences" was a potent force in the shaping of the Constitution. The conclusion seems inescapble that any interpretation of the Convention which stresses realty and personalty, large states and small states, or monarchy and democracy, but leaves slavery out, is an inadequate interpretation.

SUGGESTIONS FOR FURTHER READING

Those interested in further exploring the controversy over the Constitution should read the whole of Charles A. Beard's *An Economic Interpretation of the Constitution;* only a portion of this important book is reprinted in this volume. Among the important critiques of Beard are Forrest McDonald, *We the People: The Economic Origins of the Constitution* (Chicago, 1958), and Robert E. Brown, *Charles Beard and the Constitution* (Princeton, N.J., 1956). More in the Beardian tradition are Merrill Jensen, *The New Nation: A History of the United States During the Confederation, 1781–89* (New York, 1950), and Jackson T. Main,

* Available in paperback edition.

The Anti-Federalists: Critics of the Constitution (Chapel Hill, N.C., 1961). That the matter is far from settled may be seen by reading Jackson T. Main's review of *We the People* and McDonald's reply in *William and Mary Quarterly*, 17 (January 1960), pp. 86–102.

More of Staughton Lynd's view, which emphasizes conflict, may be found in his *Class Conflict, Slavery and the United States Constitution* (Indianapolis, 1967). Consensus and easy compromise are stressed in Carl Van Doren, *The Great Rehearsal* (New York, 1948); Benjamin F. Wright, *Consensus and Continuity, 1776–1787* (Boston, 1958); and Edmund S. Morgan, *The Birth of the Republic, 1763–1789* (Chicago, 1956).

The following articles trace differences between supporters and opponents of the Constitution to their different wartime experiences and their different attitudes toward the future possibilities of the new nation: Stanley Elkins and Eric McKitrick, "The Founding Fathers: Young Men of the Revolution," *Political Science Quarterly*, 76 (June 1961), pp. 201–16, and Cecilia M. Kenyon, "Men of Little Faith: The Anti-Federalists on the Nature of Representative Government," *William and Mary Quarterly*, 3rd ser., 12 (January 1955), pp. 38–43. Similarly, Jackson T. Main, *Political Parties before the Constitution* (Chapel Hill, N.C., 1973) and Gordon S. Wood, *The Creation of the American Republic* (Chapel Hill, N.C., 1970), emphasize conflicts stemming from differences in ideology and attitudes rather than class.

The best way to get the point of view of the founding fathers is to read their own explanation in *The Federalist Papers*, available in many editions.

4

Jeffersonians and Federalists

The ratification and general acceptance of the Constitution did not eliminate all disagreements in the new nation. Indeed, strong differences of opinion arose within George Washington's cabinet, differences that soon spread to the Congress and, through the public press, to the country at large. The economic program proposed by Washington's strong-willed secretary of the treasury, Alexander Hamilton, was soon opposed by the secretary of state, Thomas Jefferson. In less than a decade after the inauguration of the first administration under the new Constitution, disagreements had led to the formation of the nation's first organized political parties. The election of 1800 was clearly a party battle, and Jefferson's newly organized Republican party emerged victorious.

Certainly this was a time of sharp debate and furious party struggle. Yet how significant were the differences dividing the country? In his old age, looking back on the event, Thomas Jefferson called his election "the revolution of 1800," obviously an assessment that implied vast differences separating him from his opponents. Yet in his first inaugural address, Jefferson minimized the importance of the party conflict from which the country had just emerged. "We are all Republicans, we are all Federalists," he said.

Because Jefferson himself entertained two seemingly contradictory evaluations of his victory, later historians have been able to agree with him and still disagree among themselves. For some, Jefferson's victory was indeed a revolution; his administration is said to have ushered in a period of agrarian democracy; his victory signaled the defeat of an aristocratic moneyed power. Others argue that Jefferson changed little of the inheritance from the Federalists he had defeated; in truth, they maintain, Jefferson continued the Federalist program.

The existence of opposing parties, then, does not by itself prove the existence of fundamental conflict during the early years of the new nation's history. Nor does the relative ease with which the Jeffersonians established their political hegemony by itself prove that they merely absorbed the program and policies of their opponents. The historian must look deeper before he can discover whether party labels revealed a major conflict in American society or merely minor differences within a basic consensus. At the same time, he must keep in mind that the country was changing rapidly during these years and that among the changes was one that opponents and supporters alike called an expansion of democracy. To see democracy and Jeffersonianism on the one side locked in a struggle with aristocracy and Federalism on the other is to recognize a fundamental conflict. But if democracy had won the day in both parties and if party conflicts had become mainly struggles for power and office, then consensus becomes the theme for the first two or three decades of the nation's history under the new Constitution.

These problems are revealed in the following selections. The first two focus directly on Jefferson. In the first one Morton Borden finds Jefferson to be a political compromiser. He denies that Jefferson, once in power, abandoned his principles and adopted those of the opposition, arguing instead that

Jefferson and his opponents were united on fundamentals and disagreed only on details.

Lance Banning disagrees with this view. He argues that fundamental differences divided Jefferson and his opponents and denies that Jefferson compromised his principles once in office. The consensus that emerged under Jefferson's successors was the result not of compromise but rather of a combination of the victory of Jeffersonian principles and the changed conditions in the nation.

A different approach to the same problems is taken by Richard Hofstadter in the final selection. He notes that neither Jefferson nor the Federalist leaders thought of their opponents as part of the legitimate, loyal opposition. Rather, each conceived of the other as an implacable enemy of the Republic, a view that certainly points to sharp and fundamental conflict. Nevertheless, he reminds the reader, the election of 1800 was the "first election in modern history which, by popular decision, resulted in the quiet and peaceful transition of national power from the hands of one of two embattled parties to another," a development that implies the existence of a widespread consensus.

The separation of Americans into different parties and factions matched by sharp and often abusive exchanges among leaders in the newspapers of the day leaves no doubt of differences among Americans during the Age of Jefferson. But how significant were these differences? Did they arise from basic economic and social cleavages in American society and reflect fundamental class conflict based on real ideological differences? Or did they reflect only minor disagreements within a general context of fundamental agreement or consensus?

Morton Borden

Thomas Jefferson:
Political Compromiser

For twelve years the Constitution worked, after a fashion. From its inception the new document had been subjected to severe trials and divisive strains. A rebellion in Pennsylvania, a naval war with France, a demand for states' rights from Virginia and Kentucky, and various Western schemes of disunion—all had been surmounted. Had it not been for the great prestige of George Washington and the practical moderation of John Adams, America's second attempt at a federal union might have failed like the first. Partisan passions had run high in the 1790's, and any single factor on which men disagreed—Hamilton's financial plans or the French Revolution or the Sedition Act—might easily have caused a stoppage of the nation's political machinery.

The two-party system emerged during this decade, and on each important issue public opinion seemed to oscillate between Federalist and Democratic-Republican. Perhaps this was to be expected of a young nation politically adolescent. Year by year Americans were becoming more politically alert and active; if there was little room for middle ground between these two factions, yet opinions were hardly fixed and irrevocable. The culmination of partisan controversy and the test of respective strengths took place in the monumental election of 1800.

Jefferson was feared, honestly feared, by almost all Federalists. Were he to win the election, so they predicted, all the hard constructive gains of those twelve years would be dissipated. Power would be returned to the in-

Morton Borden, "Thomas Jefferson," in Morden Borden (ed.), America's Eleven Greatest Presidents, 2nd edition, © 1971, 1961 by Rand McNally & Company, Chicago, pp. 52–62. Reprinted by permission of Rand McNally College Publishing Company.

dividual states; commerce would suffer; judicial power would be lessened; and the wonderful financial system of Hamilton would be dismantled and destroyed. Jefferson was an atheist, and he would attack the churches. Jefferson was a hypocrite, an aristocrat posing as democrat, appealing to the baser motives of human beings in order to obtain votes. Jefferson was a revolutionary, a Francophile and, after ruining the Army and Navy under the guise of economy measures, might very well involve the nation in a war with England. In short, it was doubtful if the Constitution could continue its successful course under such a president.

In like manner the Republicans feared another Federalist victory. To be sure, John Adams had split with Hamilton and had earned the enmity of the Essex Junto. But would he not continue Hamilton's "moneyed system"? Did not Adams share the guilt of every Federalist for the despicable Alien and Sedition Acts? Was it not true that "His Rotundity" so admired the British system that he was really a monarchist at heart? Republicans were not engaging in idle chatter, nor were they speaking solely for effect, when they predicted many dire consequences if Adams were elected. A typical rumor had Adams uniting "his house to that of his majesty of Britain" and "the bridegroom was to be king of America."

Throughout the country popular interest in the election was intense, an intensity sustained over months of balloting. When the Republicans carried New York City, Alexander Hamilton seriously suggested that the results be voided. And when the breach between Adams and Hamilton became public knowledge. Republicans nodded knowingly and quoted the maxim: "When thieves fall out, honest men come by their own."

The Federalists were narrowly defeated. But the decision was complicated by a result which many had predicted: a tied electoral vote between the two Republican candidates, Aaron Burr and Thomas Jefferson. (Indeed, the Twelfth Amendment was adopted in 1804 to avoid any such recurrence.) A choice between the two would be made by the House of Representatives. At this moment, February, 1801, the Constitution seemed on the verge of collapse. Federalist members of the lower house united in support of Burr; Republicans were just as adamant for Jefferson. After thirty-five ballots, neither side had yet obtained the necessary majority. The issue seemed hopelessly deadlocked. What would happen on March 4, inauguration day?

One representative from Maryland, sick with a high fever, was literally carried into Congress on a stretcher to maintain the tied vote of his state. The Republican governor of Pennsylvania, Thomas McKean, threatened to march on Washington with troops if the Federalists persisted in thwarting the will of the people. Hamilton was powerless; his advice that Jefferson was the lesser evil went unheeded. So great was their hatred of the Virginian that most Federalists in Congress would have opposed him regardless of the consequences. After all, they reasoned, Jefferson would dismantle the Federal government anyway. In the end, however, patriotism and common sense prevailed. For the choice was no longer Jefferson or Burr, but Jefferson or no president at all. A few Federalists, led by James A. Bayard of Delaware, could not accept the logic of their party, and threw the election to Jefferson.

What a shock it was, then, to read Jefferson's carefully chosen words in his inaugural address:

But every difference of opinion is not a difference of principle. We have called by different names brethren of the same principle. We are all republicans—we are all federalists. If there be any among us who would wish to dissolve this Union or to change its republican form, let them stand undisturbed as monuments of the safety with which error of opinion may be tolerated where reason is left free to combat it. I know, indeed, that some honest men fear that a republican government cannot be strong; that this government is not strong enough. But would the honest patriot, in the full tide of successful experiment, abandon a government which has so far kept us free and firm, on the theoretic and visionary fear that this government, the world's best hope, may by possibility want energy to preserve itself? I trust not. I believe this, on the contrary, the strongest government on earth. I believe it is the only one where every man, at the call of the laws, would fly to the standard of the law, and would meet invasions of the public order as his own personal concern. Sometimes it is said that man cannot be trusted with the government of himself. Can he, then, be trusted with the government of others? Or have we found angels in the form of kings to govern him? Let history answer this question.

The words were greeted with applause—and confusion. It was obvious that Jefferson wanted to salve the wounds of bitter factionalism. While many Federalists remained distrustful and some even regarded it as hypocritical, most men approved the tone of their new president's message.

But what did Jefferson mean? Were there no economic principles at stake in his conflicts with Hamilton? Were there no political and constitutional principles implicit in the polar views of the respective parties? And, in the last analysis, did not these differences reflect a fundamental philosophical quarrel over the nature of human beings? Was not the election of 1800 indeed a revolution? If not, then what is the meaning of Jeffersonianism?

For two terms Jefferson tried, as best he could, to apply the standards of his inaugural address. Naturally, the Alien and Sedition Acts were allowed to lapse. The new secretary of the treasury, Albert Gallatin, was instructed to devise an easily understood program to erase the public debt gradually. Internal taxes were either abolished or reduced. Frugality and economy were emphasized to an extreme. Elegant and costly social functions were replaced by simple and informal receptions. The expense of maintaining ambassadors at the courts of Portugal, Holland, and Prussia was erased by withdrawing these missions. The Army and Navy were pared down to skeleton size. To be sure, Jefferson had to reverse himself on the matter of patronage for subordinate Government posts. Originally he planned to keep these replacements

to a minimum, certainly not to permit an individual's partisan opinions to
be a basis for dismissal unless the man manifestly used his office for partisan
purposes. This position was politically untenable, according to Jefferson's
lieutenants, and they pressed him to accept a moderate number of removals.
Indeed, Jefferson's handling of patronage is symbolic of what Hamilton once
called his "ineradicable duplicity."

The Federalist leaders cried out in anguish at every one of these policy
changes. The lowering of the nation's military strength would increase the
danger of invasion. It was a rather risky gamble to assume that peace could
be maintained while European war was an almost constant factor, and the
United States was the major neutral carrier. The abolition of the excises,
especially on distilled spirits, would force the Government to rely on tariffs,
an unpredictable source of revenue depending on the wind and waves. It was
charged that several foreign ambassadors were offended by Jefferson's rather
affected and ultrademocratic social simplicity. Most important, the ultimate
payment of the public debt would reduce national power.

This time, however, the people did not respond to the Federalist lament of impending anarchy. After all, commerce prospered throughout most
of Jefferson's administration. Somehow the churches remained standing. No
blood baths took place. The Bank of the United States still operated. Peace
was maintained. Certainly, some Federalist judges were under attack, but the
judicial power passed through this ordeal to emerge unscathed and even
enhanced. Every economic indicator—urban growth, westward expansion,
agricultural production, the construction of canals, turnpikes and bridges—
continued to rise, undisturbed by the political bickering in Washington.

At first the Federalists were confident that they would regain power.
Alexander Hamilton's elaborate scheme for an organization to espouse Christianity and the Constitution, as the "principal engine" to restore Federalist
power, was rejected out of hand. He was told that "our adversaries will soon
demonstrate to the world the soundness of our doctrines and the imbecility
and folly of their own." But hope changed to despair as the people no longer
responded; no "vibration of opinion" took place as in the 1790's. Federalism
was the party of the past, an antiquated and dying philosophy. "I will fatten
my pigs, and prune my trees; nor will I any longer . . . trouble to govern this
country," wrote Fisher Ames: "You federalists are only lookers-on." Jefferson
swept the election of 1804, capturing every state except Connecticut and
Delaware from the Federalist candidate, Charles C. Pinckney, "Federalism
is dead," wrote Jefferson a few years later, "without even the hope of a day
of resurrection. The quondam leaders indeed retain their rancour and principles; but their followers are amalgamated with us in sentiment, if not in
name."

It is the fashion of some historians to explain the Federalist demise and
Republican ascendancy in terms of a great change in Jefferson. A radical

natural law philosopher when he fought as minority leader, he became a first-rate utilitarian politician as president. The Virginian became an American. Revolutionary theory was cast aside when Jefferson faced the prosaic problem of having to run the country. He began to adopt some of the techniques and policies of the Federalists. Indeed, it is often observed that Jefferson "outfederalized the Federalists."

There is much to be said for this view. After all, less than three months after he assumed the presidency, Jefferson dispatched a naval squadron to the Mediterranean on a warlike mission, without asking the permission of Congress. Two members of his Cabinet, Levi Lincoln and Albert Gallatin, thought the action unconstitutional, and so advised the President. Almost from the moment of its birth the young nation had paid tribute, as did every European power, rather than risk a war with the Barbary pirates. But Jefferson could not abide such bribery. No constitutional scruples could delay for a moment his determination to force the issue. Later, Congress declared war, and in four years Barbary power was shattered. The United States under Jefferson accomplished an object that England, France, Spain, Portugal, and Holland had desired for more than a century—unfettered commerce in the Mediterranean. Here, then, in this episode, is a totally different Jefferson—not an exponent of states' rights and strict interpretation of the Constitution, but an American nationalist of the first order.

Perhaps the most frequently cited example of Jefferson's chameleon quality, however, was on the question of whether the United States should or should not purchase the Louisiana Territory from France. On this question the fundamental issue was squarely before Jefferson, and a choice could not be avoided. The purchase would more than double the size of the United States. Yet the Constitution did not specifically provide for such acquisition of foreign territory. Further, the treaty provided that this area would eventually be formed into states, full partners in the Union. Again, the Constitution did not specifically cover such incorporation. A broad interpretation of Article IV, Section III, however, might permit United States' ratification of the treaty. Should theory be sacrificed and an empire gained? Or were the means as important as the ends?

Broad or loose construction of the Constitution was the key to the growth of Federal power. Federalists had argued in this vein to justify most of their legislation in the 1790's. To Jefferson, individual liberty and governmental power were on opposite ends of a see-saw, which the Federalists had thrown off balance. He believed that government, especially the central government, must be restricted within rather narrow and essential limits. Only by continually and rigidly applying strict construction to the Constitution could this tendency to overweening power be controlled and individual liberty be safeguarded. As early as 1777, Jefferson, then governor of Virginia, had warned that constitutions must be explicit, "so as to exclude all possible doubt; . . . [lest] at some future day . . . power[s] should be assumed."

On the other hand, the purchase of Louisiana would fulfill a dream and solve a host of problems. Jefferson envisioned an American empire covering "the whole northern, if not the southern continent, with a people speaking the same language, governed in similar forms, and by similar laws." The purchase would be a giant step in the direction of democracy's inevitable growth. "Is it not better," asked Jefferson, "that the opposite bank of the Mississippi should be settled by our own brethren and children, than by strangers of another family?"

Of more immediate interest, Westerners would be able to ship their goods down the Mississippi without fear that New Orleans might be closed. Indian attacks undoubtedly would taper off without the Spanish to instigate them. Uppermost in Jefferson's mind, however, was the freedom from England that the purchase would assure. He did not fear Spanish ownership. A feeble, second-rate nation like Spain on the frontier offered little threat to America's future security. The continued possession of Louisiana by an imperialistic France led by the formidable Napoleon, however, might force the United States into an alliance with England. At first Jefferson thought a constitutional amendment specifically permitting the purchase might solve the dilemma. But Napoleon showed signs of wavering. The treaty had to be confirmed immediately, with no indication of constitutional doubt. Jefferson asked the Republican leaders in the Senate to ratify it "with as little debate as possible, and particularly so far as respects the constitutional difficulty."

In still other ways Jefferson's presidency was marked by Federalist policies which encouraged the growth of central power. Internal improvements loomed large in Jefferson's mind. While many turnpikes and canals were financed by private and state capital, he realized that Federal support would be necessary, especially in the western part of the nation. With the use of Federal money obtained from the sale of public lands, and (later) aided by direct congressional appropriations, the groundwork for the famous Cumberland road was established during Jefferson's administration. He enthusiastically supported Gallatin's plan to spend twenty million dollars of Federal funds on a network of national roads and canals. Other more pressing problems intervened, however, and it was left to later administrations to finance these local and interstate programs. If Hamilton had pressed for internal improvements in the 1790's (he suggested them in the *Report on Manufactures*), Jefferson probably would have raised constitutional objections.

Finally, is not Jefferson's change of tack further reflected in the political history of that era? Over the span of a few years it seemed as if each party had somehow reversed directions. In 1798–99 Jefferson and Madison penned the Virginia and Kentucky Resolutions as an answer to the Federalists' infamous Alien and Sedition Acts. In 1808–9 more radical but comparable rumblings of dissatisfaction emanated from some New England Federalists over Jefferson's Embargo Act. For the embargo, says one of Jefferson's biographers, was "the most arbitrary, inquisitorial, and confiscatory measure formulated in American legislation up to the period of the Civil War." Further, both parties splintered during Jefferson's administration. Many moderate Federalists, like John Quincy Adams, found themselves in closer harmony with Administration policy than with Essex Junto beliefs. And Jefferson's actions alienated old comrades, like John Randolph, Jr., whose supporters were called the Tertium Quids. It is interesting to note that there is no historical consensus of why, when, how, or what precipitated the break between Randolph and Jefferson. Randolph is always referred to as brilliant but erratic; and whatever immediate reason is alleged, the cause somehow has to do with Randolph's personality and Jefferson's betrayal of the true doctrines.

It is part of Jefferson's greatness that he could inspire a myth and project an image. But one must not confuse myth and reality, shadow and substance. Thomas Jefferson as he was, and Thomas Jefferson as people perceived him, are quite different. While both concepts of course, are of equal value in understanding our past, it is always the historian's task to make the distinction. Too often, in Jefferson's case, this has not been done. Too often the biographers have described the myth—have taken at face value the popular view of Jefferson and his enemies, contained in the vitriolic newspaper articles and pamphlets, the passionate debates and fiery speeches of that period—and missed or misconstrued the reality.

This is understandable. Even the principals inevitably became involved and helped to propagate the exaggerated images of the 1790's and thus misunderstood one another's aims and motives. Jefferson, according to his grandson, never considered Federalist fulminations "as abusing him; they had never known him. They had created an imaginary being clothed with odious attributes, to whom they gave his name; and it was against that creature of their imaginations they had levelled their anathemas." John Adams, reminiscing in a letter to Jefferson, wrote: "Both parties have excited artificial terrors and if I were summoned as a witness to say upon oath, which party had excited . . . the most terror, and which had really felt the most, I could not give a more sincere answer, than in the vulgar style 'Put them in a bag and shake them, and then see which comes out first.' "

On March 4, 1801, following a decade of verbal violence, many Americans were surprised to hear that "We are all republicans—we are all federalists." Some historians act as if they, too, are surprised. These historians then describe Jefferson's administration as if some great change took place in his thinking, and conclude that he "outfederalized the Federalists." This is a specious view, predicated on an ultraradical Jefferson of the 1790's in constant debate with an ultraconservative Hamilton. Certainly Jefferson as president had to change. Certainly at times he had to modify, compromise, and amend his previous views. To conclude, however, that he outfederalized the Federalists is to miss the enormous consistency of Jefferson's beliefs and practices.

Jefferson was ever a national patriot second to none, not even to Hamilton. He always conceived of the United States as a unique experiment, destined for greatness so long as a sharp line isolated American civilization from European infection. Thus he strongly advised our youth to receive their education at home rather than in European schools, lest they absorb ideas and traits he considered "alarming to me as an American." From "Notes on Virginia" to his advice at the time of Monroe's doctrine, Jefferson thought of America first. It matters not that Hamilton was the better prophet; Jefferson was the better American. The French minister Adet once reported: "Although Jefferson is the friend of liberty . . . although he is an admirer of the efforts we have made to cast off our shackles . . . Jefferson, I say, is an American, and as such, he cannot sincerely be our friend. An American is the born enemy of all the peoples of Europe."

Jefferson's nature was always more practical than theoretical, more common-sensical than philosophical. Certainly the essence of his Declaration of Independence is a Lockean justification of revolution; but, said Jefferson, "It was . . . an expression of the American mind," meant "to place before mankind the common sense of the subject." Jefferson always preferred precision to "metaphysical subtleties." The Kentucky and Virginia Resolutions can be understood only as a specific rebuttal of the Sedition Act. "I can never fear that things will go far wrong," wrote Jefferson, "where common sense has fair play."

One must also remember that Hamilton's power lessened considerably in the last four years of Federalist rule. He had a strong coterie of admirers, but the vast body of Federalists sided with John Adams. Despite all Hamilton did to insure Adams' defeat, and despite the split in Federalist ranks, the fact that Jefferson's victory in 1801 was won by a narrow margin indicated Federalist approval of Adams' actions. Certainly the people at that time— Jefferson and Adams included—regarded 1801 as the year of revolution. But if historians must have a revolution, perhaps Adams' split with the Hamiltonians is a better date. "The mid-position which Adams desired to achieve," writes Manning Dauer, "was adopted, in the main, by Jefferson and his successors."

To be sure, the two men disagreed on many matters of basic importance. Jefferson placed his faith in the free election of a virtuous and talented natural aristocracy; Adams did not. Within the constitutional balance, Jefferson emphasized the power of the lower house; Adams would give greater weight to the executive and judiciary. Jefferson, as a general rule, favored a strict interpretation of the Constitution; Adams did not fear broad construction. Both believed that human beings enjoyed inalienable rights, but only Jefferson had faith in man's perfectability. Jefferson could say, "I like a little rebellion now and then. It is like a storm in the atmosphere"; Adams had grown more conservative since 1776. Jefferson always defended and befriended Thomas Paine; Adams found Edmund Burke's position on the French Revolution more palatable.

Yet, the sages of Quincy and Monticello were both moderate and practical men. Despite the obvious and basic contrasts, both Adams and Jefferson stood side by side on certain essentials: to avoid war, to quiet factionalism, to preserve republican government. Their warm friendship, renewed from 1812 to 1826 in a remarkable and masterful correspondence, was based on frankness, honesty, and respect. "About facts," Jefferson wrote, "you and I cannot differ, because truth is our mutual guide; And if any opinions you may express should be different from mine, I shall receive them with the liberality and indulgence which I ask for my own." Jefferson and Adams represent, respectively, the quintessence of the very best in American liberalism and conservatism. Their indestructible link, then, was "a keen sense of national consciousness," a realization that America's destiny was unique. This is the meaning of Jefferson's words: "We are all republicans—we are all federalists."

Lance Banning

The Revolution of 1800 and the Principles of Ninety-Eight

I

Thomas Jefferson wrote proudly of "the revolution of 1800," calling it "as real a revolution in the principles of our government as that of 1776 was in its form." Many of his followers agreed. Today, however, most historians would probably prefer a different phrase. Too little changed—and that too slowly— to justify the connotations present in that loaded word. There were no radicals among the great triumvirate who guided the Republicans in power, as they had led them through the years of opposition. The President was bent on reconciliation with the body of his former foes. "We are all Republicans, all Federalists," he said. He wanted to detach the mass of Federalists from their former leaders, and he knew that this was incompatible with an abrupt reversal of the policies that had been followed for a dozen years. He had, in any case, no notion that his predecessors' work could be dismantled all at once. The Hamiltonian system might be hateful, but it had bound the nation to a contract it had no alternative except to honor. Madison and Gallatin, who were by instinct more conservative than Jefferson himself, were not disposed to disagree.

From the beginning of the new administration, nonetheless, Republicans insisted that a change of policies, not just of men, was necessary to return the state to its republican foundations. In his inaugural address, Jefferson announced commitment to "a wise and frugal government which shall restrain men from injuring one another, shall leave them otherwise free to regulate their own pursuits of industry and improvement, and shall not take from the

Reprinted from Lance Banning, The Jeffersonian Persuasion. Copyright © 1978 by Cornell University. Used by permission of the publisher, Cornell University Press.

mouth of labor the bread it has earned." This kind of government, he hinted, would be guided by a set of principles that could be readily distinguished from the policies of years before. Among them were

> *Peace, commerce, and honest friendship with all nations; entangling alliances with none.*
> *The support of the state governments in all their rights as the most competent administrations for our domestic concerns and the surest bulwarks against anti-republican tendencies. . . .*
> *A well disciplined militia, our best reliance in peace and for the first moments of war, till regulars may relieve them. . . .*
> *Economy in public expense, that labor may be lightly burdened*
> *The honest payment of our debts and sacred preservation of the public faith.*

Reform began while Jefferson awaited the assembly of the first Republican Congress. Pardons were issued to the few men still affected by sedition prosecutions. The diplomatic corps, a target for its costs and for the influence it was thought to give to the executive, was cut to barest bones. A few of the most active Federalists were purged from office, while the President withheld commissions signed by Adams after his defeat was known. The evolution of a partisan appointments policy was too slow for some members of the party, who argued that "no enemy to democratic government will be provided with the means to sap and destroy any of its principles nor to profit by a government to which they are hostile in theory and practice." But even the most radical were satisfied with the administration's purpose when the President announced his program to the Seventh Congress.

Jefferson's first annual message was "an epitome of republican principles applied to practical purposes." After a review of foreign policy and Indian affairs, the President suggested abolition of all internal taxes. "The remaining sources of revenue will be sufficient," he believed, "to provide for the support of government, to pay the interest on the public debts, and to discharge the principals in shorter periods than the laws or the general expectations had contemplated. . . . Sound principles will not justify our taxing the industry of our fellow citizens to accumulate treasure for wars to happen we know not when, and which might not perhaps happen but from the temptations offered by that treasure." Burdens, he admitted, could only be reduced if expenditures fell too. But there was room to wonder "whether offices or officers have not been multiplied unnecessarily." The military, for example, was larger than required to garrison the posts, and there was no use for the surplus. "For defence against invasion, their number is as nothing; nor is it conceived needful or safe that a standing army should be kept up in time of peace." The judiciary system, packed and altered by the Federalists at the close of their regime, would naturally "present itself to the contemplation of Congress." And the laws concerning naturalization might again be liberalized.

The Seventh Congress, voting usually on party lines, did everything that Jefferson had recommended. It also gave approval to a plan prepared by Gallatin, the Secretary of the Treasury, for the complete retirement of the public debt before the end of 1817. Along with its repeal of the Judiciary Act of 1800, it reduced the army to three thousand officers and men, while lowering appropriations for the navy in the face of war with Tripoli. Of all its measures, though, the abolition of internal taxes (and four hundred revenue positions) called forth the most eloquent enunciation of the principles on which the new majority thought it should act:

The Constitution is as dear to us as to our adversaries. . . . It is by repairing the breeches that we mean to save it and to set it on a firm and lasting foundation. . . . We are yet a young nation and must learn wisdom from the experience of others. By avoiding the course which other nations have steered, we shall likewise avoid their catastrophe. Public debts, standing armies, and heavy taxes have converted the English nation into a mere machine to be used at the pleasure of the crown. . . . We have had no riot act, but we have had a Sedition Act calculated to secure the executive from free and full investigation; we have had an army and still have a small one, securing to the executive an immensity of patronage; and we have a large national debt, for the payment . . . of which it is necessary to collect "yearly millions" by means of a cloud of officers spread over the face of the country. . . . Iniquitous as we deem the manner of its settlement, we mean to discharge; but we mean not to perpetuate it; it is no part of our political creed that "a public debt is a public blessing."

Before the session ended, Jefferson could tell a friend that "some things may perhaps be left undone from motives of compromise for a time and not to alarm by too sudden a reformation," but the proceedings of the Congress gave every ground for hope that "we shall be able by degrees to introduce sound principles and make them habitual." Indeed, the session was so good a start that there was little left to recommend in 1802. The effort of the next few years would be to keep the course already set.

"Revolution" may not be the proper word to characterize the changes introduced in 1801 and early 1802. "Apostasy," however, would be worse. Yet every study of the Jeffersonian ascendency must come to terms with the magnificent and multivolumed work of Henry Adams. Though now almost a century old, the scope and literary power of this classic give it influence that has lasted to the present day. And one of Adams' major themes was the abnegation of the principles of 1798 by the Republican regime. Jefferson had hoped to put an end to parties by detaching the great body of Federalists from their irreconcilable leaders. By 1804 he seemed to have approached this end. To Adams, though, his great successes were a consequence of Jefferson's abandonment of principle and single-minded quest for popularity. If party lines were melting, it had been the Jeffersonians who had compromised their principles the most:

not a Federalist measure, not even the Alien and Sedition laws, had been expressly repudiated; . . . the national debt was larger than it had ever been before, the navy maintained and energetically employed, the national bank preserved and its operations extended; . . . the powers of the national government had been increased [in the Louisiana Purchase] to a point that made blank paper of the Constitution.

It was the Federalists, not the Republicans, who now upheld the states' rights principles of 1798.

Every part of Adams' powerful indictment could be contradicted or excused. Thus, Jefferson abandoned scruple in the case of the Louisiana Purchase with reluctance and because there seemed some danger that the Emperor of France might change his mind about a bargain that could guarantee the nation's peace while promising indefinite postponement of the day when overcrowding and development might put an end to its capacity for freedom. Jefferson continued to distrust the national bank, but would not break the public's pledge by moving to revoke its charter. The party had repudiated the Sedition Law, explicitly refusing to renew it in the session that had also seen a relaxation of the naturalization law. The national debt had been considerably reduced before the purchase of Louisiana raised it once again, and it would fall much further in the years to come.

It is necessary to admit, however, that the list of Adams' charges also could be lengthened. While Jefferson himself was never reconciled, Gallatin and Madison eventually supported the Bank of the United States. While Jefferson preferred to lead by indirection, he was in fact a stronger President than either of his predecessors ever tried to be. His public messages suggested measures, but his hints were often taken as commands by party members in the Congress. Informally or through floor leaders in the House, the administration made its wishes known and drafted most of the important legislation. Finally, in 1808, in its progressively more stringent efforts to enforce the embargo, Jefferson's administration wielded powers over the daily life of Americans that far exceeded anything its predecessors ever sought, even using regulars to help enforce the law.

There were, without a doubt, occasions after 1801 when the warring parties came so close to switching sides that one might doubt that principle meant much to either group. The Federalists stood forth, when they could hope to profit, as defenders of states' rights. They shamelessly employed old opposition rhetoric to criticize the massive force of party loyalty and the influence of the President on Congress. Nor was Henry Adams first to charge the Jeffersonians with a surrender to the principles of their opponents. Jefferson and his successor faced a swelling discontent from a minority of purists among Republicans themselves.

In October, 1801, before the meeting of the Seventh Congress, Edmund Pendleton had published a widely read consideration of the policies that would be necessary to make the revolution of 1800 complete. Jefferson's election, he began, had "arrested a train of measures which were gradually conducting us towards ruin." But the election victory did not permit Republicans to rest content. It merely opened up an opportunity "to erect new barriers against folly, fraud, and ambition and to explain such parts of the Constitution as have been already or may be interpreted contrary to the intention of those who adopted it." Liberty, said Pendleton, is the "chief good" of government, but "if government is so constructed as to enable its administration to assail that liberty with the several weapons heretofore most fatal to it, the structure is defective: of this sort, standing armies—fleets—severe penal laws—war—and a multitude of civil officers are universally admitted to be." Union is a great good, but union can "only be preserved by confining . . . the federal government to the exercise of powers clearly required by the general interest . . . because the states exhibit such varieties of character and interests that a consolidated general government would . . . produce civil war and dissension." A separation of powers is necessary, but the Constitution gives the Senate a part in the exercise of powers that belong to other branches "and tends to create in that body a dangerous aristocracy." Representative government must rest on the will of the people, but the people's will can "never be expressed if their representatives are corrupted or influenced by hopes of office." "Since experience has evinced that much mischief may be done under an unwise administration," it is time to consider several amendments to the Constitution. These should make the President ineligible for a second term and give the appointment of judges and ambassadors to Congress; end the Senate's role in executive functions and shorten the Senators' terms of office; make judges and legislators incapable of accepting any federal office; subject the judges to removal by the legislature; form "some check upon the abuse of public credit"; declare that treaties relating to war or peace or requiring the expenditure of money must be ratified by the whole Congress; and define the powers of the federal government in such a way as to "defy the wiles of construction."

"The Danger Not Over" was a systematic effort to define the fundamental changes that seemed to be implicit in the principles of 1798. And as the years went by without a movement to secure the constitutional amendments it had recommended, without destruction of the national bank, without complete proscription of old Federalists from places of public trust, "there were a number of people who soon thought and said to one another that Mr. Jefferson did many good things, but neglected some better things," who came to "view his policy as very like a compromise with Mr. Hamilton's, . . . a compromise between monarchy and democracy." Strongest in Virginia and including several of the most important party writers of the 1790s—George Logan and John Taylor as well as Pendleton himself—this band of "Old Republicans" soon found an eloquent, if vitriolic and eccentric, spokesman in the Congress. In 1806, John Randolph, who had led the party's forces in the Seventh Congress, broke with the administration and commenced a systematic opposition to the moral bankruptcy and "backstairs influence" of the government. As Jefferson and Madison began to face the gravest crisis of their leadership, they were persistently annoyed by a minority of vocal critics from within their former ranks. In 1808, Monroe became the unsuccessful candidate for those expressing this variety of discontent.

*   *   *

Both [Henry] Adams and the Old Republicans identified the principles of '98 with the Virginia and Kentucky Resolutions of that year. To both, the party's creed in years of opposition centered on allegiance to states' rights. But I have tried to show that such an understanding is too narrow. Even in the crisis introduced by the repressive laws, states' rights and strict construction of the Constitution were among the means to more essential ends. The means were taken seriously, indeed, but they were never held among the absolutes. The body of the party and its most important leaders never sought, as their essential end, to hold the federal government within the narrowest of bounds. They sought, instead, a federal government that would preserve the virtues necessary to a special way of life. Their most important goal had been to check a set of policies—among them loose interpretation of the Constitution—that Republicans had seen as fundamentally destructive of the kind of government and social habits without which liberty could not survive. To judge them only on the basis of their loyalty to strict construction and states' rights is to apply a standard they had never held.

Minds changed when party leaders were confronted with responsibility. But they did not change thoroughly enough to justify the charge that they adopted principles of their opponents. The principles of the Republicans had not been Antifederalist. Republicans had traced the evils of the 1790s to the motives of the governors, not to the government itself. With few and brief exceptions, most had thought a change of policy, without a change of structure, would effect a cure. Moreover, in the last years of the decade, the development of party thought had probably persuaded many members to believe that a simple change of men might cure more evils than they once had thought.

The Republican persuasion rose, in the beginning, under circumstances that conjoined to make a reconstruction of an ideology developed in a different time and place seem relevant for the United States. The revolutionary debt to eighteenth-century opposition thought was certainly sufficient, by itself, to have assured loud echoes of the old ideas in the first years of the new republic. But this is not the lesson of this work. Republican convictions were not simply reminiscent of the old ideas. Republicans revived the eighteenth-century ideology as a coherent structure, reconstructed it so thoroughly that the persistence of an English style of argument is easily as striking as the changes we might trace to revolutionary alterations of the American polity. At least three circumstances of the 1790s had to join with expectations prompted by the heritage of revolutionary thought to generate a reconstruction so complete. None of these circumstances persisted to the decade's end. First, popular respect for Washington and ambiguity about the nature of the new executive directed discontent at the first minister. Second, Hamiltonian finance was modeled on an English prototype. And finally, an opposition first appeared in the House of Representatives.

The Republican persuasion, in its early years, attempted to alert the nation to a ministerial conspiracy that was operating through corruption to secure the revival of a British kind of constitution. Ministerial influence would subvert the independence of the Congress, which would acquiesce in constitutional constructions leading to consolidation of the states and thence to monarchy. Meanwhile, a decay of public virtue, spread by the example of the lackeys of administration and encouraged by the shift of wealth resulting from the funding plan, would ease the way for a transition to hereditary forms. With relatively minor changes, this was just the accusation that the eighteenth-century English opposition had traditionally directed at governments in power, and, like its prototype, it was, in the beginning, the weapon of a legislative group that had to reconcile its status as minority with its commitment to majority control. Legislative blocs were fluid, and the minority could understand its own position and appeal for popular support with the assistance of traditional assumptions that the influence of the Treasury, when added to an honest difference of opinion, was sufficient to account for policies with which they disagreed.

Images of conspiracy and accusations of corruption continued to provide the starting point for Republican analyses of Federalist policies, but it was not so many years before events and circumstances pushed Republican opinion away from its original foundations. First, circumstances undermined a logical necessity of neo-opposition arguments by making the Republicans a majority in the House. Then, Hamilton resigned. Concurrently, however, Jay's Treaty and the foreign war became the major issues for dispute. In other words, just when the opposition might have savored the retirement of the archconspirator, just when their logic was endangered by their own success, events conjoined to redirect attention to the powers of the Senate and the actions of the President himself. British influence and affection for the cause of monarchy displaced attachment to the funding system as the leading explanation for administration policies. But the Republicans could see that the financial structure was dependent on the British trade, and thus the Federalists' foreign policy appeared to be a new means to old ends. In this way, the Republicans continued their conspiratorial analysis into the Adams years.

Only in the last years of the decade can we see a clearer movement of Republican concerns away from the inherited foundations of their thought and toward a style of argument that seems more native. The alteration might be traced to 1794, when the Republicans began to count on a majority of Representatives. From that point forward, we have seen, party writers focused somewhat less on the corruption of the lower house and somewhat more on dangers posed by enemies of the Republic in the several branches of the government and in the country as a whole. During the first years under Adams, critics concentrated their denunciations less on the "funding and banking gentry" or the

Hamiltonian "phalanx" than on the "anglo-federal," "anglo-monarchical," or simply "tory" party. The crisis of 1798—the popular hysteria, the Quasi-War, and the Sedition Law—strengthened this trend. Such a crisis in a polity that rested on a large electorate made the administration's influence on the legislature seem less important than the efforts of a ruling party to mislead the people and destroy effective checks on Federalist abuses. Finally, the split among the Federalists confirmed the inclination to direct attacks, not at the link between the government and its dependents in the Congress—the characteristic target of the British critics of administration—but at a party that depended on its influence with the voters. During the last two years of the decade, Republican newspapers gave less space to criticism of the Congress or administration than they did to mockery of their Federalist competitors or efforts to assassinate the reputations of the leaders of the other party. The scurrility of party sheets reflected their recognition that the enemy, in the United States, was not a governmental faction of the British type, but a party with its base among the people.

When Jefferson assumed the presidential office, he and the body of his party were prepared to believe that they had wakened a majority of voters and thereby put an end to the most immediate danger to the American Republic. Removal of the enemy from power and from public trust had come to seem sufficient, by itself, to safeguard liberty while friends of freedom worked toward gradual replacement of the Hamiltonian system with one better suited to republican ways. With the conspirators deposed, the country could afford to ease toward change—and change would come more certainly that way. Still, change it must—change as rapidly as possible according to a very different vision of the good society. Republicans were still persuaded that the debt must be retired as rapidly as preexisting contracts would permit, without internal taxes. It should not be clung to for its broader economic uses. It would not be used as an excuse to push the federal government into revenue resources better left to separate states. Even here, fanaticism was eschewed by a majority. Jefferson's administration did not hesitate to borrow more for the Louisiana Purchase. But the Republicans were willing to subordinate almost all else to the reduction of the debt. Every year the debt existed meant, to them, another year that taxes would inflate the rich, another year of the increasing gap between the rich and poor, which was potentially destructive to free states. By 1812, Republican administrations had reduced the debt from $83 million, where it had climbed under the Federalists, to $27.5 million. They would have retired it completely in a few more years if war had not gotten in the way.

Reform did not go far enough to satisfy the Old Republicans. Change was incomplete enough—and leaders compromised enough—to make it possible for Henry Adams to support his accusation that the Jeffersonians surrendered to the principles of their opponents. Yet even Adams tried to have it several ways. Sometimes he condemned the Jeffersonians for lack of principle. Sometimes he accused them of a change of mind. At other times, however, he switched ground to level his attacks on their adherence to a set of principles that were ill-suited to the country's needs. The effort to retire the debt, he pointed out, committed the first $7.3 million of yearly revenues to payment of principal and interest. The remainder was too small to run the government and meet the costs of national defense. "The army was not large enough to hold the Indians in awe; the navy was not strong enough to watch the coasts. . . . The country was at the mercy of any Power which might choose to rob it." "Gallatin's economies turned on the question whether the national debt or the risk of foreign aggression were most dangerous to America." The Republicans assumed the former.

If we would choose among the different condemnations Adams made of the Republican regime, it would be better to prefer the last. Adherence to the principles of ninety-eight—a strikingly consistent effort to adopt and maintain policies implicit in the ideology of opposition days—is a better explanation for Republican actions during their years in power than any emphasis upon hypocrisy or change. The Old Republicans were worrisome beyond their numbers for no other reason than that they appealed to principles that still had the allegiance of large portions of the party. And, as Adams saw it, it was the party's loyalty to old ideas that brought the country to the edge of ruin in 1812.

II

The first years of the new republic were a time of unexampled prosperity and growth. The most important reason was the European war, which continued with few interruptions from 1790 to 1815. With France and Britain both preoccupied with warfare, a portion of the trade that they would normally have carried fell by default to neutrals. As the greatest trading neutral of the age, America had much to gain. It also risked involvement in the war, since both the European powers periodically attempted to deny the other neutral help.

During the 1790s, America's attempt to carry on a thriving commerce had nearly brought a war with Britain. The effort in fact resulted in a limited conflict with France. Thomas Jefferson came to the Presidency near the beginning of a brief respite in the European struggle, and the interlude of peace gave the Republicans a chance to apply their principles of governmental economy. In 1803, however, France and Britain resumed their titanic war. With Napoleon in power, Republicans had long since dropped their admiration of the French. But the commercial problems of the 1790s now returned with doubled force. After 1805, when Admiral Lord Nelson destroyed most of the French fleet in the Battle of Trafalgar, Britain was unchallengeable at sea, while Bonaparte was temporarily supreme on land. Both powers turned to economic warfare, catching the United States between.

For America the situation reached its worst in 1807. In that year Napoleon's Milan Decree completed a "continental system" under which the Emperor threatened to seize any neutral ship that had submitted to a British search or paid a duty in a British port. Britain replied with Orders-in-Council that promised to seize any neutral trading with the continent *unless* that ship had paid a British fee. The combined effect of French and British measures was to threaten any vessel engaged in the continental trade. To make the situation worse, in the summer of 1807, near the mouth of Chesapeake Bay, the British frigate "Leopard" fired upon the American warship "Chesapeake," forced it to submit to search, and impressed four sailors into British service. By any standard, "Leopard's" action was a cause for war.

War might have been an easy choice. There was a storm of patriotic outrage possibly a match for that following the revelation of the XYZ Affair ten years before. Particularly in the Old Northwest, where British officials in Canada soon began to give assistance and encouragement to Tecumseh and his efforts to unite the western tribes against the progress of new settlement, demands for war rose steadily from that point on. But the Republicans did not want war. They were determined to face the present troubles in the way that they believed the Federalists should have responded to similar problems in the 1790s.

Since the beginning of the party quarrel, Republicans had consistently expressed a fear of war and a profound distrust of normal preparations for defense. They were afraid of war's effects on civil liberties. They clung to the traditional distrust of standing armies. They had consistently opposed the frightful cost of navies. Their ideology identified high taxes, large armed forces, and the increase in executive authority that seemed inseparable from war as mortal dangers to republican society and government. Even preparations for hostilities would require abandonment of all the most important policies that they had followed since the triumph seven years before: low taxes, small armed forces, little governmental guidance of the nation's life, and quick retirement of the public debt.

In any case, Republicans had always argued that America possessed a weapon that provided an alternative to war, a weapon that had proven its effectiveness during the long struggle preceding independence. This weapon was its trade. Since opposition days, the party's leaders had maintained that the things America exported—mostly food and other raw materials—were necessities of life. The things America imported, on the other hand, were mostly manufactured goods and other "luxuries." In case of trouble, then, America could refuse to trade. Healthier than Europe, because it was not bound to large-scale manufacturing, America would win a test of wills, creating potent discontent and dislocation in the feebler state. Trade restrictions could secure the national interest as effectively as war and without the dangers to free government and social health that war would necessarily incur. Trade was the weapon that the Madisonians had wanted to employ against the British back in 1794. It was the weapon that Republicans preferred when difficulties once again arose. Indeed, the party held to economic warfare, to its antiwar and antipreparation ideology, so long and so stubbornly that the result was nearly a disaster for the United States.

In December, 1807, Jefferson's administration responded to the French and British decrees by placing an embargo on American trade. The embargo had a measurable effect in France and Britain. Unfortunately the economic consequences for America were even worse. Under the embargo, all American sailings overseas were halted for more than a year. The country suffered a severe depression. In New England and upstate New York, noncooperation and illegal sailings rose to such proportions that the government resorted to repressive measures so severe as to endanger the Republicans' reputation as friends of limited government and guardians of civil rights. To keep the peace within the country and to safeguard their majority, the Republicans relaxed their application of the economic weapon. As Madison succeeded Jefferson, Congress started a long search for ways to hurt the Europeans more than the United States. On the surface, this looked very like a gradual retreat. Inconsistent enforcement of changing regulations meant that pressure was repeatedly relaxed just as it began to have effect, and the Republicans' persistence simply led the warring powers to conclude that America would never fight. In 1809 the embargo was replaced with a measure confining nonintercourse to trade between America and French or British ports. In 1810 restrictions were removed completely, although it was provided that nonintercourse would be resumed against one country or the other if either of the powers would agree to end its violations of neutral rights.

Since the ending of American restrictions would benefit Great Britain, Napoleon made moves that it was possible to interpret as an exemption of American shipping from the Berlin and Milan Decrees. Madison announced that nonintercourse would be imposed against the British unless the Orders-in-Council were repealed. When they were not, restrictions were resumed.

The situation quickly passed the bounds of the absurd. By the winter of 1811–1812, four years of various experiments with commercial coercion had failed to force a change in European policies. During all that time the frontier trouble had continued, and Great Britain had persisted in its arrogant, humiliating practice of impressment. Meanwhile the Republicans had lost New England and were threatened in the middle states by the revival of a party that they still considered dangerous to the survival of a democratic way. With the people growing restless under policies that damaged their prosperity without securing change, it was increasingly apparent to most members of the party that commercial weapons would not work. The choice must be between submission to the British policies and war. Neither the people's sense of national honor nor the survival of the Republican Party—a party that believed that liberty would not be safe with its opponents—would permit submission. Madison reluctantly resigned himself to war, and younger representatives from the West and South—"war hawks" to their enemies—worked a declaration through the Congress. There were defections by Clintonians and Quids, but it was basically a party vote.

III

To anyone inclined to balance gain with loss, the War of 1812 must seem a masterpiece of folly. The god who ruled its fortunes was decidedly perverse.

Two days before the Senate completed a declaration of war, though not in time for news to cross the sea, the British government announced that the Orders-in-Council would be repealed. The battle at New Orleans was planned by generals who had not learned that peace had been agreed upon at Ghent on December 24, 1814, two weeks before. The slaughter on the Mississippi—nineteen months of warfare—ultimately went for naught. The Treaty of Ghent simply restored the situation that had existed before the war. Boundaries were unaltered. Disputes over neutral rights and impressment were left unresolved.

Contemporaries, however, were not disposed to make a practical calculation of this sort. After all, the war had not been fought for rational reasons alone. National honor, the reputation of republican government, and the continuing supremacy of the Republican party had seemed to be at stake.

National honor had been satisfied. Jackson's stunning victory at New Orleans more than redeemed earlier reverses in the field. And news of his triumph arrived in the East just before the news of peace. Americans celebrated the end of the struggle with a brilliant burst of national pride. They felt that they had fought a second war for independence, and had won. If little had been gained, nothing had been lost in a contest with the greatest imperial power on the earth.

Independence, of course, had never been literally at risk. For Britain the War of 1812 was an unwelcome outcome of a quarrel that had seemed a lesser evil than a relaxation of the struggle against Napoleon. Once Bonaparte was vanquished, little could be gained by further prosecution of the lesser war. British statesmen had no will whatever for the effort that would have been required to defeat, much less to subjugate, the United States. They preferred a quick renewal of the valuable American trade.

Nevertheless, a new American independence did follow the Treaty of Ghent. The American Revolution was, at least in one respect, an effort to break connections with a corrupt Old World. But withdrawal from European involvements had been far from complete. Americans could not be indifferent when the republican revolution promised to convert Europe in the years after 1789, and the new American republic had continued an oceanic trade that inevitably weighed in the power calculations of European states. Independence from European involvements could not be more complete until the new nation had proven its ability to survive the great wars of the French Revolution. The magnetic attraction of European developments would not be weakened until the United States stood once again as the preeminent republic in the world, its belief in European corruption once again confirmed.

* * *

In the first years of the new federal government, Alexander Hamilton had grounded his great plans on the assumption that the world was not the kind of place where republican purists could pursue their schemes in peace. Republicans had insisted that there was an alternative to the Secretary's system, one which could secure national respectability without the unacceptable risks to revolutionary accomplishments that Hamilton's seemed to entail. In the years after 1800, they had gradually dismantled much of the foundation on which the Federalists had meant to build an America that could compete with empires such as England's on English terms. They had substituted a different vision, in which a society of independent men of virtue would appear in arms when necessary to defend America's shores, but trust their influence on the course of history, more generally, to the moral force of republican example and the necessary demand for the raw materials they would produce for trade. Jefferson and Madison had also tried a different course in foreign policy. Under the pressure of Napoleonic wars, the Republican alternative had failed.

Hamilton had been right, at least in significant part. America did not have the capacity to force the great states of Europe to accept the kind of international order within which the new nation could pursue the Republican ideal, a society in which the virtue of independent farmers and craftsmen would not be threatened by great cities, large-scale industry, professional armed forces, and a polity committed to the mysteries and dangers of English-style finance. The choice did seem to lie between greater self-sufficiency and national humiliation or war. Now, implicitly, a Republican President admitted this truth.

It was not an unconditional surrender to Hamilton's ideas. Madison could hope that vast expanses of western land and the continued leadership of genuine republicans would postpone to an indefinite future the debilitating corruption that Republicans had always feared. He still had no desire to see the land become a democratic England. Yet he did suggest that old Jeffersonian principles might be tempered with a program that would resurrect an essential portion of the Hamiltonian state. In doing so, he legitimized the other side of a debate that had held the nation's attention since 1789. He hinted that America could build on an amalgam of Republican and Federalist ideas, and the majority of his party agreed. . . .

The ancient argument did not abruptly stop. . . . As the "American System" of Henry Clay, the Hamiltonian vision of a self-sufficient republic, where industrial development would provide a domestic market for agricultural goods and federal programs would tie diverse sections into an imperial whole, remained a central topic for political division and dispute. Jacksonians attacked "aristocracy" and "corruption." Whigs condemned "King Andrew." John C. Calhoun was intensely concerned with something strongly reminiscent of corrupting influence. The new Republicans who followed Lincoln celebrated virtue and the independent man. As a consequence of revolutionary hopes and thought, proponents of American grandeur have always had to answer those who worry about a loss of innocence at home. In the years around 1815, however, the context of these controversies underwent a fundamental change. Experiments with economic coercion, followed by the War of 1812, had exposed an undeniable weakness in the principles on which the Republican party had based its rule. But the war had also made it easier to contemplate a change of course. Events destroyed one of the two great parties to the long dispute over the shaping of a society and government that could make republicanism lasting and complete. Doing this, they freed the other party to turn its attention to the needs of the future. Leadership passed increasingly to younger men, whose lives had not been molded by the great Revolution that had shaped the experience of the generation before. Arguments among the younger men would still be fierce, but the edges of hysteria grew blunt. For it was now the most appropriate means of national development that seemed to be at stake, not the very meaning of America itself.

Richard Hofstadter

The Transit of Power

I

Jefferson's ideas about parties were the conventional notions of his age. . . .
No less than most of his contemporaries he was enthralled by the conviction
that the sound citizen who has the public interest at heart is normally above
and outside parties and the vices of partisanship. . . .

As the party battle began to take shape in the 1790's, Jefferson, though
himself busy stimulating party animosities, looked upon them with some misgivings. In a letter of 1792, urging Washington to accept a second term, he
argued that the President in so doing could prevent "violence or secession,"
which he feared might be the consequence of some of Hamilton's measures.
In the same letter he also stated a notion which was to become all but ob-
sessional in his correspondence for more than a quarter of a century, a notion
which indeed colored much Republican thinking about the party battle:
that the real aim of the leading Federalists was to restore monarchy on the
British model, and that therefore the basic issue between the parties was
monarchical versus republican principles.

Two conclusions, both fatal to the acceptance of a continuing party
system, seemed to follow from this idea. The first was that the Federalists,
since they harbored a goal that ran counter to the convictions of the vast
majority and flouted the explicitly republican covenant of the Constitution,
were simply not a legitimate party at all. And Jefferson's conviction of their
un-Americanism would only have been confirmed if he had known all the
details of Hamilton's uninhibited and near-treasonous intrigues with James
Beckwith and George Hammond. The second, which sustained Jefferson's
patient confidence in his party's ultimate victory, was that since the hard-core

From Richard Hofstadter, The Idea of a Party System (Berkeley, 1972), pp. 122–25,
127–41, 149–55, 161–62, 165–69. Copyright © 1969 by The Regents of the University
of California; reprinted by permission of the University of California Press.

Federalists were monarchists and the American public was doughtily republican in its sentiments, the final triumph of his own principles, given a fair chance to assert them, was secure.

If one imagined that no less fundamental a principle than monarchy versus republicanism was at stake, one could of course waive all scruples about a strong partisan allegiance. And the justice of this course would be trebly confirmed if the opposition party, by an unmistakable squint toward England, underlined its essential foreignness. By the time of the Jay Treaty, when party lines had hardened, Jefferson had no further use for equivocal men like his fellow Virginian, Edmund Randolph, whose political conduct, he thought, had not set him on a lofty perch above parties but rather in the ignominious position of a trimmer. "Were parties here divided by a greediness for office, as in England," Jefferson explained, "to take a part with either would be unworthy of a reasonable or moral man, but where the principle of difference is as substantial and as strongly pronounced as between the republicans and Monocrats of our country, I hold it as honorable to take a firm and decided part, and as immoral to pursue a middle line, as between the parties of Honest men and Rogues, into which every country is divided." By early 1796, he was referring to the Federalists as "a faction" which "has entered in a conspiracy with the enemies of their country to chain down the legislature at the feet of both." As a conspiratorial, monarchical faction, the Federalists would have no moral claim to survival, and one can only concur with Noble Cunningham's conclusion in his careful study of Republican party history that Jefferson "never recognized the validity of the Federalist party either while Adams was in office or as an opposition party during his own administration." In the intensity of his partisan conviction, Jefferson the secularist lapsed into the language of dogma and ecclesiasticism when he spoke of the views of his foes: his letters bristle with heated digs at "apostacy," "sects," "political heresies," "conversions," "bigots," "votaries," and with invocations of "the truth faith.". . .

Such, then, was Jefferson's view of the Federalists: a small faction creeping into the heart of the government under the mantle of Washington and the perverse guidance of Hamilton, addicted to false principles in politics, animated by a foreign loyalty, and given to conspiratorial schemes aiming at the consolidation of government and the return of monarchy. It was a faction which, though enjoying certain temporary advantages, would ultimately lack the power to impose its will on the great mass of loyal republicans. Here Jefferson's optimism, as always, sustained him: before long the people through their faithful representatives would take over. And at that point it would be the duty of the Republican party to annihilate the opposition—not by harsh and repressive measures like the Sedition Act, but by the more gentle means of conciliation and absorption that were available to a principled majority party. Here necessity came to fortify temperament, for the circumstances of Jefferson's election were such as to require a measure of conciliation and appeasement at the very beginning.

II

The election of 1800 was an anomalous election in a double sense: first, in that it was the first election in modern history which, by popular decision, resulted in the quiet and peaceful transition of national power from the hands of one of two embattled parties to another; second, in that it was the first of only two American elections in which, since no candidate had a majority in the Electoral College, the outcome had to be decided in the House of Representatives. The superficial circumstances of the election are quite familiar: the Constitution, written without party tickets in mind, arranged for no separate designation of presidential and vice-presidential candidates before the adoption of the Twelfth Amendment in 1804; in consequence of a lapse in party planning, the two Republican candidates, Jefferson and Burr, turned up with the same number of electoral votes, though it was clearly understood throughout the party that the Virginian was head of the ticket; when the election went to the House, where the states voted as units, the Federalists fell heir to the unhappy luxury of choosing between the two leading Republicans. The resolution of the problem is also a familiar story: how the great majority of the Federalist leaders preferred Burr; how Hamilton repeatedly pleaded that they turn from this dangerous adventurer to the more certain and predictable, as well as endurable, limitations of Jefferson; and how, in the end, under the leadership of James A. Bayard of Delaware, who swallowed Jefferson, as he wrote Adams, "so . . . as not to hazard the Constitution," the necessary portion of them abstained from voting and thus accepted Jefferson, only after an understanding, very delicate and proper and quite indirect, about the character of Jefferson's intentions had been arrived at.

Historians have spent so much effort to unravel the details of this complex election, and in particular to evaluate Burr's role and the character of the tenuous understanding or "bargain" upon which Jefferson's election depended, that some aspects of the situation which we may regard as equally significant have not yet had their due. Since the badly needed definitive account of this election remains to be written, it is necessary to proceed with caution, but it is certainly possible to examine in this event the calculations by which the two-party system in the United States took a long and decisive step forward. Here were the Federalists, many of whom, not so many months earlier, had been hoping to finish off the opposition under the pressure of a war with France and through the agency of the Alien and Sedition Acts, now quietly acquiescing in the decision of a few of their fellow partisans to put into office a man whom they had long been portraying as an atheist, a French fanatic, a libertine, a visionary; and a political incompetent. The circumstances give us a rare opportunity to look at the minds of a set of governmental leaders as they faced the loss of power, and at the interplay between the two sides as they groped for an accommodation.

Abstractly speaking, the choices opened to a defeated governmental party in a new federally organized country where the practice of legitimate opposition is still not wholly certain and where the incoming foes are profoundly suspect are three: *coup d'état*, disunion, or a resigned acceptance of their new oppositional status. Here we may begin by pointing to the central significance of something that did not happen: *violent resistance was never, at any time, discussed.* Neither was disunion discussed as a serious immediate possibility in 1801, though three years later a small but ineffectual faction of New England Federalists would lay abortive plans to bring it about. Something in the character of the American system was at work to unleash violent language but to inhibit violent solutions, and to reconcile the Federalists to the control of the government by a party they suspected of deep hostility to the Constitution. Somehow we must find a way to explain the rapid shift from the Dionysian rhetoric of American politics during the impassioned years 1795 to 1799 to the Apollonian political solution of 1800–1801.

What is observable in a wide range of Federalist letters and memoirs is a basic predisposition among the great majority of them to accept a defeat, fairly administered, even in 1800 before that defeat was a certainty. The whole historical experience of America, as well as the temperament of their class, argued against extreme or violent measures. They were conservative men, and extreme responses that might risk what they sometimes called "the public tranquillity" were not to their way of thinking. Even the instrumentalities of force were lacking in the American environment; and a class of intensely political generals, the elite corps of any *coup d'état*, was impressively absent from the American scene. Most Federalists were realistic enough to see that they were not only divided but outvoted; and none of their fulminations against democracy should blind us to the fact that they did not fancy trying to rule without a decent public mandate. Again, the federal system took some of the steam out of their frustration; in New England, where partisan feeling ran strongest among them, the Federalists were, for the time being, still in control of their own affairs at the state level. They had no reason. to believe that they would be politically suppressed, and some of them thought that before very long the incompetence of the Republicans would swing the balance back to their side. Finally, the nature of the political parties and of political careers in America took some of the sting out of defeat.

The parties, for all the intensity of their passions and the bombast of their rhetoric, were new, their organization was rudimentary, and in some parts of the country partisan loyalties were thinner and more fragile than they might seem. No one, as Paul Goodman has remarked, had been born a Federalist or a Republican, and time was to show that switches from side to side were by no means unthinkable. Also, for many of the top leaders, politics was far from an exclusive concern. Political leaders were merchants, planters, lawyers, men of affairs with wide interests and with much capacity for taking pleasure in their private lives. Many of the best of them looked upon politics as a duty and not a livelihood or a pleasure. "To Bayard," his biographer pointedly observes, "the Senate was a job and not a career, a position of dignity

and respectability rather than a battleground under observation by the nation."
After the first flush of nationalist enthusiasm under Washington, it had become increasingly difficult to find men willing to accept positions of high
responsibility and honor. Offices were refused or resigned with astonishing
frequency, and Jefferson had to offer the Secretaryship of the Navy on five
occasions to four different men before he had an acceptance. Professional
politicians were, to be sure, emerging—fewer of them among the Federalists
than among their foes—but they were somewhat looked down upon by men
of eminence. And professional officeholders were the acknowledged dregs of
the political world.

To some degree, the option between Jefferson and Burr distracted the
Federalists from facing the full significance of their loss in 1800 and eased
them into it by stages. The prevailing Federalist preference for Burr, who
was widely regarded as an adventurer without fixed principles and who was
even seen by many as being preferable to Jefferson precisely on this count,
may certainly argue for a spirit of desperation. But here again the party was
divided, and the circumstances of the affair are significant for a reading of
Federalist temperature. What the Federalist leaders had to ponder was not
simply the character of Burr as against that of Jefferson but also whether
there was enough left of the spirit of concord or patriotism after the rancor
of the preceding years to warrant thinking that they could endure Jefferson's
possession of power. While it is an interesting question whether there was a
firm, formally concluded "bargain" between the Virginian and some of his
enemies—a question answered by most writers in the negative—it is still more
interesting to note what particular assurances Hamilton suggested as necessary
and that Bayard sought for when Jefferson was subtly and indirectly sounded
about his intentions. Hamilton's advice and Bayard's terms shed much light
on the practical differences that now separated the parties, and upon the
calculations some Federalists were making about the future.

First, as to the terms: Bayard at one point approached a friend of Jefferson suggesting that if certain points of concord could be arrived at, three
decisive states would withdraw their opposition to Jefferson's election. The
points were enumerated: "First, . . . the subject of the public credit; secondly,
the maintenance of the naval system; and, lastly, that subordinate public
officers employed only in the execution of details established by law shall not
be removed from office on the ground of their political character, nor without
complaint against their conduct." These points were later reiterated to another
intimate of Jefferson's, General Samuel Smith, who then purported to have
won Jefferson's assent to them, and so gained Bayard's consent. On the second
occasion the names of some of Bayard's friends were submitted, to give substance as it were, to the point about officeholders, and specific assurances
involving them were offered in return. What is perhaps most interesting is
that Bayard's conditions, in omitting a neutrality policy, deviate on only one
count from those Hamilton proposed that the Federalists seek for: "the maintenance of the present system, especially in the cardinal articles of public

credit—a navy, neutrality." Later Hamilton added patronage: "The preservation in office of our friends, except in the great departments, in respect to which and in future appointments he ought to be at liberty to appoint his friends."

One is at first disposed to conclude that despite their public ravings about Monocrats and Jacobins, American politicians were beginning to behave like politicians. The patronage question in particular argues for this point of view. But it should be realized too that for the Federalists in 1801 the question, now raised for the first time in national politics, whether an incoming party would make a wholesale sweep of public offices and install everywhere its own partisans, involved more than solicitude for the jobs and livelihoods of their friends. Jefferson's intentions as to removals and replacements were the object of a good deal of discussion in Federalist letters of 1800–1801, whose tenor suggests that, aside from the concern for loaves and fishes which was not a negligible thing for lesser party figures, the patronage issue had two further points of significance. It was, in the first instance, a symbolic matter of decisive importance: if the Federalist followers were to be swept out of all the lesser offices, the act would be a declaration of partisan warfare suggesting that the two parties were incapable of governing in concert, and that the desire of the Jeffersonians to decide the nation's policies was coupled with a gratuitous desire to retaliate and humiliate. A policy of proscription would put an end to the harmony and balance they considered essential to the republican order. Secondly, one must reckon with the Federalists' conviction that by far the larger portion of honest and able men, competent for the public business, were in their ranks; and that hence a wholesale displacement of such men might, quite aside from differences on policies, reduce the level of civic competence to a point at which the new government, established at so much effort and sacrifice, would be ruined. As Fisher Ames put it: "The success of governments depends on the selection of the men who administer them. It seems as if the ruling system would rob the country of all chance, by excluding the only classes proper to make the selection from."

Some historians have been at pains to establish that there was in fact no explicit understanding and hence no "corrupt" bargain between Jefferson and the Federalists; and certainly the way in which he was sounded out through an intermediary, who took it upon himself to tender the desired assurances after exploring Jefferson's mind, leaves Jefferson in the clear. Yet such efforts to acquit our political heroes seem to me somewhat misplaced; we would probably have reason to think less of them if they had been incapable of arriving at some kind of understanding. After all, Jefferson was morally and constitutionally entitled to the presidency, and it was the part of statesmanship, if not indeed of wisdom and morality, to offer the Federalists some assurances about his intentions. The survival of the constitutional system was at stake, and it had become necessary for both sides, in the spirit of practical men, to step back from their partisan embroilments, take a larger look at what they were doing, and try once again to make a fresh estimate of each other.

In this respect, Hamilton's appraisal of Jefferson, expressed in the course of his efforts to persuade other Federalists to accept him rather than choose Burr, becomes most illuminating. It was not many months earlier that Hamilton, trying to persuade Governor John Jay to get New York's electoral procedures changed to increase the chances of the Federalists in the forthcoming presidential election, warned Jay once again that the Republican party was a subversive and revolutionary party, and urged that his "scruples of delicacy and propriety" be set aside: "They ought not to hinder the taking of a *legal* and *constitutional step*, to prevent an *atheist* in Religion and a fanatic in politics from getting possession of the helm of the State."

But in January 1801, faced with the alternative of Burr, Hamilton was pushing this atheist and fanatic as a much safer prospective president and portraying him in quite different terms. "I admit," he wrote to Bayard in a remarkable letter, "that his politics are tinctured with fanaticism; that he is too much in earnest with his democracy; that he has been a mischievous enemy to the principal measures of our past administration; that he is crafty and persevering in his objects; that he is not scrupulous about the means of success, nor very mindful of truth, and that he is a contemptible hypocrite—" thus far as damaging an estimate as any Burrite Federalist could have wished. But, Hamilton went on, Jefferson was really not an enemy to the power of the Executive (this would prove all too true) or an advocate of putting all the powers of government in the House of Representatives. Once he found himself by way of inheriting the executive office, he would be "solicitous to come into the possession of a good estate." And then, prefatory to a long and devastating estimate of Burr's character and talents, there occurs the strategic and prophetic appraisal of Jefferson: "Nor is it true that Jefferson is zealot enough to do anything in pursuance of his principles, which will contravene his popularity or his interest. He is as likely as any man I know to temporize; to calculate what will be likely to promote his own reputation and advantage, and the probable result of such a temper is the preservation of systems, though originally opposed, which being once established, could not be overturned without danger to the person who did it. To my mind, a true estimate of Mr. Jefferson's character warrants the expectation of a temporizing, rather than a violent system." Even Jefferson's predilection for France was based more upon the popularity of France in America than upon his own sentiment, and it would cool when that popularity waned. "Add to this, that there is no fair reason to suppose him capable of being corrupted, which is a security that he will not go beyond certain limits." After his scathing dissertation upon Burr, Hamilton reverted to some partisan considerations: if the Republicans got Jefferson, they would be responsible for him; but if the Federalists should install Burr, "they adopt him, and become answerable for him." Moreover, he would doubtless win over many of them, "and the federalists will become a disorganized and contemptible party."

Finally, Hamilton repeated to several correspondents his conviction that Burr could not be relied upon to keep any commitment he might make to the Federalists.

In repeated letters to Bayard and others deemed open to his waning influence, Hamilton hammered away at the contrast he had laid down between the temporizing, politic Jefferson, and the dangerous Burr, that "embryo Caesar," "the Catiline of America," the "most unfit man in the United States for the office of President"—a man who, he told Oliver Wolcott in a significant phrase, would call to his side "rogues of all parties, to overrule the good men of all parties." Jefferson would never know how much he owed to Burr for having provided such a chiaroscuro, for throwing him into such high and acceptable relief, if only to a decisive minority of Federalists. But Hamilton's sense of the situation, his implicit recognition that there were, after all, good men on both sides, casts a powerful shaft of light into the roiled and murky bottoms of Federalist rhetoric. There are moments of supreme illumination in history when the depth of men's belief in their own partisan gabble has to be submitted at last to the rigorous test of practical decision. For about eight years the Federalists had been denouncing Jefferson and his party, and in the last few years their accusations had mounted to the point at which the leader of the opposition, the Vice President of the United States, had been charged with Jacobinism, atheism, fanaticism, unscrupulousness, wanton folly, incompetence, personal treachery, and political treason. Now this atheist in religion and fanatic in politics was to be quietly installed in the new White House, by courtesy of a handful of Federalist Congressmen, and though there was still hardly a man in the Federalist party who trusted him, there was also not a man to raise a hand against him. The Federalists, having failed to install Burr, preferred to risk Jefferson rather than to risk the constitutional system that had been so laboriously built and launched, and the way in which they explained to each other this seeming change of heart deserves some attention.

III

There was, of course, nothing cheerful about Federalist acquiescence in the transit of power. The overwhelming party preference for an acknowledged adventurer like Burr in the face of the clear public mandate for Jefferson was a token of the persistence of the exacerbated party conflict of the past half-dozen years. The Federalists had not softened their view of Jefferson: they expected to have to endure grave evils from a Republican victory, and a few even took a stark apocalyptic view of it. . . .

But, with all this, the prevailing note among leading Federalists in 1800–1801 was one of short-run resignation and long-run hope, and it was only a few years later that many of them gave way to complete despair. They still had faith in their principles and confident knowledge of their influence among the dominant classes. They were entrenched in the judiciary, strong in the

Senate, preponderant in New England, and at competitive strength in other
states of the Union. They could hope that their continued opposition would
be powerful enough to check some disasters, or, at worst, that if Jefferson
did bring an exceptional train of evils, men everywhere would respond by
rallying to them and bringing their party back to office, unified and perhaps
stronger than ever. Hence their tactical counsel to each other during and
shortly after the election and the final balloting in the House of Representatives looked not to extreme responses but to a measured judgment of the
situation and to the means by which their interests could be protected and
their influence best made felt. Their talk was not that of conspirators planning
to react with force, but of politicians, accustomed to power, who must now
learn how to play the role of a constructive constitutional opposition. They
had lost only by a narrow margin, they were still free to organize opposition,
and they expected that they would have an excellent chance to return to
power. . . .

   After the violent and impassioned rhetoric of the preceding years, one
is impressed, then, with the readiness of leading Federalists to adapt themselves to evils they considered inevitable, to accept the position of a legitimate
opposition, and to disenthrall their practical judgment from the gaudy threats
and dire predictions with which their propaganda was so free. One of Rufus
King's correspondents, Joseph Hale, put it well in December 1800, when he
wrote: "Men of the most judgment with us do not expect those evils to
follow the adminn. of Jeff. or Burr which while they were candidates it was
thought politic to predict.". . .

IV

It was characteristic of Jefferson that he perceived the keen political conflict
of the years just preceding his election not as an opportunity but as a difficulty.
Thanks to the efforts both of his detractors and his admirers, his historical
reputation has caused us to misread him. In the Federalist tradition, later
taken up by so many historians, he was a theorist, a visionary, a radical; and
American liberals have praised him for the same qualities the Federalists
abhorred. The modern liberal mind has been bemused by his remarks about
the value of a little rebellion now and then, or watering the tree of liberty
with the blood of tyrants, or having a complete constitutional revision every
twenty or thirty years. But Jefferson's more provocative utterances, it has
been too little noticed, were in his private correspondence. His public statements and actions were colored by a relative caution and timidity that reveal
a circumspect and calculating mind—or, as so many of his contemporary
foes believed, a guileful one. He was not enraptured by the drama of un-
restrained political conflict; and with the very important exception of some
of his views on foreign policy and war, his approach to public policy was far
from utopian. He did not look forward to a vigorously innovative administration—he had seen enough of that. The most stunning achievement of his

presidential years, the Louisiana Purchase, was an accident, the outcome of the collapse of Napoleon's ambitions for a Caribbean empire—the inadvertent gift of Toussaint L'Ouverture and the blacks of Haiti to this slaveholding country. Its most stunning disaster was the embargo, and the embargo itself came from Jefferson's penchant, here misapplied, for avoiding conflict. His was, as Hamilton put it in his tardy burst of pragmatic insight, a temporizing and not a violent disposition.

This disposition dictated an initial strategy of conciliation toward the Federalists, which led to a basic acceptance of the Hamiltonian fiscal system, including even the bank, to a patronage policy which Jefferson considered to be fair and compromising and hoped would appease moderate Federalists, and to an early attempt to pursue neutrality and to eschew aggravating signs of that Francophilia and Anglophobia with which the Federalists so obsessively and hyperbolically charged him. But for our concern, it is particularly important to understand that in Jefferson's mind conciliation was not a way of arriving at coexistence or of accommodating a two-party system, but a technique of absorption: he proposed to win over the major part of the amenable Federalists, leaving the intractables an impotent minority faction rather than a full-fledged opposition party. His strategy, which aimed, once again, at a party to end parties, formed another chapter in the quest for unanimity.

"The symptoms of a coalition of parties give me infinite pleasure," wrote Jefferson less than three weeks after delivering his inaugural address. "Setting aside a few only, I have been ever persuaded that the great bulk of both parties had the same principles fundamentally, and that it was only as to our foreign relations there was any division. These I hope can be so managed as to cease to be a subject of division for us. Nothing shall be spared on my part to obliterate the traces of party and consolidate the nation, if it can be done without abandonment of principle." His inaugural address itself had been designed to strike the first conciliatory note, and on the key question of party conflict it was a masterpiece of statesmanlike equivocation. It had a number of grace notes that might be calculated to appease opposition sensibilities: a prideful reference to American commerce, a strong hint about sustaining the public credit, an injunction to "pursue our own Federal and Republican principles," the memorable promise of "peace, commerce, and honest friendship with all nations, entangling alliances with none," obeisance to the memory of Washington as "our first and greatest revolutionary character," modest remarks about the fallibility of his own judgment, a promise not only to try to hold the good opinion of his supporters but also "to conciliate that of others by doing them all the good in my power," and finally, that *sine qua non* of inaugural addresses, especially necessary from one widely deemed "an atheist in religion"—an invocation of divine aid.

But it was in speaking of American conflicts that Jefferson achieved his finest subtlety. The acerbity of American political conflict, he suggested, would deceive "strangers unused to think freely and to speak and to write what they think." But now that the issue had been decided, Americans would unite for the common good. "All, too, will bear in mind this sacred principle, that though the will of the majority is in all cases to prevail, that will to be rightful must be reasonable; that the minority possess their equal rights, to violate which could be oppression." Let us restore harmony and affection to our society, he pleaded, and banish political intolerance as we have banished religious intolerance. That the agonies and agitations of Europe should have reached our shores and divided our opinions over proper measures of national safety is hardly surprising, but "every difference of opinion is not a difference of principle. We have called by different names brethren of the same principle. We are all republicans; we are all federalists."

In expressing these healing sentiments, which set a fine precedent for other chief executives taking office after acrimonious campaigns, Jefferson succeeded at a focal moment in reassuring many Federalists. Hamilton thought the address "virtually a candid retraction of past misapprehensions, and a pledge to the community that the new President will not lend himself to dangerous innovations, but in essential points tread in the steps of his predecessors." It contained some foolish but also many good ideas, George Cabot judged. "It is so conciliatory that much hope is derived from it by the Federalists," and he thought it "better liked by our party than his own." Robert Troup, who referred to its "wonderful lullaby effect" also thought it displeasing to the "most violent of the party attached to him," as did James A. Bayard. It was well calculated, Robert Goodloe Harper reported to his constituents, "to afford the hope of such an administration as may conduce to his own glory and the public good." "A fine opening," said Manasseh Cutler.

Yet the Federalists would have been much deceived if they had imagined that the striking sentence, "We are all republicans; we are all federalists," implied that Jefferson would put the principles of the two *parties*, and hence the parties themselves, on a nearly equal footing of legitimacy. The context, as well as various private utterances, showed that he meant only that almost all Americans believed both in the federal union and in the general principles of republican government, and that therefore the two parties stood close enough to be not so much reconciled as *merged*, and merged under his own standard. One can only concur here with Henry Adams's remark that Jefferson "wished to soothe the great body of his opponents, and if possible to win them over; but he had no idea of harmony or affection other than that which was to spring from his own further triumph." Jefferson's letters substantiate this interpretation. He had hardly finished the labors of the inauguration before he was writing letters to John Dickinson, James Monroe, and General Horatio Gates in which his hopes were spelled out with great clarity. Large numbers of his fellow citizens had been "hood-winked" from their principles through an extraordinary combination of circumstances, he argued, but it was now possible to enlighten them. An incorrect idea of his own views had got about, but "I am in hopes my inaugural address will in some measure set this to rights, as it will present the leading objects to be conciliation and adherence to sound principle." The leaders of the "late faction" were, of course, "incurables" and need not be courted, but "with the main body of federalists I believe it very practicable." The XYZ affair had created a political delusion among many people, but the uncertainties of the preceding month arising from the presidential election in the House of Representatives, and the alarm over a possible constitutional crisis had produced "a wonderful effect . . . on the mass of federalists." Many wanted only "a decent excuse for coming back" to a party that represented their own deepest views, and others had come over "rather than risk anarchy." Therefore Jefferson's policies, especially as to patronage, would be prudent, and would be so designed as "to give time for a perfect consolidation." In short: "If we can hit on the true line of conduct which may conciliate the honest part of those who were called federalists, and do justice to those who have so long been excluded from it, I shall hope to be able to obliterate, or rather to unite the names of federalists and republicans. The way to effect it is to preserve principle, but to treat tenderly those who have been estranged from us, and dispose their minds to view our proceedings with candour.". . .

V

It hardly needs to be said that Jefferson's middle course did not succeed in appeasing Federalist leaders. At best it can be said that it avoided goading them into violent responses for the brief period during which he consolidated his influence; and when they awoke from the relative torpor into which they receded in 1801, it was only to find, as many of them promptly concluded, that democracy was so much in the ascendant that all hopes of an early return to power had to be given up. By 1803 most of them had decided that Jefferson was as bad as they had ever expected him to be, and some of them were lamenting that the Constitution was dead. They had been infuriated by the Jeffersonian war on the judiciary, which, beginning with the refusal of some of Adams's midnight appointments, went on early in 1802 to the repeal of the Judiciary Act of 1801, and was climaxed by the impeachments of Justices Pickering and Chase in 1804 and 1805. They were intensely discouraged by the Louisiana Purchase in 1803, which not only seemed to cut off all prospects of war with France but added immense western territories out of which they could foresee the Jeffersonians carving many new agrarian states and thus piling further gains on top of the already substantial Republican majorities. By 1804, when a few maddened New England conspirators tried to use Burr's candidacy for the governorship of New York as a pivot upon which to engineer an independent New England–New York confederacy, they were so far out of touch with reality that even some of the most stoutly parochial New England conservatives, whose support they had to have, hung back in discouragement and disapproval. George Cabot, speaking for Chief Justice Theophilus Parsons, Fisher Ames, and Stephen Higginson as well as himself, warned Timothy Pickering that secession was pointless as long as democracy remained such a general creed that even New England was thoroughly infected with it. The best hope for the Federalists, he thought, would be in the public reaction to a gratuitous war with England. . . .

As renewed party strife replaced the brief testing period that followed Jefferson's inauguration, his response to the Federalist leaders was as sharp as theirs to him, and while his public stance still invoked the restoration of harmony and affection and left open his bid for the Federalist rank and file, his private correspondence was electric with flashes of impassioned hostility to opposition leaders who would "toll us back to the times when we burnt witches," to the "ravenous crew" of his foes, the "monocrats" who "wish to sap the republic by fraud," "incurables to be taken care of in a mad house," and "heroes of Billingsgate." "I wish nothing but their eternal hatred," he flared out in one of his letters. He could find nothing legitimate or useful in the Federalist opposition. "A respectable minority," he explained to Joel Barlow in May 1802, "is useful as censors," but the present minority did not qualify because it was "not respectable, being the bitterest cup of the remains of Federalism rendered desperate and furious with despair." They would not, they should not, survive at all.

If Jefferson was winning over precious few of the Federalist leaders, he had the pleasure at least of taking away much of their following and mobilizing his own to the point of nearly total party victory. To this degree his political optimism was quite justified: he had gauged public sentiment correctly and he was giving the people what they wanted—frugal government, low taxes, fiscal retrenchment, a small army and navy, peace, and the warm sentiments of democratic republicanism. And he had behind him a party far more popular and efficient than anything the Federalists could mobilize against him. He had not been in the White House as much as a year before he was reporting to Dupont de Nemours his immense satisfaction with his efforts at conciliation and unity—by which he meant Republican preponderance. If a presidential election were held a year hence, he ventured on January 18, 1802, solely on grounds of political principle and uncomplicated by personal likes or dislikes, "the federal candidate would not get the vote of a single elector in the U.S." And indeed the Congressional elections of 1802 yielded an overwhelming Republican majority, which, though somewhat weakened later by reactions to the embargo and to the War of 1812, was never substantially endangered. In May Jefferson exulted that Republican advances had reached the point at which "candid federalists acknowledge that their party can never more raise its head." In 1804 he was re-elected with the votes of all New England except Connecticut, and given a party preponderance of four to one in the Senate and five to one in the House. In his second inaugural address he congratulated the country on "the union of sentiment now manifested so generally" and anticipated among the people an "entire union of opinion." In 1807, when the Massachusetts Federalists lost even their governorship, he saw the Federalists as "completely vanquished, and never more to take the field under their own banners." The old dream of national unanimity seemed to be coming true.

As Federalism dwindled away toward virtual impotence, Jefferson seemed to fall victim to a certain inconsistency between his passion for unanimity on one side and on the other to his long-standing philosophical conviction that free men will differ and that differences will engender parties. But he was perhaps less inconsistent than he seemed: to him achieving unanimity meant not establishing a dead level of uniform thought but simply getting rid of the deep and impassioned differences which had arisen only because the extreme Federalists had foisted upon their party a preference for England and for monarchy. Unanimity did not require eliminating various low-keyed and negotiable differences of opinion between different schools of honest republicans. The chief limit to unity now indeed seemed to stem from divisions appearing in the Republican ranks in Congress and from such intra-state factionalism as disturbed the party in Pennsylvania. But none of this worried him unduly. He understood that a party which had no opposition to fight with would develop a centrifugal tendency: "We shall now be so strong that we shall split again; for freemen thinking differently and speaking and acting as they think, will form into classes of sentiment, but it must be under another name, that of federalism is to become so scouted that no party can rise under it."

On this count we can find him prophetic. Partisan victory seems finally to have brought him back to his original understanding that party differences are founded in human nature. For him the goal of unanimity was satisfied by the elimination of Federalism, the disappearance of fundamental issues; and it may not be too fanciful to see in this some likeness to Burke's satisfaction in the disappearance of "the great parties" which was the very thing Burke thought laid a foundation for moderate party differences and justifiable party loyalties. Jefferson once observed that with "the entire prostration of federalism" the remaining Federalists might form a coalition with the Republican minority; but in this he saw no danger so long as the Republican dissidents were not—here the party obsession raises its head once again—flirting with monarchy. "I had always expected," he wrote to Thomas Cooper in 1807, "that when the republicans should have put down all things under their feet, they would schismatize among themselves. I always expected, too, that whatever names the parties might bear, the real division would be into moderate and ardent republicanism. In this division there is no great evil,—not even if the minority obtain the ascendency by the accession of federal votes to their candidate; because this gives us one shade only, instead of another, of republicanism." The notion that the animating principle behind Federalism had been a passion for monarchy, however delusive it had been, led to the comforting conclusion that the last nail had now been driven into the coffin of the hereditary principle, and hence that the country had reached a unanimity deep enough. But in 1807 neither Thomas Jefferson nor George Cabot could possibly have imagined what would come in the next few years: that Jefferson would leave the presidency with a sense of failure and with diminished popularity; that Federalism, for all this, would undergo only a modest resurgence; that a war with Great Britain would finally come under the Republicans, and that, though conducted with consummate incompetence, it would lead to the complete triumph of Republicanism and the final disappearance of the Federalist party.

SUGGESTIONS FOR FURTHER READING

Henry Adams's monumental nine-volume *History of the United States During the Administrations of Jefferson and Madison* (New York, 1889–1891) is a classic that should at least be sampled by every student of American history. Adams finds that Jefferson as President often departed radically from the theories he advanced before becoming President, but Adams is on the whole sympathetic to Jefferson. Claude Bowers in **Jefferson and Hamilton: The Struggle for Democracy in America* (Boston, 1925) has written an interpretation of the Jefferson-Hamilton struggle as a "clear-cut fight between democracy and aristocracy." Vernon L. Parrington, in his superbly written and influential **Main Currents in American Thought* (New York, 1927), builds his analysis on the fundamental disagreements between Jefferson and Hamilton. He pictures Jefferson as the philosopher of agrarian democracy, a man who had faith in the common man's ability to rule himself. Charles A. Beard in his *Economic Origins of Jeffersonian Democracy* (New York, 1915) is less emphatic about Jefferson's contribution to democracy, although he does argue that Jefferson's victory was a triumph for the agrarian interests. Hamilton is treated much more sympathetically and with much less emphasis on conflict in a number of more recent studies. See, for example, Nathan Schachner, **The Founding Fathers* (New York, 1954) and John C. Miller, **The Federalist Era, 1789–1801* (New York, 1960). A brief, provocative essay on Jefferson describing the consensus that united Jefferson and Hamilton may be found in Richard Hofstadter, **The American Political Tradition* (New York, 1948).

Leonard Levy, *Jefferson and Civil Liberties: The Darker Side* (New York, 1973), describes a perverse kind of consensus by showing that Jefferson, the ardent opponent of the Alien and Sedition Acts, used similarly repressive measures against his opponents after he came to office. David Hackett Fischer, *The Revolution of American Conservatism: The Federalist Party in the Era of Jeffersonian Democracy* (New York, 1965), finds the emergence of a new consensus not because the Jeffersonians compromised with the Federalists but because the Federalists, once out of power, compromised with the dominant Jeffersonian ideas. The "Old Republican" opposition to Jefferson from within his own party is discussed (along with many other topics) in Merrill D. Peterson, *Thomas Jefferson and the New Nation* (New York, 1970), and more fully in Norman K. Risjord, *The Old Republicans: Southern Conservatism in the Age of Jefferson*

* Available in paperback edition.

(New York, 1965). John Chester Miller, *The Wolf By the Ears: Thomas Jefferson and Slavery* (New York, 1977), describes Jefferson's ambivalent attitude toward slavery.

There is a vast literature on this subject. An introduction to some of it, along with a fascinating study of the way that Jefferson has been viewed since his death, is Merrill D. Peterson, *The Jeffersonian Image in the American Mind* (New York, 1960). Peterson's recent biography of Jefferson is warmly sympathetic: *Thomas Jefferson and the New Nation: A Biography* (New York, 1970). Fawn M. Brodie, *Thomas Jefferson: An Intimate History*, is a more personal and controversial biography.

5

BORN TO COMMAND

OF VETO MEMORY

HAD I BEEN CONSULTED

KING ANDREW THE FIRST.

The Era
of Andrew Jackson

Some men seem to so dominate the age in which they live that they become symbols of that age even during their own lifetimes. Such a man was Andrew Jackson: loved by his followers and detested by his opponents, he somehow seemed to represent both the best and the worst in America. Controversial in his own time, Jackson has since become a subject of debate among historians who seek to understand the man and the age in which he lived.

There can be no disagreement that the era of Andrew Jackson was a time of great change in America. People were moving in large numbers to the West, where they established farms and plantations and founded villages, many of which would quickly grow into thriving towns and cities. Mills and factories began to dot the landscape, especially in the East, providing an increasing supply of manufactured goods for a growing population. Steamboats, canals, and soon railroads linked the nation together and shrank the vast distances that separated East and West, North and South.

Such changes provided Americans with many new opportunities. Indeed, the life of Jackson himself seemed to symbolize these opportunities. A poor Carolina back-country farm boy, he became a wealthy Tennessee planter, a popular military hero, and finally President of the United States. Yet, change also brought new problems. If some Americans, like Jackson, grew wealthy and powerful, others—indeed, most—did not. Many people felt that a new aristocracy of wealth threatened the country.

Some of the differences among historians evaluating the Jacksonian era stem from their conflicting views as to the results of the vast changes taking place in American life during the second quarter of the nineteenth century. For some, Jacksonianism is the effort of the common man to defend his rights against the incursions of a new economic elite. In this view, Jackson becomes a charismatic leader of farmers and workers in a struggle against special privilege; his party, true to its name, becomes the party of democracy, while the Whigs—Jackson's opponents—emerge as the party of wealth and special privilege. From this perspective, Jackson's war on the Bank of the United States is a people's struggle against a powerful financial monopoly. The "spoils system" is not a cynical effort to build the party by rewarding the faithful, but rather a means to bring democracy to government; the government could—and should—be run by ordinary men who accepted the views of the majority of the population, and not by a technical, aristocratic elite.

But other historians, who point out the difficulty in most states of distinguishing Whigs from Democrats in terms of their wealth or social class, see Jackson's democratic stance as merely political opportunism, a clever method used by an astute politician to win political office. "Jackson never really championed the cause of the people; he only invited them to champion his," argued Thomas P. Abernethy. Some historians go beyond mere political infighting to argue that Jackson's politics were designed to provide opportunities for a new group of businessmen and entrepreneurs who had arisen in the wake of the nation's rapid geographic and economic expansion. Where the first group of historians sees fundamental conflict in the era of Jackson—rich versus poor, farmers versus capitalists, employees versus employers—the second group finds a greater consensus among Americans. Beneath the violent political rhetoric, they say, were much milder disagreements over the precise way in which an essentially egalitarian, business-oriented society was to work.

Varying interpretations of Jacksonianism may be seen in the following selections. Arthur Schlesinger, Jr., describes Jacksonian democracy as a part of "that enduring struggle between the business community and the rest of society." There is no doubt in his mind that there was real and important conflict in the Age of Jackson. Bray Hammond does not agree; he decides that there was little dividing the Jacksonians from their opponents. Rather than an ideological struggle between business and the rest of society, the era of Jackson was marked by a wild scramble of "expectant capitalists" for a place in the economic sun. In the final selection, Edward Pessen examines some of the recent state studies of the Jackson period and concludes that there were no great differences between the followers of Jackson and of his opponents. He also studies the Workingman's Party, whose members did think in terms of ideological and class conflict. But he concludes that perhaps the most important fact is how few Americans dissented from the Jacksonian consensus.

How, then, are we to interpret the Age of Jackson? Was the period marked by the struggle of the common man to advance democracy? Was this struggle based on fundamental conflict emanating from class and sectional differences? Or did it arise from relatively minor political differences within a basic underlying consensus? Is it meaningful to talk about Jacksonian "democracy"? If so, does this mean that democracy was won in the course of a conflict with undemocratic or aristocratic forces? These questions cannot be answered without a clear understanding of what is meant by "democracy." Does democracy imply economic as well as political rights? Can there be democracy with economic and social inequality?

Arthur M. Schlesinger, Jr.

Jacksonian Democracy vs. the Business Community

The Jacksonian revolution rested on premises which the struggles of the thirties hammered together into a kind of practical social philosophy. The outline of this way of thinking about society was clear. It was stated and restated, . . . on every level of political discourse from presidential messages to stump speeches, from newspaper editorials to private letters. It provided the intellectual background without which the party battles of the day cannot be understood.

I

The Jacksonians believed that there was a deep-rooted conflict in society between the "producing" and "non-producing" classes—the farmers and laborers, on the one hand, and the business community on the other. The business community was considered to hold high cards in this conflict through its network of banks and corporations, its control of education and the press, above all, its power over the state: it was therefore able to strip the working classes of the fruits of their labor. "Those who produce all wealth," said Amos Kendall, "are themselves left poor. They see principalities extending and palaces built around them, without being aware that the entire expense is a tax upon themselves."

If they wished to preserve their liberty, the producing classes would have to unite against the movement "to make the rich richer and the potent more powerful." Constitutional prescriptions and political promises afforded no sure protection. "We have heretofore been too disregardful of the fact," observed William M. Gouge, "that social order is quite as dependent on the laws which regulate the distribution of wealth, as on political organization." The program now was to resist every attempt to concentrate wealth and power further in a single class. Since free elections do not annihilate the opposition, the fight would be unceasing. "The struggle for power," said C. C. Cambreleng, "is as eternal as the division of society. A defeat cannot destroy the boundary which perpetually separates the democracy from the aristocracy."

The specific problem was to control the power of the capitalistic groups, mainly Eastern, for the benefit of the noncapitalist groups, farmers and laboring men, East, West and South. The basic Jacksonian ideas came naturally enough from the East, which best understood the nature of business power and reacted most sharply against it. The legend that Jacksonian democracy was the explosion of the frontier, lifting into the government some violent men filled with rustic prejudices against big business, does not explain the facts, which were somewhat more complex. Jacksonian democracy was rather a second American phase of that enduring struggle between the business community and the rest of society which is the guarantee of freedom in a liberal capitalist state.

Like any social philosophy, Jacksonian democracy drew on several intellectual traditions. Basically, it was a revival of Jeffersonianism, but the Jeffersonian inheritance was strengthened by the infusion of fresh influences; notably the antimonopolistic tradition, formulated primarily by Adam Smith and expounded in America by Gouge, Legett, Sedgwick, Cambreleng; and the pro-labor tradition, formulated primarily by William Cobbett and expounded by G. H. Evans, Ely Moore, John Ferral.

II

The inspiration of Jeffersonianism was so all-pervading and fundamental for its every aspect that Jacksonian democracy can be properly regarded as a somewhat more hard-headed and determined version of Jeffersonian democracy. But it is easy to understate the differences. Jefferson himself, though widely revered and quoted, had no personal influence on any of the leading Jacksonians save perhaps Van Buren. Madison and Monroe were accorded still more vague and perfunctory homage. The radical Jeffersonians, Taylor, Randolph and Macon, who had regarded the reign of Virginia as almost an era of betrayal, were much more vivid in the minds of the Jacksonians.

Yet even Taylor's contributions to the later period have been exaggerated. His great work, the *Inquiry into the Principles and Policy of the Government of the United States*, published in 1814 just before the Madisonian surrender, had no significant contemporary vogue except among the faithful; and its difficult style, baffling organization and interminable length prevented it ever from gaining wide currency. By Jackson's presidency it was long out of print. In 1835 it was reported unobtainable in New York and to be procured only "with great difficulty" in Virginia. There is little trace of its peculiar terminology in the Jacksonian literature.

While the *Inquiry* properly endured as the most brilliant discussion of the foundations of democracy, many of its details were in fact obsolete by 1830. It was oriented to an important degree around the use of the national debt as the mechanism of aristocracy; in Jackson's day the debt had been extinguished but the aristocracy remained. Moreover, Taylor's arguments against executive power, against the party system and for a revivified militia had lost their point for the Jacksonians. George Bancroft voiced a widely felt need when he called, in 1834, for a general work on American society. "Where doubts arise upon any point relating to the business of government," one radical wrote in response, "no dependence can be placed upon any treatise that has yet appeared which professes to discuss this subject. You must draw upon your own resources, you must think,—and think alone."

The obsolescence of Taylor was caused by the enormous change in the face of America. The period of conservative supremacy from 1816 to 1828 had irrevocably destroyed the agricultural paradise, and the Jacksonians were accommodating the insights of Jefferson to the new concrete situations. This process of readjustment involved a moderately thorough overhauling of favorite Jeffersonian doctrines.

The central Jefferson hope had been a nation of small freeholders, each acquiring thereby so much moral probity, economic security and political independence as to render unnecessary any invasion of the rights or liberties of others. The basis of such a society, as Jefferson clearly recognized, was agriculture and handicraft. What was the status of the Jeffersonian hope now that it was clear that, at best, agriculture must share the future with industry and finance?

Orestes A. Brownson exhausted one possibility in his essay on "The Laboring Classes." He reaffirmed the Jeffersonian demand: "we ask that every man become an independent proprietor, possessing enough of the goods of this world, to be able by his own moderate industry to provide for the wants of his body." But what, in practice, would this mean? As Brownson acknowledged years later, his plan would have "broken up the whole modern commercial system, prostrated the great industries, . . . and thrown the mass of the people back on the land to get their living by agricultural and mechanical pursuits." Merely to state its consequences was to prove its futility. The dominion of the small freeholder was at an end.

The new industrialism had to be accepted: banks, mills, factories, industrial capital, industrial labor. These were all distasteful realities for orthodox Jeffersonians, and, not least, the propertyless workers. "The mobs of great cities," Jefferson had said, "add just so much to the support of pure government, as sores do to the strength of the human body." The very ferocity of his images expressed the violence of his feelings. "When we get piled upon one another in large cities, as in Europe," he told Madison, "we shall become corrupt as in Europe, and go to eating one another as they do there." It was a universal sentiment among his followers. "No man should live," Nathaniel Macon used to say, "where he can hear his neighbour's dog bark."

Yet the plain political necessity of winning the labor vote obliged a change of mood. Slowly, with some embarrassment, the Jeffersonian preferences for the common man were enlarged to take in the city workers. In 1833 the *New York Evening Post*, declaring that, if anywhere, a large city of mixed population would display the evils of universal suffrage, asked if this had been the case in New York and answered: No. Amasa Walker set out the same year to prove that "great cities are not *necessarily*, as the proverb says, 'great sores,'" and looked forward cheerily to the day when they would be "great fountains of healthful moral influence, sending forth streams that shall fertilize and bless the land." The elder Theodore Sedgwick added that the cause of the bad reputation of cities was economic: "it is the sleeping in garrets and cellars; the living in holes and dens; in dirty, unpaved, unlighted streets, without the accommodations of wells, cisterns, baths, and other means of cleanliness and health"—clear up this situation, and cities will be all right.

Jackson himself never betrayed any of Jefferson's revulsion to industrialism. He was, for example, deeply interested by the mills of Lowell in 1833, and his inquiries respecting hours, wages and production showed, observers reported, "that the subject of domestic manufactures had previously engaged his attentive observation." His presidential allusions to the "producing classes" always included the workingmen of the cities. . . .

III

In several respects, then, the Jacksonians revised the Jeffersonian faith for America. They moderated that side of Jeffersonianism which talked of agricultural virtue, independent proprietors, "natural" property, abolition of industrialism, and expanded immensely that side which talked of economic equality, the laboring classes, human rights and the control of industrialism. This readjustment enabled the Jacksonians to attack economic problems which had baffled and defeated the Jeffersonians. It made for a greater realism, and was accompanied by a general toughening of the basic Jeffersonian conceptions. While the loss of "property" was serious, both symbolically and intellectually, this notion had been for most Jeffersonians somewhat submerged next to the romantic image of the free and virtuous cultivator; and the Jacksonians grew much more insistent about theories of capitalist alienation. Where, for the Jeffersonians, the tensions of class conflict tended to dissolve in vague generalizations about the democracy and the aristocracy, many Jacksonians would have agreed with A. H. Wood's remark, "It is in vain to talk of Aristocracy and Democracy—these terms are too variable and indeterminate to convey adequate ideas of the present opposing interests; the division is between the rich and the poor—the warfare is between them."

This greater realism was due, in the main, to the passage of time. The fears of Jefferson were now actualities. One handled fears by exorcism, but actualities by adjustment. For the Jeffersonians mistrust of banks and corporations was chiefly a matter of theory; for the Jacksonians it was a matter of experience. The contrast between the scintillating metaphors of John Taylor and the sober detail of William M. Gouge expressed the difference. Jefferson rejected the Industrial Revolution and sought to perpetuate the smiling society which preceded it (at least, so the philosopher; facts compelled the President toward a different policy), while Jackson, accepting industrialism as an ineradicable and even useful part of the economic landscape, sought rather to control it. Jeffersonian democracy looked wistfully back toward a past slipping further every minute into the mists of memory, while Jacksonian democracy came straightforwardly to grips with a rough and unlovely present.

The interlude saw also the gradual unfolding of certain consequences of the democratic dogma which had not been so clear to the previous generation. Though theoretically aware of the relation between political and economic power, the Jeffersonians had been occupied, chiefly, with establishing political equality. This was their mission, and they had little time to grapple with the economic questions.

But the very assertion of political equality raised inevitably the whole range of problems involved in property and class conflict. How could political equality mean anything without relative economic equality among the classes of the country? This question engaged the Jacksonians. As Orestes A. Brownson said, "A Loco-foco is a Jeffersonian Democrat, who having realized political equality, passed through one phase of the revolution, now passes on to another, and attempts the realization of social equality, so that the actual condition of men in society shall be in harmony with their acknowledged rights as citizens." This gap between Jeffersonian and Jacksonian democracy enabled men like John Quincy Adams, Henry Clay, Joseph Story and many others, who had been honest Jeffersonians, to balk at the economic extremities to which Jackson proposed to lead them.

The Jacksonians thus opened irrevocably the economic question, which the Jeffersonians had only touched halfheartedly. Yet, while they clarified these economic implications of democracy, the Jacksonians were no more successful than their predecessors in resolving certain political ambiguities. Of these, two were outstanding—the problem of the virtue of majorities, and the problem of the evil of government. . . .

IV

The radical democrats had a definite conception of their relation to history. From the Jeffersonian analysis, fortified by the insights of Adam Smith and Cobbett, they sketched out an interpretation of modern times which gave meaning and status to the Jacksonian struggles.

Power, said the Jacksonians, goes with property. In the Middle Ages the feudal nobility held power in society through its monopoly of land under feudal tenure. The overthrow of feudalism, with the rise of new forms of property, marked the first step in the long march toward freedom. The struggle was carried on by the rising business community—"commercial, or business capital, against landed capital; merchants, traders, manufacturers, artizans, against the owners of the soil, the great landed nobility." It lasted from the close of the twelfth century to the Whig Revolution of 1688 in Britain.

The aristocracy of capital thus destroyed the aristocracy of land. The business classes here performed their vital role in the drama of liberty. The victory over feudalism, as the *Democratic Review* put it, "opened the way for the entrance of the democratic principle into the Government." But the business community gained from this exploit an undeserved reputation as the champion of liberty. Its real motive had been to establish itself in power, not to free mankind; to found government on property, not on the equal rights of the people. "I know perfectly well what I am saying," cried George Bancroft, "and I assert expressly, and challenge contradiction, that in all the history of the world there is not to be found an instance of a commercial community establishing rules for self-government upon democratic principles." "It is a mistake to suppose commerce favorable to liberty," added Fenimore Cooper. "Its tendency is to a monied aristocracy." "Instead of setting man free," said Amos Kendall, it has "only increased the number of his masters."

The next great blow for liberty was the American Revolution, "effected not in favor of men in classes; . . . but in favor of men." But the work of Hamilton halted the march of democracy. "He established the money power," wrote Van Buren, "upon precisely the same foundations upon which it had been raised in England." The subsequent history of the United States was the struggle to overthrow the Hamiltonian policy and fulfill the ideals of the Revolution.

What of the future? The Jacksonians were sublimely confident: history was on their side. "It is now for the yeomanry and the mechanics to march at the head of civilization," said Bancroft. "The merchants and the lawyers, that is, the moneyed interest broke up feudalism. The day for the multitude has now dawned." "All classes, each in turn, have possessed the government," exclaimed Brownson; "and the time has come for all predominance of class to end; for Man, the People to rule."

This was not simply a national movement. It was a movement of all people, everywhere, against their masters, and the Jacksonians watched with keen interest the stirrings of revolt abroad. Jackson and his cabinet joined in the celebrations in Washington which followed the Revolution of 1830 in France; and Van Buren, as Secretary of State, ordered the new government informed that the American people were "universally and enthusiastically in favor of that change, and of the principle upon which it was effected." (The Whigs, on the other hand, in spite of Clay's support of national revolutions in Greece and South America, remained significantly lukewarm.) Lamennais, the eloquent voice of French popular aspirations, was read in Jacksonian circles. The *Paroles d'un Croyant* influenced Orestes A. Brownson, and in 1839 *Le Livre du Peuple* was published in Boston under the title of *The People's Own Book*, translated by Nathaniel Greene, postmaster of Boston, brother of Charles Gordon Greene of the *Post* and intimate of David Henshaw.

Democrats followed with similar enthusiasm the progress of the Reform Bill in England, while the Whigs sympathized with the Tories. The Chartist uprisings at the end of the decade were greeted with delight by the Democratic press. British reformers returned this interest. Not only Cobbett and Savage Landor but the veteran radical Jeremy Bentham observed Jackson's administration with approval. Bentham, a friend of John Quincy Adams, had been disappointed at the triumph in 1828 of this military hero; but early in 1830, as he huddled by his hissing steam radiator, he heard read aloud Jackson's first message to Congress. The old man was highly pleased to discover greater agreement with the new President than with the old. Later he wrote that lengthy and cryptic memorandum entitled *Anti-Senatica*, intended to aid Jackson in the problems of his administration.

Jacksonians everywhere had this faith in the international significance of their fight. For this reason, as well as from a desire to capture their votes, Democratic leaders made special appeals to newly naturalized citizens. Where many Whigs tended to oppose immigration and demand sanctions against it, Democrats welcomed the newcomers with open arms and attacked the nativist agitation. The United States must remain a refuge from tyranny. "The capitalist class," said Samuel J. Tilden, "has banded together all over the world and organized the *modern dynasty of associated wealth*, which maintains an unquestioned ascendency over most of the civilized portions of our race." America was the proving-ground of democracy, and it was the mission of American Democrats to exhibit to the world the glories of government by the people. They were on the spearhead of history. They would not be denied. "With the friends of freedom throughout the world," declared Theophilus Fisk, "let us be co-workers." "The People of the World," cried Fanny Wright, "have but one Cause."

Bray Hammond

The Jacksonians:
Expectant Capitalists

During the half century that ended with General Jackson's election, America underwent changes perhaps the most radical and sweeping it has ever undergone in so short a time. It passed the climacteric separating a modern industrial economy from an older one of handicraft; it passed from colonial weakness through bare independence to actual power and from an unjostled rural culture to the complexities of populousness, sectionalism, urban slums, mechanized industry, and monetary credit. Men who had spent their childhood in a thin line of seaboard colonies, close even in their little cities to the edge of the westward continental wilderness, spent their late years in a tamed and wealthy land spread already to the Missouri and about to extend beyond it. They lived to ride on railways and steamships, to use the products of steam-driven machinery, to dwell in metropolitan centers, and to feel within their grasp and the grasp of their sons more potential and accessible wealth than had ever before excited the enterprise of man.

An outstanding factor in the changes that came about was the flow of immigration from Europe. Between 1790 and 1840 the population grew from 4,000,000 to 17,000,000. In the latter year an average of 230 immigrants entered the country daily. Ten years later it was over 1,000 daily. The area of settlement and exploitation expanded swiftly under the pressure of this movement. While General Jackson was President the federal union came to include twice as many states as it had begun with and held territory that recently had belonged to Spain and France. It was shortly to add regions in

From Banks and Politics in America from the Revolution to the Civil War by Bray Hammond, pp. 345–350, 358–361, 326–330. Copyright © 1957 by Princeton University Press; Princeton Paperback, 1967. Reprinted by permission of Princeton University Press.

the South and West taken from Mexico and regions in the Northwest that Great Britain claimed. Its expansion seemed irresistible.

The changes in social outlook were profound. Steam was generating conceptions of life, liberty, and the pursuit of happiness that were quite alien to Thomas Jefferson's; and the newcomers pushing into the country from Europe had more impatient economic motives than their 18th-century predecessors. People were led as they had not been before by visions of money-making. Liberty became transformed into *laisser faire*. A violent, aggressive, economic individualism became established. The democracy became greedy, intolerant, imperialistic, and lawless. It opened economic advantages to those who had not previously had them; yet it allowed wealth to be concentrated in new hands only somewhat more numerous than before, less responsible, and less disciplined. There were unenterprising and unpropertied thousands who missed entirely the economic opportunities with which America was thick. There was poverty in the eastern cities and poverty on the frontier. Those who failed to hold their own in the struggle were set down as unfit.

Wealth was won and lost, lost and won. Patient accumulation was contemned. People believed it was not what they saved but what they made that counted. Jay Cooke, one of America's future millionaires, who was scarcely born poor on a farm but primitively at least, in a frontier settlement, was already on his way to fortune in a private banking firm before the age of twenty and writing home about his work with enthusiasm. This was in the winter of 1839–1840. "My bosses are making money fast," he said. "This business is always good, and those who follow it in time become rich. . . . Among our customers are men of every age and every position in society, from the hoary miser to the dashing buck who lives upon his thousands. Through all grades I see the same all-pervading, all-engrossing anxiety to grow rich." Something of the same sort, to be sure, was taking place in western Europe and especially in Great Britain. Half the people and most of the money for America's transformation came from there. But though industrial and technological revolution occurred also in the Old World, in the New, where vast resources awaited exploitation, it produced a dazzling, democratic expansion experienced nowhere else. The situation was such that the rallying cry, "*Laissez nous faire!*" expressed the views of Americans perfectly, when translated.

Socially, the Jacksonian revolution signified that a nation of democrats was tired of being governed, however well, by gentlemen from Virginia and Massachusetts. As Professor Sumner observed, what seems to have enchanted people with General Jackson when he became a candidate for President was not any principles or policies he advocated but his breaches of decorum, real or alleged. Economically, the revolution signified that a nation of potential money-makers could not abide traditionary, conservative limitations on business enterprise, particularly by capitalists in Philadelphia. The Jacksonian revolution was a consequence of the Industrial Revolution and of a farm-born people's realization that now anyone in America could get rich and through his own efforts, if he had a fair chance. A conception of earned wealth arose which rendered the self-made man as superior morally to the hereditary well-to-do as the agrarian had been. It was like the conception which led Theodoric the Great to boast that he held Italy solely by right of conquest and without the shadow of legal, that is, hereditary right. The humbly born and rugged individualists who were gaining fortunes by their own toil and sweat, or wits, were still simple Americans, Jeffersonian, anti-monopolistic, anti-governmental, but fraught with the spirit of enterprise and fired with a sense of what soon would be called manifest destiny. They envied the social and economic advantages of the established urban capitalists, mercantile and financial; and they fought these aristocrats with far more zeal and ingenuity than the agrarians ever had. They resented the federal Bank's interference with expansion of the monetary supply. They found it bestriding the path of enterprise, and with Apollyon's brag but Christian's better luck they were resolved to spill its soul. They democratized business under a great show of agrarian idealism and made the age of Jackson a festival of *laisser faire* prelusive to the age of Grant and the robber barons.

In their attack on the Bank of the United States, the Jacksonians still employed the vocabulary of their agrarian backgrounds. The phraseology of idealism was adapted to money-making, the creed of an earlier generation becoming the cant of its successor. Their terms of abuse were "oppression," "tyranny," "monied power," "aristocracy," "wealth," "privilege," "monopoly"; their terms of praise were "the humble," "the poor," "the simple," "the honest and industrious." Though their cause was a sophisticated one of enterpriser against capitalist, of banker against regulation, and of Wall Street against Chestnut, the language was the same as if they were all back on the farm. Neither the President, nor his advisers, nor their followers saw any discrepancy between the concept of freedom in an age of agrarianism and the concept of freedom in one of enterprise. Only the poets and philosophers were really aware that a discrepancy existed and though troubled by it their vision was far from clear. Notwithstanding their language, therefore, the Jacksonians' destruction of the Bank of the United States was in no sense a blow at capitalism or property or the "money power." It was a blow at an older set of capitalists by a newer, more numerous set. It was incident to the democratization of business, the diffusion of enterprise among the mass of people, and the transfer of economic primacy from an old and conservative merchant class to a newer, more aggressive, and more numerous body of business men and speculators of all sorts.

The Jacksonians were unconventional and skillful in politics. In their assault on the Bank they united five important elements, which, incongruities notwithstanding, comprised an effective combination. These were Wall Street's jealousy of Chestnut Street, the business man's dislike of the federal Bank's restraint upon bank credit, the politician's resentment at the Bank's interference with states' rights, popular identification of the Bank with the aristocracy of business, and the direction of agrarian antipathy away from banks in general to the federal Bank in particular. Destruction of the Bank ended federal regulation of bank credit and shifted the money center of the country from Chestnut Street to Wall Street. It left the poor agrarian as poor as he had been before and it left the money power possessed of more and more power than ever.

By the term "Jacksonian" I mean not merely the President's Democratic supporters, whom he still called Republican, but in particular his closest advisers and sharers in responsibility. These included most of his "Kitchen Cabinet," some of his official Cabinet, and a number of others. Those most responsible for the destruction of the Bank, without whose urgency and help it might not have been undertaken or achieved, were all either business men or closely concerned with the business world. Named in the approximate order of their appearance, they were Duff Green, Samuel Ingham, Isaac Hill, Martin Van Buren, Amos Kendall, Francis Preston Blair, Churchill C. Cambreleng, Roger B. Taney, and David Henshaw—all but Taney being or becoming men of wealth. They did not include Major William B. Lewis, a Tennessee planter, one of the General's oldest friends and the only one of his intimates not openly hostile to the Bank. Others of importance were Thomas Hart Benton, James K. Polk, Levi Woodbury, Benjamin F. Butler, Jacob Barker, Reuben M. Whitney, William Gouge, and James A. Hamilton.

* * *

With the business interests and objectives of the Jacksonians I have no quarrel save for the cant which made the conflict over the Bank of the United States appear to be one of idealism against lucre and of human rights against property rights. The Jacksonians were no less drawn by lucre than the so-called conservatives, but rather more. They had no greater concern for human rights than the people who had what they were trying to get. The millionaires created by the so-called Jacksonian revolution of "agrarians" against "capitalists"—of the democracy against the money-power—were richer than those they dispossessed, they were more numerous, they were quite as ruthless; and *laisser faire*, after destroying the monopolies and vested rights the Jacksonians decried, produced far greater ones. There was nothing sacred about the federal Bank. The defense of it is simply that it was very useful and if not perfect it could have been improved, had its enemies felt any interest in improving it. The Jacksonians paid no heed to its merits but canted virtuously about the rich and the poor, hydras, and other irrelevancies. This was good politics. But it cannot conceal the envy and acquisitiveness that were their real motives. What the Jacksonians decided on, they directed their propaganda toward, and got. What they went for, they fetched, like

Amos Kendall. An unusual number of them were not only business men but journalists, and gained both profit and influence through the press—notably Duff Green, Amos Kendall, Francis Preston Blair, Isaac Hill, and David Henshaw. They told the world it was governed too much. They vied with their great contemporary James Gordon Bennett in a glib and vigorous style. The Washington *Globe*, the organ of the administration, was attractively printed on good paper, every active Jacksonian had to take it, and, its contents aside, even the best people could feel satisfied to have it lying on the parlor table. It relied otherwise on unashamed, repetitious adulation of Andrew Jackson and defamation of his enemies. It presented matters in black and white, Bank and President, hydra and hero. "Many a time," Amos Kendall is made to say in John Pendleton Kennedy's satire, *Quod-libet*, "have I riveted by diligent hammering, a politic and necessary fabrication upon the credulity of the people—so fast that no art of my adversary could tear it away to make room for the truth. Therefore, I say to you and our democratic friends—hammer without ceasing."

Andrew Jackson himself had been lawyer, legislator, jurist, merchant, and land speculator, but principally planter and soldier. His origin was humble and agrarian. He was a self-made man. He belonged to an aristocracy of a frontier sort peculiar to the Southwest of his day—landed, proud, individualistic, slave-owning, and more bound by the cruder conventions than the politer ones. Cock-fighting, betting, horse-racing, and the punctilio of the duel seem to have satisfied its cultural needs. It was without the education and discipline of the older aristocracies of the sea-board. It possessed more of the aristocrat's assertive and obnoxious vices than his gentler, liberal virtues and stood on property and pretension rather than birth and breeding. In a quarrel General Jackson would resort to the field of honor if his enemy were a "gentleman" but merely beat him with a stick on sight if he were not. Such distinctions seem to have been lost on Albert Gallatin, an aristocrat of a different water, in whose fastidious judgment President Jackson was "a pugnacious animal."

Yet the distinction and courtesy of the General's manners took by surprise those who knew him first as President; he was by then unwell, grieving over the death of his wife, and softened besides by what age will sometimes do to men. He was not now the brawler in taverns and at racetracks. "I was agreeably disappointed and pleased," wrote William Lyon Mackenzie of Upper Canada in 1829—a man of considerable violence himself in word and deed—"to find in General Jackson great gentleness and benevolence of manner, accompanied by that good natured affability of address which will enable persons who wait upon him to feel at ease in his presence. . . ." When he chose, however, the General still could storm outrageously enough. He could simulate bursts of passion that terrified strangers, who shrank from having the President of the United States burst a blood vessel on their account, even though they were not fond of him. But his tongue seldom slipped. No one profited from blunders of his. What mistakes he made arose from a child-like trust in his friends and not from carelessness with his adversaries.

He was exceptionally susceptible to the flattery and suggestion of his friends. This did not impair his maintaining a forceful, determined leadership. He listened to his advisers individually and chose his plan of action himself. His native views were agrarian and Jeffersonian, though of Jefferson himself he could entertain very low opinions, and no one—not Alexander Hamilton himself—ever went further from the constitutional principles of Jefferson than Jackson did in his nullification proclamation of December 1832. With him, moreover, as with other self-made men of his time, agrarian and Jeffersonian views faded into *laisser faire*. He was a rugged individualist in all directions. He was no friend to the shiftless and indigent who got into debt and then could not get out. He paid his own debts, no matter how hard he found it to do so, and he expected others to pay theirs.

"Andrew Jackson was on the side of the capitalists," writes Mr Marquis James of his earlier career. "His first case in Nashville in 1788 had landed him as champion of the creditors against the debtors. Jackson desired wealth." He had been opposed to western relief measures taken on behalf of debtors in the ten years preceding his election to the Presidency. They were wicked, pernicious, profligate, and unconstitutional. Opinions like this put him logically on the side of the Bank of the United States, which was the pivotal creditor, and opposed him to the banks made of paper, such as the Bank of the Commonwealth of Kentucky, over which his kitchen adviser, Francis Preston Blair, had presided. But solecisms embarrassed the General very little. On the frontier more than elsewhere, the modification of an agrarian economy into an industrial and financial one was such, in William Lyon Mackenzie's words, as to "make speculation as extensive as life, and transform a Jeffersonian democracy into a nation of gamesters and our land into one great gaming house where all are forced to play, while but few can understand the game." General Jackson's prejudices were stronger than his convictions, and he was himself among the least consistent and stable of the Jacksonians. "Not only was Jackson not a consistent politician," says Professor Thomas P. Abernethy,

he was not even a real leader of democracy. He had no part whatever in the promotion of the liberal movement which was progressing in his own state. . . . He was a self-made man . . . he always believed in making the public serve the ends of the politician. Democracy was good talk with which to win the favor of the people and thereby accomplish ulterior objectives. Jackson never really championed the cause of the people; he only invited them to champion his. He was not consciously hypocritical in this. It was merely the usual way of doing business in these primitive and ingenuous times.

Of his election to the Presidency Professor Richard Hofstadter writes that it was not "a mandate for economic reform; no financial changes, no crusades against the national Bank, were promised. . . . Up to the time of his inauguration Jackson had contributed neither a thought nor a deed to the democratic movement, and he was elected without a platform."

What counts is that Jackson was popular. He was a picturesque folk character, and it does his memory an injustice to make him out a statesman. "All the remodelling and recoloring of Andrew Jackson," says Professor Abernethy, "has not created a character half so fascinating as he was in reality." To the dissatisfied, whether through distress or ambition, Andrew Jackson offered a distinct and attractive change from the old school of leaders the country had had—and not the least by his want of real ideas. He became the champion of the common man, even though the latter might be no longer either frontiersman or farmer but speculator, capitalist, or entrepreneur of a new, democratic sort, who in every village and township was beginning to profit by the Industrial Revolution, the growth of population, and the expanding supply of bank credit. This new common man was manufacturer, banker, builder, carrier, and promoter. He belonged to the "active and enterprising," in the luminous contrast put by Churchill C. Cambreleng, as against the "wealthier classes." And his conflict was not the traditionary one between the static rich and the static poor but a dynamic, revolutionary one between those who were already rich and those who sought to become rich.

General Jackson was an excellent leader in the revolt of enterprise against the regulation of credit by the federal Bank. Though the inferior of his associates in knowledge, he was extraordinarily effective in combat. And as a popular leader he combined the simple agrarian principles of political economy absorbed at his mother's knee with the most up-to-date doctrine of *laisser faire*. Along with several of the best constitutional authorities of his day—but not Mr Taney—General Jackson believed that the notes issued by state banks were unconstitutional. In 1820 he wrote to his friend Major Lewis: "You know my opinion as to the banks, that is, that the constitution of our state as well as the Constitution of the United States prohibited the establishment of banks in any state. Sir, the tenth section of the first article of the federal Constitution is positive and explicit, and when you read the debates in the convention you will find it was introduced to prevent a state legislature from passing such bills." Seventeen years later, in 1837, he wrote to Senator Benton: "My position now is and has ever been since I have been able to form an opinion on this subject that Congress has no power to charter a Bank and that the states are prohibited from issuing bills of credit or granting a charter by which such bills can be issued by any corporation or order." Yet in effect he did as much as could be done to augment the issue of state bank notes and was proud of what he did. Most statesmen would feel some embarrassment in such a performance.

The Jacksonians were anything but rash. Once decided that they should fight the Bank rather than wed with it, they developed their attack patiently, experimentally, shrewdly, probing the aristocratic victim and teasing public interest into action. The President himself took no unnecessary chances, but those he had to take he took without fear. He was a man of "sagacious temerity," in the words of one of his contemporaries. His attack on the Bank was like his careful slaying of Charles Dickinson in a duel thirty years before. His opponent had been formidable—much younger than he and an expert marksman, which he himself was not. Each was to have one shot. Jackson and his second had gone over the prospects carefully and decided it would be best to wait for Dickinson to fire first. For though Jackson would probably be hit, "he counted on the resource of his will to sustain him until he could aim deliberately and shoot to kill, if it were the last act of his life." So he awaited his adversary's fire and, as he had expected, he was hit. But his coat, buttoned loosely over his breast, as was his wont, had presented a deceptive silhouette, and the ball had missed his heart. He concealed his hurt and concentrated on his helpless enemy, whose life he now could take. "He stood glowering at him for an instant, and then his long pistol arm came slowly to a horizontal position." He aimed carefully and pulled the trigger. But the hammer stopped at half-cock. The seconds consulted while the principals stood, and Jackson was allowed to try again. Once more he took deliberate aim, his victim waiting in evident horror, and fired. Dickinson fell, mortally hurt. "I should have hit him," Jackson asserted later, "if he had shot me through the brain." The same mystical will power, the same canny and studious appraisal of probabilities and of relative advantages and disadvantages, weighed in the conflict with the Bank. The President tantalized the frank and impatient Mr Biddle, he waited for him to make the appropriate mistakes, and then with care and effectiveness he struck. His adversaries' weaknesses were no less at his command than his own skill. . . .

Despite the fact of a strong and determined rebellion within the business world against the Bank of the United States, the fiction that the attack on the Bank was on behalf of agrarians against capitalists, of humanity against property, of the poor against the rich, and of "the people" against "the money power," has persisted. There was, to be sure, an extremely respectable minority comprising the more conservative and thoughtful men of business, Mr Gallatin, for example, and Nathan Appleton, who defended the Bank till near the end, but it will scarcely do to say that they represented the business world while C. C. Cambreleng, David Henshaw, and Reuben Whitney did not.

It is obvious that New York, besides gaining most from a successful attack on the Bank, risked the least; for it did not need, as the South and West did, the capital brought in by the Bank's branches. The West's aversion for the federal Bank was like the nationalistic resentment in a 20th-century under-developed economy which wants and needs imported capital but growls at the "imperialism" of the country that is expected to provide it. The western enemies of the Bank were moved by complex psychological and political considerations—including past distress and present dependence— while its New York enemies were moved, much more simply, by covetousness and rivalry. This was the decisive new ingredient provided in the Jacksonian attack. The agrarian prejudice had been alive since 1791 and most dangerous to the Bank a few years past during its critical days and the distress in the Ohio valley. The state bank opposition was almost as old as the agrarian. And the relative importance of the two varied with the decline of agrarianism and the growth of enterprise. New York, now the center of enterprise, added to the long-lived antagonism a hearty and acute self-interest. That Andrew Jackson proved to be the instrument of her interest was the happy result of Mr Van Buren's skill and devotion.

It goes without saying that Andrew Jackson himself did not understand what was happening. He had started with a vague, agrarian prejudice against banking which on occasion cropped up throughout his life but never led him to deny himself the service of banks or the friendship and support of bankers.* It was no great task for his advisers to arouse this dormant distrust, nourished on what he had read about the South Sea Bubble, and focus it upon the Bank in Philadelphia, a city whence he had suffered years before, at the hands of a bankrupt merchant and speculator, a harsh financial misfortune. Nor was an elaborate plot required to be agreed upon among conspirators. The first harassment of the Bank from the administration group was evidently spontaneous and simply aimed at making the Bank Jacksonian. Some time elapsed before it got under directed control. Even then there is no reason to suppose that the program was not mainly opportunistic. In the early stages the object need have been only to make sure that the charter be not renewed. To this end the General's mind must be fixed against the Bank, and the proper improvement of opportunities could be left to the discretion of those in whose path the opportunities appeared. The adviser who influenced the General most directly or who perhaps left the best record of what he did was Roger B. Taney, though he joined the Jacksonian circle late. He succeeded in filling the General's mind with a vindictiveness that Martin Van Buren or Amos Kendall would probably not have produced. They too would have killed the Bank but with less emotion and less cant. "When a great monied institution," Mr Taney told the General, "attempts to overawe the President in the discharge of his high constitutional duties, it is conclusive evidence that it is conscious of possessing vast political power which it supposes the President can be made to feel." The Taney reasoning

---

* He did not cease transacting personal and family business with the Nashville office of the Bank of the United States, which he presumably dissociated from the main office in Philadelphia. The view was reasonable. Gravitation of the branches toward independence was a perennial source of weakness to the Bank; and eventually they became local banks in fact.

is sound, but the premises are misrepresented, and the effect was to fill the President with bitter suspicion of the Bank; though the alleged "attempts to overawe the President"—this was written in June 1832—were the reasonable attempts of Mr Biddle to gain support for the Bank, find out what the scowls and rumblings from Washington signified, and remove the doubts that he thought were troubling the President.

But thanks to the sort of thing Mr Taney kept telling him, the President by now had few doubts such as Mr Biddle imagined. He was merely considering how best to proceed against the Bank. Replacement, he realized, was necessary, and for a long time he was fumbling over unintelligible projects to that end. One of these projects, which may be intelligible to those whose understanding has not been corrupted by some knowledge and experience of the subject, was described to James A. Hamilton, 3 June 1830. The President had in mind "a national bank chartered upon the principles of the checks and balances of our federal government, with a branch in each state, the capital apportioned agreeably to representation and to be attached to and be made subject to supervision of the Secretary of the Treasury." He recalls having shown Mr Hamilton

my ideas on a bank project, both of deposit (which I think the only national bank that the government ought to be connected with) and one of discount and deposit, which from the success of the State Bank of South Carolina I have no doubt could be wielded profitably to our government with less demoralizing effects upon our citizens than the Bank that now exists. But a national Bank, entirely national Bank of deposit is all we ought to have: but I repeat a national Bank of discount and deposit may be established upon our revenue and national faith pledged and carried on by salaried officers, as our revenue is now collected, with less injury to the morals of our citizens and to the destruction of our liberty than the present hydra of corruption and all the emoluments accrue to the nation as part of the revenue.

But these ruminations belonged merely to a period of waiting. As soon as a promising arrangement offered, the President acted. He ordered the federal funds removed from the Bank and put in the banks of his friends.

Besides contributing mainly, by this course, to a shift of the money market from Chestnut Street to Wall Street, the General contributed to the inflation, the speculation, and the various monetary evils which, with a persistent agrarian bias, he blamed on banks and paper money. There were plenty of men in his own party, among them better agrarians than himself, who would have cleared his vision and tried to, but the old gentleman preferred the sycophantic advisers who stimulated his suspicions and prejudices, blinded him to facts, confused him about the nature of the federal Bank's usefulness, diverted his attention from the possibility that it be amended and corrected instead of being destroyed, and allowed him to declaim the most ignorant but popular clap-trap.

Edward Pessen

Consensus and Ideology in the Age of Jackson

Those who find striking contrasts in the beliefs and actions of the major parties tend to believe the Whigs and Democrats appealed to unlike .constituencies. In this view, Democrats were led by plebeians, Whigs by aristocrats. The Democratic rank and file, whether in city or countryside, were allegedly much poorer than their Whig counterparts. Whiggery flourished where soils were superior. In the South it was most popular in the black belt, where plantations prevailed or where slaveownership was greatest. The religious diversity of the party memberships was also believed to reflect the social gulf dividing them. Denominations of high prestige thus aligned themselves with the party of Clay while their social inferiors chose Jacksonian Democracy. And where poor or ordinary folk voted Whig, as millions of them obviously did, a traditional interpretation explained the phenomenon in terms of an "economic dependency" that drew the lower orders to support their overlords.

According to the popular interpretation of American history that stresses the twin themes of continuity and struggle, the Jackson party took up where the Jeffersonians had left off in the never ending fight of the people against the privileged few. The Democratic party of Franklin Roosevelt's time would later fight the same good fight that had been waged a century earlier by the partisans of Old Hickory. The enemies of the people—whether Federalists, Whigs, or Liberty League—were also judged to be spiritually akin. Certainly Jacksonian campaigners regularly referred to their opponents, whether Whig, Antimason, or other, as "Federalists." There is no doubt the charge was an effective one, what with the deteriorating reputation of Wash-

Excerpts from Edward Pessen, Jacksonian America: Society, Personality, and Politics (Homewood, Ill.: The Dorsey Press, 1969). © 1969 by The Dorsey Press.

ington's and Hamilton's old party after the War of 1812. What the student of history wishes to know is whether the charge was accurate. . . . The old question still stands: were the memberships of the major parties dissimilar in their social and economic backgrounds?

It is very difficult to discern any significant differences in the social composition of Democratic and Whig party leaders. Of course the situation varied from state to state. The men at the helm of the Jacksonian party in Massachusetts, for example, were outsiders, politically, and of lower status than their opposite numbers in the other party, socially, in part because the wealth of Democratic leaders was in some cases only recently come by. Yet there were Bay State Whig leaders who were also *nouveau.* The "Conscience Whigs," who emerged with the heating up of the slavery issue and who became Free Soilers after the Mexican War, were for the most part of older family and higher social status than their more expedient Whig fellows. In that state the inveterately successful Whigs reigned as the party not only of old wealth but of practically every other social stratum as well. The slight but significant differences in the social tone of major party leadership there were due essentially to the domination of state politics by one party. Whether *parvenus* or not, David Henshaw and his circle,—typically bankers or members of the boards of directors of railroads and other businesses—were not poor men.

The top and "middle grade" leadership of New York State's Democratic party were not commonfolk. Rather they were men of wealth and high status, the social and economic equal of their Whig opposite numbers. New York City's Jacksonian leaders characteristically stressed their alleged plebeian backgrounds. In fact, many of them were either wealthy businessmen, merchants, and bankers, or prominent lawyers and doctors, members all of the city's "privileged aristocracy." In the other middle states the Democratic leadership was similarly in the hands of men of unusual wealth and prominence in business affairs.

In Michigan's strategic Wayne County, leaders of the two major parties, whether of the top, middle, or intermediate grades were essentially alike in their social and economic backgrounds. Lawyers and businessmen were to be found in roughly equal numbers in the Democratic and Whig top echelons. That they evidently mingled socially without regard to party suggests something of their view of the "great" party battles in their community. Differences there were in the elites of the parties but they had to do with religion, ethnic origins, the geographical backgrounds of the native-born and how long they had lived in their Michigan residences, not with wealth or occupation. In contrast to Kentucky, Democratic leaders were less foot-loose than their Whig counterparts. In common with other states, Michigan Whig leaders were more likely to be New Englanders and of that section's predominant Protestant denominations, less likely to be foreigners or Catholics than the Democrats. In contrast to Alabama, youth was no more a characteristic of the leadership of the one party than of the other.

The socioeconomic status of Jacksonian and Whig leaders has been most fully investigated for the southern states. Of course scholars of different persuasion will either interpret the same evidence differently or focus on different facts. Thus one study notes that Whig members of the Tennessee lower house were more than twice as likely as Democrats to be lawyers. A more recent examination of Tennessee's Congressmen finds that for all their ideological differences, the men of both parties were of roughly equal wealth and professional attainment. Despite the inevitable differences in viewpoint of the men engaged in the modern research, its most amazing feature is the essential similarity it discloses in the occupations, wealth and status of Whig and Jacksonian leaders. In Louisiana, "leaders in both parties were seemingly equal in wealth and education." North Carolina's Jacksonian leaders by the early 1830's were substantial eastern elements, rather than the frontiersmen and westerners who earlier had been influential. Mississippi's Democratic activists were for the most part successful men of affairs.

Florida's party leaders have been examined closely. The Democracy's chieftains may perhaps have owned less land and fewer slaves than their Whig colleagues. Yet the "nucleus," which constituted the original Jacksonian coalition of the early 1830's, was composed of speculators, planters, bankers, and professionals. True, many of these men later deserted the Jacksonian party for the Whigs. But the residue were not poor men. The Democratic party of 1838 to 1845 was made up of farmers and planters, large and small, with merchants, rural capitalists, and village entrepreneurs having "considerable weight" in its affairs. As in Massachusetts, newer and smaller merchants were more likely than the well-established ones to be Democrats. Yet 150 Democratic leaders in Florida, when subjected to a detailed analysis, proved to be unusually wealthy men. There were "a disproportionate number of them lawyers, relatively few yeoman farmers—fourteen percent— in contrast to planters who made up close to forty percent of the group, while merchants and manufacturers constituted twenty-five percent." For all the Whig demagogy and Democratic counter-demagogy about Jacksonian leveling and affinity for the poor, the "Democratic movement in Florida was certainly no lower-class manifestation of radicalism."

An exhaustive study of the socioeconomic and family backgrounds of the more than 1,000 Alabama Congressmen and State legislators for the period 1835 to 1856 found no important differences between Democrats and Whigs. A larger percentage of Democrats had gone to college; 47.6 percent of Democrats were planters in contrast to 34.5 percent of the Whigs. Slightly more than half of the representatives of each party were lawyers. The percentage of businessmen was about equal. A "slightly higher percentage of Whigs than Democrats" were professional men. As for religion, Methodists and Baptists abounded: there were "few Episcopalians in either party." A subsequent study of several hundred Whig and Democratic local activists in Alabama found a remarkable similarity in their situations. Occupations and religious denominations were alike while they owned equal amounts of real estate and were "strikingly similar in their pattern of slaveownership."

There is little doubt that the Whig Party in the South became increasingly preoccupied with banking and business issues or that its leadership included many wealthy merchants, bankers, and professional men. As the historians of an earlier day suggested, it was also a party dominated by the planter and slaveholder, in the language of one memorable characterization, "the broad cloth and silk stocking party." A stunning word picture of a later time depicted the typical Whig leader as the man in a silk hat nearby a Negro on a cotton bale. But the painstaking modern studies of Alabama and other southern states indicate that broadcloth and silk stockings were the badge not only of Whig party leadership; "the man in a silk hat nearby a Negro on a cotton bale was by no means necessarily a Whig."

In Missouri, too, the Jackson party leadership contained more slaveholders as well as the men who owned the largest numbers of slaves. Practically no Whigs owned more than 20 slaves. While Democratic leaders were wealthier and of higher status than the average Missourian, the leaders of the Whig party of that state were typically richer, more likely to be lawyers, slightly more likely to be businessmen, and while less likely to be farmers, more likely to claim large farms than the Jacksonians. Among the top leaders of the party, more than twice as many Whigs on the average had attended college—although the rate of college attendance among the Democracy's prominent figures was between 500 and 1,000 times the national average. In the city of St. Louis both parties typically put up extremely wealthy men for Mayor and middle-class persons for the Council, although Democrats did on occasion also nominate artisans to that body. On the level of "vigilance committees" or poll watchers, essentially similar patterns prevailed, although when tavern keepers and brewers are ranked as "businessmen," there is little to choose between the party faithful. The Democracy's local activists included 21 tavern keepers or brewers while the Whigs had none. Differences there were in the social and economic positions of Missouri's party leadership, but as John Vollmer Mering has observed, they were hardly those separating an "aristocracy" from a "proletariat." . . .

There seems to be a widespread assumption that a party supported overwhelmingly by the poor or by whatever class, is the party of the poor or of the class that does support it. If this is taken to mean—as I think it often is—that a so-called party of the poor either truly serves them or that it deserves their support, then I think it is a false notion. It does not take into account the power of demagogy or the gullibility of voters. To cite a drastic example, the fact that Hitler's party may have been supported by the German workers would hardly make the Nazis the party of the poor. American history, fortunately not yielding examples so dramatic as German, also affords illustrations of the point. McKinley's party would not be the party of the poor no matter how well it might do in working class electoral districts. The determination that the Democrats were the party of this or that group must finally be made not on the basis of statistics or the degree of electoral support the Democracy got from the group in question, but according to an evaluation of the party's behavior. . . .

The complicated New York evidence revealed "that farmers, mechanics, and 'working classes' did not form the mainstay of the Democratic party." The Jacksonians' main support came not from "low-status socioeconomic groups," but rather from "relatively high-status socioeconomic groups in the eastern counties, and relatively low-status ethnocultural and religious groups in all sections of New York." Among natives, Jacksonians won small but significant majorities from "Old British," "Old German," "Dutch" and "Penn-Jerseyite" voters, and overwhelming majorities from "Catholic Irish," "French Canadian," "French" and "New German" immigrant groups. In the Empire State the Democracy attracted gamblers, bohemians, the free thinking, the free swearing. In showing that equally prosperous communities voted differently; that economically unlike communities produced strikingly similar party percentages; and the durability of party affiliations through all manner of changing economic circumstances that overtook given communities; Benson makes a shambles of the old simplistic notion that "voters vote by class."

Other detailed studies of voting in North Carolina and New York, counties in Pennsylvania and Tennessee, and of townships in New Jersey, have also demonstrated that the relative wealth or poverty of citizens seemed to have nothing to do with their party preferences. Poorer voters divided their votes among the two major parties in almost exactly the same proportions as their wealthier neighbors. Certain counties unbelievably registered exactly the same division of votes for the parties over the course of several elections, through thick and thin, despite socioeconomic changes in their electorates.

Not that the modern findings point only in one direction. In Georgia, Whig strength did appear to be greatest "where cotton growing and attendant activities were dominant interests" and in "those counties where investment in primary types of manufacturing and commercial ventures supplemented cotton growing." But as in Alabama the response in such communities came from men of all classes. An economic interpretation failed to account for the political sympathies of the many Georgians who simply admired the good sense of Whig appeals. Maryland politics may have been unideological but Jacksonian electoral support at first came from the old Republican—if not necessarily poor—districts of Baltimore and the western counties. Even T. P. Abernethy, as sharp a critic of the progressive interpretation of Jacksonian Democracy as any historian of the 20th century, conceded that in the Tennessee gubernatorial election of 1839, the "focal points of Whig strength . . . tended to radiate along the lines of communication." The Whig constituency in Florida lived in the "rich, earlier-settled, plantation areas" of middle Florida, while Democrats were in the "new, frontier, small farmer region of East and South Florida." The commercial centers, however, leaned toward the Democracy.

Less than one fifth of Missouri's 108 counties consistently voted Whig in presidential elections between 1836 and 1852. The Whigs of Thomas

Hart Benton's state were inveterate losers who as often as not chose not to run candidates. If one can therefore speak of characteristic Whig counties in such a state, he would note that they were relatively old or long-established, touched the Missouri or Mississippi river, contained unusually large farms, and were the more populous counties. (Of course many Democratic counties, in a state controlled by the Jacksonians, had similar traits.) That the Whig vote was high where slaveholding was great, does not substantiate the old Phillips-Cole thesis: John Mering, the modern historian of the Missouri party, cautions that "slavery and the interests it generated do not explain a Missouri county's Whiggery."

This tendency of relatively well-established, commercially active, "go ahead" communities to vote against Jackson has also been found to have been true in New Hampshire, at least in the presidential election of 1832. A "typical" Clay town in that state was old, prosperous, populous, connected to the outside world by many roads, near the ocean, possessed of a lively newspaper, great buildings, and a couple of Congregationalist churches. Jackson towns—and one had recently changed its name from Adams to Jackson! —were isolated, poor, "out of the mainstream" of New Hampshire life, sparsely populated, and had no church or perhaps one church, the Free Will Baptist. Small upland villages on poor soil worked by small farmers, with the exception of one district of 16 towns whose Clay vote has recently been interpreted as due to its relative prosperity and its proximity to the world outside and to areas of former Federalist influence, voted overwhelmingly for Old Hickory. The correlation between religious denomination and voting appears to have been greater than any other. For in addition to the "exceptional" Clay upland towns running from Sullivan to Amherst, the next to the poorest town in the state voted for Clay, while the second wealthiest went for Jackson by two to one. But the latter were exceptions to the New Hampshire pattern. For that matter any anti-Democratic voting seems to have been exceptional in a state whose "Concord Regency," led by the redoubtable Isaac Hill and Levi Woodbury, "had been electing Democratic Governors and Congressmen by wide margins since 1829."

Michigan voting late in the Jackson era, certainly in the towns and villages of Wayne County, sharply contradicts the older version of the nature of the major party electorates. Middle and lower-class persons who made up the great bulk of the electorate divided their votes, without reference to class, more or less equally among Democrats and Whigs. That towns were populated either by "rural lower classes" or by large proportions of "prosperous, middle-class farmers" was no clue to their political preferences. As in Lee Benson's New York, towns with similar social patterns differed sharply in their voting behavior while towns whose social elements were markedly unlike nevertheless exhibited similar voting patterns. No discernible correlations existed between economic status and party choice. The most striking correlations rather were to be found between ethnic identity and party, style of life and party, and above all between religion and party. Yankees, for example, tended only slightly to be Whigs, but Yankee Presbyterians, decisively. Evangelical sects were overwhelmingly Whig; Catholics, whether Irish or French, were Democrats. The ethnic patterns were also similar to New York State's, as were the relationships between life style and voting. Hedonists were Jacksonian; the God fearing, Whig.

In Kentucky, at least in 1828, Jackson seemed to do unusually well in "counties with high rates of population growth," and with men who had been active in the old Relief movement—albeit the latter movement was led by many well-to-do men who became repudiationists out of temporary need rather than compassion for poor debtors. In Virginia in 1828 both the Tidewater and Piedmont, "strongholds of conservative views," went heavily for Jackson. In North Carolina the Democratic party's social and geographical bases did not conform to the traditional ideas about them. Democratic strength in that state was not on the frontier but in "the North-Central counties and in the East." Democratic majorities were large in districts where slavery was most prominent. In a word, voting patterns were varied, sometimes contradictory, and give little support to the theory that clear-cut class lines divided Whig from Jacksonian voters. . . .

The closest thing to a classic ideological party in the entire antebellum period, the Working Men burst forth like a political meteor only to fall to earth in the space of a few years. Following the creation of the Philadelphia Working Men's party in 1828, groups sprang up all over the country. The modern discussion, focusing as it does on a few major cities, has perhaps obscured what Helen Sumner, one of the pioneer labor researchers working with John R. Commons, long ago discovered: the ubiquitousness of the movement. In fact recent investigations show it to have been even more widespread than Miss Sumner imagined. Operating under a variety of names, "Working Men's Parties," "Working Men's Republican Associations," "People's Parties," "Working Men's Societies," "Farmers' and Mechanics' Societies," "Mechanics and Other Working Men," and just plain "Working Men" appeared in most of the states of the Union. They took shape in such communities as Carlisle, Pennsylvania; Glens Falls, New York; Caldwell, New Jersey; Zanesville, Ohio; Dedham, Massachusetts; Lyme, Connecticut; and Calais, Vermont; as well as in such centers as New York City, St. Louis, Boston, Newark, and Philadelphia.

Almost every one of these organizations had its own press. These journals, most unlike the Regency's Albany *Argus* or the Whig *Columbian Centinel* in Boston, contained, in addition to accounts of Working Men's activities in their own and other cities and the usual advertisements and literary excerpts that then characterized journalism, "a spectrum of reform, from Pestallozzian educational ideas and cooperative store suggestions to the views of freethinkers and reprints from [English socialist] works." Typically edited by leaders of the new party, they provide the fullest contemporary account of what the Working Men's movement was about.

Many questions have been raised about the Working Men's party, the most important having to do with its authenticity. "Decayed Federal dandies!" not true workingmen, charged a New England journal, while at other times proto-Whig editors bitterly stamped the new organizations a mere front for the Democracy. The evidence is complicated, often contradictory, and suggests the wisdom of careful examination of the facts relating to each group before coming to conclusions as to whether they truly represented artisans and mechanics. According to Miss Sumner the issue that separated legitimate Working Men from fraudulent was the protective tariff. In some cases, she wrote, "advocates of a protective tariff assumed without warrant the popular name—'mechanics and working men.'" She suspected that these "associations of so-called workingmen which favored protection generally avoided committing themselves to the usual demands of the Working Men's party." But let the organization be silent on protection and approve the "usual demands" and her study accepted its *bona fides*. Modern scholars have been more skeptical and with good reason. For as one of them wrote, after noting the great wealth of the Philadelphia Working Men's candidates for office, "to believe that [such] a party . . . was really devoted to solving working class problems in the interests of the workers would seem to lay a heavy tax on credulity." And yet the record is clear: the Philadelphia Working Men's Party was no misnomer.

The party arose out of a decision by the city's Mechanics' Union of Trade Associations to enter into politics, in order to promote "the interests and enlightenment of the working classes." There can be no question of the authenticity of this latter group, "the first union of all the organized workmen of any city." Consisting of individual unions—or societies as they were then called—of journeymen bricklayers, painters, glaziers, typographers, house carpenters, and other craftsmen, its main purpose was to provide financial support to journeymen striking against their masters. An amendment to this Mechanics' Union's constitution, in 1828, provided that three months prior to the forthcoming elections, the membership should "nominate as candidates for public office such individuals as shall pledge themselves . . . to support and advance . . . the interests and enlightenment of the working classes." Shortly thereafter the *Mechanic's Free Press*, edited by a young Ricardian socialist, William Heighton, reported that "at a very large and respectable meeting of Journeymen House Carpenters held on Tuesday evening, July 1st . . . the Mechanics' Union of Trade Associations is entering into measures for procuring a nomination of candidates for legislative and other public offices, who will support the interest of the working classes." Thus was born the Philadelphia Working Men's party, in the promise made by journeymen workers to support at the polls individuals sympathetic to— not necessarily members of—the working class.

New York City's Working Men made their appearance in 1829 when their candidates for the State Assembly made a remarkable showing. Some contemporaries and later scholars alike explained this new party as nothing more than anti-Tammany dissidents, born out of "the bitter internal dissensions and schisms that were wrecking the Republican party of New York." The fact remains that the decision to run candidates on a separate Working Men's ticket was made at a meeting of mechanics on October 19, 1829, in agreement with the proposal by the executive body—the "Committee of Fifty." A number of journeymen's meetings held in April had created this Committee. Its purpose was to combat "all attempts to compel journeymen mechanics to work more than ten hours a day." It would seem that at least in its origins the New York Working Men's party was indubitably a response of workers to a threatened attack on their working conditions.

For Boston the evidence is not clear, for all the press unhappiness with the new party or the impressionistic recording by a journalist present at early meetings of the Working Men's party in the summer of 1830. He wrote that they were attended by large numbers of men who, "from appearance, were warm from their workshops and from other places of daily toil, but who bore on their countenances convictions of their wrongs, and a determination to use every proper means to have them redressed." Two years later New England workingmen and their friends formed the New England Association of Farmers, Mechanics, and Other Working Men, described as a "new type of labor organization, in part economic and in part political." This interesting organization was preoccupied with trying to achieve for New England's workers what remained a will-o'-the-wisp for most of the era—the 10 hour day. Its failures do not detract from its authenticity.

Logic as well as the historical record suggest the essential validity and independence from other political groupings of the Working Men's party— at least at its birth. The new party was a form of rejection by its members of both the Jacksonians and their major opponents. The Working Men stood for programs and called for changes in American society not dreamed of by the pragmatists at the helm of the major parties. And in view of the relatively small followings of the new organizations for all their idealism— or was it because of it?—it strains credulity to attribute to shrewd Jacksonian manipulators the formation of ostensibly single-class political organizations that exasperated both the business community and those many Americans of whatever class who under no circumstances wished to think of themselves as workers. . . .

The parties' real leaders are best studied not for their social and economic backgrounds, which were in fact diverse, but for their ideas and personal force, which actually accounted for their leadership. Unlike their contemporaries in the major parties these men were indeed radicals, certainly for this phase of their careers. There was nothing politic in adhering to essentially socialistic doctrines that most of the press savagely excoriated. Beliefs such as theirs, going beyond the patent demagogy of the day, could find no expression in the programs of the era's major parties. As to the party's rank and file constituency, apart from the sparkling successes achieved in Philadelphia and New York in 1829, it does not seem ever to have been very great. On the other hand, particularly in the latter city but in Boston, too, what electoral support it got did come primarily from poorer or working-class wards. In New York City its candidates got close to 50 percent of the vote of the five poorest wards while averaging only about 20 percent in the wealthier districts.

Their program was amazingly similar, with substantially the same measures advocated in most of the western and southern cities, as well as in New Jersey, Delaware, and New England, as were advocated in Philadelphia and New York. The original Philadelphia demands became the nucleus of the Working Men's program everywhere. They called above all for free, tax-supported school system of high quality to replace the stigmatized "pauper schools." Stephen Simpson, brilliant and unreliable one-time Jacksonian, was nominated to office by the Philadelphia Working Men and became a leading figure in the movement mainly because of his advanced educational ideas. In addition, the masthead of the *Mechanic's Free Press* urged abolition of imprisonment for debt; abolition of all licensed monopolies; an entire revision or abolition of the prevailing militia system; a less expensive legal system; equal taxation on property; no legislation on religion; and a district system of elections. The paper's columns also pressed vigorously for a mechanics' lien law to assure workers first claim to the employers' payroll, shorter hours, better working conditions, and constantly urged improved housing for workers. The major parties were regularly denounced as were city fathers who administered the city by a double standard, failing either to provide sufficient "hydrant water for the accommodation of the poor" or "to clean the streets in the remote sections of the city where the working-men reside." Political action was not considered at odds with economic, by the Working Men's leaders, for they strongly favored creation of unions. Nor does this exhaust the list even of the Philadelphia issues.

The movements in other cities added dozens of other grievances. The New York party went so far as to call for "equal property to all adults" in its early stages when the radical Thomas Skidmore was its leading figure. When he was cashiered out of the party at the end of its first year by the opportunists who had infiltrated it, with the acquiescence of the more innocent Robert Dale Owen and George Henry Evans, even the latter continued to insist, in the party's official organ, that it continued to stand for Skidmore's principles; it had only modified its tactics for achieving them. The Owen-Evans faction of the party stressed the need for a revamped educational system featured by "state guardianship" or the boarding out of working-class children in publicly-supported schools. Regional variations might call for a reform in land tenure laws or, as in the case of the New England Association, insistence on factory legislation. Abolition of capital punishment and prison reform were popular demands everywhere. In sum, Working Men's parties were champions of a great variety of political, social, economic, and educational reforms. That much of the program was not of a "bread and butter" character or that the victims of some grievances were not confined to the "laboring poor" are not valid grounds for skepticism. For it would be a most doctrinaire economic determinism indeed that insisted that authentic labor organizations confine their programs to economic issues. In that era when the diverse and youthful American labor movement was very much influenced by the radical English model, and when American work-men were as much concerned with enhanced status and educational oppor-tunity as with material gains, organizations speaking for labor quite naturally reflected this breadth of interest. Short-term, pitifully organized affairs for the most part, a major function of the new organizations was not to win elections so much as to call attention to the gamut of abuses bearing most heavily on the nation's working people.

The Working Men were essentially independent of the major parties although from time to time they cooperated with them. Certainly in choos-ing candidates they paid little attention to the previous political preferences of a nominee who was sound on an important Working Men's principle. At times, particularly during the Bank War, they cooperated closely with the Jacksonians. Stephen Simpson's refusal to issue a blanket condemnation of the "monster bank" infuriated many of his one-time admirers. The regular support given the Democracy by the Newark Working Men, their tendency, if not to hold joint nominating conventions, then to hold them on the same date and in the same town, and to approve closely similar lists of candidates, did not fail to draw the condemnation of the anti-Jacksonian press.

The New York City party broke into three pieces shortly after its 1829 success, the largest splinter supporting and subsequently being absorbed into the New York State Democratic party. New England's Working Men in 1833 threw their support in the gubernatorial campaign to Samuel Clesson Allen, champion of Andrew Jackson and enemy to Nicholas Biddle. Evidence of Working Men's collaboration with anti-Jacksonians however, as in Phila-delphia, is as easily come by. When the New England Association again nominated Allen in 1834 it condemned the candidates of both major parties. Working Men of most New Jersey towns and cities typically had as little to do with Democrats as with their opponents, while even in Newark the ro-mance was not a lasting one. It was punctuated finally by a falling out in 1836. Most of the Working Men's leaders even when cooperating with the Democrats on a particular issue, never ceased warning that the Jackson party was no different from the Clay, no more concerned with the real problems of working people.

Future studies of the Working Men's party are likely only to accentu-ate what previous work has disclosed: how hard it is to generalize about the movement as a whole. For as I have elsewhere noted, "there were Working Men and Working Men. The origin of some was obscure; of others, dubi-ous. Some arose out of economic struggles, others out of concern for status. Some came to be dominated by opportunists, other by zealots." The signifi-cant common feature of the movement as a whole was its authenticity—at least for part of its history. I regard it authentic because the parties seem to have been formed by workers and men devoted to their interests, and con-cerned themselves with the cause and welfare of workers, hoping to goad or influence the major parties into like concern. Of course the parties contained many men who by present standards would not qualify as workers. The definition of that day was less restrictive. George Henry Evans for example seemed to regard only "lawyers, bankers, and brokers as disqualified for membership." The equally radical William Heighton advised his Philadelphia party that "an employer [who] superintends his business" but "works with his own hands is a workingman." A movement in need of all the membership it could get would not permit a Skidmore to narrow down further its small chances for growth by establishing uncompromising standards for participation. The typical resolution of this problem was to ask few questions about the social position of any individual who in Heighton's words, was "willing to join us in obtaining our objects." But of course such an approach created additional problems.

In New York City, for example, by 1830 elements which not only were not themselves of the working class but which had little sympathy with its aspirations succeeded in taking over the party by the use of money, intrigue, and extralegal tactics that denied the floor to opposition, all the while paying lip service to the party program. There was nothing to prevent special pleaders from calling meetings designed to further their objects while masquerading under the banner of the new party. Much of the nation's press, Democratic and National Republican alike, nevertheless persisted in taking a dim view of a party whose own press constantly reminded its readers that this was a class society. "The very pretension to the necessity of such a party is a libel on the community," protested the editors of the Boston Courier. Shortly afterwards Edward Everett pressed home the point that rich and poor alike, all are workingmen. What need was there for a separate Working Men's party? Parties nevertheless insisted on forming, in the City of Brotherly Love obtaining the balance of power by their second electoral try, in New York winning better than 6,000 out of 21,000 votes cast in their initial effort. And yet their success was decidedly ephemeral.

Most of the Working Men's parties disappeared within five years of their birth. Among the many factors responsible for their downfall, newspaper denunciation, internal dissension in some cases introduced by infiltrators intent on taking over the party, doctrinal squabbles by party zealots, the hostility of the major parties, the increasing prosperity which, according to Miss Sumner, turned the attention of workers from "politics to trade unionism," the inexperience of their leadership, and not least the absorption of some of their program by the major parties, all played their part. Parties which sharply delineated the social and economic cleavages and disparities besetting American society on the one hand were offensive to those Americans used to more cheerful assessment, and on the other were inevitably attacked by men, newspapers, and political parties possessed of far more money, experience, and influence. And a political system which rewarded only winners of majorities or pluralities was not conducive to the perpetuation of such a movement.

Short-lived though they were the Working Men's parties were a significant phenomenon. They played an important part in the achievement of a number of the era's reforms. Particularly outstanding was their contribution to the movement for a democratic and public educational system. They agitated not only for broadened opportunities for the poor but for surprisingly sophisticated modifications in curriculum and teacher training. A final significance of the movement was its indirect testimony that even in the age of optimism, speculation, and major party demagogy, a significant number of Americans were disenchanted with their society and responsive to the voice of radical dissent. . . .

On the national level, particularly in 1844, and on the local and state levels throughout the era, a number of the third parties at times held the balance of political power. In view of the nearly equal followings of the great major parties, a minor party whose own voting support was minuscule could nevertheless manage to determine the outcome of an election. The major significance of the dissenting parties however was in other things than their occasional fateful effect on the party battles between the giants. Their very existence highlighted the nonideological nature of the Democracy and Whiggery. The absorption of parts of their program and their memberships by the major parties was one more revelation of the political knowhow of the latter. Small memberships and highly localized centers of support testified to the indifference most American voters felt toward the politics of principle and zeal. For if the very existence of third parties showed that the Jacksonian consensus was not universally subscribed to, the most revealing feature of the situation was how few Americans dissented from it.

SUGGESTIONS FOR FURTHER READING

Arthur Schlesinger, Jr.'s book *The Age of Jackson* (Boston, 1945), a portion of which is reprinted here, deserves to be read in its entirety. A critical review by Bray Hammond may be found in *Journal of Economic History*, 6 (May 1946), pp. 79–84. Hammond's important book, from which the selection here has been taken, also deserves careful attention by any serious student: *Banks and Politics in America from the Revolution to the Civil War* (Princeton, N.J., 1957). John William Ward finds that the image of Jackson helped to define a consensus in his *Andrew Jackson: Symbol for an Age* (New York, 1955). Richard Hofstadter's chapter on Andrew Jackson in his *American Political Tradition* (New York, 1948) is a perceptive and subtle interpretation in the consensus tradition. The notion of paradox appears in Marvin Meyers's book *The Jacksonian Persuasion* (Stanford, 1957). A very different view may be found in Michael A. Lebowitz, "The Jacksonians: Paradox Lost?" in Barton J. Bernstein, ed., *Towards a New Past: Dissenting Essays in American History* (New York, 1968), pp. 65–89. Lebowitz argues that Jackson appealed to "farmers in relatively declining regions."

Edward Pessen, *Jacksonian America: Society, Personality and Politics* (Homewood, Ill., 1969) summarizes most of the recent research and emerges with a balanced but generally consensus interpretation. Lee Benson, *The Concept of Jacksonian Democracy: New York as a Test Case* (Princeton, N.J., 1961) argues on the basis of much statistical evidence that the concept of Jacksonian democracy has little validity. Politics are the concern of Herbert Ershkowitz and William G. Shade, "Consensus or Conflict? Political Behavior in the State Legislatures during the Jacksonian Era," *Journal of American History*, 8 (December 1971), pp. 591–621. They conclude that party differences "represented contrasting belief systems" and that political battles concerned far more than "the spoils of office," a view that challenges, among others, Richard P. McCormick, *The Second American Party System: Party Formation in the Jacksonian Era* (Chapel Hill, N.C., 1966).

A good collection of some of the interesting new research is Edward Pessen, ed., *New Perspectives on Jacksonian Parties and Politics* (Boston, 1969). Other good general works on the subject are Robert V. Remini, *The Election of Andrew Jackson* (Philadelphia, 1963), and Glyndon G. Van Deusen, *The Jacksonian Era* (New York, 1959). Both contain useful bibliographies. Michael Paul Rogin, *Fathers and Children: Andrew Jackson and the Subjugation of the American Indian* (New York, 1975), is a psychological interpretation.

Two useful historiographic essays on Jacksonian politics are Charles Grier Sellers, Jr., "Andrew Jackson versus the Historians," *Mississippi Valley Historical Review*, 44 (March 1958), pp. 615–34 and Ronald P. Formisano, "Toward a Reorientation of Jacksonian Politics: A Review of the Literature, 1959–1975," *Journal of American History*, 63 (June 1976), pp. 42–65.

* Available in paperback edition.

6

Women in Antebellum Society

Women have usually been left out of American history, perhaps because that history has most often been written by men. But there is also another reason; until recently history has been the story of explorers, politicians, generals, industrialists, and others who achieved fame, fortune, or notoriety. Women, with a few exceptions, stayed at home or in any case remained anonymous and powerless in American society. In the last few years the contemporary feminist movement and a greater concern for the social history of ordinary Americans have focused attention on the role and status of women in the past.

In colonial America women had few rights (though their rights and opportunities may have been greater than those possessed by European women). Married women could not own property, could not sign contracts, had no legal right even to their own inheritance. Divorce was rarely granted and then only for the most flagrant abuses. Few women were educated beyond the elementary level, and almost all professional roles were closed to them. Woman's place was in the home; but, with the exception of a few upper-class ladies, women worked in the home and on the farm. They not only raised and prepared the food and cared for large families, but they often ran a domestic factory as well, producing cloth, soap, butter, and almost all the necessities of life. Childbirth and disease made the life expectancy of a woman several years shorter than a man's. On the frontier woman's role became even more arduous, and the slave woman, of course, faced the most difficult and hopeless task of all.

There were exceptions to the pattern that made women powerless and without rights. Occasionally women such as Anne Hutchison in colonial Massachusetts achieved some status (and notoriety) by challenging and confronting the Puritan leaders on matters of theology and politics, and a number of widows of plantation owners, farmers, and merchants took over their husbands' businesses, competing successfully in what was assumed to be a man's world. Other women achieved some status as school teachers, midwives, or occasionally as writers, but almost all women were spiritually and legally subservient to their fathers, brothers, husbands, and sons.

The American Revolution, which stimulated movements for freedom and equality in many areas of American life, had little impact on the status of women. Despite the plea of Abigail Adams to her husband, John Adams, in 1777 to "remember the ladies and be more generous and favorable to them than your ancesters," the revolutionary generation took no action to extend the rights of women.

The period from 1800 to 1860 witnessed the consolidation of the idea that the proper sphere for women was in the home, and that she should be domestic, submissive, subservient, even an invalid; but this same period also saw the beginning of the women's rights movement. Women like Emma Willard, who founded the Troy Female Seminary and Mary Lyon, who established Mount Holyoke College, pushed for equal educational opportunities for women. Women such as Margaret Fuller, writer, lecturer, and author of Women in the Nineteenth Century, and Frances Wright, editor, reformer, and founder of a utopian community, were the intellectual equals of the best minds of their generation. Other women, such as Angelina and Sarah Grimké, daughters of a South Carolina slaveowner, and blacks, such as Harriet Tubman and Sojourner Truth, became important leaders in the abolitionist movement. Women were active in the temperance movement, the prison reform movement, and the peace movement, and many were influenced by religious revivalism. But most of the women reformers eventually became involved in the movement for women's rights.

The beginnings of the women's rights movement in America can be dated in a number of ways. Perhaps it began at the World Anti-Slavery Convention in London in 1840 when two American delegates, Lucretia Mott, a Quaker school teacher, and Elizabeth Cady Stanton, a young abolitionist, were refused seats because they were women. Or perhaps the beginning was a few years later in 1848 at Seneca Falls, New York, when these two women and a few others declared their militant opposition to the powerless condition of women by holding a Woman's Rights Convention where they solemnly amended the Declaration of Independence: "We hold these truths to be self-evident: that all men and women are created equal. . . . The history of mankind is a history of repeated injuries and usurpations on the part of man toward woman, having in direct object the establishment of absolute tyranny over her." The fight was carried on by other women—lecturers like Lucy Stone, organizers and strategists like Susan B. Anthony, and many others. A few states passed married women's property laws, and it became a little less unusual to find a woman lecturer or writer. But before the Civil War the victories were rare indeed, and the movement for women's rights touched only a few.

How should we judge the role and status of women in the pre-Civil War years? In the first selection Barbara Welter defines the consensus and the norm for most women as the "cult of true womanhood." While men built bridges and railroads and became lawyers and doctors, women, she argues, were expected to be pious, pure, submissive, and domestic. In the second selection Gerda Lerner traces the changing status of women in the North from the colonial period to about 1840. She tells a more complex story. Women, she contends, saw their status decline in some respects and rise in others. But she especially emphasizes the difference in status and role between the working-class women and the ladies of the middle and upper classes. Working women were in many ways untouched by the "cult of true womanhood." Yet all women had something in common; they were a part of the "largest disfranchised group in the nation's history." In the final selection Carroll Smith Rosenberg describes a group of women who found a way to express their resentment against their powerless roles in a male-dominated society through militant rebellion and an all-out attempt to reform American sexual mores.

In seeking to understand the role of women in American society before the Civil War, should we emphasize those few militant reformers who rebelled against their subservient position and took part in other crusades to change society? Or should we stress the prevailing idea that woman's place was in the home, that she should be seen but not heard, that she should "suffer and be still"? Did the early feminist movement pose a fundamental challenge to American society? Why did not more women join the movement? Why were most men so vehemently opposed to it? To what extent is the nineteenth-century view that women should be pious, pure, submissive, and domestic still believed in today? To what extent has the fight for equality for women, begun in the nineteenth century, been successful today?

Barbara Welter

The Cult of True Womanhood: 1820-1860

The nineteenth-century American man was a busy builder of bridges and railroads, at work long hours in a materialistic society. The religious values of his forebears were neglected in practice if not in intent, and he occasionally felt some guilt that he had turned this new land, this temple of the chosen people, into one vast countinghouse. But he could salve his conscience by reflecting that he had left behind a hostage, not only to fortune, but to all the values which he held so dear and treated so lightly. Woman, in the cult of True Womanhood presented by the women's magazines, gift annuals and religious literature of the nineteenth century, was the hostage in the home. In a society where values changed frequently, where fortunes rose and fell with frightening rapidity, where social and economic mobility provided instability as well as hope, one thing at least remained the same—a true woman was a true woman wherever she was found. If anyone, male or female, dared to tamper with the complex of virtues which made up True Womanhood, he was damned immediately as an enemy of God, of civilization and of the Republic. It was a fearful obligation, a solemn responsibility, which the nineteenth-century American woman had—to uphold the pillars of the temple with her frail white hand.

The attributes of True Womanhood, by which a woman judged herself and was judged by her husband, her neighbors and society could be divided into four cardinal virtues—piety, purity, submissiveness and domesticity. Put them all together and they spelled mother, daughter, sister, wife —woman. Without them, no matter whether there was fame, achievement or wealth, all was ashes. With them she was promised happiness and power.

Religion or piety was the core of woman's virtue, the source of her

From American Quarterly, 18 (Summer 1966), pp. 151–66, 171–74. Published by the University of Pennsylvania; copyright, 1966, Trustees of the University of Pennsylvania.

strength. Young men looking for a mate were cautioned to search first for piety, for if that were there, all else would follow. Religion belonged to woman by divine right, a gift of God and nature. This "peculiar susceptibility" to religion was given her for a reason: "the vestal flame of piety, lighted up by Heaven in the breast of woman" would throw its beams into the naughty world of men. So far would its candle power reach that the "Universe might be Enlightened, Improved, and Harmonized by WOMAN!!" She would be another, better Eve, working in cooperation with the Redeemer, bringing the world back "from its revolt and sin." The world would be reclaimed for God through her suffering, for "God increased the cares and sorrows of woman, that she might be sooner constrained to accept the terms of salvation." A popular poem by Mrs. Frances Osgood, "The Triumph of the Spiritual Over the Sensual" expressed just this sentiment, woman's purifying passionless love bringing an erring man back to Christ.

Dr. Charles Meigs, explaining to a graduating class of medical students why women were naturally religious, said that "hers is a pious mind. Her confiding nature leads her more readily than men to accept the proffered grace of the Gospel." Caleb Atwater, Esq., writing in *The Ladies' Repository*, saw the hand of the Lord in female piety: "Religion is exactly what a woman needs, for it gives her that dignity that best suits her dependence." And Mrs. John Sandford, who had no very high opinion of her sex, agreed thoroughly: "Religion is just what woman needs. Without it she is ever restless or unhappy. . . ." Mrs. Sandford and the others did not speak only of that restlessness of the human heart, which St. Augustine notes, that can only find its peace in God. They spoke rather of religion as a kind of tranquilizer for the many undefined longings which swept even the most pious young girl, and about which it was better to pray than to think.

One reason religion was valued was that it did not take a woman away from her "proper sphere," her home. Unlike participation in other societies or movements, church work would not make her less domestic or submissive, less a True Woman. In religious vineyards, said the *Young Ladies' Literary and Missionary Report*, "you may labor without the apprehension of detracting from the charms of feminine delicacy." Mrs. S. L. Dagg, writing from her chapter of the Society in Tuscaloosa, Alabama, was equally reassuring: "As no sensible woman will suffer her intellectual pursuits to clash with her domestic duties" she should concentrate on religious work "which promotes these very duties."

The women's seminaries aimed at aiding women to be religious, as well as accomplished. Mt. Holyoke's catalogue promised to make female education "a handmaid to the Gospel and an efficient auxiliary in the great task of renovating the world." The Young Ladies' Seminary at Bordentown, New Jersey, declared its most important function to be "the forming of a sound and virtuous character." In Keene, New Hampshire, the Seminary tried to instill a "consistent and useful character" in its students, to enable them in this life to be "a good friend, wife and mother but more important, to qualify them for "the enjoyment of Celestial Happiness in the life to come." And Joseph M' D. Mathews, Principal of Oakland Female Seminary in Hillsborough, Ohio, believed that "female education should be preeminently religious."

If religion was so vital to a woman, irreligion was almost too awful to contemplate. Women were warned not to let their literary or intellectual pursuits take them away from God. Sarah Josepha Hale spoke darkly of those who, like Margaret Fuller, threw away the "One True Book" for others, open to error. Mrs. Hale used the unfortunate Miss Fuller as fateful proof that "the greater the intellectual force, the greater and more fatal the errors into which women fall who wander from the Rock of Salvation, Christ the Saviour. . . ."

One gentleman, writing on "Female Irreligion" reminded his readers that "Man may make himself a brute, and does so very often, but can woman brutify herself to his level—the lowest level of human nature—without exerting special wonder?" Fanny Wright, because she was godless, "was no woman, mother though she be." A few years ago, he recalls, such women would have been whipped. In any case, "woman never looks lovelier than in her reverence for religion" and, conversely, "female irreligion is the most revolting feature in human character."

Purity was as essential as piety to a young woman, its absence as unnatural and unfeminine. Without it she was, in fact, no woman at all, but a member of some lower order. A "fallen woman" was a "fallen angel," unworthy of the celestial company of her sex. To contemplate the loss of purity brought tears; to be guilty of such a crime, in the women's magazines at least, brought madness or death. Even the language of the flowers had bitter words for it: a dried white rose symbolized "Death Preferable to Loss of Innocence." The marriage night was the single great event of a woman's life, when she bestowed her greatest treasure upon her husband, and from that time on was completely dependent upon him, an empty vessel, without legal or emotional existence of her own.

Therefore all True Women were urged, in the strongest possible terms, to maintain their virtue, although men, being by nature more sensual than they, would try to assault it. Thomas Branagan admitted in *The Excellency of the Female Character Vindicated* that his sex would sin and sin again, they could not help it, but woman, stronger and purer, must not give in and let man "take liberties incompatible with her delicacy." "If you do," Branagan addressed his gentle reader, "You will be left in silent sadness to bewail your credulity, imbecility, duplicity, and premature prostitution."

Mrs. Eliza Farrar, in *The Young Lady's Friend*, gave practical logistics to avoid trouble: "Sit not with another in a place that is too narrow; read not out of the same book; let not your eagerness to see anything induce you to place your head close to another person's."

If such good advice was ignored the consequences were terrible and inexorable. In *Girlhood and Womanhood: Or Sketches of My Schoolmates*, by

Mrs. A. J. Graves (a kind of mid-nineteenth-century *The Group*), the bad
ends of a boarding school class of girls are scrupulously recorded. The worst
end of all is reserved for "Amelia Dorrington: The Lost One." Amelia died
in the almshouse "the wretched victim of depravity and intemperance" and
all because her mother had let her be "high-spirited not prudent." These
girlish high spirits had been misinterpreted by a young man, with disastrous
results. Amelia's "thoughtless levity" was "followed by a total loss of virtuous principle" and Mrs. Graves editorializes that "the coldest reserve is more
admirable in a woman a man wishes to make his wife, than the least approach to undue familiarity.". . .

If, however, a woman managed to withstand man's assaults on her virtue, she demonstrated her superiority and her power over him. Eliza Farn-
ham, trying to prove this female superiority, concluded smugly that "the
purity of women is the everlasting barrier against which the tides of man's
sensual nature surge." . . .

Men could be counted on to be grateful when women thus saved them
from themselves. William Alcott, guiding young men in their relations with
the opposite sex, told them that "Nothing is better calculated to preserve a
young man from contamination of low pleasures and pursuits than frequent
intercourse with the more refined and virtuous of the other sex." And he
added, one assumes in equal innocence, that youths should "observe and
learn to admire, that purity and ignorance of evil which is the characteristic
of well-educated young ladies, and which, when we are near them, raises us
above those sordid and sensual considerations which hold such sway over men
in their intercourse with each other."

The Rev. Jonathan F. Stearns was also impressed by female chastity in
the face of male passion, and warned woman never to compromise the source
of her power: "Let her lay aside delicacy, and her influence over our sex is
gone."

Women themselves accepted, with pride but suitable modesty, this
priceless virtue. *The Ladies' Wreath*, in "Woman the Creature of God and
the Manufacturer of Society" saw purity as her greatest gift and chief means
of discharging her duty to save the world: "Purity is the highest beauty—
the true pole-star which is to guide humanity aright in its long, varied, and
perilous voyage."

Sometimes, however, a woman did not see the dangers to her treasure.
In that case, they must be pointed out to her, usually by a male. In the
nineteenth century any form of social change was tantamount to an attack
on woman's virtue, if only it was correctly understood. For example, dress
reform seemed innocuous enough and the bloomers worn by the lady of that
name and her followers were certainly modest attire. Such was the reasoning
only of the ignorant. In another issue of *The Ladies' Wreath* a young lady
is represented in dialogue with her "Professor." The girl expresses admiration
for the bloomer costume—it gives freedom of motion, is healthful and attractive. The "Professor" sets her straight. Trousers, he explains, are "only

one of the many manifestations of that wild spirit of socialism and agrarian radicalism which is at present so rife in our land." The young lady recants immediately: "If this dress has any connexion with Fourierism or Socialism, or fanaticism in any shape whatever, I have no disposition to wear it at all . . . no true woman would so far compromise her delicacy as to espouse, however unwittingly, such a cause." . . .

Submission was perhaps the most feminine virtue expected of women. Men were supposed to be religious, although they rarely had time for it, and supposed to be pure, although it came awfully hard to them, but men were the movers, the doers, the actors. Women were the passive, submissive responders. The order of dialogue was, of course, fixed in Heaven. Man was "woman's superior by God's appointment, if not in intellectual dowry, at least by official decree." Therefore, as Charles Elliott argued in *The Ladies' Repository*, she should submit to him "for the sake of good order at least." In *The Ladies Companion* a young wife was quoted approvingly as saying that she did not think woman should "feel and act for herself" because "When, next to God, her husband is not the tribunal to which her heart and intellect appeals—the golden bowl of affection is broken." Women were warned that if they tampered with this quality they tampered with the order of the Universe. . . .

"True feminine genius," said Grace Greenwood (Sara Jane Clarke) "is ever timid, doubtful, and clingingly dependent; a perpetual childhood." And she advised literary ladies in an essay on "The Intellectual Woman"—"Don't trample on the flowers while longing for the stars." A wife who submerged her own talents to work for her husband was extolled as an example of a true woman. In *Women of Worth: A Book for Girls*, Mrs. Ann Flaxman, an artist of promise herself, was praised because she "devoted herself to sustain her husband's genius and aid him in his arduous career."

Caroline Gilman's advice to the bride aimed at establishing this proper order from the beginning of a marriage: "Oh, young and lovely bride, watch well the first moments when your will conflicts with his to whom God and society have given the control. Reverence his *wishes* even when you do not his *opinions*."

Mrs. Gilman's perfect wife in *Recollections of a Southern Matron* realizes that "the three golden threads with which domestic happiness is woven" are "to repress a harsh answer, to confess a fault, and to stop (right or wrong) in the midst of self-defense, in gentle submission." Woman could do this, hard though it was, because in her heart she knew she was right and so could afford to be forgiving, even a trifle condescending. "Men are not unreasonable," averred Mrs. Gilman. "Their difficulties lie in not understanding the moral and physical nature of our sex. They often wound through ignorance, and are surprised at having offended." Wives were advised to do their best to reform men, but if they couldn't, to give up gracefully. "If any habit of his annoyed me, I spoke of it once or twice, calmly, then bore it quietly." . . .

Woman then, in all her roles, accepted submission as her lot. It was a lot she had not chosen or deserved. As *Godey's* said, "the lesson of submission is forced upon woman." Without comment or criticism the writer affirms that "To suffer and to be silent under suffering seems the great command she has to obey." George Burnap referred to a woman's life as "a series of suppressed emotions." She was, as Emerson said, "more vulnerable, more infirm, more mortal than man." The death of a beautiful woman, cherished in fiction, represented woman as the innocent victim, suffering without sin, too pure and good for this world but too weak and passive to resist its evil forces. The best refuge for such a delicate creature was the warmth and safety of her home.

The true woman's place was unquestionably by her own fireside—as daughter, sister, but most of all as wife and mother. Therefore domesticity was among the virtues most prized by the women's magazines. "As society is constituted," wrote Mrs. S. E. Farley, on the "Domestic and Social Claims on Woman," "the true dignity and beauty of the female character seem to consist in a right understanding and faithful and cheerful performance of social and family duties." Sacred Scripture re-enforced social pressure: "St. Paul knew what was best for women when he advised them to be domestic," said Mrs. Sandford. "There is composure at home; there is something sedative in the duties which home involves. It affords security not only from the world, but from delusions and errors of every kind.". . .

One of the most important functions of woman as comforter was her role as nurse. Her own health was probably, although regrettably, delicate. Many homes had "little sufferers," those pale children who wasted away to saintly deaths. And there were enough other illnesses of youth and age, major and minor, to give the nineteenth-century American woman nursing experience. The sickroom called for the exercise of her higher qualities of patience, mercy and gentleness as well as for her housewifely arts. She could thus fulfill her dual feminine function—beauty and usefulness.

The cookbooks of the period offer formulas for gout cordials, ointment for sore nipples, hiccough and cough remedies, opening pills and refreshing drinks for fever, along with recipes for pound cake, jumbled stewed calves head and currant wine. *The Ladies' New Book of Cookery* believed that "food prepared by the kind hand of a wife, mother, sister, friend" tasted better and had a "restorative power which money cannot purchase."

A chapter of *The Young Lady's Friend* was devoted to woman's privilege as "ministering spirit at the couch of the sick." Mrs. Farrar advised, a soft voice, gentle and clean hands, and a cheerful smile. She also cautioned against an excess of female delicacy. That was all right for a young lady in the parlor, but not for bedside manners. Leeches, for example, were to be regarded as "a curious piece of mechanism . . . their ornamental stripes should recommend them even to the eye, and their valuable services to our feelings." And she went on calmly to discuss their use. Nor were women to shrink from medical terminology, since "If you cultivate right views of the wonderful structure of the body, you will be as willing to speak to a physician of the bowels as the brains of your patient."

Nursing the sick, particularly sick males, not only made a woman feel useful and accomplished, but increased her influence. In a piece of heavy-handed humor in *Godey's* a man confessed that some women were only happy when their husbands were ailing that they might have the joy of nursing him to recovery "thus gratifying their medical vanity and their love of power by making him more dependent upon them." In a similar vein a husband sometimes suspected his wife "almost wishes me dead—for the pleasure of being utterly inconsolable."

In the home women were not only the highest adornment of civilization, but they were supposed to keep busy at morally uplifting tasks. Fortunately most of housework, if looked at in true womanly fashion, could be regarded as uplifting. Mrs. Sigourney extolled its virtues: "The science of housekeeping affords exercise for the judgment and energy, ready recollection, and patient self-possession, that are the characteristics of a superior mind." According to Mrs. Farrar, making beds was good exercise, the repetitiveness of routine tasks inculcated patience and perseverance, and proper management of the home was a surprisingly complex art: "There is more to be learned about pouring out tea and coffee, than most young ladies are willing to believe." *Godey's* went so far as to suggest coyly, in "Learning vs. House-wifery" that the two were complementary, not opposed: chemistry could be utilized in cooking, geometry in dividing cloth, and phrenology in discovering talent in children. . . . The female was dangerously addicted to novels, according to the literature of the period. She should avoid them, since they interfered with "serious piety." If she simply couldn't help herself and read them anyway, she should choose edifying ones from lists of morally acceptable authors. She should study history since it "showed the depravity of the human heart and the evil nature of sin." On the whole, "religious biography was best."

The women's magazines themselves could be read without any loss of concern for the home. *Godey's* promised the husband that he would find his wife "no less assiduous for his reception, or less sincere in welcoming his return" as a result of reading their magazine. *The Lily of the Valley* won its right to be admitted to the boudoir by confessing that it was "like its name-sake humble and unostentatious, but it is yet pure, and, we trust, free from moral imperfections."

No matter what later authorities claimed, the nineteenth century knew that girls *could* be ruined by a book. The seduction stories regard "exciting and dangerous books" as contributory causes of disaster. The man without honorable intentions always provides the innocent maiden with such books as a prelude to his assault on her virtue. Books which attacked or seemed to attack woman's accepted place in society were regarded as equally dangerous. A reviewer of Harriet Martineau's *Society in America* wanted it kept out of the hands of American women. They were so susceptible to persuasion, with their "gentle yielding natures" that they might listen to "the bold ravings of the hard-featured of their own sex." The frightening result: "such reading will unsettle them for their true station and pursuits, and they will throw the world back again into confusion.". . .

Marriage was seen not only in terms of service but as an increase in authority for woman. Burnap concluded that marriage improves the female character "not only because it puts her under the best possible tuition, that of the affections, and affords scope to her active energies, but because it gives her higher aims, and a more dignified position." *The Lady's Amaranth* saw it as a balance of power: "The man bears rule over his wife's person and conduct. She bears rule over his inclinations: he governs by law; she by persuasion. . . . The empire of the woman is an empire of softness . . . her commands are caresses, her menaces are tears."

Woman should marry, but not for money. She should choose only the high road of true love and not truckle to the values of a materialistic society. A story "Marrying for Money" (subtlety was not the strong point of the ladies' magazines) depicts Gertrude, the heroine, rueing the day she made her crass choice: "It is a terrible thing to live without love. . . . A woman who dares marry for aught but the purest affection, calls down the just judgments of heaven upon her head."

The corollary to marriage, with or without true love, was motherhood, which added another dimension to her usefulness and her prestige. It also anchored her even more firmly to the home. "My Friend," wrote Mrs. Sigourney, "If in becoming a mother, you have reached the climax of your happiness, you have also taken a higher place in the scale of being . . . you have gained an increase of power." The Rev. J. N. Danforth pleaded in *The Ladies' Casket*, "Oh, mother, acquit thyself well in thy humble sphere, for thou mayest affect the world." A true woman naturally loved her children; to suggest otherwise was monstrous.

America depended upon her mothers to raise up a whole generation of Christian statesmen who could say "all that I am I owe to my angel mother." The mothers must do the inculcating of virtue since the fathers, alas, were too busy chasing the dollar. Or as *The Ladies' Companion* put it more effusively, the father "weary with the heat and burden of life's summer day, or trampling with unwilling foot the decaying leaves of life's autumn, has forgotten the sympathies of life's joyous springtime. . . . The acquisition of wealth, the advancement of his children in worldly honor—these are his self-imposed tasks." It was his wife who formed "the infant mind as yet untainted by contact with evil . . . like wax beneath the plastic hand of the mother."

The Ladies' Wreath offered a fifty-dollar prize to the woman who submitted the most convincing essay on "How May An American Woman Best Show Her Patriotism." The winner was Miss Elizabeth Wetherell who provided herself with a husband in her answer. The wife in the essay of course asked her husband's opinion. He tried a few jokes first—"Call her eldest son George Washington," "Don't speak French, speak American"—but then got down to telling her in sober prize-winning truth what women could do for their country. Voting was no asset, since that would result only in "a vast increase of confusion and expense without in the smallest degree affecting the result." Besides, continued this oracle, "looking down at their child," if "we were to go a step further and let the children vote, their first act would be to vote their mothers at home." There is no comment on this devastating male logic and he continues: "most women would follow the lead of their fathers and husbands," and the few who would "fly off on a tangent from the circle of home influence would cancel each other out."

The wife responds dutifully: "I see all that. I never understood so well before." Encouraged by her quick womanly perception, the master of the house resolves the question—an American woman best shows her patriotism by staying at home, where she brings her influence to bear "upon the right side for the country's weal." That woman will instinctively choose the side of right he has no doubt. Besides her "natural refinement and closeness to God" she has the "blessed advantage of a quiet life" while man is exposed to conflict and evil. She stays home with "her Bible and a well-balanced mind" and raises her sons to be good Americans. The judges rejoiced in this conclusion and paid the prize money cheerfully, remarking "they deemed it cheap at the price.". . .

The American woman had her choice—she could define her rights in the way of the women's magazines and insure them by the practice of the requisite virtues, or she could go outside the home, seeking other rewards than love. It was a decision on which, she was told, everything in her world depended. "Yours it is to determine," the Rev. Mr. Stearns solemnly warned from the pulpit, "whether the beautiful order of society . . . shall continue as it has been" or whether "society shall break up and become a chaos of disjointed and unsightly elements." If she chose to listen to other voices than those of her proper mentors, sought other rooms than those of her home, she lost both her happiness and her power—"that almost magic power, which, in her proper sphere, she now wields over the destinies of the world."

But even while the women's magazines and related literature encouraged this ideal of the perfect woman, forces were at work in the nineteenth century which impelled woman herself to change, to play a more creative role in society. The movements for social reform, westward migration, missionary activity, utopian communities, industrialism, the Civil War—all called forth responses from woman which differed from those she was trained to believe were hers by nature and divine decree. The very perfection of True Womanhood, moreover, carried within itself the seeds of its own destruction. For if woman was so very little less than the angels, she should surely take a more active part in running the world, especially since men were making such a hash of things.

Real women often felt they did not live up to the ideal of True Womanhood: some of them blamed themselves, some challenged the standard, some tried to keep the virtues and enlarge the scope of womanhood. Somehow through this mixture of challenge and acceptance, of change and continuity, the True Woman evolved into the New Woman—a transformation as startling in its way as the abolition of slavery or the coming of the machine age. And yet the stereotype, the "mystique" if you will, of what woman was and ought to be persisted, bringing guilt and confusion in the midst of opportunity.

The women's magazines and related literature had feared this very dislocation of values and blurring of roles. By careful manipulation and interpretation they sought to convince woman that she had the best of both worlds—power and virtue—and that a stable order of society depended upon her maintaining her traditional place in it. To that end she was identified with everything that was beautiful and holy. . . .

Gerda Lerner

The Lady and the Mill Girl: Changes in the Status of Women in the Age of Jackson

The period 1800–1840 is one in which decisive changes occurred in the status of American women. It has remained surprisingly unexplored. With the exception of a recent, unpublished dissertation by Keith Melder and the distinctive work of Elisabeth Dexter, there is a dearth of descriptive material and an almost total absence of interpretation.[1] Yet the period offers essential clues to an understanding of later institutional developments, particularly the shape and nature of the woman's rights movement. This analysis will consider the economic, political, and social status of women and examine the changes in each area. It will also attempt an interpretation of the ideological shifts which occurred in American society concerning the "proper" role for women.

Periodization always offers difficulties. It seemed useful here, for purposes of comparison, to group women's status before 1800 roughly under the "colonial" heading and ignore the transitional and possibly atypical shifts which occurred during the American Revolution and the early period of nationhood.

From Gerda Lerner, The Majority Finds Its Past: Placing Women in History (New York: Oxford University Press, 1979). Copyright © 1969 by American Studies, Inc., and copyright © 1979 by Gerda Lerner. Reprinted by permission of Gerda Lerner c/o International Creative Management.

This article first appeared in American Studies, Vol. 10, No. 1, Spring 1969. Research for this article was facilitated by a research grant provided by Long Island University, Brooklyn, N.Y., which is gratefully acknowledged.

The generalizations in this article are based on extensive research in primary sources, including letters and manuscripts of the following women: Elizabeth Cady Stanton, Susan B. Anthony, Abby Kelley, Lucretia Mott, Lucy Stone, Sarah and Angelina Grimké, Maria Weston Chapman, Lydia Maria Child, and Betsey Cowles. Among the organizational records consulted were those of the Boston Female Anti-Slavery Society, the Philadelphia Female Anti-Slavery Society, Anti-Slavery Conventions of American Women, all the Woman's Rights Conventions prior to 1870, and the records of various female charitable organizations.

Also, regional differences were largely ignored. The South was left out of consideration entirely because its industrial development occurred later.

The status of colonial women has been well studied and described and can briefly be summarized for comparison with the later period. Throughout the colonial period there was a marked shortage of women, which varied with the regions and always was greatest in the frontier areas.[2] This (from the point of view of women) favorable sex ratio enhanced their status and position. The Puritan world view regarded idleness as sin; life in an underdeveloped country made it absolutely necessary that each member of the community perform an economic function. Thus work for women, married or single, was not only approved, it was regarded as a civic duty. Puritan town councils expected single girls, widows, and unattached women to be self-supporting and for a long time provided needy spinsters with parcels of land. There was no social sanction against married women working; on the contrary, wives were expected to help their husbands in their trade and won social approval for doing extra work in or out of the home. Needy children, girls as well as boys, were indentured or apprenticed and were expected to work for their keep.

The vast majority of women worked within their homes, where their labor produced most articles needed for the family. The entire colonial production of cloth and clothing and in part that of shoes was in the hands of women. In addition to these occupations, women were found in many different kinds of employment. They were butchers, silversmiths, gunsmiths, upholsterers. They ran mills, plantations, tan yards, shipyards, and every kind of shop, tavern and boarding house. They were gate keepers, jail keepers, sextons, journalists, printers, "doctoresses," apothecaries, midwives, nurses, and teachers. Women acquired their skills the same way as did the men, through apprenticeship training, frequently within their own families.[3]

Absence of a dowry, ease of marriage and remarriage, and a more lenient attitude of the law with regard to women's property rights were manifestations of the improved position of wives in the colonies. Under British common law, marriage destroyed a woman's contractual capacity; she could not sign a contract even with the consent of her husband. But colonial authorities were more lenient toward the wife's property rights by protecting her dower rights in her husband's property, granting her personal clothing, and upholding pre-nuptial contracts between husband and wife. In the absence of the husband, colonial courts granted women "femme sole" rights, which enabled them to conduct their husband's business, sign contracts, and sue. The relative social freedom of women and the esteem in which they were held was commented upon by most early foreign travelers in America.[4]

But economic, legal, and social status tells only part of the story. Colonial society as a whole was hierarchical, and rank and standing in society depended on the position of the men. Women did not play a determining role in the ranking pattern; they took their position in society through the men of their own family or the men they married. In other words, they participated in the hierarchy only as daughters and wives, not as individuals. Similarly, their occupations were, by and large, merely auxiliary, designed to contribute to family income, enhance their husbands' business or continue it in case of widowhood. The self-supporting spinsters were certainly the exception. The underlying assumption of colonial society was that women ought to occupy an inferior and subordinate position. The settlers had brought this assumption with them from Europe; it was reflected in their legal concepts, their willingness to exclude women from political life, their discriminatory educational practices. What is remarkable is the extent to which this felt inferiority of women was constantly challenged and modified under the impact of environment, frontier conditions, and a favorable sex ratio.

By 1840 all of American society had changed. The Revolution had substituted an egalitarian ideology for the hierarchical concepts of colonial life. Privilege based on ability rather than inherited status, upward mobility for all groups of society, and unlimited opportunities for individual self-fulfillment had become ideological goals, if not always realities. For men, that is; women were, by tacit consensus, excluded from the new democracy. Indeed, their actual situation had in many respects deteriorated. While, as wives, they had benefitted from increasing wealth, urbanization, and industrialization, their role as economic producers and as political members of society differed sharply from that of men. Women's work outside of the home no longer met with social approval; on the contrary, with two notable exceptions, it was condemned. Many business and professional occupations formerly open to women were now closed, many others restricted as to training and advancement. The entry of large numbers of women into low status, low pay, and low skill industrial work had fixed such work by definition as "woman's work." Women's political status, while legally unchanged, had deteriorated relative to the advances made by men. At the same time the genteel lady of fashion had become a model of American femininity, and the definition of "woman's proper sphere" seemed narrower and more confined than ever.

Within the scope of this essay only a few of these changes can be more fully explained. The professionalization of medicine and its impact on women may serve as a typical example of what occurred in all the professions.

In colonial America there were no medical schools, no medical journals, few hospitals, and few laws pertaining to the practice of the healing arts. Clergymen and governors, barbers, quacks, apprentices, and women practiced medicine. Most practitioners acquired their credentials by reading Paracelsus and Galen and serving an apprenticeship with an established practitioner. Among the semi-trained "physics," surgeons, and healers, the occasional "doctoress" was fully accepted and frequently well rewarded. County records of all the colonies contain references to the work of the female physicians. There was even a female Army surgeon, a Mrs. Allyn, who served during King Philip's war. Plantation records mention by name several slave women who were granted special privileges because of their useful service as midwives and "doctoresses." [5]

The period of the professionalization of American medicine dates from

1765, when Dr. William Shippen began his lectures on midwifery in Philadelphia. The founding of medical faculties in several colleges, the standardization of training requirements, and the proliferation of medical societies intensified during the last quarter of the 18th century. The American Revolution dramatized the need for trained medical personnel, afforded first-hand battlefield experience to a number of surgeons and brought increasing numbers of semi-trained practitioners in contact with the handful of European-trained surgeons working in the military hospitals. This was an experience from which women were excluded. The resulting interest in improved medical training, the gradual appearance of graduates of medical colleges, and the efforts of medical societies led to licensing legislation. In 1801 Maryland required all medical practitioners to be licensed; in 1806 New York enacted a similar law, followed by all but three states.[6] This trend was reversed in the 1830s and 40s when most states repealed their licensure requirements. This was due to pressure from eclectic, homeopathic practitioners, the public's dissatisfaction with the "heroic medicine" then practiced by licensed physicians, and to the distrust of state regulation, which was widespread during the Age of Jackson. Licensure as prime proof of qualification for the practice of medicine was reinstituted in the 1870s.

In the middle of the 19th century it was not so much a license of an M.D. which marked the professional physician as it was graduation from an approved medical college, admission to hospital practice and to a network of referrals through other physicians. In 1800 there were four medical schools, in 1850, forty-two. Almost all of them excluded women from admission. Not surprisingly, women turned to eclectic schools for training. Harriot Hunt, a Boston physician, was trained by apprenticeship with a husband and wife team of homeopathic physicians. After more than twenty years of practice she attempted to enter Harvard Medical school and was repeatedly rebuffed. Elizabeth Blackwell received her M.D. from Geneva (New York) Medical College, an eclectic school. Sarah Adamson found all regular medical schools closed against her and earned an M.D. in 1851 from Central College at Syracuse, an eclectic institution. Clemence Lozier graduated from the same school two years later and went on to found the New York Medical College and Hospital for women in 1862, a homeopathic institution which was later absorbed into the Flower-Fifth Avenue Hospital.

Another way in which professionalization worked to the detriment of women can be seen in the cases of Drs. Elizabeth and Emily Blackwell, Marie Zakrzewska, and Ann Preston, who despite their M.D.s and excellent training were denied access to hospitals, were refused recognition by county medical societies, and were denied customary referrals by male colleagues. Their experiences were similar to those of most of the pioneer women physicians. Such discrimination caused the formation of alternate institutions for the training of women physicians and for hospitals in which they might treat their patients.[7] The point here is not so much that any one aspect of the process of professionalization excluded women but that the process, which took place over the span of almost a century, proceeded in such a way as to institutionalize an exclusion of women, which had earlier been accomplished irregularly, inconsistently, and mostly by means of social pressure. The end result was an *absolute* lowering of status for all women in the medical profession and a *relative* loss. As the professional status of all physicians advanced, the status differential between male and female practitioners was more obviously disadvantageous and underscored women's marginality. Their vital exclusion from the most prestigious and lucrative branches of the profession and their concentration in specializations relating to women and children made such disadvantaging more obvious by the end of the 19th century.

This process of pre-emption of knowledge, of institutionalization of the profession, and of legitimation of its claims by law and public acceptance is standard for the professionalization of the sciences, as George Daniels has pointed out.[8] It inevitably results in the elimination of fringe elements from the profession. It is interesting to note that women had been pushed out of the medical profession in 16th-century Europe by a similar process.[9] Once the public had come to accept licensing and college training as guarantees of up-to-date practice, the outsider, no matter how well qualified by years of experience, stood no chance in the competition. Women were the casualties of medical professionalization.

In the field of midwifery the results were similar, but the process was more complicated. Women had held a virtual monopoly in the profession in colonial America. In 1646 a man was prosecuted in Maine for practicing as a midwife.[10] There are many records of well-trained midwives with diplomas from European institutions working in the colonies. In most of the colonies midwives were licensed, registered, and required to pass an examination before a board. When Dr. Shippen announced his pioneering lectures on midwifery, he did it to "combat the widespread popular prejudice against the man-midwife" and because he considered most midwives ignorant and improperly trained.[11]

Yet he invited "those women who love virtue enough, to own their Ignorance, and apply for instruction" to attend his lectures, offering as an inducement the assurance that female pupils would be taught privately. It is not known if any midwives availed themselves of the opportunity.[12]

Technological advances, as well as scientific, worked against the interests of female midwives. In 16th-century Europe the invention and use of obstetrical forceps had for three generations been the well-kept secret of the Chamberlen family and had greatly enhanced their medical practice. Hugh Chamberlen was forced by circumstances to sell the secret to the Medical College in Amsterdam, which in turn transmitted the precious knowledge to licensed physicians only. By the time the use of the instrument became widespread, it had become associated with male physicians and male midwives. Similarly in America, introduction of the obstetrical forceps was associated with the practice of male midwives and served to their advantage. By the end of the 18th century a number of male physicians advertised their practice of midwifery.

Shortly thereafter female midwives also resorted to advertising, probably in an effort to meet the competition. By the early 19th century male physicians had virtually monopolized the practice of midwifery on the Eastern seaboard. True to the generally delayed economic development in the Western frontier regions, female midwives continued to work on the frontier until a much later period. It is interesting to note that the concepts of "propriety" shifted with the prevalent practice. In 17th-century Maine the attempt of a man to act as a midwife was considered outrageous and illegal; in mid-19th-century America the suggestion that women should train as midwives and physicians was considered equally outrageous and improper.[13]

Professionalization, similar to that in medicine with the elimination of women from the upgraded profession, occurred in the field of law. Before 1750, when law suits were commonly brought to the courts by the plaintiffs themselves or by deputies without specialized legal training, women as well as men could and did act as "attorneys-in-fact." When the law became a paid profession and trained lawyers took over litigation, women disappeared from the court scene for over a century.[14]

A similar process of shrinking opportunities for women developed in business and in the retail trades. There were fewer female storekeepers and business women in the 1830s than there had been in colonial days. There was also a noticeable shift in the kind of merchandise handled by them. Where previously women could be found running almost every kind of retail shop, after 1830 they were mostly found in businesses which served women only.[15]

The only fields in which professionalization did not result in the elimination of women from the upgraded profession were nursing and teaching. Both were characterized by a severe shortage of labor. Nursing lies outside the field of this inquiry, since it did not become an organized profession until after the Civil War. Before then, it was regarded peculiarly as a woman's occupation, although some of the hospitals and the Army during wars employed male nurses. These bore the stigma of low skill, low status, and low pay. Generally, nursing was regarded as simply an extension of the unpaid services performed by the housewife—a characteristic attitude that haunts the profession to this day.

Education seems, at first glance, to offer an entirely opposite pattern from that of the other professions. In colonial days women had taught "Dame schools" and grade schools during summer sessions. Gradually, as educational opportunities for girls expanded, they advanced just a step ahead of their students. Professionalization of teaching occurred between 1820 and 1860, a period marked by a sharp increase in the number of women teachers. The spread of female seminaries, academies, and normal schools provided new opportunities for the training and employment of female teachers.

This trend, which runs counter to that found in the other professions, can be accounted for by the fact that women filled a desperate need created by the challenge of the common schools, the ever-increasing size of the student body, and the westward growth of the nation. America was committed to educating its children in public schools, but it was insistent on doing so as cheaply as possible. Women were available in great numbers, and they were willing to work cheaply. The result was another ideological adaptation: in the very period when the gospel of the home as woman's only proper sphere was preached most loudly, it was discovered that women were the natural teachers of youth, could do the job better than men, and were to be preferred for such employment. This was always provided, of course, that they would work at the proper wage differential—30 to 50 per cent of the wages paid male teachers was considered appropriate. The result was that in 1888 in the country as a whole 63 per cent of all teachers were women, while the figure for the cities only was 90.04 per cent.[16]

It appeared in the teaching field, as it would in industry, that role expectations were adaptable provided the inferior status group filled a social need. The inconsistent and peculiar patterns of employment of black labor in the present-day market bear out the validity of this generalization.

There was another field in which the labor of women was appreciated and which they were urged to enter—industry. From Alexander Hamilton to Matthew Carey and Tench Coxe, advocates of industrialization sang the praises of the working girl and advanced arguments in favor of her employment. The social benefits of female labor particularly stressed were those bestowed upon her family, who now no longer had to support her. Working girls were "thus happily preserved from idleness and its attendant vices and crimes," and the whole community benefitted from their increased purchasing power.[17]

American industrialization, which occurred in an underdeveloped economy with a shortage of labor, depended on the labor of women and children. Men were occupied with agricultural work and were not available or were unwilling to enter the factories. This accounts for the special features of the early development of the New England textile industry: the relatively high wages, the respectability of the job and relatively high status of the mill girls, the patriarchal character of the model factory towns, and the temporary mobility of women workers from farm to factory and back again to farm. All this was characteristic only of a limited area and of a period of about two decades. By the late 1830s the romance had worn off: immigration had supplied a strongly competitive, permanent work force willing to work for subsistence wages; early efforts at trade union organization had been shattered, and mechanization had turned semi-skilled factory labor into unskilled labor. The process led to the replacement of the New England-born farm girls by immigrants in the mills and was accompanied by a loss of status and respectability for female workers.

The lack of organized social services during periods of depression drove ever greater numbers of women into the labor market. At first, inside the factories distinctions between men's and women's jobs were blurred. Men and women were assigned to machinery on the basis of local need. But as more women entered industry the limited number of occupations open to them tended to increase competition among them, thus lowering pay standards.

Generally, women regarded their work as temporary and hesitated to invest in apprenticeship training, because they expected to marry and raise families. Thus they remained untrained, casual labor and were soon, by custom, relegated to the lowest paid, least skilled jobs. Long hours, overwork, and poor working conditions would characterize women's work in industry for almost a century.[18]

Another result of industrialization was in increasing differences in life styles between women of different classes. When female occupations, such as carding, spinning, and weaving, were transferred from home to factory, the poorer women followed their traditional work and became industrial workers. The women of the middle and upper classes could use their newly gained time for leisure pursuits: they became ladies. And a small but significant group among them chose to prepare themselves for professional careers by advanced education. This group would prove to be the most vocal and troublesome in the near future.

As class distinctions sharpened, social attitudes toward women became polarized. The image of "the lady" was elevated to the accepted ideal of femininity toward which all women would strive. In this formulation of values, lower-class women were simply ignored. The actual lady was, of course, nothing new on the American scene; she had been present ever since colonial days. What was new in the 1830s was the cult of the lady, her elevation to a status symbol. The advancing prosperity of the early 19th century made it possible for middle-class women to aspire to the status formerly reserved for upper-class women. The "cult of true womanhood" of the 1830s became a vehicle for such aspirations. Mass circulation newspapers and magazines made it possible to teach every woman how to elevate the status of her family by setting "proper" standards of behavior, dress, and literary tastes. *Godey's Lady's Book* and innumerable gift books and tracts of the period all preach the same gospel of "true womanhood"—piety, purity, domesticity.[19] Those unable to reach the goal of becoming ladies were to be satisfied with the lesser goal—acceptance of their "proper place" in the home.

It is no accident that the slogan "woman's place is in the home" took on a certain aggressiveness and shrillness precisely at the time when increasing numbers of poorer women *left* their homes to become factory workers. Working women were not a fit subject for the concern of publishers and mass media writers. Idleness, once a disgrace in the eyes of society, had become a status symbol. Thorstein Veblen, one of the earliest and sharpest commentators on the subject, observed that it had become almost the sole social function of the lady "to put in evidence her economic unit's ability to pay." She was "a means of conspicuously unproductive expenditure," devoted to displaying her husband's wealth.[20] Just as the cult of white womanhood in the South served to preserve a labor and social system based on race distinctions, so did the cult of the lady in an egalitarian society serve as a means of preserving class distinctions. Where class distinctions were not so great, as on the frontier, the position of women was closer to what it had been in colonial days; their economic contribution was more highly valued, their opportunities were less restricted, and their positive participation in community life was taken for granted.

In the urbanized and industrialized Northeast the life experience of middle-class women was different in almost every respect from that of the lower-class women. But there was one thing the society lady and the mill girl had in common—they were equally disfranchised and isolated from the vital centers of power. Yet the political status of women had not actually deteriorated. With very few exceptions women had neither voted nor stood for office during the colonial period. Yet the spread of the franchise to ever wider groups of white males during the Jacksonian age, the removal of property restrictions, the increasing numbers of immigrants who acquired access to the franchise, made the gap between these new enfranchised voters and the disfranchised women more obvious. Quite naturally, educated and propertied women felt this deprivation more keenly. Their own career expectations had been encouraged by widening educational opportunities; their consciousness of their own abilities and of their potential for power had been enhanced by their activities in the reform movements of the 1830s; the general spirit of upward mobility and venturesome entrepreneurship that pervaded the Jacksonian era was infectious. But in the late 1840s a sense of acute frustration enveloped these educated and highly spirited women. Their rising expectations had met with frustration, their hopes had been shattered; they were bitterly conscious of a relative lowering of status and a loss of position. This sense of frustration led them to action; it was one of the main factors in the rise of the woman's rights movement.[21]

The women, who at the first woman's rights convention at Seneca Falls, New York, in 1848 declared boldly and with considerable exaggeration that "the history of mankind is a history of repeated injuries and usurpations on the part of man toward woman, having in direct object the establishment of an absolute tyranny over her," did not speak for the truly exploited and abused working woman.[22] As a matter of fact, they were largely ignorant of her condition and, with the notable exception of Susan B. Anthony, indifferent to her fate. But they judged from the realities of their own life experience. Like most revolutionaries, they were not the most downtrodden but rather the most status-deprived group. Their frustrations and traditional isolation from political power funneled their discontent into fairly utopian declarations and immature organizational means. They would learn better in the long, hard decades of practical struggle. Yet it is their initial emphasis on the legal and political "disabilities" of women which has provided the framework for most of the historical work on women.* For almost a hundred years sympathetic historians have told the story of women in America by deriving from the position of middle-class women a generalization concerning all American women. To avoid distortion, any valid generalization concerning American women after the 1830s should reflect a recognition of class stratification.

* To the date of the first printing of this article (1969).

For lower-class women the changes brought by industrialization were actually advantageous, offering income and advancement opportunities, however limited, and a chance for participation in the ranks of organized labor.* They, by and large, tended to join men in their struggle for economic advancement and became increasingly concerned with economic gains and protective labor legislation. Middle- and upper-class women, on the other hand, reacted to actual and fancied status deprivation by increasing militancy and the formation of organizations for woman's rights, by which they meant especially legal and property rights.

The four decades preceding the Seneca Falls Convention were decisive in the history of American women. They brought an actual deterioration in the economic opportunities open to women, a relative deterioration in their political status, and a rising level of expectation and subsequent frustration in a privileged elite group of educated women. It was in these decades that the values and beliefs that clustered around the assertion "Woman's place is in the home" changed from being descriptive of an existing reality to becoming an ideology. "The cult of true womanhood" extolled woman's predominance in the domestic sphere, while it tried to justify women's exclusion from the public domain, from equal education, and from participation in the political process by claims to tradition, universality, and a history dating back to antiquity, or at least to the *Mayflower*. In a century of modernization and industrialization, women alone were to remain unchanging, embodying in their behavior and attitudes the longing of men and women caught in rapid social change for a mythical archaic past of agrarian family self-sufficiency. In preindustrial America the home was indeed the workplace for both men and women, although the self-sufficiency of the American yeoman, whose economic well-being depended on a network of international trade and mercantilism, was even then more apparent than real. In the 19th and 20th centuries, the home was turned into the realm of woman, while the workplace became the public domain of men. The ideology of "woman's sphere" sought to upgrade women's domestic function by elaborating the role of mother, turning the domestic drudge into a "homemaker" and charging her with elevating her family's status by her exercise of consumer functions and by her display of her own and her family's social graces. These prescribed roles never were a reality. In the 1950s Betty Friedan would describe this ideology and rename it "the feminine mystique," [23] but it was no other than the myth of "woman's proper sphere" created in the 1840s and updated by consumerism and the misunderstood dicta of Freudian psychology.

The decades 1800–1840 also provide the clues to an understanding of the institutional shape of the later women's organizations. These would be led by middle-class women whose self-image, life experience, and ideology had largely been fashioned and influenced by these early, transitional years. The concerns of middle-class women—property rights, the franchise, and moral uplift—

---

* In 1979, I would not agree with this optimistic generalization.

would dominate the woman's rights movement. But side by side with it, and at times co-operating with it, would grow a number of organizations serving the needs of working women.

American women were the largest disfranchised group in the nation's history, and they retained this position longer than any other group. Although they found ways of making their influence felt continuously, not only as individuals but as organized groups, power eluded them. The mill girl and the lady, both born in the age of Jackson, would not gain access to power until they learned to cooperate, each for her own separate interests. It would take almost six decades before they would find common ground. The issue around which they finally would unite and push their movement to victory was the "impractical and utopian" demand raised at Seneca Falls—the means to power in American society—female suffrage.

NOTES

1. Keith E. Melder, "The Beginnings of the Women's Rights Movement in the United States: 1800–1840" (Dissertation, Yale, 1963); Elisabeth A. Dexter, *Colonial Women of Affairs: Women in Business and Professions in America before 1776* (Boston, 1931) and *Career Women of America: 1776–1840* (Francestown, N.H., 1950).

2. Herbert Moller, "Sex Composition and Corresponding Culture Patterns of Colonial America," *William and Mary Quarterly*, Ser. 3, II (April 1945), 113–53.

3. The summary of the status of colonial women is based on the following sources: Mary Benson, *Women in 18th Century America: A Study of Opinion and Social Usage* (New York, 1935); Arthur Calhoun, *A Social History of the American Family* (3 vols.; Cleveland, 1918); Dexter, *Colonial Women*; Dexter, *Career Women*; Edmund S. Morgan, *Virginians at Home: Family Life in the 18th Century* (Williamsburg, 1952); Julia C. Spruill, *Women's Life and Work in the Southern Colonies* (Chapel Hill, 1938).

4. E. M. Boatwright, "The Political and Legal Status of Women in Georgia: 1783–1860," *Georgia Historical Quarterly*, XXV (April 1941); Richard B. Morris, *Studies in the History of American Law* (New York, 1930), chap. 3. A summary of travelers' comments on American women may be found in: Jane Mesick, *The English Traveler in America: 1785–1835* (New York, 1922), pp. 83–99.

5. For facts on colonial medicine the following sources were consulted: Wyndham B. Blanton, *Medicine in Virginia* (3 vols.; Richmond, 1930); N. S. Davis, M.D., *History of Medical Education and Institutions in the United States . . .* (Chicago, 1851); Dexter, *Career Women*; K. C. Hurd-Mead, M.D., *A History of Women in Medicine: from the Earliest Times to the Beginning of the 19th Century* (Haddam, Conn., 1938); Geo. W. Norris, *The Early History of Medicine in Philadelphia* (Philadelphia, 1886); Joseph M. Toner, *Contributions to the annals of Medical Progress in the United States before and during the War of Independence* (Washington, D.C., 1874). The citation regarding Mrs. Allyn is from Hurd-Mead, *Women in Medicine*, p. 487.

6. Fielding H. Garrison, M.D., *An Introduction to the History of Medicine* (Philadelphia, 1929). For licensing legislation: Davis, Mc 88–103; see also: Martin Kaufman, "American Medical Diploma Mills," *The Bulletin of the Tulane University Medical Faculty*, vol. 26, no. 1 (Feb. 1967), 53–57.

7. Among the alternate institutions founded are: New England Female Medical College (1848); Female (later Women's) Medical College of Philadelphia (1850); Women's Medical College and New York Infirmary for Women (1865); Woman's Hospital of Philadelphia (1861); New England Hospital for Women and Children (1862).

   For information on the training of pioneer women physicians see: James R. Chadwick, M.D., *The Study and Practice of Medicine by Women* (New York, 1879).

   For instances of discrimination see: Harriot K. Hunt, M.D., *Glances and Glimpses or Fifty Years Social Including Twenty Years Professional Life* (Boston, 1856); Elizabeth Blackwell, *Pioneer Work in Opening the Medical Profession to Women* (New York, 1865); "Preamble and Resolution of the Philadelphia County Medical Society Upon the Status of Women Physicians with A Reply by a Woman" (Philadelphia, 1867), pamphlet.

   See also biographies of women physicians in Edward and Janet James (eds.), *Notable American Women, 1607–1950: A Biographical Dictionary* (3 vols.; Cambridge, Mass., 1972).

   For a recent work offering a somewhat different interpretation see Mary Roth Walsh, *Doctors Wanted: No Women Need Apply: Sexual Barriers in the Medical Profession, 1835–1975* (New Haven, 1977).

8. George Daniels, "The Professionalization of American Science: The Emergent Period, 1820–1860," paper delivered at the joint session of the History of Science Society and the Society of the History of Technology, San Francisco, December 28, 1965.

9. Hurd-Mead, *Women in Medicine*, p. 391.

10. *Ibid.*, p. 486.

11. Betsy E. Corner, *William Shippen Jr.: Pioneer in American Medical Education* (Philadelphia, 1951), p. 103.

12. *Ibid.*

13. Benjamin Lee Gordon, *Medieval and Renaissance Medicine* (New York, 1959), pp. 689–91. Blanton, *Medicine*, II, 23–24; Hurd-Mead, *Women in Medicine*, pp. 487–88; Annie Nathan Meyer, *Woman's Work in America* (New York, 1891); Harriot K. Hunt, M.D., *Glances* . . . pp. 127–40; Eleanor Flexner, *Century of Struggle: The Woman's Rights Movement in the United States* (Cambridge, Mass., 1959), pp. 115–19.

14. Sophie H. Drinker, "Women Attorneys of Colonial Times," *Maryland Historical Society Bulletin*, vol. LVI, no. 4 (Dec. 1961).

15. Dexter, *Colonial Women*, pp. 34–35, 162–65.

16. Harriet W. Marr, *The Old New England Academies* (New York, 1959), chap. 8; Thomas Woody, *A History of Women's Education in the United States* (2 vols.; New York, 1929), pp. 100–109, 458–60, 492–93.

17. Matthew Carey, *Essays on Political Economy* . . . (Philadelphia, 1822), p. 459.

18. The statements on women industrial workers are based on the following sources: Edith Abbot, *Women in Industry* (New York, 1910), pp. 66–80,

and "Harriet Martineau and the Employment of Women in 1836," *Journal of Political Economy*, XIV (Dec. 1906), 614–26; Matthew Carey, *Miscellaneous Essays* (Philadelphia, 1830), pp. 153–203; Helen L. Sumner, *History of Women in Industry in the United States*, in *Report on Condition of Woman and Child Wage-Earners in the United States* (19 vols., Washington, D.C., 1910), IX; also: Elizabeth F. Baker, *Technology and Woman's Work* (New York, 1964), chaps. 1–5.

19. Emily Putnam, *The Lady: Studies of Certain Significant Phases of Her History* (New York, 1910), pp. 319–20; Barbara Welter, "The Cult of True Womanhood: 1820–1860," *American Quarterly*, vol. XVIII, no. 2, part 1 Summer 1966), 151–74.

20. Veblen generalized from his observations of the society of the Gilded Age and fell into the usual error of simply ignoring the lower-class women, whom he dismissed as "drudges . . . fairly content with their lot," but his analysis of women's role in "conspicuous consumption" and of the function of women's fashions is unsurpassed. For references see: Thorstein Veblen, *The Theory of the Leisure Class* (New York, 1962, first printing, 1899), pp. 70–71, 231–32, and "The Economic Theory of Woman's Dress," *Essays in Our Changing Order* (New York, 1934), pp. 65–77.

21. Like most groups fighting status oppression women formulated a compensatory ideology of female superiority. Norton Mezvinsky has postulated that this was clearly expressed only in 1874; in fact this formulation appeared in the earliest speeches of Elizabeth Cady Stanton and in the speeches and resolutions of the Seneca Falls convention and other pre-Civil War woman's rights conventions. Rather than a main motivating force, the idea was a tactical formulation, designed to take advantage of the popularly held male belief in woman's "moral" superiority and to convince reformers that they needed the votes of women. Those middle-class feminists who believed in woman's "moral" superiority exploited the concept in order to win their major goal—female equality. For references see: Norton Mezvinsky, "An Idea of Female Superiority," *Midcontinent American Studies Journal*, vol. II, no. 1 (Spring 1961), 17–26; Stanton et al., *HWS*, I, 72, 479, 522, 529, and passim; Alan P. Grimes, *The Puritan Ethic and Woman Suffrage* (New York, 1967), chaps. 2 and 3.

22. Stanton et al., *HWS*, I, 70.

23. Betty Friedan, *The Feminine Mystique* (New York, 1963).

Carroll Smith-Rosenberg

Beauty, the Beast and the Militant Woman in Jacksonian America

American society from the 1830s to the 1860s was marked by advances in political democracy, by a rapid increase in economic, social and geographic mobility, and by uncompromising and morally relentless reform movements. Though many aspects of Jacksonianism have been subjected to historical investigation, the possibly stressful effects of such structural change upon family and sex roles have not. The following pages constitute an attempt to glean some understanding of women and women's role in antebellum America through an analysis of a self-consciously female voluntary association dedicated to the eradication of sexual immorality.

Women in Jacksonian America had few rights and little power. Their role in society was passive and sharply limited. Women were, in general, denied formal education above the minimum required by a literate early industrial society. The female brain and nervous system, male physicians and educators agreed, were inadequate to sustained intellectual effort. They were denied the vote in a society which placed a high value upon political participation; political activity might corrupt their pure feminine nature. All professional roles (with the exception of primary school education) were closed to women. Even so traditional a female role as midwife was undermined as male physicians began to establish professional control over obstetrics. Most economic alternatives to marriage (except such burdensome and menial tasks as those of seamstress or domestic) were closed to women. Their property rights were still restricted and females were generally considered to be the legal wards either of the state or of their nearest male rela-

From American Quarterly, 23 (October 1971), pp. 562–84. Published by the University of Pennsylvania; copyright, 1971, Trustees of the University of Pennsylvania.

tive. In the event of divorce, the mother lost custody of her children—even when the husband was conceded to be the erring party. Women's universe was bounded by their homes and the career of father or husband; within the home it was woman's duty to be submissive and patient.

Yet this was a period when change was considered a self-evident good, and when nothing was believed impossible to a determined free will, be it the conquest of a continent, the reform of society or the eternal salvation of all mankind. The contrast between these generally accepted ideals and expectations and the real possibilities available to American women could not have been more sharply drawn. It is not implausible to assume that at least a minority of American women would find ways to manifest a discontent with their comparatively passive and constricted social role.

Only a few women in antebellum America were able, however, to openly criticize their socially defined sexual identity. A handful, like Fanny Wright, devoted themselves to overtly subversive criticism of the social order. A scarcely more numerous group became pioneers in women's education. Others such as Elizabeth Cady Stanton, Lucretia Mott and Susan B. Anthony founded the women's rights movement. But most respectable women —even those with a sense of ill-defined grievance—were unable to explicitly defy traditional sex-role prescriptions.

I would like to suggest that many such women channeled frustration, anger and a compensatory sense of superior righteousness into the reform movements of the first half of the 19th century; and in the controversial moral reform crusade such motivations seem particularly apparent. While unassailable within the absolute categories of a pervasive evangelical worldview, the Female Moral Reform Society's crusade against illicit sexuality permitted an expression of anti-male sentiments. And the Society's "final solution"—the right to control the mores of men—provided a logical emotional redress for those feelings of passivity which we have suggested. It should not be surprising that between 1830 and 1860 a significant number militant women joined a crusade to establish their right to define—and limit —man's sexual behavior.

Yet adultery and prostitution were unaccustomed objects of reform even in the enthusiastic and millennial America of the 1830s. The mere discussion of these taboo subjects shocked most Americans; to undertake such a crusade implied no ordinary degree of commitment. The founders of the Female Moral Reform Society, however, were able to find both legitimization for the expression of grievance normally unspoken and an impulse to activism in the moral categories of evangelical piety. Both pious activism and sex-role anxieties shaped the early years of the Female Moral Reform Society. This conjunction of motives was hardly accidental.

The lady founders of the Moral Reform Society and their new organization represented an extreme wing of that movement within American Protestantism known as the Second Great Awakening. These women were intensely pious Christians, convinced that an era of millennial perfection awaited human effort. In this fervent generation, such deeply felt millennial possibilities made social action a moral imperative. Like many of the abolitionists, Jacksonian crusaders against sexual transgression were dedicated activists, compelled to attack sin wherever it existed and in whatever form it assumed—even the unmentionable sin of illicit sexuality.

New Yorkers' first awareness of the moral reform crusade came in the spring of 1832 when the New York Magdalen Society (an organization which sought to reform prostitutes) issued its first annual report. Written by John McDowall, their missionary and agent, the report stated unhesitatingly that 10,000 prostitutes lived and worked in New York City. Not only sailors and other transients, but men from the city's most respected families, were regular brothel patrons. Lewdness and impurity tainted all sectors of New York society. True Christians, the report concluded, must wage a thoroughgoing crusade against violators of the Seventh Commandment.

The report shocked and irritated respectable New Yorkers—not only by its tone of righteous indignation and implied criticism of the city's old and established families. The report, it seemed clear to many New Yorkers, was obscene, its author a mere seeker after notoriety. Hostility quickly spread from McDowall to the Society itself; its members were verbally abused and threatened with ostracism. The society disbanded.

A few of the women, however, would not retreat. Working quietly, they began to found church-affiliated female moral reform societies. Within a year, they had created a number of such groups, connected for the most part with the city's more evangelical congregations. These pious women hoped to reform prostitutes, but more immediately to warn other God-fearing Christians of the pervasiveness of sexual sin and the need to oppose it. Prostitution was after all only one of many offenses against the Seventh Commandment; adultery, lewd thoughts and language, and bawdy literature were equally sinful in the eyes of God. These women at the same time continued unofficially to support their former missionary, John McDowall, using his newly established moral reform newspaper to advance their cause not only in the city, but throughout New York State.

After more than a year of such discreet crusading, the women active in the moral reform cause felt sufficiently numerous and confident to organize a second city-wide moral reform society, and renew their efforts to reform the city's prostitutes. On the evening of May 12, 1834, they met at the Third Presbyterian Church to found the New York Female Moral Reform Society. . . .

The program adopted by the Female Moral Reform Society in the spring of 1834 embraced two quite different, though to the Society's founders quite consistent, modes of attack. One was absolutist and millennial, an attempt to convert all of America to perfect moral purity. Concretely the New York women hoped to create a militant nationwide women's organization to fight the double standard and indeed any form of licentiousness—beginning of course in their own homes and neighborhoods. Only an organization of women, they contended, could be trusted with so sensitive and yet monumental a task. At the same time, the Society sponsored a parallel and somewhat more pragmatic attempt to convert and reform New York City's prostitutes. Though strikingly dissimilar in method and geographic scope, both efforts were unified by an uncompromising millennial zeal and by a strident hostility to the licentious and predatory male.

The Society began its renewed drive against prostitution in the fall of 1834 when the executive committee appointed John McDowall their missionary to New York's prostitutes and hired two young men to assist him. The Society's three missionaries visited the female wards of the almshouse, the city hospital and jails, leading prayer meetings, distributing Bibles and tracts. A greater proportion of their time, however, was spent in a more controversial manner, systematically visiting—or, to be more accurate, descending upon—brothels, praying with and exhorting both the inmates and their patrons. The missionaries were especially fond of arriving early Sunday morning—catching women and customers as they awoke on the traditionally sacred day. The missionaries would announce their arrival by a vigorous reading of Bible passages, followed by prayer and hymns. At other times they would station themselves across the street from known brothels to observe and note the identity of customers. They soon found their simple presence had an important deterring effect, many men, with doggedly innocent expressions, pausing momentarily and then hastily walking past. Closed coaches, they also reported, were observed to circle suspiciously for upwards of an hour until, the missionary remaining, they drove away.

The Female Moral Reform Society did not depend completely on paid missionaries for the success of such pious harassment. The Society's executive committee, accompanied by like-thinking male volunteers, regularly visited the city's hapless brothels. (The executive committee minutes for January 1835, for example, contain a lengthy discussion of the properly discreet makeup of groups for such "active visiting.") The members went primarily to pray and to exert moral influence. They were not unaware, however, of the financially disruptive effect that frequent visits of large groups of praying Christians would have. The executive committee also aided the concerned parents (usually rural) of runaway daughters who, they feared, might have drifted to the city and been forced into prostitution. Members visited brothels asking for information about such girls; one pious volunteer even pretended to be delivering laundry in order to gain admittance to a brothel suspected of hiding such a runaway.

In conjunction with their visiting, the Moral Reform Society opened a House of Reception, a would-be refuge for prostitutes seeking to reform. The Society's managers and missionaries felt that if the prostitute could be convinced of her sin, and then offered both a place of retreat and an economic alternative to prostitution, reform would surely follow. Thus they envisioned their home as a "house of industry" where the errant ones would be taught new trades and prepared for useful jobs—while being instructed in morality and religion. When the managers felt their repentant charges prepared to return to society, they attempted to find them jobs with Christian families—and, so far as possible, away from the city's temptations.

Despite their efforts, however, few prostitutes reformed; fewer still appeared, to their benefactresses, to have experienced the saving grace of conversion. Indeed, the number of inmates at the Society's House of Reception was always small. In March 1835, for instance, the executive committee reported only fourteen women at the House. A year later, total admissions had reached but thirty—only four of whom, were considered saved. The final debacle came that summer when the regular manager of the House left the city because of poor health. In his absence, the executive committee reported unhappily, the inmates seized control, and discipline and morality deteriorated precipitously. The managers reassembled in the fall to find their home in chaos. Bitterly discouraged, they dismissed the few remaining unruly inmates and closed the building.

The moral rehabilitation of New York's streetwalkers was but one aspect of the Society's attack upon immorality. The founders of the Female Moral Reform Society saw as their principal objective the creation of a woman's crusade to combat sexual license generally and the double standard particularly. American women would no longer willingly tolerate that traditional—and role-defining—masculine ethos which allotted respect to the hearty drinker and the sexual athlete. This age-old code of masculinity was as obviously related to man's social preeminence as it was contrary to society's explicitly avowed norms of purity and domesticity. The subterranean mores of the American male must be confronted, exposed and rooted out. . . .

The founders and supporters of the Female Moral Reform Society entertained several primary assumptions concerning the nature of human sexuality. Perhaps most central was the conviction that women felt little sexual desire; they were in almost every instance induced to violate the Seventh Commandment by lascivious men who craftily manipulated not their sensuality, but rather the female's trusting and affectionate nature. A woman acted out of romantic love, not carnal desire; she was innocent and defenseless, gentle and passive. "The worst crime alleged against [the fallen woman] in the outset," the *Advocate's* editors explained, "is . . . 'She is without discretion.' She is open-hearted, sincere, and affectionate. . . . She trusts the vows of the faithless. She commits her all into the hands of the deceiver."

The male lecher, on the other hand, was a creature controlled by base sexual drives which he neither could nor would control. He was, the *Advocate's* editors bitterly complained, powerful and decisive; unwilling (possibly unable) to curb his own willfulness, he callously used it to coerce the more passive and submissive female. This was an age of rhetorical expansiveness, and the *Advocate's* editors and correspondents felt little constraint in their delineation of the dominant and aggressive male. "Reckless," "bold," "mad," "drenched in sin" were terms used commonly to describe erring males; they "robbed," "ruined" and "rioted." But one term above all others seemed most fit to describe the lecher—"The Destroyer."

A deep sense of anger and frustration characterized the *Advocate's* discussion of such all-conquering males, a theme reiterated again and again in the letters sent to the paper by rural sympathizers. Women saw themselves with few defenses against the determined male; his will was far stronger than that of woman. Such letters often expressed a bitterness which seems directed not only against the specific seducer, but toward all American men. One representative rural subscriber complained, for example: "Honorable men; they would not plunder; . . . an imputation on their honour might cost a man his life's blood. And yet they are so passingly mean, so utterly contemptible, as basely and treacherously to contrive . . . the destruction of happiness, peace, morality, and all that is endearing in social life; they plunge into degradation, misery, and ruin, those whom they profess to love. O let them not be trusted. Their 'tender mercies are cruel.'"

The double standard seemed thus particularly unjust; it came to symbolize and embody for the Society and its rural sympathizers the callous indifference—indeed at times almost sadistic pleasure—a male-dominated society took in the misfortune of a passive and defenseless woman. The respectable harshly denied her their friendship; even parents might reject her. Often only the brothel offered food and shelter. But what of her seducer? Conventional wisdom found it easy to condone his greater sin: men will be men and right-thinking women must not inquire into such questionable matters.

But it was just such matters, the Society contended, to which women must address themselves. They must enforce God's commandments despite hostility and censure. "Public opinion must be operated upon," the executive committee decided in the winter of 1835, " by endeavoring to bring the virtuous to treat the guilty of both sexes alike, and exercise toward them the same feeling." "Why should a female be trodden under foot," the executive committee's minutes questioned plaintively, "and spurned from society and driven from a parent's roof, if she but fall into sin—while common consent allows the male to habituate himself to this vice, and treats him as not guilty. Has God made a distinction in regard to the two sexes in this respect? The guilty woman too should be condemned, the Moral Reform Society's quarterly meeting resolved in 1838: "But let not the most guilty of the two—the deliberate destroyer of female innocence—be afforded even an 'apron of fig leaves' to conceal the blackness of his crimes."

Women must unite in a holy crusade against such sinners. The Society called upon pious women throughout the country to shun all social contact with men suspected of improper behavior—even if that behavior consisted only of reading improper books or singing indelicate songs. Churchgoing women of every village and town must organize local campaigns to outlaw such men from society and hold them up to public judgment. "Admit him not to your house," the executive committee urged, "hold no converse with him, warn others of him, permit not your friends to have fellowship with him, mark him as an evildoer, stamp him as a villain and exclaim, 'Behold the Seducer.'" The power of ostracism could become an effective weapon in the defense of morality.

A key tactic in this campaign of public exposure was the Society's willingness to publish the names of men suspected of sexual immorality. The *Advocate*'s editors announced in their first issue that they intended to pursue this policy, first begun by John McDowall in his *Journal*. "We think it proper," they stated defiantly, "even to expose names, for the same reason that the names of thieves and robbers are published, that the public may know them and govern themselves accordingly. We mean to let the licentious know, that if they are not ashamed of their debasing vice, we will not be ashamed to expose them. . . . It is a justice which we owe each other." Their readers responded enthusiastically to this invitation. Letters from rural subscribers poured into the *Advocate*, recounting specific instances of seduction in their towns and warning readers to avoid the men described. The editors dutifully set them in type and printed them. . . .

Ostracism, exposure and statutory enactment offered immediate, if unfortunately partial, solutions to the problem of male licentiousness. But for the seduced and ruined victim such vengeance came too late. The tactic of preference, women moral reformers agreed, was to educate children, especially young male children, to a literal adherence to the Seventh Commandment. This was a mother's task. American mothers, the *Advocate*'s editors repeated endlessly, must educate their sons to reject the double standard. No child was too young, no efforts too diligent in this crucial aspect of socialization. The true foundations of such a successful effort lay in an early and highly pietistic religious education and in the inculcation of a related imperative—the son's absolute and unquestioned obedience to his mother's will. "Obedience, entire and unquestioned, must be secured, or all is lost." The mother must devote herself whole-heartedly to this task for self-will in a child was an ever-recurring evil. "Let us watch over them continually. . . . Let us . . . teach them when they go out and when they come in—when they lie down, and when they rise up. . . ." A son must learn to confide in his mother instinctively; no thought should be hidden from her.

Explicit education in the Seventh Commandment itself should begin quite early for bitter experience had shown that no child was too young for such sensual temptation. As her son grew older, his mother was urged to instill in him a love for the quiet of domesticity, a repugnance for the unnatural excitements of the theater and tavern. He should be taught to prefer home and the companionship of pious women to the temptations of bachelor life. The final step in a young man's moral education would come one evening shortly before he was to leave home for the first time. That night, the *Advocate* advised its readers, the mother must spend a long earnest time at his bedside (ordinarily in the dark to hide her natural blushes) discussing the importance of maintaining his sexual purity and the temptations he would inevitably face in attempting to remain true to his mother's religious principles.

Mothers, not fathers, were urged to supervise the sexual education of sons. Mothers, the Society argued, spent most time with their children; fathers were usually occupied with business concerns and found little time for their children. Sons were naturally close to their mothers and devoted maternal supervision would cement these natural ties. A mother devoted to the moral reform cause could be trusted to teach her son to reject the traditional ethos of masculinity and accept the higher—more feminine—code of Christianity. A son thus educated would be inevitably a recruit in the women's crusade against sexual license.

The Society's general program of exposure and ostracism, lobbying and education depended for effectiveness upon the creation of a national association of militant and pious women. In the fall of 1834, but a few months after they had organized their Society, its New York officers began to create such a woman's organization. At first they worked through the *Advocate* and the small network of sympathizers John McDowall's efforts had created. By the spring of 1835, however, they were able to hire a minister to travel through western New York State "in behalf of Moral Reform causes." The following year the committee sent two female missionaries, the editor of the Society's newspaper and a paid female agent, on a thousand-mile tour of the New England states. Visiting women's groups and churches in Brattleboro, Deerfield, Northampton, Pittsfield, the Stockbridges and many other towns, the ladies rallied their sisters to the moral reform cause and helped organize some forty-one new auxiliaries. Each succeeding summer saw similar trips by paid agents and managers of the Society throughout New York State and New England. By 1839, the New York Female Moral Reform Society boasted some 445 female auxiliaries, principally in greater New England. So successful were these efforts that within a few years the bulk of the Society's membership and financial support came from its auxiliaries. In February 1838, the executive committee voted to invite representatives of these auxiliaries to attend the Society's annual meeting. The following year the New York Society voted at its annual convention to reorganize as a national society—the American Female Moral Reform Society; the New York group would be simply one of its many constituent societies. . . .

The New York Female Moral Reform Society quite consciously sought to inspire in its members a sense of solidarity in a cause peculiar to their sex, and demanding total commitment, to give them a sense of worthiness and autonomy outside woman's traditionally confining role. Its members, their officers forcefully declared, formed a united phalanx twenty thousand strong, "A UNION OF SENTIMENT AND EFFORT AMONG . . . VIRTUOUS FEMALES FROM MAINE TO ALABAMA." The officers of the New York Society were particularly conscious of the emotional importance of female solidarity within their movement—and the significant role that they as leaders played in the lives of their rural supporters. "Thousands are looking to us," the executive committee recorded in their minutes with mingled pride and responsibility, "with the expectation that the principles we have adopted, and the example we have set before the world will continue to be held up & they reasonably expect to witness our *united onward* movements till the conflict shall end in Victory.". . .

In some ways, indeed, the New York Female Moral Reform Society could be considered a militant woman's organization. Although it was not overtly part of the woman's rights movement, it did concern itself with a number of feminist issues, especially those relating to woman's economic role. Society, the *Advocate*'s editors argued, had unjustly confined women to domestic tasks. There were many jobs in society that women could and should be trained to fill. They could perform any light indoor work as well as men. In such positions—as clerks and artisans—they would receive decent wages and consequent self-respect. And this economic emphasis was no arbitrary or inappropriate one, the Society contended. Thousands of women simply had to work; widows, orphaned young women, wives and mothers whose husbands could not work because of illness or intemperance had to support themselves and their children. Unfortunately, they had now to exercise these responsibilities on the pathetically inadequate salaries they received as domestics, washerwomen or seamstresses—crowded, underpaid and physically unpleasant occupations. By the end of the 1840s, the Society had adopted the cause of the working woman and made it one of their principal concerns—in the 1850s even urging women to join unions and, when mechanization came to the garment industry, helping underpaid seamstresses rent sewing machines at low rates.

The Society sought consciously, moreover, to demonstrate woman's ability to perform successfully in fields traditionally reserved for men. Quite early in their history they adopted the policy of hiring only women employees. From the first, of course, only women had been officers and managers of the Society. And after a few years, these officers began to hire women in preference to men as agents and to urge other charitable societies and government agencies to do likewise. (They did this although the only salaried charitable positions held by women in this period tended to be those of teachers in girls' schools or supervisors of women's wings in hospitals and homes for juvenile delinquents.) In February 1835, for instance, the executive committee hired a woman agent to solicit subscriptions to the *Advocate*. That summer they hired another woman to travel through New England and New York State organizing auxiliaries and giving speeches to women on moral reform. In October of 1836, the executive officers appointed two women as editors of their journal—undoubtedly among the first of their sex in this country to hold such positions. In 1841, the executive committee decided to replace their male financial agent with a woman bookkeeper. By 1843 women even set type and did the folding for the Society's journal. All these jobs, the ladies proudly, indeed aggressively stressed, were appropriate tasks for women.

The broad feminist implications of such statements and actions must have been apparent to the officers of the New York Society. And indeed the Society's executive committee maintained discreet but active ties with the broader woman's rights movement of the 1830s, 40's and 50s; at one point at least, they flirted with official endorsement of a bold woman's rights position. Evidence of this flirtation can be seen in the minutes of the executive committee and occasionally came to light in articles and editorials appearing in the Advocate. As early as the mid-1830s, for instance, the executive committee began to correspond with a number of women who were then or were later to become active in the woman's rights movement. Lucretia Mott, abolitionist and pioneer feminist, was a founder and secretary of the Philadelphia Female Moral Reform Society; as such she was in frequent communication with the New York executive committee. Emma Willard, a militant advocate of women's education and founder of the Troy Female Seminary, was another of the executive committee's regular correspondents. Significantly, when Elizabeth Blackwell, the first woman doctor in either the United States or Great Britain, received her medical degree, Emma Willard wrote to the New York executive committee asking its members to use their influence to find her a job. The Society did more than that. The Advocate featured a story dramatizing Dr. Blackwell's struggles. The door was now open for other women, the editors urged; medicine was a peculiarly appropriate profession for sensitive and sympathetic womankind. The Society offered to help interested women in securing admission to medical school.

One of the most controversial aspects of the early woman's rights movement was its criticism of the subservient role of women within the American family, and of the American man's imperious and domineering behavior toward women. Much of the Society's rhetorical onslaught upon the male's lack of sexual accountability served as a screen for a more general—and less socially acceptable—resentment of masculine social preeminence. Occasionally, however, the Advocate expressed such resentment overtly. An editorial in 1838, for example, revealed a deeply felt antagonism toward the power asserted by husbands over their wives and children. "A portion of the inhabitants of this favored land," the Society admonished, "are groaning under a despotism, which seems to be modeled precisely after that of the Autocrat of Russia. . . . We allude to the tyranny exercised in the HOME department, where lordly man, 'clothed with a little brief authority,' rules his trembling subjects with a rod of iron, conscious of entire impunity, and exalting in his fancied superiority." The Society's editorialist continued, perhaps even more bitterly: "Instead of regarding his wife as a help-mate for him, an equal sharer in his joys and sorrows, he looks upon her as a useful article of furniture, which is valuable only for the benefit derived from it, but which may be thrown aside at pleasure." Such behavior, the editorial carefully emphasized, was not only commonplace, experienced by many of the Society's own members—even the wives of "Christians" and of ministers—but was accepted and even justified by society; was it not sanctioned by the Bible? . . .

The membership of the New York Female Moral Reform Society chose not to openly espouse the woman's rights movement. Yet many interesting emotional parallels remain to link the moral reform crusade and the suffrage movement of Elizabeth Cady Stanton, the Grimké sisters and Susan B. Anthony. In its own way, indeed, the war for purification of sexual mores was far more fundamental in its implications for woman's traditional role than the demand for woman's education—or even the vote.

Many of the needs and attitudes, moreover, expressed by suffragette leaders at the Seneca Falls Convention and in their efforts in the generation following are found decades earlier in the letters of rural women in the *Advocate of Moral Reform*. Both groups found woman's traditionally passive role intolerable. Both wished to assert female worth and values in a heretofore entirely male world. Both welcomed the creation of a sense of feminine loyalty and sisterhood that could give emotional strength and comfort to women isolated within their homes—whether in a remote farmstead or a Gramercy Park mansion. And it can hardly be assumed that the demand for votes for women was appreciably more radical than a moral absolutism which encouraged women to invade bordellos, befriend harlots and publicly discuss rape, seduction and prostitution.

It is important as well to re-emphasize a more general historical perspective. When the pious women founders of the Moral Reform Society gathered at the Third Free Presbyterian Church, it was fourteen years before the Seneca Falls Convention—which has traditionally been accepted as the beginning of the woman's rights movement in the United States. There simply was no woman's movement in the 1830s. The future leaders were either still adolescents or just becoming dissatisfied with aspects of their role. Women advocates of moral reform were among the very first American women to challenge their completely passive, home-oriented image. They were among the first to travel throughout the country without male chaperones. They published, financed, even set type for their own paper and defied a bitter and long-standing male opposition to their cause. They began, in short, to create a broader, less constricted sense of female identity. Naturally enough, they were dependent upon the activist impulse and legitimating imperatives of evangelical religion. This was indeed a complex symbiosis, the energies of pietism and the grievances of role discontent creating the new and activist female consciousness which characterized the history of the American Female Moral Reform Society in antebellum American. Their experience, moreover, was probably shared, though less overtly, by the thousands of women who devoted time and money to the great number of reform causes which multiplied in Jacksonian America. Women in the abolition and the temperance movements (and to a less extent in more narrowly evangelical and religious causes) also developed a sense of their ability to judge for themselves and of their right to publicly criticize the values of the larger society. The lives and self-image of all these women had changed—if only so little— because of their new reforming interests.

SUGGESTIONS FOR FURTHER READING

After years of neglect the field of women in American history is now booming, and every month several new titles come from the publishers. Bookstores often have special sections of material for Women's Studies. It is becoming difficult to separate the important from the trivial. Perhaps the best place to start reading on the woman movement is Eleanor Flexner, *Century of Struggle: The Woman's Rights Movement in the United States* (Cambridge, Mass., 1959), which emphasizes the role of a few feminists in working for women's rights. This may be supplemented by a lively account, Andrew Sinclair, *The Emancipation of the American Woman* (New York, 1965).

Ellen Carol DuBois, *Feminism and Suffrage: The Emergence of an Independent Women's Movement* (Ithaca, 1978) is a recent and more detailed study. Nancy F. Cott, *The Bonds of Womanhood: Woman's Sphere in New England, 1780–1835* (New Haven, 1977), extends Barbara Welter's thesis and makes it more complex. Ann Douglas, *The Feminization of American Culture* (New York, 1977), uses a variety of sources including fiction to argue that middle-class women and liberal clergymen created a feminine consensus. Linda Gordon, *Woman's Body, Woman's Right: Birth Control in America* (New York, 1976), finds conflict between the sexes and between those favoring birth control and the rest of society. An important article is Carroll Smith-Rosenberg, "The Female World of Love and Ritual," *Signs: A Journal of Women in Culture and Society I* (1975) 1–29.

Two general accounts of the women's movement are Mary P. Ryan, *Womanhood in America: From Colonial Times to the Present* (New York, 1975), and Carol Ruth Berkin and Mary Beth Norton, *Women of America: A History* (Boston, 1979). Two books of documents, both with interesting and perceptive introductions, are especially recommended. Nancy F. Cott, *Root of Bitterness: Documents of the Social History of American Women* (New York, 1972) republishes material from women of all classes and describes the condition of women as well as their rebellion against that condition. Alice S. Rossi, *The Feminist Papers: From Adams to de Beauvoir* (New York, 1973) republishes some of the most important documents from the women's movement, but the introductions fit the documents into the social context. Martha Vicinus, ed., *Suffer and Be Still: Women in the Victorian Age* (Bloomington, 1973) is a collection of essays on the condition of women in England and America. Anne Firor Scott, *The Southern Lady: From Pedestal to Politics 1830–1930* (Chicago, 1970) explores the myth and the reality of being a lady in the South.

* Available in paperback edition.

The Black Response to Slavery

The first blacks in the English colonies of North America arrived in 1619; John Rolfe recorded that in that year a Dutch ship "sold" twenty Negroes in Virginia. While there is some dispute about when the institution of slavery was actually established—the early arrivals were probably indentured servants with limited terms of servitude—it is quite clear that by 1660 the black had become a slave. Servitude had become permanent, and children of slaves, according to law, themselves became slaves. In the years that followed, slaves increased in numbers, gradually displacing indentured servants as the primary form of labor on Southern plantations.

Declining profits in tobacco culture in the late eighteenth century, combined with the nagging contradiction between human bondage and colonial proclamations of liberty and human rights, led some Americans to foresee an early end to slavery. These expectations dissolved, however. Eli Whitney's invention of the cotton gin in 1793 made commercial cotton growing economically feasible and suddenly Southern planters found a new and profitable use for their slaves.

In the North, slavery gradually disappeared, but in the South the number of slaves grew rapidly as planters and farmers moved west, carving plantations and farms out of the wilderness. By 1860 the nation had some four million slaves, most of them living in the cotton-growing areas. Slavery had become the South's "peculiar institution."

The existence of slavery produced a number of contradictions in American society. Many felt that the holding of human beings as property offended their religious scruples and their democratic inclinations, and often such people became militant abolitionists. Others, sure that slavery was a menace to free labor everywhere, fought the extension of slavery into new territories. Some charged that servile labor held back economic development and consigned the South to poverty.

But perhaps the most potent of the contradictions was that between the slave and his owner. The slave was restricted in his movements, forced to work for little more than subsistence, subjected to corporal punishment, and afforded little or no legal redress for grievances. It might be expected that such conditions in the midst of an essentially democratic society would have induced longings for freedom as well as resentments provoking servile insurrections. Slaves who escaped from the South often wrote of their experiences in slavery in just such terms; and the elaborate precautions Southerners took to prevent revolt reflected their concern.

Yet there was another side to the question. Even as they spoke of the dangers of slave revolts, Southerners argued that the slaves were happy in their condition. On the one hand, it was explained, slaves were better treated than abolitionists and antislavery proponents charged; indeed, black slaves were far better off than the white "wage slaves" of the North. On the other hand, defenders of slavery insisted that the black was incapable of understanding and appreciating freedom. He was said to be inferior to the white man and had to be forced to work under direction in order to survive.

Thus debate on the black's response to slavery is as old as the peculiar institution itself. Until relatively recently, historians have discussed the matter in much the same way as did the pro- and anti-slavery advocates of the ante-bellum years. Many modern historians, however, have shifted the emphasis significantly. They deny that the black's response to servitude must be seen as either docile acceptance or militant opposition. Some note that slaves effectively resisted their status in ways short of armed rebellion, while others argue that even within the restricted confines of a barbaric system, slaves found ways to protect themselves, to maintain their cultural identity, and to mitigate the rigors of their servitude. Although this shift in emphasis has provided important new insights, it has not stilled the debate, as the following selections make clear.

Kenneth M. Stampp finds the slave restive under his bondage, seeking always to lessen its restraints, willing to chance punishment in order to escape, and at times even attempting outright rebellion. Implicit in his approach to the black in this selection is a point of view that he expresses explicitly in the preface to the book from which the selection is taken: "I have assumed that the slaves were merely ordinary human beings, that innately Negroes are, after all, only white men with black skins, nothing more, nothing less."

In the next selection, Robert William Fogel and Stanley L. Engerman argue that the slaves were efficient and productive workers largely because of the effective organization of plantation work, which was very often directed by the slaves themselves. The slaves were successful workers not because they were happy with their lot but because this course was the best available to them: ". . . though they longed for freedom, slaves could strive to develop and improve themselves in the only way that was open to them."

Eugene D. Genovese argues that the work rhythms of the slaves were those of the preindustrial system in which they lived. Moreover, he continues, the slaves, within the limitations imposed by a barbaric system, were able to develop their own work ethic, which was a part of the unique black culture that they were able to carve out for themselves under slavery. For Genovese blacks under slavery were able to forge a culture that provided them with living space within the system, a culture that remains the property of blacks today.

As these selections make clear, the response of blacks to slavery cannot be assessed simply by counting the numbers of armed revolts. We must look more deeply into the problem of how the experience of slavery affected the blacks themselves. Did the slaves respond to a system that they were powerless to alter by becoming highly motivated and efficient workers in hopes that this would mitigate the rigors of the system? Did the conditions of slavery produce resentments, frustrations, and a will to resist that led to day-to-day resistance and, when the possibility arose, to armed conflict and rebellion? Did the conflict between master and slave create an identifiable black identity and culture that became the means for black resistance to servitude?

Kenneth M. Stampp

A Troublesome Property

Slaves apparently thought of the South's peculiar institution chiefly as a system of labor extortion. Of course they felt its impact in other ways—in their social status, their legal status, and their private lives—but they felt it most acutely in their lack of control over their own time and labor. If discontented with bondage, they could be expected to direct their protests principally against the master's claim to their work. Whether the majority were satisfied with their lot, whether they willingly obeyed the master's commands, has long been a controversial question.

It may be a little presumptuous of one who has never been a slave to pretend to know how slaves felt; yet defenders of slavery did not hesitate to assert that most of them were quite content with servitude. Bondsmen generally were cheerful and acquiescent—so the argument went—because they were treated with kindness and relieved of all responsibilities; having known no other condition, they unthinkingly accepted bondage as their natural status. "They find themselves first existing in this state," observed a Northerner who had resided in Mississippi, "and pass through life without questioning the justice of their allotment, which, if they think at all, they suppose a natural one."[1] Presumably they acquiesced, too, because of innate racial traits, because of the "genius of African temperament," the Negro being "instinctively . . . contented" and "quick to respond to the stimulus of joy, quick to forget his grief." Except in rare instances when he was cruelly treated, his "peaceful frame of mind was not greatly disturbed by the mere condition of slavery."[2]

From The Peculiar Institution, by Kenneth M. Stampp. Copyright © 1956 by Kenneth M. Stampp. Reprinted by permission of Alfred A. Knopf, Inc.

1 [Ingraham], South-West, II, p. 201.
2 Francis P. Gaines, The Southern Plantation: A Study in the Development and the Accuracy of a Tradition (New York, 1924), p. 244.

Though sometimes asserted with such assurance, it was never proved that the great majority of bondsmen had no concept of freedom and were therefore contented. It was always based upon inference. Most masters believed they understood their slaves, and most slaves apparently made no attempt to discourage this belief. Instead, they said the things they thought their masters wanted to hear, and they conformed with the rituals that signified their subservience. Rare, no doubt, was the master who never heard any of his humble, smiling bondsmen affirm their loyalty and contentment. When visitors in the South asked a slave whether he wished to be free, he usually replied: "No, massa, me no want to be free, have good massa, take care of me when I sick, never 'buse nigger; no, me no want to be free."[3]

This was dubious evidence, as some slaveholders knew and others learned. (They would have acknowledged the validity of an affirmation later to be made by a post-bellum South Carolinian: "the white man does not know the Negro so well as he thinks he does."[4]) A Virginia master believed that slaves had their faculties "sharpened by constant exercise" and that their perceptions were "extremely fine and acute." An overseer decided that a man who "put his confidence in a Negro . . . was simply a Damned Fool." A Georgia planter concluded: "So deceitful is the Negro that as far as my own experience extends I could never in a single instance decipher his character. . . . We planters could never get at the truth."[5] When advertising for runaways, masters repeatedly confirmed these opinions by describing them as being "very artful," as acting and conversing in a way "calculated to deceive almost any one," and (most frequently) as possessing a "pretty glib and plausible tongue." Yet proslavery writers swallowed whole the assurances of contentment which these glib-tongued "scoundrels" gave them.

Since there are few reliable records of what went on in the minds of slaves, one can only infer their thoughts and feelings from their behavior, that of their masters, and the logic of their situation. That they had no understanding of freedom, and therefore accepted bondage as their natural condition, is hard to believe. They had only to observe their masters and the other free men about them to obtain a very distinct idea of the meaning and advantages of freedom. All knew that some Negroes had been emancipated; they knew that freedom was a *possible* condition for any of them. They "continually have before their eyes, persons of the same color, many of whom they have known in slavery . . . freed from the control of masters, working where they please, going whither they please, and expending their money how they please." So declared a group of Charleston whites who

---

[3] Ethan A. Andrews, *Slavery and the Domestic Slave Trade in the United States* (Boston, 1836), pp. 97–99.

[4] Mason Crum, *Gullah: Negro Life in the Carolina Sea Islands* (Durham, 1940), p. 80.

[5] Abdy, *Journal*, II, pp. 216–17; Manigault Ms. Plantation Records, summary of plantation events, May 1863–May 1864; entry for March 22, 1867.

petitioned the legislature to expel all free persons of color from South Carolina.[6]

Untutored slaves seldom speculated about freedom as an abstraction. They naturally focused their interest upon such immediate and practical benefits as escaping severe discipline and getting increased compensation for less labor. An ex-slave explained simply what freedom meant to her: "I am now my own mistress, and need not work when I am sick. I can do my own thinkings, without having any to think for me,—to tell me when to come, what to do, and to sell me when they get ready."[7] Though she may never have heard of the doctrine of natural rights, her concept of freedom surely embraced more than its incidental aspects.

If slaves had some understanding of the pragmatic benefits of freedom, no doubt most of them desired to enjoy these benefits. Some, perhaps the majority, had no more than a vague, unarticulated yearning for escape from burdens and restraints. They submitted, but submission did not necessarily mean enjoyment or even contentment. And some slaves felt more than a vague longing, felt a sharp pang and saw a clear objective. They struggled toward it against imposing obstacles, expressing their discontent through positive action.

Were these, the actively discontented, to be found only among slaves exposed to great physical cruelty? Apparently not. Slaves of gentle masters might seek freedom as eagerly as those of cruel ones. Frederick Douglass, the most famous refugee from slavery, testified: "Beat and cuff your slave, keep him hungry and spiritless, and he will follow the chain of his master like a dog; but feed and clothe him well,—work him moderately—surround him with physical comfort,—and dreams of freedom intrude. Give him a *bad* master, and he aspires to a *good* master; give him a good master, and he wishes to become his *own* master."[8] Here was a problem confronting conscientious slaveholders. One confessed that slaveownership subjected "the man of care and feeling to more dilemmas than perhaps any other vocation he could follow. . . . To moralize and induce the slave to assimilate with the master and his interest, has been and is the great desideratum aimed at; but I am sorry to say I have long since desponded in the completion of this task."[9] Another slaveholder who vaguely affirmed that his bondsmen were "as contented as their nature will permit" was in reality agreeing with what a white man once bluntly stated before the Louisiana Supreme Court: The desire for freedom "exists in the bosom of every slave—whether the recent captive, or him to whom bondage has become a habit."[10]

---

6 Phillips (ed.), *Plantation and Frontier*, II, pp. 108–11.
7 Drew, *The Refugee*, p. 177.
8 Douglass, *My Bondage*, pp. 263–64.
9 *Southern Agriculturist*, III (1830), p. 238.
10 Ebenezer Pettigrew to Mrs. Mary Shepard, September 22, 1847, Pettigrew Family Papers; Catterall (ed.), *Judicial Cases*, III, p. 568.

Slaves showed great eagerness to get some—if they could not get all—
of the advantages of freedom. They liked to hire their own time, or to work
in tobacco factories, or for the Tredegar Iron Company, because they were
then under less restraint than in the fields, and they had greater opportunities to earn money for themselves. They seized the chance to make their
condition approximate that of freedmen.

But they were not satisfied with a mere loosening of the bonds. Former
slaves affirmed that one had to "know the *heart* of the poor slave—learn
his secret thoughts—thoughts he dare not utter in the hearing of the white
man," to understand this. "A man who has been in slavery knows, and no
one else can know, the yearnings to be free, and the fear of making the
attempt." While he was still in bondage Douglass wondered how white
people knew that God had made black people to be slaves. "Did they go up
in the sky and learn it? or, did He come down and tell them so?"[11] A slave
on a Louisiana sugar plantation assured Olmsted that slaves did desire freedom, that they talked about it among themselves, and that they speculated
about what they would do if they were emancipated. When a traveler in
Georgia told a slave he understood his people did not wish to be free, "His
only answer was a short, contemptuous laugh."[12]

If slaves yielded to authority most of the time, they did so because they
usually saw no other practical choice. Yet few went through life without
expressing discontent somehow, some time. Even the most passive slaves,
usually before they reached middle age, flared up in protests now and then.
The majority, as they grew older, lost hope and spirit. Some, however, never
quite gave in, never stopped fighting back in one way or another. The "bad
character" of this "insolent," "surly," and "unruly" sort made them a lia-
bility to those who owned them, for a slave's value was measured by his
disposition as much as by his strength and skills. Such rebels seldom won
legal freedom, yet they never quite admitted they were slaves.

Slave resistance, whether bold and persistent or mild and sporadic,
created for all slaveholders a serious problem of discipline. As authors or as
readers they saw the problem discussed in numberless essays with such titles
as "The Management of Negroes," essays which filled the pages of southern
agricultural periodicals. Many masters had reason to agree with the owner
of a hundred slaves who complained that he possessed "just 100 troubles,"
or with the North Carolina planter who said that slaves were "a troublesome
property."[13]

The record of slave resistance forms a chapter in the story of the end-

---

[11] Northup, *Twelve Years a Slave*, pp. 206–207; Drew, *The Refugee*, pp. 43, 115;
Douglass, *My Bondage*, pp. 89–91.
[12] Olmsted, *Seaboard*, pp. 679–80; James Stirling, *Letters from the Slave States* (London,
1857), p. 201.
[13] Gustavus A. Henry to his wife, November 25, 1849, Henry Papers; William S. Pettigrew
to James C. Johnston, January 6, 1947 (copy), Pettigrew Family Papers.

less struggle to give dignity to human life. Though the history of southern bondage reveals that men *can* be enslaved under certain conditions, it also demonstrates that their love of freedom is hard to crush. The subtle expressions of this spirit, no less than the daring thrusts for liberty, comprise one of the richest gifts the slaves have left posterity. In making themselves "troublesome property," they provide reassuring evidence that slaves seldom wear their shackles lightly.

The record of the minority who waged ceaseless and open warfare against their bondage makes an inspiring chapter, also, in the history of Americans of African descent. True, these rebels were exceptional men, but the historian of any group properly devotes much attention to those members who did extraordinary things, men in whose lives the problems of their age found focus, men who voiced the feelings and aspirations of the more timid and less articulate masses. As the American Revolution produced folk heroes, so also did southern slavery—heroes who, in both cases, gave much for the cause of human freedom. . . .

The masses of slaves, for whom freedom could have been little more than an idle dream, found countless ways to exasperate their masters—and thus saw to it that bondage as a labor system had its limitations as well as its advantages. Many slaves were doubtless pulled by conflicting impulses; a desire for the personal satisfaction gained from doing a piece of work well, as against a desire to resist or outwit the master by doing it badly or not at all. Which impulse dominated a given slave at a given time depended upon many things, but the latter one was bound to control him at least part of the time. Whether the master was humane or cruel, whether he owned a small farm or a large plantation, did not seem to be crucial considerations, for almost all slaveholders had trouble in managing this kind of labor.

Not that every malingering or intractable bondsman was pursuing a course calculated to lead toward freedom for his people, or at least for himself. He was not always even making a conscious protest against bondage. Some of his "misdeeds" were merely unconscious reflections of the character that slavery had given him—evidence, as one planter explained, that slavery tended to render him "callous to the ideas of honor and even honesty" (as the master class understood those terms). "Come day, go day, God send Sunday," eloquently expressed the indifference of the "heedless, thoughtless," slave.[14]

But the element of conscious resistance was often present too; whether or not it was the predominant one the master usually had no way of knowing. In any case, he was likely to be distressed by his inability to persuade his slaves to "assimilate" their interest with his. "We all know," complained one slaveholder, that the slave's feeling of obligation to his master "is of so

---

[14] Johnson, *Ante-Bellum North Carolina*, p. 496; W. P. Harrison, *The Gospel Among the Slaves* (Nashville, 1893), p. 103.

flimsy a character that none of us rely upon it."[15]

Slaveholders disagreed as to whether "smart" Negores or "stupid" ones caused them the greater trouble. A Mississippian told Olmsted that the "smart" ones were "rascally" and constantly "getting into scrapes," and a Louisianian confessed that his slave Lucy was "the greatest rascal" and the "smartest negro of her age" he had ever known.[16] On the other hand, many masters were annoyed by the seeming stupidity of some of their slaves, by their unwillingness to "think for themselves." A Negro recently imported from Africa was said to be especially prone to this kind of stubborn obtuseness: "let a hundred men shew him how to hoe, or drive a wheelbarrow, he'll still take the one by the Bottom and the other by the Wheel."[17]

According to a former slave, the bondsmen had good reason for encouraging their master to underrate their intelligence. Ignorance was "a high virtue in a human chattel," he suggested, and since it was the master's purpose to keep his bondsmen in this state, they were shrewd enough to make him think he succeeded.[18] A Virginia planter concluded from his own long experience that many slaveholders were victimized by the "sagacity" of Negroes whom they mistakenly thought they understood so well. He was convinced that the slaves, "under the cloak of great stupidity," made "dupes" of their masters: "The most general defect in the character of the negro, is hypocrisy; and this hypocrisy frequently makes him pretend to more ignorance than he possesses; and if his master treats him as a fool, he will be sure to act the fool's part. This is a very convenient trait, as it frequently serves as an apology for awkwardness and neglect of duty."[19]

Slaveowners generally took it as a matter of course that a laborer would shirk when he could and perform no more work than he had to. They knew that, in most cases, the only way to keep him "in the straight path of duty" was to watch him "with an eye that never slumbers."[20] They frequently used such terms as "slow," "lazy," "wants pushing," "an eye servant," and "a trifling negro" when they made private appraisals of their slaves. "Hands won't work unless I am in sight," a small Virginia planter once wrote angrily in his diary. "I left the Field at 12 [with] all going on well, but very little done after [that]."[21] Olmsted, watching an overseer riding among the slaves on a South Carolina plantation, observed that he was "constantly directing and encouraging them, but . . . as often as he visited one end of the line of operations, the hands at the other end would discontinue their labor, until

[15] James W. Bell to William S. Pettigrew, May 3, 1853, Pettigrew Family Papers.
[16] Olmsted, *Back Country*, pp. 154–55; Edwin A. Davis (ed.), *Plantation Life in the Florida Parishes of Louisiana, 1836–1846. As Reflected in the Diary of Bennet H. Barrow* (New York, 1943), p. 164.
[17] E. B. R. to James B. Bailey, March 24, 1856, James B. Bailey Papers; Gray, *History of Agriculture*, I, p. 519.
[18] Douglass, *My Bondage*, p. 81.
[19] Farmers' Register, V (1837), p. 32.
[20] William S. Pettigrew to [James C. Johnston], October 3, 1850, Pettigrew Family Papers.
[21] William C. Adams Ms. Diary, entries for July 18, 20, 1857.

he turned to ride towards them again." Other visitors in the South also noticed "the furtive cessation from toil that invariably took place, as the overseer's eye was turned from them."[22]

Slaves sought to limit the quantity of their services in many different ways. At cotton picking time they carried cotton from the gin house to the field in the morning to be weighed with the day's picking at night. They concealed dirt or rocks in their cotton baskets to escape punishment for loafing. They fixed their own work quotas, and masters had to adopt stern measures to persuade them that they had been unduly presumptuous. Where the task system was used, they stubbornly resisted any attempt to increase the size of the daily tasks fixed by custom.[23] Athletic and muscular slaves, as Frederick Douglass recalled, were inclined to be proud of their capacity for labor, and the master often sought to promote rivalry among them; but they knew that this "was not likely to pay," for "if, by extraordinary exertion, a large quantity of work was done in one day, the fact becoming known to the master, might lead him to require the same amount every day." Some refused to become skilled craftsmen, for, as one of them explained, he would gain nothing by learning a craft.[24] Few seemed to feel any personal shame when dubbed "eye servants."

Slaves retaliated as best they could against those who treated them severely, and sometimes their reprisals were at least partly successful. Experience taught many slaveholders "that every attempt to force a slave beyond the limit that he fixes himself as a sufficient amount of labor to render his master, instead of extorting more work, only tends to make him unprofitable, unmanageable, a vexation and a curse. If you protract his regular hours of labor, his movements become proportionally slower." The use of force might cause him to work still more slowly until he fell "into a state of impassivity" in which he became "insensible and indifferent to punishment, or even to life."[25] After a slave was punished in the Richmond tobacco factories, the other hands "gave neither song nor careless shout for days, while the bosses fretted at slackened production."[26]

Besides slowing down, many slaves bedeviled the master by doing careless work and by damaging property. They did much of this out of sheer irresponsibility, but they did at least part of it deliberately, as more than one master suspected. A Louisiana doctor, Samuel W. Cartwright, attributed their work habits to a disease, peculiar to Negroes, which he called *Dysaethesia Æthiopica* and which overseers "erroneously" called "rascality." An African who suffered from this exotic affliction was "apt to do much mis-

22 Olmsted, *Seaboard*, pp. 387–88; Abdy, *Journal*, II, p. 214; William Chambers, *Things as They Are in America* (London, 1854), pp. 269–70.
23 [Ingraham], *South-West*, II, p. 286; Hammond Diary, entries for October 23, 24, 1834; Olmsted, *Seaboard*, pp. 434–36.
24 Douglass, *My Bondage*, pp. 261–62; Catterall (ed.), *Judicial Cases*, II, pp. 73–74, 210–11.
25 *De Bow's Review*, VII (1849), p. 220; XVII (1854), p. 422; XXV (1858), p. 51.
26 Joseph C. Robert, *The Story of Tobacco in America* (New York, 1949), p. 89.

chief" which appeared "as if intentional." He destroyed or wasted everything he touched, abused the livestock, and injured the crops. When he was driven to his labor he performed his tasks "in a headlong, careless manner, treading down with his feet or cutting with his hoe the plants" he was supposed to cultivate, breaking his tools, and "spoiling everything." This, wrote the doctor soberly, was entirely due to "the stupidness of mind and insensibility of the nerves induced by the disease."[27]

But slaveowners ignored this clinical analysis and persisted in diagnosing the disease as nothing but "rascality." To overcome it, they had to supervise the work closely. They searched for methods to prevent slaves from abusing horses and mules, plowing and hoeing "badly," damaging tools, killing young plants, and picking "trashy cotton." James H. Hammond noted in his diary: "I find [hoe-hands] chopping up cotton dreadfully and begin to think that my stand has every year been ruined in this way." A Louisiana sugar planter advised his son to turn to cotton production, because it was "trouble enough to have to manage negroes in the simplest way, without having to overlook them in the manufacture of sugar and management of Machinery."[28] "Rascality" was also a major problem for those who employed slaves in factories.

Olmsted found slaveholders fretting about this problem everywhere in the South. In Texas an angry mistress complained that her domestics constantly tracked mud through the house: "What do they care? They'd just as lief clean the mud after themselves as [do] anything else—*their time isn't any value to themselves.*" A Virginia planter said that he grew only the coarser and cheaper tobaccos, because the finer varieties "required more pains-taking and discretion than it was possible to make a large gang of negroes use." Another Virginian complained that slaves were "excessively careless and wasteful, and, in various ways . . . subject us to very annoying losses." Some masters used only crude, clumsy tools, because they were afraid to give their hands better ones.[29] One slaveholder felt aggrieved when he saw that the small patches which his Negroes cultivated for themselves were better cared for and more productive than his own fields.[30]

Masters were also troubled by the slave who idled in the quarters because of an alleged illness or disability. They often suspected that they were being victimized, for feigning illness was a favorite method of avoiding labor. Olmsted found one or more bondsmen "complaining" on almost every plantation he visited, and the proprietor frequently expressed "his suspicion that the invalid was really as well able to work as anyone else." Some masters and overseers believed that they could tell when a slave was deceiving them, but others were afraid to risk permanent injury to their human property. Ac-

---

[27] *De Bow's Review*, XI (1851), pp. 333–34.
[28] Hammond Diary, entry for June 7, 1839; Lewis Thompson to Thomas Thompson, December 31, 1858, Lewis Thompson Papers.
[29] Olmsted, *A Journey Through Texas* (New York, 1857), p. 120; *id.*, *Seaboard*, pp. 44–45, 91, 480–82.
[30] *American Farmer*, 4th Ser., I (1846), p. 295.

cording to one overseer, trying to detect those who were "shamming illness" was "the most disagreeable duty he had to perform. Negroes were famous for it."[31]

Slave women had great success with this stratagem. The overseer on Pierce Butler's Georgia plantation reported that they were constantly "shamming themselves into the family-way in order to obtain a diminution of their labor." One female enjoyed a "protracted pseudo-pregnancy" during which she "continued to reap increased rations as the reward of her expectation, till she finally had to disappoint and receive a flogging."[32] A Virginian asserted that a slave woman was a less profitable worker after reaching the "breeding age," because she so often pretended to be suffering from what were delicately called "female complaints." "You have to take her word for it . . . and you dare not set her to work; and so she will lay up till she feels like taking the air again, and plays the lady at your expense."[33]

Almost every slaveholder discovered at one time or another that a bondsman had outwitted him by "playing possum" or by some ingenious subterfuge. One Negro spread powdered mustard on his tongue to give it a foul appearance before he was examined by a doctor. Another convinced his owner that he was totally disabled by rheumatism, until one day he was discovered vigorously rowing a boat. A master found two of his slaves "grunting" (a common term), one affecting a partial paralysis and the other declaring that he could not walk; but he soon learned that they "used their limbs very well when they chose to do so." For many years a slave on a Mississippi plantation escaped work by persuading his master that he was nearly blind. After the Civil War, however, he produced "no less than eighteen good crops for himself" and became one of "the best farmers in the country."[34]

In these and other ways a seemingly docile gang of slaves drove an inefficient manager well nigh to distraction. They probed for his weaknesses, matched their wits against his, and constantly contrived to disrupt the work routine. An efficient manager took cognizance of the fact that many of his bondsmen were "shrewd and cunning," every ready to "disregard all reasonable restraints," and eager "to practice upon the old maxim, of 'give an inch and take an ell.' "[35] This was the reason why the owner of a small cotton plantation rejoiced when at last he could afford to employ an overseer: "I feel greatly relieved at the idea of getting a lazy trifling set of negroes off my hands. . . . They have wearied out all the patience I had with them."[36] . . .

For the most part the slaves who thus provoked masters and overseers were the meek, smiling ones whom many thought were contented though

[31] Olmsted, Seaboard, pp. 186–90; id., Back Country, pp. 77–79.

[32] Frances Anne Kemble, Journal of a Residence on a Georgian Plantation in 1838–1839 (New York, 1863), pp. 135–36, 235.

[33] Olmsted, Seaboard, pp. 188–90.

[34] Buckingham, Slave States, I, pp. 135, 402; Clement Claiborne Clay to Clement Comer Clay, April 19, 1846, Clement C. Clay Papers; Smedes, Memorials, p. 80.

[35] Southern Cultivator, VII (1849), p. 140; XII (1854), p. 206.

[36] John W. Brown Diary, entry for January 24, 1854.

irresponsible. They were not reckless rebels who risked their lives for freedom; if the thought of rebellion crossed their minds, the odds against success seemed too overwhelming to attempt it. But the inevitability of their bondage made it none the more attractive. And so, when they could, they protested by shirking their duties, injuring the crops, feigning illness, and disrupting the routine. These acts were, in part, an unspectacular kind of "day to day resistance to slavery."[37]

According to Dr. Cartwright, there was a . . . disease peculiar to Negroes which he called *Drapetomania:* "the disease causing negroes to run away." Cartwright believed that it was a "disease of the mind" and that with "proper medical advice" it could be cured. The first symptom was a "sulky and dissatisfied" attitude. To forestall the full onset of the disease, the cause or discontent must be determined and removed. If there were no ascertainable cause, then "whipping the devil out of them" was the proper "preventive measure against absconding."[38]

Though Cartwright's dissertations on Negro diseases are mere curiosities of medical history, the problem he dealt with was a real and urgent one to nearly every slaveholder. Olmsted met a few planters, large or small, who were not more or less troubled by runaways. A Mississippian realized that his record was most unusual when he wrote in his diary: "Harry ran away; *the first* negro that ever ran from me." Another slaveholder betrayed his concern when he avowed that he would "rather a negro would do anything Else than runaway."[39]

The number of runaways was not large enough to threaten the survival of the peculiar institution, because slaveholders took precautions to prevent the problem from growing to such proportions. But their measures were never entirely successful, as the advertisements for fugitives in southern newspapers made abundantly clear. Actually, the problem was much greater than these newspapers suggested, because many owners did not advertise for their absconding property. (When an owner did advertise, he usually waited until his slave had been missing for several weeks.) In any case, fugitive slaves were numbered in the thousands every year. It was an important form of protest against bondage.

Who were the runaways? They were generally young slaves, most of them under thirty, but occasionally masters searched for fugitives who were more than sixty years old. The majority of them were males, though female runaways were by no means uncommon. It is not true that most of them were mulattoes or of predominantly white ancestry. While this group was well represented among the fugitives, they were outnumbered by slaves who were described as "black" or of seemingly "pure" African ancestry. Domes-

---

[37] Raymond A. and Alice H. Bauer, "Day to Day Resistance to Slavery," *Journal of Negro History,* XXVII (1942), pp. 388–419.

[38] *De Bow's Review,* XII (1851), pp. 331–33.

[39] Olmsted, *Back Country,* p. 476; Newstead Plantation Diary, entry for June 7, 1860; Davis (ed.), *Diary of Bennet H. Barrow,* p. 165.

tics and skilled artisans—the ones who supposedly had the most intimate ties with the master class—ran away as well as common field-hands. . . .

"His look is impudent and insolent, and he holds himself straight and walks well." So a Louisiana master described James, a runaway slave.[40] There were always bondsmen like James. In 1669, a Virginia statute referred to "the obstinacy of many of them"; in 1802, a South Carolina judge declared that they were "in general a headstrong, stubborn race of people"; and in 1859, a committee of a South Carolina agricultural society complained of the "insolence of disposition to which, as a race, they were remarkably liable." An overseer on a Louisiana plantation wrote nervously about the many "outrageous acts" recently committed by slaves in his locality and insisted that he scarcely had time to eat and sleep: "The truth is no man can begin to attend to Such a business with any Set of negroes, without the Strictest vigilance on his part."[41] It was the minority of slaves whom his discipline could not humble (the "insolent," "surly," and "unruly" ones) that worried this overseer—and slaveholders generally. These were the slaves whose discontent drove them to drastic measures.

Legally the offenses of the rebels ranged from petty misdemeanors to capital crimes, and they were punished accordingly. The master class looked upon any offense as more reprehensible (and therefore subject to more severe penalties) when committed by a slave than when committed by a free white. But how can one determine the proper ethical standards for identifying undesirable or even criminal behavior among slaves? How distinguish a "good" from a "bad" slave? Was the "good" slave the one who was courteous and loyal to his master, and who did his work faithfully and cheerfully? Was the "bad" slave the one who would not submit to his master, and who defiantly fought back? What were the limits, if any, to which a man deprived of his freedom could properly go in resisting bondage? How accountable was a slave to a legal code which gave him more penalties than protection and was itself a bulwark of slavery? This much at least can be said: many slaves rejected the answers which their masters gave to questions such as these. The slaves did not thereby repudiate law and morality: rather, they formulated legal and moral codes of their own.

The white man's laws against theft, for example, were not supported by the slave's code. In demonstrating the "absence of moral principle" among bondsmen, one master observed: "To steal and not to be detected is a merit among them." Let a master turn his back, wrote another, and some "cunning fellow" would appropriate part of his goods. No slave would betray another, for an informer was held "in greater detestation than the most notorious thief."[42]

40 New Orleans *Picayune*, November 4, 1851.
41 Hurd, *Law of·Freedom and Bondage*, I, p. 232; Catterall (ed.), *Judicial Cases*, II, pp. 281–82; *De Bow's Review*, XXVI (1859), p. 107, Moore Rawls to Lewis Thompson, May 9, 1858, Lewis Thompson Papers.
42 Harrison, *Gospel Among the Slaves*, p. 103; *Farmers' Register*, V (1837), p. 302.

If slaveholders are to be believed, petty theft was an almost universal "vice"; slaves would take anything that was not under lock and key. Field-hands killed hogs and robbed the corn crib. House servants helped themselves to wines, whiskey, jewelry, trinkets, and whatever else was lying about. Fugitives sometimes gained from their master unwilling help in financing the journey to freedom, the advertisements often indicating that they absconded with money, clothing, and a horse or mule. Thefts were not necessarily confined to the master's goods: any white man might be considered fair game.

Some bondsmen engaged in theft on more than a casual and petty basis. They made a business of it and thus sought to obtain comforts and luxuries which were usually denied them. A South Carolina master learned his house servants had been regularly looting his wine cellar and that one of them was involved in an elaborate "system of roguery." A planter in North Carolina found that three of his slaves had "for some months been carrying on a robbery" of meat and lard, the leader being "a young carpenter, remarkable for smartness . . . and no less worthy for his lamentable deficiency in common honesty."[43]

If the stolen goods were not consumed directly, they were traded to whites or to free Negroes. This illegal trade caused masters endless trouble, for slaves were always willing to exchange plantation products for tobacco, liquor, or small sums of money. Southern courts were kept busy handling the resulting prosecutions. One slaveholder discovered that his bondsmen had long been engaged in an extensive trade in corn. "Strict vigilance," he concluded, was necessary "to prevent them from theft; particularly when dishonesty is inherent, as is probably the case with some of them."[44] Dishonesty, as the master understood the term, indeed seemed to be a common if not an inherent trait of southern slaves.

The slaves, however, had a somewhat different definition of dishonesty in their own code, to which they were reasonably faithful. For appropriating their master's goods they might be punished and denounced by him, but they were not likely to be disgraced among their associates in the slave quarters, who made a distinction between "stealing" and "taking." Appropriating things from the master meant simply taking part of his property for the benefit of another part or, as Frederick Douglass phrased it, "taking his meat out of one tub, and putting it in another." Thus a female domestic who had been scolded for the theft of some trinkets was reported to have replied: "Law, mam, don't say I's wicked; ole Aunt Ann says its allers right for us poor colored people to 'popiate whatever of de wite folk's blessings de Lord puts in our way." Stealing, on the other hand, meant appropriating something

---

[43] Hammond Diary, entry for October 16, 1835; William S. Pettigrew to (James C. Johnston), October 3, 1850, Pettigrew Family Papers.
[44] William S. Pettigrew to J. Johnston Pettigrew, March 9, 1840, Pettigrew Family Papers; Catterall (ed.), *Judicial Cases, passim.*

that belonged to another slave, and this was an offense which slaves did not condone.[45]

The prevalance of theft was a clear sign that slaves were discontented, at least with the standard of living imposed upon them. They stole food to increase or enrich their diets or to trade for other coveted commodities. Quite obviously they learned from their masters the pleasures that could be derived from the possession of worldly goods; and when the opportunity presented itself, they "took" what was denied them as slaves.

Next to theft, arson was the most common slave "crime," one which slaveholders dreaded almost constantly. Fire was a favorite means for aggrieved slaves to even the score with their master. Reports emanated periodically from some region or other that there was an "epidemic" of gin-house burnings, or that some bondsman had taken his revenge by burning the slave quarters or other farm buildings. More than one planter thus saw the better part of a year's harvest go up in flames.[46] Southern newspapers and court records are filled with illustrations of this offense, and with evidence of the severe penalties inflicted upon those found guilty of committing it.

Another "crime" was what might be called self-sabotage, a slave deliberately unfitting himself to labor for his master. An Arkansas slave, "at any time to save an hour's work," could "throw his left shoulder out of place." A Kentucky slave made himself unserviceable by downing medicines from his master's dispensary (thus showing a better understanding of the value of these nostrums than his owner). A slave woman was treated as an invalid because of "swillings in her arms"—until it was discovered that she produced this condition by thrusting her arms periodically into a beehive. Yellow Jacob, according to his master's plantation journal, "had a kick from a mule and when nearly well would bruise it and by that means kept from work."[47] Another Negro, after being punished by his owner, retaliated by cutting off his right hand; still another cut off the fingers of one hand to avoid being sold to the Deep South.[48]

A few desperate slaves carried this form of resistance to the extreme of self-destruction. Those freshly imported from Africa and those sold away from friends and relatives were especially prone to suicide.[49] London, a slave on a Georgia rice plantation, ran to the river and drowned himself after be-

[45] Douglass, My Bondage, pp. 189–91; Austin Steward, Twenty-Two Years a Slave (Canandaigua, N.Y., 1856), p. 29; Olmsted, Seaboard, pp. 116–17; Sellers, Slavery in Alabama, p. 257.

[46] Davis (ed.), Diary of Bennet H. Barrow, p. 131 n.; Rachel O'Conner to David Weeks, June 16, 1833, Weeks Collection; S. Porcher Gaillard Ms. Plantation Journal, entry for May 9, 1856.

[47] Helena (Ark.) Southern Shield, July 23, 1853; Buckingham, Slave States, I, p. 402; Gaillard Plantation Journal, entry for May 9, 1856.

[48] Harriet Martineau, Society in America (New York, 1837), II, p. 113; Drew, The Refugee, p. 178.

[49] Phillips (ed.), Plantation and Frontier, II, p. 31; Catterall (ed.), Judicial Cases, II, pp. 425–26; III, pp. 216–17; Drew, The Refugee, p. 178.

ing threatened with a whipping. His overseer gave orders to leave the corpse untouched "to let the [other] negroes see [that] when a negro takes his own life they will be treated in this manner." A Texas planter bewailed the loss of a slave woman who hanged herself after two unsuccessful breaks for freedom: "I had been offered $900.00 for her not two months ago, but damn her . . . I would not have had it happened for twice her value. *The fates pursue me.*"[50]

Some runaways seemed determined to make their recapture as costly as possible and even resisted at the risk of their own lives. One advertisement, typical of many, warned that an escaped slave was a "resolute fellow" who would probably not be taken without a "show of competent force." When, after a day-long chase, three South Carolina fugitives were cornered, they "fought desperately," inflicted numerous wounds upon their pursuers with a barrage of rocks, and "refused to surrender until a force of about forty-five or fifty men arrived."[51] In southern court records there are numerous cases of runaway slaves who killed whites or were themselves killed in their frantic efforts to gain freedom.

In one dramatic case, a Louisiana fugitive was detected working as a free Negro on a Mississippi River flatboat. His pursuers, trailing him with a pack of "Negro dogs," finally found him "standing at bay upon the outer edge of a large raft of drift wood, armed with a club and pistol." He threatened to kill anyone who got near him. "Finding him obstinately determined not to surrender, one of his pursuers shot him. He fell at the third fire, and so determined was he not to be captured, that when an effort was made to rescue him from drowning he made battle with his club, and sunk waving his weapon in angry defiance."[52]

An effort to break up an organized gang of runaways was a dangerous business, because they were often unwilling to surrender without a fight. The fugitives in one well-armed band in Alabama were building a fort at the time they were discovered. Their camp was destroyed after a "smart skirmish" during which three of them were killed.[53] Such encounters did not always end in defeat for the slaves; some runaway bands successfully resisted all attempts at capture and remained at large for years.

Ante-bellum records are replete with acts of violence committed by individual slaves upon masters, overseers, and other whites. A Texan complained, in 1853, that cases of slaves murdering white men were becoming "painfully frequent." "Within the last year or two many murders have taken place, by negroes upon their owners," reported a Louisiana newspaper. And

---

[50] Phillips (ed.), *Plantation and Frontier*, II, p. 94; John R. Lyons to William W. Renwick, April 4, 1854, William W. Renwick Papers.

[51] Petition of William Boyd to South Carolina legislature, November 29, 1858, in South Carolina Slavery Manuscripts Collection.

[52] *Feliciana Whig*, quoted in Olmsted, *Back Country*, p. 474.

[53] Phillips (ed.), *Plantation and Frontier*, II, pp. 90–91; Bassett, *Plantation Overseer*, pp. 78–79.

a Florida editor once wrote: "It is our painful duty to record another instance of the destruction of the life of a white man by a slave."[54]

Many masters owned one or more bondsmen whom they feared as potential murders. A Georgia planter remembered Jack, his plantation carpenter, "the most notoriously bad character and worst Negro of the place." Jack "was the only Negro ever in our possession who I considered capable of Murdering me, or burning my dwelling at night, or capable of committing any act."[55]

Slaves like Jack could be watched closely; but others appeared to be submissive until suddenly they turned on their masters. Even trusted house servants might give violent expression to long pent up feelings. One "first rate" female domestic, while being punished, abruptly attacked her mistress, "threw her down, and beat her unmercifully on the head and face." A "favorite body servant" of a "humane master who rarely or never punished his slaves" one day became insolent. Unwilling to be disciplined, this slave waylaid his owner, "knocked him down with a whiteoak club, and beat his head to a pumice."[56] Here was another reason why it seemed foolish for a master to put his "confidence in a Negro."

At times these acts of violence appeared to be for "no cause"—that is, they resulted from a slave's "bad disposition" rather than from a particular grievance. But more often they resulted from a clash of personalities, or from some specific incident. For example, a slave who had been promised freedom in his master's will, poisoned his master to hasten the day of liberation. A South Carolina bondsman was killed during a fight with an overseer who had whipped his son. In North Carolina a slave intervened while the overseer was whipping his wife, and in the ensuing battle the overseer met his death.[57]

The most common provocation to violence was the attempt of a master or overseer either to work or to punish slaves severely. An Alabama bondsman confessed killing the overseer because "he was a hard down man on him, and said he was going to be harder." Six Louisiana slaves together killed an overseer and explained in their confession that they found it impossible to satisfy him. Three North Carolina slaves killed their master when they decided that "the old man was too hard on them, and they must get rid of him."[58] During one of these crises an overseer called upon his hands to help him punish an "unmanageable" slave: "not one of them paid the least attention to me but kept on at their work." These encounters did not always

54 Austin *Texas State Gazette*, September 3, 1853; Alexandria (La.), *Red River Republican*, April 24, 1852, Pensacola Gazette, May 4, 1839.
55 Manigault Plantation Records, entry for March 22, 1867.
56 Rachel O'Conner to A. T. Conrad, May 26, 1836, Weeks Collection; Austin *Texas State Gazette*, September 23, 1854.
57 Martineau, *Society in America*, II, pp. 110–11; Catterall (ed.), *Judicial Cases*, II, pp. 206–207, 434–35.
58 Catterall (ed.), *Judicial Cases*, III, pp. 238–41; Reuben Carnal to Lewis Thompson, June 17, 1855, Lewis Thompson Papers; Hardy Hardison to William S. Pettigrew, February 11, 1858, Pettigrew Family Papers.

lead to death, but few plantations escaped without at least one that might easily have ended in tragedy. "Things move on here in the old Style except that now and then a refractory negro has to be taken care of," was the off-hand comment of a planter.[59]

Sometimes a slave who showed sufficient determination to resist punishment managed to get the best of his owner or overseer. A proud bondsman might vow that, regardless of the consequences, he would permit no one to whip him.[60] An overseer thought twice before precipitating a major crisis with a strong-willed slave, he might even overlook minor infractions of discipline.

But an impasse such as this was decidedly unusual; if it had not been, slavery itself would have stood in jeopardy. Ordinarily these clashes between master and slave were fought out to a final settlement, and thus a thread of violence was woven into the pattern of southern bondage. Violence, indeed, was the method of resistance adopted by the boldest and most discontented slaves. Its usual reward, however, was not liberty but death!

No ante-bellum Southerner could ever forget Nat Turner. The career of this man made an impact upon the people of this section as great as that of John C. Calhoun or Jefferson Davis. Yet Turner was only a slave in Southampton County, Virginia—and during most of his life a rather unimpressive one at that. He was a pious man, a Baptist exhorter by avocation, apparently as humble and docile as a slave was expected to be. There is no evidence that he was underfed, overworked, or treated with special cruelty. If Nat Turner could not be trusted, what slave could? That was what made his sudden deed so frightening.

Somehow Turner came to believe that he had been divinely chosen to deliver his people from bondage, and he persuaded several other slaves to assist him. In due time he saw the sign for which he had waited, and early in the morning of August 22, 1831, he and his followers rose in rebellion. They began by killing the family to whom Turner belonged. As they marched through the Southampton countryside they gained additional recruits, making a total of about seventy. (Others seemed ready to join if the rebels came their way. The slave Jacob, for example, proclaimed "that if they came by he would join them and assist in killing all the white people.") Within two days they killed nearly sixty whites. They could have killed more. They left undisturbed at least one poor white family, "because they thought no better of themselves than they did of the negroes." To justify the killings, members of Turner's band declared that they had had enough of punishment, or that they now intended to be as rich as their masters. One rebel demonstrated his new status by walking off in his late owner's shoes and socks.

The Nat Turner rebellion lasted only forty-eight hours. Swiftly mobilizing in overwhelming strength, the whites easily dispersed the rebels. Then

[59] Taylor, "Negro Slavery in Louisiana," pp. 258–59; Charles L. Pettigrew to William S. Pettigrew, October 9, 1837, Pettigrew Family Papers.
[60] Douglass, *My Bondage*, pp. 95, 242–46; Brown, *Narrative*, pp. 17–18.

followed a massacre during which not only the insurrectionists but scores of innocent bondsmen were slaughtered. Others, charged with "feloniously consulting, advising and conspiring . . . to rebel . . . and making insurrection and taking the lives of divers free white persons of this Commonwealth," were tried before a court of oyer and terminer during the months of September and October. Some were executed, others transported. Most of those transported had not actively participated in the rebellion; they had merely expressed sympathy for the rebels.

Nat Turner himself was not captured until October 30, more than two months after the uprising. He was brought to trial on November 5, convicted the same day, and hanged six days later.[61] Thus ended an event which produced in the South something resembling a mass trauma, from which the whites had not recovered three decades later. The danger that other Nat Turners might emerge, that an even more serious insurrection might some day occur, became an enduring concern as long as the peculiar institution survived. Proslavery writers boldly asserted that Southerners did not fear their slaves, that a rebellion of the laboring class was more likely to transpire in the North than in the South; but the fear of rebellion, sometimes vague, sometimes acute, was with them always.

Though it was the most disastrous (for both slaves and masters), Nat Turner's was not the first insurrection. Several earlier conspiracies, which narrowly missed being carried into execution might easily have precipitated rebellions much more extensive than that of Turner.[62] These uprisings and conspiracies began as early as the seventeenth century and kept Southerners apprehensive throughout the colonial period. The preamble to the South Carolina statute of 1740 defining the duties of slave patrols stated that many "horrible and barbarous massacres" had been committed or plotted by the slaves who were "generally prone to such cruel practices."[63] On the eve of the American Revolution a Charlestonian wrote about a "disturbance" among the bondsmen who had "mimicked their betters in crying Liberty." In 1785, a West Florida slaveholder was dismayed to learn that several of his slaves were involved in an insurrection plot: "Of what avail is kindness and good usage when rewarded by such ingratitude . . . [?]"[64] Such incidents set the pattern for the nineteenth century.

61 Details of the Turner insurrection can be found in contemporary Richmond newspapers, and in the manuscript records of the trials in Southampton County Minute Book, 1830–1835. See also William S. Drewry, The Southampton Insurrection (Washington, D.C., 1900); Thomas R. Gray, The Confessions of Nat Turner (Baltimore, 1831).

62 Herbert Aptheker, American Negro Slave Revolts (New York, 1943) presents evidence of many conspiracies and a few rebellions, each involving ten or more slaves, from the colonial period to the end of the Civil War. See also Joseph C. Carroll, Slave Insurrections in the United States, 1800–1865 (Boston, 1938); Harvey Wish, "American Slave Insurrections before 1861," Journal of Negro History, XXII (1937), pp. 299–320.

63 Hurd, Law of Freedom and Bondage, I, p. 308.

64 Henry Laurens to J. Gervais, January 29, 1766, Henry Laurens Ms. Letter Book, 1762–1766, Historical Society of Pennsylvania, Philadelphia (copy in possession of Professor Carl Bridenbaugh); Sellers, Slavery in Alabama, pp. 13–14.

The new century opened with the Gabriel Conspiracy (August, 1800) in Henrico County, Virginia, in which at least a thousand slaves were implicated. The warnings of two bondsmen and a severe storm enabled the whites to forestall a projected march upon Richmond. A decade later some five hundred slaves in St. John the Baptist Parish, Louisiana, armed with cane knives and other crude weapons, advanced toward New Orleans. But the planters and a strong detachment of troops put them to flight. In 1822, Denmark Vesey, a free Negro in Charleston, planned a vast conspiracy which came to nothing after it was given away by a slave. These and other plots were invariably followed by severe reprisals, including the indiscriminate killing of slaves as well as mass executions after regular trials. The heads of sixteen Louisiana rebels were stuck upon poles along the Mississippi River as a grim warning to other slaves. After the Vesey conspiracy, Charlestonians expressed disillusionment with the idea that by generous treatment the slaves "would become more satisfied with their condition and more attached to the whites."[65]

The shock of Nat Turner caused Southerners to take preventive measures, but these never eliminated their apprehension or the actual danger. Hardly a year passed without some kind of alarming disturbance somewhere in the South. When no real conspiracy existed, wild rumors often agitated the whites and at times came close to creating an insurrection panic. The rumors might be entirely unfounded, or they might grow out of some local incident which was magnified by exaggeration. Even the historian cannot always distinguish between the rumors and the facts. Most of the stories seem to have had a foundation in at least a minor disturbance, limited perhaps to a single plantation where the slaves suddenly became insubordinate, or to a whole neighborhood where they showed signs of becoming restive. Whether caused by rumor or fact, the specter of rebellion often troubled the sleep of the master class.

The Turner rebellion itself produced an insurrection panic that swept the entire South. A Richmond editor wondered whether the southern press was trying to give the slaves "false conceptions of their numbers and capacity, by exhibiting the terror and confusion of the whites, and to induce them to think that practicable, which they see is so much feared by their superiors."[66] In eastern North Carolina the panic caused the arrest of scores of slaves and the execution of more than a dozen. A South Carolinian reported that there was "considerable alarm" in his state too and that some slaves were hanged to prevent a rumored uprising.[67] The excitement spread into the Southwest where it was feared that the bondsmen would become "troublesome." A Mississippian, confessing "great apprehension," noted that

---

[65] Aptheker, *American Negro Slave Revolts*, pp. 209–92; Taylor, "Negro Slavery in Louisiana," pp. 268–74; Phillips, *Plantation and Frontier*, II, pp. 103–104.
[66] Richmond *Whig*, quoted in Alexandria (Va.) *Phenix Gazette*, September 6, 1831.
[67] Johnson, *Acute-Bellum North Carolina*, pp. 519–20; Rosannah P. Rogers to David S. Rogers, October 29, 1831, Renwick Papers.

"within 4 hours march of Natchez" there were "2200 able bodied male slaves." He warned: "It behooves [us] to be vigilent—but silent."[68]

Similar insurrection panics developed from time to time thereafter. In 1835, one of these frightful disturbances centered in Mississippi and Louisiana; before it subsided, numerous bondsmen had been legally or extralegally executed. This panic even spread into Roane County in East Tennessee, though that county contained a very small slave population. There was "a great deal of talk and some dread of the negroes rising at Christmas or new year," reported a local slaveholder. "I can not say that I have had much fear of their rising here, but have thought it right to be careful and watchful. It is a disagreeable state of living to be ever suspicious of those with whom we live."[69] This point was illustrated by a not uncommon incident in a small village on the Eastern Shore of Virginia. One night in 1849, the firing of guns "alarmed the people very much. They at once thought that the Slaves had risen to murder the white people. Many immediately left their houses and fled to the woods. . . . But it was afterwards ascertained that it was a false alarm."[70] This was indeed a "disagreeable state of living"!

The most acute and widespread insurrection panics, after the Turner rebellion, occurred in 1856 and 1860, each of them resulting in part from the rise of the Republican party and the exciting political campaigns. On both occasions alarming stories of huge conspiracies spread through every slave state, stories frequently mentioning "unscrupulous" white men (presumably abolitionist emissaries like John Brown) who were "tampering" with the Negroes and encouraging them to rebel. "All at once, in Kentucky, Tennessee, Missouri, Arkansas, Louisiana and Texas, it is discovered that the slaves are meditating schemes of insurrection," proclaimed a Richmond newspaper in a hysterical editorial. "From almost every point in the Southwest, rumors of insurrectionary movements among the negroes come upon us with more or less distinct and authentic detail." In Virginia, as a slaveholder noted, "reports of negro plots" had "induced proper measures of vigilance."[71] A South Carolinian observed privately that there was "a good deal of anxiety," but little was being said about it, "as every one felt it should not be the subject of general talk." In Texas, one of the principal centers of these insurrection panics, vigilance committees were hastily formed to deal with the expected emergency.[72] On these occasions, as on others, there was some substance to the rumors, however much they were exaggerated. In 1856 slave unrest did

---

[68] Nevitt Plantation Journal, entry for October 28, 1831; Stephen Duncan to Thomas Butler, October 4, 1831, Butler Family Papers.

[69] William D. Lenoir to Thomas Lenoir, December 27, 1835, Lenoir Family Papers.

[70] J. Milton Emerson Ms. Journal, entry for September 29, 1849.

[71] Richmond *Enquirer*, December 16, 1856; Edmund Ruffin Ms. Diary, entry for December 25, 1856.

[72] Easterby (ed.), *South Carolina Rice Plantation*, p. 136; Austin *Texas State Gazette*, November 15, 22, 29, 1856; Harvey Wish, "The Slave Insurrection Panic of 1856," *Journal of Southern History*, V (1939), pp. 206–22.

increase noticeably in certain areas, including Texas, where there was at least one well authenticated conspiracy.[73]

Sometimes rebellions took odd forms. The Seminole War in Florida was in part a slave revolt, for many fugitive Negroes fought alongside the Indian warriors. In 1841, a group of slaves being carried from Virginia to New Orleans on the brig *Creole* rose in rebellion, seized the ship, and sailed it to the Bermudas. In 1848, about seventy-five slaves from Fayette County, Kentucky, led by a white man, made a break for the Ohio River. They waged a brisk battle with their pursuers before they were forced to surrender. More than forty of them were tried for "most wickedly, seditiously, and rebelliously" making a "public insurrection." Three of the slaves were executed, and their white leader was sentenced to twenty years in prison.[74]

One of the last ante-bellum slave conspiracies occurred in October, 1860, in the neighborhood of Plymouth, in eastern North Carolina. It began when a score of slaves met in a swamp to plan an insurrection. Their plan was to persuade several hundred bondsmen to join them in a march on Plymouth; they would kill all the whites they met on the road, burn the town, take money and weapons, and escape by ship through Albemarle Sound. The plot was betrayed by a slave, and once again panic spread throughout the neighborhood. "When I reached Plymouth," wrote a local planter, "the town was in the greatest of commotion, and, as even calm persons thought, with some reason." The country people were "so much excited and alarmed as to vow themselves as ready to slaughter the negroes indiscriminately." This planter believed that during an insurrection panic "the negroes are in much more danger from the non slave holding whites than the whites are from the negroes."[75] He was probably right, though the slaveholders were hardly less inclined, on that account, to be ruthless whenever rumors of rebellion swept through the land.

That there was no slave conspiracy comparable to Denmark Vesey's and no rebellion comparable to Nat Turner's, during the three decades before the Civil War, has been explained in many ways. The explanations, however, do not sufficiently emphasize the impact which the Turner rebellion had on the slaves themselves. The speed with which it was crushed and the massacre that followed were facts soon known, doubtless, to every slave in Virginia and, before long, to almost every slave in the South. Among the Negroes everywhere, news generally spread so far and so fast as to amaze the whites. The Turner story was not likely to encourage slaves to make new attempts to win their freedom by fighting for it. They now realized that they would face a united white community, well armed and quite willing to annihilate as much of the black population as might seem necessary.

[73] Aptheker, *American Negro Slave Revolts*, pp. 325–58; Wendell G. Addington, "Slave Insurrections in Texas," *Journal of Negro History*, XXXV (1950), pp. 408–35.
[74] Porter, "Florida Slaves and Free Negroes in the Seminole War, 1835–1842," *loc. cit.*, pp. 420–21; Catterall (ed.), *Judicial Cases*, III, pp. 565–67; Coleman, *Slavery Times in Kentucky*, pp. 88–92.
[75] William S. Pettigrew to James C. Johnston, October 25, 1860, Pettigrew Family Papers.

In truth, no slave uprising ever had a chance of ultimate success, even though it might have cost the master class heavy casualties. The great majority of the disarmed and outnumbered slaves, knowing the futility of rebellion, refused to join in any of the numerous plots. Most slaves had to express their desire for freedom in less dramatic ways. They rarely went beyond disorganized individual action—which, to be sure, caused their masters no little annoyance. The bondsmen themselves lacked the power to destroy the web of bondage. They would have to have the aid of free men inside or outside the South.

The survival of slavery, then, cannot be explained as due to the contentment of slaves or their failure to comprehend the advantages of freedom. They longed for liberty and resisted bondage as much as any people could have done in their circumstances, but their longing and their resistance were not enough even to render the institution unprofitable to most masters. The masters had power and, as will be seen, they developed an elaborate technique of slave control. Their very preoccupation with this technique was, in itself, a striking refutation of the myth that slavery survived because of the cheerful acquiescence of the slaves.

Robert William Fogel and Stanley L. Engerman

The Quality of Slave Labor and Racism

Perhaps the most important technological advance within the agricultural sector of the South after 1800 was in the realm of management, particularly in the development of organizational methods which permitted southern planters to capture the potential benefits of economies of large-scale operation. It must be remembered that the shift from the production of grain and tobacco to cotton, sugar, and rice coincided with a substantial increase in the average size of slaveholdings. The optimal farm size appears to have differed by crop. There is little evidence of economies of scale in grain production; and economies of scale appear to have been fairly limited in tobacco production. Thus, farms located in counties specializing in these crops grew little between 1790 and 1860. On the eve of the Civil War the average size of Virginia slaveholdings was still only 18.8, while the county averages in the alluvial regions of short-staple cotton production ranged as high as one hundred and twenty-five slaves per holding. By the last decade prior to the Civil War the optimal size (minimum size of the most efficient farms) had increased to approximately fifty slaves in the cotton lands of the black belt and to over two hundred slaves in counties of the alluvial lands along the Mississippi. Indeed by the last decade of the slave era, the ability to provide efficient management appears to have become the main constraint on the optimal size of plantations.

One should not leap to the conclusion that this finding supports the stereotype of planters as a class of "idlers" who lacked "steady habits and frugal instincts," and who usually entrusted the primary management of their plantations to inept, cruel overseers while they indulged their taste for pleasure in various cities of the South, the North, or of Europe. No doubt such planters existed. But they were a distinct minority. Among moderate-sized holdings (sixteen to fifty slaves) less than one out of every six plantations used a white overseer. On large slaveholdings (over fifty slaves) only one out of every four owners used white overseers. Even on estates with more than one hundred slaves, the proportion with white overseers was just 30 percent, and on many of these the planters were usually in residence.

The continual discussions of problems of plantation management in the agricultural journals of the South were not evidence of the failure of southern planters but of the earnestness with which they approached their tasks. Far from being cavalier fops, the leading planters were, on the whole, a highly self-conscious class of entrepreneurs who generally approached their governmental responsibilities with deliberation and gravity—a manner which accorded with their self-image. They strove to become steeped in the scientific agricultural literature of the day; they organized agricultural societies as a means of disseminating information on the "best practices" in various aspects of farming, and in order to encourage experimentation in animal husbandry, agronomy, horticulture, and related matters; and they established journals in which they could report their findings as well as debate the full range of problems that they encountered in plantation management.

No question was treated with more gravity than that of labor management. Planters recognized that this was the critical issue. Economic success rode or fell with it. No aspect of slave management was considered too trivial to be omitted from consideration or debate. Details of housing, diet, medical care, marriage, child rearing, holidays, incentives and punishments, alternative methods of organizing field labor, the duties of managerial personnel, and even the manner or air to be assumed by a planter in his relationship with his slaves were all deemed worthy of debate. Discussions of diet included such matters as the balance between meat, vegetables, grains, and dairy products, the virtues of fat versus lean meats, and the optimum method of food distribution and preparation. With respect to housing, planters debated the respective merits of single- and multi-family dwellings, the benefits and costs of various types of building materals, the design of chimneys, and the optimum spatial distribution of slave houses and other buildings. On marriage and the family, the debate included such issues as whether or not slaves should be permitted to marry across plantations, and the latitude to be allowed to drivers and overseers in the mediation of intra- as well as interfamily disputes. Debates around the incentive structure turned on such matters as the relative advantages of gifts or cash bonuses versus allotments of plots of land, the types of crops that slaves could grow on their individual plots, whether or not slaves should be permitted to have quasi-property rights in the small livestock, and whether slaves should be permitted to market their own crops and livestock or should be required to sell them to the planter at prevailing market prices.

Whatever the differences among planters in the resolution of these particular issues, there was widespread agreement that the ultimate objective of slave management was the creation of a highly disciplined, highly specialized, and well-coordinated labor force. Specialization and interdependence were the hallmarks of the medium- and large-sized plantations. On family-sized farms, each worker had to fulfill a multiplicity of duties according to a pace and pattern which were quite flexible and largely independent of the activities of others. On plantations, the hands were as rigidly organized as in a factory. Each hand was assigned to a set of tasks which occupied him throughout the year, or at least through particular seasons of the year. There were drivers, plowmen, hoe hands, harrowers, seed sowers, coverers, sorters, ginners, packers, milkmaids, stock minders, carpenters, blacksmiths, nurses, and cooks—to give only a partial listing.

With respect to field labor, the various hands were formed into gangs or teams in which the interdependence of labor was a crucial element. During the planting period the interdependence arose largely from within each gang. A planting gang consisted of five types of hands who followed one another in a fixed procession. Leading off the procession were plowmen who ridged up the unbroken earth; then came harrowers who broke up the clods; then drillers who created the holes to receive the seeds, each hole a prescribed distance apart from the next one; then droppers who planted the seeds in the holes; and finally rakers who covered up the holes. The intensity of the pace of these gangs was maintained in three ways:

First, by choosing as the plowmen and harrowers who led off the planting operation the strongest and ablest hands.

Second, by the interdependence of each type of hand on the other. (For as on an assembly line, this interdependence generated a pressure on all those who worked in the gang to keep up with the pace of the leaders.)

Third, by assigning drivers or foremen who exhorted the leaders, threatened the laggards, and did whatever was necessary to ensure both the pace and the quality of each gang's labor.

During the period of cultivation, this interdependence, and the productive tension which it created, stemmed to a considerable extent from the interaction between gangs. Field hands were divided into two groups: the hoe gang and the plow gang. The hoe hands chopped out the weeds which surrounded the cotton plants as well as excessive sprouts of cotton plants. The plow gangs followed behind, stirring the soil near the rows of cotton plants and tossing it back around the plants. Thus the hoe and plow gangs each put the other under an assembly-line type of pressure. The hoeing had to be completed in time to permit the plow hands to carry out their tasks. At the same time the progress of the hoeing, which entailed lighter labor than plowing, set a pace for the plow gang. The drivers or overseers moved back and forth between the two gangs, exhorting and prodding each to keep up with the pace of the other, as well as inspecting the quality of the work.

This feature of plantation life—the organization of slaves into highly disciplined, interdependent teams capable of maintaining a steady and intense rhythm of work—appears to be the crux of the superior efficiency of large-scale operations on plantations, at least as far as fieldwork was concerned. It is certainly the factor which slaveowners themselves frequently singled out as the key to the superiority of the plantation system of organization. Although Olmsted repeatedly reported that planters preferred slave labor to white labor because slaves "could be driven," the significance of these statements completely eluded him. White men, said one planter, "are not used to steady labour; they work reluctantly, and will not bear driving; they cannot be worked to advantage with slaves, and it is inconvenient to look after them, if you work them separately." A slaveholder who listened to Olmsted's report of his conversation with Griscom, the Northerner who claimed that slave laborers produced only one fourth as much output per day as northern laborers, responded that these slaves "could not have been well 'driven.' " Another reported that "he would never have white people at ordinary work, because he couldn't drive them." Still another said: "You never could depend on white men, and you couldn't *drive* them any; they wouldn't stand it. Slaves were the only reliable laborers. . . ." The conclusion that Olmsted drew from such reports was not that slave labor in the plantation context was of a superior quality, but that southern free laborers must have been extremely lazy, inept, and of low quality compared to northern laborers.

Even on those few occasions when Olmsted actually witnessed gangs working in the field, he failed to appreciate the significance of slave teamwork, coordination, and intensity of effort, although he faithfully recorded these features of their work. The hoe gang, he reported on one of these instances, "numbered nearly two hundred hands (for the force of two plantations was working together), moving across the field in parallel lines, with a considerable degree of precision. I repeatedly rode through the lines at a canter, with other horsemen, often coming upon them suddenly, without producing the smallest change or interruption in the dogged action of the labourers, or causing one of them, so far as I could see, to lift an eye from the ground." What conclusion did Olmsted draw from this experience? Did he view it as a remarkable demonstration of the teamwork of black laborers and of the intensity of their concentration on the task at hand? The "stupid, plodding, machine-like manner in which they labour," said Olmsted, "is painful to witness." While Olmsted was willing to concede that these slave hands probably worked "harder, and more unremittingly," than northern laborers, he still doubted that "they accomplish as much in the same time as agricultural labourers at the North usually do."

Harvest operations in cotton do not appear to have offered the opportunities for division of labor and specialization that existed during the planting and cultivation seasons (although such opportunities do appear to have existed in sugar harvesting). In the absence of an interdependence that could be exploited to promote an intense rhythm of work, planters attempted to achieve the same objective by dividing harvest hands into competing groups. There were daily as well as weekly races, with prizes (bonuses) offered to the winning team and to the leading individual picker. There were daily weigh-ins of the cotton picked, and those who did not respond to the positive incentive had to face the abuse, verbal or physical, of the driver, if they fell too far below the expected pace.

The so-called "task method" was still another means of promoting the intensity of labor during the harvest season. Under this method, slaves were assigned given plots of land which were to be picked each day. Intensity of labor was promoted by permitting the slave to use his time for his own purposes when the task was completed. One way of ensuring that the work was done well under this system was to reassign the same plot to the same slave in each of the successive rounds of picking. Daily weighing of cotton also served as a check on performance.

Specialization and division of labor were not limited to fieldwork. They carried over into domestic aspects of plantation life. Certain domestic tasks were socialized to a considerable extent. This was true of child rearing and, to a lesser extent, of the production of clothing and of cooking. It was women, predominantly, who specialized in these employments. Most large plantations maintained nurseries. These were supervised by one or more of the older women, depending on the size of the plantation, who generally were assisted by older children. Women who worked in the fields, or at other assignments, deposited their children in the morning and picked them up in the evening. Nursing mothers returned to the nursery three or four times per day for feedings.

The production of clothing was, in varying degrees, carried out on most plantations. Some had loom houses in which most of the cloth consumed on plantations was woven. Others limited production to the sewing of purchased cloth. Sometimes these tasks were carried out by women in their own houses, when the weather was inclement or during slack seasons. In other cases, a permanent staff was assigned to a special building. Olmsted described the loom-house staff on one very large plantation. Of the dozen hands so employed, one "was insane, and most of the others were crippled, invalids with chronic complaints, or unfitted by age, or some infirmity, for field work."

Olmsted's description points to another aspect of the efficiency of plantations—the extraordinarily high labor-force participation rate (share of the population in the labor force). In the free economy—North and South— approximately one third of the population was in the labor force. Among slaves, the labor-force participation rate was two thirds. Virtually every slave capable of being in the labor force was in it. This was due largely to the inability of slaves, particularly women and children, to choose leisure, education, or work at home, if they preferred it, to work in fields or other assigned tasks. It was partly due to institutional arrangements which permitted plantations to find methods of employing those who would, to a large extent, be unemployable in free societies, particularly in free urban societies—the mentally retarded, the crippled, the aged.

Plantations not only brought a larger share of the population into the labor force, but they were also able to move closer to "full-capacity" utilization of the labor potential than was true of the free economy. This was not because slaves worked more hours per day or more days per week than free farmers. The best available evidence is that both slaves and free farmers averaged approximately 70–75 hours of work per week during the peak labor periods of planting, cultivation, and harvesting. Nor does it appear that slaves worked more days per year. In addition to having Sundays off, slaves had all or part of half of their Saturdays free, most of these being concentrated in the off-peak periods of farming. There was also up to a week or so of additional holidays, some at predesignated times, as during Christmas or in the interstice between the end of cultivation and the beginning of the harvest, some as unscheduled rewards for work well done. About a dozen days per year were lost due to illness. Thus the work year appears to have consisted of roughly 265–275 days.

The higher rate of the utilization of labor capacity was partly due to what was, by the usual standards of farmers, an extraordinary intensity of labor. Far from being "ordinary peasants" unused to "pre-industrial rhythms of work," black plantation agriculturalists labored under a regimen that was more like a modern assembly line than was true of the routine in many of the factories of the antebellum era. It was often easier for factory workers to regulate the pace of machines to their accustomed rhythm than for slaves to regulate the pace set by drivers. For much of antebellum manufacturing was still operated on the work patterns of the handicrafts. Division of labor was still at relatively low levels and interdependence of operations was still limited. Just as the great plantations were the first large, scientifically managed business enterprises, and as planters were the first group to engage in large-scale, scientific personnel management, so, too, black slaves were the first group of workers to be trained in the work rhythms which later became characteristic of industrial society. It was not the slaves but men like Olmsted who retained a "pre-industrial peasant mentality," who viewed the teamwork, coordination, and intensity of effort achieved by black field hands as "stupid, plodding, machine-like," and "painful to witness." While Olmsted's revulsion is quite understandable, he was nevertheless wrong in concluding that the gang system was inefficient, and his belittling of the quality of slave labor was unwarranted. . . .

The large slave plantations were about 34 percent more efficient than free southern farms. This advantage was not due to some special way in which land or machinery was used, but to the special quality of plantation labor. It is true that large plantations used more land and equipment (by value) per worker than small plantations. However, this feature was taken into account in computing the efficiency indexes. In other words, even after one adjusts for the fact that on large plantations slaves generally worked on better land than free southern farmers and had more equipment, large plantations were still some 34 percent more efficient than free farms.

The advantage of plantations, at least that part which has been measured thus far, was due to the combination of the superior management of planters and the superior quality of black labor. In a certain sense, all, or nearly all, of the advantage is attributable to the high quality of slave labor, for the main thrust of management was directed at improving the quality of labor. How much of the success of this effort was due to the management, and how much to the responsiveness of the workers is an imperative question, but its resolution lies beyond the range of current techniques and available data.

Whatever the contribution of management, however, it should not all be assigned to white planters and overseers. For blacks—though slaves, though severely limited in the extent to which they could climb the economic ladder of antebellum society—were a vital part of the management of plantations and, in this capacity, of the economic success of the plantation.

Slaves entered into plantation management at two levels. As drivers or gang foremen they were ubiquitous on medium and large plantations. In the fields the drivers were responsible for ensuring that each gang achieved its daily objectives and, if the gang was operating on the task system, for determining the daily tasks of particular hands. Gang objectives were sometimes established either by the plantation owner or overseer. In other instances the establishment of these objectives was left to the discretion of the drivers.

Slaves also operated at the highest level of plantation supervision, short of actual ownership, as overseers or general managers. When acting as overseers, slaves were responsible not only for the overall direction of the labor force but for various entrepreneurial decisions, including the scheduling of the particular field operations and the purchasing of supplies. In such cases the burden of the success or failure of the entire production side of plantation operations rested on these slaves. Much of the attention of owners was directed to the commercial aspects of operations—the marketing of the crops, the purchase of equipment, the acquisition of new lands, the construction of new buildings, the negotiation of loans—or to other nonagricultural enterprises in which they were engaged.

Various scholars have recognized that slaves *sometimes* acted as overseers or general managers. But it has been assumed that this was rare, that on most large plantations the general management *of production* was in the hands of white overseers. The white overseer is assumed to have been a ubiquitous figure, present on virtually all plantations of one hundred or more slaves and on the majority of those with fifty to one hundred slaves. As pointed out previously, data in the census manuscripts clearly invalidates this assumption. Only 30 percent of plantations with one hundred or more slaves employed white overseers. On smaller plantations the proportion was even lower.

It might be thought that on many of the large plantations sons of planters took over the functions of the overseer. The data in the manuscript schedules of the census rules this possibility out in most cases. Among large plantations without overseers, 61 percent had only one adult male over age nineteen in the planter's family. In these cases the planter was the only adult male in his family who was in residence, or else the father was absent or dead and his only resident son was running the plantation. In any event there was no second male family member to take up the duties of the overseer. On 6 percent of the large plantations there were two adults over age nineteen, but the second of these persons was at least seventy years of age, and hence was probably too old to be actively involved in the business affairs of the plantation. Another 9 percent of the plantations had no male at all over age nineteen in residence. Thus, for 75 percent of the plantations without overseers there were no sons or other males who could have assumed the duties of the overseer. The conclusion indicated by these findings is startling: On a majority of the large plantations, the top nonownership management was black.

The question that begs to be explained is how so many scholars could have been so badly misled on this issue? Part of the explanation turns on a methodological consideration. To a considerable extent, the views of historians regarding the nature of plantation management are based on inferences from correspondence between owners and overseers. However, such correspondence (including instructions to overseers) was most likely to arise when owners did not reside on their plantations. Thus, previous historians based their conclusions on a biased sample of evidence, on a relatively small group of plantations which were unrepresentative of the whole. It is probable that absentee owners relied on white overseers to a much greater extent than did resident owners, among other reasons, because laws made it illegal to leave slaves exclusively under their own supervision.

Part of the explanation also turns on the way in which many historians have accepted the arguments of the authors of the economic indictment of slavery. One would hardly expect a system in which even the masters were cavalier fops and idlers to produce a high-quality class of slave managers. Nor was a mass of blacks "incapable of all but the rudest forms of labour," "evasive," incapable of maintaining "a steady routine," "incorrigibly indolent," "wanting in versatility," and unsuited for any activity that requires "the slightest care, forethought, or dexterity" likely to throw up any considerable number of able managers. If one accepts the premise that the system crushed all opportunity for the personal and intellectual development of slaves, mere consistency requires one also to expect to find that slaves were debarred from virtually all positions of responsibility.

Interestingly enough, Olmsted did not show such consistency of mind. Despite his low opinion of the quality of the black masses, he had a high opinion of the quality of blacks who functioned as drivers.

In the selection of drivers, regard seems to be had to size and strength—at least, nearly all the drivers I have seen are tall and strong men—but a great deal of judgment, requiring greater capacity of mind than the ordinary slave is often supposed to be possessed of, is certainly needed in them. A good driver is very valuable and usually holds office for life. His authority is not limited to the direction of labour in the field, but extends to the general deportment of the negroes. He is made to do the duties of policeman, and even of police magistrate. It is his duty, for instance, on Mr. X's estate, to keep order in the settlement; and, if two persons, men or women, are fighting, it is his duty to immediately separate them, and then to "whip them both."

Before any field of work is entered upon by a gang, the driver who is to superintend them has to measure and stake off the tasks. To do this at all accurately, in irregular-shaped fields, must require considerable powers of calculation. A driver with a boy to set the stakes, I was told, would accurately lay out forty acres a day, in half-acre tasks. The only instrument used is a five-foot measuring rod. When the gang comes to the field, he points out to each person his or her duty for the day, and then walks about among them, looking out that each proceeds properly. If, after a hard day's labour, he sees that the gang has been over-tasked, owing to a miscalculation of the difficulty of the work, he may excuse the completion of the tasks; but he is not allowed to extend them. In the case of uncompleted tasks, the body of the gang begin new tasks the next day, and only a sufficient number are detailed from it to complete, during the day, the unfinished tasks of the day before. The relation of the driver to the working hands seems to be similar to that of the boatswain to the seamen in the navy, or of the sergeant to the privates in the army.

Having generally had long experience on the plantation, the advice of the drivers is commonly taken in nearly all the administration, and frequently they are, de facto, the managers. Orders on important points of the plantation economy, I have heard given by the proprietor directly to them, without the overseer's being consulted or informed of them; and it is often left with them to decide when and how long to flow the rice-grounds—the proprietor and overseer deferring to their more experienced judgment. Where the drivers are discrete, experienced, and trusty, the overseer is frequently employed merely as a matter of form, to comply with the laws requiring the superintendence or presence of a white man among every body of slaves; and his duty is rather to inspect and report than to govern. Mr. X considers his overseer an uncommonly efficient and faithful one, but he would not employ him, even during the summer, when he is absent for several months, if the law did not require it. He has sometimes left his plantation in care of one of the drivers for a considerable length of time, after having discharged an overseer; and he thinks it has then been quite as well conducted as ever. His overseer consults the drivers on all important points, and is governed by their advice.

"Mr. X" was not the only planter who frequently consulted with his slave managers and who deferred to their judgment, or insisted that his overseers do so. Nor was Olmsted the only one to note the high quality of black managers. When McBride, the owner of the Hickory Hill plantation, left on a long trip, he wrote detailed instructions to his overseer on the method of planting and cultivating various crops. In the case of rice, however, McBride said he was too ill-informed on that crop to offer advice and suggested that the overseer consult the driver who was "an old rice planter." Similarly, Charles Manigault instructed his overseer to "be careful not to interfere too much with the beating and management of the Rice Mill" since "the Negroes in charge have much experience therein." Indirect testimony of the high regard which planters had for the intelligence and good judgment of their slave drivers and other lower echelon personnel comes from the frequent complaints of white overseers that direct consultations between planters and drivers or other respected slaves were undermining their authority. No doubt some drivers deliberately provoked tests of strength between themselves and the overseers. In many such instances they were successful, and the overseer was fired or left of his own volition. On many of those plantations which did make use of white overseers, the turnover rate of overseers was quite high.

That the quality of slaves, both as ordinary workers and as managers, could have been so completely misrepresented by the antebellum critics of slavery is testimony to the extent of their racist myopia. What bitter irony it is that the false stereotype of black labor, a stereotype which still plagues blacks today, was fashioned not primarily by the oppressors who strove to keep their chattel wrapped in the chains of bondage, but by the most ardent opponents of slavery, by those who worked most diligently to destroy the chains of bondage.

While keenly aware of the torment which these false stereotypes of incompetence have helped to impose on blacks for more than a century, we are, as social scientists, impressed by this exceptional demonstration of the power of ideology to obliterate reality, and we view it as an unparalleled opportunity to investigate the complex interrelationships between ideas and the material circumstances of life. What is at issue here is not only how these false stereotypes regarding blacks came into being, but how they could have persisted for so long. Resolution of the first issue involves consideration of the intricate ways in which variations of racist viewpoints among critics and defenders of slavery, among northern and southern whites—for with very few exceptions they were all racists—interacted with each other to create an almost indestructible image of black incompetence. Resolution of the second issue involves consideration of why it has been so difficult for the many historians and social scientists who have studied slave society to penetrate this image and to discover the reality which it hid.

Much as we desire to do so, we cannot settle these issues—not merely because they lie beyond the scope of this book, or even because they require skills which go beyond our special areas of expertise, but because much research is still required before the various aspects of these questions can be treated adequately. Nevertheless, we cannot resist the opportunity to suggest some considerations which we believe ought to enter into the ultimate resolution.

One point on which there can be little doubt is that the belief in Negro incompetence was given a powerful fillip by the racial theories that came into prominence during the first half of the nineteenth century. These theories were embraced by Northerners as well as Southerners, by critics of slavery as well as its defenders. The theories asserted that blacks and whites were of different species or at least that blacks were an "inferior variety" of the human species. The African origins of blacks were thought to have contributed to the biological defects. Some attributed the racial differences to geographic factors. Thus, Negroes had "a dull torpid brain," a feature thought to be characteristic of "inhabitants of the warmer climates." Others saw Negro backwardness as being rooted in their savage ancestry. Whatever the cause, the innate inferiority of the Negro race was said to manifest itself in laziness, limited intellectual capacity, a childlike simplicity, docility, sensuousness, and tempestuousness. It is important to stress that these racist views were not embraced merely in popular thought. They were the reigning tenets of mid-nineteenth-century anthropology, in Europe as well as in the United States.

Although both critics and defenders of slavery believed in the innate inferiority of Negroes, there were important differences between them in assessing the effect of slavery on the natural endowments of Negroes. Critics of slavery believed that bondage had not only retarded the development of blacks but had exacerbated the baser features of their nature. Slavery had encouraged blacks to be slovenly, to prefer indolence to industry, to be evasive, to lie, and to steal. Abolitionists believed that slavery retarded black development because it was incapable of recognizing individual accomplishment and rewarding it, because it relied on the lash to elicit effort, thus identifying labor with pain. They also believed that the plantation form of organization kept blacks relatively isolated from contacts with whites and hindered their capacity to assimilate the higher white culture. Hence they drew a distinction between house servants and field hands, assuming the former were more highly developed intellectually and culturally because of their more intimate association with whites.

Defenders of slavery argued that their system not only had a beneficial development on blacks but was, indeed, pushing them to the outer limits of their capacity. Despite the fact that they were of an inferior race, under the slave system of labor organization blacks were induced to work harder and produce more than white labor. Not only was the natural indolence of blacks thus thwarted, but the most talented of their number were trained in the handicrafts and in other higher arts, thus achieving a status under slavery which was not only "elevated from the condition in which God first created them" but was clearly more lofty than anything that might be obtained under freedom. For everybody knew that slave labor was "vastly more efficient and productive than the labor of free blacks."

Obviously a debate cast along the lines just described could only serve to reinforce the stereotype of Negro incompetence. For neither side ever called the alleged natural incompetence of the Negro into question. Quite the contrary—each new round of debate served to raise the proposition of natural incompetence to the status of an axiomatic truth. Critics of slavery emphasized the failings of southern production, attributing these to a system which was not only based on an inferior variety of human labor but which degarded all labor, reducing in quality not only the effort of blacks but of whites as well. Defenders of slavery attributed outstanding accomplishments in production not to the high quality of black labor but to the success of the system of slavery which enabled the South to achieve as much as it did from what was basically inferior human material.

That Olmsted fully accepted the racial views of his day is clearly evident in his books. The Germans appear as the only whites in the South capable of resisting the degrading effects of slavery on white labor. They are invariably portrayed as industrious and efficient—the very models of enterprising, thrifty, and ambitious small proprietors. On the other hand, the only Jews that Olmsted encountered in the South were moneylenders "of no character" who charged extortionate interest rates ("often . . . not less than 25 percent per annum"), who lived in squalid homes, and who engaged "in an unlawful trade with the simple negroes." Similarly, the Irish were "dumb Paddies" who easily succumbed to the degrading southern attitude toward labor and usually fell to a level that made their labor even less desirable than that of slaves. Olmsted's northern chauvinism came to the fore whenever he compared the quality of northern and southern laborers. Few northern employers would have recognized their employees from his description of them. Northern workers were almost invariably portrayed as highly motivated, diligent, self-propelled, and polite, even when being fired for some infraction of their normally high standards of behavior. There can be little doubt that Olmsted's jaundiced views of black relative to white labor, and of southern relative to northern labor, were influenced by the racial presuppositions that he brought with him on his travels through the South.

But to leave the matter there is to grossly oversimplify the issue. For whatever his prejudices, Olmsted was an extremely keen and diligent observer who was striving to discover those characteristics which distinguished the system of slave labor and which differentiated it from the system of free labor. While his prejudices undoubtedly predisposed him toward misinterpreting what he in fact observed, or had reported to him, it is not likely that he would have fallen into these errors if there had not been mitigating circumstances that made his misinterpretations plausible—if there had not been substantial elements which lent support, or at least appeared to lend support, to his conclusions. . . .

The issue which probably confused Olmsted more than any other one came to the fore during his very first visit to a slave plantation—a wheat farm in Maryland which he examined on December 14, 1852. The slaves he saw there were not engaged in the fields but were at work in the neighborhood of the plantation buildings. The owner of the plantation told Olmsted that while he had employed white laborers on several occasions for digging ditches, he would not think of using whites "for common farm-labor, and made light of their coming in competition with slaves. Negroes at hoeing and any steady field work, he assured me, would 'do two to their one'. . . .''

Olmsted did not press the planter further. He clearly did not accept such a high appraisal of the quality of the planter's black labor force. Olmsted characterized the slaves on this farm as "stupid and dilatory in executing any orders given to them." "Those I saw at work," he said, "appeared to me to move very slowly and awkwardly, as did also those engaged in the stable."

This Maryland wheat plantation was not a run-down, piddling farm operated by a "mean white." It was, in Olmsted's words, a "fine farm," over two thousand acres in extent, run under "excellent management," with a main house which had "somewhat the look of an old French chateau," with "well-secured, wire fences," with a "nicely graveled and rolled" road, with "thorough-bred Shorthorns" as the milking stock ("I have seldom seen a better lot of milkers," said Olmsted), and with drains on the farm's lowlands that were so well built that they lasted "twenty years without failing." The planter's experiments with fertilizers so impressed Olmsted that he singled them out. How could so keen a planter, a man whose excellence in farm management had won him "a national reputation," have deceived himself so badly about the quality of his laborers? And how had he been able to prosper with workers who were "stupid and dilatory," who moved "very slowly" and who "must" have been "very difficult to direct efficiently"?

The mistake was Olmsted's. What he observed on this plantation was the easy-going rhythm of slaves during the winter interstice. The planting of winter wheat had been completed more than a month before Olmsted's arrival and the fall harvesting of other crops, such as corn, had also been completed well before his visit. This was a period for putting things in order—repairing fences, thoroughly cleaning stables, rerolling of roads—important tasks all, but not the type that called for intensive effort. The high-pressure tasks of planting, cultivating, and harvesting were either over, or not yet at hand. As we have previously stated. Olmsted's itinerary during his first trip kept him squarely in the interstice between harvesting and planting. As he moved south and westward into cotton country, he generally moved toward both later completion of the harvest and later resumption of the date of planting. By the time he arrived in Georgia, Alabama, and Louisiana, states in which he might still have observed the picking of cotton in mid-December, he was already into February. He left Louisiana well before the onset of the new planting season, which began during the last days of March or early in April.

Thus, Olmsted's opinion of the typical work rhythms of slaves, an opinion in which he gained more and more confidence as he traveled through the "Seaboard States," was once again based on an unrepresentative sample of evidence. Olmsted appears to have made the mistake of assuming that the leisurely work pace of slaves during the southern agricultural interstice prevailed throughout the balance of the year. In his subsequent two trips, Olmsted did, of course, witness the typical rhythms of planting and cultivating.

But by then he had become so convinced that the pace he had observed during his first trip was the norm, that he invariably classified his later encounters with intense labor as exceptions.

Toward an Explanation for the Persistence of the Myth of Black Incompetence

The principal cause of the persistence of the myth of black incompetence in American historiography is racism. Perhaps no single history book written during the twentieth century has had a greater impact on the interpretation of slave life than U. B. Phillips's *American Negro Slavery*. To point out that this volume was deeply marred by its author's adherence to the proposition that Negroes were racially inferior to whites would hardly evoke controversy among historians today. This point is now emphasized not only by the critics of Phillips but also his defenders.

How different the situation was when *American Negro Slavery* was published in 1918. Of the principal reviewers of the book, only two attacked Phillips's treatment of Negroes—and they were not in the mainstream of the historical profession as it was then constituted. One of these reviewers was W. E. B. Du Bois, the director of publicity and research for the N.A.A.C.P. and the editor of its journal, *Crisis*. Du Bois found *American Negro Slavery* "curiously incomplete and unfortunately biased."

The Negro as a responsible human being has no place in the book. To be sure individual Negroes are treated here and there but mainly as exceptional or as illustrative facts for purposes outside themselves. Nowhere is there any adequate conception of "darkies," "niggers" and "negroes" (words liberally used throughout the book) as making a living mass of humanity with all the usual human reactions. . . .

Mr. Phillips recurs again and again to this inborn character of Negroes: they are "submissive," "light-hearted" and "ingratiating" (p. 342), very "fond of display" (pp. 1, 291), with a "proneness to superstition" and "acceptance of subordination" (p. 291); "chaffing, and chattering" (p. 292) with "humble nonchalance and a freedom from carking care" (p. 416). From the fourteenth to the twentieth century Mr. Phillips sees no essential change in these predominant characteristics of the mass of Negroes; and while he is finishing his book in a Y.M.C.A. army hut in the South all he sees in the Negroe soldier is the "same easy-going amiable serio-comic obedience," and all he hears is the throwing of dice (pp. viii, ix). This Negro nature is, to Mr. Phillips, fixed and unchangeable. A generation of freedom has brought little change (p. ix). Even the few exceptional Negroes whom he mentions are of interest mainly because of their unexpected "ambition" and not for any especial accomplishment (p. 432). The fighting black maroons were overcome by "fright" (p. 466), and the Negroes' part in the public movements like the Revolution was "barely appreciable" (p. 116); indeed his main picture is of "inert Negroes, the majority of whom are as yet perhaps less efficient in freedom than their forbears were as slaves" (p. 396)!

Brilliant as it was, Du Bois's critique fell largely on deaf ears. It could hardly have been otherwise during an era when the pseudoscientific racial theories which still dominated anthropology were widely accepted in scholarly circles. Indeed, more than two decades elapsed before scholars in the mainstream of the history profession began to press the theme enunciated by Du Bois.

While not unanticipated by others, the flag of general revolt against the Phillips school was raised by Richard Hofstadter in a 1944 paper entitled "U. B. Phillips and the Plantation Legend." Hofstadter attacked Phillips for exaggerating the paternalistic impulses of the planter, for painting too "rosy" a portrait of the material conditions of slave life, and for depicting the Negro as "a singularly contented and docile 'serio-comic' creature." The real nature of the treatment of slaves, said Hofstadter, was far more cruel than admitted by Phillips, slave health was much poorer than Phillips admitted, and slaves were more often left to the mercy of harsh overseers by their absentee owners than Phillips admitted. Hofstadter also charged Phillips with having underestimated the extent, and having distorted the nature of, "the slave's resistance to slavery." He chided Phillips for stressing a benign type of "give-and-take process between master and slave," for failing to appreciate "the extent to which the easement of the slave's condition came not from the master's benevolence but from the slave's resistance." Hofstadter ended his essay with a call for the rewriting of the history of slavery from the "viewpoint of modern cultural anthropology"; by this he meant the new view on race, pioneered by Franz Boas, which held that racial factors were unimportant in determining intellectual capacity.

Hofstadter's rebellion was far less sweeping than might appear. Hofstadter did not challenge Phillips on the general profitability and viability of slavery. Neither did he take issue with him on the quality of slave labor, on the economic efficiency of slavery, or on the effect of slavery on southern economic growth. Indeed, Hofstadter confined his attack to just four of the twenty-three chapters of *American Negro Slavery*, specifically excluding from consideration those which dealt with the issues of profitability, efficiency, and growth.

The limited nature of Hofstadter's attack on Phillips is not difficult to explain. Like so many others, Hofstadter's conception of slavery was developed largely from his reading of Olmsted. Hofstadter excoriated Phillips for not having made greater use of the work of this witness and critic. "Olmsted was not only an honest but an unusually acute observer," said Hofstadter, "and I believe that a fuller and more accurate knowledge of the late antebellum South can be obtained from the volumes of Olmsted than from Professor Phillips's own writings." But Phillips, despite his mistrust for the man, had read Olmsted with care and made great use of him. On the issues of the profitability and efficiency of slavery, as well as on the quality of slave labor and the effect of slavery on southern economic growth, Phillips was pure Olmsted. And on some of these issues Phillips merely paraphrased Olmsted. (Olmsted: "slaves thus get a fictitious value like stocks 'in a corner.'"

Phillips: "when the supply [of slaves] was 'cornered' it was unavoidable that the price should be bid up to the point of overvaluation.")

Despite Phillips's pretensions to a revolutionary break with James Ford Rhodes, the dominant historian in the interpretation of southern slavery at the time Phillips was a graduate student, and despite Hofstadter's claims to a revolutionary break with Phillips, all three men—and the schools of historical writing on the antebellum South which they symbolize—were adherents to what we have termed the "traditional interpretation" of the slave economy. That interpretation is the one which emerged from the economic indictment of slavery described in chapter 5. It consists of five main propositions. These are: 1, that slavery was generally an unprofitable investment, or depended on a trade in slaves to be profitable, except on new, highly fertile land; 2, that slavery was economically moribund; 3, that slave labor, and agricultural production based on slave labor, was economically inefficient; 4, that slavery caused the economy of the South to stagnate, or at least retarded its growth, during the antebellum era; 5, that slavery provided extremely harsh material conditions of life for the typical slave.

Phillips accepted all of these propositions except the last. When he claimed he was revolutionizing the interpretation of the antebellum South, he was referring only to point five, the harsh treatment of slaves, and to the shadow which that treatment cast on the character of slaveholders. Phillips did not have to overturn Rhodes on the character of blacks and the quality of their labor. Rhodes's views on the character of slaves and on the quality of their labor were fully congenial to Phillips. Rhodes described slaves as "indolent and filthy"; their expression was "besotted and generally repulsive"; on their "brute-like countenances . . . were painted stupidity, indolence, duplicity, and sensuality"; their labor was "stupid, plodding, machine-like"; licentiousness and indifference to chastity were "a natural inclination of the African race" which was further fostered by slavery; as women displayed "an entire lack of chastity," the men displayed "an entire lack of honesty"; and slave women yielded "without objection, except in isolated cases, to the passion of their master." In Rhodes's view the error of southern apologists was not in the claim that blacks were inferior, but in the manner in which they sought to cope with the problem created by this inferiority. "So long as Southern reasoners maintained that the negro race was inferior to the Caucasian, their basis was scientific truth, although their inference that this fact justified slavery was cruel as well as illogical."

The irony of Hofstadter's call for a rejection of the Phillips position on treatment, without a simultaneous attack on the other four points, is that it led in the direction of the re-establishment of the pre-Phillips or "pure" version of the traditional interpretation of the economics of slavery. As long as historians remained locked in combat on the issue of treatment, explicitly accepting all other aspects of the economic indictment of slavery, the myth of Negro incompetence continued to reign supreme—just as it had in the antebellum era when critics of slavery and apologists debated over whether slavery had exacerbated or ameliorated the "natural" inferiority of blacks.

We do not mean that Hofstadter, or that scholars who responded to his call, aimed to re-establish the theories of the racial inferiority of Negroes as they existed in Rhodes or as in Clay, Helper, and Olmsted. Quite the contrary, as both Hofstadter and those who rallied to his banner have made clear, their aim was the unequivocal and complete rout of the racist myths that lingered on in the historiography of the antebellum South. What they failed to appreciate was that these racist myths drew sustenance not merely from one of the five points in the traditional interpretation of slavery but from each of them.

This was true even of Kenneth Stampp who . . . went further than any other post-Phillips scholar, except perhaps Lewis C. Gray, in rejecting the traditional interpretation of slavery. In *The Peculiar Institution*, Stampp argued that investments in slaves were quite generally profitable, indeed, highly profitable for most planters. He also rejected the contention that economic forces would by themselves have led to the demise of slavery, even in the upper South. Nor did Stampp find any evidence to support the claim that slavery prevented industrialization and economic growth. He pointed to "innumerable experiments" which "demonstrated that slaves could be employed profitably in factories," arguing that slaveholders preferred to operate in agriculture because, for the South, agriculture "seemed to be the surest avenue to financial success."

Stampp even expressed doubts about the fourth proposition in the traditional interpretation—that slavery was less efficient than an economic system based on free labor. "Slavery's economic critics overlooked the fact," he said, "that physical coercion, or the threat of it, proved to be a rather effective incentive, and that the system did not prevent masters from offering tempting rewards for the satisfactory performance of assigned tasks."

At this point, however, Stampp faltered. He hesitated to go on to the conclusion that slaves were equal to free men in the efficiency of their labor. He conceded that slave productivity was sharply reduced by "the slave's customary attitude of indifference toward his work, together with the numerous methods he devised to resist his enslavement." Stampp was able to hold on to his contention that slavery was profitable only by arguing that there were other "advantages" which "more than compensated for whatever superiority free labor had in efficiency." These "advantages" included longer hours of work, more complete exploitation of women and children, and lower real wages for slaves than for free men.

Why did Stampp, who broke with so much of the traditional interpretation and who came so close to rejecting the myth of the incompetence of slave labor, fail to do so? Why did he, as it were, pull back just as he seemed about to do so?

The answer lies in Stampp's preoccupation with the refutation of Phillips on point five, the nature of the treatment of slaves. Surely Phillips's idyllic portrait needed correction. In reacting against the Rhodes treatment of plantations as houses of immorality and unmitigated terror run by men who were not only brutal but corrupt, Phillips substituted a near-paradise— at least as much of a paradise on earth as was reasonable to expect from a "primitive" race whose "savage" instincts had to be kept in check and which had to be trained to overcome a "natural ineptitude" and "indolence." In Phillips's reconstruction, planters emerged not merely as good men but, to use Du Bois's word, as supermen. Slavery became "less a business than a life." The objective of planters was not so much to make a profit as to make men.

Recoiling from such apologetics, Stampp provided testimony that cruelty was indeed an ingrained feature of the treatment of slaves. The cases of cruelty which Phillips regarded as unusual, as outside the unwritten rules of the master class, emerged as a common pattern of white behavior in *The Peculiar Institution*. Cruelty, Stampp said, "was endemic in all slave-holding communities"; even those "who were concerned about the welfare of slaves found in difficult to draw a sharp line between acts of cruelty and such measures of physical force as were an inextricable part of slavery." For Stampp, cruelty arose not because of the malevolent nature of the slaveholders but because of the malevolent nature of the system—because a master could brook nothing less from his slave than "perfect" submission. To achieve that goal masters were impelled, regardless of their humanity in other respects, to develop in the Negro "a paralyzing fear of white men," to "impress upon him his innate inferiority," and to "instill in him a sense of complete dependence." While Stampp did not employ the concentration camp analogy later set forth by Stanley Elkins, his plantation strongly suggested a prison with cruel wardens.

From this point the argument could have gone—and did in fact go— in two directions. One was the direction taken by Elkins, who argued that a system as cruel as the one described by Stampp must have had a devastating impact on the personality of slaves. No one could live under so brutal a regime without succumbing to it. Negroes were not supermen, any more than were the Jews in Hitler's concentration camps. Although plantations were not concentration camps, the masters who ran the plantations had as much absolute power over slaves as Hitler's gauleiters had over the Jews, and as much determination to crush their spirit. What emerged from the process was "Sambo, the typical plantation slave . . . docile but irresponsible, loyal but lazy, humble but chronically given to lying and stealing." Sambo's "behavior was full of infantile silliness" and his "relationship with his master was one of utter dependence and childlike attachment."

Stampp decided to move in a direction that, on the surface, appears quite different from the one Elkins chose. He argued that slaves did not succumb; they resisted. Resistance did not generally take the form of revolution or strikes. Such open forms of resistance were sheer suicide. There were no rebellions among U.S. slaves comparable to those in Jamaica or Brazil;

there was no protracted guerrilla warfare. Resistance in the U.S. took a much more subtle form; it came in guises so innocent that masters and overseers failed even to recognize it. The participants in this resistance movement "were the meek, smiling ones whom many thought were contented though irresponsible."

They were not reckless rebels who risked their lives for freedom; if the thought of rebellion crossed their minds, the odds against success seemed too overwhelming to attempt it. But the inevitability of their bondage made it none the more attractive. And so, when they could, they protested by shirking their duties, injuring the crops, feigning illness, and disrupting the routine. These acts were, in part, an unspectacular kind of "day to day resistance to slavery."

What, of course, is common to both Stampp and Elkins is agreement on the characteristic of slave behavior: slaves lie, steal, feign illness, behave childishly, and shirk their duties. Indeed, this characterization has been one of the enduring constants in the literature on slavery. By whatever path they moved, writers on slavery usually returned to the theme of the inferiority of slave labor. To Olmsted, Rhodes, and Phillips the inferiority was due to racial factors. To Cairnes, inferiority was sociological in origin. To Elkins, the cause was psychological. To Stampp, the inferiority was due to "day to day resistance." Paradoxically, it was the slaveholders who were least inhibited in acknowledging that blacks were better workers than whites, although they attributed this superiority to themselves rather than to their bondsmen.

Stampp hesitated to make the leap required to recognize the superior quality of slave labor because he remained too enmeshed in the debate between the critics of slavery and the apologists, and he overestimated the cruelty of the slave system. The logic of his position made it difficult to acknowledge that ordinary slaves could be diligent workers, imbued like their masters with a Protestant ethic, or that, even though they longed for freedom, slaves could strive to develop and improve themselves in the only way that was open to them.

Eugene D. Genovese

The Black Work Ethic

It goes without saying that "niggers are lazy": the planters always said so, as did the "poor white trash," whose own famous commitment to hard and steady work doubtless assured their entrance into John Calvin's Kingdom of Heaven. Some of the refrain may be dismissed as obvious ideological rationalization and self-serving cant or a distorted interpretation of the effects of a lack of adequate incentives. Yet much more needs to be said, for the slaves themselves sang at their work:

> Nigger mighty happy when he layin' by the corn,
> Nigger mighty happy when he hear dat dinner horn;
> But he more happy when de night come on,
> Dat sun's a slantin', as sho's you born!
> Dat old cow's a shakin' dat great big bell,
> And de frogs tunin' up. 'cause de dew's done fell.[1]

"The white men," Johann David Schoepf observed on his travels during the 1780s, "are all the time complaining that the blacks will not work, and they themselves do nothing." Virginia's great humorist, George W. Bagby, once reflected on the complacency and self-satisfaction of antebellum life: "Time was abundant in those days. It was made for slaves, and we had the slaves."[2]

The slaveholders presided over a plantation system that constituted a halfway house between peasant and factory cultures. The tobacco and cotton

[1] Rawick, ed., Texas Narr., V (4), 54.
[2] Johann David Schoepf, Travels in the Confederation, 1783–1784 (2 vols.; trans. A. J. Morrison; Philadelphia, 1911), II, 118. The Bagby quotation is from Bancroft, Slave Trading, p. 88.

plantations, which dominated the slave economy in the United States, ranged closer to the peasant than the factory model, in contradistinction to the great sugar plantations of the Caribbean, which in some respects resembled factories in the field; but even the small holders pushed their laborers toward modern work discipline. The planters' problem came to this: How could they themselves preserve as much as possible of that older way of life to which they aspired and yet convince their slaves to repudiate it? How could they instill factorylike discipline into a working population engaged in a rural system that, for all its tendencies toward modern discipline, remained bound to the rhythms of nature and to traditional ideas of work, time, and leisure?

They succeeded in overcoming this contradiction only to the extent that they got enough work out of their slaves to make the system pay at a level necessary to their survival as a slaveholding class in a capitalist world market. But they failed in deeper ways that cast a shadow over the long-range prospects for that very survival and over the future of both blacks and whites in American society. Too often they fell back on the whip and thereby taught and learned little. When they went to other incentives, as fortunately most tried to do, they did get satisfactory economic results, but at the same time they reinforced traditional attitudes and values instead of replacing them with more advanced ones.

The black work ethic grew up within a wide Protestant Euro-American community with a work ethic of its own. The black ethic represented at once a defense against an enforced system of economic exploitation and an autonomous assertion of values generally associated with preindustrial peoples. As such, it formed part of a more general southern work ethic, which developed in antagonism to that of the wider American society. A Euro-American, basically Anglo-Saxon work ethic helped shape that of southerners in general and slaves in particular and yet, simultaneously, generated a profound antithesis. . . .

The setting remained rural, and the rhythm of work followed seasonal fluctuations. Nature remained the temporal reference point for the slaves. However much the slaveholders might have wished to transform their slaves into clock-punchers, they could not, for in a variety of senses both literal and metaphoric, there were no clocks to punch.[3] The planters, especially the resident planters of the United States and Brazil but even the typical West Indian agents of absentee owners, hardly lived in a factory world themselves and at best could only preach what the most docile or stupid slave knew very well they did not and could not practice. Since the plantation economy required extraordinary exertion at critical points of the year, notably the harvest, it required measures to capitalize on the slaves' willingness to work in spurts rather than steadily. The slaveholders turned the inclinations of the

---

[3] "We didn't own no clocks in dem days. We just told de time by de sun in de day and de stars at night. If it was clouded we didn't know what time it was" (Jane Simpson, ex-slave, in Yetman, ed., *Life Under the "Peculiar Institution,"* p. 279); also Fisk University, *Unwritten History of Slavery*, p. 146.

slaves to their own advantage, but simultaneously they made far greater concessions to the value system and collective sensibility of the quarters than they intended.

The slaveholders, as usual, had their way but paid a price. The slaves, as usual, fell victim to the demands of their exploiters but had some success in pressing their own advantage. Thus, the plantation system served as a halfway house for Africans between their agricultural past and their imposed industrial future. But, it froze them into a position that allowed for their exploitation on the margins of industrial society. The advantage of this compromise, from the black point of view, lay in the protection it provided for their rich community life and its cultural consolidation. The disadvantage lay in its encouragement of a way of life that, however admirable intrinsically, ill prepared black people to compete in the economic world into which they would be catapulted by emancipation. . . .

The black view of time, conditioned by the plantation slave experience, has provided a great source of strength for a people at bay, as one of Bishop A. G. Dunston's sermons makes clear:

You know, that's the way God does it. Same as you can't hurry God—so why don't you wait, just wait. Everybody's ripping and racing and rushing. And God is taking his time. Because he knows that it isn't hurtin' neary so bad as you and I think it's hurtin'—and that is the way he wants us to go. But by and by he brings relief. . . .[4]

Black people, in short, learned to take the blow and to parry it as best they could. They found themselves shut out by white racism from part of the dominant culture's value system, and they simultaneously resisted that system both by historically developed sensibility and by necessity. Accordingly, they developed their own values as a force for community cohesion and survival, but in so doing they widened the cultural gap and exposed themselves to even harder blows from a white nation that could neither understand their behavior nor respect its moral foundations. . . .

The slaves' world outlook, as manifested in their attitude toward work, has usually been treated as a mechanism of resistance to labor or to the demoralization occasioned by an especially oppressive labor system. Older and openly racist writers like Ulrich Bonnell Phillips or A. H. Stone accounted for it primarily by reference to "Negro traits." Ironically, W. E. B. Du Bois, the one scholar who attacked the question without bias and with sympathetic care, came out closer to the white racists than to the liberals, for he too proclaimed profound cultural differences; but he simultaneously stripped away the racists' distortions and, as it were, turned their arguments back on them. Any consideration of this question—indeed, any consideration of any question concerning slave life—must begin with a careful reconsideration of Dr. Du Bois's great work.

[4] Quoted in H. H. Mitchell, *Black Preaching*, p. 131.

Perhaps Dr. Du Bois's best discussion of the black work ethic is the one in The Gift of Black Folk:

The black slave brought into common labor certain new spiritual values not yet fully realized. As a tropical product with a sensuous receptivity to the beauty of the world, he was not as easily reduced to be the mechanical draft-horse which the northern European laborer became. He was not easily brought to recognize any ethical sanctions in work as such but tended to work as the results pleased him and refused to work or sought to refuse when he did not find the spiritual returns adequate, thus he was easily accused of laziness and driven as a slave when in truth he brought to modern manual labor a renewed valuation of life.

And again:

Many a northern manager has seen the contradiction when, facing the apparent laziness of Negro hands, he has attempted to drive them and found out that he could not and at the same time has afterward seen someone used to Negro labor get a tremendous amount of work out of the same gangs. The explanation of all this is clear and simple: the Negro laborer has not been trained in modern organized industry but rather in a quite different school.[5]

Dr. Du Bois located the difference in the attitudes of Euro-American and Afro-American workers in the difference between the bourgeois social system of the one and the ostensibly "communistic" social system of the other. The white worker worked hard not only to avoid starvation but to avoid disgracing himself and his family, whereas the black worker "looked upon work as a necessary evil and maintained his right to balance the relative allurements of leisure and satisfaction at any particular day, hour, or season."[6] Ever alert to complexities, Dr. Du Bois suggested that the white worker brought to America the habit of regular toil as a great moral duty and used it to make America rich, whereas the black worker brought the idea of work as a necessary evil and could, if allowed, use it to make America happy.

There is much that is wise as well as humane in Dr. Du Bois's point of view, and it seems incomprehensible that it should so long have been ignored, if only because it raises so many questions of a kind that now threaten to tear the country apart generationally as well as racially. Santayana, with whom Dr. Du Bois studied at Harvard, once wrote: "Certain moralists, without meaning to be satirical, often say that the sovereign cure for unhappiness is work. Unhappily, the work they recommend is better fitted to dull pain than to remove its cause. It occupies the faculties without rationalising the life."[7] Notwithstanding the great merit of Dr. Du Bois's interpretation, its historical specifics cannot go unchallenged. The blacks may indeed be seen as "a tropical product with a sensuous receptivity to the beauty of the world."

[5] Du Bois, Gift of Black Folk, pp. 14, 29.
[6] Ibid., p. 30.
[7] Santayana, Life of Reason, Vol. II, Reason in Religion, p. 132.

Despite appearances, there is nothing mystical here—merely a proper concern for the impact of physical environment on the historically developed, collective sensibilities of peoples. But, Dr. Du Bois made a costly error in assuming that white European workers came to the United States after having internalized the Puritan work ethic, and he thereby drew attention away from the central character of the slave experience and moved it to the African experience, which was only a special case in the general immigrant experience.

The immigrants who filled the ranks of the unskilled labor force during the nineteenth century came, to a great extent, from peasant societies with a rural work ethic reinforced by Roman Catholicism. The Sicilians and East Europeans who followed did not bring the maxims of Benjamin Franklin with them. Each wave of immigrants had to undergo a process of acculturation that meant a harsh struggle to break down an established set of values and the slow inculcation of those values we associate with specifically industrial discipline. Moreover, as E. P. Thompson has so well demonstrated, the English working class itself had arisen from the countryside amidst the bitter contention of rival value systems in general and work ethics in particular. Thus, the contribution of Africa came not from some supposed communistic tradition but from its particular participation in a much broader tradition that we associate with most agrarian peoples. But whereas the Europeans found themselves drawn into an industrial system that slowly transformed them into suitable industrial workers, the Africans found themselves drawn into a plantation system that, despite certain similarities to an industrial setting, immensely reinforced traditional values and also added elements of corruption and degradation.

The African tradition, like the European peasant tradition, stressed hard work and condemned and derided laziness in any form.[8] Not hard work but steady, routinized work as moral duty was discounted. In this attitude African agriculturalists resembled preindustrial peoples in general, including urban peoples. The familiar assertion that certain people would work only long enough to earn the money they needed to live was leveled not only against day laborers but against the finest and most prestigious artisans in early modern Europe.[9]

Olmsted reported that the slaves could be and often were driven into hard, unremitting toil but that they responded with a dull, stupid, plodding effort which severely reduced their productive contribution.[10] The slaves, he added, "are far less adapted for steady, uninterrupted labor than we are, but excel us in feats demanding agility and tempestuous energy." Olmsted's argument became standard among postbellum employers who were trying to

---

[8] For a brief discussion and references to the literature see by *Political Economy of Slavery*, Ch. 3. Also Mendras, *Vanishing Peasant*, p. 69. The Africans might well have agreed with the French peasants that a brave man (*courageux*) is by definition a hard worker. See also the interesting comparison of the Irish and Africans in Abraham, *Mind of Africa*, pp. 98–99.

[9] See Menéndez Pidal, *Spaniards in Their History*, p. 21.

[10] Olmsted, *Back Country*, p. 81.

rebuild with a labor force of freedmen. As one farmer in North Carolina told John Richard Dennett in 1865, "You know how it is with them—for about three days it's work as if they'd break everything to pieces; but after that it's go out late and come in soon."[11] Ironically, this distinction parallels precisely the one made by proslavery ideologues who wished to describe the cultural differences between themselves and the Yankees. It is also the distinction made by scholars in describing the position of southern blacks who went north to cities like Chicago during the twentieth century.[12]

What did the blacks themselves say? Isaac Adams, who had been a slave on a big plantation in Louisiana, recalled that most of the blacks remained there when the Yankees emancipated them. "But," he added, "they didn't do very much work. Just enough to take care of themselves and their white folks."[13] Frank Smith, an ex-slave who went north from Alabama to Illinois, complained: "I didn't lak de Yankees. Dey wanted you to wuk *all de time*, and dat's sump'n I hadn't been brung up to do."[14] Colin Clark and Margaret Haswell may have a point when they argue, in *The Economics of Subsistence Agriculture*, that subsistence laborers will overcome their attachment to leisure and work steadily once they have been brought into contact with communities and values strong enough to stimulate their wants.[15] But powerful cultural resistance to any such tendency must be overcome, and the projected outcome of such a confrontation is not inevitable. In part the outcome must depend on the extent to which the more traditional group has organized itself into a community rather than continuing as a conglomerate of individuals and on the extent to which assimilation to the more economically advanced community is blocked by discrimination.

The slaves' willingness to work extraordinarily hard and yet to resist the discipline of regularity accompanied certain desires and expectations. During Reconstruction the blacks sought their own land; worked it conscientiously when they could get it; resisted being forced back into anything resembling gang labor for the white man; and had to be terrorized, swindled, and murdered to prevent their working for themselves.[16] This story was prefigured in antebellum times when slaves were often allowed garden plots for their families and willingly worked them late at night or on Sundays in order to provide extra food or clothing. The men did not generally let their families

---

11 *Ibid.*, p. 106; Frederick Law Olmsted, *Journey Through Texas: Or, A Saddle Trip on the Southwestern Frontier* (New York, 1969 [1859]), p. 33; Dennett, *South as It Is*, p. 114. See André Hodeir, *Jazz: Its Evolution and Essence* (trans. D. Noakes; New York, 1961), p. 240, for a description of the structure of jazz that parallels these facets of the work ethic.

12 See, e.g., Allan H. Spear, *Black Chicago: The Making of the Negro Ghetto, 1890–1920* (Chicago, 1967), p. 156.

13 Yetman, ed., *Life Under the "Peculiar Institution,"* p. 10.

14 Rawick, ed., *Ala. Narr.*, VI (1), 347.

15 Colin Clark and Margaret Haswell, *The Economics of Subsistence Agriculture* (4th ed.; London, 1970), pp. 139–141.

16 See esp. Rose, *Rehearsal for Reconstruction,* and Bleser, *Promised Land;* also S. Andrews, *South Since the War,* pp. 97–98, 206, 221–222, 339; *Journal of Charlotte Forten,* p. 178.

subsist on the usual allotments of pork and corn. In addition to working with their wives in the gardens, they fished and hunted and trapped animals. In these and other ways they demonstrated considerable concern for the welfare of their families and a strong desire to take care of them. But in such instances they were working for themselves and at their own pace. Less frequently, slaves received permission to hire out their own time after having completed the week's assigned tasks. They were lured, not by some internal pressure to work steadily, but by the opportunity to work for themselves and their families in their own way.[17]

Many slaves voluntarily worked for their masters on Sundays or holidays in return for money or goods. This arrangement demonstrated how far the notion of the slaves' "right" to a certain amount of time had been accepted by the masters; how readily the slaves would work for themselves; and how far the notion of reciprocity had entered the thinking of both masters and slaves.

The slaves responded to moral as well as economic incentives. They often took pride in their work, but not necessarily in the ways most important to their masters. Solomon Northup designed a better way to transport lumber only to find himself ridiculed by the overseer. In this case it was in the master's interest to intervene, and he did. He praised Northup and adopted the plan. Northup comments: "I was not insensible to the praise bestowed upon me, and enjoyed especially, my triumph over Taydem [the overseer], whose half-malicious ridicule had stung my pride."[18]

From colonial days onward plantation slaves, as well as those in industry, mining, and town services, received payments in money and goods as part of a wider system of social control.[19] These payments served either as incentive bonuses designed to stimulate productivity, or more frequently, as a return for work done during the time recognized as the slaves' own. Many planters, including those who most clearly got the best results, used such incentives. Bennet H. Barrow of Louisiana provides a noteworthy illustration, for he was not a man to spare the whip. Yet his system of rewards included frequent holidays and dinners, as well as cash bonuses and presents for outstanding work. In Hinds County, Mississippi, Thomas Dabney gave small cash prizes— a few cents, really—to his best pickers and then smaller prizes to others who worked diligently even if they could not match the output of the leaders. In Perry County, Alabama, Hugh Davis divided his workers into rival teams and had them compete for prizes. He supplemented this collective competition with individual contests. In North Carolina at the end of the eighteenth

[17] See the account of Clara Brim of Louisiana in Rawick, ed., *Texas Narr.*, IV (1), 148.
[18] Northup, *Twelve Years a Slave*, p. 99.
[19] For the historical growth of this practice in industry, as well as for a vigorous insistence that it strengthened rather than weakened the system of social control, see Starobin, *Industrial Slavery*; also S. Sydney Bradford, "The Negro Ironworker in Ante-bellum Virginia," in Meier and Rudwick, eds., *Making of Black America*, p. 142; Fletcher M. Green, "Gold Mining in Ante Bellum Virginia," *VMHR*, XLV (July, Oct., 1937), 227–235; 357–366.

century Charles Pettigrew, like many others before and after him, paid slaves for superior or extra work.[20]

The amounts sometimes reached substantial proportions. Captain Frederick Marryat complained that in Lexington, Kentucky, during the late 1830s a gentleman could not rent a carriage on Sundays because slaves with ready money invariably rented them first for their own pleasure. Occasionally, plantation records reported surprising figures. One slave in Georgia earned fifty to sixty dollars per year by attending to pine trees in his off hours. Others earned money by applying particular skills or by doing jobs that had to be done individually and carefully without supervision. Amounts in the tens and even hundreds of dollars, although not common, caused no astonishment.[21]

The more significant features of these practices, for the society as a whole if not for the economy in particular, was the regularity—almost the institutionalization—of payments for work on Sundays or holidays. Apart from occasional assignments of Sunday or holiday work as punishment and apart from self-defeating greed, not to say stupidity, which led a few masters to violate the social norm, Sunday was the slaves' day by custom as well as law.[22] The collective agreement of the slaveholders on these measures had its origin in a concern for social peace and reflected a sensible attitude toward economic efficiency. But once the practice took root, with or without legal sanction, the slaves transformed it into a "right." So successfully did they do so that the Supreme Court of Louisiana ruled in 1836: "According to . . . law, slaves are entitled to the produce of their labor on Sunday; even the master is bound to remunerate them, if he employs them." Here again the slaves turned the paternalist doctrine of reciprocity to advantage while demonstrating the extent to which that doctrine dominated the lives of both masters and slaves.[23]

Ralph Ellison writes of his experience as a boy: "Those trips to the cotton patch seemed to me an enviable experience because the kids came back with such wonderful stories. And it wasn't the hard work which they stressed, but the communion, the playing, the eating, the dancing and the singing."[24] A leading theme in the blues tradition of black "soul" music is "Do your best." The emphasis in both performance and lyrics rests not on

---

[20] E. A. Davis, ed., *Plantation Life in the Florida Parishes of Louisiana;* also on Barrow see Eaton, *Growth of Southern Civilization,* p. 61; Smedes, *Southern Planter,* p. 31; W. T. Jordan, *Hugh Davis,* pp. 105–107; Wall, "Founding of Pettigrew Plantations," *NCHR,* XXVII (Oct., 1950), 409.

[21] Frederick Marryat, *A Diary in America* (Paris, 1839), p. 186; Bonner, ed., "Plantation Experiences of a New York Woman," *NCHR,* XXXIII (July, 1956), 395; Phillips, *Life and Labor,* p. 283. In a typical performance for planters as a group, William Ethelbert Ervin of Lowndes County, Miss., paid thirty-five slaves $63.10 for work done during the Christmas holiday of 1846; Ervin Journal, Dec. 31, 1846, and entries for the subsequent years. See also Fisk University, *God Struck Me Dead,* p. 121.

[22] The special conditions of the sugar harvest often required Sunday work and the postponement of the Christmas holiday until sometime in January. In such cases, slaves were generally compensated in time and presents.

[23] *Rice v. Cade, et al.,* 1836, in Catterall, ed., *Judicial Cases,* III, 512.

[24] Ellison, *Shadow and Act,* p. 27.

the degree of success but on the extent and especially the sincerity of effort.[25] Underlying black resistance to prevailing white values, then, has been a set of particular ideas concerning individual and community responsibility. It is often asserted that blacks spend rather than save as someone else thinks they should. But the considerable evidence for this assertion must be qualified by the no less considerable evidence of the heartbreaking scraping together of nickels and dimes to pay for such things as the education of children, which will generally draw Anglo-Saxon applause, and the provision of elaborate funerals, which generally will not but which for many peoples besides blacks constitutes a necessary measure of respect for the living as well as the dead.

The slaves could, when they chose, astonish the whites by their work-time élan and expenditure of energy. The demands of corn shucking, hog killing, logrolling, cotton picking, and especially sugar grinding confronted the slaves with particularly heavy burdens and yet drew from them particularly positive responses.

With the exception of the Christmas holiday—and not always that—former slaves recalled having looked forward to corn shucking most of all.[26] Sam Colquitt of Alabama explained:

Next to our dances, de most fun was corn-shucking. Marsa would have de corn hauled up to de crib, and piled as a house. Den he would invite de hands 'round to come and hope shuck it. Us had two leaders or generals and choose up two sides. Den us see which side would win first and holler and sing. . . . Marsa would pass de jug around too. Den dey sho' could work and dat pile'd just vanish.[27]

Some ex-slaves remembered corn shuckings as their only good time, but many more said simply that they were the best. Occasionally a sour note appeared, as when Jenny Proctor of Alabama said, "We had some co'n shuckin's sometimes but de white folks gits de fun and de nigger gits de work."[28] For the vast majority, however, they were "de big times."

The descriptions that have been preserved provide essential clues for an understanding of plantation life and its work rhythms. According to Robert Shepherd of Kentucky:

[25] For a good discussion see Keil, Urban Blues, pp. 170–171.
[26] The account of corn shucking draws most heavily on the following: Bremer, Homes of the New World, I, 370–371—note esp. her remarks on the songs as "histories" and her account of courtship patterns; Yetman, ed., Life Under the "Peculiar Institution," pp. 62, 70, 267, 314; Fisk University, Unwritten History of Slavery, pp. 46, 50, 69, 148, 150. Relevant material in Rawick, ed., American Slave, may be found as follows: S.C. Narr., II (1), 23; III (1), 283–284; III (4), 89–90; Texas Narr., IV (1), 112, 118, 206, 260, 261; IV (2), 175; V (3), 119, 214, 266; V (4), 53, 104–105, 197–198; Ala. Narr., VI (1), 49, 89, 193, 216, 280, 360, 412; Okla. Narr., VII (1), 136, 230; Ark. Narr., IX (3), 68, 291; Ga. Narr., XII (1), 71, 99; XIII (4), 19. See also George Teamoh Journal, Pts. 1–2, pp. 14–15, in the Woodson Papers.
[27] Rawick, ed., Ala. Narr., VI (1), 89.
[28] Rawick, ed., Texas Narr., V (3), 214.

Dem corn shuckin's was sure 'nough big times. When us got all de corn gathered up and put in great long piles, den de gettin' ready started. Why, dem womans cooked for days, and de mens would get de shoats ready to barbecue. Master would send us out to get de slaves from de farms round about dere. De place was all lit up with light-wood knot torches and bonfires, and dere was 'citement a-plenty when all niggers get to singin' and shoutin' as dey made de shucks fly.[29]

An ex-slave from Georgia recalled:

In corn shucking time no padderollers would ever bother you. We would have a big time at corn shuckings. They would call up the crowd and line the men up and give them a drink. I was a corn general—would stand out high above every-body, giving out corn songs and throwing down corn to them. There would be two sides of them, one side trying to outshuck the other. Such times we have.[30]

White contemporaries provided comments that complement those of former slaves. Fredrika Bremer, one of the more astute and thoughtful travelers to the South, wrote that corn shuckings "are to the negroes what the harvest-home is to our [Swedish] peasants."[31]

Certainly, the slaves had some material incentives. The best shuckers would get a dollar or a suit of clothes, as might those who found a red ear. But these incentives do not look impressive and do not loom large in the testimony. Those plantations on which the prize for finding a red ear consisted of a dollar do not seem to have done any better than those on which the prize consisted of an extra swig of whiskey or a chance to kiss the prettiest girl. The shucking was generally night work—overtime, as it were—and one might have expected the slaves to resent it and to consider the modest material incentives, which came to a special dinner and dance and a lot of whiskey, to be inadequate.

The most important feature of these occasions and the most important incentive to these long hours of extra work was the community life they called forth. They were gala affairs. The jug passed freely, although drunkenness was discouraged; the work went on amidst singing and dancing; friends and acquaintances congregated from several plantations and farms; the house slaves joined the field slaves in common labor; and the work was followed by an all-night dinner and ball at which inhibitions, especially those of class and race, were lowered as far as anyone dared.

Slavery, a particularly savage system of oppression and exploitation, made its slaves victims. But the human beings it made victims did not consent to be just that; they struggled to make life bearable and to find as much joy in it as they could. Up to a point even the harshest of masters had to help

[29] Yetman, ed., *Life Under the "Peculiar Institution,"* p. 267.
[30] Fisk University, *Unwritten History of Slavery,* p. 50.
[31] Bremer, *Homes of the New World,* I, 370. These huskings were rooted in English tradition and became major events among the white servants and black slaves in New England. See William Dawson Johnston, *Slavery in Rhode Island, 1775–1776* (Providence, R.I., 1894), p. 138.

them do so. The logic of slavery pushed the masters to try to break their slaves' spirit and to reconstruct it as an unthinking and unfeeling extension of their own will, but the slaves' own resistance to dehumanization compelled the masters to compromise in order to get an adequate level of work out of them.

The combination of festive spirit and joint effort appears to have engaged the attention of the slaves more than anything else. Gus Brown, an ex-slave from Alabama, said simply, "On those occasions we all got together and had a regular good time." The heightened sense of fellowship with their masters also drew much comment. Even big slaveholders would join in the work, as well as in the festivities and the drinking, albeit not without the customary patriarchal qualifications. They would demand that the slaves sing, and the slaves would respond boisterously. Visitors expressed wonder at the spontaneity and improvisation the slaves displayed. The songs, often made up on the spot, bristled with sharp wit, both malicious and gentle. The slaves sang of their courtships and their lovers' quarrels; sometimes the songs got bawdy, and the children had to be hustled off to bed. They sang of their setbacks in love:

> When I'se here you calls me honey.
> When I'se gone you honies everybody.

They sang of their defeats in competition:

> You jumped and I jumped;
> Swear by God you outjumped me,
> Huh, huh, round de corn, Sally.

and of their victories:

> Pull de husk, break de ear
> Whoa, I'se got de red ear here.

But the songs also turned to satire. White participation in these festivals was always condescending and self-serving, and the slaves' acceptance of it displayed something other than childlike gratitude for small favors. They turned their wit and incredible talent for improvisation into social criticism. Occasionally they risked a direct, if muted, thrust in their "corn songs," as they came to be called.

> Massa in the great house, counting out his money,
> Oh, shuck that corn and throw it in the barn.
> Mistis in the parlor, eating bread and honey,
> Oh, shuck that corn and throw it in the barn.

More often, they used a simpler and safer technique. Ole Massa was always God's gift to humanity, the salt of the earth, de bestest massa in de whole wide worl'. But somehow, one or more of his neighbors was mighty bad buckra.

I

Massa's niggers am slick and fat,
   Oh! Oh! Oh!
Shine jes like a new beaver hat,
   Oh! Oh! Oh!

Refrain: Turn out here and shuck dis corn.
   Oh! Oh! Oh!
Biggest pile o' corn since I was born,
   Oh! Oh! Oh!

II

Jones' niggers am lean an po'
   Oh! Oh! Oh!
Don't know whether they git 'nough ter eat or no,
   Oh! Oh! Oh![32]

Blacks—any blacks—were not supposed to sass whites—any whites; slaves—any slaves—were not supposed to sit in judgment on masters—any masters. By the device of a little flattery and by taking advantage of the looseness of the occasion, they asserted their personalities and made their judgments.

A curious sexual division of labor marked the corn shuckings. Only occasionally did women participate in the shucking. The reason for the exclusion is by no means clear. Field women matched the men in hard work, not only in picking cotton but in rolling logs, chopping wood, and plowing. Yet at corn shuckings they divided their time between preparing an elaborate spread for the dinner and taking part in quilting bees and the like. As a result, the corn shuckings took on a peculiarly male tone, replete with raucous songs and jokes not normally told in front of women, as well as with those manifestations of boyish prancing associated with what is called—as if by some delightful Freudian slip—a "man's man."

The vigor with which the men worked and the insistence on a rigid sexual separation raise the central question of the slaves' attitude toward work in its relationship to their sense of family and community. The sense of community established by bringing together house and field slaves and especially slaves from several plantations undoubtedly underlay much of the slaves' positive response, and recalled the festivities, ceremonials, and rituals of traditional societies in a way no office Christmas party in an industrial firm

---

[32] For "Massa in the Great House" see Southern, *Music of Black Americans*, p. 181; for "Massa's Niggers Am Slick and Fat" see Doyle, *Etiquette of Race Relations*, pp. 22–23.

has ever done. And corn shucking, like hog killing, had a special meaning, for at these times the slaves were literally working for themselves. The corn and pork fed them and their families; completion of these tasks carried a special satisfaction.

From this point of view the sexual division of labor, whatever its origins, takes on new meaning. In a limited way it strengthened that role of direct provider to which the men laid claim by hunting and fishing to supplement the family diet. Even the less attractive features of the evening in effect reinforced this male self-image. Nor did the women show signs of resentment. On the contrary, they seem to have grasped the opportunity to underscore a division of labor and authority in the family and to support the pretensions of their men. Slavery represented a terrible onslaught on the personalities and spirit of the slaves, and whatever unfairness manifested itself in this sexual bias, the efforts of male and female slaves to create and support their separate roles provided a weapon for joint resistance to dehumanization.

Hog-killing time rivaled corn shucking as a grand occasion. Consider two accounts from Virginia—one from J. S. Wise's well-known memoir, *The End of an Era*, and the other from Joseph Holmes's account of his life as a slave.[33] First, Wise:

Then there was hog-killing time, when long before day, the whole plantation force was up with knives for killing, and seething cauldrons for scalding, and great doors for scraping, and long racks for cooling the slaughtered swine. Out to the farmyard rallied all the farm hands. Into the pens dashed the boldest and most active. Harrowing was the squealing of the victims; quick was the stroke that slew them, and quicker the sousing of the dead hog into the scalding water; busy the scraping of his hair away; strong the arms that bore him to the beams, and hung him there head downward to cool; clumsy the old woman who brought tubs to place under him; deft the strong hands that disemboweled him.

And now, Joseph Holmes:

Dat was de time of times. For weeks de mens would haul wood an' big rocks, an' pile 'em together as high as dis house, an' den have several piles, lak dat 'roun' a big hole in de groun' what has been filled wid water. Den jus' a little atter midnight, de boss would blow de ole hawn, an' all de mens would git up an' git in dem big pens. Den dey would sot dat pile of wood on fire an' den start knockin' dem hogs in de haid. Us neber shot a hog lak us does now; us always used an axe to kill 'em wid. Atter knockin' de hog in de haid, dey would tie a rope on his leg an' atter de water got to de right heat, fum dose red-hot rocks de hog would be throwed in an' drug aroun' a while, den taken out an' cleaned. Atter he was cleaned he was cut up into sections an' hung up in de smoke house. Lawsie, lady, dey don't cure meat dese days; dey jus' uses some kind of liquid to bresh over it. We useta have sho' nuff meat.

33 Wise, *End of an Era*, pp. 44–45; Rawick, ed., *Ala. Narr.*, VI (1), 193; also VI (1), 183; Smedes, *Southern Planter*, pp. 47, 126. See also C. S. Davis, *Cotton Kingdom in Alabama*, p. 67.

The slaves enjoyed a special and delightful inducement here, for they could eat as they worked and could display pride in their individual skills within the totality of a community effort. As in corn shucking, they did this work for themselves and poured enthusiasm into it.

Logrollings called forth some of the same festive spirit but came less frequently. They had some direct reference to the slaves' own life when they contributed to building the quarters. Women worked along with the men, and teams competed against each other. In other respects the event had the same style as the corn shuckings. As Frank Gill, an ex-slave from Alabama, recalled:

Talkin' 'bout log rollin', dem was great times, 'ca'se if some ob dem neighborin'' plantations wanted to get up a house, dey would invite all de slaves, men and women, to come wid dere masters. De women would help wit de cookin' an' you may be shore dey had something to cook. Dey would kill a cow, or three or four hogs, and den hab peas, cabbage, an' everything lack grows on de farm.[34]

The evidence from the sugar plantations is especially instructive. Louisiana's sugar planters reputedly drove their slaves harder than any others in the slave states. Such reputations are by no means to be accepted at face value, but they certainly drove them hard during the grinding season. Yet, slaves took to the woods as limited and local runaways more often during the spring and summer months than during the autumn grinding season, when the work reached a peak of intensity and when the time for rest and sleep contracted sharply.[35] Once again, the small material incentives cannot account for the slaves' behavior.[36]

The slaves brought to their labor a gaiety and élan that perplexed observers, who saw them work at night with hardly a moment to catch their breath. Many, perhaps most, found themselves with special tasks to perform and special demands upon them; by all accounts they strained to rise to the occasion. The planters, knowing that the season lasted too long to sustain a fever pitch of effort, tried to break it up with parties and barbecues and at the very least promised and delivered a gala dinner and ball at the end. Ellen Betts, an ex-slave from Texas, recalled: "Massa sho' good to dem gals and bucks what cuttin' de cane. Whey dey git done makin' sugar, he give a

---

[34] Rawick, ed., *Ala. Narr.*, VI (1), pp. 150–151. See also *Texas Narr.*, IV (1), 158; Fisk University, *Unwritten History of Slavery*, p. 4.

[35] J. G. Taylor, *Negro Slavery in Louisiana*, p. 77. The Rice Coast of Georgia and South Carolina had a similar experience; see Heyward, *Seed from Madagascar*, p. 25. For Jamaica, see H. O. Patterson, *Sociology of Slavery*, p. 68.

[36] See esp. Moody, *Slavery on Louisiana Sugar Plantations*, pp. 77–78; J. G. Taylor, *Negro Slavery in Louisiana*, pp. 77–78; Sitterson, *Sugar Country*, pp. 132–136; Ingraham, *South-West*, I, 240–241. For particularly useful sets of plantation papers see those of R. R. Barrow, *Residence Journal*, esp. Dec. 13, 1857; and Bond Diary, Dec., 1861, and Jan., 1862. For a striking English parallel see E. P. Thompson, "Time, Work Discipline and Industrial Capitalism," *Past and Present*, No. 38 (Dec., 1967), pp. 56–97. For similar conditions in the hemp region see Hopkins, *Hemp Industry in Kentucky*, pp. 61–63.

drink called 'Peach 'n' Honey' to de women folk and whiskey and brandy to de men." Another ex-slave, William Stone of Alabama, said that the slaves were "happy" to work during the sugar harvest " 'cause we knowed it mean us have plenty 'lasses in winter."[37]

Still, the demands of the sugar crop meant the sacrifice of some Sundays and even the Christmas holiday. The slaves showed no resentment at the postponement of the holiday. It would come in due time, usually in mid-January, and the greater their sacrifices, the longer and fuller the holiday would likely be. For the slaves on the sugar plantations Christmas did not mean December 25; it meant the great holiday that honored the Lord's birth, brought joy to His children, and properly fell at the end of the productive season.

Cotton picking was another matter. One ex-slave recalled cotton-picking parties along with corn-shucking parties but added, "Dere wasn't so much foolishness at cotton pickin' time." The slaves missed, in particular, the fellowship of slaves from other plantations. An exchange of labor forces on a crash basis sometimes occurred, and ex-slaves remembered precisely those times warmly. The planters had to have their cotton picked at about the same time and could not easily exchange labor forces. But the neighborly tradition was too strong to be denied entirely, and when a planter fell dangerously behind, others would come to his aid. Unable to take time away from their own work unless well ahead of schedule, friendly planters had to send their slaves after hours to pick by moonlight. The slaves, instead of becoming indignant over the imposition, responded with enthusiasm and extra effort. Many of them later recalled this grueling all-night work as "big times," for they were helping their own friends and combining the work with festivity. Bonuses, parties, and relaxed discipline rewarded their cooperation. Scattered evidence suggests less whipping and harsh driving during the cotton-picking season on some plantations but the opposite on others.[38]

Some planters congratulated themselves on their success in getting a good response during the critical cotton harvest. Virginia Clay visited Governor Hammond's noteworthy plantation in South Carolina and enthusiastically reported on the magnificent singing and general spirit of the slaves, and Kate Stone was sure that "the Negroes really seemed to like the cotton picking best of all." Henry William Ravenel, in his private journal, made an interesting observation that provides a better clue to the slaves' attitude. Writing in 1865, immediately after their emancipation, he declared that the slaves had always disliked planting and cultivating cotton and would now

[37] Rawick, ed., *Texas Narr.*, IV (1), 79; V (4), 65.
[38] Rawick, ed., *Ala. Narr.*, VI (1), 151. For comments by South Carolina ex-slaves that suggest a holiday view of cotton picking see *S.C. Narr.*, III (3), 62; III (3), 115; III (4), 89–90; *Ga. Narr.*, XII (2), 6, 228, 348; XIII (3), 63, 100; Yetman, ed., *Life Under the "Peculiar Institution,"* pp. 62–63. For corroboration see the reviews of plantation records in J. G. Taylor, *Negro Slavery in Louisiana*, p. 66; C. S. Davis, *Cotton Kingdom in Alabama*, p. 64. But also see the opposite accounts in Sydnor, *Slavery in Mississippi*, pp. 103–104; J. B. Sellers, *Slavery in Alabama*, p. 267.

prefer almost any alternative labor.[39] The picking season must have struck the slaves as a mixed affair. It meant hard and distasteful work and sometimes punishment for failure to meet quotas, but also the end of a tough season, prizes for good performances, and the prelude to relaxation and a big celebration. Yet, the special spirit of the season was not strong enough to carry the slaves through the rigors of labor; the whip remained the indispensable spur.

Some anthropologists and cultural historians, noting the tradition of collective work among West Africans, have suggested its continuing influence among Afro-Americans. The Yoruba, for example, ingeniously combine community spirit and individual initiative by organizing hoeing in a line, so that everyone works alongside someone else and yet has his own task. But evidence of direct influence remains elusive, and, as William R. Bascom points out, collective patterns of work abounded in medieval Europe too.[40] Whatever the origins of the slaves' strong preference for collective work, it drew the attention of their masters, who knew that they would have to come to terms with it. Edmund Ruffin, the South's great soil chemist and authority on plantation agriculture, complained that the pinewoods of North Carolina were set afire every spring by inconsiderate poor whites who cared nothing for the damage they did in order to provide grazing land for their few cows. He added that the slaves also set many fires because they intensely disliked collecting turpentine from the trees. This work was light and easy in Ruffin's estimation, but the slaves resisted it anyway because it had to be performed in isolation. "A negro," Ruffin explained from long experience, "cannot abide being alone and will prefer work of much exposure and severe toil, in company, to any lighter work, without any company."[41]

This preference for work in company manifested itself in a readiness to help each other in field labor. Richard Mack, among others, recalled that he could finish a given task quickly and would then help others so that they would avoid punishment. This attitude, by no means rare, led another ex-slave, Sylvia Durant of South Carolina, to protest in the 1930s, "Peoples used to help one another out more en didn't somebody be tryin' to pull you down all de time."[42]

Mrs. Durant's lament, common in the testimony of ex-slaves, hints at an anomaly reminiscent of the attitude of the Russian peasants who left the mir. The powerful community spirit and preference for collective patterns of

[39] Virginia Clay-Clopton, *A Belle of the Fifties* (New York, 1905), p. 220; Kate Stone, *Brokenburn*, p. 4; *Private Journal of H. W. Ravenel*, p. 252; J. G. Taylor, *Negro Slavery in Louisiana*, p. 66; Rawick, ed., *Texas Narr.*, IV (2), 16; *Ala. Narr.*, VI (1), 151, 365.

[40] William R. Bascom, "Acculturation Among the Gullah Negroes," *American Anthropologist*, LXIII (1941), 43–50. For a good general discussion see Rawick, *Sundown to Sunup*, pp. 17, 27–28.

[41] Scarborough, ed., *Diary of Edmund Ruffin*, April 5, 1857 (I, 52); also Botume, *First Days Amongst the Contrabands*, p. 80; Higginson, *Army Life*, p. 250. See also the remarks of Mamadou Dia on African traditions of collective work: *Réflexions sur l'économie de l'Afrique noire* (Paris, 1961), p. 27.

[42] Rawick, ed., *S.C. Narr.*, III (3), 152–153; II (1), 345; *Ark. Narr.*, X (5), 143; Martineau, *Society in America*, II, 157.

working and living had their antithesis in an equally powerful individualism, manifested most attractively during and after Reconstruction in an attempt to transform themselves into peasant proprietors. This particular kind of individualism has also had less attractive manifestations, from the creation of the ghetto hustler and the devil-take-the-hindmost predator to the creation of a set of attitudes that many blacks hold responsible for a chronic lack of political unity. Certainly, the old collective spirit remains powerful, as the very notion of a black "brotherhood" demonstrates, but it does rest on a contradictory historical base. The work ethic of the slaves provided a firm defense against the excesses of an oppressive labor system, but like the religious tradition on which it rested, it did not easily lend itself to counterattack. Once the worst features of the old regime fell away, the ethic itself began to dissolve into its component parts. Even today we witness the depressing effects of this dissolution in a futile and pathetic caricature of bourgeois individualism, manifested both in the frustrated aspirations so angrily depicted in E. Franklin Frazier's *Black Bourgeoisie* and in violent, antisocial nihilism. But we also witness the continued power of a collective sensibility regarded by some as "race pride" and by others as a developing black national consciousness.

The slaves expressed their attitude in song. The masters encouraged quick-time singing among their field slaves, but the slaves proved themselves masters of slowing down the songs and the work. They willingly sang at work, as well as going to work, coming from work, and at almost any time. While assembling for field work they might sing individually.

> Saturday night and Sunday too
> Young gals on my mind.
> Monday morning 'way 'fore day,
> Old master's got me gwine.
> Peggy, does you love me now?

But whenever possible they sang collectively, in ways derived from Africa but rooted in their own experience. When they had to work alone or when they felt alone even in a group, they "hollered." Imamu Amiri Baraka's extraordinary analysis of the historical development of black music, however controversial, speculative, and tentative it may be judged, remains the indispensable introduction to the subject. He remarks on the roots of the blues: "The shouts and hollers were strident laments, more than anything. They were also chronicles but of such a mean kind of existence that they could not assume the universality any lasting musical form must have."[43] Imamu Baraka traces the spread of hollers during and after Reconstruction when work patterns fragmented; but even during slavery a large portion of the slaves worked in isolation on small farms. Their hollers provided a counterpart to

[43] LeRoi Jones, *Blues People*, pp. 17–18, 41, 61, 67.

plantation work songs, but ranged beyond a direct concern with labor to a concern with the most personal expressions of life's travail. As such, they created a piercing history of the impact of hardship and sorrow on solitary black men. Their power notwithstanding, they represented a burning negative statement of the blacks' desire for community in labor as well as in life generally. As positive expression, both in themselves and in the legacy they left for blues singers to come, they contributed to the collective in a strikingly dialectical way, for they provided a form for a highly individualistic self-expression among a people whose very collectivity desperately required methods of individual self-assertion in order to combat the debilitating thrust of slavery's paternalistic aggression.

SUGGESTIONS FOR FURTHER READING

The first systematic study of slavery by a modern American scholar is Ulrich B. Phillips, *American Negro Slavery* (New York, 1918; paperback edition, Baton Rouge, 1966). This book exerted an enormous influence on later scholarship; most modern historians must take Phillips's work into consideration if only to attempt to refute it. Indeed, Kenneth Stampp's work, a portion of which is reprinted above, is in many ways an attempted refutation of Phillips. Its influence has also been profound. Herbert Aptheker's pioneering work *American Negro Slave Revolts* (New York, 1943, 1963) finds discontent and rebellion to be characteristic among slaves. Stanley M. Elkins, *Slavery* (Chicago, 1959) depicts slavery as a total, closed, repressive system that had devastating effects on the black personality and effectively destroyed any indigenous black culture.

Recent scholarship has questioned Elkins's assessment. John W. Blassingame, *The Slave Community* (New York, 1972); George P. Rawick, *From Sundown to Sunup* (Westport, Conn., 1972); Eugene D. Genovese, *Roll, Jordan, Roll* (New York, 1974), a portion of which is reprinted above; Leslie Howard Owens, *This Species of Property: Slave Life and Culture in the Old South* (New York, 1976); and Nathan Irvin Huggins, *Black Odyssey: The Afro-American Ordeal in Slavery* (New York, 1977)—all find evidence of a viable black culture developing under slave conditions, although all are not in agreement as to the nature of that culture. Herbert G. Gutman, *The Black Family in Slavery and Freedom, 1750–1925* (New York, 1976), argues that blacks under slavery developed a unique family and kinship structure which, like much else in their culture, was not merely a reflection of the dominant white culture. Gutman's study is an attempt at a direct historical refutation of Daniel P. Moynihan's *The Negro Family in America: The Case for National Action* (printed in Lee Rainwater and William L. Yancey, *The Moynihan Report and the Politics of Controversy* [Cambridge, Mass., 1967]) and E. Franklin Frazier, *The Negro Family in the United States* (Chicago, 1939). Robert W. Fogel and Stanley L. Engerman, *Time on the Cross* (Boston, 1974), a portion of which is reprinted above, is a general revisionist study of the whole question of the economics of black slavery. The Fogel and Engerman book stirred an enormous controversy, a taste of which may be seen in Paul A. David et al., *Reckoning with Slavery* (New York, 1976).

* Available in paperback edition.

Genovese's views on the nature of Southern society may be followed in his *The Political Economy of Slavery* (New York, 1965) and *The World the Slaveholders Made* (New York, 1969). For important investigations of the effects of slavery on particular aspects of Southern society see Richard C. Wade, *Slavery in the Cities* (New York, 1964), and Robert S. Starobin, *Industrial Slavery in the Old South* (New York, 1970). Not all Southern blacks were slaves; for a fine study of those who were not, see Ira Berlin, *Slaves Without Masters: The Free Negro in the Antebellum South* (New York, 1974). Outstanding studies of the responses of western Europeans and Americans to black slavery are two volumes by David Brion Davis: *The Problem of Slavery in Western Culture* (Ithaca, N.Y., 1966) and *The Problem of Slavery in the Age of Revolution* (Ithaca, N.Y., 1975).

8

The
Abolitionists

The age of Jackson was also an age of reform. If it was a time of optimism, intellectual ferment, and growing nationalism, it was also a time when a large number of men and women discovered that America had many problems. A religious revival (The Second Great Awakening), led by ministers like Charles Grandison Finney, spread across the land, leaving in its wake an army of converts ready to drive sin from the face of the earth. But not all reformers were motivated by religious zeal; some were influenced by a rational belief that men could improve their world. Like most Americans these reformers had faith in progress, and they were confident that they could speed the way toward a perfect social order.

The reform impulse took many forms. Some men founded utopian communities, such as Brook Farm near Boston, in order to experiment with new ways of organizing society. Perhaps these utopians were trying to escape the complicated problems of a country just beginning to be transformed by the revolutions in industry and transportation, but they sincerely believed that they were forerunners of a new order and that the world would follow their lead. Although there were a few eccentrics like Sylvester Graham, who was confident that he could change the world by getting everyone to eat "Graham Crackers," most were sincere men and women who set out to promote peace, to improve education, to secure the more humane treatment of prisoners, to win more opportunities and more rights for women, and to prohibit the use of alcoholic beverages. But the greatest reform of all was the crusade against slavery.

There had been opposition to slavery before the 1830s. The Quakers had been one of the few groups that had consistently opposed slavery in the colonial period; but the Revolution, with its emphasis on the rights of "life, liberty and the pursuit of happiness" for all men, initiated a more general movement that resulted by 1804 in the end of slavery, or provision for its abolition, in all Northern states. Even in the South there were many who favored gradual emancipation or who supported the American Colonization Society (organized 1817), which projected an eventual solution to the problem by shipping freed slaves to Africa.

The antislavery movement changed dramatically about 1830 with the emergence of a small group of abolitionists led by William Lloyd Garrison, Theodore Weld, and other militant radicals who denounced slavery as a crime and demanded immediate emancipation. They were willing to disrupt the Union and to incite riot and even war to get rid of human bondage. The abolitionists, always in the minority, often did not agree among themselves, but they uniformly spoke the language of conflict. "I do not wish to think or speak or write with moderation," Garrison announced. "I will not retreat a single inch, and I will be heard."

The abolitionists were promptly labeled dangerous radicals and fanatics who overemphasized the evils of slavery, ignored the progress being made towards reform, and stirred up passions that endangered the Union. They responded that the system of human bondage was shameful and criminal, that such organizations as the American Colonization Society were really attempts to avoid, rather than face, the problem, and that a union with slavery was a union with the devil.

Controversial in their own time, the abolitionists have continued to arouse disagreement among historians who have tried to determine who the abolitionists were, what motivated them to risk life and limb, and what effects they had. The selections that follow show some of the disagreements historians have in dealing with a group of militant agitators who believed in conflict —or at least were willing to accept it—in order to eradicate evil.

In the first selection Ronald G. Walters argues that the abolitionists were moralistic reformers whose basic religious and economic values were consonant with those of the majority of Northern whites. Most Northerners, however, turned against the abolitionists through latent racism and their fear that abolitionism would destroy the Union. Eventually, in ways the abolitionists could not foresee, the slavery issue became linked with expansion, and "free soil" became a popular political issue. Abolitionist goals and rhetoric became acceptable, even if the abolitionists did not.

David Donald analyzes the leaders of the abolitionist movement. He suggests that the reason they became militant reformers was not so much that slavery was evil, but rather that the abolitionists themselves were "an elite without function," suffering because the industrial revolution had displaced them from their positions of leadership in society. "Basically," Donald concludes, "abolitionism should be considered the anguished protest of an aggrieved class against a world they never made." Donald implies that although there was conflict between the abolitionists and the South, the conflict was essentially the product of the reformers' failure to adjust to changes in their society and had little to do with the evils of slavery.

Martin Duberman, one of several historians who are reexamining the antislavery movement from the perspective of the present, views the abolitionists in a broader context and is concerned with why the North did not accept the abolitionists' militant solution. He suggests that any radical attack on social problems tends to compromise the national optimism, and, therefore, the majority of Americans find it necessary to label "extreme" any movement that calls for large-scale readjustments in society. Duberman also strikes out at those historians who suggest that any individual who protests strongly against social injustice is disturbed or fanatical. Those who fail to protest strongly against an institution as inhuman as slavery are the real "neurotics," he suggests.

What, then, was the abolitionist movement? Was it a useless crusade led by fanatics or a displaced elite? Or was it a radical and rational attempt to end a great evil—human slavery? The abolitionists believed in conflict, but why did not most Northerners accept their interpretation of the situation? Was the conflict and the antagonism fostered and encouraged by the abolitionists unnecessary and tragic?

Ronald G. Walters

Antislavery Reformers

* * *

On January 1, 1831, William Lloyd Garrison, a young native of Newburyport, Massachusetts, published the first issue of the Liberator. During its thirty-five-year run, the Boston newspaper would be abrasive, vituperative, and consistent in its loathing of slavery. It would never have a large circulation nor would Garrison ever represent the whole of abolitionism—the movement was diverse and decentralized. Still, more than any other event, the founding of the Liberator marked the beginning of a variety of antislavery that was new in tone, social composition, and doctrine.

Before 1831 opposition to slavery had taken several forms. From the outset blacks made their feelings clear by fleeing bondage, by day-to-day resistance, and by staging occasional insurrections. In the eighteenth century—and especially by the time of the Revolution—increasing numbers of whites were preaching abolition, inspired by religion, Enlightenment humanitarianism, and their own egalitarian rhetoric. Most Northern states ended slavery before 1800. Abolition sentiment, however, was on the wane by then and the institution, if anything, was becoming more strongly entrenched in the lower South, as the newly invented cotton gin and population growth pushed cotton production farther west.

Organized antislavery, although subdued, persisted in the early nineteenth century and differed strikingly from the caustic brand Garrison and his colleagues would promote after 1830. It was concentrated in the upper South,

From Ronald G. Walters, American Reformers, 1815–1860, pp. 77–100. Reprinted with the permission of Hill and Wang (now a division of Farrar, Straus & Giroux, Inc.) from American Reformers by Ronald G. Walters. Copyright © 1978 by Ronald G. Walters.

was conciliatory to the master, and had minimal sympathy for blacks. Above all, there was no particular urgency to it. Prior to 1831 most critics of slavery assumed that manumission would be gradual and ought not to cause social or economic dislocation. No organization better typified such an approach than the American Colonization Society, which was founded in 1816. Its mission was to send ex-bondsmen out of the country, preferably to its African outpost, Liberia. The society's supporters included slaveholders, prominent politicians, and distinguished men of the sort who would later shun abolitionism. Their motives were varied and conflicted. Some genuinely hated slavery, but believed the races could never coexist without it. Their solution was to get rid of black people. Other colonizationists were proslavery and were merely determined to dispose of the small free black population of the South and to eliminate bondsmen who might become a burden on their owners or society. Without much consistency, idealism, or practicality to recommend it, the Colonization Society nevertheless profited from this ability to satisfy contradictory viewpoints. It sent few black people to Africa but it attracted generally favorable attention, discharged white anxieties about slavery and race, and otherwise did well in the 1820s.

Most post-1830 abolitionists regarded colonization as their great enemy. Their hostility was comprised of a combination of disillusion—many of them had once believed in it—and tactical necessity. From personal experience they knew how powerful its appeal was and how difficult it would be to get whites to accept a truer, more demanding antislavery position. Yet even allowing for some understandable exaggeration, later abolitionists were right to contrast their crusade with colonization and everything else that had come before. The platform Garrison proclaimed on New Year's Day, 1831, was different. It would find no favor in the South. It made few concessions to the sensibilities of slaveholders (they were "oppressors," "man-stealers," "despots," and "tyrants"). Although tainted with streaks of racism, post-1830 abolitionists like Garrison dismissed any thoughts of exiling blacks, accepted the idea of civil equality for them, and greeted the slave as "A Man and a Brother" or "A Woman and a Sister," phrases borrowed from British abolitionism. Most important, antislavery after 1831 repudiated what Garrison called the "pernicious doctrine of *gradual* abolition." "Immediate emancipation" became the new battle cry.

The phrase was ambiguous. Abolitionists—even Garrison—seldom insisted that it meant slavery should cease right away. More often, they intended it as a demand for people to decide instantly to renounce slaveholding. Abolitionists admitted that, for the sake of master and slave alike, emancipation might take time to complete. Immediatism, however, tolerated no delay in beginning the process, as earlier, gradualistic approaches had. It was a call to break off an evil practice without hesitation or equivocation, just as sinners, when saved, utterly repudiated sin. The revivalism of the 1820s encouraged abolitionists and most other antebellum crusaders to see reform as something akin to an act of repentance. That approach to problems slighted social, political, and economic factors, and it could be narrow and self-righteous; but it had a passion and moral firmness badly needed when men and women agitated unpopular issues in a society where the instinct to compromise was second nature. Instead of describing a well-worked-out plan, "immediate emancipation" served to jolt people out of their complacency and to infuse abolitionism with a fervor it seldom had before 1831.

Immediatism quickly made converts in New England, New York City and upstate New York, Pennsylvania, and Ohio. The first organization based upon the doctrine was the New-England Anti-Slavery Society (1832). Nearly two years later, in December 1833, delegates from several states gathered in Philadelphia and created the American Anti-Slavery Society. For the next half decade it would play a crucial role in spreading abolitionism throughout the North.

Garrison had been instrumental in founding the American Anti-Slavery Society, but control of it passed to able and dedicated men at its New York headquarters. Chief among them was Lewis Tappan, blessed with ample financial resources and a fine managerial experience gained as a leader of the "benevolent empire" of Protestant charities. He and several energetic co-workers marshaled support for the cause and guided a remarkable outpouring of antislavery activity up to 1837 (when internal disputes and hard times slowed the crusade down temporarily). Affluent members like Tappan himself subsidized the printing and distribution of a wide range of American Anti-Slavery Society publications (at least three quarters of a million pieces of propaganda by 1838). In 1835 the organization flooded the mails with this literature, in an attempt to reach, and presumably persuade, clergy, editors, and other influential people in every state, particularly in the South. Two years later the society began to encourage and coordinate the circulation of antislavery petitions directed at Congress. Abolitionists—especially female ones—were so diligent in collecting signatures that they gathered over 400,000 by 1838.

Among the national organization's most significant enterprises during Tappan's stewardship was the recruitment of agents. These were zealous young men, charged with carrying abolitionism across the American countryside. Like Theodore Dwight Weld, their greatest orator, many were would-be, or former, ministers; several had been brought into the abolitionist fold during highly emotional debates over slavery at Lane Theological Seminary in Ohio in 1834. Whatever their background, the agents sparked controversy and inspired the rapid formation of town, county, and state antislavery groups. By 1838 the American Anti-Slavery Society claimed a membership of a quarter of a million and over 1,300 auxiliaries. Once begun, these local organizations worked in cooperation with the parent society, published newspapers of their own, and waged campaigns of special importance to their areas (including challenges to segregation and racist legislation in the North). Before the 1830s were over, immediatism had passed into the hinterland and the agency system had served its purpose.

Neither its success, nor the bureaucratic expertise of Tappan, nor the blistering rhetoric of Garrison can entirely explain what drew men and women to antislavery. It is easier to understand the motives of the many black people who participated in the movement, sometimes in alliance with whites, sometimes independently. Those from free families often lived in fairly comfortable circumstances and risked retaliation from hostile whites for their public stand; but slavery and prejudice were intolerable insults to their pride in themselves and their race. Other blacks had even more immediate reasons for becoming abolitionists. They were among the thousands of escaped slaves who carved out new, precarious lives for themselves in the North. The most famous of them were Frederick Douglass and two remarkable women, Sojourner Truth and Harriet Tubman (the latter courageously assisted hundreds of runaways fleeing the South). Their firsthand knowledge, and that of their fellow fugitives, made them bitter opponents of slavery and effective propagandists.

More puzzling is the reason why thousands of whites dedicated themselves to immediate emancipation and to achieving justice for black people. As best we can tell, most came from highly moralistic families, influenced by evangelical Protestantism, Quakerism, or Unitarianism. In their own accounts, they made much of the discrepancies between the way the United States was and the religious and political ideals they held. In itself, that described rather than accounted for their objections to slavery. Thousands of equally moralistic Americans, from the same areas and same sorts of families and maintaining the same values, felt no urge to attack the institution. It is difficult to say, with great confidence, what caused such people to ignore slavery while others, very much like them, condemned it.

For those who did become abolitionists, exposure to antislavery agitation often came at a crucial moment in their lives and helped them find direction, meaning, and companionship. To be an abolitionist was to declare allegiance to the principles of brotherhood and equality of opportunity, to suffer for those ideals, and to band together with like-minded individuals. It was to find a moral community in a society that appeared increasingly immoral.

Antislavery also attracted support because it spoke to a complex set of hopes and fears about the future. These were social in origin and they were expressed forcefully in a kind of moral drama present in much abolitionist propaganda. The chief protagonists in it were the master and the slave. The former was lustful and tyrannical; dominion over others, not greed, was what abolitionists usually regarded as his primary motive. The slave, on the other hand, was the epitome of powerlessness: his or her degradation came not primarily from cruelty, but from the loss of the right to exercise choice. Real freedom, abolitionists maintained, meant the absence, as much as possible, of external restraints on one's behavior. Only then could people be morally responsible for their actions and justly rewarded for their labor.

Most of those assumptions were familiar to Americans and permeated other reforms of the day. There was nothing novel about the abolitionist notion that restraint was the mark of a virtuous person, nor were a fear of power and a desire for individual autonomy unique to antislavery. Those attitudes had been current at least since the eighteenth century. Conditions in the 1820s and 1830s, however, gave them special urgency and made it easier for abolitionists to see them reflected in slavery and other evils. By the antebellum period, Americans had become mobile, energetic, and heterogeneous; they capitalized on the opportunities put before them and paid scant attention to anything except personal advantage. Religious and political leaders, according to abolitionists, did little to make the situation better; they were either ineffective or corrupt, or both. Reformers thought it necessary to find some means to make certain that virtue was not trampled in the rush to get ahead. One half of the abolitionist answer was not to trust anyone with too much power, lest he turn it to his advantage at the expense of everyone else. The other half was for people to be sufficiently self-disciplined to do what was right and resist what was wrong without help from ministers or politicians.

Abolitionists aimed that message at all Americans. In their bleak images of the slaveholder, the slave, and the South, they constructed a model of what happened when any people did not conquer their worst cravings. The slave states, according to antislavery rhetoric, were characterized by laziness, contempt for honest work, insolvency, violence, licentiousness, irreligion, and disrespect for the family. Tyranny and disorder prevailed. Moral desolation turned the South into a cursed land, upon which God showered few material blessings. It lacked such signs of progress as railroads, factories, public schools, and other benefits of Yankee culture. Abolitionists, however, refused to let Northerners take too much comfort in the contrast between their "civilization" and the "barbarism" of the South. The cardinal sin of Southerners—loss of moral control—appeared in the North in the guise of social turmoil and rampant selfishness; surely the free states would be punished for their transgressions just as severely as the slave ones were, unless repentance came in time. In an unconscious way, abolitionists were using the South as a mirror for their concerns about their own region and about people like themselves.

Although the values behind that view were old, abolitionists were applying them in a manner that would have been unthinkable in the eighteenth century, before economic growth sharpened differences between the sections. Only after slavery vanished in the North, and after factories and cities blossomed there, was it possible to believe that the free states represented a higher level of development than the South. Antislavery men and women, naturally, did not entirely endorse the emerging urban and industrial order of their region—its excesses were what they had in mind when arguing that Northerners were in danger of losing self-control and becoming like Southerners. Yet abolitionists accepted many of the assumptions of Northern capitalism, particularly when they insisted that liberty meant the ability to buy and sell property and labor (although not humans) without hindrance. They used that definition to indict slavery and, to their credit, they worried about the consequences of economic individualism even while they promoted it. They always insisted that entrepreneurship had to conform to Christian morality and they declared that the free market had to be opened to blacks on an equal footing with whites. Far from being uncritical apologists for their section, they demanded that the North live up to its best standards and fulfill its greatest promises.

Race prejudice prevented the majority of Northern whites from acknowledging how thoroughly antislavery expressed many of their own cherished economic and religious beliefs. But there must have been some recognition of the fact: much of the strength of abolitionism was in cities, towns, and rural areas swept by commerce and evangelical Protestantism.

The spread of immediatism in the mid-1830s came in the face of suppression. Defenders of slavery saw abolitionism as a dangerous assault on the status quo and believed it had to be stopped by all possible means. Their response, in retrospect, seems out of proportion to the actual threat—at the time supporters of antislavery were a tiny minority in the North. There were, nonetheless, reasons to be outraged and fearful. Many abolitionists did indeed proclaim radical social doctrines, including the heretical notion that blacks ought to be equal, under the law, with whites. If that idea ever became current, the system of race relations in the South (and in the North, for that matter) would come tumbling down. Moreover, the most terrifying North American slave uprising, Nat Turner's Revolt, occurred just seven months after Garrison began to publish the *Liberator*. Many white Southerners were wrongly convinced that the two events were related and that "agitation" from the North was bound to produce further rebellions. Abolitionists denied the charge and countered by saying that the only way to ensure the safety of Southern whites was for them to free blacks, words which did nothing to calm the defenders of slavery.

White Southerners and their Northern allies were especially adept at using force and the political system to thwart abolitionists in the 1830s. The American Anti-Slavery Society's postal campaign of 1835, for instance, prompted a mob in Charleston, South Carolina, to break into the post office to steal, and later burn, antislavery publications. Instead of deploring this clearly illegal act, public officials in the South, and some in the North, applauded. President Andrew Jackson put his seal of approval on the Charleston riot when he suggested, some months later, that the real problem was with antislavery propaganda and that it ought to be banned from the mails. No such bill ever passed but proslavery forces were soon to be successful in stopping Congress from considering antislavery petitions. In 1836 the House of Representatives resolved that all of them should "be laid upon the table, and that no further action whatever shall be had thereon." Some form of this "gag resolution" remained in effect until December 1844.

Repression was not confined to Congress and the South. Connecticut in the mid-1830s passed legislation to outlaw racially mixed schools and to silence antislavery lecturers. Although politicians in other Northern states were similarly inclined to give the South a helping hand, there was very little they actually could do. Mobs proved to be much more of a danger—from 1834 through 1838 abolitionists were the victims of several major riots. One occurred in Boston in 1835 (the crowd led Garrison through the streets by a rope) and on the same day a similar fracas took place in Utica, New York. In yet another violent episode two years later, Elijah Lovejoy, an antislavery editor, lost his life while defending his press in Alton, Illinois. As abolitionists were fond of noting, substantial citizens—"gentlemen of property and standing"—were prominent in creating most of these disturbances. Such people cared less about the South's "peculiar institution" than about the federal Union and the nation's racial and social hierarchy, both of which they thought the abolitionists were out to destroy.

Although fierce, efforts to stop antislavery agitation probably were more effective in making converts than in slowing down the crusade. Among those joining the movement in the 1830s were people who dated their commitment from revulsion at some piece of anti-abolition mayhem. Abolitionists well appreciated that and made much out of incidents like the slaying of Lovejoy and passage of the "gag resolution." (The American Anti-Slavery Society's great petition campaign, in fact, got under way *after* the first gag resolution passed.) Besides providing opportunities for publicity, repression strengthened the resolve of abolitionists and confirmed, in their minds, two cardinal tenets of their propaganda. The first was a belief that American institutions were dominated by the "slave power" (an alleged conspiracy of slaveholders and their Northern lackeys). The second was an insistence that proslavery men had no respect for the civil liberty of whites. Congress, President Jackson, and mobs seemed to prove that every time they denied white abolitionists their right to free speech and to petition the government.

Abolitionists may have been helped by their enemies, but the results were less beneficial when they began battling each other, as they did with increasing frequency after 1836. The issues were seldom as clearly defined as the warring factions thought they were, and both geographical distance and irascible personalities played a significant part in dividing abolitionists. These disagreements, nonetheless, were severe enough to break the movement into fragments in 1840, a feat no amount of proslavery violence had been able to accomplish.

William Lloyd Garrison was the center around which most internal conflict revolved. He was deeply disturbed by mobs, by the mindlessness of partisan politics, and by the reluctance of well-established ministers to endorse antislavery. There was nothing unusual about Garrison's perception of things: most abolitionists shared his disgust with the level of public morality in the country and with the weak-willed performance of politicians and of many clergymen. But where other abolitionists tried to purge the churches and the government of corruption, the Boston editor sought alternatives. Disillusion and his own spiritual restlessness made him uncommonly susceptible to theological and social notions that upset his straitlaced contemporaries.

Within a short span of time in the mid-1830s Garrison did indeed adopt an impressive number of unconventional positions. He questioned whether

Sunday ought to be celebrated as the Sabbath (all days should be holy, he maintained). He denounced both the Protestant denominations and the majority of clergy for "sectarianism"—the sin of putting selfish interests ahead of morality. In addition, Garrison came to believe in a form of Christian anarchism known as nonresistance. It involved repudiating all varieties of force, among which Garrison included laws and governments. As we shall see . . . , nonresistance was subtle beyond simple summary and rooted in evangelical Protestantism. Yet neither its complexity nor its origins made it acceptable to most Americans or to many within the antislavery movement. Along with the rest of Garrison's crusades, it struck the public as silly at best, horrifying at worst.

But there was more. At the very moment that Garrison's multiple heresies were offending many former supporters, he added woman's rights to the controversial causes he favored. Garrison himself had no particular responsibility for raising the issue, which largely grew out of the activities of female abolitionists. By the mid-1830s women had become deeply involved in antislavery agitation, working within separate organizations affiliated with those run by men. That kind of arrangement was common in the antebellum period and suited contemporary notions of propriety. What some antislavery women did, nevertheless, was not so consistent with a Victorian sense of decorum. For instance, they welcomed blacks as equals (thereby stirring white fears of miscegenation), and they left the family circle (supposedly their "sphere") for such unladylike ventures as petitioning the government to end slavery. Women chafed at opposition from the public and at the condescending attitudes of their male comrades. Yet despite the discontent that had been simmering, it took an unforeseen event to elevate the "woman question" into a matter of open contention among abolitionists and further to alienate Garrison from some of his colleagues.

The catalyst was a lecture tour of New England, undertaken in 1837 by two sisters who were valuable and unusual additions to the antislavery crusade, Angelina and Sarah Grimké. Unlike most abolitionists, they were Southerners, members of a prominent South Carolina slaveholding family. Their public appearances drew curiosity seekers. Originally, the Grimkés were to talk only to female audiences—it was generally thought improper for women to address "promiscuous assemblies" (those with both sexes in attendance). Men frustrated the sisters' intentions by sneaking into antislavery gatherings to see them and to hear what they had to say. This outrage to public decency attracted the attention of New England clergy, ever vigilant to spot sin and preserve the social order. A grandiose Pastoral Letter, circulated to the Congregationalist churches, chastised the sisters. It declared that women should not speak in public and should obey men, rather than lecture to them. Some abolitionists shared the clergy's consternation over the Grimkés' tour, while others, perhaps a majority, had trouble arriving at a consistent view of the matter. They could not entirely repudiate the sisters nor could they endorse the Pastoral Letter, which made extreme claims for ministerial authority; yet they were unwilling to fly in the face of public opinion on issues other than slavery. Garrison, characteristically, was not the least uncertain. He argued that there was nothing immoral about the sisters, or any woman, participating in public life or addressing men. Like many other abolitionists, he was in the process of shaking loose from his old assumptions about feminine roles and beginning to comprehend, in quite sweeping terms, the injustices done to women.

Taken along with his other enthusiasms, Garrison's support of the Grimkés convinced many abolitionists that he was either abandoning antislavery or taking it straight to ruin by associating it with strange crusades and by assaulting the sensibilities of decent folk. Garrison responded that expediency should never prevent a person from speaking out against evil and, moreover, that his views on questions other than slavery were his own, not an essential part of the crusade for abolition. He advocated an "open platform" where all who believed in immediate emancipation were welcome, no matter what their differences were on other social or theological questions. That point was lost on anti-abolitionists, who saw Garrison as representative of the cause and who cited him to show that the movement consisted of dangerous crackpots. Some of his colleagues felt they had to put distance between themselves and him simply to refute such charges and to gain respectability and credibility. Garrison, meanwhile, subtly closed the "open platform" and frittered away support by using harsh language to describe allies who disagreed with him. By 1838 he had repelled many admirers while retaining an intensely loyal cluster of followers, concentrated in New England and labeled "Garrisonians." They were diverse in religion, had a high proportion of women, were flamboyant in their tactics, and were extreme on social issues.

Abolitionist opponents of Garrison were not of one mind, nor did they ever form a coherent group. They included a great number of evangelical Protestants who were put off by Garrison's heterodoxy and who believed that the clergy and other influential men, if approached tactfully, would provide greater support for the movement (a notion many of them lost with time). Some, like Lewis Tappan, were quite traditional regarding the role of women, while others, like Theodore Dwight Weld—who married Angelina Grimké— took a woman's rights position but felt it should not be proclaimed openly, lest it detract from abolitionism.

Divisive as Garrison and the "woman question" were, the most serious dispute among abolitionists came over politics. From the beginning antislavery had been non-partisan, as well as non-sectarian. Abolitionists did, however, expect to have political influence by acting as a pressure group, by changing public opinion, and by extracting pledges from major-party candidates for office. In the late 1830s a number of abolitionists in New York and Ohio, led by such men as James G. Birney, Myron Holley, and Henry B. Stanton, became dissatisfied with those tactics. They recognized that abolitionists were being taken in by wily politicians who found promises easier to make than to keep. Politicking, moreover, seemed a good way to focus abolitionist energies and to give publicity to the cause. Since many abolitionists regarded the

Whigs and Democrats as hopelessly corrupt and chained to Southern votes, the logical conclusion was to form a separate antislavery political organization, with its own electioneering apparatus and candidates. After months of talk, the Liberty Party emerged in time to run Birney for the presidency in 1840.

Garrisonians opposed the move on practical and philosophical grounds. Politics, they felt, demanded unacceptable moral compromises as the price of success. They further argued that an antislavery party would do poorly in elections (they were right) and that it would actually diminish the influence of abolitionists votes since the major parties would no longer bother to compete for them in close elections. Even if they had swallowed those objections, many Garrisonians would not have joined the Liberty Party under any circumstances. As Christian anarchists, they believed the proper course of action was *not* to vote or to have anything else to do with human governments, which they regarded as inherently sinful. Yet Garrison and his followers did not entirely reject political means—for others. Garrison frequently said that he expected antislavery to be manifested at the ballot box. He added that it would only get there if abolitionists kept their moral purity (which meant staying clear of party politics) and if they persuaded public opinion of the evils of slavery. What Garrison failed to see was that the Liberty Party did not necessarily have to make moral compromises or to win elections in order to have a purpose: in a highly political nation, electioneering and losing can serve as a valuable form of propaganda.

Well before the Liberty Party materialized, cracks in antislavery unity became too obvious to ignore. The worst of the early breaches appeared in Garrison's home territory. In 1838 his critics organized an alternative organization to the Massachusetts Anti-Slavery Society (which he dominated). In the meantime, politically minded abolitionists like Henry B. Stanton and James G. Birney pressed for resolutions defining the voting obligations of antislavery men. Although Garrisonians suggested compromise declarations, Birney and his allies stuck to a formula calculated to purge the movement of nonresistants and of abolitionists who wanted to stay within the Whig or the Democratic Party. The "woman question" also remained a source of irritation. It nearly broke up the American Anti-Slavery Society in 1839, when female delegates were admitted for the first time on equal terms with men.

The following year the American Anti-Slavery Society did indeed split under the accumulated weight of all the disputes. With the election of a woman, Abby Kelley, to serve on a previously all-male committee, a substantial minority of delegates walked out of the annual meeting. Some of the seceders left to work primarily within the Liberty Party; others joined Lewis Tappan in a new, largely ineffective venture, the American and Foreign Anti-Slavery Society.

The schism might have been averted. When the positions taken by Garrison and his critics appeared in various state and local organizations they often did not cause any comparable disruption. Abolitionists in places remote from the battles in Boston and New York commonly regarded the feuding as silly and refused to take sides. The antagonists, and historians, nevertheless persisted in blaming the division of 1840 on drastic and irreconcilable differences in world-views between the factions. Supposedly, it was Garrison, the radical, opposed by moderates who accepted Protestant orthodoxy and the legitimacy of American institutions. That interpretation, however, fails to acknowledge that Garrison's "radicalism" grew out of the values of the day (it stemmed from Protestant perfectionism and millennialism) and that he was capable of altering it with circumstances—in spite of his pacifism and anarchism, for example, he accepted the Civil War and the Republican Party as means of achieving reform goals. His abolitionist opponents, furthermore, were not always so "moderate" as they seemed to Garrison. They, too, made drastic criticisms of the political system and of American religion (James G. Birney called it the "bulwark" of slavery). Non-Garrisonians also had visions of a society morally transformed and they endorsed causes in addition to antislavery, although usually in more temperate fashion than the Boston editor. Indeed, all factions recognized that the basic principles of abolitionism—control of one's self and one's labor, personal moral responsibility, human brotherhood, and so on—applied to a great many situations beyond the institution of slavery. Still, whatever underlying agreement there was among abolitionists, their personality conflicts and disagreements over tactics made a parting of the ways difficult to prevent by 1840.

The schism seemed a major tragedy to Garrison, who blamed it on "traitors" and insisted that it was a blow to the cause of antislavery. The results were less dramatic than he made them out to be. Neither the American Anti-Slavery Society nor the American and Foreign Anti-Slavery Society was especially effective in coordinating abolitionist efforts after 1840; yet the movement may no longer have needed firm central direction. The American Anti-Slavery Society seems to have been past its prime before the division occurred. The Panic of 1837 dried up funds for major undertakings of the sort it mounted earlier. More important, the functions of the national society were already being passed down to the auxiliaries—probably a healthy thing since local control permitted maximum participation in decision making and allowed abolitionists to modify tactics to suit circumstances in their areas.

Whether for better or worse, the fate of the American Anti-Slavery Society paralleled that of other reform organizations in the antebellum decades. National voluntary societies were a relatively new and exciting development, a product of early-nineteenth-century improvements in communication and transportation. Virtually every antebellum movement generated its own central organization, although some, like phrenology, did so belatedly. Virtually every such organization fell apart within a short span of years. National reform institutions—national institutions of any sort—were hard to maintain in a country as diverse and with such a tradition of localism as the United States. Yet few crusades seem to have suffered irreparable damage from lack of central direction (the exception may have been labor reform, which needed to be able to control wages and working conditions over a broad area). More remarkable than the failure of organizations like the American Anti-Slavery Society is the fact that antebellum Americans were able to build them in the first place.

After 1840 Garrisonians continued to rely on "moral suasion," believing that slavery would end when Americans were convinced of its sinfulness. But they did shift tactics, most notably when they endorsed "disunionism," the idea that the free states ought to secede from the Southern ones. First promoted by Garrison in 1842 and officially proclaimed by the American Anti-Slavery Society in 1844, disunionism had several things to recommend it. It shocked public opinion, got publicity, and provoked defenders of slavery into behaving foolishly. It also fit well with the "ultraist" desire, prevalent among antebellum reformers, to be cut off from anything impure.

Disunionism, finally, expressed a principle abolitionists had long been trying to establish—that slavery was the responsibility of all Americans, not just Southerners. To a degree, abolitionists had to make that argument or find some other line of work since they had no audience among whites in the South. But they sincerely believed that slavery depended upon Northern military might, available to put down slave insurrections, and upon Northern economic assistance. Remove these, Garrisonians argued, and the institution must fall. In its own fashion, disunionism was both a politically sophisticated tactic and an affirmation of American nationhood—a curious thing coming from the branch of abolitionism which seemed most nonpolitical and most sectional. (The real irony was that the South, not the North, made disunionism a reality in 1860, and in the name of preserving slavery.)

After 1840 non-Garrisonians worked to free slaves in their own fashion, with little sympathy for disunionism. Lewis Tappan corresponded with foreign abolitionists, financed propaganda, and mounted religious and legal campaigns to help blacks. Liberty men continued electioneering, with minimal success, until 1848, when the thrust of political antislavery was drastically redirected.

Even earlier, there were stresses and strains apparent within the Liberty Party. The lines of conflict crisscrossed in complicated ways and, as usual, personality conflicts figured in. Some members were dissatisfied with Birney, the presidential candidate in 1840 and 1844—he spent much of his first campaign for office in London and was given to casting aspersions upon the morality of the electorate, neither of which did much to stir enthusiasm. Matters of more substance also divided Liberty men. There were debates over whether to stay with the one issue of slavery or to add others in an effort to apply abolitionist ideals to all social problems and thus to become a party with a broad platform. There was disagreement over the constitutionality of slavery and over Congress's power to touch the institution. And there were those who wanted to keep to the purest possible antislavery position and those who were willing to make concessions in order to attract moderate, even racist, voters.

These quarrels continued among abolitionists into the 1850s, but by the late 1840s events had upset the calculations of Liberty men and Garrisonians alike. At first the trouble had to do with Texas. In the 1830s American settlers there declared independence from Mexico and set up their own republic, sparking controversy over whether Texas ought to join the Union. To bring it into the United States meant adding slave-state representation in Congress and shifting the delicate balance there. Not to bring Texas in implied a censure of slavery and denied political and economic advantages to the South. Texas was eventually annexed in 1845, although through a devious procedure which reinforced the abolitionist suspicion that Southerners secretly controlled the federal government.

The worst was yet to come. Shortly after annexation, the United States and Mexico went to war over a disputed boundary. Although the war was not glorious, the United States won. The total amount of real estate acquired from Mexico (counting Texas) came to over a million square miles, including what is now the state of California.

The war disturbed many Northerners who cared nothing for black people and who were not especially hostile to the South. So long as slavery stayed where it was, they could tolerate it and comfort themselves by believing it would die a natural death. They were not prepared to see it expand and they were uneasy about the acquisition of fresh soil for the South's "peculiar institution." In 1846 David Wilmot, a Pennsylvania congressman, spoke for them. A piece of legislation he sponsored—the Wilmot Proviso—demanded that slavery be prohibited in territories taken from Mexico as a result of the war. The upshot was sharp sectional conflict in Congress (where the South defeated the Proviso in the Senate) and, through a long chain of circumstances, the emergence of a new force in American politics. In 1848 an odd coalition— disaffected Democrats, Liberty men, and a few stray politicians looking for a home—formed the Free Soil Party. Its candidate was ex-President Martin Van Buren, once an obnoxious figure to abolitionists. Its platform advocated the non-extension of slavery, the position of the Wilmot Proviso.

The Free Soil Party posed an intellectual problem for all abolitionists and a tactical one for Liberty men. It was far from being truly antislavery: it did not demand immediate emancipation, nor did it propose to touch slavery where it already existed. It depended, as the Colonization Society did, on an alliance of ardent racists and genuine racial egalitarians. To the former, it promised that Northern whites could preserve western land for themselves and keep blacks out. To the latter, it offered the possibility of a broadly based coalition capable of checking the power of slaveholders in government. Perhaps because of its ideological adaptability, the Free Soil Party met with far greater success than the Liberty Party. It drew 10 percent of the presidential vote in 1848, a respectable showing for a hastily assembled organization, and it elected candidates to state and national offices.

Quick to point out the Party's moral lapses and personally unable to endorse it, Garrisonians were cheered nonetheless. They interpreted Free Soil gains as encouraging signs that the Northern public was slowly moving toward abolitionism and that the South would soon be at bay. Many Liberty men agreed and a few prominent ones such as Salmon P. Chase of Ohio were among the party's founders and most diligent supporters. James G. Birney and some other key Liberty men, however, saw Free Soil as a betrayal of the cause and had nothing to do with it. They persisted in waging hopeless, but morally pure, campaigns of their own in the 1850s, running as self-styled "radical political abolitionists." Free Soil further fragmented the abolitionists at the very time public controversy over slavery was reaching its peak.

The question of the territories remained unresolved throughout 1849, only to be "settled" in the Compromise of 1850, which created new tensions while trying to soothe old ones. The terms of the Compromise cost the South a bit of political leverage. Until then the number of states—hence the number of U.S. senators—had been evenly balanced between slave and free. The admission of California in 1850 as a free state changed that. In return for accepting its new minority status in the Senate, the South received concessions. The most significant of these was a Fugitive Slave Act to assist masters in retrieving their runaway property, some of whom were providing Northern audiences with eyewitness testimony about the South. The law was not the first of its kind, but it was offensive because, contrary to the principles of Anglo-American justice, it stacked the deck against the accused and because it gave Northerners direct responsibility for helping to retake bondsmen. As almost no other piece of legislation could have done, the Act gave credence to the abolitionist argument that slavery rested on a total disrespect for civil liberties and that it could not survive without the support of Northerners, who were now called upon to do the slaveholder's dirty work for him.

The Act probably captured more headlines than fugitives. It led to well-publicized episodes of civil disobedience—blacks and whites fought slave catchers, rescued fugitives from courtrooms and jails, and broke the law in the name of a higher law. Abolitionists made the most of these incidents and wrote movingly of the runaways and their quest for freedom. Beyond that, the Act inspired the single most effective piece of antislavery propaganda, *Uncle Tom's Cabin*, published in 1852 by Harriet Beecher Stowe, who was more of a colonizationist than an abolitionist. With its vivid cast of characters, the novel was wildly popular in the North and was quickly transformed into countless stage productions (leading one abolitionist to note wryly that the theater became antislavery before many churches did).

It is in the nature of compromises to outrage people at the extremes, to please no one fully, and yet to work, at least for a while. Despite the furor over the Fugitive Slave Act, the Compromise of 1850 undercut abolitionism by settling the fate of slavery in the territories, seemingly in favor of freedom. The Free Soil Party did poorly in the election of 1852.

The relative calm was easily shattered. In 1854 a Democratic senator from Illinois, Stephen A. Douglas, introduced legislation to organize territory west of Iowa and Missouri. In order to secure Southern support for the Kansas-Nebraska Act (as it was known), he wrote in the principle that settlers ought to be able to decide for themselves whether the newly formed territories would be slave or free. He graced this notion with a glittering phrase, "popular sovereignty." The problem, so far as Northerners were concerned, was that this changed the rules of the game. According to the Missouri Compromise of 1819–20, slavery had been prohibited from much of the area. Now, with passage of the Act, slavery might gain a foothold there.

Dismay over this brought together ex-Free Soilers, a few old Liberty men, a smattering of disaffected Democrats, and many onetime antislavery Whigs, who created the Republican Party. Like its predecessor, the Free Soil Party, it stood for the non-extension of slavery while professing not to want to harm the institution in the Southern states. Even so, the party's rhetoric was bound to make white Southerners edgy. In addition to criticizing slavery, Republicans (again like Free Soilers) envisioned a nation consisting of independent, prosperous white property holders. That image implied a criticism of the Southern way of life and was powerfully appealing to Northern voters. In a short time the Republicans made remarkable gains and threatened to win the presidency and control Congress without having any support in the South.

These events of the mid- and late-1850s partially vindicated abolitionists, and then passed them by. As Garrison and others predicted, slavery had become something the major parties could not ignore: it broke up the Whigs, divided the Democrats, and produced the Republicans. Southern aggressiveness and political maneuvering also made it appear that abolitionists had been right in their charge that there was a sinister conspiracy in the government, hell-bent on promoting the interests of slavery. The actions of Southerners and their Northern supporters, furthermore, lent weight to the abolitionist argument that the institution was a national evil. The Fugitive Slave Act, of course, did that, as did a Supreme Court decision in the case of Dred Scott. (It appeared to write slavery and racial discrimination into the Constitution.) Yet even while Northerners slipped closer to abolitionist views, older members of the antislavery vanguard had little to do with guiding public affairs. Initiative and leadership belonged to people like Charles Sumner and Henry Wilson (senators from Massachusetts), Salmon P. Chase, and others. Many of these men were ex-Whigs, some former Free Soilers; all were antislavery politicians and Republican stalwarts. Few came out of the original abolitionist organizations.

That was not especially disturbing to the older abolitionists. None expected popularity and most had always assumed their greatest effect would come from persuading others. Many, including Garrison, were pleasantly surprised to find a politician as righteous as Sumner winning office and they had cordial feelings for such men (even while being critical of their public stands and suspicious of their involvement in partisan activities). For abolitionists the unsettling thing about Republican victories was their partial nature. Northern voters were indeed beginning to elect moderately abolitionist candidates. They were also beginning to see slavery as a threat to the republic and to the civil liberties of whites. They were not, however, convinced of the utter sinfulness of slavery, ready to demand its immediate extinction in the South, and prepared to accept black people as fellow citizens. Clearly there was a great deal left to do before the abolitionist message got through to the white public in its entirety.

Yet the time for propaganda seemed to be passing: violence, not moral suasion, was the order of the day in the late 1850s. Vicious guerrilla warfare raged in Kansas between free- and slave-state settlers, each exercising "popular sovereignty" with firearms rather than honest ballots. Violence even invaded the chambers of the United States Senate. A speech made by Sumner in 1856 maligned slavery, administration policy toward Kansas, and, almost incidentally, a fellow senator from South Carolina. The senator's kinsman Preston Brooks (himself a representative from South Carolina) approached Sumner, then seated at his desk, and used a cane to administer a savage beating, presumably vindicating the honor of Brooks's relative and his region. Feelings about slavery were running so high that each man became a hero to many. Sumner was glorified as a martyr to Southern brutality; Brooks, whose cane broke over Sumner's skull, received a fine collection of replacements from well-wishers.

The bloodiest and most ominous episode of the late 1850s was the work of John Brown, a strange old man and a veteran of antislavery battles in Kansas. In October, 1859, he and a small band of black and white followers attacked the Federal Arsenal at Harpers Ferry, Virginia. Most of his men were killed or captured. Brown survived, only to be tried and executed soon after. In the minds of Southerners the raid raised the nightmarish prospect of future slave revolts in which Northern whites might similarly assist blacks in the carnage. Northerners, abolitionists among them, had a harder time interpreting the meaning of Brown's actions. Insurrection was abhorrent to them; yet Brown had taken up weapons in order to strike down evil—a noble gesture, many thought. A failure in most things in his life, Brown helped his reputation in the North by dying well: he accepted his fate with eloquence and dignity. He was an avenging angel. Admiration for the old man appeared even among pacifists like Garrison and Transcendentalist intellectuals like Henry David Thoreau, who had not previously committed himself unreservedly to antislavery.

From the beginning abolitionists had advocated peaceful means to end slavery; but they also predicted it would die violently if emancipation did not come quickly. Kansas, the beating of Sumner, and Brown's raid appeared to justify their darkest fears. Some of them began to wonder, in the bleak days of the 1850s, whether America's sins might not be so horrible that they would have to be washed away in blood.

They were. On December 20, 1860, South Carolina responded to the election of Abraham Lincoln, the Republican presidential candidate, by declaring that the Union between it and the other states was "dissolved." Four months later the Civil War began. As usual, abolitionists were divided. Consistent with their pacifism (and with Garrisonian nonresistance), many believed the Southern states should be allowed—even encouraged—to secede.

Others endorsed the use of force to prevent them from going. Abolitionists were far more agreed upon the moral inadequacy of Lincoln's position, which was that the North was fighting only to preserve the Union, not to meddle with Southern institutions. Opposition to the war, however, faded as the Emancipation Proclamation (to take effect in 1863) and the course of events made it impossible to deny that the conflict was over slavery after all. In 1864 Garrison, for thirty years a nonvoter and nonresistant, cast a ballot for Lincoln.

The war did end slavery. Many abolitionists, pleased with the North's victory, were aging and ready for retirement. A weary Garrison published the last issue of the *Liberator* and left the American Anti-Slavery Society in 1865. The organization continued another five years until the Fifteenth Amendment to the Constitution promised to guarantee civil liberties for blacks. Yet even in 1870 there was much left undone: racism lived on, although slavery did not.

A few abolitionists did recognize that only the first battle had been won and continued throughout the rest of the nineteenth century to press for equal justice. They, however, were not intellectually prepared to agitate for the freedman with the same passion and thoroughness they had brought to the cause of the slave. In common with most antebellum reformers, abolitionists tended to believe that both evil and success were problems of the human spirit, not matters of economics and social structure. Blacks, they felt, needed opportunity, not help. With freedom, ex-slaves could fend for themselves. Those who were virtuous would succeed; those who were not would fail. Although some former abolitionists recognized the weaknesses in that line of reasoning, it was a common one and it tragically underestimated the economic, psychological, and social damage slavery inflicted on both sections and both races.

It is difficult to gauge precisely the importance of the antislavery crusade. Unlike temperance and school reformers, abolitionists were not directly responsible for any great amount of legislation, nor did the original band of abolitionists ever wield much influence in government, although such antislavery politicians as Charles Sumner eventually did. Propaganda campaigns, nevertheless, have an effect. Reformers often find that they remain personally unpopular while voters and leaders come, in time, to accept much of what they have to say. Certainly antislavery images and language passed into common usage and into the rhetoric of elected officials. When that happened, it was because abolitionists phrased things in a manner making sense out of events and speaking to general concerns of the day. In the best example, antislavery talk about a conspiracy of slaveholders gained currency by playing to American fears of arbitrary power and by seeming to describe the actual behavior of Southerners. The importance of antislavery (or any antebellum reform) came through a similar ability to help the public perceive situations, or institutions like slavery, in a new, emotionally charged way. The pity is that abolitionists could not communicate their entire vision: slavery was ended, but largely as a boon to whites. The higher goals of racial harmony and of a society ruled by God's law remained elusive.

David Donald

The Abolitionists:
A Displaced Elite

The abolitionist . . . was a special type of antislavery agitator, and his crusade
was part of that remarkable American social phenomenon which erupted in
the 1830's, "freedom's ferment," the effervescence of kindred humanitarian
reform movements—prohibition; prison reform; education for the blind,
deaf, dumb; world peace; penny postage; women's rights; and a score of lesser
and more eccentric drives.

Historians have been so absorbed in chronicling what these movements
did, in allocating praise or blame among squabbling factions in each, and
in making moral judgments on the desirability of various reforms that they
have paid surprisingly little attention to the movement as a whole. Few
serious attempts have been made to explain why humanitarian reform appeared in America when it did, and more specifically why immediate abolitionism, so different in tone, method, and membership from its predecessors
and its successor, emerged in the 1830's.

The participants in such movements naturally give no adequate explanation for such a causal problem. According to their voluminous memoirs and
autobiographies, they were simply convinced by religion, by reading, by
reflection that slavery was evil, and they pledged their lives and their sacred
honor to destroy it. Seeing slavery in a Southern state, reading an editorial
by William Lloyd Garrison, hearing a sermon by Theodore Dwight Weld—
such events precipitated a decision made on the highest of moral and ethical
planes. No one who has studied the abolitionist literature can doubt the
absolute sincerity of these accounts. Abolitionism was a dangerous creed of

devotion, and no fair-minded person can believe that men joined the movement for personal gain or for conscious self-glorification. In all truth, the decision to become an antislavery crusader was a decision of conscience.

But when all this is admitted, there are still fundamental problems. Social evils are always present; vice is always in the saddle while virtue trudges on afoot. Not merely the existence of evil but the recognition of it is the prerequisite for reform. Were there more men of integrity, were there more women of sensitive conscience in the 1830's than in any previous decade? A generation of giants these reformers were indeed, but why was there such a concentration of genius in those ten years from 1830 to 1840? If the individual's decision to join the abolitionist movement was a matter of personality or religion or philosophy, is it not necessary to inquire why so many similar personalities or religions or philosophies appeared in America simultaneously? In short, we need to know why so many Americans in the 1830's were predisposed toward a certain kind of reform movement.

Many students have felt, somewhat vaguely, this need for a social interpretation of reform. Little precise analysis has been attempted, but the general histories of antislavery attribute the abolitionist movement to the Christian tradition, to the spirit of the Declaration of Independence, to the ferment of Jacksonian democracy, or to the growth of romanticism. That some or all of these factors may have relation to abolitionism can be granted, but this helps little. Why did the "spirit of Puritanism," to which one writer attributes the movement, become manifest as militant abolitionism in the 1830's although it had no such effect on the previous generation? Why did the Declaration of Independence find fulfillment in abolition during the sixth decade after its promulgation, and not in the fourth or the third?

In their elaborate studies of the antislavery movement, Gilbert H. Barnes and Dwight L. Dumond have pointed up some of the more immediate reasons for the rise of American abolitionism. Many of the most important antislavery leaders fell under the influence of Charles Grandison Finney, whose revivalism set rural New York and the Western Reserve ablize with religious fervor and evoked "Wonderful outpourings of the Holy Spirit" throughout the North. Not merely did Finney's invocation of the fear of hell and the promise of heaven rouse sluggish souls to renewed religious zeal, but his emphasis upon good works and pious endeavor as steps toward salvation freed men's minds from the bonds of arid theological controversies One of Finney's most famous converts was Theodore Dwight Weld, the greatest of the Western abolitionists, "eloquent as an angel and powerful as thunder," who recruited a band of seventy antislavery apostles, trained them in Finney's revivalistic techniques, and sent them forth to consolidate the emancipation movement in the North. Their greatest successes were reaped in precisely those communities where Finney's preaching had prepared the soil.

Barnes and Dummond also recognized the importance of British influence upon the American antislavery movement. The connection is clear and easily traced: British antislavery leaders fought for immediate emancipation in the West Indies; reading the tracts of Wilberforce and Clarkson converted William Lloyd Garrison to immediate abolitionism at about the same time that Theodore Weld was won over to the cause by his English friend Charles Stuart; and Weld in turn gained for the movement the support of the Tappan brothers, the wealthy New York merchants and philanthropists who contributed so much in money and time to the antislavery crusade. Thus, abolition had in British precedent a model, in Garrison and Weld leaders, and in the Tappans financial backers.

Historians are deeply indebted to Professors Barnes and Dumond, for the importance of their studies on the antislavery movement is very great. But perhaps they have raised as many questions as they have answered. Both religious revivalism and British antislavery theories had a selective influence in America. Many men heard Finney and Weld, but only certain communities were converted. Hundreds of Americans read Wilberforce, Clarkson, and other British abolitionists, but only the Garrisons and the Welds were convinced. The question remains: Whether they received the idea through the revivalism of Finney or through the publications of British antislavery spokesmen, why were some Americans in the 1830's for the first time moved to advocate immediate abolition? Why was this particular seed bed ready at this precise time?

I believe that the best way to answer this difficult question is to analyze the leadership of the abolitionist movement. There is, unfortunately, no complete list of American abolitionists, and I have had to use a good deal of subjective judgment in drawing up a roster of leading reformers. From the classified indexes of the *Dictionary of American Biography* and the old Appleton's *Cyclopaedia of American Biography* and from important primary and secondary works on the reform generation, I made a list of about two hundred and fifty persons who seemed to be identified with the antislavery cause. This obviously is not a definitive enumeration of all the important abolitionists; had someone else compiled it, other names doubtless would have been included. Nevertheless, even if one or two major spokesmen have accidentally been omitted, this is a good deal more than a representative sampling of antislavery leadership.

After preliminary work I eliminated nearly one hundred of these names. Some proved not to be genuine abolitionists but advocates of colonizing the freed Negroes in Africa; others had only incidental interest or sympathy for emancipation. I ruthlessly excluded those who joined the abolitionists after 1840, because the political antislavery movement clearly poses a different set of causal problems. After this weeding out, I had reluctantly to drop other names because I was unable to secure more than random bits of information about them. Some of Weld's band of seventy agitators, for instance, were so obscure that even Barnes and Dumond were unable to identify them. There remained the names of one hundred and six abolitionists, the hard core of active antislavery leadership in the 1830's.

Most of these abolitionists were born between 1790 and 1810, and when the first number of the *Liberator* was published in 1831, their median age was twenty-nine. Abolitionism was thus a revolt of the young.

My analysis confirms the traditional identification of radical antislavery with New England. Although I made every effort to include Southern and Western leaders, eighty-five percent of these abolitionists came from Northeastern states, sixty percent from New England, thirty percent from Massachusetts alone. Many of the others were descended from New England families. Only four of the leaders were born abroad or were second-generation immigrants.

The ancestors of these abolitionists are in some ways as interesting as the antislavery leaders themselves. In the biographies of their more famous descendants certain standard phrases recur: "of the best New England stock," "of Pilgrim descent," "of a serious, pious household." The parents of the leaders generally belonged to a clearly defined stratum of society. Many were preachers, doctors, or teachers; some were farmers and a few were merchants; but only three were manufacturers (and two of these on a very small scale), none was a banker, and only one was an ordinary day laborer. Virtually all the parents were staunch Federalists.

These families were neither rich nor poor, and it is worth remembering that among neither extreme did abolitionism flourish. The abolitionist could best appeal to "the substantial men" of the community, thought Weld, and not to "the *aristocracy* and fashionable worldliness" that remained aloof from reform. In *The Burned-Over District*, an important analysis of reform drives in western New York, Whitney R. Cross has confirmed Weld's social analysis. In New York, antislavery was strongest in those counties which had once been economically dominant but which by the 1830's, though still prosperous, had relatively fallen behind their more advantageously situated neighbors. As young men the fathers of abolitionists had been leaders of their communities and states; in their old age they were elbowed aside by the merchant prince, the manufacturing tycoon, the corporation lawyer. The bustling democracy of the 1830's passed them by; as the Reverend Ludovicus Weld lamented to his famous son Theodore: "I have . . . felt like a stranger in a strange land."

If the abolitionists were descendants of old and distinguished New England families, it is scarcely surprising to find among them an enthusiasm for higher education. The women in the movement could not, of course, have much formal education, nor could the three Negroes here included, but of the eighty-nine white male leaders, at least fifty-three attended college, university, or theological seminary. In the East, Harvard and Yale were the favored schools; in the West, Oberlin; but in any case the training was usually of the traditional liberal-arts variety.

For an age of chivalry and repression there was an extraordinary proportion of women in the abolitionist movement. Fourteen of these leaders were women who defied the convention that the female's place was at the fireside, not in the forum, and appeared publicly as antislavery apostles. The Grimké sisters of South Carolina were the most famous of these, but most of the antislavery heroines came from New England.

It is difficult to tabulate the religious affiliations of antislavery leaders. Most were troubled by spiritual discontent, and they wandered from one sect to another seeking salvation. It is quite clear, however, that there was a heavy Congregational-Presbyterian and Quaker preponderance. There were many Methodists, some Baptists, but very few Unitarians, Episcopalians, or Catholics. Recent admirable dissertations on the antislavery movement in each of the Western states, prepared at the University of Michigan under Professor Dumond's supervision, confirm the conclusion that, except in Pennsylvania, it is correct to consider humanitarian reform and Congregational-Presbyterianism as causally interrelated.

Only one of these abolitionist leaders seems to have had much connection with the rising industrialism of the 1830's, and only thirteen of the entire group were born in any of the principal cities of the United States. Abolition was distinctly a rural movement, and throughout the crusade many of the antislavery leaders seemed to feel an instinctive antipathy toward the city. Weld urged his following: "Let the great cities *alone*; they must be burned down by *back fires*. The springs to touch in order to move them *lie in the country*."

In general the abolitionists had little sympathy or understanding for the problems of an urban society. Reformers though they were, they were men of conservative economic views. Living in an age of growing industrialization, of tenement congestion, of sweat-shop oppression, not one of them can properly be identified with the labor movement of the 1830's. Most would agree with Garrison, who denounced labor leaders for trying "to inflame the minds of our working classes against the more opulent, and to persuade men that they are contemned and oppressed by a wealthy aristocracy." After all, Wendell Phillips assured the laborers, the American factory operative could be "neither wronged nor oppressed" so long as he had the ballot. William Ellery Channing, gentle high priest of the Boston area, told dissatisfied miners that moral self-improvement was a more potent weapon than strikes, and he urged that they take advantage of the leisure afforded by unemployment for mental and spiritual self-cultivation. A Massachusetts attempt to limit the hours of factory operatives to ten a day was denounced by Samuel Gridley Howe, veteran of a score of humanitarian wars, as "emasculating the people" because it took from them their free right to choose their conditions of employment.

The suffering of laborers during periodic depressions aroused little sympathy among abolitionists. As Emerson remarked tartly, "Do not tell me . . .

of my obligation to put all poor men in good situations. Are they my poor? I tell thee, thou foolish philanthropist, that I grudge the dollar, the dime, the cent I give to such men. . . ."

Actually it is clear that abolitionists were not so much hostile to labor as indifferent to it. The factory worker represented an alien and unfamiliar system toward which the antislavery leaders felt no kinship or responsibility. Sons of the old New England of Federalism, farming, and foreign commerce, the reformers did not fit into a society that was beginning to be dominated by a bourgeoisie based on manufacturing and trade. Thoreau's bitter comment, "We do not ride on the railroads; they ride on us," was more than the acid aside of a man whose privacy at Walden had been invaded; it was the reaction of a class whose leadership had been discarded. The bitterest attacks in the Journals of Ralph Waldo Emerson, the most pointed denunciations in the sermons of Theodore Parker, the harshest philippics in the orations of Charles Sumner were directed against the "Lords of the Loom," not so much for exploiting their labor as for changing the character and undermining the morality of old New England.

As Lewis Tappan pointed out in a pamphlet suggestively titled *Is It Right to Be Rich?*, reformers did not obect to ordinary acquisition of money. It was instead that "eagerness to amass property" which made a man "selfish, unsocial, mean, tyrannical, and but a nominal Christian" that seemed so wrong. It is worth noting that Tappan, in his numerous examples of the vice of excessive accumulation, found this evil stemming from manufacturing and banking, and never from farming or foreign trade—in which last occupation Tappan himself flourished.

Tappan, like Emerson, was trying to uphold the old standards and to protest against the easy morality of the new age. "This invasion of Nature by Trade with its Money, its Credit, its Steam, its Railroads," complained Emerson, "threatens to upset the balance of man, and establish a new universal monarchy more tyrannical than Babylon or Rome." Calmly Emerson welcomed the panic of 1837 as a wholesome lesson to the new monarchs of manufacturing: "I see good in such emphatic and universal calamity. . . ."

Jacksonian democracy, whether considered a labor movement or a triumph of laissez-faire capitalism, obviously had little appeal for the abolitionist conservative. As far as can be determined, only one of these abolitionist leaders was a Jacksonian; nearly all were strong Whigs. William Lloyd Garrison made his first public appearance in Boston to endorse the arch-Whig Harrison Gray Otis; James G. Birney campaigned throughout Alabama to defeat Jackson; Henry B. Stanton wrote editorials for anti-Jackson newspapers. Not merely the leaders but their followers as well seem to have been hostile to Jacksonian democracy, for it is estimated that fifty-nine out of sixty Massachusetts abolitionists belonged to the Whig party.

Jacksonian Democrats recognized the opposition of the abolitionists and accused the leaders of using slavery to distract public attention from more immediate economic problems at home. "The abolitionists of the North have mistaken the color of the American slaves," Theophilus Fisk wrote tartly; "all the real Slaves in the United States have pale faces. . . . I will venture to affirm that there are more slaves in Lowell and Nashua alone than can be found South of the Potomac."

Here, then, is a composite portrait of abolitionist leadership. Descended from old and socially dominant Northeastern families, reared in a faith of aggressive piety and moral endeavor, educated for conservative leadership, these young men and women who reached maturity in the 1830's faced a strange and hostile world. Social and economic leadership was being transferred from the country to the city, from the farmer to the manufacturer, from the preacher to the corporation attorney. Too distinguished a family, too gentle an education, too nice a morality were handicaps in a bustling world of business. Expecting to lead, these young people found no followers. They were an elite without function, a displaced class in American society.

Some—like Daniel Webster—made their terms with the new order and lent their talents and their family names to the greater glorification of the god of trade. But many of the young men were unable to overcome their traditional disdain for the new money-grubbing class that was beginning to rule. In these plebeian days they could not be successful in politics; family tradition and education prohibited idleness; and agitation allowed the only chance for personal and social self-fulfillment.

If the young men were aliens in the new industrial society, the young women felt equally lost. Their mothers had married preachers, doctors, teachers, and had become dominant moral forces in their communities. But in rural New England of the 1830's the westward exodus had thinned the ranks of eligible suitors, and because girls of distinguished family hesitated to work in the cotton mills, more and more turned to schoolteaching and nursing and other socially useful but unrewarding spinster tasks. The women, like the men, were ripe for reform.

They did not support radical economic reforms because fundamentally these young men and women had no serious quarrel with the capitalistic system of private ownership and control of property. What they did question, and what they did rue, was the transfer of leadership to the wrong groups in society, and their appeal for reform was a strident call for their own class to re-exert its former social dominance. Some fought for prison reform; some for women's rights; some for world peace; but ultimately most came to make that natural identification between moneyed aristocracy, textile-manufacturing, and Southern slave-grown cotton. An attack on slavery was their best, if quite unconscious, attack upon the new industrial system. As Richard Henry Dana, Jr., avowed: "I am a Free Soiler, because I am . . . of the stock of the old Northern gentry, and have a particular dislike to any subserviency on the part of our people to the slave-holding oligarchy"—and, he might have added, to their Northern manufacturing allies.

   With all its dangers and all its sacrifices, membership in a movement like abolitionism offered these young people a chance for a reassertion of their traditional values, an opportunity for association with others of their kind, and a possibility of achieving that self-fulfillment which should traditionally have been theirs as social leaders. Reform gave meaning to the lives of this displaced social elite. "My life, what has it been?" queried one young seeker;

the panting of a soul after eternity—the feeling that there was nothing here to fill the aching void, to provide enjoyment and occupation such as my spirit panted for. The world, what has it been? a howling wilderness. I seem to be just now awakened . . . to a true perception of the end of my being, my duties, my responsibilities, the rich and perpetual pleasures which God has provided for us in the fulfillment of duty to Him and to our fellow creatures. Thanks to the A[nti]. S[lavery]. cause, it first gave an impetus to my palsied intellect. . . .

   Viewed against the backgrounds and common ideas of its leaders, abolitionism appears to have been a double crusade. Seeking freedom for the Negro in the South, these reformers were also attempting a restoration of the traditional values of their class at home. Leadership of humanitarian reform may have been influenced by revivalism or by British precedent, but its true origin lay in the drastic dislocation of Northern society. Basically, abolitionism should be considered the anguished protest of an aggrieved class against a world they never made.

Martin Duberman

The Northern Response to Slavery

The abolitionist movement never became the major channel of Northern antislavery sentiment. It remained in 1860 what it had been in 1830: the small but not still voice of radical reform. An important analytical problem thus arises: why did most Northerners who disapproved of slavery become "nonextensionists" rather than abolitionists? Why did they prefer to attack slavery indirectly, by limiting its spread, rather than directly, by seeking to destroy it wherever it existed?

On a broad level, the answer involves certain traits in the national character. In our society of abundance, prosperity has been the actual condition—or the plausible aspiration—of the majority. Most Americans have been too absorbed in the enjoyment or pursuit of possessions to take much notice of the exactions of the system. Even when inequalities have become too pronounced or too inclusive any longer to be comfortably ignored, efforts at relief have usually been of a partial and half-hearted kind. Any radical attack on social problems would compromise the national optimism; it would suggest fundamental defects, rather than occasional malfunctions. And so the majority has generally found it necessary to label "extreme" any measures which call for large-scale readjustment. No one reasonably contented welcomes extensive dislocation; what seems peculiarly American is the disbelief, under *all* circumstances, in the necessity of such dislocation.

Our traditional recoil from "extremism" can be defended. Complex problems, it might be said, require complex solutions; or, to be more precise, complex problems have no solutions—at best, they can be but partially adjusted. If even this much is to be possible, the approach must be flexible, piecemeal, pragmatic. The clear-cut blueprint for reform, with its utopian demand for total solution, intensifies rather than ameliorates disorder.

There is much to be said for this defense of the American way—in the abstract. The trouble is that the theory of gradualism and the practice of it have not been the same. Too often Americans have used the gradualist argument as a technique of evasion rather than as a tool for change, not as a way of dealing with difficult problems slowly and carefully, but as an excuse for not dealing with them at all. We do not want time for working out our problems—we do not want problems, and we will use the argument of time as a way of not facing them. As a chosen people, we are meant only to have problems which are self-liquidating. All of which is symptomatic of our conviction that history is the story of inevitable progress, that every day in every way we *will* get better and better even though we make no positive efforts toward that end.

Before 1845, the Northern attitude toward slavery rested on this comfortable belief in the benevolence of history. Earlier, during the 1830's, the abolitionists had managed to excite a certain amount of uneasiness about the institution by invoking the authority of the Bible and the Declaration of Independence against it. Alarm spread still further when mobs began to prevent abolitionists from speaking their minds or publishing their opinions, and when the national government interfered with the mails and the right of petition. Was it possible, men began to ask, that the abolitionists were right in contending that slavery, if left alone, would not die out but expand, would become more not less vital to the country's interests? Was it possible that slavery might even end by infecting free institutions themselves?

The apathetic majority was shaken, but not yet profoundly aroused; the groundwork for widespread anti-slavery protest was laid, but its flowering awaited further developments. The real watershed came in 1845, when Texas was annexed to the Union, and war with Mexico followed. The prospect now loomed of a whole series of new slave states. It finally seemed clear that the mere passage of time would not bring a solution; if slavery was ever to be destroyed, more active resistance would be necessary. For the first time large numbers of Northerners prepared to challenge the dogma that slavery was a local matter in which the free states had no concern. A new era of widespread, positive resistance to slavery had opened.

Yet such new resolve as had been found was not channeled into a heightened demand for the abolition of the institution, but only into a demand that its further extension be prevented. By 1845 Northerners may have lost partial, but not total confidence in "Natural Benevolence"; they were now wiser Americans perhaps, but Americans nonetheless. More positive action against slavery, they seemed to be saying, was indeed required, but nothing too positive. Containing the institution would, in the long run, be tantamount to destroying it; a more direct assault was unnecessary. In this sense, the doctrine of nonextension was but a more sophisticated version of the standard faith in "time."

One need not question the sincerity of those who believed that nonextension would ultimately destroy slavery, in order to recognize that such a belief partook of wishful thinking. Even if slavery was contained, there remained large areas in the Southern states into which the institution could still expand; even without further expansion, there was no guarantee that slavery would cease to be profitable; and finally, even should slavery cease to be profitable, there was no certainty that the South, psychologically, would feel able to abandon it. Nonextension, in short, was hardly a fool-proof formula. Yet many Northerners chose to so regard it. And thus the question remains: why did not an aroused antislavery conscience turn to more certain measures and demand more unequivocal action?

To have adopted the path of direct abolition, first of all, might have meant risking individual respectability. The unsavory reputation of those already associated with abolitionism was not likely to encourage converts to it. Still, if that doctrine had been really appealing, the disrepute of its earlier adherents could not alone have kept men from embracing it. Association with the "fanatics" could have been smoothed simply by rehabilitating their reputations; their notoriety, it could have been said, had earlier been exaggerated —it had been the convenient invention of an apathetic majority to justify its own indifference to slavery. When, after 1861, public opinion did finally demand a new image of the abolitionists, it was readily enough produced. The mere reputation of abolitionism, therefore, would not have been sufficient to repel men from joining its ranks. Hostility to the movement had to be grounded in a deeper source—fear of the doctrine of "immediatism" itself.

Immediatism challenged the Northern hierarchy of values. To many, a direct assault on slavery meant a direct assault on private property and the Union as well. Fear for these values clearly inhibited antislavery fervor (though possibly a reverse trend operated as well—concern for property and Union may have been stressed in order to justify the convenience of "going slow" on slavery).

As devout Lockeans, Americans did believe that the sanctity of private property constituted the essential cornerstone for all other liberties. If property could not be protected in a nation, neither could life nor liberty. And the Constitution, so many felt, had upheld the legitimacy of holding property in men. True, the Constitution had not mentioned slavery by name, and had not overtly declared in its favor, but in giving the institution certain indirect guarantees (the three-fifths clause; noninterference for twenty-one years with the slave trade; the fugitive slave proviso), the Constitution had seemed to sanction it. At any rate no one could be sure. The intentions of the Founding Fathers remained uncertain, and one of the standing debates of the antebellum generation was whether the Constitution had been meant by them to be a pro- or an antislavery document. Since the issue was unresolved,

Northerners remained uneasy, uncertain how far they could go in attacking slavery without at the same time attacking property.

Fear for property rights was underscored by fear for the Union. The South had many times warned that if her rights and interests were not heeded, she would leave the Union and form a separate confederation. The tocsin had been sounded with enough regularity so that to some it had begun to sound like hollow bluster. But there was always the chance that if the South felt sufficiently provoked she might yet carry out the threat.

It is difficult today fully to appreciate the horror with which most Northerners regarded the potential breakup of the Union. The mystical qualities which surrounded "Union" were no less real for being in part irrational. Lincoln struck a deep chord for his generation when he spoke of the Union as the "last best hope of earth"; that the American experiment was thought the "best" hope may have been arrogant, a hope at all, naïve, but such it was to the average American, convinced of his own superiority and the possibility of the world learning by example. Today, more concerned with survival than improvement, we are bemused (when we are not cynical) about "standing examples for mankind," and having seen the ghastly deeds done in the name of patriotism, we are impatient at signs of national fervor. But 100 years ago, the world saw less danger in nationalism, and Americans, enamored with their own extraordinary success story, were especially prone to look on love of country as one of the noblest of human sentiments. Even those Southerners who had ceased to love the Union had not ceased to love the idea of nationhood; they merely wished to transfer allegiance to a more worthy object.

Those who wanted to preserve the old Union acted from a variety of motives: the Lincolns, who seem primarily to have valued its spiritual potential, were joined by those more concerned with maintaining its power potential; the Union was symbol of man's quest for a benevolent society—and for dominion. But if Northerners valued their government for differing reasons, they generally agreed on the necessity for preserving it. Even so, their devotion to the Union had its oscillations. In 1861 Lincoln and his party, in rejecting the Crittenden Compromise, seemed willing to jeopardize Union rather than risk the further expansion of slavery (perhaps because they never believed secession would really follow, though this complacency, in turn, might only have been a way of convincing themselves that a strong antislavery stand would not necessarily destroy the Union). After war broke out the value stress once more shifted: Lincoln's party now loudly insisted that the war was indeed being fought to preserve the Union, not to free the slaves. Thus did the coexisting values of Union and antislavery tear the Northern mind and confuse its allegiance.

The tension was compounded by the North's ambivalent attitude toward the Negro. The Northern majority, unlike most of the abolitionists, did not believe in the equality of races. The Bible (and the new science of anthropology) seemed to suggest that the Negro had been a separate, inferior creation meant for a position of servitude. Where there was doubt on the doctrine of racial equality, its advocacy by the distrusted abolitionists helped to settle the matter in the negative.

It was possible, of course, to disbelieve in Negro equality, and yet disapprove of Negro slavery. Negroes were obviously men, even if an inferior sort, and as men they could not in conscience (the Christian-Democratic version) be denied the right to control their own souls and bodies. But if anti-Negro and antislavery sentiments were not actually incompatible, they were not mutually supportive either. Doubt of the Negro's capacity for citizenship continually blunted the edge of antislavery fervor. If God had intended the Negro for some subordinate role in society, perhaps a kind of benevolent slavery was, after all, the most suitable arrangement; so long as there was uncertainty, it might be better to await the slow unfolding of His intentions in His good time.

And so the average Northerner, even after he came actively to disapprove of slavery, continued to be hamstrung in his opposition to it by the competitive pull of other values. Should prime consideration be given to freeing the slaves, even though in the process the rights of property and the preservation of the Union were threatened? Should the future of the superior race be endangered in order to improve the lot of a people seemingly marked by Nature for a degraded station? Ideally, the North would have liked to satisfy its conscience about slavery and at the same time preserve the rest of its value system intact—to free the Negro and yet do so without threatening property rights or dislocating the Union. This struggle to achieve the best of all possible worlds runs like a forlorn hope throughout the ante-bellum period—the sad, almost plaintive quest by the American Adam for the perfect world he considered his birthright.

The formula of nonextension did seem, for a time, the perfect device for balancing these multiple needs. Nonextension would put slavery in the course of ultimate extinction without producing excessive dislocation; since slavery would not be attacked directly, nor its existence immediately threatened, the South would not be unduly fearful for her property rights, the Union would not be needlessly jeopardized, and a mass of free Negroes would not be precipitously thrust upon an unprepared public. Nonextension, in short, seemed a panacea, a formula which promised in time to do everything while for the present risking nothing. But like all panaceas, it ignored certain hard realities: would containment really lead to the extinction of slavery? would the South accept even a gradual dissolution of her peculiar institution? would it be right to sacrifice two or three more generations of Negroes in the name of uncertain future possibilities? Alas for the American Adam, so soon to be expelled from Eden.

The abolitionists, unlike most Northerners, were not willing to rely on future intangibles. Though often called impractical romantics, they were in some ways the most tough-minded of Americans. They had no easy faith in the benevolent workings of time or in the inevitable triumphs of gradualism. If change was to come, they argued, it would be the result of man's effort to produce it; patience and inactivity had never yet helped the world's ills. Persistently, sometimes harshly, the abolitionists denounced delay and those who advocated it; they were tired, they said, of men using the councils of moderation to perpetuate injustice.

In their own day, and ever since, the abolitionists have faced a hostile majority; their policies have been ridiculed, their personalities reviled. Yet ridicule, like its opposite, adoration, is usually not the result of analysis but a substitute for it. Historians have for so long been absorbed in denouncing the abolitionists, that they have had scant energy left over for understanding them. The result is that we still know surprisingly little about the movement, and certainly not enough to warrant the general assumptions so long current in the historical profession.

Historians have assumed that the abolitionists were unified in their advocacy of certain broad policies—immediate emancipation, without compensation—and also unified in refusing to spell out details for implementing these policies. To some extent this traditional view is warranted. The abolitionists did agree almost unanimously (Gerrit Smith was one of the few exceptions) that slaveholders must not be compensated. One does not pay a man, they argued, for ceasing to commit a sin. Besides, the slaveholder had already been paid many times over in labor for which he had never given wages. Defensible though this position may have been in logic or morals, the abolitionists should perhaps have realized that public opinion would never support the confiscation of property, and should have modified their stand accordingly. But they saw themselves as prophets, not politicians; they were concerned with what was "right," not with what was possible, though they hoped that if men were once made aware of the right, they would find some practical way of implementing it.

The abolitionists were far less united on the doctrine of immediate emancipation—at least in the 1830's, before Southern intransigence and British experience in the West Indies, convinced almost all of them that gradualism was hopeless. But during the 1830's, there was a considerable spectrum of opinion as to when and how to emancipate the slave. Contrary to common myth, some of the abolitionists did advocate a period of prior education and training before the granting of full freedom. Men like Weld, Birney, and the Tappans, stressing the debasing experience of slavery, insisted only that gradual emancipation be immediately begun, not that emancipation itself be at once achieved. This range of opinion has never been fully appreciated. It has been convenient, then and now, to believe that all abolitionists always advocated instantaneous freedom, for it thus became possible to denounce any call for emancipation as "patently impractical."

By 1840, however, most abolitionists had become immediatists, and that position, "practical" or not, did have a compelling moral urgency. Men learned how to be free, the immediatists argued, only by being free; slavery, no matter how attenuated, was by its very nature incapable of preparing men for those independent decisions necessary to adult responsibility. Besides, they insisted, the Negro, though perhaps debased by slavery, was no more incapacitated for citizenship than were many poor whites, whose rights no one seriously suggested curtailing.

The immediatist position was not free of contradiction. If slavery had been as horrendous as the abolitionists claimed, it was logical to expect that its victims would bear deep personality scars—greater than any disabilities borne by a poor white, no matter how degraded his position. Either slavery had not been this deadly, or, if it had, those recently freed from its toils could not be expected to move at once into the responsibilities of freedom. This contradiction was apparent to some immediatists, but there was reason for refusing to resolve it. Ordinarily, they said, a system of apprenticeship might be desirable, but if conditions to emancipation were once established, they could be used as a standing rationale for postponement; the Negro could be kept in a condition of semislavery by the self-perpetuating argument that he was not yet ready for his freedom.

Moreover, any intermediary stage before full freedom would require the spelling out of precise "plans," and these would give the enemies of emancipation an opportunity to pick away at the impracticality of this or that detail. They would have an excuse for disavowing the broader policy under the guise of disagreeing with the specific means for achieving it. Better to concentrate on the larger issue and force men to take sides on that alone, the abolitionists argued, than to give them a chance to hide their opposition behind some supposed disapproval of detail. Wendell Phillips, for one, saw the abolitionists' role as exclusively that of agitating the broader question. Their primary job, Phillips insisted, was to arouse the country's conscience rather than to spell out to it precise plans and formulas. After that conscience had been aroused, it would be time to talk of specific proposals; let the moral urgency of the problem be recognized, let the country be brought to a determination to rid itself of slavery, and ways and means to accomplish that purpose would be readily enough found.

No tactical position could really have saved the abolitionists from the denunciation of those hostile to their basic goal. If the abolitionists spelled out a program for emancipation, their enemies would have a chance to pick at details; if they did not spell out a program, they could then be accused of vagueness and impracticality. Hostility can always find its own justification.

A second mode of attack on the abolitionists has centered on their personalities rather than their policies. The stereotype which long had currency sees the abolitionist as a disturbed fanatic, a man self-righteous and self-deceived, motivated not by concern for the Negro, as he may have believed, but by an unconscious drive to gratify certain needs of his own. Seeking to discharge either individual anxieties or those frustrations which came from membership in a "displaced élite," his antislavery protest was, in any case, a mere disguise for personal anguish.

A broad assumption underlies this analysis which has never been made explicit—namely, that strong protest by an individual against social injustice is ipso facto proof of his disturbance. Injustice itself, in this view, is apparently never sufficient to arouse unusual ire in "normal" men, for normal men, so goes the canon, are always cautious, discreet, circumspect. Those who hold to this model of human behavior seem rarely to suspect that it may tell us more about their hierarchy of values than about the reform impulse it pretends to describe. Argued in another context, the inadequacies of the stereotype become more apparent: if normal people do not protest "excessively" against injustice, then we should be forced to condemn as neurotic all those who protested with passion against the Nazi persecution of the Jews.

Some of the abolitionists, it is true, were palpable neurotics, men who were not comfortable within themselves and therefore not comfortable with others, men whose "reality-testing" was poor, whose life styles were pronouncedly compulsive, whose relationships were unusual compounds of demand and phantasy. Such neurotics were in the abolitionist movement—the Parker Pillsburys, Stephen Fosters, Abby Folsoms. Yet even here we must be cautious, for our diagnostic accuracy can be blurred if the life style under evaluation is sharply different from our own. Many of the traits of the abolitionists which today "put us off" were not peculiar to them, but rather to their age—the declamatory style, the abstraction and idealization of issues, the tone of righteous certainty, the religious context of argumentation. Thus the evangelical rhetoric of the movement, with its thunderous emphasis on sin and retribution, can sound downright "queer" (and thus "neurotic") to the 20th century skeptic, though in its day common enough to abolitionists and nonabolitionists alike.

Then, too, even when dealing with the "obvious" neurotics, we must be careful in the link we establish between their pathology and their protest activity. It is one thing to demonstrate an individual's "disturbance" and quite another then to explain all of his behavior in terms of it. Let us suppose, for example, that Mr. Jones is a reformer; he is also demonstrably "insecure." It does not necessarily follow that he is a reformer *because* he is insecure. The two may seem logically related (that is, if one's mind automatically links "protest" with "neurosis"), but we all know that many things can be logical without being true.

Even if we establish the neurotic behavior of certain members of a group, we have not, thereby, established the neurotic behavior of *all* members of that group. The tendency to leap from the particular to the general is always tempting, but because we have caught one benighted monsignor with a boy scout does not mean we have conclusively proved that all priests are pederasts. Some members of every group are disturbed; put the local police force, the Medal of Honor winners, or the faculty of a university under the Freudian microscope, and the number of cases of "palpable disturbance" would probably be disconcertingly high. But what *precisely* does their disturbance tell us about the common activities of the group to which they belong—let alone about the activities of the disturbed individuals themselves?

Actually, behavioral patterns for many abolitionists do *not* seem notably eccentric. Men like Birney, Weld, Lowell, Quincy—abolitionists all—formed good relationships, saw themselves in perspective, played and worked with zest and spontaneity, developed their talents, were aware of worlds beyond their own private horizons. They all had their tics and their traumas—as who does not—but the evidence of health is abundant and predominant. Yet most historians have preferred to ignore such men when discussing the abolitionist movement. And the reason, I believe, is that such men conform less well than do the Garrisons to the assumption that those who become deeply involved in social protest are necessarily those who are deeply disturbed.

To evaluate this assumption further, some effort must be made to understand current findings in the theory of human motivation. This is difficult terrain for the historian, not made more inviting by the sharp disagreements which exist among psychologists themselves (though these disagreements do help to make us aware of the complexities involved). Recent motivational research, though not conclusive, throws some useful new perspectives on "reformers."

A reaction has currently set in among psychologists against the older behaviorist model of human conduct. The behaviorists told us that men's actions were determined by the nature of the stimulus exerted upon them, and that their actions always pointed towards the goal of "tension reduction." There was little room in behaviorist theory for freedom of choice, for rationality, or for complex motives involving abstract ideas as well as instinctive drives.

Without denying the tension-reducing motives of certain kinds of human behavior, a number of psychologists are now insisting on making room for another order of motivation, involving more than the mere "restoration of equilibrium." Mature people, they believe—that is, those who have a realistic sense of self—can act with deliberation and can exercise control over their actions. This new view presumes an active intellect, an intellect capable of interpreting sensory data in a purposive way. The power of reflection, of self-objectification, makes possible a dynamic as opposed to a merely instinctive life. Men, in short, need not be wholly driven by habit and reflex; they need not be mere automatons who respond in predictable ways to given stimuli. Rather, they can be reasoning organisms capable of decision and choice. Among the rational choices mature men may make is to commit themselves to a certain set of ethical values. They are not necessarily forced to such a commitment by personal or social tensions (of which they are usually unaware), but may come to that commitment deliberately, after reflective consideration.

The new psychology goes even one step further. It suggests that the very definition of maturity may be the ability to commit oneself to abstract ideals, to get beyond the selfish, egocentric world of children. This does not mean that every man who reaches outward does so from mature motives; external involvement may also be a way of acting out sick phantasies. The point is only that "commitment" need not be a symptom of personality disturbance. It is just as likely to be a symptom of maturity and health.

It does not follow, of course, that all abolitionists protested against slavery out of mature motives; some may have been, indeed were, "childish neurotics." But if we agree that slavery was a fearful injustice, and if motivational theory now suggests that injustice will bring forth protest from mature men, it seems reasonable to conclude that at least some of those who protested strongly against slavery must have done so from "healthy" motives.

The hostile critic will say that the abolitionists protested *too* strongly to have been maturely motivated. But when is a protest *too* strong? For a defender of the status quo, the answer (though never stated in these terms) would be: when it succeeds. For those not dedicated to the current status, the answer is likely to be: a protest is too strong when it is out of all proportion to the injustice it indicts. Could any verbal protest have been too strong against holding fellow human beings as property? From a moral point of view, certainly not, though from a practical point of view, perhaps. That is, the abolitionist protest might have been *too* strong if it somehow jeopardized the very goal it sought to achieve—the destruction of human slavery. But no one has yet shown this to have been the case.

At any rate, current findings in motivational theory suggest that at the very least we must cease dealing in blanket indictments, in simple-minded categorizing and elementary stereotyping. Such exercises may satisfy our present-day hostility to "reformers," but they do not satisfy the complex demands of historical truth. We need an awareness of the wide variety of human beings who became involved in the abolitionist movement, and an awareness of the complexity of human motivation sufficient to save us from summing up men and movements in two or three unexamined adjectives.

Surely there is now evidence enough to suggest that commitment and concern need not be aberrations; they may represent the profoundest elements of our humanity. Surely there are grounds for believing that those who protested strongly against slavery were not all misguided fanatics or frustrated neurotics—though by so believing it becomes easier to ignore the injustice against which they protested. Perhaps it is time to ask whether the abolitionists, in insisting that slavery be ended, were indeed those men of their generation furthest removed from reality, or whether that description should be reserved for those Northerners who remained indifferent to the institution, and those Southerners who defended it as a "positive good." From the point of view of these men, the abolitionists were indeed mad, but it is time we questioned the sanity of the point of view.

Those Northerners who were not indifferent to slavery—a large number after 1845—were nonetheless prone to view the abolitionist protest as "excessive," for it threatened the cherished values of private property and Union. The average Northerner may have found slavery disturbing, but convinced as he was that the Negro was an inferior, he did not find slavery monstrous. Certainly he did not think it an evil sufficiently profound to risk, by "precipitous action," the nation's present wealth or its future power. The abolitionists were willing to risk both. They thought it tragic that men should weigh human lives in the *same* scale as material possessions and abstractions of government. It is no less tragic that we continue to do so.

SUGGESTIONS FOR FURTHER READING

Louis Filler, *The Crusade Against Slavery (New York, 1960), is a balanced account that takes the abolitionists seriously and makes connections between the movement and the other reforms of the period. Gilbert H. Barnes, *The Antislavery Impulse, 1830–1844 (New York, 1933), emphasizes the importance of religious revivalism, and especially the leadership of Theodore Weld for the movement. Dwight L. Dumond, *Anti-Slavery Origins of the Civil War in the United States (Ann Arbor, 1939), is a sympathetic account stressing the moral basis for the crusade against slavery. Richard O. Curry, *The Abolitionists: Reformers or Fanatics (New York, 1965), is a convenient collection of essays. William H. and Jane H. Pease, *The Anti-Slavery Argument (New York, 1965), and Louis Ruchames, *The Abolitionists: A Collection of Their Writings (New York, 1963) are collections of documents.

Avery Craven, *The Coming of the Civil War (Chicago, 1957), argues that the abolitionists were maladjusted, misguided fanatics who provoked a conflict that was unnecessary and tragic. A similar view may be found in William B. Hesseltine, *The South in American History* (New York, 1936).

For a criticism of Donald's method see Robert A. Skotheim, "A Note on Historical Method: David Donald's 'Toward a Reconsideration of Abolitionists,'" *Journal of Southern History*, 25 (1959), pp. 356–65. Frederick Douglass, *Life and Times of Frederick Douglass (Hartford, Conn., 1882), is the autobiography of the best-known black abolitionist. Leon L. Litwack, *North of Slavery: The Negro in the Free States, 1790–1860 (Chicago, 1961), shows that Northern racism was pervasive, even affecting many abolitionists. On this question see also William H. and Jane H. Pease, "Antislavery Ambivalence: Immediatism, Expediency, Race," *American Quarterly*, 17 (Winter 1965).

Some important work may be found in a fascinating group of essays edited by Martin Duberman, *The Antislavery Vanguard: New Essays on the Abolitionists (Princeton, 1965). Aileen S. Kraditor, *Means and Ends in American Abolitionism (New York, 1969), is a brilliant study of abolitionist tactics. Leonard

* Available in paperback edition.

L. Richards, *Gentlemen of Property and Standing: Anti-Abolition Mobs in Jacksonian America* (New York, 1970), describes some of the conflict and violence directed against the abolitionists in the North. Benjamin Quarles, **Black Abolitionists* (New York, 1969), traces the contributions of blacks to the movement. Gerald Sorin, **Abolitionism: A New Perspective* (New York, 1972), argues that the abolitionists were agitators who viewed slavery as morally wrong. James Brewer Stewart, *Holy Warriors: Abolitionists and American Slavery* (New York, 1976), is a fine survey of the movement with an interpretation similar to that of Ronald G. Walters. Ronald G. Walters's essay (reprinted above) is from his general study of American reform, **American Reformers, 1815–1860* (New York, 1978). The same author's *The Antislavery Appeal: American Abolitionism After 1830* (Baltimore, 1976) minimizes the differences among the abolitionists and describes an antislavery consensus.

9

The Civil War

Americans have found their Civil War to be more interesting than any other event in their history. Even the Revolution that marked the birth of the republic cannot compete in popularity with the bloody fratricidal conflict of 1861–1865. The popular imagination has been fed by thousands of books and articles, movies and television performances. Commemorative monuments, museums, parks, and cemeteries dot every state that saw battle. No skirmish, however minor, lacks at least one historical marker to remind visitors of the event, and every state that raised troops has its mementos—flags, uniforms, guns, and equipment—which it treasures. And it is only in recent years that anniversary dates were not marked by the appearance of an old veteran, willing to recount his experiences—real and imagined—in the war.

The historian has not been immune to this fascination with our Civil War. He has recounted the battles many times over and has described, defended, and attacked the actions of the important actors (and many not so important) on both sides of the conflict.

One million casualties, including a half million deaths, and millions of dollars in destroyed property are ample evidence that the Civil War marked a sharp conflict in American history. But how significant were the differences that led to war between North and South in 1861? In October 1858 William H. Seward, a prominent New York Republican leader, declared that the struggle over slavery dividing North and South was "an irrepressible conflict." Earlier that same year an Illinois Republican politician, Abraham Lincoln, had enunciated similar beliefs: "A house divided against itself cannot stand. I believe this government cannot endure permanently, half-slave and half-free."

Taking their lead from such statements, some historians have argued that the Civil War revealed deep and abiding differences in American society. So significant were the disagreements between North and South that compromise became impossible. The gulf that separated the sections had become so wide that a bridge of consensus could not be built; conflict in the form of organized warfare was inevitable. Moreover, the defeat and subjugation of the South, many of these scholars argue, marked a fundamental turning point in American history. The victory of the Northern troops led to the victory of the Northern point of view; compromise, which had been impossible, now had become unnecessary.

Other historians dispute this interpretation. The nation had lived with slavery for many generations, they argue; and, when disputes arose between the sections, they had repeatedly been resolved through compromise. While Lincoln made it clear that he did not like slavery, he also made it clear that he would not interfere with it in the South. War was not inevitable; on the contrary it could have been prevented. That it was not prevented was not the result of fundamental differences between North and South, but rather the result of what one historian has called the failures of a "blundering generation."

The three selections that follow give very different evaluations of the significance of the Civil War. For Charles and Mary Beard the Civil War was a struggle for political power waged by representatives of two economic systems. The war was an "irrepressible conflict" between the industrial North and the agricultural South; the prize for which they contended was political domination of the nation. When the North won on the battlefields, the industrialists won in Congress. The domination of the country by the agricultural interests was at an end; and, as such, the Civil War, was "a Second American Revolution," the Beards conclude.

Like the Beards, Eric Foner argues that the Civil War resulted from a basic conflict in American society. But he rejects the notion that the conflict was between industrialism and agrarianism. For Foner, the key issue was slavery, not merely as a moral issue (as some historians have argued), but as the basis of a complex web of ideas that led both sides to accept ideologies, or world views, which they were convinced put them in "sharp, perhaps mortal, conflict with one another." This interpretation is in direct contrast to that of Daniel J. Boorstin, who is struck by what he considers to be the essential "continuity" in American thought—North and South—throughout the period of the Civil War. He finds both sides more alike than different in their arguments about institutions and politics.

It would seem that the American people would turn to war as a way of settling their differences only after every other means of settlement had proved ineffective. Can we say, then, that the Civil War arose because the differences between North and South were so great and so fundamental that compromise had become impossible? If so, what were these differences? Why were they so great that they could not be compromised and had instead to be settled on the battlefield? On the other hand, few modern social scientists would deny the role of irrational factors in motivating human behavior. Can such factors explain the Civil War? Were Americans, North and South, so blinded by irrational emotionalism that they lost sight of their common interests and of the compromise and accommodation available to them and utilized by them many times before 1861? Clearly, a bloody civil war is a national tragedy. But when such a war could have been avoided had the participants acted more wisely, the tragedy is compounded.

Charles and Mary Beard

The Second
American Revolution

Had the economic systems of the North and the South remained static or
changed slowly without effecting immense dislocations in the social structure, the balance of power might have been maintained indefinitely by
repeating the compensatory tactics of 1787, 1820, 1833, and 1850; keeping
in this manner the inherent antagonisms within the bounds of diplomacy.
But nothing was stable in the economy of the United States or in the moral
sentiments associated with its diversities.

Within each section of the country, the necessities of the productive
system were generating portentous results. The periphery of the industrial
vortex of the Northeast was daily enlarging, agriculture in the Northwest
was being steadily supplemented by manufacturing, and the area of virgin
soil open to exploitation by planters was diminishing with rhythmic regularity
—shifting with mechanical precision the weights which statesmen had to
adjust in their efforts to maintain the equilibrium of peace. Within each of
the three sections also occurred an increasing intensity of social concentration
as railways, the telegraph, and the press made travel and communication cheap
and almost instantaneous, facilitating the centripetal process that was drawing
people of similar economic status and parallel opinions into cooperative
activities. Finally the intellectual energies released by accumulating wealth
and growing leisure—stimulated by the expansion of the reading public and
the literary market—developed with deepened accuracy the word-patterns
of the current social persuasions, contributing with galvanic effect to the
consolidation of identical groupings.

As the years passed, the planting leaders of Jefferson's agricultural party insisted with mounting fervor that the opposition, first of the Whigs and then of the Republicans, was at bottom an association of interests formed for the purpose of plundering productive management and labor on the land. And with steadfast insistence they declared that in the insatiable greed of their political foes lay the source of the dissensions which were tearing the country asunder.

"There is not a pursuit in which man is engaged (agriculture excepted)," exclaimed Reuben Davis of Mississippi in 1860,

which is not demanding legislative aid to enable it to enlarge its profits and all at the expense of the primary pursuit of man—agriculture. . . . Those interests, having a common purpose of plunder, have united and combined to use the government as the instrument of their operation and have thus virtually converted it into a consolidated empire. Now this combined host of interests stands arrayed against the agricultural states; and this is the reason of the conflict which like an earthquake is shaking our political fabric to its foundation.

The furor over slavery is a mere subterfuge to cover other purposes. "Relentless avarice stands firm with its iron heel upon the Constitution." This creature, "incorporated avarice," has chained "the agricultural states to the northern rock" and lives like a vulture upon their prosperity. It is the effort of Prometheus to burst his manacles that provokes the assault on slavery. "These states struggle like a giant," continued Davis, "and alarm these incorporated interests, lest they may break the chain that binds them to usurpation; and therefore they are making this fierce onslaught upon the slave property of the southern states."

The fact that free-soil advocates waged war only on slavery in the territories was to Jefferson Davis conclusive proof of an underlying conspiracy against agriculture. He professed more respect for the abolitionist than for the freesoiler. The former, he said, is dominated by an honest conviction that slavery is wrong everywhere and that all men ought to be free; the latter does not assail slavery in the states—he merely wishes to abolish it in the territories that are in due course to be admitted to the Union.

With challenging directness, Davis turned upon his opponents in the Senate and charged them with using slavery as a blind to delude the unwary:

What do you propose, gentlemen of the Free-Soil party? Do you propose to better the condition of the slave? Not at all. What then do you propose? You say you are opposed to the expansion of slavery. . . . Is the slave to be benefited by it? Not at all. It is not humanity that influences you in the position which you now occupy before the country. . . . It is that you may have an opportunity of cheating us that you want to limit slave territory within circumscribed bounds. It is that you may have a majority in the Congress of the United States and convert the Government into an engine of northern aggrandizement. It is that your section may grow in power and prosperity upon treasures unjustly taken from the South, like the vampire bloated and gorged with the blood which it has secretly sucked from its victim. . . . You desire to weaken the political power of the southern states; and why? Because you want, by an unjust system of legislation, to promote the industry of the New England states, at the expense of the people of the South and their industry.

Such in the mind of Jefferson Davis, fated to be president of the Confederacy, was the real purpose of the party which sought to prohibit slavery in the territories; that party did not declare slavery to be a moral disease calling for the severe remedy of the surgeon; it merely sought to keep bondage out of the new states as they came into the Union—with one fundamental aim in view, namely, to gain political ascendancy in the government of the United States and fasten upon the country an economic policy that meant the exploitation of the South for the benefit of northern capitalism.

But the planters were after all fighting against the census returns, as the phrase of the day ran current. The amazing growth of northern industries, the rapid extension of railways, the swift expansion of foreign trade to the ends of the earth, the attachment of the farming regions of the West to the centers of manufacture and finance through transportation and credit, the destruction of state consciousness by migration, the alien invasion, the erection of new commonwealths in the Valley of Democracy, the nationalistic drive of interstate commerce, the increase of population in the North, and the southward pressure of the capitalistic glacier all conspired to assure the ultimate triumph of what the orators were fond of calling "the free labor system." This was a dynamic thrust far too powerful for planters operating in a limited territory with incompetent labor on soil of diminishing fertility. Those who swept forward with it, exulting in the approaching triumph of machine industry, warned the planters of their ultimate subjection.

To statesmen of the invincible forces recorded in the census returns, the planting opposition was a huge, compact, and self-conscious economic association bent upon political objects—the possession of the government of the United States, the protection of its interests against adverse legislation, dominion over the territories, and enforcement of the national fugitive slave law throughout the length and breadth of the land. No phrase was more often on the lips of northern statesmen than "the slave power." The pages of the Congressional Globe bristled with references to "the slave system" and its influence over the government of the country. But it was left for William H. Seward of New York to describe it with a fullness of familiar knowledge that made his characterization a classic.

Seward knew from experience that a political party was no mere platonic society engaged in discussing abstractions. "A party," he said, "is in one sense a joint stock association, in which those who contribute most direct the action and management of the concern. The slaveholders contributing in an overwhelming proportion to the capital strength of the Democratic party, they necessarily dictate and prescribe its policy. The inevitable caucus system enables them to do this with a show of fairness and justice." This class of slaveholders, consisting of only three hundred and forty-seven thousand persons, Seward went on to say, was spread from the banks of the Delaware to the banks of the Rio Grande; it possessed nearly all the real estate in that section, owned more than three million other "persons" who were denied all civil and political rights, and inhibited "freedom of speech, freedom of press, freedom of the ballot box, freedom of education, freedom of literature, and freedom of popular assemblies. . . . The slaveholding class has become the governing power in each of the slaveholding states and it practically chooses thirty of the sixty-two members of the Senate, ninety of the two hundred and thirty-three members of the House of Representatives, and one hundred and five of the two hundred and ninety-five electors of the President and Vice-President of the United States."

Becoming still more concrete, Seward accused the President of being "a confessed apologist of the slave-property class." Examining the composition of the Senate, he found the slave-owning group in possession of all the important committees. Peering into the House of Representatives he discovered no impregnable bulwark of freedom there. Nor did respect for judicial ermine compel him to spare the Supreme Court. With irony he exclaimed:

How fitting does the proclamation of its opening close with the invocation: "God save the United States and this honorable court". . . . The court consists of a chief justice and eight associate justices. Of these five were called from slave states and four from free states. The opinions and bias of each of them were carefully considered by the President and Senate when he was appointed. Not one of them was found wanting in soundness of politics, according to the slaveholder's exposition of the Constitution, and those who were called from the free states were even more distinguished in that respect than their brethren from the slaveholding states.

Seward then analyzed the civil service of the national government and could descry not a single person among the thousands employed in the post office, the treasury, and other great departments who was "false to the slaveholding interest." Under the spoils system, the dominion of the slavocracy extended into all branches of the federal administration. "The customshouses and the public lands pour forth two golden streams—one into the elections to procure votes for the slaveholding class; and the other into the treasury to be enjoyed by those whom it shall see fit to reward with places in the public service." Even in the North, religion, learning, and the press were under the spell of this masterful class, frightened lest they incur its wrath.

Having described the gigantic operating structure of the slavocracy, Seward drew with equal power a picture of the opposing system founded on "free labor." He surveyed the course of economy in the North—the growth of industry, the spread of railways, the swelling tide of European immigration, and the westward roll of free farmers—rounding out the country, knitting it together, bringing "these antagonistic systems" continually into closer contact. Then he uttered those fateful words which startled conservative citizens from Maine to California—words of prophecy which proved to be brutally true—"the irrepressible conflict."

This inexorable clash, he said, was not "accidental, unnecessary, the work of interested or fanatical agitators and therefore ephemeral." No. "It is an irrepressible conflict between opposing and enduring forces." The hopes of those who sought peace by appealing to slave owners to reform themselves were as chaff in a storm. "How long and with what success have you waited already for that reformation? Did any property class ever so reform itself? Did the patricians in old Rome, the noblesse or clergy in France? The landholders in Ireland? The landed aristocracy in England? Does the slaveholding class even seek to beguile you with such a hope? Has it not become rapacious, arrogant, defiant?" All attempts at compromise were "vain and ephemeral." There was accordingly but one supreme task before the people of the United States—the task of confounding and overthrowing "by one decisive blow the betrayers of the Constitution and freedom forever." In uttering this indictment, this prophecy soon to be fulfilled with such appalling accuracy, Seward stepped beyond the bounds of cautious politics and read himself out of the little group of men who were eligible for the Republican nomination in 1860. Frantic efforts to soften his words by explanations and additions could not appease his critics.

Given an irrepressible conflict which could be symbolized in such unmistakable patterns by competent interpreters of opposing factions, a transfer of the issues from the forum to the field, from the conciliation of diplomacy to the decision of arms was bound to come. Each side obdurately bent upon its designs and convinced of its rectitude, by the fulfillment of its wishes precipitated events and effected distributions of power that culminated finally in the tragedy foretold by Seward. Those Democrats who operated on historic knowledge rather than on prophetic insight, recalling how many times the party of Hamilton had been crushed at elections, remembering how the Whigs had never been able to carry the country on a cleancut Webster-Clay program, and counting upon the continued support of a huge array of farmers and mechanics marshaled behind the planters, imagined apparently that politics—viewed as the science of ballot enumeration—could resolve the problems of power raised by the maintenance of the Union.

And in this opinion they were confirmed by the outcome of the presidential campaign in 1852, when the Whigs, with General Winfield Scott, a hero of the Mexican war, at their head, were thoroughly routed by the Democratic candidate, General Franklin Pierce of New Hampshire. Indeed the verdict of the people was almost savage, for Pierce carried every state but four, receiving 254 out of 296 electoral votes. The Free-Soil party that branded slavery as a crime and called for its prohibition in the territories scarcely made a ripple, polling only 156,000 out of more than three million votes, a figure below the record set in the previous campaign.

With the Whigs beaten and the Free-Soilers evidently a dwindling handful of negligible critics, exultant Democrats took possession of the Executive offices and Congress, inspired by a firm belief that their tenure was secure. Having won an overwhelming victory on a definite tariff for revenue and pro-slavery program, they acted as if the party of Hamilton was for all practical purposes as powerless as the little band of abolitionist agitators. At the succeeding election in 1856 they again swept the country—this time with James Buchanan of Pennsylvania as their candidate. Though his triumph was not as magisterial as that of Pierce it was great enough to warrant a conviction that the supremacy of the Democratic party could not be broken at the polls.

During these eight years of tenure, a series of events occurred under Democratic auspices, which clinched the grasp of the planting interest upon the country and produced a correlative consolidation of the opposition. One line of development indicated an indefinite extension of the slave area; another the positive withdrawal of all government support from industrial and commercial enterprise. The first evidence of the new course came in the year immediately following the inauguration of Pierce. In 1854, Congress defiantly repealed the Missouri Compromise and threw open to slavery the vast section of the Louisiana Purchase which had been closed to it by the covenant adopted more than three decades before. On the instant came a rush of slavery champions from Missouri into Kansas determined to bring it into the southern sphere of influence. Not content with the conquest of the forbidden West, filibustering parties under pro-slavery leaders attempted to seize Cuba and Nicaragua and three American ministers abroad flung out to the world a flaming proclamation, known as the "Ostend Manifesto," which declared that the United States would be justified in wresting Cuba from Spain by force—acts of imperial aggression which even the Democratic administration in Washington felt constrained to repudiate.

Crowning the repeal of the Missouri Compromise came two decisions of the Supreme Court giving sanction to the expansion of slavery in America and assuring high protection for that peculiar institution even in the North. In the Dred Scott case decided in March, 1857, Chief Justice Taney declared in effect that the Missouri Compromise had been void from the beginning and that Congress had no power under the Constitution to prohibit slavery in the territories of the United States anywhere at any time. This legal triumph for the planting interest was followed in 1859 by another decision in which the Supreme Court upheld the fugitive slave law and all the drastic procedure provided for its enforcement. To the frightened abolitionists it seemed that only one more step was needed to make freedom unconstitutional throughout the country.

These extraordinary measures on behalf of slavery were accompanied by others that touched far more vitally economic interests in the North. In 1859, the last of the subsidies for trans-Atlantic steamship companies was ordered discontinued by Congress. In 1857, the tariff was again reduced, betraying an unmistakable drift of the nation toward free trade. In support of this action, the representatives of the South and Southwest were almost unanimous and they gathered into their fold a large number of New England congressmen on condition that no material reductions should be made in duties on cotton goods. On the other hand, the Middle States and the West offered a large majority against tariff reduction so that the division was symptomatic.

Immediately after the new revenue law went into effect an industrial panic burst upon the country, spreading distress among business men and free laborers. While that tempest was running high, the paper money anarchy let loose by the Democrats reached the acme of virulence as the notes of wildcat banks flooded the West and South and financial institutions crashed in every direction, fifty-one failing in Indiana alone within a period of five years. Since all hope of reviving Hamilton's system of finance had been buried, those who believed that a sound currency was essential to national prosperity were driven to the verge of desperation. On top of these economic calamities came Buchanan's veto of the Homestead bill which the impatient agrarians had succeeded in getting through Congress in a compromise form —an act of presidential independence which angered the farmers and mechanics who regarded the national domain as their own inheritance. . . .

The amazing acts of mastery—legislative, executive, judicial—committed by the federal government in the decade between 1850 and 1860 changed the whole political climate of America. They betrayed a growing consolidation in the planting group, its increased dominance in the Democratic party, and an evident determination to realize its economic interests and protect its labor system at all hazards. In a kind of doom, they seemed to mark the final supremacy of the political army which had swept into office with Andrew Jackson. During the thirty-two years between that event and the inauguration of Lincoln, the Democrats controlled the Presidency and the Senate for twenty-four years, the Supreme Court for twenty-six years, and the House of Representatives for twenty-two years. By the end of the period, the old farmer-labor party organized by Jackson had passed under the dominion of the planting interest and the farming wing of the North was confronted with the alternative of surrender or secession.

In this shift of power the Whigs of the South, discovering the tendencies of the popular balloting, moved steadily over into the Democratic camp. Though unavoidable, the transfer was painful; the planting Whigs, being rich and influential, had little affection for the white farmers who rallied around the Jacksonian banner. According to the estimate of a southern newspaper in 1850, the Whigs owned at least three-fourths of all the slaves in the country and it was a matter of common knowledge that leaders among them disliked wildcat banking as much as they hated high duties on the manufactured goods they bought. Indeed to a southern gentleman of the old school the radical agrarianism of Andrew Jackson was probably more odious than the tariff schedules devised by Daniel Webster. It was said that one of them, when asked whether a gentleman could be a Democrat, snapped back the tart reply: "Well, he is not apt to be; but if he is, he is in damned bad company."

But the rich planters were relatively few in numbers and virtue was subject to the law of necessity; the populace had the votes, northern manufacturers were demanding protection, abolitionists were agitating, and in the end all but the most conservative remnant of the southern Whigs had to go over to the party that professed the dangerous doctrines of Jackson. The achievements of the years that lay between 1850 and 1860 seemed to justify the sacrifice.

Though the drift toward the irrepressible conflict was steady and strong, as events revealed, the politics of the decade had the outward semblances of dissolution. The abolitionists and free-soilers, while a mere minority as we have seen, were able to worry the politicians of both parties in the North. Largely deserted by their southern cohorts, the Whigs, whose organization had always been tenuous at best, could discover no way of mustering a majority of votes on the bare economic policies of Hamilton and Webster. Their two victories—in 1840 and 1848—had been dubious and their only hope for a triumph at the polls lay in a combination with other factors. . . .

The signal for a general realignment of factions and parties was given by the passage of the Kansas-Nebraska bill of 1854 repealing the Missouri Compromise. In fact, while that measure was pending in Congress a coalescing movement was to be observed: northern Whigs persuaded that their old party was moribund, Democrats weary of planting dominance, and free-soilers eager to exclude slavery from the territories began to draw together to resist the advance of the planting power. In February of that year, a number of Whigs and Democrats assembled at Ripon, Wisconsin, and resolved that a new party must be formed if the bill passed.

When the expected event occurred, the Ripon insurgents created a fusion committee and chose the name "Republican" as the title of their young political association. In July, a Michigan convention composed of kindred elements demanded the repeal of the Kansas-Nebraska act, the repeal of the fugitive slave law, and the abolition of slavery in the District of Columbia. This convention also agreed to postpone all differences "with regard to political economy or administrative policy" and stay in the field as a "Republican" party until the struggle against slavery extension was finished. All over the country similar meetings were mustered and the local cells of the new national party rose into being. Meanwhile the old Whigs who wanted peace and prosperity were floating about looking for any drifting wreckage that might hold them above the waves. . . .

"The Government has fallen into the hands of the Slave Power completely," wrote Wendell Phillips in 1854.

So far as national politics are concerned, we are beaten—there's no hope. We shall have Cuba in a year or two, Mexico in five, and I should not wonder if efforts were made to revive the slave trade, though perhaps unsuccessfully, as the northern slave states, which live by the export of slaves, would help us in opposing that. Events hurry forward with amazing rapidity; we live fast here. The future seems to unfold a vast slave empire united with Brazil and darkening the whole West. I hope I may be a false prophet, but the sky was never so dark.

Three years later, when the inauguration of Buchanan had turned discouragement into despair, the only strategic stroke that Phillips and his colleagues could invent was to hold an abolition convention in Massachusetts and adopt a solemn slogan calling for the disruption of the Union with the slave states. And the events of the swiftly flowing months that followed, as we have already indicated, merely seemed to confirm the belief of Phillips in the supremacy of the Democratic party led by the indomitable planting interest; events such as the downward revision of the tariff, the withdrawal of the ship subsidies, and the Dred Scott decision opening the territories to slavery.

All the while the conflict was growing more furious. Advocates of protection, taking advantage of the panic which followed the tariff revision, organized a stirring campaign to wean workingmen from their allegiance to a free-trade Democracy. Advocates of a sound currency protested against the depreciated notes and the wildcat banks that spread ruin through all sections of the land. The abolitionists maintained their fusillade, Garrison and Phillips, despite their pessimism, resting neither day nor night. Going beyond the bounds of mere agitation, the slavery faction of Missouri in its grim determination to conquer Kansas for bondage and northern abolitionists in their equally firm resolve to seize it for freedom convulsed the country by bloody deeds and then by bloody reprisals. In a powerful oration, "The Crime against Kansas," done in classical style but bristling with abuse of the slavery party, Charles Sumner threw Congress into a tumult in 1856 and provided a text for the free-soilers laboring to wrest the government from the planting interest. Before the public excitement caused by this speech had died away, the attention of the nation was arrested by a series of debates between Lincoln and Douglas held in Illinois in 1858—debates which set forth in clear and logical form the program for excluding slavery from the territories and the squatter-sovereignty scheme for letting the inhabitants decide the issue for themselves.

Then came the appalling climax in 1859 when John Brown, after a stormy career in Kansas, tried to kindle a servile insurrection in the South. In the spring of that year, Brown attended an anti-slavery convention from which he went away muttering: "These men are all talk; what we need is action— action!" Collecting a few daring comrades he made a raid into Harpers Ferry for the purpose of starting a slave rebellion. Though his efforts failed, though he was quickly executed as a "traitor to Virginia," the act of violence rocked the continent from sea to sea.

In vain did the Republicans try to treat it as the mere work of a fanatic and denounce it as "among the gravest of crimes." In vain did Lincoln attempt to minimize it as an absurd adventure that resulted in nothing note-worthy except the death of Brown. It resounded through the land with the clangor of an alarm bell, aggravating the jangling nerves of a people already excited by fears of a race war and continued disturbances over the seizure of slaves under the fugitive slave act—disorders which sometimes assumed the form of menacing riots.

The turmoil in the country naturally found sharp echoes in the halls of Congress. Buchanan's policy of aiding the slavery party in its efforts to get possession of Kansas and the taunting action of the free-soilers in their de-termination to save it for liberty, gave abundant occasions for debates that grew more and more acrimonious. Indeed the factions in Congress were now almost at swords' points, passion in argument and gesture becoming the commonplace of the day.

When Senator Sumner made a vehement verbal attack on Senator Butler of South Carolina in 1856, Preston Brooks, a Representative from the same state and a relative of the latter, replied in terms of physical force, catch-ing Sumner unawares and beating his victim senseless with a heavy cane. Though the act was not strictly chivalrous—for Sumner, wedged in between his chair and his desk, could not defend himself—admiring South Carolinians gave Brooks a grand banquet and presented him with a new cane bearing the words: "Use knockdown arguments." On both sides of the Senate chamber all the arts of diplomacy were discarded, and the meanest weapons of personal abuse brought into play. Douglas called Sumner a perjurer who spat forth malignity upon his colleagues. The prim, proud Senator from Massachusetts, conscious of possessing a mellow culture, replied by likening Douglas to a "noisome, squat and nameless animal" that filled the Senate with an offensive odor.

Things were even worse in the lower house. Again and again debate was on the verge of physical combat, for which members equipped themselves with knives and revolvers. A Representative from Pennsylvania and another from North Carolina had to be put under bonds to keep the peace. A general mêlée occurred in the spring of 1860 when Lovejoy, whose brother had been shot by a pro-slavery mob in Illinois, made an unbridled attack on slave owners and Democrats, advanced to their side of the house shaking his fists in a terrible rage, and threw the whole chamber into such a confusion that all the resources of experienced leaders were needed to prevent bloodshed then and there. Without exaggeration did Jefferson Davis exclaim that members of Congress were more like the agents of belligerent states than men assembled in the interest of common welfare—an utterance that was startlingly accurate—born of prophetic certainty. After a few fleeting days, the irrepressible conflict that had so long been raging was actually to pass from the forum to the battlefield, to that court where the only argument was the sword and where the one answer that admitted of no appeal was death.

Every shocking incident on the one side only consolidated the forces on the other. By 1860 leaders of the planting interest had worked out in great detail their economic and political scheme—their ultimatum to the serried opposition—and embodied it in many official documents. The economic elements were those made familiar to the country through twenty years of agitation: no high protective tariffs, no ship subsidies, no national banking and currency system; in short, none of the measures which business enterprise deemed essential to its progress. The remaining problem before the planting interest, namely, how to clinch its grip and prevent a return to the Hamilton-Webster policy as the industrial North rapidly advanced in wealth and population, was faced with the same penchant for definition.

Plans for accomplishing that purpose were mapped out by able spokesmen from the South in a set of Senate resolutions adopted on May 24–25, 1860: slavery is lawful in all the territories under the Constitution; neither Congress nor a local legislature can abolish it there; the federal government is in duty bound to protect slave owners as well as the holders of other forms of property in the territories; it is a violation of the Constitution for any state or any combination of citizens to intermeddle with the domestic institutions of any other state "on any pretext whatever, political, moral, or religious, with a view to their disturbance or subversion"; open or covert attacks on slavery are contrary to the solemn pledges given by the states on entering the Union to protect and defend one another; the inhabitants of a territory on their admission to the Union may decide whether or not they will sanction slavery thereafter; the strict enforcement of the fugitive slave law is required by good faith and the principles of the Constitution.

In brief, the federal government was to do nothing for business enterprise while the planting interest was to be assured the possession of enough political power to guarantee it against the reënactment of the Hamilton-Webster program. Incidentally the labor system of the planting interest was not to be criticized and all runaway property was to be returned. Anything short of this was, in the view of the planting statesmen, "subversive of the Constitution."

The meaning of the ultimatum was not to be mistaken. It was a demand upon the majority of the people to surrender unconditionally for all time to the minority stockholders under the Constitution. It offered nothing to capitalism but capitulation; to the old Whigs of the South nothing but submission. Finally—and this was its revolutionary phase—it called upon the farmers and mechanics who had formed the bulk of Jacksonian Democracy in the North to acknowledge the absolute sovereignty of the planting interest. Besides driving a wedge into the nation, the conditions laid down by the planters also split the Democratic party itself into two factions.

Soon after the Democratic convention assembled at Charleston in April, 1860, this fundamental division became manifest. The northern wing, while entirely willing to indorse the general economic program of the planters, absolutely refused to guarantee them sovereignty in the party and throughout the country. Rejecting the proposal of the southern members to make slavery obligatory in the territories, it would merely offer to "abide by the decisions of the Supreme Court on all questions of constitutional law." Since the Dred Scott case had opened all the territories to slavery, that tender seemed generous enough but the intransigent representatives of the planting interest would not accept it as adequate. Unable to overcome the majority commanded in the convention by the northern group, they withdrew from the assembly, spurning the pleas of their colleagues not to break up the union of hearts on "a mere theory" and countering all arguments with a declaration of finality: "Go your way and we will go ours."

After balloting for a time on candidates without reaching a decision under the two-thirds rule, the remaining members of the Charleston conference adjourned to meet again at Baltimore. When they reassembled, they nominated Stephen A. Douglas of Illinois, the apostle of "squatter sovereignty," who was ready to open the territories to slavery but not to guarantee the planting interest unconditional supremacy in the Democratic party and the Union. Determined to pursue their separate course to the bitter end, the Charleston seceders adopted the platform rejected by the Douglas faction and chose as their candidate, John C. Breckinridge of Kentucky, an unyielding champion of planting aristocracy and its labor system. The union of farmers and slave owners was thus severed: the Republicans had carried off one large fragment of the northern farmers in 1856; Douglas was now carrying off another.

During the confusion in the Democratic ranks, the Republicans, in high glee over the quarrels of the opposition, held their convention in Chicago —a sectional gathering except for representatives from five slave states. Among its delegates the spirit of opposition to slavery extension, which had inspired the party assembly four years before, was still evident but enthusiasm on that ticklish subject was neutralized by the prudence of the practical politicians who, sniffing victory in the air, had rushed to the new tent. Whigs, whose affections were centered on Hamilton's program rather than on Garrison's scheme of salvation, were to be seen on the floor. Advocates of a high protective tariff and friends of free homesteads for mechanics and farmers now mingled with the ardent opponents of slavery in the territories. With their minds fixed on the substance of things sought for, the partisans of caution were almost able to prevent the convention from indorsing the Declaration of Independence. Still they were in favor of restricting the area of slavery; they had no love for the institution and its spread helped to fasten the grip of the planting interest on the government at Washington. So the Republican convention went on record in favor of liberty for the territories, free homesteads for farmers, a protective tariff, and a Pacific railway. As the platform was read, the cheering became especially loud and prolonged when the homestead and tariff planks were reached. Such at least is the testimony of the stenographic report.

Since this declaration of principles was well fitted to work a union of forces, it was essential that the candidate should not divide them. The protective plank would doubtless line up the good old Whigs of the East but tender consideration had to be shown to the Ohio Valley, original home of Jacksonian Democracy, where national banks, tariffs, and other "abominations" still frightened the wary. Without Ohio, Indiana, and Illinois, the Republican managers could not hope to win and they knew that the lower counties of these states were filled with settlers from the slave belt who had no love for the "money power," abolition, or anything that savored of them. In such circumstances Seward, idol of the Whig wing, was no man to offer that section; he was too radical on the slavery issue and too closely associated with "high finance" in addition. "If you do not nominate Seward, where will you get your money?" was the blunt question put by Seward's loyal supporters at Chicago. The question was pertinent but not fatal.

Given this confluence of problems, a man close to the soil of the West was better suited to the requirements of the hour than a New York lawyer with somewhat fastidious tastes, obviously backed by fat purses. The available candidate was Abraham Lincoln of Illinois. Born in Kentucky, he was of southern origin. A son of poor frontier parents, self-educated, a pioneer who in his youth had labored in field and forest, he appealed to the voters of the backwoods. Still by an uncanny genius for practical affairs, he had forged his way to the front as a shrewd lawyer and politician. In his debates with Douglas he had shown himself able to cope with one of the foremost leaders in the Democratic party. On the tariff, bank, currency, and homestead issues he was sound. A local railway attorney, he was trusted among business men.

On the slavery question Lincoln's attitude was firm but conservative. He disliked slavery and frankly said so; yet he was not an abolitionist and he saw no way in which the institution could be uprooted. On the contrary, he favored enforcing the fugitive slave law and he was not prepared to urge even the abolition of slavery in the District of Columbia. His declaration that a house divided against itself could not stand had been counterbalanced by an assertion that the country would become all free or all slave—a creed which any southern planter could have indorsed. Seward's radical doctrine that there was a "higher law" than the Constitution, dedicating the territories to freedom, received from the Illinois lawyer disapproval, not commendation.

Nevertheless Lincoln was definite and positive in his opinion that slavery should not be permitted in the territories. That was necessary to satisfy the minimum demands of the anti-slavery faction and incidentally it pleased those Whigs of the North who at last realized that no Hamiltonian program could be pushed through Congress if the planting interest secured a supremacy, or indeed held an equal share of power, in the Union. Evidently Lincoln was the man of the hour: his heritage was correct, his principles were sound, his sincerity was unquestioned, and his ability as a speaker commanded the minds and hearts of his auditors. He sent word to his friends at Chicago that, although he did not indorse Seward's higher-law doctrine, he agreed with him on the irrepressible conflict. The next day Lincoln was nominated amid huzzas from ten thousand lusty throats.

A large fraction of Whigs and some fragments of the Know Nothing, or American, party, foreseeing calamity in the existing array of interests, tried to save the day by an appeal to lofty sentiments without any definitions. Assuming the name of Constitutional Unionists and boasting that they represented the "intelligence and respectability of the South" as well as the lovers of the national idea everywhere, they held a convention at Baltimore and nominated John Bell of Tennessee and Edward Everett of Massachusetts for President and Vice-President. In the platform they invited their countrymen to forget all divisions and "support the Constitution of the country, the union of the states, and the enforcement of the laws." It was an overture of old men— men who had known and loved Webster and Clay and who shrank with horror from agitations that threatened to end in bloodshed and revolution —a plea for the maintenance of the status quo against the whims of a swiftly changing world.

A spirited campaign followed the nomination of these four candidates for the presidency on four different platforms. Huge campaign funds were raised and spent. Beside pursuing the usual strategy of education, the Republicans resorted to parades and the other spectacular features that had distinguished the log-cabin crusade of General Harrison's year. Emulating the discretion of the Hero of Tippecanoe, Lincoln maintained a judicious silence at Springfield while his champions waged his battles for him, naturally tempering their orations to the requirements of diverse interests. They were fully conscious, as a Republican paper in Philadelphia put it, that "Frémont had tried running on the slavery issue and lost." So while they laid stress on it in many sections, they widened their appeal.

In the West, a particular emphasis was placed on free homesteads and the Pacific railway. With a keen eye for competent strategy, Carl Schurz carried the campaign into Missouri where he protested with eloquence against the action of the slave power in denying "the laboring man the right to acquire property in the soil by his labor" and made a special plea for the German vote on the ground that the free land was to be opened to aliens who declared their intention of becoming American citizens. Discovering that the homestead question was "the greatest issue in the West," Horace Greeley used it to win votes in the East. Agrarians and labor reformers renewed the slogan: "Vote yourself a farm."

In Pennsylvania and New Jersey, protection for iron and steel was the great subject of discussion. Curtin, the Republican candidate for governor in the former state, said not a word about abolishing slavery in his ratification speech but spoke with feeling on "the vast heavings of the heart of Pennsylvania whose sons are pining for protection to their labor and their dearest interests." Warming to his theme, he exclaimed: "This is a contest involving protection and the rights of labor. . . . If you desire to become vast and great, protect the manufactures of Philadelphia. . . . All hail, liberty! All hail, freedom! Freedom to the white man! All hail freedom general as the air we breathe!" In a fashion after Curtin's own heart, the editor of the Philadelphia *American* and *Gazette*, surveying the canvass at the finish, repudiated the idea that "any sectional aspect of the slavery question" was up for decision and declared that the great issues were protection for industry, "economy in the conduct of the government, homesteads for settlers on the public domain, retrenchment and accountability in the public expenditures, appropriation for rivers and harbors, a Pacific railroad, the admission of Kansas, and a radical reform in the government."

With a kindred appreciation of practical matters, Seward bore the standard through the North and West. Fully conversant with the Webster policy of commercial expansion in the Pacific and knowing well the political appeal of Manifest Destiny, he proclaimed the future of the American empire —assuring his auditors that in due time American outposts would be pushed along the northwest coast to the Arctic Ocean, that Canada would be gathered into our glorious Union, that the Latin-American republics reorganized under our benign influence would become parts of this magnificent confederation, that the ancient Aztec metropolis, Mexico City, would eventually become the capital of the United States, and that America and Russia, breaking their old friendship, would come to grips in the Far East—"in regions where civilization first began." All this was involved in the election of Lincoln and the triumph of the Republican party. Webster and Cushing and Perry had not wrought in vain.

The three candidates opposed to Lincoln scored points wherever they could. Douglas took the stump with his usual vigor and declaimed to throngs in nearly every state. Orators of the Breckinridge camp, believing that their extreme views were sound everywhere, invaded the North. Bell's champions spoke with dignity and warmth about the dangers inherent in all unwise departures from the past, about the perils of the sectional quarrel. When at length the ballots were cast and counted, it was found that the foes of slavery agitation had carried the country by an overwhelming majority. Their combined vote was a million ahead of Lincoln's total; the two Democratic factions alone, to say nothing of Bell's six hundred thousand followers, outnumbered the Republican army. But in the division and uproar of the campaign Lincoln, even so, had won the Presidency; he was the choice of a minority—a sectional minority at that—but under the terms of the Constitution, he was entitled to the scepter at Washington.

From what has just been said it must be apparent that the forces which produced the irrepressible conflict were very complex in nature and yet the momentous struggle has been so often reduced by historians to simple terms that a re-examination of the traditional thesis has become one of the tasks of the modern age. On the part of northern writers it was long the fashion to declare that slavery was the cause of the conflict between the states. Such for example was the position taken by James Ford Rhodes and made the starting point of his monumental work.

Assuming for the moment that this assertion is correct in a general sense, it will be easily observed even on a superficial investigation that "slavery" was no simple, isolated phenomenon. In itself it was intricate and it had filaments through the whole body economic. It was a labor system, the basis of planting, and the foundation of the southern aristocracy. That aristocracy, in turn, owing to the nature of its economic operations, resorted to public policies that were opposed to capitalism, sought to dominate the federal government, and, with the help of free farmers also engaged in agriculture, did at last dominate it. In the course of that political conquest, all the plans of commerce and industry for federal protection and subvention were overborne. It took more than a finite eye to discern where slavery as an ethical question left off and economics—the struggle over the distribution of wealth—began.

On the other hand, the early historians of the southern school, chagrined by defeat and compelled to face the adverse judgment of brutal fact, made the "rights of states"—something nobler than economics or the enslavement of Negroes—the issue for which the Confederacy fought and bled. That too like slavery seems simple until subjected to a little scrutiny. What is a state? At bottom it is a majority or perhaps a mere plurality of persons engaged in the quest of something supposed to be beneficial, or at all events not injurious, to the pursuers. And what are rights? Abstract, intangible moral values having neither substance nor form? The party debates over the economic issues of the middle period answer with an emphatic negative. If the southern planters had been content to grant tariffs, bounties, subsidies, and preferences to northern commerce and industry, it is not probable that they would have been molested in their most imperious proclamations of sovereignty.

But their theories and their acts involved interests more ponderable than political rhetoric. They threatened the country with secession first in defying the tariff of abominations and when they did secede thirty years later it was in response to the victory of a tariff and homestead party that proposed nothing more dangerous to slavery itself than the mere exclusion of the institution from the territories. It took more than a finite eye to discern where their opposition to the economic system of Hamilton left off and their affection for the rights of states began. The modern reader tossed about in a contrariety of opinions can only take his bearings by examining a few indubitable realities.

With reference to the popular northern view of the conflict, there stands the stubborn fact that at no time during the long gathering of the storm did Garrison's abolition creed rise to the dignity of a first-rate political issue in the North. Nobody but agitators, beneath the contempt of the towering statesmen of the age, ever dared to advocate it. No great political organization even gave it the most casual indorsement.

When the abolitionists launched the Liberty party in the campaign of 1844 to work for emancipation, as we have noted, the voters answered their plea for "the restoration of equality of political rights among men" in a manner that demonstrated the invincible opposition of the American people. Out of more than two and a half million ballots cast in the election, only sixty-five thousand were recorded in favor of the Liberty candidate. That was America's answer to the call for abolition; and the advocates of that policy never again ventured to appeal to the electorate by presenting candidates on such a radical platform.

No other party organized between that time and the clash of arms attempted to do more than demand the exclusion of slavery from the territories and not until the Democrats by repealing the Missouri Compromise threatened to extend slavery throughout the West did any party poll more than a handful of votes on that issue. It is true that Van Buren on a free-soil platform received nearly three hundred thousand votes in 1848 but that was evidently due to personal influence, because his successor on a similar ticket four years afterward dropped into an insignificant place.

Even the Republican party, in the campaign of 1856, coming hard on the act of defiance which swept away the Missouri compact, won little more than one-third the active voters to the cause of restricting the slavery area. When transformed after four more years into a homestead and high tariff party pledged merely to liberty in the territories, the Republicans polled a million votes fewer than the number cast for the opposing factions and rode into power on account of the divided ranks of the enemy. Such was the nation's reply to the anti-slavery agitation from the beginning of the disturbance until the cannon shot at Sumter opened a revolution.

Moreover not a single responsible statesman of the middle period committed himself to the doctrine of immediate and unconditional abolition to be achieved by independent political action. John Quincy Adams, ousted from the Presidency by Jacksonian Democracy but returned to Washington as the Representative of a Massachusetts district in Congress, did declare that it was the duty of every free American to work directly for the abolition of slavery and with uncanny vision foresaw that the knot might be cut with the sword. But Adams was regarded by astute party managers as a foolish and embittered old man and his prophecy as a dangerous delusion.

Practical politicians who felt the iron hand of the planters at Washington—politicians who saw how deeply intertwined with the whole economic order the institution of slavery really was—could discover nothing tangible in immediate and unconditional abolition that appealed to reason or came within the range of common sense. Lincoln was emphatic in assuring the slaveholders that no Republican had ever been detected in any attempt to disturb them. "We must not interfere with the institution of slavery in the states where it exists," he urged, "because the Constitution forbids it and the general welfare does not require us to do so."

Since, therefore, the abolition of slavery never appeared in the platform of any great political party, since the only appeal ever made to the electorate on that issue was scornfully repulsed, since the spokesman of the Republicans emphatically declared that his party never intended to interfere with slavery in the states in any shape or form, it seems reasonable to assume that the institution of slavery was not the fundamental issue during the epoch preceding the bombardment of Fort Sumter.

Nor can it be truthfully said, as southern writers were fond of having it, that a tender and consistent regard for the rights of states and for a strict construction of the Constitution was the prime element in the dispute that long divided the country. As a matter of record, from the foundation of the republic, all factions were for high nationalism or low provincialism upon occasion according to their desires at the moment, according to turns in the balance of power. New England nullified federal law when her commerce was affected by the War of 1812 and came out stanchly for liberty and union, one and inseparable, now and forever, in 1833 when South Carolina attempted to nullify a tariff act. Not long afterward, the legislature of Massachusetts, dreading the overweening strength of the Southwest, protested warmly against the annexation of Texas and resolved that "such an act of admission would have no binding force whatever on the people of Massachusetts."

Equally willing to bend theory to practical considerations, the party of the slavocracy argued that the Constitution was to be strictly and narrowly construed whenever tariff and bank measures were up for debate; but no such piddling concept of the grand document was to be held when a bill providing for the prompt and efficient return of fugitive slaves was on the carpet. Less than twenty years after South Carolina prepared to resist by arms federal officers engaged in collecting customs duties, the champions of slavery and states' rights greeted with applause a fugitive slave law which flouted the precious limitations prescribed in the first ten Amendments to the Constitution—a law which provided for the use of all the powers of the national government to assist masters in getting possession of their elusive property —which denied to the alleged slave, who might perchance be a freeman in spite of his color, the right to have a jury trial or even to testify in his own behalf. In other words, it was "constitutional" to employ the engines of the federal authority in catching slaves wherever they might be found in any northern community and to ignore utterly the elementary safeguards of liberty plainly and specifically imposed on Congress by language that admitted of no double interpretation.

On this very issue of personal liberty, historic positions on states' rights were again reversed. Following the example of South Carolina on the tariff, Wisconsin resisted the fugitive slave law as an invasion of her reserved rights —as a violation of the Constitution. Alarmed by this action, Chief Justice Taney answered the disobedient state in a ringing judicial decision announcing a high nationalism that would have delighted the heart of John Marshall, informing the recalcitrant Wisconsin that the Constitution and laws enacted under it were supreme; that the fugitive slave law was fully authorized by the Constitution; and that the Supreme Court was the final arbiter in all controversies over the respective powers of the states and the United States. "If such an arbiter had not been provided in our complicated system of government, internal tranquility could not have been preserved and if such controversies were left to the arbitrament of physical force, our Government, State and National, would cease to be a government of laws, and revolution by force of arms would take the place of courts of justice and judicial decisions." No nullification here; no right of a state to judge for itself respecting infractions of the Constitution by the federal government; federal law is binding everywhere and the Supreme Court, a branch of the national government, is the final judge.

And in what language did Wisconsin reply? The legislature of the state, in a solemn resolution, declared that the decision of the Supreme Court of the United States in the case in question was in direct conflict with the Constitution. It vowed that the essential principles of the Kentucky doctrine of nullification were sound. Then it closed with the rebel fling: "that the several states . . . being sovereign and independent, have the unquestionable right to judge of its [the Constitution's] infraction and that a positive defiance by those sovereignties of all unauthorized acts done or attempted to be done under color of that instrument is the rightful remedy."

That was in 1859. Within two years, men who had voted for that resolution and cheered its adoption were marching off in martial array to vindicate on southern battlefields the supremacy of the Union and the sovereignty of the nation. By that fateful hour the southern politicians who had applauded Taney's declaration that the Supreme Court was the final arbiter in controversies between the states and the national government had come to the solemn conclusion that the states themselves were the arbiters. Such words and events being facts, there can be but one judgment in the court of history; namely, that major premises respecting the nature of the Constitution and deductions made logically from them with masterly eloquence were minor factors in the grand dispute as compared with the interests, desires, and passions that lay deep in the hearts and minds of the contestants.

Indeed, honorable men who held diametrically opposite views found warrant for each in the Constitution. All parties and all individuals, save the extreme abolitionists, protested in an unbroken chant their devotion to the national covenant and to the principles and memory of the inspired men who framed it. As the Bible was sometimes taken as a guide for theologians traveling in opposite directions, so the Constitution was the beacon that lighted the way of statesmen who differed utterly on the issues of the middle period. . . .

When the modern student examines all the verbal disputes over the nature of the Union—the arguments employed by the parties which operated and opposed the federal government between the adoption of the Constitution and the opening of the Civil War—he can hardly do otherwise than conclude that the linguistic devices used first on one side and then on the other were not derived from inherently necessary concepts concerning the intimate essence of the federal system. The roots of the controversy lay elsewhere—in social groupings founded on differences in climate, soil, industries, and labor systems, in divergent social forces, rather than varying degrees of righteousness and wisdom, or what romantic historians call "the magnetism of great personalities."

In the spring of 1861 the full force of the irrepressible conflict burst upon the hesitant and bewildered nation and for four long years the clash of arms filled the land with its brazen clangor. For four long years the anguish, the calamities, and the shocks of the struggle absorbed the energies of the multitudes, blared in the headlines of the newspapers, and loomed impressively in the minds of the men and women who lived and suffered in that age.

Naturally, therefore, all who wrote of the conflict used the terms of war. In its records, the government of the United States officially referred to the contest as the War of the Rebellion, thus by implication setting the stigma of treason on those who served under the Stars and Bars. Repudiating this brand and taking for his shield the righteousness of legitimacy, one of the leading southern statesmen, Alexander H. Stephens, in his great history of the conflict, called it the War between the States. This, too, no less than the title chosen by the federal government, is open to objections; apart from the large assumptions involved, it is not strictly accurate for, in the border states, the armed struggle was a guerrilla war and in Virginia the domestic strife ended in the separation of several counties, under the aegis of a new state constitution, as West Virginia. More recently a distinguished historian, Edward Channing, entitled a volume dealing with the period The War for Southern Independence—a characterization which, though fairly precise, suffers a little perhaps from abstraction.

As a matter of fact all these symbols are misleading in that they overemphasize the element of military force in the grand denouement. War there was unquestionably, immense, wide-sweeping, indubitable, as Carlyle would say. For years the agony of it hung like a pall over the land. And yet with strange swiftness the cloud was lifted and blown away. Merciful grass spread its green mantle over the cruel scars and the gleaming red splotches sank into the hospitable earth.

It was then that the economist and lawyer, looking more calmly on the scene, discovered that the armed conflict had been only one phase of the cataclysm, a transitory phase; that at bottom the so-called Civil War, or the War between the States, in the light of Roman analogy, was a social war, ending in the unquestioned establishment of a new power in the government, making vast changes in the arrangement of classes, in the accumulation and distribution of wealth, in the course of industrial development, and in the Constitution inherited from the Fathers. Merely by the accidents of climate, soil, and geography was it a sectional struggle. If the planting interest had been scattered evenly throughout the industrial region, had there been a horizontal rather than a perpendicular cleavage, the irrepressible conflict would have been resolved by other methods and accompanied by other logical defense mechanisms.

In any event neither accident nor rhetoric should be allowed to obscure the intrinsic character of that struggle. If the operations by which the middle classes of England broke the power of the king and the aristocracy are to be known collectively as the Puritan Revolution, if the series of acts by which the bourgeois and peasants of France overthrew the king, nobility, and clergy is to be called the French Revolution, then accuracy compels us to character-ize by the same term the social cataclysm in which the capitalists, laborers, and farmers of the North and West drove from power in the national govern-ment the planting aristocracy of the South. Viewed under the light of universal history, the fighting was a fleeting incident; the social revolution was the essential, portentous outcome.

To be sure the battles and campaigns of the epoch are significant to the military strategist; the tragedy and heroism of the contest furnish inspiration to patriots and romance to the makers of epics. But the core of the vortex lay elsewhere. It was in the flowing substance of things limned by statistical reports on finance, commerce, capital, industry, railways, and agriculture, by provisions of constitutional law, and by the pages of statute books—prosaic muniments which show that the so-called civil war was in reality a Second American Revolution and in a strict sense, the First. . . .

Eric Foner

Slavery and the
Republican Ideology

I

"Of the American Civil War," James Ford Rhodes wrote over a half a century ago, "it may safely be asserted that there was a single cause, slavery." In this opinion, Rhodes was merely echoing a view which seemed self-evident to Abraham Lincoln and many other participants in the sectional conflict. Their interpretation implicitly assumes that the ante-bellum Republican party was primarily a vehicle for anti-slavery sentiment. Yet partly because historians are skeptical of explanations made by participants of their own behavior, Rhodes' view quickly fell under attack. Even before Rhodes wrote, John R. Commons had characterized the Republicans as primarily a homestead party, and Charles and Mary Beard later added the tariff as one of its fundamental concerns. More recently, historians have stressed aversion to the presence of blacks—free or slave—in the western territories as the Republicans' motive for opposing the extension of slavery. Because the Republicans disavowed the intention of attacking slavery in states where it already existed by direct federal action, their anti-slavery declarations have been dismissed by some historians as hypocritical. And recently, a political analyst, not a professional historian, revealed how commonplace a cynical attitude toward the early Republican party has become when he wrote: "The Republican Party succeeded by soft-pedalling the issue of slavery altogether and concentrating on economic issues which would attract Northern businessmen and Western farmers."

From Free Soil, Free Labor, Free Men: The Ideology of the Republican Party Before the Civil War, by Eric Foner. Copyright © 1970 by Eric Foner. Reprinted by permission of Oxford University Press, Inc.

Controversy over the proper place of anti-slavery in the Republican ideology is hardly new. During the 1850's, considerable debate occurred within abolitionist circles on the proper attitude toward Republicanism. In part, this was simply an extension of the traditional schism between political and non-political abolitionists, and it is not surprising that William Lloyd Garrison and his followers should have wasted little enthusiasm on the Republicans. Yet many abolitionists who had no objection on principle to political involvements considered the anti-slavery commitment of the Republican party insufficient to merit their support. Gerrit Smith and William Goodell, for example, who had been instrumental in organizing the Liberty party in New York State, declared that they could not support a party which recognized the constitutionality of slavery anywhere in the Union. The Republican party, Smith charged, "refuses to oppose slavery where it is, and opposes it only where it is not," and he continuously urged radicals like Chase and Giddings to take an abolitionist stance. Theodore Parker made the same criticism. When Chase declared in the Senate that the federal government would not interfere with slavery in the states, Parker wrote that while he did not object to attacking slavery one step at a time, he "would not promise *not to take other steps.*"

Yet it is important to remember that despite their criticisms of the Republican party, leading abolitionists maintained close personal relations with Republican leaders, particularly the radicals. The flow of letters between Chase and Smith, cordial even while each criticized the attitude of the other, is one example of this. Similarly, Parker kept up a correspondence with Henry Wilson, Charles Sumner, and William Seward as well as Chase. And he and Wendell Phillips, both experts at the art of political agitation, recognized the complex interrelationship between abolitionist attempts to create a public sentiment hostile to slavery, and the political anti-slavery espoused by Republicans. "Our agitation, you know, helps keep yours alive in the rank and file," was the way Wendell Phillips expressed it to Sumner. And Seward agreed that the abolitionists played a vital role in awakening the public conscience—"open[ing] the way where the masses can follow." For their part, abolitionists like Theodore Parker were happy to borrow statistics and arguments from the anti-slavery speeches of politicians.

The evidence strongly suggests that outside of Garrison's immediate circle, most abolitionists voted with the Republican party despite their wish that the party adopt a more aggressive anti-slavery position. Indeed, abolitionist societies experienced financial difficulties in the late 1850's, as former contributors began giving their money to the Republicans. Even Gerrit Smith, who insisted he could "never vote for any person who recognizes a law for slavery," contributed five hundred dollars to the Frémont campaign. The attitude of many abolitionists was summed up by Elizur Wright, a proponent of Smith and Goodell's brand of political anti-slavery who nonetheless voted for Lincoln in 1860. While Wright criticized the Republicans for their shortcomings on slavery, he acknowledged that "the greatest recommendation of the Republican Party is, that its enemies do not quite believe its disclaimers, while they do believe that [it is] sincerely opposed to slavery as far as it goes." Prophetically, he added: "Woe to the slave power under a Republican President if it strikes the first blow."

The fact that so many abolitionists, not to mention radical Republicans, supported the Republican party, is an indication that anti-slavery formed no small part of the Republican ideology. Recent historians have concluded, moreover, that writers like Beard greatly overestimated the importance of economic issues in the elections of 1856, 1858, and 1860. We have already seen how tentative was the Republican commitment to the tariff. As for the homestead issue, Don E. Fehrenbacher has pointed out that the Republicans carried most of the Northwest in 1856 when free land was not a political issue, and that in 1860, Douglas Democrats supported the measure as ardently as Republicans. More important, it would have been suicidal for the Republicans to have put their emphasis on economic policies, particularly the neo-Whiggism described by Beard. If one thing is evident after analyzing the various elements which made up the party, it is that anti-slavery was one of the few policies which united all Republican factions. For political reasons, if for no other, the Republicans were virtually obliged to make anti-slavery the main focus of their political appeal. Such questions as the tariff, nativism, and race were too divisive to be stressed, while the homestead issue could be advanced precisely because it was so non-controversial in the North.

Conservative Republicans and radicals, ex-Democrats and former Whigs, all agreed that slavery was the major issue of the 1850's. It was not surprising that Giddings should insist that "there is but one real issue between the Republican party and those factions that stand opposed to it. That is the question of slavery," or that Salmon P. Chase should declare that the election of 1860 had not turned on "subordinate questions of local and temporary character," but had vindicated the principle of "the restriction of slavery within State limits." But Orville H. Browning, as conservative as Giddings and Chase were radical, appraised the politics of 1860 in much the same way. "It is manifest to all," he declared, "that there is an unusual degree of political interest pervading the country—that the people, everywhere, are excited, . . . and yet, from one extremity of the Republic to the other, scarcely any other subject is mentioned, or any other question discussed . . . save the question of negro slavery. . . ." Ex-Democrats in the Republican party fully agreed. Both Francis Spinner and Preston King rejected suggestions that Democratic economic policies be engrafted onto the Republican platform, on the ground that these must await settlement until the slavery issue had been decided. As Spinner tersely put it, "Statesmen cannot make issues for the people. As live men we must take the issues as they present themselves." The potency of the slavery issue, and the way in which it subordinated or absorbed all other political questions, was noted by the anti-Lecompton Democrat from New York, Horace Clark, on the eve of the 1860 campaign:

It is not to be controverted that the slavery agitation is not at rest. It has absorbed and destroyed our national politics. It has overrun State politics. It has even invaded our municipalities; and now, in some form or other, everywhere controls the elections of the people.

In a recent study of Civil War historiography, Roy F. Nichols observed that we still do not know whether either section had reached its own consensus on major issues by 1861. Some historians have interpreted the strong showing of Stephen A. Douglas in the free states as proof that a substantial portion of the electorate rejected the Republican brand of anti-slavery. Though there is some truth in this view, it is important to remember that by 1860 the Douglas Democrats shared a good many of the Republicans' attitudes toward the South. One of the most striking aspects of the Democratic debate over the Lecompton constitution was the way in which the Douglasites echoed so many of the anti-southern views which anti-Nebraska Democrats had expressed only a few years earlier. There is a supreme irony in the fact that the same methods which Douglas had used against dissident Democrats in 1854 were now turned against him and his supporters. Buchanan applied the patronage whip ruthlessly, and anti-Lecompton Democrats complained that a new, pro-slavery test had suddenly been imposed upon the party. And like the anti-Nebraska Democrats, who were now members of the Republican party, the Douglasites insisted that they commanded the support of most northern Democrats. Historians have tended to agree with them. Roy Nichols suggests that the enthusiasm Douglas's anti-southern stand aroused among rank and file Democrats was one reason why he refused to accept the compromise English bill to settle the Lecompton controversy, and recent students of Pennsylvania and Indiana politics agree that the vast majority of the Democrats in those states favored Douglas against the administration.

The bitterness of Douglas Democrats against the South did not abate between 1858 and 1860. They believed that the South had embarked upon a crusade to force slavery into all the territories, and protested that endorsement of such a goal would destroy the northern Democracy. "We have confided in their honor, their love of justice, their detestation of what is wrong," Henry Payne, a prominent Ohio Democrat, said of his southern colleagues in 1858, "but we can do it no more." And many Republicans believed that, even if Douglas made his peace with the Democratic organization, many of his followers had acquired "a feeling against Slavery and its arrogant demands which if cherished will prevent their going back. . . ." A few Democrats did defect to the Republican party in 1858, 1859, and 1860, including a former chairman of the Iowa Democrats, several anti-Lecompton Congressmen, and F. P. Stanton, the former Democratic governor of Kansas. That there were not more defections largely reflected the continuation into 1860 of Douglas's contest with the administration, which increasingly took on what one historian calls "a semi-free-soil" tone. And when the 1860 Democratic national convention broke up over the South's insistence on a platform guaranteeing slavery in the territories, the bitterness of the Douglasites knew no bounds. The reporter Murat Halstead observed that he had "never heard Abolitionists talk more rancorously of the people of the South than the Douglas men here." For their part, southerners insisted they would not accept popular sovereignty since this would be as effective as the Wilmot Proviso in barring slavery from the territories.

There were, of course, many important differences between the Douglasites and Republicans. Douglas still insisted in 1860 that the slavery question was not important enough to risk the disruption of the Union, he was much more inclined to use racism as a political weapon, and, as one Republican newspaper put it, in words echoed by several recent scholars, Douglas "does not recognize the moral element in politics. . . ." Yet in their devotion to the Union and their bitter opposition to southern domination of the government, Republicans and Douglasites stood close together in 1860. There was much truth in the observation of one Republican that "the rupture between the northern and southern wing of the democracy, is permanent with the masses . . . ," and the experiences of the Douglas Democrats in the years preceding the Civil War go a long way toward explaining the unanimity of the North's response to the attack on Fort Sumter.

II

The attitude of the Douglasites toward the South on the eve of the Civil War partially reflected their assessment of northern opinion regarding slavery. Politicians of all parties agreed that northerners opposed slavery as an abstract principle, although they disagreed on the intensity of this sentiment. John C. Calhoun had estimated in 1847 that while only 5 percent of northerners supported the abolitionists, more than 66 percent viewed slavery as an evil, and were willing to oppose its extension constitutionally. Similarly, a conservative Republican declared in 1858, "There is no man [in the North] who is an advocate of slavery. There is no man from that section of the country who will go before his constituents and advocate the extension of slavery." Northern Democrats had the same perception of northern sentiments. Even the Hunkers of New York, who consistently opposed the Wilmot Proviso, refused to say "that they are not opposed to slavery." For as William L. Marcy declared in 1849, "In truth we all are."

Anti-slavery as an abstract feeling had long existed in the North. It had not, however, prevented abolitionists from being mobbed, nor anti-slavery parties from going down to defeat. Democrats and Whigs had long been able to appeal to devotion to the Union, racism, and economic issues, to neutralize anti-slavery as a political force. "The anti-slavery sentiment," Hamilton Fish explained in 1854, "is inborn, and almost universal at the North . . . but it is only as a *sentiment* that it generally pervades; it has not and cannot be inspired with the activity that even a very slight interest excites." But Fish failed to foresee the fundamental achievement of the Republican party before the Civil War: the creation and articulation of an ideology which blended personal and sectional interest with morality so perfectly that it became the most potent political force in the nation. The free labor assault upon slavery and southern society, coupled with the idea that an aggressive Slave Power was threatening the most fundamental values and interests of the free states, hammered the slavery issue home to the northern public more emphatically than an appeal to morality alone could ever have done.

To agree with Rhodes that slavery was ultimately the cause of the Civil War, therefore, is not to accept the corollary that the basis of the Republican opposition to slavery was simple moral fervor. In a speech to the Senate in 1848, John M. Niles listed a dozen different reasons for his support of the Wilmot Proviso—but only once did he mention his belief that slavery was morally repugnant. And thirteen years later, George William Curtis observed that "there is very little moral mixture in the 'Anti-Slavery' feeling of this country. A great deal is abstract philanthropy; part is hatred of slaveholders; a great part is jealousy for white labor, very little is consciousness of wrong done and the wish to right it." The Republican ideology included all these elements, and much more. Rhodes argued that northerners wished to preserve the Union as a first step toward abolition. A more accurate formulation would reverse the equation and say that many Republicans were anti-slavery from the conviction that slavery threatened the Union. Aside from some radicals, who occasionally flirted with disunion, most Republicans were united by the twin principles of free soil and Unionism. Cassius M. Clay even suggested that the Free-Soilers in 1851 adopt the name "Liberty and Union" party, in order to impress their essential goals upon the electorate. The New York *Times* emphasized this aspect of Republican thought in 1857: "The barbaric institution of slavery will become more and more odious to the northern people because it will become more and more plain . . . that the States which cling to Slavery thrust back the American idea, and reject the influences of the Union."

Still, Unionism, despite its importance to the mass of northerners, and obviously crucial to any explanation of the Republicans' decision to resist secession, was only one aspect of the Republican ideology. It would have been just as logical to compromise on the slavery question if the preservation of the Union were the paramount goal of Republican politics. Nor should Republicanism be seen merely as the expression of the northern drive toward political power. We have seen, to be sure, that resentment of southern power played its part, that many Democratic-Republicans had watched with growing jealousy the South's domination of the Democratic party and the national government, and that many former Whigs were convinced that the South was blocking economic programs essential for national economic development.

But there is more to the coming of the Civil War than the rivalry of sections for political power. (New England, after all, could accept its own decline in political power without secession.)

In short, none of these elements can stand separately; they dissolve into one another, and the total product emerges as ideology. Resentment of southern political power, devotion to the Union, anti-slavery based upon the free labor argument, moral revulsion to the peculiar institution, racial prejudice, a commitment to the northern social order and its development and expansion—all these elements were intertwined in the Republican world-view. What they added up to was the conviction that North and South represented two social systems whose values, interests, and future prospects were in sharp, perhaps mortal, conflict with one another. The sense of difference, of estrangement, and of growing hostility with which Republicans viewed the South, cannot be overemphasized. Theodore Sedgwick of New York perhaps expressed it best when he declared during the secession crisis: "The policy and aims of slavery, its institutions and civilization, and the character of its people, are all at variance with the policy, aims, institutions, education, and character of the North. There is an irreconcilable difference in our interests, institutions, and pursuits; in our sentiments and feelings." Greeley's *Tribune* said the same thing more succinctly: "We are not one people. We are two peoples. We are a people for Freedom and a people for Slavery. Between the two, conflict is inevitable." An attack not simply on the institution of slavery, but upon southern society itself, was thus at the heart of the Republican mentality. Of all historians, I think Avery Craven caught this feature best: "By 1860, slavery had become the symbol and carrier of *all* sectional differences and conflicts." Here and elsewhere, Craven describes the symbolic nature of the slavery controversy, reflected as it was in the widespread acceptance among Republicans of the Slave Power idea—a metaphor for all the fears and resentments they harbored toward the South. But Craven did leave out something crucial. Slavery was not only the symbol, but also the real basis of sectional conflict, for it was the foundation of the South's economy, social structure, aspirations, and ideology.

"Why do we Meddle with Slavery?" the New York *Times* asked in an 1857 editorial. The answer gives us a penetrating insight into the Republican mind on the eve of Civil War:

The great States of the North are not peopled exclusively by quidnuncs and agitators. . . . Nevertheless, we do give ourselves great and increasing concern about the existence of Slavery in States over whose internal economy we have no right and no wish to exercise any control whatever. Nevertheless, we do feel, and the feeling is growing deeper in the northern heart with every passing year, that our character, our prosperity, and our destiny are most seriously involved in the question of the perpetuation or extinction of slavery in those States.

What is striking about this statement is a concern directed not only against the extension of slavery, but against its very existence. Lincoln put the same concern even more succinctly to a Chicago audience in 1859, "Never forget," he said, "that we have before us this whole matter of the right or wrong of slavery in this Union, though the immediate question is as to its spreading out into new Territories and States."

Lincoln and the editors of the *Times* thus made explicit that there was more to the contest over the extension of slavery than whether the institution should spread to the West. As Don E. Fehrenbacher puts it, the territorial question was the "skirmish line of a more extensive struggle." Only by a comprehension of this total conflict between North and South, between Republican and southern ideologies, can the meaning of the territorial issue be fully grasped. Its importance went even beyond the belief shared widely in both sections that slavery required expansion to survive, and that confinement to the states where it already existed would kill it. For in each ideology was the conviction that its own social system must expand, not only to insure its own survival but to prevent the expansion of all the evils the other represented. We have already seen how Republicans believed that free society, with its promise of social mobility for the laborer, required territorial expansion, and how this was combined with a messianic desire to spread the benefits of free society to other areas and peoples. Southerners had their own grandiose design. "They had a magnificent dream of empire," a Republican recalled after the war, and such recent writers as C. Stanley Urban and Eugene Genovese have emphasized how essential expansionism was in the southern ideology. The struggle for the West represented a contest between two expansive societies, only one of whose aspirations could prevail. The conflict was epitomized by two statements which appeared in the Philadelphia *North American* in 1856. Slavery, the *North American* argued, could not be allowed to expand, because it would bring upon the West "a blight whose fatal influence will be felt for centuries." Two weeks later the same paper quoted a southern journal, which, in urging slavery expansionism, used precisely this logic in reverse. Such expansion, the southern paper argued, would "forbid the extension of the evils of free society to new people and coming generations."

Here then was a basic reason why the South could not accept the verdict of 1860. In 1848, Martin Van Buren had said that the South opposed the principle of free soil because "the prohibition carries with it a reproach to the slaveholding states, and . . . submission to it would degrade them." Eight years later, the Richmond *Enquirer* explained that for the South to abandon the idea of extending slavery while accepting Republican assurances of noninterference in the states would be "pregnant with the admission that slavery is wrong, and but for the constitution should be abolished." To agree to the containment of slavery, the South would have had to abandon its whole ideology, which had come to view the institution as a positive good, the basis of an enlightened form of social organization.

III

Although it has not been the purpose of this study to examine in any detailed way the southern mind in 1860, what has been said about the Republican ideology does help to explain the rationale for secession. The political wars of the 1850's, centering on the issue of slavery extension, had done much to erode whatever good feeling existed between the sections. The abolitionist Elihu Burrit suggested in 1857 that a foreigner observing American politics would probably conclude "that the North and South were wholly occupied in gloating upon each others' faults and failings." During the 1856 campaign, Burrit went on, sectional antagonisms had been brought "to a pitch of rancor, never reached before" in American politics. This was precisely the reason that Union-loving conservatives like Hamilton Fish dreaded the mounting agitation. "I cannot close my eyes to the fact which all history shows," Fish wrote Thurlow Weed in 1855, "that every physical revolution (of governments) is preceded by a moral revolution. [Slavery agitation] leads to estrangement first, and next to hostility and hatred which end inevitably in separation." By the time of the secession crisis another former Whig could observe that "the people of the North and of the South have come to hate each other worse than the hatred between any two nations in the world. In a word the moral basis on which the government is founded is all destroyed."

It is thus no mystery that southerners could not seriously entertain Republican assurances that they would not attack slavery in the states. For one thing, in opposing its extension, Republicans had been logically forced to attack the institution itself. This, indeed, was one of the reasons why radicals accepted the emphasis on non-extension. "We are disposed to select this single point," Sumner explained to Chase, "because it has a peculiar practical issue at the present moment, while its discussion would, of course, raise the whole question of slavery." Frederick Douglass agreed that agitation for the Wilmot Proviso served "to keep the subject before the people—to deepen their hatred of the system—and to break up the harmony between the Northern white people and the Southern slaveholders. . . ." As we have seen, many Republicans, both radicals and moderates, explicitly stated that non-extension was simply the first step, that there would come a day when slavery would cease to exist.

As southerners viewed the Republican party's rise to power in one northern state after another, and witnessed the increasingly anti-southern tone of the northern Democrats, they could hardly be blamed for feeling apprehensive about the future. Late in 1859, after a long talk with the moderate Unionist Senator from Virginia, R. M. T. Hunter, Senator James Dixon of Connecticut reported that the Virginian was deeply worried. "What seems to alarm Hunter is the *growth* of the Anti-slavery feeling at the North." Southerners did not believe that this anti-slavery sentiment would be satisfied with the prohibition of slavery in the territories, although even that would be bad enough. They also feared that a Republican administration would adopt the radicals' program of indirect action against slavery. This is why continued Democratic control of Congress was not very reassuring, for executive action could implement much of the radicals' program. Slavery was notoriously weak in the states of Missouri, Maryland, and Delaware. With federal patronage, a successful emancipation movement there might well be organized. And what was more dangerous, Lincoln might successfully arouse the poor whites in other states against the slaveholders. "Cohorts of Federal office-holders, Abolitionists, may be sent into [our] midst," a southern Senator warned in January 1861; ". . . Postmasters . . . controlling the mails, and loading them down with incendiary documents," would be appointed in every town. One southern newspaper declared that "the great lever by which the abolitionists hope to extirpate slavery in the states, is the aid of the non-slaveholding citizens of the South." The reply of Republicans to these warnings was hardly reassuring. Commenting on one southern editorial, the Cincinnati *Commercial* declared that the spread of anti-slavery sentiment among southern poor whites was "an eventuality against which no precautions can avail." And by December 1860, Republican Congressmen were already receiving applications for office from within the slave states.

For many reasons, therefore, southerners believed that slavery would not be permanently safe under a Republican administration. Had not William H. Seward announced in 1858, "I know, and you know, that a revolution has begun. I know, and all the world knows, that revolutions never go backward." Did not Republican Congressmen openly express their conviction that "slavery must die"? The Republican policy of preventing the spread of slavery, one southerner wrote to William T. Sherman, "was but the entering wedge to overthrow it in the States."

The delegates to South Carolina's secession convention, in their address to the people of the state, explained why they had dissolved the state's connection with the Union:

If it is right to preclude or abolish slavery in a Territory, why should it be allowed to remain in the States? . . . In spite of all disclaimers and professions, there can be but one end by the submission of the South to the rule of a sectional anti-slavery government at Washington; and that end, directly or indirectly, must be— the emancipation of the slaves of the South.

Emancipation might come in a decade, it might take fifty years. But North and South alike knew that the election of 1860 had marked a turning point in the history of slavery in the United States. To remain in the Union, the South would have had to accept the verdict of "ultimate extinction" which Lincoln and the Republicans had passed on the peculiar institution.

The decision for civil war in 1860–61 can be resolved into two questions —why did the South secede, and why did the North refuse to let the South secede? As I have indicated, I believe secession should be viewed as a total and logical response by the South to the situation which confronted it in the election of Lincoln—logical in the sense that it was the only action consistent with its ideology. In the same way, the Republicans' decision to maintain the Union was inherent in their ideology. For the integrity of the Union, important as an end in itself, was also a prerequisite to the national greatness Republicans felt the United States was destined to achieve. With his faith in progress, material growth, and the spread of both democratic institutions and American influence throughout the world, William Seward brought the Republican ideology to a kind of culmination. Although few Republicans held as coherent and far-reaching a world view as he, most accepted Lincoln's more modest view that the American nation had a special place in the world, and a responsibility to prove that democratic institutions were self-sustaining. Much of the messianic zeal which characterized political anti-slavery derived from this faith in the superiority of the political, social, and economic institutions of the North, and a desire to spread these to their ultimate limits.

When a leading historian says, therefore, that the Republican party in 1860 was bound together "by a common enmity rather than a common loyalty," he is, I believe, only half right. For the Republicans' enmity toward the South was intimately bound up with their loyalty to the society of small-scale capitalism which they perceived in the North. It was its identification with the aspirations of the farmers, small entrepreneurs, and craftsmen of northern society which gave the Republican ideology much of its dynamic, progressive, and optimistic quality. Yet paradoxically, at the time of its greatest success, the seeds of the later failure of that ideology were already present. Fundamental changes were at work in the social and economic structure of the North, transforming and undermining many of its free-labor assumptions. And the flawed attitude of the Republicans toward race, and the limitations of the free labor outlook in regard to the Negro, foreshadowed the mistakes and failures of the post-emancipation years.

Daniel J. Boorstin

The Civil War and the
Spirit of Compromise

As the American Revolution had been a struggle within a long-established colonial framework, so the Civil War was a struggle within a working federal system. The two events were to have analogous consequences in hedging in our political reflection, and in identifying the special institutions of this country with the normal conditions of life on this continent. Whatever theoretical debate went on, with few exceptions, was concerned not with the nature of governments but rather with the nature of this particular government.

That the Civil War was a federal conflict, like the colonial character of our Revolution, seems, perhaps, too obvious to require elaboration. But some of our ablest recent historians have given currency to an emphasis which has tended to obscure, or even to displace, the obvious.

In their brilliant *Rise of American Civilization*, Charles A. and Mary R. Beard christened the Civil War "The Second American Revolution." The phrase and the idea have had wide appeal. It has suited our current attitudes to suspect that the actual subject of debate was not the real cause of the conflict. The battle itself, supposedly, was but a symptom of deeper forces: "the social cataclysm in which the capitalists, laborers, and farmers of the North and West drove from power in the national government the planting aristocracy of the South . . . the social revolution was the essential, portentous outcome." Without denying that such a social revolution was taking place, we can recall that there was another side to the conflict. If we turn our attention from inevitable forces to human debate, we must look primarily

Reprinted from The Genius of American Politics by Daniel J. Boorstin, pp. 119–132. By permission of The University of Chicago Press. Copyright 1953 by The University of Chicago.

at a different aspect of the struggle. This is only appropriate, since we are concerned with the place of theory in our conscious political life.

The name "The Second American Revolution" given by the Beards and their disciples, is misleading. They (and others who find the center of change in economic events) would thus emphasize the *discontinuity* of our history: the Civil War as a hiatus in our development, a gulf between an agricultural-commercial and an industrial society. But to those students who, like me, are impressed by the extraordinary continuity of our history, such an emphasis seems distortion. As we all know, the great economic developments are slow, evolutionary, and sometimes imperceptible; their triumphs are not self-announced in manifestoes. The Industrial Revolution was a matter of centuries, and the kind of revolution to which the Beards refer must also have been a matter of decades.

But *political* history (such events as go by the name of "revolution" and "civil war") has the abruptness of mutation. It is therefore in this area that it would be especially significant to note that what is called a great gulf in our history may not be so great as has been supposed. One of the remarkable characteristics of our Civil War, as contrasted with civil wars of recent European history (excepting possibly the English Civil War), is that ours did *not* significantly interrupt the continuity of our thinking about institutions.

From the point of view of political and constitutional thought, we might do better to call our Civil War "The Second War of Independence." I have already mentioned Guizot's remark that the English Revolution succeeded twice, once in England in the seventeenth century and a second time in America in the eighteenth. We might go further and say that, from the point of view of constitutional law and political theory, the Revolution occurred a third time, namely, in the middle of the nineteenth century. For the relation of the ancient rights of Englishmen to federalism, which was only partly redefined in the course of the American Revolution, was more extensively explored and settled during the Civil War.

That continuity of our political thought which, as we have seen, had been expressed in the legalistic character of the American Revolutionary debate was also expressed later in much of the argument over the Civil War. There is even less evidence here for the pattern which Carl Becker saw in the Revolution. The main current did not seem to rise above the "provincial" level of constitutionalism to the more "cosmopolitan" atmosphere of natural law. Indeed, we find something of the opposite of what Becker remarks as the increasing abstractness of Revolutionary debate. In the South at least, as the crisis proceeded the debate seemed to become more and more legalistic, reaching its climax actually after the war was over. The legal debate never rose to the realm of natural law, not even to the extent found in the American Revolution.

The North and the South each considered that it was fighting primarily for its legal rights under the sacred federal Constitution. A man like Thoreau probably stood only for himself and a few fire-eating abolitionists. On neither side do we hear much of the sort of argument familiar in European civil wars: that the existing federal constitution was bad and ought to be changed, and that was what one should fight for. On the contrary, each side purported to represent the authentic original doctrine, to be *defending* the Constitution.

Calhoun, who was by far the most profound of the southern writers on the subject, shows this peculiarity. His major theoretical work, not published until after his death in 1850, consists of two parts: "A Disquisition on Government" and "A Discourse on the Constitution and Government of the United States." It is on these that his growing reputation as a political philosopher largely depends. These works taken together (as Calhoun intended that they should be) admirably illustrate the point of view I have been describing.

The "Disquisition," an essay of about a hundred pages, though starting from some general principles of psychology and political theory, is primarily a defense of Calhoun's principle of the "concurrent majority" and an exposition of his objections to governments based on the "numerical majority." In a closely reasoned argument, Calhoun points out the dangers of uncontrolled majority rule. The only safeguard, he insists, is a system of constitutionalism which will allow each separate interest a veto on all legislation to which it objects. Such a system, he urges, results in moderation and compromise and still can leave government strong enough to combat enemies from without. He supports his argument by the experience of Rome, Poland, and Great Britain.

"A Discourse on the Constitution and Government of the United States," a work about three times the length of the "Disquisition," is the sequel. In it Calhoun tries to show that

it was the object of the framers of the constitution, in organizing the government, to give to the two elements [the states as units and the voting population], of which it is composed, separate, but concurrent action; and, consequently, a veto on each other, whenever the organization of the department, or the nature of the power would admit: and when this could not be done, so to blend the two, as to make as near an approach to it, in effect, as possible. It is, also, apparent, that the government, regarded apart from the constitution, is the government of the concurrent, and not of the numerical majority (Works, I, 181).

By reference to the proceedings of the Philadelphia convention and of the ratifying conventions, Calhoun demonstrates that, through a happy coincidence, the true and original conception of the federal Constitution was actually nothing but a design for the attainment of his ideal government. The departure from his ideal, the gradual growth of a consolidated national government, and the development of means by which one section could dominate another were all to be explained as departures from the true intent of the Framers.

> To the one, or to the other,—to monarchy, or disunion it must come, if not
> prevented by strenuous and timely efforts. And this brings up the question,—How
> is it to be prevented? How can these sad alternatives be averted? For this purpose,
> it is indispensable that the government of the United States should be restored to
> its federal character. Nothing short of a perfect restoration, as it came from the
> hands of its framers, can avert them [Works, I, 381].

This restoration was to be effected by getting rid of certain perversions which
had been introduced after the adoption of the Constitution. Calhoun urges,
for example, the repeal of Section 25 of the Judiciary Act of 1789, and of the
Act of 1833; "the repeal of all acts by which the money power is carried
beyond its constitutional limits"; the confining of the president to those
powers expressly conferred on him by the Constitution and by acts of Congress; the return in practice to the original way of electing the president and
vice-president.

Such means as these—together with a few reforms like the introduction
of a plural executive—would, in Calhoun's phrase, "complete the work
of restoration." We are never allowed to forget that what Calhoun aims at is
not revolution but *restoration*.

A Conflict of Orthodoxies

Here, once again, was a competition between constitutional orthodoxies. As
often in American history, a great political conflict was taking the form not
of a struggle between essentially different political theories but between
differences of constitutional emphasis. There was a striking, if obvious,
parallel to the epoch of the Revolution. But the South was now even more
conservative than the Revolutionaries had been. It found no reason to issue
a Declaration of Independence. The colonists had set themselves up as
defenders of the British constitution and contended that it was not they but
the parliament who were actually the revolutionaries. So now, champions of
the South could—and did—argue that it was not they, but the northerners,
who were, properly speaking, the revolutionaries. Each accused the other of
seeking to overthrow the established doctrine of the federal Constitution, the
ideas of the Founding Fathers.

The Civil War secessionist argument—like that of the Revolution—
could be carried on in such a conservative vocabulary because both events
were, theoretically speaking, only surface breaches in a firm federal framework. Because of this, they both implied, win or lose, the continued acceptance of the existing structure of local government. Thus in the Civil War
southern partisans, like the Americans in the Revolution, could continue to
profess loyalty to the theory of the Union. As a New Yorker championing
the Southern cause declared in 1860:

> The South views the matter in the spirit of Patrick Henry. "The object is

now, indeed, small, but the shadow is large enough to darken all this fair land."
They can have no faith in men who profess what they think a great moral principle, and deny that they intend to act upon it. It was the principle of taxation
without representation that the colonies resisted, and it is the principle of the
"irrepressible conflict," based avowedly on a "higher law," that the South resists.
She is now in the position of the Colonies eighty-four years ago, and is adopting
the same measures that they adopted. . . . A prompt retreat from this dangerous
agitation within the shadow of the Constitution, is the only means of realizing the
rich future, which will be the reward only of harmony, good faith, and loyalty to
the Constitution [Thomas P. Kettell, Southern Wealth and Northern Profits (New
York, 1860), p. 5].

On the other side, Lincoln, in nearly every one of his principal speeches,
appealed to the authentic Revolutionary tradition. His most succinct statement was, of course, in the familiar opening of the Gettysburg Address, to
which I have already referred in another connection. But he rang all the
rhetorical changes on this appeal, as, for example, in his speech at Peoria in
1854:

Our republican robe is soiled and trailed in the dust. Let us repurify it. Let us
turn and wash it white in the spirit, if not the blood, of the Revolution. Let us turn
slavery from its claims of "moral right" back upon its existing legal rights and its
argument of "necessity." Let us return it to the position our fathers gave it, and
there let it rest in peace. Let us readopt the Declaration of Independence, and with
it the practices and policy which harmonize with it.

Statesmen of the North were perhaps more inclined to appeal to the
Declaration of Independence, while those of the South leaned more heavily
on the Constitution. But both had in common the assumption that the pretty
homogeneous philosophy of the Founding Fathers was what they were being
called upon to vindicate. Fitzhugh did, to be sure, characterize the Declaration as "exhuberantly false, and arborescently fallacious." Yet even the
Declaration of Independence was by no means generally rejected by southern
advocates. Some southerners, for example, Chief Justice Taney in the Dred
Scott decision, even argued that their position had been well stated in the
Declaration. They adduced historical proof (in my opinion convincing) that
the authors of the sacred document had intended that Negroes be excluded
from their professions of "equality." Another remarkable feature of the Dred
Scott decision for us is the frankness with which it takes a preformation or a
static view of the Constitution. Chief Justice Taney seemed to assume that
the legal question of Negro status could be resolved by accurate historical
definition of the original meaning of the Declaration of Independence and
the Constitution, considered together.

Few documents could be more interesting in this connection than one
which nowadays is almost never read. For there is probably no more authentic

index to the theoretical conservatism of the "rebel" cause than the Constitution of the Confederate States of America. President Jefferson Davis boasted that the document proved the "conservative" temper of the people of the Confederate States. Alexander Stephens, his vice-president, declared that the form of the document showed that "their only leading object was to sustain, uphold, and perpetuate the fundamental principles of the Constitution of the United States." Closely following the original in organization, the Confederate constitution is almost a verbatim copy of the federal Constitution.

Its differences consist mainly in that it incorporates into the body of the document some of the principal amendments to the federal Constitution (the Bill of Rights, for example, being absorbed into Art. I, sec. 9); and it explicitly resolves certain ambiguities (for example, those concerning slavery and the federal principle generally) in the sense which the South believed to have been the original intent of the authors. The Preamble, for example, reads:

> We, the People of the Confederate States, each State acting in its sovereign and independent character, in order to form a permanent Federal Government, establish justice, insure domestic tranquility, and secure the blessings of liberty to ourselves and our posterity—invoking the favor and guidance of Almighty God— do ordain and establish this Constitution for the Confederate States of America.

It is of great significance that in our bloody Civil War the so-called "rebel" side produced, through two of its best minds, treatises on the origin and nature of our Constitution which deserve to stand, alongside *The Federalist* and Adams' *Defence of the Constitutions*, on the small shelf of basic books about the American political system. The first, of course, is Calhoun's "Discourse on the Constitution and Government of the United States" (1851), which I have already described. The second is Alexander H. Stephens' *Constitutional View of the Late War between the States* (1868–70).

We cannot be surprised that the South, weaker in economy and in arms, found an incentive to be stronger in legal debate. But it remains a curiosity of political thought, as well as a pregnant fact of American history, that the principal theoretical defense of the southern position should have been a treatise on the origin of the federal Constitution, produced actually after the South had lost the last battle. Stephens' work was dedicated to "All true friends of the Union under the Constitution of the United States, throughout their entire limits, without regard to present or past party associations." The conflict, Stephens emphasized, was not basically over slavery but over two "different and opposing ideas as to the nature of what is known as the General Government. The contest was between those who held it to be strictly Federal in its character, and those who maintained that it was thoroughly National." The work is historical: a documented demonstration that the Constitution was intended to set up a *federal* government.

We can begin to grasp the true proportions of what I have called the continuity of the history of the United States, as contrasted with that of the countries of western Europe, if we try to imagine the leader of a defeated party in any of the recent European civil wars producing a heavy scholarly treatise proving that he had been in the right *strictly from the point of view of constitutional theory.* George Fitzhugh in 1857 and Jefferson Davis in 1881 both earnestly wished for the "strength and perpetuity" of the Union.

In virtually every one of the recent domestic struggles in Europe, the conflict has been so basic that only one side could conceivably have set itself up as the champion of existing legal institutions. The other has proudly stood for a new concept of government, for a new constitution, and another basis of law. Hitler's cynicism toward the German constitution is typical of this frame of mind. Yet in the American Civil War, after hundreds of thousands of lives had been lost, both sides were still thinking on similar constitutional assumptions. An intelligent and realistic critic like Alexander Stephens still after the war considered it possible that his image of the original doctrine (that the Union was a federal and not a national government) might eventually prevail. This hope would have been hardly conceivable, had not both parties to the conflict accepted the same premises of political theory, had they not preserved a common devotion to a hypothetically perfect original theory. This is what I mean by the idea of "preformation."

For the reasons which I have mentioned, the legacy of the Civil War to American thought has been one of sectionalism and constitutional debate rather than of dogmatic nationalism and "return to fundamentals." The tendency of sectionalism has been to reinforce our awareness of variety within our national culture and of the desirability and inevitability of preserving it. The tendency of the continuous constitutional tradition has been to give the defeated cause, the South, a legitimate theoretical position within the federal system.

The South, except in its romantic literature of chivalry and mint juleps, is now no champion of a different concept of life but rather of a different constitutional emphasis. The South remains, as it is desirable that someone should always be, champion of the states'-rights, local-autonomy principle of our federal Constitution. The South can still debate about what it once gave its lives to defend, for it has never lost essential devotion to the constitutional spirit and its pure original image. What Lincoln called "the spirit of concession and compromise, that spirit which has never failed us in past perils, and which may be safely trusted for all the future"—that spirit can survive precisely because the Civil War was poor in political theory. Notwithstanding the abolitionists and people like Garrison who wished to burn the Constitution, the war did not represent a quest for a general redefinition of political values.

Whatever the crimes, the senseless bitterness, that were visited on the South in the era of reconstruction, they were committed in a vindictive or narrowly provincial spirit. The triumph of the national emphasis in the federal structure did not carry with it victory of a nationalist philosophy. In Lincoln's phrase, "the Union"—not any self-conscious national culture—was what was to be preserved. This distinguished him sharply from his contemporaries like Bismarck and Cavour. The remarkable reintegration of the South into our constitutional system is the best evidence of the community of certain assumptions. The Civil War emerged, then, as a struggle over complicated matters, on which everyone knew there had been a long series of compromises, beginning with the Declaration of Independence and the Constitution themselves. Such a controversy could have happened only within the framework of going federal institutions.

Not the least remarkable feature of the Civil War—apart from the fact that it occurred at all—is that it was so unproductive of political theory. This, the bloodiest single civil war of the nineteenth century, was also perhaps the least theoretical. The sectional character of the conflict had tended to make sociology—the description of things as they were—take the place of the uncharted exploration of things as they ought to be. It also prevented the crisis from propagating panaceas. This was another example of the recurrent tendency in American history to identify the "is" with the "ought," to think of values and a theory of society as implicit in facts about society. The era was strikingly lacking in romanticism of the Rousseauistic brand. The romantics of the day were the Thaddeus Stevenses—the bearers of fire and sword.

At the same time, the federal character of the struggle, the fact that it took place within a functioning federal order, confined much of the theoretical discussion within the area of constitutional law, of the search for the true original image of the Constitution. This, too, discouraged American thinkers of the age (excepting a vagrant Thoreau) from making confusion in the market place an excuse for going off into the solitude of the woods to rethink the whole problem of institutions. The sense of "givenness" was reinforced. In this case it meant the empirical tradition, the reliance on constitutionalism, and an unwillingness to remake institutions out of whole cloth.

The continuity of American political thought—which included the American way of *not* philosophizing about politics—was to stay. The mere fact that the nation had survived the ordeal of civil war seemed itself to prove the strength of the thread which bound the present to the past and to confirm the common destiny of the nation.

SUGGESTIONS FOR FURTHER READING

Charles and Mary Beard's description of the Civil War as a "revolution" is supported by Louis M. Hacker, *The Triumph of American Capitalism* (New York, 1940). Arthur C. Cole finds the Civil War to be *The Irrepressible Conflict, 1850–*

1865 (New York, 1934), and Robert R. Russel describes some Southern economic grievances in his *Economic Aspects of Southern Sectionalism, 1840–61* (Urbana, Ill., 1924).

Arthur Schlesinger, Jr. has argued that slavery was a fundamental moral issue dividing the sections, an issue that could not be compromised. See his "The Causes of the Civil War: A Note on Historical Sentimentalism," *Partisan Review*, XVI (October 1949), pp. 969–981. Avery Craven, in *An Historian and the Civil War* (Chicago, 1964) and *The Coming of the Civil War* (Chicago, 1942), takes a very different view. He argues that prejudices, misconceptions, and emotionalism blinded Americans. When political issues became moral absolutes, compromise became impossible. David Donald has argued perceptively against both the Craven and the Beards' points of view in "An Excess of Democracy: The American Civil War and the Social Process," Chapter XI of his *Lincoln Reconsidered* (New York, 1961). A discussion of Southern society and the sources of its ideology that would support Eric Foner's essay is Eugene D. Genovese, *The Political Economy of Slavery* (New York, 1965).

David Donald, *Liberty and Union: The Crisis of Popular Government* (Boston, 1978), tells the story of these years of crisis mostly in terms of harmony and consensus. David M. Potter, *The Impending Crisis, 1848–1861* (New York, 1976), is a fine, balanced survey of the coming of the Civil War which traces the growing conflicts stemming from northern and southern nationalism, slavery, and political differences. Roy F. Nichols, *The Disruption of American Democracy* (New York, 1948), sketches the political realignments arising from sectional conflicts, 1856–1861; he finds the heightened emotionalism of the times rather than fundamental class or ideological differences to be the cause of this political disruption. William L. Barney, *The Road to Secession* (New York, 1972), describes the course of secession and the conflicts over this issue in the South.

No subject has received more attention than the Civil War; the bibliography is endless. Those wishing to delve into the literature may start with Thomas J. Pressly, *Americans Interpret Their Civil War* (Princeton, 1954). A more recent survey containing a number of perceptive insights is Eric Foner, "The Causes of the American Civil War: Recent Interpretations and New Directions," *Civil War History*, XX (September 1974), 197–214. A convenient collection of primary and secondary sources on the war may be found in Edwin C. Rozwenc, ed., *The Causes of the American Civil War* (Boston, 1961).

* Available in paperback edition.

10

Reconstruction

The Civil War has had an endless fascination for Americans, who usually see it as a time of great heroism and idealism on the part of both sides in the conflict. But no such rosy aura surrounds the years after the war, the years when an attempt was made to reconstruct the nation and heal the wounds of war. If the Civil War made heroes, Reconstruction produced villains; if the war was marked by tragic idealism, Reconstruction was characterized by venal corruption. Even those historians who find much beneficial in Reconstruction conclude that the period ended in dismal failure.

The basic problem facing Northern leaders after the war was how to restore national unity after a bitter and bloody sectional conflict. But there was sharp disagreement as to how this could be best accomplished. Should the Confederacy be treated as a conquered province, or should the Southern states be welcomed back into the Union as wayward but repentant members of the family? What kind of changes should the ex-Confederate states accept before being allowed to participate once again in the political process?

Even during the war there was disagreement between President Lincoln, who favored treating the seceded states leniently, and some congressional leaders, who argued for harsher peace terms. This executive-legislative battle continued after the assassination of Lincoln, but the mid-term elections of 1866, favorable to the so-called "radicals," made it possible for Congress to pass legislation concerning the South over the opposition and vetoes of President Andrew Johnson. Congress quickly passed the Civil Rights Bill, the Freedman's Bureau Bill, and, finally, the Reconstruction Acts of 1867. The Southern states were put under military rule until they approved new constitutions guaranteeing Negro suffrage, ratified the Fourteenth Amendment, and in other ways satisfied the radical majority in Congress.

As new governments were set up under congressional tutelage in each Southern state, they were declared reconstructed and their representatives and senators admitted to Congress. For the first time, blacks voted and held office, some even serving as their state's senators and representatives in Congress. The Republican-dominated state governments were often marked by corruption and inefficiency, but they also instituted significant and needed reforms in education and welfare. All of them faced sharp and often violent opposition, and one by one they fell from power. None remained when the last troops were removed from the South in 1877

No period has evoked more impassioned and opinionated historical writing than has Reconstruction. Some historians, seeing the South as victim, have called it a "tragic era," a period during which the defeated South was put to the torture by a vindictive victor. Others, sensitive to the position of the black population, have depicted it as a betrayal when opportunistic Northerners abandoned the black to racist violence and a life of discrimination and fear. One way into the maze of historical writing on Reconstruction is to see it in terms of the Civil War. The following selections show

how interpretations of the causes of the Civil War can color the interpretations of its aftermath, Reconstruction.

If we adopt the Beards' analysis that the war was the result of a struggle between industrial and agrarian interests, we could expect that Reconstruction policies would reflect the victory of Northern industrialists. Such is the view presented in the first selection, by William B. Hesseltine. He argues that Reconstruction was simply "the method by which the 'Masters of Capital' sought to secure their victory over the vanquished 'Lords of the Manor.'" Reconstruction was abandoned, he concludes, not because the goal changed, but because of a change in method.

On the other hand, if slavery is seen as a key issue in the coming of the Civil War, then Reconstruction must be viewed in the context of the end of slavery. But here details will depend on how one assesses Northern war aims. Did abolitionism carry with it a promise to open the doors to full equality of opportunity for the black? If so, then Reconstruction, as James M. McPherson argues in the second selection, was an incomplete revolution, a revolution that achieved only part of its goal.

In the third selection, Grady McWhiney views Reconstruction in the context of a general political consensus, much as Daniel J. Boorstin did in his discussion of the Civil War. Interestingly enough, however, McWhiney's view in some ways resembles that of Hesseltine. He maintains that white Southerners were never very different from the Yankees, and that once the war was over they quickly accepted Yankee ideology. He adds that even blacks, although "relegated to a subservient position . . . , pursued the goal of material progress."

Obviously, the Reconstruction period was marked by political and often physical conflict. But did this conflict reveal fundamental differences? Is the essence of Reconstruction class conflict and race conflict? Or was Reconstruction essentially a conservative phenomenon in which there was little meaningful conflict over race and class issues? Finally, how is the legacy, or aftermath, of Reconstruction to be evaluated? Did a post-Civil War consensus merely delay and perhaps magnify significant racial conflicts?

William B. Hesseltine

Reconstruction: Changing Revolutionary Tactics

By common consent, President Rutherford B. Hayes's withdrawal of the federal troops from the South has been accepted as the end of reconstruction. The President's action, however, was but the outward and visible symbol of an already accomplished revolution in northern sentiment. For a number of years the northern voters had been coming to realize that the effort to force the South into the northern political mold was both costly and futile.

Commentators on the politics of the Reconstruction period have ascribed this reversal of opinion to the rise of new interests among the northern electorate, or have dismissed it with a remark that the people had grown tired of the southern question in politics. Such an interpretation fails to consider that reconstruction itself was an economic as well as a political problem, and that it was not until the political program failed to bring economic results that the control of the South was returned to the southern white man.

Fundamentally, reconstruction was the method by which the "Masters of Capital" sought to secure their victory over the vanquished "Lords of the Manor," and through which they expected to exploit the resources of the southern states. Long before the war was over cotton speculators, acting as the vanguard of an economic army, followed the advancing federal armies and annoyed commanders from the Red River to the Potomac by their persistent efforts to carry on trade with the South. Behind the lines, less

From William B. Hesseltine, "Economic Factors in the Abandonment of Reconstruction," Mississippi Valley Historical Review, XXII (September 1935), pp. 191–220, excluding footnotes. Reprinted by permission of the Organization of American Historians.

mobile entrepreneurs calculated the possibility of carrying the northern economic system into the South at the close of hostilities. In the first months after Appomattox, business men in the North looked for immediate profits from the return of peace and endorsed General Ulysses S. Grant's leniency and President Andrew Johnson's plans for a speedy restoration of the southern states. One of Grant's aides-de-camp found that in the summer of 1865 "all the sober, substantial men" of New York, St. Louis, and Washington were in favor of Johnson's policy. Impressed with the necessity for southern industrial rehabilitation, the New York *Commercial and Financial Chronicle* ingratiatingly assured the South that the northern people contemplated no oppression but would accord the southern states an early readmission to the Union.

Totally ignoring the psychoses of the conquered southerners, northern financial circles seemed to believe that the South would "treat political questions as secondary" until industrial recuperation had been accomplished. This recovery, of course, would be the result of northern capital, in the hands of northern men, flowing into the South. "There can be no way so sure to make the late rebels of the South loyal men and good citizens," declared the New York organ of the financiers, "as to turn their energies to the pursuits of peace, and the accumulation of wealth." When goods from southern factories appeared in the New York markets, they caused this journal to remember that in 1860 there had been 350 woolen mills and 180 cotton mills in the South and that the total value of southern manufactured goods had been over $238,000,000! "Now," proclaimed the hopeful editor, "Northern men, accustomed to business, have gone South and will give a new impetus" to industrial development.

In order to encourage northern men to migrate to the South, commercial newspapers began to advertise the South as the nation's new land of opportunity. The abundance of land, the manufacturing possibilities, the climate, soil, water-power, and timber of the South came in for extensive exposition, and the figures of the South's exports in 1860—over two hundred million dollars—was dangled before the eyes of the northern people. The South was assured that an immigration of new and energetic people would begin as soon as the Johnsonian governments were fully established.

Such roseate dreams of a golden harvest in the South were rudely shattered when the southerners began to take stock of their own position. In the first days after the war planters welcomed ex-officers of the Union armies who came to purchase cotton plantations, but few of these adventurers were successful either in handling negroes or in living harmoniously with their white neighbors. Political differences which engendered social ostracism and even physical violence soon developed, and the northerners returned to their homes none the richer for their experience. Instead of welcoming immigrants and making provisions to receive migrating capitalists, the provisional governments under Johnson's program showed more interest in attempting to solve the economic problems of an agrarian area.

Some efforts, however, were made by several of the states to attract immigrants, and boards of immigration were set up by the Reconstruction governments. But only in Tennessee was there a real enthusiasm for the task. There the East Tennesseans, who had never been a part of the cotton kingdom but had long nursed secret ambitions to become industrialized, controlled the state and made a serious effort to entice northern capital. Newspapers appealed to Tennesseans to advertise their lands, mill and factory sites, and mines in order to attract merchants, manufacturers, and bankers —"the very class of men . . . whose help is needed in developing the wealth of our great State." The legislature generously chartered a number of "immigration" companies in order to assist expected immigrants, and in December, 1867, a State Board of Immigration was established. The board employed an energetic commissioner to advertise the state's resources in the North and in Europe. In radical Missouri there was also a welcome to immigrants, but in other parts of the South a suspicion of the political motives of the migrants caused them to be either ostracized or mistreated.

The attitude of the southerners was not long in being reported to Congress. "Loyal" citizens, Unionists, and northern immigrants appealed to congressmen for protection against the "frightful spirit of lawlessness extant among the late rebels." From Virginia to Texas plaintive letters to congressmen told the story of bad treatment. Already the Radicals in Congress had determined to force Negro suffrage on the South in order to maintain the Republican party in power. Under the added stimulus of the anguished cries of business men both North and South the congressional program of reconstruction was formulated. The Fourteenth Amendment would protect the property of Union men in the South and by disfranchising the leaders of the old agricultural South would enable "loyal" men and Negroes to enact the legislation which would protect the northern capitalist in exploiting the South. When the southern states rejected the amendment, Congress proceeded to carry its program into effect. Only radical Tennessee, whose arms were outstretched in welcome to invading capital, was admitted to representation in Congress.

The passage of the Reconstruction Act of March 2, 1867, renewed the hope of a migration of capital and labor to the South. Union men in Virginia looked forward to the migration of "Northern men with capital and enterprise to develop the resources of our fields and forests." Moreover a political purpose would be served for such people, wrote a citizen of Richmond, "by their social intercourse and votes . . . would do much to neutralize the prejudices and influence of parties inimical to the Government." When General James A. Longstreet renounced his Confederate heresies in favor of southern prosperity, Massachusett's Ben Butler hastened to welcome him to the radical fold. If all southerners would take Longstreet's views, Butler foresaw that "harmony of feeling, community of interest, unity of action as well as homogeneity of institutions" would follow to produce national well being.

But Longstreet was almost alone in his decision to "accept the results of the war" and the military governments in the South could do little to further the North's exploitation of its southern colony. Men who had gone South for economic reasons took advantage of the changed situation to recoup their losses in politics, and others came from the North solely for the plums of office. But the Union men and northerners in the South continued to find themselves at a disadvantage. The property of loyalists was not safe in the courts, and Ben Butler soon heard appeals from the Unionists to turn the courts over to loyal men. "The Northern man will not come here unless his capital is safe," declared one of Butler's Georgia informants. From Texas it was reported that rebel leaders were growing rich but that there was no hope for Union men. On the advice of the "best financiers" Butler decided to abandon his own extensive investments in the South, although he contemplated, according to one newspaper, a bill which would prevent disfranchised rebels from holding office on railroads or chartered companies.

The New York *Commercial and Financial Chronicle*, a consistent supporter of Johnson's policy, soon found that Congressional Reconstruction was paralyzing business and unnecessarily prolonging southern industrial prostration. If Negro majorities controlled the state legislatures, the paper warned, capital would stay out of the section. Despite this analysis, the Radicals pursued their course and blamed bad conditions on President Johnson. When the Tennessee legislature met in December, 1867, Governor William G. Brownlow, the "Fighting Parson," reported that "men of capital and enterprise" had not come into the state in the expected numbers. This was due to Andrew Johnson's "insane policy" of holding out to "pestilential disloyalists" the hope that they would be restored to power. Butler agreed with this contention and declared that only a new president could insure the property rights of northerners in the South.

During the campaign of 1868 Democratic orators took pains to assert that peace and prosperity could only come through the abandonment of Congressional Reconstruction, but Republicans, saying little of the economic rehabilitation of the South, made much of the southerner's vindictiveness towards the Union men and loyal Negroes of the South. Ku Klux outrages and Democratic murders constituted the main theme of the Republicans, despite the fact that these very stories would serve as a deterrent to capital seeking southern investments. In their belief, interest in manufactures and agriculture would "supersede the excitement of the caucus" and the South would "turn all her energies to . . . developing her immense resources" as soon as the election was over. When friction ceased, business would "spring to its feet . . . manufacture . . . unchain her idle wheels," and "the cotton and rice plantations of the South . . . vie with the cornfields of the West." In the end, the business man of the North voted for the Republicans, not because he was convinced by this reasoning but because the party stood for the payment of the national debt in gold.

Republican success in the election of 1868 was widely interpreted as settling the disorders in the South. "The election of Grant and Colfax means peace," cried Tennessee's Brownlow. "It means that carpetbaggers are not to be molested in Tennessee; that capital, coming to us from abroad, whether of brains or hands, or money, is not to be spurned, prescribed, persecuted, because it comes from north of a given line." According to Horace Greeley, immigrants could now be safely invited into the country, and two-thirds of them would "go to build up the waste places of the South." Greeley also noticed that the election would insure the reconstruction of Virginia where northern capital was waiting for a favorable government before it advanced money for the completion of a railroad from the Ohio to the Chesapeake Bay. Even from ex-Confederates in the South there came echoes of the same conclusion. One Alabamian, who had served in the Confederate army and had voted against Grant, wrote to Butler that his state wanted to "induce men of capital and skill" to come in. "If you are desirous for the welfare of the South, and wish to be personally highly remunerated and at the same time become a public benefactor, you can accomplish these objects better than in any other manner by inducing your men of means and skill to invest their money and skill" in the South. John Letcher, erstwhile war-governor of Virginia, looked forward to a speedy settlement of the political controversies in order that the prosperity of his section might be assured.

President Grant entered office determined to end the conflict in the South. His first action on reconstruction was to submit the constitutions of Virginia, Texas, and Mississippi to a vote without the obnoxious clauses which disfranchised the Confederate leaders. This action was immediately hailed with satisfaction, and northern business men looked to the completion of political reconstruction as the beginning of southern prosperity. In Virginia, the Conservatives of the state rapidly formed a party pledged to the acceptance of the Fifteenth Amendment, to the development of industry, and to the encouragement of immigration. "In short," commented Greeley, "Virginia, having had enough of Civil War and devastation, is about to subordinate political strife to industrial progress and material prosperity, and thus advance to a future of power and wealth undreamed of in her past." On the eve of the Virginia election, General J. D. Imboden, who had served his state from Bull Run to Appomattox, wrote to the *Tribune* that northern men were safe and welcome in Virginia. Millions of white men were needed to develop the state's resources. There was no doubt that Virginia was succumbing to the lure of profits. In May, 1869, General Lee visited Washington on railroad business, and called at the White House to assure Grant that Virginia favored the Fifteenth Amendment and Negro suffrage!

The Virginia elections were the quietest that had taken place in the South since secession, but the resultant Conservative victory struck terror into the ranks of the radical Republican politicians. On economic issues the newly elected governor, Gilbert C. Walker, was in thorough accord with the masters of capital who were backing the Republican party in the North. His party accepted Negro suffrage and stood for the industrialization of the state, yet there was little doubt that the Virginia Conservatives would unite with the northern Democracy in national elections. Faced with this certainty, Republican politicians sought for an excuse to keep the state under military government, while Walker hurried to Washington to lay his case before Grant and to promise that the Conservatives would not recant on their promises to ratify the Fifteenth Amendment.

The dissatisfaction of the politicians with this development was soon revealed. Although the politicians represented the masters of capital who were interested in tariffs, railroads, and the exploitation of the South, they were themselves more interested in the preservation of their party in power. The only member of Grant's cabinet who was a politician was Secretary of the Treasury George S. Boutwell, who immediately declared his unalterable opposition to the Virginia results. Publicly, he counselled caution, taking, according to the disgusted Greeley, "more account of the unity and coherence of the Republican party than of the triumph of its cardinal principle." Intent upon preventing a repetition of this miscarriage Boutwell condemned the Conservative party in Mississippi and persuaded Grant to repudiate his brother-in-law, Louis Dent, whom the Conservatives had nominated for governor. So great was the pressure of the politicians that Grant yielded to their wishes in Texas and threw the weight of the administration's influence into the scales against the Conservative candidate.

Boutwell's attitude foreshadowed the imminent separation between those who would exploit the South for political advantage and those who who sought a field for economic expansion. Moderate Republicans, such as James A. Garfield, deplored the violence that existed in Texas and Mississippi at the same time they commended the peaceful reconstruction of Virginia. Radicals of the Butler stripe, on the other hand, were convinced that Virginia had deceived the Republican party. The victory of the Conservatives in Tennessee in 1869 and the action of the Georgia legislature in expelling its Negro members seemed to them sufficient indication that the South was not yet reconciled to the Union. Butler's own losses in three southern investments had convinced him that capital was not yet safe in the South.

After the election of 1868 Horace Greeley had become the principal exponent of northern infiltration into the South. In much the same manner that he had formerly urged the male youth to seek the West, he now devoted the columns of the powerful New York *Tribune* to urging groups to settle in the South. Southern land which had been worth twenty dollars an acre before the war and would soon be worth that again could be bought for one or two dollars an acre. Advising settlement in colonies, Greeley estimated that three thousand colonists in Florida, five thousand each in Alabama, Louisiana, Arkansas, and Mississippi, and ten thousand each in Virginia, North Carolina, and Texas would make the South Republican and deliver it from "the nightmare which now oppresses . . . politics and industry." Within the South, said Greeley, there was a division between two classes on the issues of reconstruction. The "landholders, merchants and men of property, with all who are inclined to industry and thrift" were opposed by a "decreasing faction of sore-heads and malignants." In issue after issue of his paper, the expansionist editor carried articles by the first class of southerners setting forth the advantages of various sections of the South for immigrants and for capital investments. As the Virginia question arose, Greeley reiterated that the South was begging for immigrants and for northern capital and a *Tribune* correspondent wandered through the South gathering details of the wealth awaiting northern enterprise. North Carolina offered cheap land, docile laborers, ample timber resources, and political peace. In South Carolina there were woolen mills and cotton factories. Tennessee had blast furnaces already established by northern capital and there were rich opportunities for investment in mines of iron, coal, zinc, and copper. The South, editorialized the *Tribune*, had shown a general willingness to come back into the Union on the Greeley platform of "universal amnesty and universal suffrage."

The fundamental issues between the politicians and the business men were clearly brought out in an open letter from Greeley to Butler. Appealing to Butler's practical sense, the editor showed that the Radical program of proscription and disfranchisement had retarded business. In reply, Butler declared that Greeley's course had encouraged the rebels so that they had gained the upper hand in Tennessee and Georgia. In these states, the people had deceived the Republican party. Conditions would have been better if a a half dozen leading rebels had been hung at the end of the war.

In the winter of 1869–70 these divergent views were advanced in the debates over the admission of Virginia and over the treatment to be accorded to recalcitrant Georgia. In the end, Virginia was admitted, although the Radicals had many misgivings. Georgia was remanded to military rule. Not even Greeley could defend the action of the "rebel element" in Georgia and both Moderates and Radicals were agreed that outrages against Republicans in the South should stop. As a means of stopping them, both elements heralded the ratification of the Fifteenth Amendment and supported the "Force Bill" of 1870 which would guarantee the right of suffrage to the Negroes. To the Radicals the martial law in Georgia and the Enforcement Act were means of getting Republican majorities in the South; to the Moderates, the hope of eventual peace carried with it the promise of a prosperous infiltration of northern business in the South. In Greeley's opinion, it was time to "have done with Reconstruction." "The country is . . . sick of it," he added. "So long as any State is held in abeyance, it will be plausibly urged that the Republicans are afraid to trust the People. Let us give every State to herself, and then punish any who violate or defy the guaranties of public and personal rights now firmly imbedded in the Constitution."

Although Moderates and Radicals had agreed on the Fifteenth Amendment and the Enforcement Act there were differences between them on the method to be pursued in the future. Radical politicians of the school of Conkling, Morton, Chandler, and Butler looked to the power of the president to enforce the law, while Greeley and the Moderates continued to appeal to the South's hopes of prosperity as a means of producing peace. The advantages of immigration, the possibility of industrial development, and the potentialities of the South's mineral wealth were constantly kept before the southerners.

Despite Greeley's appeals, the majority of the southern states offered few inducements to northern migrants. The competition of western lands prevented new agricultural groups entering the South, while cases of violence were constantly reported which discouraged those who might have thought of carrying their capital into southern industry. Greeley's Washington correspondent suspected that most of the outrage stories were "manufactured and published in the North to further the personal designs of unscrupulous and ambitious men." Yet a *Tribune* agent in the South in the summer of 1870 found the Ku Klux in undeniable operation. Throughout the congressional campaigns the North was flooded with atrocity stories, and a congressional investigation in the succeeding winter gave ample evidence that the Klan was terrorizing the South. The result of these outrages was the passage of two more acts which would keep the South orderly: the Federal Elections Act of February 28, and the Ku Klux Act of April 20, 1871.

In contemplating the southern scene, Moderates found themselves forced to admit that violence and political murders prevented business recovery and impelled the government to take action. Greeley, however, continued to advise moderation and amnesty as a more suitable means of inducing the southerners to accept a real economic reconstruction. In Congress, Garfield doubted the constitutionality of the "Force Acts" and declared that the legislation was "working on the very edge of the Constitution." Nevertheless, he found that a "kind of party terrorism" forced all Republicans to vote for the measures. To J. D. Cox, Grant's former secretary of the interior, it seemed that Congress was pursuing the wrong course in attempting to conquer the South. "Capital and intelligence must lead," he told Garfield. "Only Butler and W. Philips would make a wilderness and call it peace." The party should organize and appeal to the "thinking and influential native Southerners"—the "intelligent, well-to-do, and controlling class" of southern whites.

Soon after the passage of the Ku Klux Act, Greeley sent correspondents into the South to study conditions. The reporters found that the Klan was overrunning South Carolina, but that the carpetbaggers, who were levying high taxes upon industry and wealth, were giving partial justification for the outrages. Late in May, Greeley himself traveled through the Southwest to speak on the glories of industry at the Texas State Fair. The New Yorker's speeches inspired the editor of the New Orleans *Price Current* to comment that the industrial doctrines of Greeley and Seward had conquered the South. "It is the true duty of the South," declared the New Orleans editor, "to cultivate all those industries the want of which has enslaved her." But Greeley had concluded from his observations that the South would not be prosperous until the carpetbaggers with their taxes and the Ku Klux with its violence had both been driven out. The South, said Greeley, was suffering from "decayed aristocracy and imported rascality."

From the time of his southern trip Greeley was a candidate for the presidency. From what he had seen in the South, however, he changed his earlier ideas that capital would enter the South. The high taxes which the carpetbag and negro governments had imposed was sufficient to prevent the migration of capital, but the editor believed that prosperity might yet come through the efforts of the southerners themselves. There were millions of acres in the South which might be sold to immigrants, and the proceeds devoted to the development of local resources. The primary needs of the South, as Greeley came to see it, were more people, more skill, more energy, and greater thrift. The South did not need more capital than would naturally flow into it if the people should use their available resources. To his earlier program of universal amnesty and universal suffrage, the editor added the proposal that the South should work out its own salvation by encouraging northern immigration and, by driving out carpetbaggers, make a land free from oppressive taxes upon industry.

Opposed to these ideas, which were politically adopted by the Liberal Republicans, the regular Republicans insisted upon the necessity of maintaining control of the politics of the southern states in order to protect migrating capital and people. Social ostracism and personal violence, said President Grant in his message of 1871, prevented "immigration and the flow of much-needed capital into the States lately in rebellion." The South, echoed the New York *Times* in the midst of the campaign, needed local governments which would protect citizens. Only the Republican party could assure solid achievement and national prosperity and "restrain with firmness any resistance to the new order of things." The South had always depended upon outside capital and the war had destroyed whatever accumulation might have existed. "Industry is sluggish, trade creeps from point to point, manufactures are feeble and few," cried the administration journal as it demanded a continuation of the policy which held out "every encouragement . . . to Northern and foreign capitalists." As the campaign went on Greeley's *Tribune* carried more items concerning available southern farm lands and showed that "had it not been for carpetbag mismanagement, this country today would be filled with millions of Northern or foreign yeomanry carving out farms, or working in . . . iron, copper, coal, and marble." At the same time, Secretary Boutwell went into North Carolina to sing the praises of the carpetbaggers, and assure the North Carolinians that neither immigrants nor capital could be safe in Democratic regions. "The business men of the South," wrote a carpetbagger to the Republican National Committee, "want stability in business, which the election of Greeley . . . will not insure."

Although other factors combined to prevent Greeley's election, his southern program had made considerable impression on the voters. The carpetbaggers had received much unfavorable publicity during the campaign, and the idea that the friction between the races in the South was caused by dishonest adventurers who drove out industry, was widely spread over the North. In the next few years the horrors of carpetbaggery were to be proclaimed by the "liberal" and Democratic press until the masters of capital were convinced that only the removal of this "swarm of locusts" would make possible the economic exploitation of the section.

At the close of the election, Greeley sadly turned to advise the southerners to accept the situation, and "set to work to build up their section's industrial and commercial prosperity." This advice, said the defeated candidate, would sound harsh to men who were unable to pay the enormous taxes imposed by the carpetbaggers. How little encouragement the South might receive from the government in such an effort was evident from the attitude of the administration press. The New York *Times* ridiculed Greeley's efforts to advise his supporters, and the administration organ in Washington announced that the South was responsible for any misfortunes which had come upon it. Acceptance of Republicanism, the paper implied, was the only hope for the section.

The country had not long to wait for the development of the Republican policy in the South. Following immediately upon the election there ensued a struggle between two groups of carpetbaggers for the control of Louisiana. Although President Grant attempted to remain impartial between the contending factions, the New York *Tribune*, continuing its rôle as the Bible of the industrialists, lost no opportunity to point out the intimate connection between Republican policies and the disordered commonwealth. It spoke feelingly about the "plundered community," showed that its government was founded upon fraud, and declared that the dispute "prostitutes the business of the State." Louisiana finances were kept before the eye of the northern people, and the "moneyed interests of the country" were warned against investments in a state whose governor could sell its railroad interests without consulting the legislature and which had a debt of twenty-four millions.

At the same time that Louisiana was troubling the political waters other points of the South were contributing testimony to the economic derangements attendant upon carpetbag governments. In Arkansas there were quarrels between factions of the Republican party comparable to those in Louisiana, whilst the debts and taxes of the state were rising. The *Tribune* published a traveller's account of the corruption and the absurdities of the "prostrate State" of South Carolina where a handful of unscrupulous whites controlled the Negro legislature. If anything were needed to impress the lesson it was furnished by the condition in the District of Columbia. At the beginning of reconstruction, Congress had granted the suffrage to the Negroes of the District. Designed as an experiment to show the capacity of the Negro for citizenship, it soon showed the reverse. Under "Boss" Shepherd's direction the Negroes voted for new bond issues and went to the polls to approve the valiant plans which the District governor was making to pull the capital city out of the mud. But the property holders and tax payers of the District, outvoted by the Negroes, ignored the improvements to gaze with horrible forebodings upon the mounting debt. This was sufficiently close to the northern voter and tax payer to clarify his view on the Radical program in the South. Perhaps an underlying fear, which few dared to express, was the danger which was involved in the rising movement of the lower classes throughout the country. The Granger movement in the West was assailing the citadels of private monopoly, and there was a conceivable connection between these elements and the "bottom rails" who had gotten on top in the South. Two years before, one observer had noticed that there were six thousand native adult whites in Georgia "who cannot read or write, and if to them were added the whole bulk of the Negro population, so vast a mass of ignorance would be found that, if combined for any political purpose it would sweep away all opposition the intelligent class might make. Many thoughtful men are apprehensive that the ignorant voters will, in the future, form a party by themselves as dangerous to the interests of society as the communists of France."

Evidence of a growing reaction in the North came simultaneously with these troubles in the South. In May, 1873, Senator Matt Carpenter, long a supporter of the extreme Radical position, visited Louisiana with a congressional committee. To the people of New Orleans the Wisconsin Senator promised a better government and urged that they turn their attention from politics to trade and business. Eugene Hale, a member of Congress from Maine, presiding over his state's Republican convention, announced that he was "tired and sick of some of the carpet-bag governments." Generally, men were coming to the belief that the poverty of the southern states was due to the villainies of the carpetbaggers, and they were coming to perceive that this had a national significance. The "withdrawal of taxes, which the Southern States might pay under favorable circumstances, throws just that additional burden upon the tax-paying property of the North," announced the *Tribune*. Even George F. Hoar came to admit that the character of the carpetbaggers was such that they would not have been tolerated in the North.

With the development of a sentiment of opposition to the carpetbaggers, there came a new hope that a change of policy might throw the South open for migration of capital and for manufacturing. Surveying the situation, it was noticed that only South Carolina and Louisiana were still in 1873 oppressed by excessive taxes, while the other states might welcome northern mills and factories. Virginia, for example, had accepted reconstruction, avoided carpetbaggers, and proceeded forward steadily in industrial development. The lesson was obvious—if the government abandoned its policy of upholding carpetbaggers, prosperity would come to the South. Propositions for moving New England cotton mills to the South were reported and discussed in the press and on the floors of Congress. Even southerners took a new hope from the renewed discussion of capital moving South.

Standing in the way of a change of policy stood the fact that stories of southern outrages had been the stock in trade of the Radicals since 1866 and the politicians had no thought of abandoning so profitable a source of political ammunition. But even the "outrage business" received a death blow in the congressional campaign of 1874. In the midst of the campaign an Alabama congressman published a list of murders and acts of violence which had recently taken place in his state. Long suspicious of such stories, the New York *Tribune* immediately investigated and found no substantial basis for the congressman's charges. Thereafter the accumulating atrocity stories were received dubiously by the northern people. However, the southern carpetbaggers were merely goaded into action by this exposure and a hastily called convention of Republican politicians assembled in Chattanooga to prepare an authentic list of atrocities for the benefit of the northern voter and to convince Congress that further protection should be given at elections. But the convention proved abortive. While a number of the delegates came prepared to contribute atrocity stories and demand more federal interference, a larger number were found to have come to the convention to prevent a "new flood of misrepresentations" which would "frighten men and capital from their neglected fields and factories." This latter class was composed of men who had become identified with the material interests of the South. Delegates from North Carolina were ready to declare that they had not heard of a political assault in their state for more than a year. The convention appointed a committee on "Facts and Statistics" which never reported, and passed general resolutions asserting that violence toward loyal men was common, but the total effect of their meeting was to give the South a clean bill of health. With the "outrage" business played out, the Republicans were deprived of their leading arguments for continuing in power, while the Democrats and the Liberal Republicans insisted that business was injured by the plundering governments of the southern states. Testimony was sedulously gathered by the *Tribune* to show that there were no outrages in Tennessee or Kentucky and that migrating capital was safe in those states.

The eventual victory of those who preferred the economic to the political exploitation of the South was foreshadowed in the election returns. The Democrats won control of Congress, and Republican politicians turned to a new stock taking. "We have got a hard lot from the South," said Postmaster-General Marshall Jewell as he surveyed the carpetbag governments, "and the people will not submit to it any longer, nor do I blame them." To Jewell's mind the carpetbaggers did not have "among them one really first class man." A consul in Germany thought it "too d—d bad that our party should be ruined and have to go to the wall through the careless labors of such cattle" as the Louisiana carpetbaggers. But, said this observer, the people were "tired out with this wornout cry of 'Southern Outrages!!!' Hard times and heavy taxes make them wish the 'nigger' 'everlasting nigger' were in — or Africa. . . . It is amazing the change that has taken place in the last two years in public sentiment." Even Vice-President Wilson concluded that the Republican party would have to change its policy, and noticed, after a trip through the South, that business conditions had improved and a spirit of industry was spreading among the southern whites. Wisconsin's Senator Howe ruefully regarded the wreck of Republican hopes and suddenly remembered that the war was not "fought for the 'nigger' " and the Negro was not "the end and aim of all our effort."

The congressional elections of 1874 marked the abandonment of political reconstruction by the northern voters. The repudiated Radicals continued their course until after they had delivered the presidency to Hayes, but the popular vote in the North was cast in 1876 for Tilden and for a different method of exploiting the South. With the withdrawal of the federal troops from the South, the masters of capital embarked upon a policy of conciliating their former enemies and of slow infiltration into their conquered but stubborn provinces.

A single glimpse at the situation a decade later will suffice to illustrate the new technique which the North came to employ in dealing with the South. In 1885 young William McKinley went to plead with the people of Virginia to send a protectionist to the Senate. "Do you imagine that anybody is coming to Virginia with his money to build a mill, or a factory, or a furnace, and develop your coal and your ore, bring his money down here, when you vote every time against his interests. . . .?" he asked. "If you think so, you might just as well be undeceived now, for they will not come. . . .

Be assured that the Republicans of the North harbor no resentments—only ask for the results of the war. They wish you the highest prosperity and the greatest development." The change from the method of coercion to that of appeal was great, but the hope was still alive that in spite of the abandonment of political reconstruction the South would receive the master of capital with his promises of prosperity.

James M. McPherson

Reconstruction:
A Revolution Manqué

More than forty years ago Charles Beard, one of the country's leading historians, described the Civil War era as the Second American Revolution. Beard maintained that Northern victory transferred political and economic power from the old Southern planter aristocracy to the new Northern industrial plutocracy and set in motion the explosive economic growth of the last third of the nineteenth century. Whatever the validity of Beard's argument (it has been challenged by several economic historians), there is no doubt that in the field of race relations the Civil War and Reconstruction did produce revolutionary changes. In a period of less than ten years, four million slaves were emancipated by the force of arms, enfranchised by the national government, and granted equal civil and political rights by the United States Constitution. But this was an aborted revolution; the promise of racial equality was never fully implemented even during Reconstruction; and after 1877, black Americans were gradually repressed into second-class citizenship, from which they are emerging slowly and painfully in our own time. This essay will try to describe the potential revolution of racial equality a century ago and to analyze the reasons for its failure.

Northern war aims evolved through three stages during the Civil War. The earliest and most important war aim, of course, was restoration of the Union. Until late in 1862 this meant the Union "as it was"—with slavery still in it. The North did not go to war to abolish slavery, and it took more than a year of discussion and agitation to bring the government to a policy of emancipation. Despite his own abhorrence of slavery, Abraham Lincoln was sensitive to the pressures of proslavery conservatives in the North and the need to keep the border slave states in the Union. The election of 1860 had shown that most Northerners, although opposed to the expansion of slavery into new territories, were not in favor of abolishing it where it already existed. The Constitution protected slavery; and Lincoln hoped that he could bring about restoration of the Union constitutionally with a demonstration of federal force and a short war, followed by political negotiations and compromise.

But there were a good many people in the North who wanted to make emancipation a second war aim. These abolitionists (black and white), and Radical Republicans, believed that slavery had caused the war and that Union victory was impossible without elimination of this festering sore. The Radicals, joined by a growing number of moderates, argued with telling effect that emancipation was a military necessity. They pointed out that the 3½ million slaves in the Confederacy constituted more than one-third of its population, raised most of the food and fiber for the South, and did most of the digging, hauling, and construction work for the Confederate army. A blow against slavery would cripple the Southern war effort and attract thousands of freed blacks to the side of the North, where they could work and fight, not only for their own freedom, but for the Union as well.

The military necessity thesis was the most compelling argument for emancipation, but abolitionists also emphasized political and moral considerations. Politically, an antislavery policy would strengthen the Union's diplomatic efforts to keep Great Britain from helping the South, for English public opinion would not tolerate its government's intervention on the side of slavery against freedom. The Radicals also pointed out that even if the Union could be restored by negotiation and compromise, slavery would remain a source of future strife. There could be no internal peace in America, they argued, while four million people were in bondage. Moreover, the North professed to be fighting for the preservation of democratic government; the national anthem declared the Union to be the "land of the free and the home of the brave." But the Northern policy of fighting for the restoration of a slave-holding Union, said the abolitionists, made a mockery of this profession.

By 1862, mainly as a result of developments in the war itself, these arguments began to gain converts. The Confederacy won most of the major battles in the first seventeen months of the war, and a serious danger of British intervention on the side of the South existed in 1862. War weariness and defeatism lowered Northern morale. Lincoln's conservative policy toward slavery alienated the Radical wing of his party. As these pressures built up Lincoln and the Republican Congress took timid and then decisive action against slavery in the second year of the war. Congress passed a series of antislavery and confiscation acts, and in September of 1862 the President issued a preliminary Emancipation Proclamation, stating that all the slaves in states still in rebellion on January 1, 1863, would be freed. The South was still in rebellion on that date, so Lincoln issued his final Emancipation Proclamation. Henceforth, the North officially fought for freedom as well as Union.

Thus the second war aim was proclaimed, to be confirmed by Northern victory and the adoption of the Thirteenth Amendment in 1865. Well before the end of the war, however, Radicals began calling for a third war aim: civil equality for the freedmen. The antislavery ideals of abolitionists and Radical Republicans envisioned not only freedom for black people, but a positive guarantee of equal rights as well. Gradually, fitfully, haltingly, and with doubtful conviction, the North groped toward a commitment to equality as its third war aim; but never was equality so important an objective as Union and emancipation. Many Northerners who supported or accepted emancipation as a military necessity were notably unenthusiastic about this third war aim. It is necessary, not only for a comprehension of the Civil War and Reconstruction but also of the race problem in our own time, to understand the incomplete and halting efforts a century ago to implement equality and the reasons why they failed.

The first step toward equality was the enlistment of black men in the Union army. As Frederick Douglass put it: "Once let the black man get upon his person the brass letters, U.S., let him get an eagle on his button, and a musket on his shoulder and bullets in his pocket, and there is no power on earth which can deny that he has earned the right to citizenship." Undertaken tentatively as an experiment late in 1862, the employment of Negro soldiers proved a success and was prosecuted on a full scale in the last two years of the war. In a sense, this result was a logical outgrowth of emancipation; for one of the purposes of freeing the slaves was to deprive the Confederacy of a vital manpower resource and utilize that resource for the Union, not only by getting black men to dig trenches and haul supplies for the Northern armies (the sort of work slaves did for the South), but by putting them into uniform to fight for Union and freedom.

Despite the initial skepticism of many Northerners, including President Lincoln, black men demonstrated impressive fighting qualities. In a series of battles all over the South in the last two years of war, Negro troopers proved their courage and determination. Thirty-eight black regiments fought in the Union armies that invaded Virginia in 1864, helping to deliver the hammer blows that finally drove Lee's forces to surrender. Negroes were the first soldiers to enter Charleston and Richmond when these important strongholds fell late in the war. By the time the war was over, about 180,000 black men, most of them former slaves, had fought for the Union army, and another 25,000 had served in the navy. More than 37,000 black soldiers lost their lives in the defense of union and freedom. Twenty-one Negroes won Congressional Medals of Honor for their courage on the field of battle. Black troops numbered nearly 10 percent of the total Union forces and constituted an even higher percentage of the Northern armies in the final, decisive year of war. As early as August 1863 General Ulysses S. Grant and President Lincoln declared that the enlistment of black regiments was "the heaviest blow yet dealt to the rebellion." After the war was over, the influential New York *Tribune* said that the use of Negro troops had shortened the war by a year. The performance of black soldiers earned new respect for their race, made emancipation secure, and helped push the North toward a commitment to equality. The contribution of the Negro to the Union war effort created a debt that could be paid only by granting full citizenship to the race.

The drive for equal rights began in the North itself. Before the war, black men did not enjoy first-class citizenship in most Northern states. Several states had "black laws" that barred Negroes from immigration into the state, prohibited testimony by blacks against whites in courts, and otherwise discriminated against people with dark skin. In many parts of the North public accommodations, transportation facilities, hotels, and theaters were off-limits to Negroes. During the war black soldiers were thrown off the horse-drawn streetcars of Washington, Philadelphia, and New York on several occasions. Public schools in most parts of the North were segregated, and in some areas black children were barred from schools altogether. Blacks in Northern cities were frequently threatened by mob violence. In 1862 and 1863 white workingmen, fearful that emancipation would bring a horde of freedmen northward to compete for jobs, killed scores of Negroes in several urban race riots, climaxed by the New York Draft Riots of July 1863.

But the impetus of emancipation and the reputation of black soldiers began to break down racial discrimination in the North. Blacks were admitted to Congressional galleries and to White House receptions for the first time in 1864. A Negro lawyer was granted a license to present cases before the Supreme Court of the United States in 1865, just eight years after Roger B. Taney, as Chief Justice, had declared, in the Dred Scott decision, that black men had no rights that white men were bound to respect. Congress passed a series of laws forbidding discrimination against Negroes in the federal courts, the post office department, and on Washington streetcars. Northern states with "black laws" repealed them during, or shortly after, the war. In the postwar decades many states took even greater steps toward equal rights. Massachusetts passed a public accommodations law in 1865. Several other states followed suit in the 1870s and 1880s. Most Northern states abolished *de jure* school segregation. This equalitarian legislation was honored more in the breach than in practice, and a great deal of discrimination remained in the North despite the laws, but at least a beginning was made.

The question of Negro suffrage became the major issue of Reconstruction. The right to vote is a basic right of citizenship in a democracy, and the issue of black voters, especially in the South, where Negroes were a majority of the population in three states and a minority of more than 40 percent in three others, generated more conflict, controversy, and dissension than any other single question in the fifteen years after the Civil War. By the end of 1865, most members of the Radical wing of the Republican party were committed to some kind of effort to secure equal voting rights for the freedmen; and by 1867, the moderate majority of the party had also come around to this position.

The prospect of Negro suffrage presented a good many practical difficulties. The four million freedmen were for the most part illiterate, penniless, and totally without political experience. The institution of slavery had crippled the self-reliance, initiative, pride, and manhood of many Negroes. The black people emerging from slavery did not have the social, economic, and educational resources to make themselves the instant equals of their old masters.

Although Radical Republicans were concerned about these problems, most of them suppressed their doubts and emphasized the positive arguments for Negro suffrage as a cornerstone of Reconstruction. The very logic of the Union war effort seemed to require the granting of equal citizenship to the Negro, who had fought not only for his own freedom but for the cause of the North. To have sloughed off these important allies into second-class citizenship would have been a repudiation of the debt that many people thought the Union owed the black man. Moreover, as a practical matter, it became clear that the freedmen would need the ballot to protect their basic civil rights. Republicans feared that if emancipated slaves were left without political power they would be reduced to some form of quasi-slavery or serfdom. The "black codes" passed by most Southern states in the months after the war confirmed this fear. Some of these codes required the arrest of black vagrants (the question of vagrancy to be determined by white sheriffs) and their lease for specified periods of time to white planters, apprenticed black children to white "masters" in certain circumstances, prohibited Negroes in some states from buying or renting land, or in other ways fastened a subordinate legal status upon the freedmen. The black codes presented the Radicals with dramatic evidence of the need for federal protection and political rights for the freedmen.

Many Republicans also feared that if the Southern states were readmitted to the Union without Negro suffrage, they would send Democratic congressmen to Washington and reduce the Republican party once again to to a minority party. Thus the ballot for freedmen became something of a political necessity for the Republicans. But it was not only expediency or partisanship that motivated Republican thinking on this issue. Most Southern Democrats and a sizable proportion of their Northern brethren had been Confederates or Confederate sympathizers. They had fought a bitter war to destroy the Union and preserve slavery, causing 350,000 Northern deaths. Thus it was easy, and not entirely specious, for Northern Republicans (and most Northern voters) to identify the Democratic party with treason and the Republican party with union and freedom. The Northern mood of 1865–69 would not stand for any policy that readmitted the Democratic South to the Union with undiminished political power, thereby "letting the fruits of victory slip from our grasp." In such circumstances, the enfranchisement of the freedmen (who were expected, with good reason, to vote Republican) was patriotic as well as good politics for the Republicans.

There was also a punitive motive for Negro suffrage. Many Northerners, bitter toward "traitors" and "rebels," wanted to destroy the political basis of the Southern "aristocracy" they believed had caused the war and punish the Confederates by temporarily disfranchising them and permanently enfranchising their former slaves, thereby destroying the old political power structure of the South and creating a new Republican coalition of unionist whites and black freedmen.

Thus, for a variety of reasons, including equalitarianism, patriotism, political partisanship, and bitterness, the Radical wing of the Republican party pushed for enfranchisement of the freedmen as the cornerstone of their Reconstruction policy. In some cases this required political courage by Republicans who represented districts where racism was still a potent force. Despite the changes in Northern attitudes toward the Negro caused by the war, latent, and often overt, prejudice was still widespread. Blacks could not vote in most Northern states at the end of the war; many white voters, in spite of their hatred of the South, disliked the prospect of black equality and feared that freedmen's suffrage would be a major step toward equal rights in the North as well as in the South. For this reason, as well as their skepticism about the freedmen's qualifications for the ballot, moderate Republicans (a majority in the party) shied away from Negro suffrage in 1865–66 and tried to find a middle ground between black enfranchisement and readmission of the South with no federal protection at all for the freedmen. Their solution was the Fourteenth Amendment to the Constitution, proposed in 1866, which guaranteed citizenship and civil rights to the freedmen and reduced the representation of Southern states in Congress by the proportion of their adult male citizens who could not vote. Thus the South's political power was reduced, while an inducement was offered for voluntary enfranchisement of the freedmen.

This moderate proposal was sabotaged by President Andrew Johnson and by the short-sighted intransigence of the South. Johnson was a Tennessee Democrat, who remained loyal to the Union during the war and was rewarded with the 1864 vice-presidential nomination of the "Union Party,"a wartime coalition of Republicans and War Democrats. After Lincoln's assassination, Johnson gradually gravitated back to his Democratic allegiance, urged the readmission of the Southern states with minimum conditions, and defied the policy of the Republican majority in Congress. With remarkable political ineptitude, Johnson vetoed moderate Congressional legislation, encouraged the Southern states to refuse ratification of the Fourteenth Amendment, alienated the moderate Republicans, and drove them closer to the Radical wing of the party. In the 1866 Congressional elections the Northern voters overwhelmingly repudiated Johnson's policies and gave the Republicans a mandate to push through their Reconstruction program over the President's vetoes.

In the spring of 1867, Congress passed a series of Reconstruction Acts that provided for military administration of the South until new state constitutions could be drawn up instituting universal manhood suffrage. Only after the state governments elected under these constitutions had ratified the Fourteenth Amendment would their representatives be readmitted to Congress. By the end of 1868, eight of the former Confederate states had been restored to the Union under these conditions; in 1869 Congress adopted the Fifteenth Amendment, prohibiting voting discrimination on grounds of race, and required the remaining three Southern states to ratify it before returning to the Union. By 1870, all the ex-Confederate states were under Republican control, with several black officeholders; the Fourteenth and Fifteenth Amendments were in the Constitution; the Union was restored; and the third Northern war aim of equality was achieved.

Or was it? Despite appearances, Radical Reconstruction rested on a weak foundation. During the 1870s the foundation gradually crumbled, and the walls came tumbling down. The framework of the Fourteenth and Fifteenth Amendments remained in the Constitution, to become the basis for the Negro Revolution of the mid-twentieth century; but in the 1870s the nation failed to carry out the promises of equality contained in these amendments.

There were several reasons for this failure. In the first place, most Northern whites were only superficially committed to the equalitarian purposes of Reconstruction, and many were openly hostile. From 1865 to 1869 there was a temporary radicalization of Northern public opinion that made possible the passage of Reconstruction measures enfranchising the freedmen, but this was the result more of war-born anti-Southern sentiment than of genuine pro-Negro feeling. In 1867, when the Reconstruction Acts instituted Negro suffrage in the South, black men could vote in only seven of the twenty Northern states and in none of the four border states. Several times, from 1865 to 1868, Northern voters rejected Negro suffrage amendments to their own state constitutions. Not until the Fifteenth Amendment went into effect in 1870, three years after the Southern freedmen had been enfranchised, did most Negroes in the North have the right to vote. The Northern hostility or indifference to equal rights betokened ill success for an equalitarian Reconstruction policy, which required a strong national commitment if it was to succeed.

A second reason for the failure of Reconstruction was the bitter, sometimes violent, and always well-organized opposition of most Southern whites. Confederate veterans, accustomed to the use of violence to attain political ends, formed such organizations as the Ku Klux Klan, the White League, the Red Shirts, and numerous "rifle clubs" to terrorize Republicans, especially black Republicans, as a means of breaking down and destroying the party in the South. The federal government made several efforts between 1870 and 1874 to enforce equal rights against this Southern counterrevolution. The "Ku Klux Act" of 1871 gave the President sweeping powers to use the armed forces and courts to suppress white terrorist organizations; and this law, when enforced vigorously in 1871–72, was successful in temporarily quelling Southern anti-Republican violence. But a combination of factors after 1873 caused a decline in federal enforcement efforts: Financial depression, which diverted national attention to economic issues; Democratic victory in the Congressional elections of 1874; adverse Supreme Court decisions that stripped enforcement legislation of much of its power; and growing Northern disillusionment with the whole experiment of Reconstruction, which produced diminishing enthusiasm among Republicans for the party's Southern policy. Actually, even with the best of intentions, the federal government could not have completely suppressed the Ku Klux Klan and its sister organizations, since the number of troops in the army was inadequate for the purpose and most of the regiments were on the frontier fighting Indians.

Another dimension of Southern white resistance was the refusal or inability of many property-owning whites (and whites owned most of the property) to pay taxes to the "alien" Republican state governments. During Reconstruction most of the Southern states built public school systems almost from scratch, constructed new charitable and welfare institutions, and undertook ambitious programs of railroad building, aided by state grants and loans. All of this cost money, more money than the South had been accustomed to paying for public and social services, more than property owners were willing or able to pay in taxes, especially when they were opposed, as some of them were, to such innovations as public schools or when they believed that much of the revenue went into the pockets of corrupt officials. The Southern state governments, in some cases, were too weak or unstable to compel payment of taxes, and the resulting deficits were another reason for the collapse of Republican regimes as the 1870s wore on.

A third reason for the failure of Reconstruction was the illiteracy, inexperience, and poverty of the freedmen. It had been illegal to teach slaves (and free blacks, in some states) to read or write. The institution of slavery trained black people to dependence and denied them the opportunity and responsibilities of freedom. It would have been criminal of the North merely to emancipate the slaves, give them equal rights on paper, and then say: "All right, you're on your own—root hog, or die." And to the credit of some Northern people and the federal government, efforts were made to educate and assist the freedmen in their difficult transition from slavery to freedom. In one of the major outpourings of idealism and missionary zeal in American history, freedmen's aid societies in the North sent thousands of teachers to the South to bring literacy to the Negroes. The federal government created the Freedmen's Bureau in 1865. More than a thousand freedmen's schools, supported by Northern philanthropy and aided by the Bureau, were in operation by 1870; and the new public school system of the South was built on the foundation provided by these mission schools. After 1870, the missionary societies concentrated their efforts on secondary schools and colleges to train the teachers, ministers, and leaders of the new black generation. The major institutions of higher learning for Negroes evolved out of these freedmen's schools: Howard, Fisk, and Atlanta Universities; Morehouse, Spelman, and Talladega Colleges; Hampton Institute; Meharry Medical College; and many others. But despite the admirable efforts of the crusade for freedmen's education, 70 percent of Southern blacks were still illiterate in 1880. An effective crash program to educate and train four million freed slaves would have required a far greater commitment of national resources than was undertaken. The mission societies did their best; but after the expiration of the Freedmen's Bureau in 1870, they received no more federal aid. Black Southerners remained at a large educational disadvantage in their relations with white Southerners.

Another facet of the black man's disadvantage was his poverty. Most emancipated slaves owned little more than the clothes on their backs when freedom came. Unless they received some kind of massive economic assistance, it was clear they would remain an economically subordinate class, dependent on whites for employment. Many abolitionists and Radical Republicans believed that there must be an economic reconstruction of the South if civil and political reconstruction were to succeed. The great abolitionist orator, Wendell Phillips, Congressman Thaddeus Stevens, and others urged the adoption of a thorough program of land reform as a basis of Reconstruction. They called for the confiscation of plantations owned by former Confederates, and the redistribution of the land in forty-acre plots to the freedmen. But this proposal threatened the sanctity of private property as a basis of society and was too radical for most Northerners. A small amount of Confederate property was expropriated during the war, and some of these lands found their way to black ownership; but there was no major program of agrarian reform. Most blacks became wage-earners, sharecroppers, or tenant farmers, rather than independent landowning farmers. The South was not reconstructed economically, and consequently political reconstruction rested on an unstable foundation.

Because of educational and economic disadvantages, black people lacked the social and psychological resources to sustain their equal rights in the face of Southern white counterrevolution. This is not to deny that there were effective Negro leaders during Reconstruction. In fact, one of the remarkable things about the era was that this largely uneducated and propertyless people could produce such a group of able leaders. Twenty black men were elected to the national House of Representatives and two to the Senate after the war. Several Negroes served as lieutenant governors, secretaries of state, superintendents of education, and treasurers of Southern states. No black man was elected governor, but one Negro lieutenant-governor, Pinckney B. S. Pinchback, served for a month as acting Governor of Louisiana. Blanche K. Bruce was an outstanding black senator from Mississippi; Robert B. Elliott, of South Carolina, and John R. Lynch, of Mississippi, were talented black congressmen. These men and others provided strong leadership for their race, but they could not overcome the determined white power structure. At least 100,000 black veterans of the Union army lived in the South during Reconstruction. Republican state governors enrolled many of them in state militia regiments to protect the freedmen's rights against terrorism. But there were four or five times as many white veterans of the Confederate army in the South, many of them enrolled in the Ku Klux Klan and similar organizations. These men were better armed and better led than the black militiamen; and in the pitched battles of the violence-wracked years of Reconstruction, the white para-military groups usually prevailed.

One other major reason for the failure of Reconstruction was the instability of the coalition called the Republican Party in the South. This coalition was composed of a small number of Northern whites ("carpetbaggers"), Southern whites ("scalawags"), and the freedmen. Some of the carpetbaggers and scalawags deserved the pejorative connotations of these words, invented by their opponents, but others were honest, sincere men who wanted to make interracial democracy work. Inevitably there was friction among the three components of the Republican coalition. Native white Republicans shared some of the region's dislike for "outsiders," and there were power struggles within the Republican Party that pitted carpetbagger against scalawag. Though blacks provided most of the Republican votes, whites held most of the offices, which produced a growing demand by Negro leaders for greater representation and power in party councils. Many scalawags could not transcend their Southern upbringing and were uncomfortable in a predominantly black party, especially when blacks tried to move into positions of power. Some of the carpetbaggers also had difficulty transcending deeply ingrained racial prejudices. The Southern Democrats, increasingly united and strong under the banner of "home rule and white supremacy," took advantage of racial and other tensions in the Republican Party, and, by a combination of inducements and threats, brought many scalawags over from the "black Republicans" to the "white man's party." The unstable Republican coalition broke into squabbling factions in several Southern states in the 1870s, making it easier for the Democrats, aided by the terrorization of black voters, to gain control of one state after another.

How did the North react to crumbling Republican power in the South? Many Northerners had hoped that with the passage of the Reconstruction Acts and adoption of the Fourteenth and Fifteenth Amendments, the task of restoring the South to the Union and ensuring equal rights would be completed. The North wanted to turn its attention to other issues. As reports of corruption, conflict, and violence filtered up from the South, however, it was clear that Reconstruction was not yet accomplished, and that continuous and vigorous national effort would be required to maintain Negro rights against Southern counterrevolution. But disillusionment and indifference sapped the Northern will. As early as 1870, Horace Greeley's New York *Tribune*, which had been one of the foremost advocates of Radical Reconstruction a few years earlier, declared that it was time to "have done with Reconstruction. The country is sick of it." In the 1870s, *The Nation*, an independent liberal weekly with great influence among Northern intellectuals, became increasingly disenchanted with the results of Negro suffrage. *The Nation* declared that the Republican state governments of South Carolina and Louisiana were "a gang of robbers making war on civilization and morality," and concluded that the average black man "as regards the right performance of a voter's duty is as ignorant as a horse or a sheep." By 1876, *The Nation* had decided that the North should never have attempted "the insane task of making newly-emancipated field hands, led by barbers and barkeepers, fancy they knew as much about government and were as capable of administering it, as the whites."

Many Northern journalists visited the South during the 1870s and wrote feature stories that were increasingly sympathetic to the white viewpoint. James Shepherd Pike, a reporter for the New York *Tribune*, gathered his articles into a book published in 1874 with the title *The Prostrate State: South Carolina Under Negro Government*. This book and others portrayed a South ruled and ruined by "Carpetbag-Negro government." Under the impact of this journalistic barrage, Northern public opinion gradually became indifferent, and even hostile, to the plight of freedmen and Republicans in the South. There was a growing consensus that Reconstruction was a mistake, that the federal government ought to cease its "misguided efforts" to enforce equal rights in the South, and that the Southern people should be left alone to work out the race problem on their own terms. "The whole public are tired of these annual autumnal outbreaks in the South," wrote the United States Attorney General, in refusing a request from the Republican Governor of Mississippi for federal troops to protect Negro voters in 1875. Mississippi was captured by the Democrats in the election, and the Attorney General's remark symbolized Northern indifference to this development.

Widespread reports of Republican corruption, incompetence, and misgovernment were one of the most important factors in turning Northern opinion against Reconstruction. It would be foolish to deny that there was corruption in the South. Like all myths, the myth of greedy, rapacious carpetbaggers, jackal-like scalawags, and incompetent, bribe-taking politicians is based on a modicum of truth. But reality bore only slight relation to the grotesque picture depicted by contemporary journalists and echoed by many historians. Disorder and mistakes inevitably accompany rapid social change such as occurred in the postwar South. The building of railroads, the construction of a public school system, the physical rehabilitation of a region scarred by war, and the democratization of the Southern political system could not have been achieved without a dislocation of values and standards. And the Southern situation should be placed in national perspective. The post-Civil War era was an age of corruption, bribery, and swindling in Northern as well as Southern states and in the federal government itself. All the Southern state governments combined probably did not steal as much from the public treasury as the Tweed Ring in New York City. Even the South Carolina and Louisiana legislatures could scarcely match the brazen bribery that took place in Albany, New York. One contemporary critic charged that the Standard Oil Company could do anything it wanted with the Pennsylvania legislature except refine it.

Despite the propaganda of Southern whites, it was not so much dishonest Republican government that they opposed as it was any Republican government at all, honest or dishonest. The Reconstruction government of Mississippi was clean and honest, yet it, too, was overthrown by terror and intimidation. Why, then, did influential segments of Northern opinion accept the journalistic descriptions of Southern corruption? Primarily because the North, in spite of its superficially pro-Negro attitude of 1865–69, had never really been converted to a genuine belief in racial equality. The Northern radicalism of 1865–69 was produced mainly by war-born hatred for Southern whites and temporary gratitude to black soldiers who had fought for the Union, but as the memories and passions of war faded in the 1870s the underlying racism of the North reasserted itself. Thus the Northern people were willing to believe exaggerated stories of the incompetence and corruption of "Negro-Carpetbag" governments. As the 1876 centennial of American independence approached there was a movement toward sectional reconciliation and a rededication to national unity. This was all very well, but the freedmen became victims of this "clasping of hands across the bloody chasm." The price of reconciliation was "home rule" for the South and a cessation of Northern interference in Southern "domestic affairs."

With the exception of some of the old Radical Republicans and abolitionists still alive in 1876, the North was prepared to retreat from Reconstruction. It was a Presidential election year, and all signs pointed to a Democratic victory. Capitalizing on the economic depression, widespread disgust with the scandals of the Grant administration, and disillusionment with Reconstruction, Democrats hoped to expand their 1874 capture of the House of Representatives into occupation of the White House. The disputed Presidential election of 1876 resulted in one of the most bizarre political crises of American history. Democrat Samuel J. Tilden won a majority of the popular vote, and was only one electoral vote short of victory, with the outcome in the three Southern states still controlled by Republicans—South Carolina, Florida, and Louisiana—in dispute. Two sets of electoral returns were submitted from each state. If Tilden won any of these votes, he was elected; Republican Rutherford B. Hayes needed the electoral votes of all three states to become the nineteenth President. With the Democratic House and Republican Senate deadlocked over the issue, there could be no Congressional counting of electoral votes, as specified by the Constitution. Passions ran high, many feared another civil war, and there was a real danger that no President would be inaugurated on March 4, 1877. Finally, Congress appointed a special commission to canvass the disputed votes. The commission, by a partisan vote, awarded all the electors to Hayes, thereby making him President. Angry Democrats in the House charged fraud and threatened a filibuster to prevent completion of the electoral count. Behind the scenes, however, several Southern Democrats were in consultation with Hayes's lieutenants, and a series of agreements was worked out whereby the Southerners promised to allow a completion of the vote in return for commitments from Hayes to withdraw the last federal troops from South Carolina and Louisiana (where the federal presence was the only power keeping duly elected Republican governments in office), to give political patronage to Southern Democrats, and to use his influence in behalf of appropriations for Southern internal improvements. This "Compromise of 1877" ended the electoral crisis. Hayes took office and promptly withdrew the troops from South Carolina and Louisiana. The Republican governments immediately collapsed and the South became solidly Democratic.

Some Republicans and former abolitionists charged that the compromise was a sellout of the freedmen; in a sense they were right. Hayes's withdrawal of the troops brought an end to meaningful national efforts to enforce the Fourteenth and Fifteenth Amendments in the South until the 1950s. In the three decades after 1877, Southern blacks were gradually disfranchised, Jim-Crowed, and reduced to a degraded second-class citizenship. But Hayes really had had no choice in 1877. Democrats controlled the House and threatened to block appropriations if he tried to use the army in the South; the North had already given up its moral commitment to Reconstruction; and the overthrow of Southern Republican governments was a virtual *fait accompli* by the time Hayes took office.

The Civil War and Reconstruction, therefore, were a revolution manqué. The Union was restored and the slaves freed, but the Negro did not achieve equality. There was a period of bright promise in the late 1860s, but it flickered out in the backlash of the 1870s. A genuine revolution of equality would have required a revolution in institutions and attitudes which did not occur. Despite the enfranchisement of the freedmen, the basic institutional structure of Southern society remained unchanged: The whites retained most of the wealth, property, education, power, and experience. The racial attitudes of both North and South bent just enough to accept (sometimes reluctantly) emancipation, but remained basically opposed to genuine equality. The revolution of racial equality was a failure.

And yet not quite a failure. The Civil War–Reconstruction era produced the system of public schools and private colleges for Negroes that brought literacy to the race and trained future generations of leaders. From the colleges founded by Northern abolitionists and missionaries after the war were graduated, among others, W. E. B. DuBois, Walter White, Thurgood Marshall, Martin Luther King, James Farmer, and Stokely Carmichael. The Fourteenth and Fifteenth Amendments were permanent results of Reconstruction, and in our own time the fusion of educated black leadership and reinvigoration of these Amendments has generated a Second Reconstruction that may produce the racial equality envisaged by the first.

Grady McWhiney

Reconstruction: Index of Americanism

Until thirty years ago scholars agreed that the decade following the Civil War was a tragic era, especially in the South. Ruled by carpetbaggers, Negroes, and renegade scalawags instead of by "decent white men," that section of the country was "reduced to the very abomination of desolation." "It was the most soul-sickening spectacle that Americans had ever been called upon to behold," wrote John W. Burgess. "Every principle of the old American policy was here reversed. In place of government by the most intelligent and virtuous part of the people for the benefit of the governed, here was government by the most ignorant and vicious part of the population for the benefit, the vulgar, materialistic, brutal benefit of the governing set."

Today most historians still consider the postwar period a tragic one, but usually for a different reason. Products of an age that is not shocked by Negro suffrage, they are inclined to deny that Reconstruction was an unmitigated disaster for the South. Revisionists have taught them to see some evidence of democratic advance in the achievements of the Reconstruction regimes in the fields of public education and internal improvements.

But the democratic advance seems to many a modern eye to have been painfully limited and compromised. The real tragedy, in this revisionist view, was that the national reconstruction program was only insincerely democratic. It gave the Negro nominal political power without giving him economic power, and so condemned him to virtual reenslavement. The tragedy of Reconstruction was that it did not really reconstruct.

One may well puzzle over this peculiar Reconstruction that did not reconstruct, with its peculiar Southerners (presumably feudal-minded racists)

From Charles Grier Sellers, Jr., ed., The Southerner As American (Chapel Hill: University of North Carolina Press, 1960). Reprinted by permission.

who accepted more colorblind democracy than they could have been expected to, and who would have accepted more than they were forced to, and with its peculiar Yankees (presumably democratic idealists) who abandoned all too quickly any effort to make colorblind democracy stick. If one puzzles long enough, he may begin to perceive that these Southerners and these Yankees were acting in peculiarly similar ways. He may begin to suspect that Reconstruction was not so peculiar after all, that it may not have been so tragic after all—except as a reflection of the contradictions of Americanism.

Today Americans are remarkably alike. Their values and aspirations are similar. With few exceptions, they believe in democracy, progress, success, universal education, equal opportunities for all citizens, Mother, God, and country. Their tastes in literature, art, music, food, drink, clothing, houses, furniture, automobiles, and entertainment vary only slightly. According to the Kinsey reports even their sex lives are similar.

American society is so mobile that economic, social, or intellectual status is frequently difficult or impossible to determine. Salesmen dress like celebrities. Cadillacs are accessible to plumbers. By following advice readily available in newspapers and magazines, garbage collectors can learn to dress, talk, and even smell like bankers. A coal miner can fly to South Bend for a football game between Pitt and Notre Dame and, if his fingernails are clean, be mistaken for an industrialist. Fashion journals tell secretaries how to outdress executives' daughters. For a nominal price every American can obtain a product which allegedly prevents tooth decay.

Such opportunities were not always present. Nor was such homogeneity. In colonial America a man's class could be recognized by his dress and, as late as 1815, gentlemen still wore ruffles and silk stockings. Nineteenth-century technological developments, however, soon allowed the poor to ape the rich. The presidency of James Monroe marked the end of an era. He was the last chief executive to wear a wig. By the end of the ante-bellum period nearly all Americans dressed alike.

Aiding technology in effecting this revolution were two of the most pervasive themes in American history: the ideology of progress and the democratic dogma. Brought to the colonies by Europeans, both doctrines were subtly shaped by Americans and have enjoyed almost universal approval since the Jacksonian period. The majority of Americans, without having heard of the Enlightenment, accepted unquestioningly the belief that men and institutions (especially American men and institutions) could attain here on earth a state of perfection once thought possible only for Christians in a state of grace, and for them only after death. Not to believe in both material and individual progress quickly became un-American. By hard work any man could become successful. The newer religions even promised earthly salvation for the most miserable sinner. A man born in a log cabin could become president. Indeed, for a time, it was hard for a man not born in a log cabin to become president.

Complementing the ideology of progress was the liberating tendency of American democracy. To develop their talents, it was argued, men must be free from traditional restraints. They must have freedom to get ahead, to make something of themselves, to start a new business, religion, or political party. But democracy was also a leveling process. If the race to perfection was to be run fairly, the participants must start together. Men must have equal opportunities.

Combined, the progressive and democratic doctrines have encouraged (among other things): the accumulation of wealth, westward expansion, "manifest destiny," immigration from Europe, extension of the suffrage, political demagoguery, "common man" culture, crime and violence, religious diversity and religious conformity, erosion of the family unit, sundry reform movements, and technological development.

*   *   *

. . . In most ways faith in democracy developed in the South as it did in other parts of America. Southerners were likewise just as devoted as other Americans to progress, especially material progress. The whole colonial experience of Southerners was one of improving themselves by acquiring farms near the Atlantic coast, or moving westward. The westward trek of Southerners continued throughout the ante-bellum years. Like their Yankee cousins, southern migrants were men on the make, driven to the frontier by the ideology of progress and the liberating theme of democracy. They knew that in America individual progress was measured in dollars and cents, and they had faith in their ability to succeed in the virgin land beyond the Appalachians. The industrious and lucky ones were not disappointed. Aided by technological discoveries which improved agriculture, transportation, and manufacturing, many Southerners prospered during the ante-bellum period. Particularly in the lower South, cotton was a great democratizing influence before 1860. It could be cultivated profitably on a few acres by one man, or on large plantations by many slaves. Men could climb to riches over bales of cotton.

Southerners joined other Americans in the Jacksonian rebellion against entrenched privilege. In fact, Andrew Jackson received some of his largest majorities in the South, where popular culture, universal suffrage for white males, and other leveling developments also won victories. Before the Civil War southern "men of the people" like W. R. W. Cobb, Alabama's "friend of the poor against the rich," who sang such original compositions as "Uncle Sam is rich enough to give us all a farm," were unbeatable politicians. According to recent studies, by 1860 white Southerners enjoyed a large measure of political, social, and economic democracy.

If most Southerners believed in progress and democracy, why were Negroes denied liberty and equality in the Old South? Part of the answer is that throughout the nineteenth century there was an aberration in the thinking of all white Americans about the Negro. Nowhere is this better demonstrated than in the diaries and letters of Union soldiers. Although considered human, "colored" peoples (such as Negroes, Indians, and Orientals) were regarded as inferiors by most Americans. Ironically, Americans believed in equality, but they also believed that some men were more equal than others. This perversion of the doctrine of equality was more apparent in the South because of its large Negro population, but it also existed in the North.

Knowing that few Yankees practiced equalitarianism, Southerners nevertheless had an uneasy conscience. True, they sought religious, philosophical, scientific, historical, and sociological justification for slavery. But the Southerner was too American to be convinced by his own arguments. One thing he did know, however: slavery was profitable. Without slaves, Southerners were certain they would fall behind the rest of America in the progressive race. As businessmen, they did not want to lose their investments or gamble with the uncertainties of a free labor supply. They were as grasping as their northern kinsmen. The indulgent master, the fabled southern planter of cavalier extravagance existed more in the mind of Henry Timrod than in fact. Plantation mansions were exceptions in the architectural pattern of the Old South; most planters lived in rather crude houses and enjoyed few luxuries. None were as wealthy as the richest Northerners. Southern slaveholders were not knights of the round table, but men of the market place. Intellectually, their culture was as sterile as the dreary romances their wives and daughters read. Planters damned the dry or rainy weather when they met, and talked about the price of staples, land, and slaves, not about the philosophy of Plato or Aristotle. Clearly, ante-bellum Southerners were men of progress. They favored better methods of cultivation, improvements in transportation and technology, and higher profits. "No class of people in the world are so dependent on Science . . . as the planter," wrote a slaveholder in 1859.

The great majority of Southerners owned no slaves (nearly three-fourths of all free Southerners had no connection with slavery through either family ties or direct ownership), yet even these non-slaveholders had practical, thoroughly American reasons for defending the "peculiar institution" to the end. Owning slaves was the way to wealth and success in the ante-bellum South, and men who did not own slaves hoped to acquire human chattels some day. In a real sense, emancipation would endanger their chance of success. Thus, Southerners faced an intellectual dilemma: how to be at the same time progressive and democratic and yet dominate the Negro.

Ironically, one reason why Southerners lost their struggle to preserve slavery was because they were too democratic. "Universal suffrage—furloughs & whiskey, have ruined us," wrote a high-ranking Confederate general. The extreme liberty practiced by state rightists, the frequently malicious criticism of civil and military officials by the unmuzzled Confederate press, the lack of discipline in the army (fostered by the election of numerous officers), and the high rate of desertion by soldiers and disaffection by civilians contributed more to the destruction of the Confederacy than stronger northern armies. Superior to the South in resources, the North could afford democracy. Lacking a distinct nationalism, the South could not.

Throughout their entire history down to Appomattox, then, Southerners had shown an unshakable devotion to both democracy and material progress, and, in case of conflict between the two, a disposition to bend their democratic ideals to accommodate their progressive appetites. But were the Yankees so different? While marching to "The Battle Hymn of the Republic" it had been easy for them to picture the Civil War as a struggle between their own democratic idealism and the South's materialistically-based racism. But Appomattox was not the end of the story; in a sense it was but the prelude to its climactic and most revealing phase. For in the sequel of Reconstruction white Northerners and white Southerners discovered a spiritual brotherhood which, however unedifying to a later generation, resulted in a durable reunion. In this spiritual brotherhood material progress took precedence over democracy.

Southerners opened the drama of Reconstruction by manifesting a disposition—such was the paradoxical situation created by defeat—to accept a large measure of democratization, including a goodly dose of colorblind democracy, in order to get back on the progress road. "The war being at an end, . . . and the questions at issue . . . having been decided, I believe it to be the duty of every one to unite in the restoration of the country, and the reestablishment of peace and harmony," wrote General Robert E. Lee. "By doing this and encouraging our citizens to engage in the duties of life with all their heart and mind . . . our country will not only be restored in material prosperity, but will be advanced in science, in virtue and in religion."

Southerners were so anxious for a share in American material prosperity that they complied with every demand made upon them for readmission to the Union. Arguing that actually they had never been out of the Union, they renounced secession, abolished slavery, repudiated the Confederate debt, and, as a result of demands by such determined congressional leaders as Thaddeus Stevens and Charles Sumner, even temporarily consented to try Negro suffrage. "I was not disappointed at the result of the war," wrote a Georgian. "Thad. Stevens would be as safe here as in Pennsylvania," said a Virginian. "Should you visit Mississippi I would be pleased to have you at my house," a stranger informed Senator John Sherman. James L. Alcorn, a former brigadier who had suffered financial ruin during the war, admitted: ". . . you were right Yankee! You have established your power; . . . we are and ever have been in the Union; secession was a nullity. We will now take the oath to support the Constitution and the laws of the United States. . . ." As proof of his sincerity, Alcorn became the Republican governor of Mississippi in 1869 and a Republican member of the United States Senate in 1871. He also recouped his financial losses and increased his property holdings.

Of course, not all Southerners were as easily reconstructed as Alcorn. Many able men were disenfranchised and prohibited from holding office. Some, like Judah P. Benjamin, left the South and found economic opportunities abroad. Edmund Ruffin, one of the most determined secessionists, committed suicide; John J. Pettus, Mississippi's war governor, spent the remaining two years of his life as a disillusioned recluse.

But Ruffin and Pettus were exceptions. Eventually, only seventy-one of the 656 prominent Confederates who lived long enough to make postwar readjustments "failed to recover a substantial portion of the position and prestige they had enjoyed at the Confederacy's peak." Denied the right to hold public office, Jefferson Davis sought to rehabilitate himself economically. For a time he served as president of a life insurance company. When it went bankrupt, he tried to start a steamship line. Only after repeated economic failure did he return to his plantation and devote himself to glorifying the Old South and the Lost Cause.

A number of leaders joined the carpetbag and Negro governments and returned to power sooner than others. In Mississippi Albert G. Brown, a former governor, advocated political expediency and submission to Radical Reconstruction. By 1868 such prominent Alabama Democrats as Lewis E. Parsons, Alexander McKinstry, Judge Samuel F. Rice, and Alexander White had joined the Republican party. Motivated partly by personal political ambition, they also believed that as Republicans they could best help their own as well as their state's economic recovery. General William C. Wickham, of Virginia, endorsed the Republican party less than a month after Appomattox. He soon became president of the Virginia Central Railroad, and three years later president of the Chesapeake and Ohio. In New Orleans General James Longstreet actually led an army of Negroes against Confederate veterans. His reward was lucrative posts from successive Republican administrations. James L. Orr, of South Carolina, marched into the National Union Convention in 1866 arm in arm with a Massachusetts general. When President Andrew Johnson's candidates lost the fall congressional elections, however, Orr changed his allegiance to the victorious Radicals. In North Carolina James G. Ramsey, Richmond M. Pearson, and General Rufus Barringer were early advocates of Negro suffrage and industrialization. General George Maney, of Tennessee, became president of the Tennessee and Pacific Railroad and a Republican.

Clearly, not all of these scalawags were renegade "poor whites." Many of them were former Whigs, seeking a new political home. Others were simply trying to adjust to the new order or to get ahead politically and financially. That they were not always concerned with the means by which success was obtained is illustrated by the case of Josephus Woodruff. A native South Carolinian, Woodruff deserted the Democratic party to become clerk of the state senate, and to insure that his company received all the state's official printing business. In 1874 he confided to his diary a conversation in which the influential Negro legislator Robert Smalls "Said if anyone was to offer him $50,000 to vote against me he would indignantly decline." Woodruff replied that he "Was pleased to hear it, but would be glad to see the offer made and accepted, and the amount equally divided between us." Three years later Smalls was convicted of having accepted a $5,000 bribe from Woodruff to vote for a printing bill.

The Radical regimes in the South lasted only a few years, however, and many scalawags either lost their positions of power and privilege or in order to save them were forced to become Democrats. After abandoning the Republican party Joseph E. Brown not only weathered investigations of his honesty, but remained one of the most powerful politicians in Georgia and one of the leading industrialists in the South. Generals P. G. T. Beauregard and Jubal A. Early had yielded to the blandishments of the Republican-supported Louisiana Lottery Company and received substantial sums for presiding over the drawings. "Ever since Longstreet feathered his nest, there has been an itching about Beauregard's stern for a similar application, and, to those who know him, it was evident time would find him in the radical camp," wrote an impoverished Confederate general. Yet both Beauregard and Early managed to retain their posts after the Democrats returned to power in Louisiana.

Without consistent Federal support, torn by internal conflicts within their own state parties, and hurt by a nation-wide depression, Republican officeholders were driven from the South in the 1870s. Charged with fraud and corruption, they were ousted by pragmatic Democrats who did not shrink from using violence, intimidation, and stuffed ballot boxes.

The Radical Reconstruction experiment failed for a number of reasons, but foremost, perhaps, was northern disillusionment with the Negro. "In spite of all their efforts, the abolitionists . . . failed to create widespread determination in any part of the nation to grant to the freedman social or political or economic equality," writes a perceptive scholar. For the most part Negro suffrage was a political expedient which was endorsed by northern voters only because politicians "waved the bloody shirt." Senator T. O. Howe wrote in 1875 that the Civil War was not "fought for the 'nigger' " and the Negro was not "the end and aim of all our effort." James H. Paine tried to insert a promise of suffrage for southern Negroes into the platform of the Wisconsin Republican Convention in 1865, but the delegates voted overwhelmingly against his proposal.

When Northerners discovered that former Confederates would defend Yankee railroad and industrial interests as vigorously as they fought Yankee armies, the Negro vote became less important. "There can be no way so sure to make the late rebels of the South loyal men and good citizens," declared the New York *Commercial and Financial Chronicle* in 1865, "as to turn their energies to the pursuits of peace, and the accumulation of wealth." By the 1870s Southerners had proved that they were willing to help bring the American dream of a materialistic utopia to fulfillment. Newspapers throughout the South reflected and helped shape their readers' enthusiastic devotion to material progress. "Country papers gave those patron saints of the New South . . . a wide reading public. Liberal news space was devoted to excerpts from the *Manufacturer's Record.* In many areas . . . there was something of religious fervor in the numerous editorials on immigration and on exploitation of land, timber, and mineral resources. Since 1867 country editors have told their readers that they were living in a land of golden opportunity. Their section . . . needed only population, capital, industry, and mechanical knowledge to make it wealthy."

The struggle for power in the South, as well as in the rest of the country, during the Reconstruction period should not be treated as a contest between the forces of good and evil. Rather it should be considered as an encounter between rival economic interests seeking exclusive privileges and trying to control the various states through two different political parties. After 1868 financiers, not radicals, dominated southern politics. According to Horace Mann Bond, "the Louisville and Nashville Railroad, the Alabama and Chattanooga Railroad, . . . the banking houses of the Cookes, of Russell Sage, of the Morgans and the Drexels, loom more significantly in Alabama Reconstruction than do the time-honored figures of the history books." In the struggle for state bonds and land grants, Democrats supported the L. & N., whose president was backed by August Belmont, national chairman of the Democratic party and the American agent for the Rothschilds. In turn, Republicans supported the A. & C., which had the backing of Russell Sage, Henry Clews, and William D. ("Pig Iron") Kelley. Initially, the L. & N. got the upper hand, but after Republicans took over the state the A. & C. put pressure on them to eliminate the L. & N. During the depression of the 1870s, however, the A. & C. went bankrupt, and when the Democrats returned to power in 1874, the L. & N. was assured of success.

In Virginia railroad promoters also played an important role in the state's reconstruction. One of the leading figures in this struggle for power was General William Mahone, who in order to protect his railroad interests successively shifted his political allegiance from the Radicals, to the Conservatives (Democrats), to the Readjusters. Even General Robert E. Lee, who was named president of the Valley Railroad a few months before his death in 1870, succumbed to the promotion fever.

By the time the Reconstruction experiment ended, Southerners were thoroughly Americanized. Every southern state was controlled by businessmen or the friends of business. The dream of an industrial millennium captivated nearly every mind. "The South found her jewel in the toad's head of defeat," said the most famous southern apostle of progress. The Lost Cause was not forgotten, but the Yankee was forgiven. Instead of lynching Congressman Lucius Q. C. Lamar for eulogizing Charles Sumner, Mississippians made him a United States senator.

Though the Negro once again was relegated to a subservient position in the South, he too pursued the goal of material progress. Booker T. Washington, the most famous Southerner of his day, advised his people: "Cast down your bucket where you are—cast it down in making friends in every manly way of the people of all races by whom we are surrounded. Cast it down in agriculture, mechanics, in commerce, in domestic service, and in the professions. And in this connection it is well to bear in mind that whatever other sins the South may be called to bear, when it comes to business, pure and simple, it is

in the South that the Negro is given a man's chance in the commercial world."
If Washington's thoroughly American and materialistic plan to raise his race
to equality was not entirely successful, it was nevertheless applauded by white
Southerners.

Twentieth-century international developments have helped shape a New
Reconstruction program. Today many Americans, aware that their future prosperity as well as the fate of their country may well be determined by an overwhelmingly "colored" world, insist that national survival depends upon practicing colorblind democracy. A number of white Southerners recognize the
logic of this argument, but most of them are still too American either to endorse racial equality or to renounce their democratic pretenses. Like most
Americans, they boast of being common men while they admire eliteness.
They see no inconsistency between the doctrine of personal equality and the
selecting of beauty queens. They admire the Queen of England more than the
wife of their own chief executive. They send their children to schools that do
not educate so that they will not be maladjusted in a society that reveres television and movie stars. They suspect that integration is a diabolical scheme to
destroy not only their present social and economic status but their chance of
future success. The white ladies of Montgomery, Alabama, who chauffeured
their bus-boycotting maids to and from work, are merely comfort-loving Americans, not integrationists.

Aware that white northerners also indulge in democratic hypocrisy, white
Southerners fear that they will be jim-crowed by other Americans if Negro
equality is practiced in the South. Subconsciously, Southerners realize that
the genius of America is inequality. They will accept colorblind democracy
only if convinced that the alternative is loss of status and the chance of future
success. Briefly this was the situation during the Old Reconstruction, when the
white Southerner was ready to acquiesce in Negro suffrage; and now the New
Reconstruction seems to promise a similar but more lasting acquiescence in a
limited amount of school desegregation. The great segregationists' bastion at
Little Rock has fallen because those ultra-typical Americans, the members of
the Downtown Businessmen's Association, hold racial exclusiveness less dear
than the good name and the continued growth and prosperity of their fair city.
For Governor Faubus' constituents, like other Southerners and other Americans, are more devoted to the ideology of material progress than to either racial
superiority or the democratic dogma.

SUGGESTIONS FOR FURTHER READING

Claude G. Bowers, *The Tragic Era: The Revolution After Lincoln* (Boston, 1929)
argues that during Reconstruction "The Southern people literally were put to the
torture" by a "brutal, hypocritical, and corrupt" leadership in the North. E. Merton
Coulter perpetuates these views in his more recent *The South During Reconstruc-*

* Available in paperback edition.

tion (Baton Rouge, 1947). But the best introduction to the anti-radical position is the older and very influential William A. Dunning, *Reconstruction, Political and Economic* (New York, 1907).

Howard K. Beale, *The Critical Year: A Study of Andrew Jackson and Reconstruction* (Baton Rouge, 1947) stresses the connection between Radical Republicans and the industrial business interests of the North. W. E. B. DuBois, *Black Reconstruction* (New York, 1935) is a direct answer to the position taken by William A. Dunning and his many students. His stress is on the accomplishments of the Republican Reconstruction governments in the South. The emphasis, however, is on class, not racial, conflict. A similar emphasis on class conflict may be found in James S. Allen, *Reconstruction: The Battle for Democracy* (New York, 1937), an attempt at a Marxist interpretation.

More recent important interpretations include John Hope Franklin, *Reconstruction After the Civil War* (Chicago, 1961); Kenneth M. Stampp, *The Era of Reconstruction* (New York, 1965); James M. McPherson, *The Struggle for Equality: Abolitionists and the Negro in the Civil War and Reconstruction* (Princeton, 1964); and Willie Lee Rose, *Rehearsal for Reconstruction: The Port Royal Experiment* (Indianapolis, 1964). McKitrick's view may be found more fully stated in his *Andrew Johnson and Reconstruction* (Chicago, 1960). A description of efforts to remake an American consensus after the war can be found in Paul H. Buck, *The Road to Reunion* (Boston, 1937).

Easily available collections of recent writing are Kenneth M. Stampp and Leon F. Litwack, eds., *Reconstruction: An Anthology of Revisionist Writings* (Baton Rouge, 1969) and Staughton Lynd, ed., *Reconstruction* (New York, 1967).

Some of the most recent studies have been concerned with what may be called economic and social reconstruction, emphasizing the effects of emancipation and the postwar settlement on the life and labor of the landlord, the yeoman farmer, and the freed slave. Varying views on this question may be found in Jonathan M. Wiener, *Social Origins of the New South* (Baton Rouge, 1978); Gavin Wright, *The Political Economy of the Cotton South* (New York, 1978), Chapter VI; Jay R. Mandle, *The Roots of Black Poverty* (Durham, N.C., 1978); Roger L. Ransom and Richard Sutch, *One Kind of Freedom* (Cambridge, England, 1977); Robert Higgs, *Competition and Coercion* (Cambridge, England, 1977).